11e

Business English

Mary Ellen Guffey
Emerita Professor of Business
Los Angeles Pierce College

Carolyn M. Seefer
Professor of Business
Diablo Valley College

SOUTH-WESTERN
CENGAGE Learning

Australia • Brazil • Japan • Korea • Mexico • Singapore • Spain • United Kingdom • United States

Business English, Eleventh Edition
Mary Ellen Guffey & Carolyn M. Seefer

Senior Vice President, LRS/Acquisitions & Solutions Planning: Jack W. Calhoun

Editorial Director, Business & Economics: Erin Joyner

Acquisitions Editor: Jason Fremder

Sr. Developmental Editor: Mary H. Emmons

Editorial Assistant: Megan Fischer

Brand Manager: Kristen Hurd

Sr. Content Project Manager: Tamborah Moore

Media Editor: John Rich

Manufacturing Planner: Ron Montgomery

Production Service: S4Carlisle Publishing Services

Sr. Art Director: Stacy Shirley

Cover and Internal Designer: Lou Ann Thesing

Cover Image: © Viktor Fischer/Alamy

Sr. Rights Acquisitions Specialist: Deanna Ettinger

Image permissions researcher: Terri Miller

Text permissions researcher: PMG/Christina Taylor

For product information and technology assistance, contact us at
Cengage Learning Customer & Sales Support, 1-800-354-9706

For permission to use material from this text or product, submit all requests online at **www.cengage.com/permissions**
Further permissions questions can be emailed to
permissionrequest@cengage.com

ExamView® is a registered trademark of eInstruction Corp. Windows is a registered trademark of the Microsoft Corporation used herein under license. Macintosh and Power Macintosh are registered trademarks of Apple Computer, Inc. used herein under license.

Cengage Learning WebTutor™ is a trademark of Cengage Learning.

Library of Congress Control Number: 2012940493

SE Package ISBN-13: 978-1-133-62750-0
SE Package ISBN-10: 1-133-62750-1

Student Edition ISBN 13: 978-1-133-62756-2
Student Edition ISBN 10: 1-133-162756-0

South-Western
5191 Natorp Boulevard
Mason, OH 45040
USA

Cengage Learning is a leading provider of customized learning solutions with office locations around the globe, including Singapore, the United Kingdom, Australia, Mexico, Brazil, and Japan. Locate your local office at: **www.cengage.com/global**

Cengage Learning products are represented in Canada by Nelson Education, Ltd.

For your course and learning solutions, visit **www.cengage.com**

Purchase any of our products at your local college store or at our preferred online store **www.cengagebrain.com**

Printed in the United States of America
1 2 3 4 5 6 7 16 15 14 13 12

Business English, 11e

Dear Students:

Many of you will be entering or returning to the world of work soon, and you want to improve your language skills. *Business English* can help you refresh your knowledge of grammar and usage so that you will be professional, competent, and confident in today's workplace where communication skills are increasingly important. Within the textbook, you will find the following tried-and-true learning tools and features to ensure that you improve your language skills:

Mary Ellen Guffey

- **Three-level approach** presents grammar guidelines in segments proceeding from easier, more frequently used concepts to less frequently used concepts. These small learning chunks proceeding from simple to complex help you understand and remember.

- **Ample end-of-chapter reinforcement exercises** enable you to apply your learning so that you can internalize and retain your new skills.

- **Pretests, posttests, and unit reviews** keep you informed about your needs and your progress.

- **Self-help exercises** give you even more opportunities to improve through practice.

- **Frequently asked questions** present everyday language queries such as those you might face in your career—with answers from the authors.

- **Writer's Workshops** offer guidelines, model documents, and writing tips necessary to compose e-mails, memos, letters, and short reports.

- **Chat About It** promotes classroom and distance-learning discussions related to chapter concepts.

- **Emphasis on Current Business Concepts and Terms.** As you apply grammar guidelines, you will also be learning about current business happenings and using business vocabulary in chapter pretests, posttests, illustrations, and exercises so that you become familiar with today's workplace.

- **Exceptional Web Resources** include chapter quizzes, PowerPoint reviews, flash cards, Ms. Grammar tutorial program, and more at www.cengagebrain.com. Access is available to those with new books; others may purchase access.

Carolyn M. Seefer

Business English reviews the grammar, punctuation, and usage guidelines necessary for you to succeed in your business or professional career. The textbook is not only a friendly teaching and learning tool but also a great reference for you to keep handy on the job.

One student remarked, "*Business English* is a gift to any student who really wants to learn how to use the English language proficiently."

Cordially,

Mary Ellen Guffey   *Carolyn M. Seefer*

Learning With Guffey/Seefer

...It's Just That Easy!

You will find multiple resources to help make learning business English easier. From the three-level approach to new digital resources, Guffey/Seefer have updated and created new ways to keep you interested and engaged. With all of these options, learning can be *just that easy.*

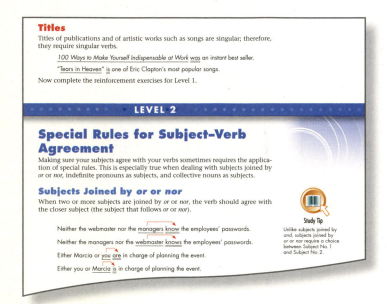

POPULAR THREE-LEVEL APPROACH

Guffey/Seefer's approach to learning grammar starts with a solid foundation of basic information and then progresses to more complex concepts step-by-step. When using this approach, you build your confidence by learning small, easily mastered learning segments. Reinforcement exercises, self-checks, and writing exercises will help you along the way.

Lively Reinforcement Exercises The authors know that you learn by doing. That's why each chapter of *Business English* includes a variety of tools, including self-help exercises aligned with the three-level approach.

Self-Check Exercises and Unit Reviews. The first exercise in each level of each chapter is self-checked to help you determine immediately whether you comprehend the concepts just presented.

Self-Help Exercises. Special worksheets enable you to check your own learning as you review and internalize chapter concepts.

Writing Exercises. Each chapter includes a short writing exercise that encourages you to apply chapter concepts in composing sentences.

Hands-On Writer's Workshops. Six workshops feature composition tips and techniques necessary to develop work-related writing skills.

" *I love learning from* **Business English** *because of its clear layout and great examples showing how to write correctly."*

— MARI MANSKER
STUDENT, DES MOINES AREA
COMMUNITY COLLEGE, IOWA

Learning With Guffey/Seefer

...It's Just That Easy!

FREQUENTLY ASKED QUESTIONS

One of the most popular features of *Business English* has been its questions and answers patterned on those received at grammar hotline services across the country. These questions—and suggested answers from Dr. Guffey and Professor Seefer—illustrate everyday communication problems encountered in the contemporary work world.

FAQs

About Business English

Courtesy of Mary Ellen Guffey

Courtesy of Carolyn M. Seefer

Dr. Guffey   **Professor Seefer**

Q: My uncle insists that *none* is singular. My English book says that it can be plural. Who's right?

A: Times are changing. Several years ago *none* was almost always used in a singular sense. Today, through usage, *none* may be singular or plural depending on what you wish to emphasize. For example, *None are more willing than we*. But, *None of the students is* (or *are* if you wish to suggest many students) *failing*.

Q: Is there a difference between the words *premier* and *premiere*? How can I decide which to use?

A: These words are the masculine (*premier*) and feminine (*premiere*) forms of "first" in the French language. However, they have different meanings in English. *Premier* can be used as an adjective meaning "first in position, rank, importance, or time" (*Google is one of the premier Web search tools*). As a noun, *premier* refers to "the prime minister of a parliamentary government" (*The premier spoke to a large crowd*). The word *premiere* can serve as a noun or verb. As a noun, *premiere* means "a first performance or exhibition" (*The Hollywood premiere was an exciting event*). As a verb, *premiere* means "to give a first public performance" (*The film will premiere in New York City*) or "to appear for the first time as a performer" (*Johnny Depp premiered in the film* A Nightmare on Elm Street).

Q: Are there two meanings for the word *discreet*?

A: You are probably confusing the two words *discreet* and *discrete*. *Discreet* means "showing good judgment" and "prudent" (*the witness gave a discreet answer, avoiding gossip and hearsay*). The word *discrete* means "separate" or "noncontinuous" (*Alpha, Inc., has installed discrete computers rather than a network computer system*). You might find it helpful to remember that the *e*'s are separate in *discrete*.

Q: When should I write *cannot* as one word, and when should I write it as two words?

A: The word *cannot* is always written as one word.

Q: I just checked the dictionary and found that *cooperate* is now written as one word. It seems to me that years ago it was *co-operate* or *coöperate*. Has the spelling changed?

A: Yes, it has. And so has the spelling of many other words. As new words become more familiar, their spelling tends to become more simplified. For example, *per cent* and *good will* ar[...] most dictionaries a[...]

© iStockphoto.com/Pavel Khorenyan

New Features With Guffey/Seefer

...It's Just That Easy!

MORE BLOOPERS!

Because students and instructors loved our Spot the Blooper feature in previous editions, we have expanded the number of bloopers from newspapers, magazines, and other sources. You'll see real examples of mangled sentences, misused words, and creative punctuation. You are challenged to explain the mishaps and correct them.

SPOT THE Blooper

Using the skills you are learning in this class, try to identify why the following items are bloopers. Consult your textbook, dictionary, or reference manual as needed. To see if you recognized the blooper, go to **www.cengagebrain.com** and use your access code to see the Spot the Blooper key.

Blooper 1: Article in the *Cape Cod Times*: "None of this is to say hard work, education, and following your dreams and passions isn't the thing to do—for it's own sake." [Did you spot two bloopers?]

Blooper 2: From an article in *The Dupont Current* [Washington, DC]: "Google wants to try out the new fiber-to-home connections in select cities and communities, and many are anxious to serve as test subjects."

Blooper 3: In the University of St. Thomas *Daily Bulletin*: "Tim Scully's Videography class will present its world premier of music videos."

Blooper 4: In an article in *The Times-Union* [Albany, New York], the interim superintendent of schools said: "A large number of students arrives without the basic skills we expect them to have."

Blooper 5: Message printed on a Gap T-shirt: "The Days of This Society Is Numbered."

nner welcoming Super Bowl fans to Tampa: "Welcome to Downtown ere's so many reasons to like it."

n *The New York Times* reporting that the firing of Merrill Lynch's chair was partly because of the company's depressed stock price: "Last stock sunk to as low as $59 a share."

Chat About It ◀◀

Your instructor may assign any of the following topics for you to discuss in class, an online chat room, or on an online discussion board. Some of the discussion to may require outside research. You may also be asked to read and respond to postin made by your classmates.

Discussion Topic 1: A study tip in this chapter said the following: "Nothing reveals a person's education, or lack thereof, so quickly as verbs that don't agree with subjects." Do you agree with this statement? Why or why not?

Discussion Topic 2: What have you learned so far in this class that will help you sound educated and professional on the job? Why do you think it is important to sound this way in the workplace?

Discussion Topic 3: You learned in this chapter that American and British English rules treat collective nouns differently. Americans generally treat collective nouns as singular, whereas the English generally treat collective nouns as plural. What do you think accounts for this

difference? What other diff ticed between American

Discussion Topic 4: In learned that each year app new words are introduced t language. Of those, about 1 used, and roughly 200 of th a part of our permanent voc do you think so many word never become a permanent our vocabulary?

Discussion Topic 5: Amer lotte Perkins Gilman said, " do you think she meant by Why or why not? Share you thoughts with your classma

CHAT ABOUT IT

To encourage classroom discussion and build online rapport among distance learners, the Eleventh Edition provides Chat About It. Each chapter offers five questions that encourage you to discuss chapter concepts and express your ideas orally or in written comments at the student course site.

TRIVIA TIDBITS

This edition provides marginal notes with captivating factoids about the history and use of the language.

Trivia Tidbit

In the United States, collective nouns are almost always considered to be singular (*The staff is...*). In Britain, however, collective nouns are usually plural (*The staff are...*).

Digital Tools With Guffey/Seefer

...It's Just That Easy!

Guffey/Seefer help you learn to communicate effectively and professionally in today's workplace, no matter what career path you choose to follow. The exciting, new *Business English*, 11e, is packed with resources to make learning easier and more enjoyable. The premium student website houses powerful resources to help make learning... *just that easy.*

Student Support Website

Guffey/Seefer's premium student website gives you one convenient place to find the support you need. You can study with self-teaching grammar/mechanics activities, PowerPoint slides, interactive review quizzes, and other valuable study tools.

Access the premium website through **www.cengagebrain.com.**

Digital Tools With Guffey/Seefer

...It's Just That Easy!

The following features are part of the Guffey/Seefer premium student website. Visit **www.cengagebrain.com** to use these tools today!

Chapter Review Quizzes highlight chapter concepts and give you immediate feedback with explanations for right and wrong responses.

Ms. Grammar strengthens language skills with chapter synopses and interactive exercises.

PowerPoint chapter slides provide a quick review of chapter concepts.

SpeakRight! helps you learn to pronounce 50 frequently mispronounced words.

SpellRight! provides interactive exercises that review all 400 words in Appendix A of the textbook.

Self-Check Diagnostic Grammar Quiz assesses strengths and weaknesses. Different from the diagnostic test in the textbook, this quiz is meant to pique interest.

Flash Cards and Glossary review key terms from each chapter and help you internalize concepts.

Bonus Bloopers supply even more language mishaps from actual written and oral expression that challenge you to detect the problems and remedy them.

Writing Help in the form of links to OWLs (online writing labs) guides you to the best Internet grammar services where you will find exercises, handouts, and writing advice.

CENGAGE**brain**.com

How do you access the Guffey/Seefer premium website?

1 To register a product using the access code found in your textbook, go to: www.cengagebrain.com.

2 Register as a new user or log in as an existing user if you already have an account with Cengage Learning or CengageBrain.com

3 Follow the prompts.

Note: If you did not buy a new textbook, the access code may have been used. You can either buy a new book or purchase access to the Guffey/Seefer Premium website at **www.cengagebrain.com**.

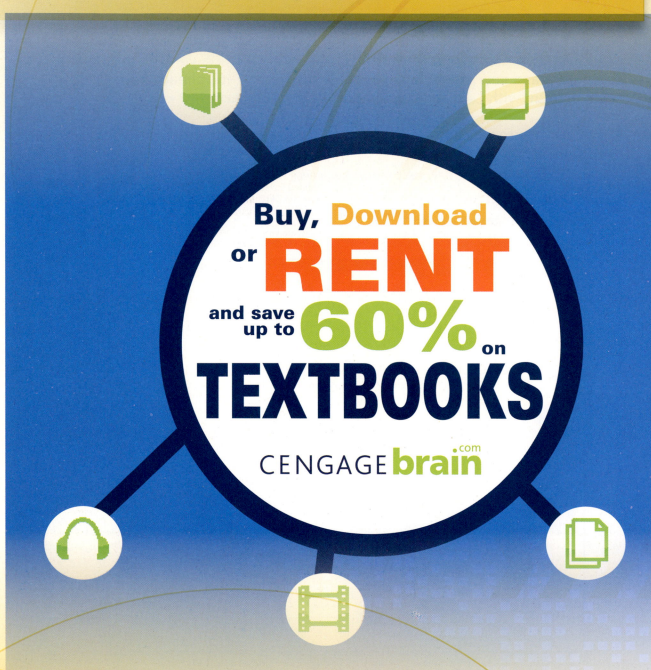

Acknowledgments

We are indebted to many individuals for the continuing success of *Business English*. Instructors across the country have acted as reviewers or have sent us excellent ideas, constructive insights, and supportive comments. We are particularly grateful for the consultation of the following people:

Paige P. Baker, *Trinity Valley Community College*

Joan W. Bass, *Clayton State University*

Julie G. Becker, *Three Rivers Community College*

Amy Beitel, *Cambria-Rowe Business College*

Margaret Britt, *Copiah-Lincoln Community College*

Leila Chambers, *Cuesta College*

Connie Jo Clark, *Lane Community College*

Robin Cook, *Sawyer School*

Maria S. Damen, *University of Cincinnati/ Raymond Walters College*

Betty Dooley, *Clark State Community College*

Cathy Dropkin, *Eldorado Colleges*

Judy Ehresman, *Mercer County Community College*

Valerie Evans, *Cuesta College*

Diane J. Fisher, *The University of Southern Mississippi*

Marye B. Gilford, *St. Philips College*

Barbara Goza, *South Florida Community College*

Margaret E. Gorman, *Cayuga Community College*

Helen Grattan, *Des Moines Area Community College*

Ginger Guzman, *J. Sargeant Reynolds Community College*

Joy G. Haynes, *Chaffey College*

Marilyn Helser, *Lima Technical College*

Nancy A. Henderson, *North Harris College*

Janet L. Hough, *Spokane Community College*

Marilynne Hudgens, *Southwestern College*

Iva A. Upchurch Jeffreys, *Ventura Community College*

Edna V. Jellesed, *Lane Community College*

Tina Johnson, *Lake Superior College Evelyn A. Katusak, Broome Community College*

Lydia J. Keuser, *San Jose City College*

Marilyn Kilbane, *Cuyahoga Community College*

Donna Kimmerling, *Indiana Business College*

Jared H. Kline, *Southeastern Community College*

Ann Marie Klinko, *Northern Virginia Community College*

Shelley Konishi, *Kauai Community College*

Linell Loncorich, *Hutchinson Technical College*

Jane Mangrum, *Miami-Dade Community College*

Shirley Mays, *Hinds Community College*

Darlene McClure, *College of the Redwoods*

Timothy A. Miank, *Lansing Community College*

Carol Vermeere Middendorff, *Clackamas Community College*

Anita Musto, *Utah Valley State College*

Paul W. Murphey, *Southwest Wisconsin Technical College*

Jaunett S. Neighbors, *Central Virginia Community College*

Mary Nerburn, *Moraine Valley Community College*

Jackie Ohlson, *University of Alaska*

Mary Quimby, *Southwestern College*

Jana Rada, *Western Wisconsin Technical College*

Susan Randles, *Vatterott College*

Carol Jo Reitz, *Allentown Business School*

Judith R. Rice, *Chippewa Valley Technical College*

Kathie Richer, *Edmonds Community College*

Benelle Robinson, *Ventura Community College*

Maria Robinson, *Columbia College*

Sally Rollman, *Shoreline Community College*

Jan Sales, *Merced College*

Linda Serra, *Glendale Community College*

Mageya R. Sharp, *Cerritos College*

Susan Simons, *Edmonds Community College*

Marilyn Simonson, *Lakewood Community College*

Lynn E. Steffen, *College of Lake County*

Letha Strain, *Riverside College*

Susan Sutkowski, *Minneapolis Technical College*

Evelyn Taylor, *Cincinnati Bible College*

Michelle Taylor, *Ogeechee Technical College*

Robert Thaden, *Tacoma Community College*

Dorothy Thornhill, *Los Angeles Trade Technical College*

James A. Trick, *Newport Business Institute*

Susan Uchida, *Kauai Community College*

June Uharriet, *East Los Angeles Community College*

Lois A. Wagner, *Southwest Wisconsin Technical College*

Fred Wolven, *Miami-Dade Community College*

Many professionals at South-Western, a part of Cengage Learning, have helped propel *Business English* to its prominent position in the field. For their contributions in producing the Eleventh Edition, we sincerely thank Jack Calhoun, Erin Joyner, Jason Fremder, John Rich, Tamborah Moore, Stacy Shirley, and especially Mary Emmons, our incomparable developmental editor. Special thanks go to Jane Flesher, Chippewa Valley Technical College, and Claudia Eckelmann, Diablo Valley College, for their enormous help in preparing student testing and online materials.

Dr. Mary Ellen Guffey
Emerita Professor of Business
Los Angeles Pierce College

Professor Carolyn M. Seefer
Professor of Business
Diablo Valley College

© iStockphoto.com/Pavel Khorenyan

CONTENTS

© iStockphoto.com/Jacob Wackerhausen

© Yuri Arcurs/Alamy

© iStockphoto.com/nyul

© iStockphoto.com/Su Min-Hsuan

© Dmitriy Shironosov/Shutterstock.com

© Corbis Super RF/Alamy

© iStockphoto.com/Clerkenwell_Images

© iStockphoto.com/Joshua Hodge Photography

© Helder Almeida/Shutterstock.com

© iStockphoto.com/Courtney Keating

© Dmitriy Shironosov/Shutterstock.com

© Corbis RF/Alamy

© Blend Images/Getty Images

© GlowImages/Alamy

In the following sentences, you will find faulty grammar, punctuation, spelling, capitalization, and number expression. For each sentence underline any error. Then write a corrected form in the space provided. If you add punctuation, also show the word that appears immediately before the necessary punctuation mark. If the sentence is correct, mark *C*.

Example: Designers know that the size and design of a product like the iPod <u>is</u> influential in its success.　　　　　　_____ are _____

LEVEL 1

1. All of the attornies were searching for administrative assistants with excellent communication skills. _____

2. A network software workshop scheduled for the fall in Scottsdale, Arizona will be valuable to some staff members. _____

3. In it's latest online announcement, our Information Technology Department said that even the best-protected data sometimes is lost, erased, or corrupted. _____

4. Rachel and I certainly appreciate your taking our calls for us when her and I are away from the office. _____

5. A list with all of our customers' comments for the past month were given to the manager and her last week. _____

6. Our job application form, along with other important documents and officers' statements, are available at our company website. _____

7. For you, Mr. Rivera, we recommend a one-year subscription rather than the two-year subscription. _____

8. We feel badly about your missing the deadline, but the application has been lying on your desk for 15 days. _____

9. We couldn't hardly believe our colleagues when they agreed to the plan. _____

10. In the spring Susan took courses in history, english, and management. _____

LEVEL 2

11. Please collect all of the graduates names and e-mail addresses so that we can keep them informed of job opportunities. _____

12. Either Jason or he will be working at the counter on the next two Friday's. _____

13. Of the forty-six orders placed by customers last week, only 9 were filled on time. _____

14. If you expect a three-week vacation, you must speak with the Manager immediately. _____

15. Either of the two job applicants are acceptable because they both have exceptional communication skills. _____

16. Your job interview with the manager and her will last for a hour. _____

17. Before her trip to the East last summer, my mother bought an Olympus Camera. _____

18. We need only 20 50-cent postage stamps to finish the mailing. _____

19. Your account is now 90 days overdue, therefore, we are submitting it to an agency for collection. _____

20. We are seeking a more faster Internet connection for video downloads, but we don't want to spend too much. _____

LEVEL 3

21. Under the circumstances, we can give you only 90 days time in which to sell the house and its contents. _____

22. The cost of the coast-to-coast flight should be billed to whomever made the airline reservation. _____

23. Los Angeles is larger than any city on the West Coast. _____

24. The number of suggestions made by employees are increasing each month as employees become more involved. _____

25. Our school's alumni are certainly different than its currently enrolled students. _____

26. Courtney is one of those efficient, competent managers who is able to give sincere praise for work done well. _____

27. You should have saw the warehouse before its contents were moved to 39th Street. _____

28. If I were him, I would call the Cortezes' attorney at once. _____

29. Three employees will be honored, namely, Lucy Lee, Tony Waters, and Jamie Craig. _____

30. If you drive a little further, you will come to the library on the right side of the street. _____

Laying a Foundation

1 **Parts of Speech**

2 **Sentences: Elements, Varieties, Patterns, Types, Faults**

1 Parts of Speech

© iStockphoto.com/Jacob Wackerhausen

Whatever your program in college, be sure to include courses in writing and speaking. Managers must constantly write instructions, reports, memos, letters, and survey conclusions. If this comes hard to you, it will hold you back.

—James A. Newman and Alexander Roy

Objectives

When you have completed the materials in this chapter, you will be able to do the following:

1. Understand the content of business English and its relevance to you and your career.

2. Define the eight parts of speech.

3. Recognize how parts of speech function in sentences.

4. Use words in a variety of grammatical roles.

Circle art: © iStockphoto.com/Pavel Khorenyan

Study the following sentence and identify selected parts of speech. For each word listed, underline the correct part of speech. Compare your answers with those at the bottom of the page.

The accountant and I carefully verified figures in the company financial statements.

1. **The**   a. preposition   b. pronoun   c. conjunction   d. adjective
2. **accountant** a. noun   b. pronoun   c. verb   d. adjective
3. **and**   a. preposition   b. conjunction   c. adjective   d. adverb
4. **I**   a. noun   b. pronoun   c. interjection   d. adjective
5. **carefully**   a. adjective   b. conjunction   c. preposition   d. adverb
6. **verified**   a. adverb   b. noun   c. verb   d. adverb
7. **figures**   a. pronoun   b. adjective   c. verb   d. noun
8. **in**   a. preposition   b. conjunction   c. adjective   d. adverb
9. **company**   a. noun   b. adverb   c. pronoun   d. adjective
10. **statements** a. pronoun   b. noun   c. adjective   d. verb

Business English is the study of the language fundamentals needed to communicate effectively in today's workplace. These fundamentals include grammar, usage, punctuation, capitalization, number style, and spelling. Because businesspeople must express their ideas clearly and correctly, language fundamentals are critical.

Why Study Business English?

What you learn in this class will help you communicate more professionally when you write and when you speak. These skills will help you get the job you want, succeed in the job you have, or prepare for promotion to a better position. Good communication skills can also help you succeed in the classroom and in your personal life, but we will be most concerned with workplace applications.

Increasing Emphasis on Workplace Communication

In today's workplace you can expect to be doing more communicating than ever before. You will be participating in meetings, writing business documents, and using technology such as e-mail, text messaging, and social media to communicate with others. Communication skills are more important than ever before, and the emphasis on writing has increased dramatically. Businesspeople who never expected to be doing much writing on the job find that e-mail, the Web, and social media force everyone to exchange written messages. As a result, businesspeople are increasingly aware of their communication skills. Misspelled words, poor grammar, sloppy punctuation—all of these faults stand out glaringly when they are in print or displayed online. Not only are people writing more, but their messages travel farther. Messages are seen by larger audiences than ever before.

1.d 2.a 3.b 4.b 5.d 6.c 7.d 8.a 9.d 10.b

Because of the growing emphasis on exchanging information, your language skills are especially important in today's dynamic and often digital workplace.

Workplace communication is important for many reasons:

- When you write or speak on the job, you are representing your company. No company wants to send out messages that contain errors, nor does a company want its employees making errors when speaking with customers or giving business presentations. Such errors cause customers and others outside the company to question the organization's competence and professionalism. No one wants to invest in or purchase products or services from a company that can't get it right.

- When you speak or write on the job, you are also representing yourself. Errors in your presentations, e-mail messages, online postings, memos, and other documents will cause others to question your education, your competence, and your professionalism.

- Those who can write and speak well and accurately are the ones who are noticed in the workplace. They are the ones who are hired, promoted, and valued in the workplace.

- When you know that your writing and expression are clear, professional, and accurate, you feel good about yourself and your abilities. Yes, it feels good to be able to get it right!

What Does This Mean for You?

As a businessperson or professional, you want to feel confident about your writing and speaking skills. This textbook and this course can sharpen your skills and greatly increase your confidence in expressing ideas. Improving your language skills is the first step toward success in your education, your career, and your life. It may not be easy, but the payoffs will be enormous!

The Eight Parts of Speech

This book focuses on the study of the fundamentals of grammar, current usage, and appropriate business and professional style. Such a study logically begins with the eight parts of speech, the building blocks of our language. This chapter provides a brief overview of the parts of speech. In future chapters you will learn about each part of speech in greater detail.

Why is it important to learn to identify the eight parts of speech? Learning the eight parts of speech helps you develop the working vocabulary necessary to discuss and study the language. You especially need to recognize the parts of speech in the context of sentences. That is because many words function in more than one role. Only by analyzing the sentence at hand can you see how a given word functions. Your boss is unlikely to ask you to identify the parts of speech in a business document. Being able to do so, however, will help you punctuate correctly and choose precise words for clear, powerful writing. Using the parts of speech correctly will also help you sound more professional and intelligent on the job. In addition, understanding the roles different parts of speech play in written and oral communication will be helpful if you learn another language.

Nouns

In elementary school you probably learned that a **noun** refers to a person, place, or thing. In addition, nouns name qualities, feelings, concepts, activities, and measures. Nouns can be proper or common. **Proper nouns** are capitalized, and

common nouns are not, as you can see in the following list. You will learn more about this concept in Chapter 3.

Persons:	Stephanie, Dr. Hudson, accountant, supervisor
Places:	New Orleans, Charles de Gaulle Airport, hospital, river
Things:	iPad, BlackBerry, automobile, pillow
Qualities:	impatience, honesty, initiative, enthusiasm
Feelings:	happiness, anger, disbelief, euphoria
Concepts:	knowledge, freedom, friendship, patriotism
Activities:	tweeting, investing, management, eating
Measures:	month, thousand, inch, kilometer

Nouns are important words in our language. Sentences revolve around nouns because these words function both as subjects and as objects of verbs. To determine whether a word is really a noun, try using it with the verb *is* or *are*. Notice that all the nouns listed here would make sense if used in this way: *Stephanie is excited*, *New Orleans is in Louisiana*, *iPads are popular*, *tweeting is fun*, and so on. In Chapter 3 you will learn about the rules for making nouns plural. You will also learn how to show that a noun possesses something.

Pronouns

Pronouns are words used in place of nouns. As noun substitutes, pronouns provide variety and efficiency to your writing. Compare these two versions of the same sentence:

Without Pronouns:	Mitch forwarded the message to Kristi so that Kristi could read the message before the meeting.
With Pronouns:	Mitch forwarded the message to Kristi so that *she* could read *it* before the meeting.

In sentences pronouns may function as subjects of verbs (such as *I, we, they*) or as objects of verbs (*me, us, them*). They may act as connectors (*that, which, who*), and they may show possession (*mine, ours, hers, theirs*). Only a few examples are given here. More examples, along with the functions and classifications of pronouns, will be presented in Chapter 4. You will also learn to use pronouns in Chapter 4.

Please note that words such as *his, my, her,* and *its* are classified as adjectives when they describe nouns (*his car, my desk, its engine*). This concept will be explained more thoroughly in Chapters 4 and 7.

Verbs

A **verb** expresses an action, an occurrence, or a state of being.

Aaron *created* a compelling business Facebook page. (Action)

It *contains* valuable information. (Occurrence)

He *is* proud of it. (State of being)

An **action verb** shows the physical or mental action of the subject of a sentence. Some action verbs are *run, study, work,* and *dream*. **Linking verbs** express a state of being and generally link to the subject words that describe or rename them. Some linking verbs are *am, is, are, was, were, be, being,*

Study Tip

To test whether a word is truly a verb, try using it with a noun or pronoun, such as *Mark studies, he seems,* or *it is. He food* doesn't make sense because *food* is not a verb.

and *been*. Other linking verbs express the senses: *feels, appears, tastes, sounds, seems, looks*.

Verbs will be discussed more fully in Chapters 5 and 6. At this point it is important that you be able to recognize verbs so that you can determine whether sentences are complete. All complete sentences must have at least one verb; many sentences will have more than one verb. Verbs may appear singly or in phrases. When verbs are used in verb phrases, **helping verbs** are added.

Diana *submitted* her application to become a paralegal. (Action verb)

Her résumé *is* just one page long. (Linking verb)

She *has been training* to become a paralegal. (Verb phrase; helping verbs *has* and *been* are added.)

Diana *feels* bad that she *will be leaving* her current colleagues. (Linking verb and verb phrase; helping verbs *will* and *be* are added.)

Adjectives

Words that describe nouns or pronouns are **adjectives**. They often answer the questions *What kind?*, *How many?*, and *Which one?* The adjectives in the following sentences are italicized. Observe that the adjectives all answer questions about the nouns they describe.

Small, independent credit unions are becoming *popular*. (What kinds of credit unions?)

We have *six* franchises in *four* states. (How many franchises? How many states?)

That chain of coffee shops started as a *small* operation. (Which chain? What kind of operation?)

He is *personable* and *outgoing*, while she is *energetic* and *confident*. (What pronouns do these adjectives describe?)

Adjectives usually precede the nouns they describe. They may, however, follow the words they describe, especially when used with linking verbs, as shown in the first and last of the preceding examples. Here is a brief list of words used as adjectives:

efficient	humorous	mature
forceful	intelligent	responsive
green	little	successful

Three words (*a*, *an*, and *the*) form a special group of adjectives called **articles**. Adjectives will be discussed more thoroughly in Chapter 7.

Adverbs

Words that modify (describe or limit) verbs, adjectives, or other adverbs are **adverbs**. Adverbs often answer the questions *When?*, *How?*, *Where?*, and *To what extent?*

Study Tip

To remember more easily what an *adverb* does, think of its two syllables: *ad* suggests that you will be adding to or amplifying the meaning of a *verb*. Hence, adverbs often modify verbs.

Tomorrow we must submit the paperwork. (Must submit the paperwork *when*?)

Rudy began his presentation *enthusiastically*. (Began *how*?)

She seems *especially* competent. (*How* competent?)

Did you see the schedule *there*? (*Where*?)

The prosecutor did not question him *further*. (Questioned him *to what extent*?)

Following are examples of commonly used adverbs:

absolutely	now	today
carefully	only	too
greatly	really	very

Many, but not all, words ending in *ly* are adverbs. Exceptions are *friendly*, *costly*, and *ugly*, all of which are adjectives. Adverbs will be discussed in greater detail in Chapter 7.

Prepositions

Prepositions join nouns and pronouns to other words in a sentence. As the word itself suggests (*pre* meaning "before"), a preposition is a word in a position *before* its object. The **object of a preposition** is a noun or pronoun. Prepositions are used in phrases to show a relationship between the object of the preposition and another word in the sentence. In the following sentences, notice how the preposition changes the relation of the object (*Ms. Lopez*) to the verb (*talk*):

> Austin often talks *with* Ms. Lopez
>
> Austin often talked *about* Ms. Lopez.
>
> Austin often talks *to* Ms. Lopez.

Some of the most frequently used prepositions are *at, by, for, from, in, of, to,* and *with.* A more complete list of prepositions can be found in Chapter 8. You should learn to recognize objects of prepositions so that you won't confuse them with sentence subjects. You will learn more about the difference between verb subjects and objects in Chapter 6.

Conjunctions

Words that connect other words or groups of words are **conjunctions**. The most common conjunctions are *and, but, or,* and *nor.* These are called **coordinating conjunctions** because they join equal (coordinate) parts of sentences. Other kinds of conjunctions will be presented in Chapter 9. Study the examples of coordinating conjunctions shown here:

> Danielle, Mark, *and* Huong are all looking for jobs. (The conjunction *and* joins equal words.)
>
> You may be interviewed by an HR officer *or* by a supervisor. (The conjunction *or* joins equal groups of words.)

Interjections

Words expressing strong feelings, but usually unconnected grammatically to the sentence, are **interjections**. Interjections standing alone are followed by exclamation marks. When woven into a sentence, they are usually followed by commas.

> *Wow!* Did you see her most recent Facebook status update? (Interjection standing alone)
>
> *Oh,* I should have known this would happen. (Interjection woven into a sentence)

Career Tip

To sound professional, credible, and objective, most business writers avoid interjections and exclamation marks in business and professional messages.

Summary

The following sentence illustrates all eight parts of speech.

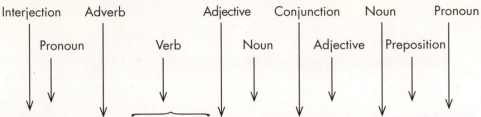

Interjection   Adverb   Adjective   Conjunction   Noun   Pronoun

Pronoun   Verb   Noun   Adjective   Preposition

Oh, I certainly will submit a résumé and cover letter to them.

You need to know the functions of these eight parts of speech in order to understand the rest of this textbook and to benefit from your study of language basics. The explanation of the parts of speech has been kept simple so far. This chapter is meant to serve as an introduction to later, more fully developed chapters about the different parts of speech. At this stage you should not expect to be able to identify the functions of *all* words in *all* sentences.

A word of caution: English is a wonderfully flexible language. As noted earlier, many words in our language serve as more than one part of speech. Notice how flexible the word *mail* is in these sentences:

Our *mail* is late today. (Noun—serves as subject of sentence.)

This pile of *mail* must be delivered today. (Noun—serves as object of preposition.)

Please read your *mail* soon. (Noun—serves as object of verb.)

Mail the letter today. (Verb—serves as action word in sentence.)

The *mail* system in the United States is efficient. (Adjective—used to describe *system*, which serves as subject of sentence.)

Courtesy of Mary Ellen Guffey

Courtesy of Carolyn M. Seefer

Dr. Guffey   Professor Seefer

Businesspeople and professionals are very concerned about appropriate and professional English usage, grammar, and style. This concern is evident in the number and kinds of questions posted to discussion boards, websites, blogs, and Facebook pages devoted to proper English usage. Among the users of these Web and social media sites are business supervisors, managers, executives, professionals, secretaries, clerks, administrative assistants, and word processing specialists. Writers, teachers, librarians, students, and other community members also seek answers to language questions. The questions that are asked online are often referred to as **Frequently Asked Questions**, or **FAQs** (pronounced "facks").

Selected questions and answers from Dr. Guffey and Professor Seefer will be presented at the end of each chapter. In this way, you, as a student of the language, will understand the kinds of everyday communication problems encountered in business and professional environments.

Representative questions come from a variety of reputable grammar-related websites and social media sites. You can locate sites that present these FAQs by using the search phrase *grammar FAQs* in Google.

Q: We're having a big argument in our office. What's correct? *E-mail, e-mail, email, or Email? On-line or online? Website, Web site, web site, or website?*

A: In the early days of computing, people capitalized *E-mail* and hyphenated *on-line*. With increased use, however, both of these forms have been simplified to *e-mail* and *online*. The letter *e* in *e-mail* should be capitalized only if the word is first in a sentence. In regard to *Web site,* we recommend the lowercase one-word form (*website*). You might want to check your company's in-house style manual for its preferred style for all of these words.

Q: Should I capitalize the word *Internet?* I see it written both ways and am confused.

A: We recommend writing the word with a capital *I* (*Internet*). However, we are in a time of change with regard to the proper spelling and writing of Web-related words. For example, *Wired News* was the first to spell *Internet* using lowercase letters, and others have followed. For now, though, you should continue to capitalize *Internet* because that is the format many style manuals and dictionaries recommend.

Q: What is the name of a group of initials that forms a word? Is it an abbreviation?

A: A word formed from the initial letters of an expression is called an **acronym** (pronounced ACK-ro-nim). Examples: *scuba* from *self-contained underwater breathing apparatus,* and *PIN* from *personal identification number.* Another example of an acronym is *OSHA* (pronounced *Oh-shah*), which stands for *Occupational Safety and Health Administration.* Acronyms are pronounced as single words and are different from abbreviations. Expressions such as *FBI* and *NFL* are **abbreviations**, not acronyms. Notice that an abbreviation is pronounced letter by letter (*F, B, I*), whereas an acronym is pronounced as a word. Shortened versions of words such as *dept.* and *Ms.* are also considered abbreviations.

Circle art: © iStockphoto.com/Pavel Khorenyan

Q: What's the difference between *toward* and *towards*?

A: None. They are interchangeable in use. However, we recommend using the shorter word *toward* because it is more efficient. *Toward* is also more common in the United States, whereas *towards* is more common in Great Britain.

Q: Is *every day* one word or two in this case? *We encounter these problems every day.*

A: In your sentence it is two words. When it means "ordinary," it is one word (*she wore everyday clothes*). If you can insert the word *single* between *every* and *day* without altering your meaning, you should be using two words, as in your sentence.

Q: Should an e-mail message begin with a salutation or some kind of greeting? Should I type my name and contact information at the bottom of a message?

A: When e-mail messages are sent to company insiders, a salutation may be omitted; however, including a salutation will personalize your message. When e-mail messages travel to outsiders, omitting a salutation seems curt and unfriendly. Because the message is more like a letter, a salutation is appropriate (such as *Dear Courtney; Hi, Courtney; Greetings;* or just *Courtney*). Including a salutation is also a visual cue that identifies the beginning of the message. Some writers prefer to incorporate the name of the recipient in the first sentence (*Thanks, Courtney, for responding so quickly.*) You should also type your name at the bottom of all e-mail messages you send to personalize them. If your message is being sent outside your organization, you might also include your contact information in the closing.

Q: In e-mail messages is it acceptable to use abbreviations such as *IMHO* (*in my humble opinion*), *LOL* (*laughing out loud*), *BTW* (*by the way*), and *TIA* (*thanks in advance*)?

A: Among close friends who understand their meaning, such abbreviations are certainly acceptable. But in business messages, these abbreviations are too casual and too obscure. Many readers would have no idea what they mean. **Emoticons** (or smileys) such as :-) are also too casual for business messages. Worst of all, abbreviations and emoticons make business messages look immature and unprofessional.

Q: Tell me it's not true! I just heard that the abbreviations *LOL* and *OMG* and the words *retweet* and *sexting* were recently added to the *Oxford English Dictionary*. Surely this is an urban legend.

A: It's true. The abbreviations *LOL* and *OMG* and the words *retweet* and *sexting* were recently added to the *Oxford English Dictionary*, long considered the foremost authority on the English language. Its editors decided that these abbreviations and words are so universally accepted that they warranted formal recognition. This certainly proves what an effect popular culture and technology have on our language. However, keep in mind that not all words appearing in dictionaries are appropriate for business messages.

Q: I just included this sentence in a cover letter and am wondering whether it is correct: *Your ad for a Web content specialist peaked my interest.*

A: We hope you haven't sent this letter yet! In this sentence you should have used *piqued* instead of *peaked*. The verb *pique* comes from a French word that means "to excite or arouse," as in "to pique your curiosity." Also don't confuse these two words with *peek*, which means "to take a brief look."

Q: Is there a difference between the words *forward* and *foreword*? How do I decide which to use?

A: The word *forward* has many uses. As an adverb it means "toward or at a place, point, or time in advance" (*from this day forward*). As an adjective it means "presumptuous or bold" (*it was forward of her to ask whether she got the job*). As a verb it means "to transmit" (*please forward the message to me*). The word *foreword*, on the other hand, can be used only as a noun, meaning "the preface or introduction of a book" (*the famous scholar wrote the foreword*).

SPOT THE Blooper

What is a **blooper**? Television producer Kermit Schaefer first defined the word *blooper* to describe mistakes made on television, in radio, and in films. Today the word *blooper* is used to describe any embarrassing blunder. In this textbook we use the word *blooper* to refer to language mistakes made in writing and speech. At the end of each chapter, you will find a list of written and spoken bloopers. Many of these bloopers appeared in prestigious publications or were spoken by highly respected individuals. Using the skills you are learning in this class, try to identify why the following items are bloopers. Consult your textbook, dictionary, or reference manual as needed. Also think about what part of speech each blooper demonstrates. To see if you recognized the blooper, go to **www.cengagebrain.com** and use your access code to see the Spot the Blooper key.

Blooper 1: Statements that appeared in résumés sent to Robert Half International, the world's largest specialist staffing firm: "Instrumental in ruining entire operation for a Midwest chain of stores." "Here are my qualifications for you to overlook." "Hope to hear from you shorty." "I'm a rabid typist."

Blooper 2: Sign in a souvenir shop in York Beach [Maine]: "You brake it, you pay for it."

Blooper 3: Magazine advertisement for a dentist in Monterey, California: "You wear your smile everyday. Make it the best!"

Blooper 4: From *The Wall Street Journal* comes a report that Marshall Field's, the big Chicago retailer, announced it would serve hot chocolate to "tiresome" shoppers.

Blooper 5: Letter to the editor of the *San Francisco Chronicle*: "Me and my siblings are not thugs and gangsters. We all have degrees and are doctors, technology workers, DNA researchers—the people who are defining the future."

Blooper 6: In a *Washington Post* article: "What drains out is an intensely sweet juice that is fermented into a pricey wine found on the desert lists of the finest restaurants."

Blooper 7: From the website of Ipsos, a company that conducts online consumer surveys: "Here are just a few highlights to peak your interest."

Blooper 8: In a column in *The Denver Post,* columnist Julia Martinez discussed a proposed history of Denver for which the city's mayor "is supposed to write the forward."

Blooper 9: When the great American opera singer Beverly Sills died, *The New York Times* said that she made her debut in 1969 "at the most scared of all Italian opera houses, La Scala."

Blooper 10: An editorial in *The New York Times* about the state of the schools in Washington, DC: "The imbalance is particularly disturbing, given that the District's children fair worse at school than children in other big cities."

1   Reinforcement Exercises

Note: At the beginning of every set of reinforcement exercises, a self-check exercise is provided so that you will know immediately whether you understand the concepts presented in the chapter. Do not look at the answers until you have completed the exercise. Then compare your responses with the answers shown at the bottom of the page. If you have more than three incorrect responses, reread the chapter before continuing with the other reinforcement exercises.

A. Self-Check. Parts of Speech. Choose the correct answer.

   1. Words that express an action, an occurrence, or a state of being are *(a) verbs, (b) nouns, (c) adverbs, (d) interjections.*   *a*

   2. Names for persons, places, things, qualities, feelings, concepts, activities, and measures are *(a) verbs, (b) adjectives, (c) nouns, (d) pronouns.*   *c*

   3. Words such as *I, you, they,* and *hers,* which substitute for nouns, are *(a) adverbs, (b) adjectives, (c) interjections, (d) pronouns.*   *d*

   4. The part of speech that answers the questions *What kind?* and *How many?* is a(n) *(a) adverb, (b) adjective, (c) preposition, (d) conjunction.*   *b*

   5. Words such as *slowly, very,* and *tomorrow* that answer the questions *How?* and *When?* are *(a) adverbs, (b) adjectives, (c) nouns, (d) conjunctions.*   *a*

   6. *Wow* and *oh* are examples of *(a) pronouns, (b) prepositions, (c) interjections, (d) adjectives.*   *c*

   7. *And, or, nor,* and *but* are *(a) adverbs, (b) prepositions, (c) interjections, (d) conjunctions.*   *d*

   8. Words such as *by, in,* and *of* that join noun or pronoun objects to other words in sentences are *(a) adverbs, (b) prepositions, (c) conjunctions, (d) adjectives.*   *b*

   9. *The, a,* and *an* are a special group of adjectives called *(a) joiners, (b) articles, (c) limiters, (d) descriptors.*   *b*

  10. Nouns that are capitalized are known as *(a) common nouns, (b) proper nouns, (c) pronouns, (d) articles.*   *b*

Check your answers below.

B. Recognizing Parts of Speech. In each sentence, identify the italicized word(s).

 11. Savvy job seekers today *include* an app for their iPhone or iPad.

    a. noun   **b.** pronoun   **c.** verb   **d.** adverb   *c*

 12. Apps offer *help* with planning and researching a job search.

    a. noun   **b.** pronoun   **c.** verb   **d.** adverb   *a*

 13. An app can provide tips for *nearly* every hurdle a job seeker faces.

    a. noun   **b.** pronoun   **c.** verb   **d.** adverb   *d*

1.a 2.c 3.d 4.b 5.a 6.c 7.d 8.b 9.b 10.b

14. One section, for example, prompts *you* to identify prospective employers.

    a. noun   **b.** pronoun   **c.** verb   **d.** adverb   _____

15. Once you identify prospective employers, the app *then* seeks relevant mobile Web pages for that company.

    a. noun   **b.** pronoun   **c.** verb   **d.** adverb   _____

16. The app *can provide* questions you would like to ask the interviewer.

    a. noun   **b.** pronoun   **c.** verb   **d.** adverb   _____

17. You can save questions in a research folder for a *particular* job interview.

    a. noun   **b.** pronoun   **c.** verb   **d.** adjective   _____

18. The interview section begins with *brain* teasers to sharpen your mind.

    a. noun   **b.** pronoun   **c.** verb   **d.** adjective   _____

19. The last *section* is devoted to essential but easy-to-remember points.

    a. noun   **b.** pronoun   **c.** verb   **d.** adjective   _____

20. *Wow!* This app sounds as if it is really worth the investment.

    a. noun   **b.** interjection   **c.** verb   **d.** adverb   _____

C. **Parts of Speech.** In each of the following groups of sentences, the same word functions differently. For each sentence indicate the part of speech for the italicized word.

Examples:

We don't have much *time* to prepare our presentation.

a. noun   **b.** adjective   **c.** verb   **d.** preposition   ___a___

Officials will *time* the runners in the marathon.

a. adjective   **b.** noun   **c.** verb   **d.** interjection   ___c___

Factory workers must punch a *time* clock.

a. verb   **b.** noun   **c.** adverb   **d.** adjective   ___d___

21. Performers *dance* at every evening ceremony.

    a. noun   **b.** adjective   **c.** verb   **d.** preposition   _____

22. A new *dance* club opened right next to our office.

    a. adjective   **b.** adverb   **c.** verb   **d.** noun   _____

23. Their first *dance* at their wedding was to the song "Always and Forever."

    a. verb   **b.** noun   **c.** interjection   **d.** conjunction   _____

24. Brandon prefers a casual *work* environment.

    a. noun   **b.** adjective   **c.** verb   **d.** preposition   _____

25. Annette Jenkins arrives at *work* early each morning.

    a. preposition   **b.** verb   **c.** noun   **d.** adjective   _____

26. The entire department will *work* overtime to finish the project.

    a. noun   **b.** adjective   **c.** verb   **d.** adverb   _____

27. Volunteers do important *work* in the community.

    a. noun   **b.** adjective   **c.** verb   **d.** preposition   _____

28. Advertisements promised instruction from a *master* teacher.

    a. noun   **b.** adverb   **c.** verb   **d.** adjective   _____

29. Few students can *master* Web design in a short course.

    a. verb   **b.** noun   **c.** adverb   **d.** pronoun   _____

30. Warren Buffet is a *master* in the field of investing.

    a. pronoun   **b.** noun   **c.** adjective   **d.** adverb   _____

D. Parts of Speech. Depending on their use in sentences, words may function as different parts of speech. This writing exercise gives you an opportunity to use the same word differently.

Write complete sentences using the word *contract* as the part of speech indicated.

31. (noun) _____

32. (verb) _____

33. (adjective) _____

Write complete sentences using the word *set* as the part of speech indicated.

34. (noun) _____

35. (verb) _____

36. (adjective) _____

Write complete sentences using the word *desert* as the part of speech indicated.

37. (noun) _____

38. (verb) _____

39. (adjective) _____

Write a complete sentence using the word *dessert* as the part of speech indicated.

40. (noun) _____

E. Parts of Speech. Read the following sentences and, taking into account the function of each word within each sentence, identify the part of speech of each word shown. Use a dictionary if necessary.

The e-mail message contained a virus, but it was quickly deleted.

41. The _____   **46.** but _____

42. e-mail _____   **47.** it _____

43. message _____   **48.** was _____

44. contained _____   **49.** quickly _____

45. virus _____   **50.** deleted _____

Wow! He immediately discovered the reason for the quarterly operating loss.

51. Wow! _____   **56.** reason _____

52. He _____   **57.** for _____

53. immediately _____   **58.** quarterly _____

54. discovered _____   **59.** operating _____

55. the _____   **60.** loss _____

F.   Verbs. In each of the following sentences, identify the verb and tell whether it is an action or linking verb.

Example: Jason is the new marketing manager.

a. Jason   **b.** is   **c.** new   **d.** manager   **b (linking)** _____

61. Some job applicants now prepare video résumés for posting on YouTube.

    a. applicants   **b.** prepare   **c.** résumés   **d.** posting   _____

62. Google Earth provides satellite images of geographic areas around the world.

    a. provides   **b.** satellite   **c.** images   **d.** world   _____

63. The hotel manager selected four trainees from many applicants.

    a. manager   **b.** selected   **c.** trainees   **d.** applicants   _____

64. Her outgoing voice mail message sounds professional.

    a. outgoing   **b.** mail   **c.** message   **d.** sounds   _____

65. Please submit your proposal before October 4.

    a. Please   **b.** submit   **c.** proposal   **d.** before   _____

66. The vice president and the controller analyzed the accounting figures carefully.

    a. controller   **b.** analyzed   **c.** accounting   **d.** carefully   _____

67. Words are the most powerful drug in the world.

    a. Words   **b.** are   **c.** powerful   **d.** drug   _____

68. Brandon felt bad about the company's quarterly loss.

    a. felt   **b.** bad   **c.** quarterly   **d.** loss   _____

69. She dreams about a bright future.

    a. She   **b.** dreams   **c.** bright   **d.** future   _____

70. I am very pleased about your new job!

    a. am   **b.** pleased   **c.** your   **d.** job   _____

G.   Writing Exercise. Parts of Speech. In three or four complete sentences, explain why it is important to understand the parts of speech for this course and later on the job.

_____

_____

_____

_____

In three or four complete sentences, explain the difference between nouns and verbs. Which do you think is more important to a writer?

_____

_____

_____

_____

H. FAQs About Business English Review. Choose the correct answer.

71. Many businesspeople begin their research on the *(a) internet, (b) Internet, (c) InterNet.* _____

72. Experts suggest that users check their *(a) Email, (b) E-mail, (c) email, (d) e-mail* at regular intervals. _____

73. Customers can receive live *(a) on-line, (b) online, (c) on line* technical support. _____

74. All computer files must be backed up *(a) everyday, (b) every day, (c) every-day* to prevent possible loss. _____

75. Backing up files is an *(a) everyday, (b) every day, (c) every-day* occurrence in most organizations. _____

76. Which of the following is an acronym? *(a) CIA, (b) IRS, (c) PIN, (d) RSVP* _____

77. Which of the following is an abbreviation? *(a) laser, (b) OSHA, (c) radar, (d) NBA* _____

78. Your statement during the interview has *(a) piqued, (b) peaked, (c) peeked* my curiosity. _____

79. When you receive the announcement, please *(a) foreword, (b) forward, (c) for-ward* it to me. _____

80. Stephen Colbert wrote the *(a) foreword, (b) forward, (c) for-ward* to the book *Tall Tales* by Al Jaffe. _____

Chat About It ◀◀

At the end of each chapter in this textbook, you will find five discussion questions related to the chapter material. Your instructor may assign these topics to you to discuss in class, in an online chat room, or on an online discussion board. Some of the discussion topics may require outside research. You may also be asked to read and respond to postings made by your classmates.

Discussion Topic 1: Prepare an introduction to deliver to your classmates so they can get to know you. Include the following in your introduction: your name, where you live, where you work, information about your family and friends, why you are taking the class, what you hope to learn, your major, your career goals, and anything else of interest.

Discussion Topic 2: Why do you think excellent communication skills are in such demand in today's workplace? How will these skills help you succeed on the job? How will understanding the fundamentals of business English help you to communicate more effectively?

Discussion Topic 3: For this discussion assignment, you will be sharing your favorite acronyms and abbreviations with the class. Select five acronyms and five abbreviations. Label each item clearly to show whether it is an acronym or an abbreviation. For each item provide the following information: what the acronym or abbreviation represents, the phonetic pronunciation (if necessary), and a brief description. All acronyms and abbreviations must be written in the correct format, including proper use of lowercase letters, capital letters, and periods. Consult your dictionary or reference manual if needed.

Discussion Topic 4: As mentioned in Chapter 1, a palindrome is a word, phrase, or sentence that reads the same backward and forward, such as *civic*, *mom*, *dad*, and *level*. Palindromes can be single words, phrases, complete sentences, poems, names, or long blocks of text; and palindromes exist in almost every language. Do a Web search to find an interesting palindrome, and then share it with your classmates. If you are creative, you could even try writing your own!

Discussion Topic 5: One of the goals of your education is to know where to find answers. You should also know how to interpret the information you find. Experts do not know all the answers. Attorneys refer to casebooks. Doctors consult their medical libraries. And you, as a student of language, must develop skill and confidence in using reference materials such as dictionaries, thesauruses, and office reference manuals. Many references are now available online. For this discussion find one online reference that would be helpful for business English students. Share the following information about the reference with the class: the complete title of the reference, the website address (URL), a brief description of the reference and why you chose it, and an explanation of how you would use the online reference on the job and/or why business English students would find it beneficial.

Posttest

Identify the parts of speech in this sentence by underlining the correct choice. Compare your answers with those at the bottom of the page.

Peter eagerly waited for the moment when **he** would become **a college graduate.**

1. **Peter**   a. pronoun   b. interjection   c. noun   d. adjective
2. **eagerly**   a. adverb   b. adjective   c. verb   d. conjunction
3. **waited**   a. adverb   b. verb   c. preposition   d. adjective
4. **for**   a. conjunction   b. pronoun   c. preposition   d. interjection
5. **the**   a. adverb   b. conjunction   c. interjection   d. adjective
6. **moment**   a. verb   b. noun   c. adverb   d. adjective
7. **he**   a. pronoun   b. verb   c. noun   d. adjective
8. **a**   a. adverb   b. adjective   c. preposition   d. interjection
9. **college**   a. adjective   b. adverb   c. noun   d. verb
10. **graduate** a. adverb   b. verb   c. pronoun   d. noun

1.c 2.a 3.b 4.c 5.d 6.b 7.a 8.b 9.a 10.d

Sentences: Elements, Varieties, Patterns, Types, Faults

©Yuri Arcurs/Alamy

I'm not a very good writer, but I'm an excellent rewriter.

—James Michener, famous American author

Objectives

When you have completed the materials in this chapter, you will be able to do the following:

1. Recognize basic sentence elements including subjects and predicates.

2. Differentiate among phrases, dependent clauses, and independent clauses.

3. Understand how to use simple, compound, complex, and compound-complex sentences.

4. Identify four basic sentence patterns.

5. Punctuate statements, questions, commands, and exclamations.

6. Use techniques to avoid basic sentence faults such as fragments, comma splices, and run-on sentences.

Circle art: © iStockphoto.com/Pavel Khorenyan

Pretest

Write the correct letter after each of the following items to identify it. End punctuation has been omitted. Then compare your answers with those below.

a. phrase   **c. independent clause**
b. dependent clause

1. Pakistan relies on its citizens to find websites to block   _____
2. Even though countries like China use the government to censor the Web   _____
3. In the course of one day   _____
4. Students and religious figures tend to be most active in flagging offensive sites   _____
5. From different continents of the world   _____

Write the correct letter after each of the following groups of words to identify it. Then compare your answers with those below.

a. correctly punctuated sentence   **c. comma splice**
b. fragment   **d. run-on sentence**

6. Amanda who was recently hired as a summer intern.   _____
7. Groupon's stock price increased this year, Yelp's decreased.   _____
8. On the ground floor of our building are a café and a bookstore.   _____
9. Some employers monitor their employees' Web use others do not want to bother.   _____
10. Although many employees start at 6 a.m., which explains the empty parking lot.   _____

To be a good writer, you must be able to construct effective sentences. **Sentences** are groups of words that express complete thoughts. In this chapter you will review the basic elements of every sentence. In addition, you will learn to recognize sentence patterns and types, and you will learn how to differentiate among phrases and clauses. This knowledge will be especially helpful in punctuating sentences and avoiding common sentence faults. The Writer's Workshop following this chapter introduces proofreading marks, which are useful in revising messages.

Sentence Elements

Understanding the important role of sentence elements—including subjects, predicates, phrases, and clauses—is the first step toward writing complete and correct sentences.

Writing Complete Sentences

To be complete, sentences must have subjects and predicates, and they must make sense.

Career Tip

You may be worth an additional $5,000 or more to your employer (and to yourself) if you have writing skills, says one communications expert. Because many companies can no longer afford expensive on-site training, employees with already developed skills are much more valuable to employers.

1. c 2. b 3. a 4. c 5. a 6. b 7. c 8. a 9. d 10. b

Must Have a Subject

Every sentence must have a subject. A **simple subject** is a noun or pronoun that tells who or what the sentence is about. The **complete subject** of a sentence includes the simple subject and all of its **modifiers** (words that describe or limit). You can locate the subject in a sentence by asking, *Who or what is being discussed?*

> *Melissa* will spend a semester studying abroad. (Who is being discussed? *Melissa*)
>
> *Positions* in many companies are advertised online. (What is being discussed? *Positions*)

Must Have a Predicate

Every sentence must have a predicate. A **simple predicate** is a verb or verb phrase that tells what the subject is doing or what is being done to the subject. The **complete predicate** includes the verb or verb phrase and its modifiers, objects, and complements. Objects and complements will be explained in more detail later in this chapter.

In the complete sentences shown here, the simple subject in each sentence is underlined once. The simple predicate is underlined twice. Notice that a sentence can have more than one simple subject and more than one simple predicate.

Simple Subject	Simple Predicate
The new <u>CEO</u> of the company	<u>introduced</u> herself and <u>outlined</u> her future plans.
All <u>students</u> in the class	<u>will attend</u> the symposium.
<u>He</u> and <u>I</u>	<u>will be presenting</u> information about new benefits.
The <u>person</u> who left the comment	<u>might have been</u> a client.

Notice in the preceding examples that the verbs in the predicate may consist of one word (*introduced*) or several (*will be presenting*). In a **verb phrase** such as *will be presenting*, the **principal verb** is the final one (*presenting*). The other verbs are **helping**, or **auxiliary**, **verbs**. The most frequently used helping verbs are *am, is, are, was, were, been, have, has, had, must, ought, can, might, could, would, should, will, do, does,* and *did.*

Must Make Sense

In addition to a subject and a predicate, a group of words must possess one additional element to qualify as a sentence. The group of words must be complete and make sense. Observe that the first two groups of words that follow express complete thoughts and make sense; the third does not. In the following examples, the simple subjects are underlined once; and the simple predicates are underlined twice.

> Athletic shoe <u>makers</u> <u>convinced</u> us to buy $200 running shoes. (Subject plus predicate making sense = sentence.)
>
> <u>Anthony</u> now <u>owns</u> different athletic shoes for every sport. (Subject plus predicate making sense = sentence.)
>
> Although sports shoe <u>manufacturers</u> <u>promote</u> new versions with new features (Subject plus predicate but NOT making sense = no sentence.)

Study Tip

Many linking verbs also serve as helping verbs. Note that a verb phrase is *linking* only when the final verb is a linking verb, such as in the phrase *might have been*.

Recognizing Phrases and Clauses

Sentences are made up of phrases and clauses. Learning to distinguish phrases and clauses will help you build complete sentences, use a variety of patterns, and avoid common sentence faults in your speaking and writing.

Phrases

A group of related words without a subject and a verb is called a **phrase**. You have already been introduced to verb phrases and prepositional phrases. It is not important that you be able to identify the other kinds of phrases (infinitive, gerund, participial); however, being able to distinguish phrases from clauses is very important to a business writer.

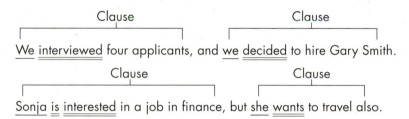

Verb phrase   Prepositional phrase   Prepositional phrase

The conference attendees *were coming* from different parts of the country.

Clauses

A group of related words including a subject and a verb is a **clause**.

| Clause | Clause |

We interviewed four applicants, and we decided to hire Gary Smith.

| Clause | Clause |

Sonja is interested in a job in finance, but she wants to travel also.

Clauses may be divided into two groups: independent and dependent. **Independent clauses** are grammatically complete. **Dependent clauses** depend for their meaning on independent clauses. Dependent clauses are often introduced by words such as *if, when, because,* and *as.*

Dependent clause   Independent clause

When employees need help, Alex solves their technology problems.

Sentence Varieties

Sentences may be divided into four groups: simple, complex, compound, and compound-complex. One important way to improve your writing is to use a variety of these kinds of sentences.

A **simple sentence**, shown in the following example, contains one independent clause (complete thought) with a subject (underlined once) and predicate (underlined twice):

Our team completed the project.

A **compound sentence** contains two complete but related thoughts. The two independent clauses may be joined by a (a) conjunction such as *and, but,* or *or*; (b) semicolon; or (c) conjunctive adverb such as *however, consequently,* and *therefore.* You will learn more about conjunctive adverbs in Chapter 9. You will also learn to use semicolons properly in Chapters 9 and 11. Compare the punctuation in these examples:

The team project was challenging, and we were happy with the results.

The team project was challenging; we were happy with the results.

The team project was challenging; however, we were happy with the results.

Trivia Tidbit

The English language has about three times as many words as any other language on Earth. English is estimated to include approximately 600,000 words. German has about 185,000; Russian, 130,000; and French, 100,000.

Study Tip

Clauses have subjects and verbs. Phrases do not. Clauses may have phrases within them.

A **complex sentence** contains an independent clause and a dependent clause (a thought that cannot stand by itself). Dependent clauses are often introduced by words such as *although*, *since*, *because*, *when*, and *if*. When dependent clauses precede independent clauses, they always are followed by a comma.

When we finished the team project, we held a team party.

A **compound-complex sentence** contains at least two independent clauses and one dependent clause. Because these sentences are usually long, use them sparingly.

Although this team project is completed, soon we will begin work on another; however, it will be less challenging.

Sentence Patterns

Another way business communicators can add variety to their writing is to use different sentence patterns. Four basic patterns express thoughts in English sentences. As a business or professional writer, you will most often use Patterns 1, 2, and 3 because readers usually want to know the subject first. For variety and emphasis, however, you can use introductory elements and inverted order in Pattern 4.

Pattern No. 1: Subject–Verb

In the most basic sentence pattern, the verb follows its subject. The sentence needs no additional words to make sense and be complete.

Subject	Verb
We	traveled.
Everyone	is surprised.
He	should have agreed.
Employees	are being informed.

Pattern No. 2: Subject–Action Verb–Object

When sentences have an object, the pattern is generally subject, action verb, and object. Objects of action verbs can be direct or indirect. A **direct object** is a noun or pronoun that answers the question *What?* or *Whom?*

Subject	Action Verb	Direct Object
Clarissa	asked	a good question. (Asked *what*?)
He and a colleague	interviewed	an expert. (Interviewed *whom*?)
The accountant	provided	accurate data. (Provided *what*?)

Pattern No. 2 may also use an **indirect object** that answers the question *To whom?, To what?, For whom?,* or *For what?* Notice that a sentence can have both an indirect object and a direct object.

Subject	Action Verb	Indirect Object	Direct Object
This provider	promises	customers	reliable service.
The salesperson	handed	her	the smartphone.
The technician	gave	the device	a check-up.

Pattern No. 3: Subject–Linking Verb–Complement

In Pattern No. 3, the subject comes before a linking verb and its complement. Recall from Chapter 1 that common linking verbs are *am, is, are, was, were, be, being*, and *been*. Other linking verbs express the senses: *feels, appears, tastes, sounds, seems, looks*. A **complement** is a noun, pronoun, or adjective that renames or describes the subject. A complement *completes* the meaning of the subject and always follows a linking verb.

Subject	Linking Verb	Complement	
The professor	was	Claudia Eckelmann.	(Noun complement)
Teri Harbacheck	will be	our team leader.	
Your supervisor	is	he.	(Pronoun complement)
The visitors	might have been	they.	
My job	is	challenging.	(Adjective complement)
My colleagues	are	friendly.	

Pattern No. 4: Inverted Order

In **inverted sentences** the verb comes before the subject. You might use inverted order for variety or emphasis in your sentences.

> Driving the company car is Kelli.

> Working hardest was the marketing team.

In questions, the verb may come before the subject or may be interrupted by the subject.

> What is his e-mail address?

> Where should the invoice be sent?

In sentences beginning with *here* or *there*, the normal word order is also inverted.

> Here are three proposals.

> There were nine employees absent today.

Punctuating Four Sentence Types

Because sentences express complete thoughts, they must include **end punctuation**. The punctuation you choose to end a sentence depends on whether the sentence is a statement, question, command, or exclamation.

Statements

A **statement** makes an assertion and ends with a period.

> Laws require truth in advertising.

> Manufacturers today must label the contents of packages.

Study Tip

Don't be tempted to punctuate statements as questions. For example, *I wonder whether he called* is a statement, not a question.

Questions

A **direct question** uses the exact words of the speaker and requires an answer. It is followed by a question mark.

How many websites <u>do</u> <u>you</u> <u>access</u> each day?

What <u>are</u> your favorite <u>sites</u>?

Commands

A **command** gives an order or makes a direct request. Commands end with periods or, occasionally, with exclamation points. Note that the subject in all commands is understood to be *you*. The subject *you* is not normally stated in the command.

<u>Lock</u> the front door. ([<u>You</u>] <u>lock</u> the front door.)

<u>Insure</u> your home against fire loss. ([<u>You</u>] <u>insure</u> your home . . .)

Exclamations

An **exclamation** shows surprise, disbelief, or strong feeling. An exclamation may or may not be expressed as a complete thought. Both subject and predicate may be implied.

What a great job <u>he</u> <u>did</u>!

Wow! <u>We</u> just <u>had</u> an earthquake!

How extraordinary [<u>that</u> <u>is</u>]!

Sentence Faults

Writing complete and grammatically correct sentences can be challenging. To be successful in your career, you must be able to write complete sentences that avoid three common faults: fragments, comma splices, and run-ons. You can eliminate these sentence faults by recognizing them and applying the revision techniques described here.

Trivia Tidbit

A *portmanteau* is created when two words are combined to form one word. Two common portmanteaus are *brunch* (*breakfast + lunch*) and *motel* (*motor + hotel*). Can you think of others?

Fragment

A **sentence fragment** is an incomplete sentence. It may be a phrase or a clause punctuated as if it were a complete sentence. Fragments are often broken off from preceding or succeeding sentences. Avoid fragments by making certain that each sentence contains a subject and a verb and makes sense by itself. You can remedy fragments by (a) joining them to complete sentences or (b) adding appropriate subjects and verbs. In the following examples, the fragments are italicized.

Fragment: *Because Zara controls every link of its supply chain.* That is why it has become one of the world's biggest clothing retailers.

Revision: Because Zara controls every link of its supply chain, it has become one of the world's biggest clothing retailers. (Join the fragment to the following complete sentence.)

Fragment: We are looking for a new wireless carrier. *One that offers unlimited minutes on a 4G network.*

Revision: We are looking for a new wireless carrier that offers unlimited minutes on a 4G network. (Join the fragment to the preceding sentence.)

Fragment:	My university offers many majors in business administration. *Such as accounting, finance, management, and marketing.*
Revision:	My university offers many majors in business administration such as accounting, finance, management, and marketing. (Join the fragment to the preceding sentence.)
Fragment:	The deadline for the project was moved up three days. *Which means that our team must work overtime.*
Revision:	The deadline for the project was moved up three days, which means that our team must work overtime. (Join the fragment to the preceding sentence.)

Comma Splice

A **comma splice** results when two sentences or independent clauses are incorrectly joined or spliced together with a comma. Remember that commas alone cannot join two sentences or independent clauses. Comma splices can usually be repaired by (a) adding a conjunction, (b) separating the thoughts into two sentences, or (c) changing the comma to a semicolon.

Comma Splice:	Groupon went public in 2011, Yelp started selling its stock soon after.
Revision:	Groupon went public in 2011, *and* Yelp started selling its stock soon after. (Add a conjunction.)
Comma Splice:	Let us help you find out what you are worth, visit us at Salary.com.
Revision:	Let us help you find out what you are worth. Visit us at Salary.com. (Separate into two sentences.)
Comma Splice:	No stock prices were available today, the market was closed for the holiday.
Revision:	No stock prices were available today; the market was closed for the holiday. (Change the comma to a semicolon.)
Comma Splice:	Many applicants responded to our advertisement, however, only one had the required certification.
Revision:	Many applicants responded to our advertisement; however, only one had the required certification. (Change the comma to a semicolon.)

Run-On Sentence

A **run-on sentence** joins two independent clauses without proper punctuation. Run-on sentences can usually be repaired by (a) separating the thoughts into two sentences, (b) adding a comma and a conjunction, or (c) adding a semicolon.

Run-On:	The work ethic in America is not dead it is deeply ingrained in most people.
Revision:	The work ethic in America is not dead. It is deeply ingrained in most people. (Separate into two sentences.)
Run-On:	Sachi thought she had gone over her credit limit she was wrong.
Revision:	Sachi thought she had gone over her credit limit, but she was wrong. (Add a comma and a conjunction.)
Run-On:	Many freelance workers take part in "coworking" this allows them to share office space and socialize with other freelancers.
Revision:	Many freelance workers take part in "coworking"; this allows them to share office space and socialize with other freelancers. (Add a semicolon.)

Career Tip

"What I know about grammar is its infinite power. To shift the structure of a sentence alters the meaning of the sentence, as definitely and inflexibly as the position of a camera alters the meaning of the subject photographed. Many people know camera angles now, but not so many know about sentences."

—Joan Didion, author of *The Year of Magical Thinking*

Courtesy of Mary Ellen Guffey

Courtesy of Carolyn M. Seefer

Dr. Guffey   Professor Seefer

Q: This sentence doesn't sound right to me, but I can't decide how to improve it: *The reason I am applying is because I enjoy editing.*

A: The problem lies in this construction: *the reason . . . is because. . . .* Only nouns or adjectives may act as complements following linking verbs. In your sentence an adverbial clause follows the linking verb and sounds awkward. One way to improve the sentence is to substitute a noun clause beginning with *that: The reason I am applying is that I enjoy editing.* An even better way to improve the sentence would be to make it a direct statement: *I am applying because I enjoy editing.*

Q: My colleague says that this sentence is correct: *Please complete this survey regarding your satisfaction at our dealership, return it in the enclosed addressed envelope.* I think something is wrong, but I'm not sure what.

A: You're right! This sentence has two independent clauses, and the writer attempted to join them with a comma. But this construction produces a comma splice. You can correct the problem by adding *and* between the clauses, starting a new sentence, or using a semicolon between the clauses.

Q: Which word is correct in this sentence? *The officer (cited, sited, sighted) me for speeding.*

A: Your sentence requires *cited*, which means "to summon" or "to quote." *Site* means "a location," as in a *construction site* or a *website*. *Sight* means "a view" or "to take aim," as in *the building was in sight*. The word *sight* also refers to "the ability to see."

Q: At the end of a letter I wrote: *Thank you for recommending me to this company.* Should I hyphenate *thank you?*

A: Do not hyphenate *thank you* when using it as a verb (*thank you for recommending me*). Do use hyphens when using *thank you* as an adjective (*I sent a thank-you note*) or as a noun (*I sent four thank-yous*). Because *thank you* is used as a verb in your sentence, do not hyphenate it. Notice that *thank you* is never written as a single word.

Q: A fellow worker insists on saying, *I could care less.* It seems to me that it should be *I couldn't care less.* Who is right?

A: You are right. The phrase *I couldn't care less* has been in the language a long time. It means, of course, "I have little concern about the matter." Recently, though, people have begun to use *I could care less* with the same meaning. Most careful listeners realize that the latter phrase says just the opposite of its intent. Although both phrases are clichés, stick with *I couldn't care less* if you want to be clear.

Q: How should I address a person who signed a letter *J. R. Henderson?* I don't know whether the person is a man or a woman, and I don't want to offend anyone.

A: When you can't determine the gender of your reader, include the entire name in the salutation and omit the personal title (*Mr., Ms.*). In your letter you should use *Dear J. R. Henderson.*

Q: My friend insists that the combination *all right* is shown in her dictionary as one word. I say that it's two words. Who's right?

A: *All right* is the only acceptable spelling. The listing *alright* is shown in many dictionaries to guide readers to the acceptable spelling, *all right.* Do not use *alright.* By the way, some people remember that *all right* is two words by associating it with *all wrong.*

Q: If I have no interest in something, am I *disinterested*?

A: No. If you lack interest, you are *uninterested.* The word *disinterested* means "unbiased" or "impartial" (*the judge was disinterested in the cases before him*).

Q: I have always spelled *alot* as one word. Is that acceptable?

A: No, this word should always be written as two words: *a lot.* In fact, the word *alot* (written as one word) does not exist. Also, don't confuse this word with the verb *allot,* which means "to assign as a share or portion" or "to distribute."

Q: I used the word *thru* in a proposal, and my boss told me to change it to *through.* What is wrong with using *thru*?

A: Some people use *thru* as a variant of *through*; however, this usage is informal and should be avoided in business writing. Your boss was correct to have you change it.

SPOT THE Blooper

Using the skills you are learning in this class, try to identify why the following items are bloopers. Consult your textbook, dictionary, or reference manual as needed. To see if you recognized the blooper, go to **www.cengagebrain.com** and use your access code to see the Spot the Blooper key.

Blooper 1: Headline in *The Washington Post*: "Woman Attacked by King Street Station."

Blooper 2: Cover of *Bloomberg BusinessWeek*: "The Kids Are Not Alright."

Blooper 3: Menu at Pizzagram Plus in Guilderland, New York: "Our food is cooked to order. We appreciate your patients."

Blooper 4: In an article in the *Statesman-Journal* [Salem, Oregon]: "Three people were arrested after an early morning robbery at a Mission Street coffee shop in a London double-decker bus."

Blooper 5: Public meeting notice in *The Newport Daily Express* [Newport, Vermont]: "Interrupters will be there to help the deaf community."

Blooper 6: Filene's Department Store ran an ad that said "One Day Sale—This Friday, Saturday, and Sunday."

Blooper 7: In an article in *Sporting News*: "Jazz musician Wayne Tisdale will make his first musical appearance since having a portion of his right leg amputated at halftime of the Sooners basketball game against Virginia Commonwealth next month."

Blooper 8: A *San Francisco Chronicle* photo caption: "Bruce Springsteen denies rumors that he and his wife, Patti Scialfa, are splitting up on his website."

Blooper 9: A wedding announcement in *The Houston Chronicle*: "Amber was escorted by her father wearing a strapless silk wedding gown designed by Marianne Lanting carrying a tropical floral bouquet." [Did you spot two bloopers?]

Blooper 10: Photo caption in the *Lodi News-Sentinel* [Lodi, California]: "Remains of buildings, including the house George Washington lived in when he was president, are seen at the sight of an archaeological dig in Philadelphia."

2 Reinforcement Exercises

A. Self-Check. Sentences. Indicate whether the following statements are true (*T*) or false (*F*).

1. The subject of a sentence indicates the person or thing being talked about. _____T_____

2. A group of words with a subject and a predicate is automatically a complete sentence. _____F_____

3. The simple subject of a sentence includes a noun or pronoun and all its modifiers. _____F_____

4. Two complete sentences incorrectly joined by a comma create a *comma splice.* _____T_____

5. You can locate the predicate in a sentence by asking who or what is being discussed. _____F_____

6. Independent clauses are grammatically complete and can stand on their own. _____T_____

7. Phrases contain subjects and verbs. _____F_____

8. A compound sentence is made up of two independent clauses. _____T_____

9. Sentences that show strong feeling are usually concluded with question marks. _____F_____

10. Sentence fragments may be repaired by joining them to complete sentences or by adding appropriate subjects and verbs. _____T_____

Check your answers below.

B. Sentence Elements. Choose the correct answers.

11. In the sentence *All employees in our firm receive health insurance and vacation time,* the simple subject is *(a) employees, (b) firm, (c) insurance, (d) time.* _____

12. In the sentence *Excellent communication skills can help you get a job,* the simple subject is *(a) communication, (b) skills, (c) you, (d) job.* _____

13. In the sentence *Some recent graduates worked as interns during the summer,* the simple subject is *(a) Some, (b) graduates, (c) interns, (d) summer.* _____

14. In the sentence *Job applicants with excellent communication skills are more likely to be hired,* the simple subject is *(a) Job, (b) applicants, (c) skills, (d) hired.* _____

15. In the sentence *First in line for a parking permit was Shaun,* the simple subject is *(a) First, (b) line, (c) permit, (d) Shaun.* _____

16. In the sentence *Dario operates a successful restaurant in San Francisco,* the simple predicate is *(a) Dario, (b) operates, (c) restaurant, (d) San Francisco.* _____

17. In the sentence *The name of the restaurant is Tommaso's,* the simple predicate is *(a) name, (b) of, (c) restaurant, (d) is.* _____

18. In the sentence *Tommaso's offers authentic Italian food,* the simple predicate is *(a) Tommaso's, (b) offers, (c) authentic, (d) food.* _____

19. In the sentence *Customers appreciate the atmosphere of the venue,* the simple predicate is *(a) Customers, (b) appreciate, (c) atmosphere, (d) venue.* _____

20. In the sentence *Dario is a dynamic entrepreneur,* the simple predicate is *(a) Dario, (b) is, (c) dynamic, (d) entrepreneur.* _____

1.T 2.F 3.F 4.T 5.F 6.T 7.F 8.T 9.F 10.T

C. Phrases and Clauses. Indicate whether the following word groups are phrases (*P*), independent clauses (*I*), or dependent clauses (*D*). (Remember that phrases do not have both subjects and verbs.) Capitalization and end punctuation have been omitted.

Example: in the fall of next year	P

21. when you prepare for your job search _____

22. Facebook and Google+ compete in the social media market _____

23. recently Twitter redesigned its website _____

24. before anyone had an opportunity to examine it carefully _____

25. during the middle of the four-year fiscal period from 2012 through 2016 _____

26. if you want to stay in touch _____

27. the merger was approved by stockholders _____

28. should have acted more professionally _____

29. because we recommend new tax regulations _____

30. is counting on a raise _____

D. Sentence Varieties. A **simple sentence** has one independent clause. A **compound sentence** has two or more independent clauses. A **complex sentence** has an independent clause and a dependent clause. Indicate whether the following sentences, all of which are punctuated correctly, are simple, compound, or complex. **Hint:** A sentence is not compound unless the words preceding and following a conjunction form independent clauses. If these groups of words could not stand alone as sentences, the group of words is not compound.

31. Susan Kunich conducted research on stock options and shared her findings with other executive board members. _____

32. Susan Kunich conducted research on stock options, and she shared her findings with other executive board members. _____

33. Management trainees are sent to all our branch offices in this country and to some of the branch offices in Asia and South America. _____

34. Fill in all answer blanks on the application, and send the completed form to the human resources director. _____

35. When you receive a response, please let me know. _____

36. In 1994 Southwest Airlines issued the industry's first e-ticket. _____

37. Before they arrive at the airport, many airline passengers now check in online for their flights. _____

38. Captain Chesley Sullenberger maintained control of his disabled US Airways plane and successfully landed it in the Hudson River. _____

39. If you have sensitive data on your mobile phone, erase or encrypt it before throwing or giving the phone away. _____

40. The most successful individuals embrace their mistakes and learn from them. _____

E. Writing Exercise. Sentence Patterns. Study the following examples. Then fill in the words necessary to complete the four sentence patterns.

Sentence Pattern No. 1: Subject–Verb

Add a verb or verb phrase to complete the sentence.

Example: The boss   called.   **Example:** The blog   was updated.

41. The soccer team   _____   **44.** Health costs   _____

42. Our office   _____   **45.** The committee   _____

43. Managers   _____   **46.** The company   _____

Sentence Pattern No. 2: Subject–Action Verb–Object

Add a noun or pronoun to complete the sentence.

Example: Accountants use   spreadsheets.

47. Daphne answered the   _____   **50.** Congress passes   _____

48. UPS delivers   _____   **51.** Stocks pay   _____

49. The employee corrected   _____   **52.** Students threw a   _____

Sentence Pattern No. 3: Subject–Linking Verb–Complement

Add a <u>noun or pronoun</u> complement to complete the sentence.

Example: The manager is   Malcolm.   **Example:** The recipient was   she.

53. The applicant was   _____   **55.** The caller was   _____

54. Chandra is the new   _____   **56.** The president is   _____

Add an <u>adjective</u> complement to complete the sentence.

Example: The salary is   reasonable.

57. My investment was   _____   **59.** Our supervisor is   _____

58. London is   _____   **60.** The report could have been   _____

Sentence Pattern No. 4: Inverted Order

Add a noun, pronoun, or verb as needed to complete the sentence.

Example: Presenting first is   Roberto.   **Example:** Across the street   sits   a café.

61. How are   _____   **64.** There _____ too many rules.

62. Where are your   _____   **65.** Here _____ the items you ordered.

63. There are five   _____   **66.** Next door to me _____ a nice family.

F. Sentence Types. From the following list, select the letter that accurately describes each of the following sentences and add appropriate end punctuation.

a. statement   c. question
b. command   d. exclamation

Example: Take appropriate steps to prevent identity theft.   b

67. Does your company offer a wellness program   _____

68. School and work holidays should always be scheduled on Mondays and Fridays _____

69. How entertaining that movie was   _____

70. Use Google to receive tens of thousands of hits in a nanosecond   _____

71. We wonder whether our new marketing campaign will be successful   _____

72. What a terrific view we have from the observatory on the tenth floor   _____

73. Do you know whether Licia Capone was offered the position   _____

74. Turn off the lights, close the windows, and lock the doors before you leave _____

75. Many college students spend a semester studying abroad   _____

76. To succeed in the job interview, research the company thoroughly   _____

G. Sentence Faults. For each of the following groups of words, write the correct letter to indicate one of the following:

a. correctly punctuated   c. comma splice
b. fragment   d. run-on sentence

Example: Because nonsmokers take fewer sick days.   b

77. Anyone doing business in another country should learn about the cultural norms in that country. _____

78. Russian children usually open gifts in private, however, Russian adults usually open gifts in front of their gift givers. _____

79. In El Salvador white flowers are not a proper gift because they are associated with funerals. _____

80. Because a large percentage of all U.S. corporate profits are now generated through international trade. _____

81. Making eye contact in America is a sign of confidence and sincerity. _____

82. Although Italians, Middle Easterners, and Latin Americans stand very close to each other when talking. _____

83. Which means that we will have to learn how to negotiate when in Turkey. _____

84. Being on time is important in North America in other countries time is less important. _____

85. Filipinos take pride in their personal appearance, they believe a person's clothing indicates social position. _____

86. In many countries people do not address each other by given names unless they are family members or old friends. _____

H. Writing Exercise. Sentence Fragments. Revise the following sentence fragments.

> **Example:** If I had planned ahead. I could have taken advantage of the sales promotion.
>
> *If I had planned ahead, I could have taken advantage of the sales promotion.*

87. Because I am looking for a position in social media management. That's why I am interested in your job posting.

_____

88. We are seeking a social media manager. Someone who has not only good communication skills but also technical expertise.

_____

_____

89. During job interviews candidates must provide details about their accomplishments. Which is why they should rehearse answers to expected questions.

_____

_____

90. Although an interviewer will typically start with general questions about your background. Be careful to respond with a brief history.

_____

_____

I. Writing Exercise. Sentence Varieties, Patterns, and Types. On a separate sheet, write complete sentences illustrating each of the following ten forms: a simple sentence, a compound sentence, a complex sentence, a sentence with a direct object, a sentence with a complement, a sentence in inverted order, a statement, a question, a command, and an exclamation. Identify each sentence.

J. FAQs About Business English Review. Choose the correct answer.

91. We visited the construction *(a) sight, (b) cite, (c) site* to perform an inspection. _____

92. I *(a) could, (b) couldn't* care less whether Clint Eastwood's latest film wins an Oscar. _____

93. Is it *(a) all right, (b) alright* if I leave work early today? _____

94. It is important to have a(n) *(a) uninterested, (b) disinterested* judge during a trial. _____

95. We would like to *(a) thank-you, (b) thank you, (c) thankyou* for your application. _____

96. Always send a *(a) thank-you, (b) thank you, (c) thankyou* note after a job interview. _____

97. Luckily the officer did not *(a) sight, (b) cite, (c) site* him for speeding. _____

98. I am completely *(a) uninterested, (b) disinterested* in reading romance novels. _____

99. The male Italian singer Andrea Bocelli was visually challenged from birth and completely lost his *(a) sight, (b) cite, (c) site* at age twelve. _____

100. She put *(a) alot, (b) allot, (c) a lot* of careful preparation into her résumé. _____

Chat About It ◀◀

Your instructor may assign any of the following topics for you to discuss in class, in an online chat room, or on an online discussion board. Some of the discussion topics may require outside research. You may also be asked to read and respond to postings made by your classmates.

Discussion Topic 1: Why is it important to write in complete sentences when communicating professionally? What does writing proper sentences communicate about you to others in the workplace?

Discussion Topic 2: Conduct Web research to find out four interesting facts about your major, program of study, or career. Write one sentence about each fact (four total sentences) using each of the four sentence patterns (Pattern No. 1, Pattern No. 2, Pattern No. 3, and Pattern No. 4). Label each sentence for clarity. Share your sentences with your classmates, and be prepared to critique your classmates' sentences.

Discussion Topic 3: What technology and social media tools do you use to communicate in writing on the job and in your personal life?

When using these tools, do you write in complete sentences? Why or why not?

Discussion Topic 4: Marilyn vos Savant, an American writer and magazine columnist, said, "When our spelling is perfect, it's invisible. But when it's flawed, it prompts strong negative associations." Do you agree? Why or why not?

Discussion Topic 5: As mentioned in this chapter, a *portmanteau* is created when two words are combined to form one word. Two common portmanteaus are *brunch* (*breakfast + lunch*) and *motel* (*motor + hotel*). Can you think of others? Do a Web search to find five interesting portmanteaus, and then share them with your classmates. Try to find words that are unique and have not yet been shared by others in your class.

Identify the sentence type of each of the following numbered items. Then compare your answers with those below.

a. simple **c. complex**
b. compound **d. compound-complex**

1. If you are going to be late for the interview, please call immediately. _____

2. Many Americans have gotten rid of their landlines and are using mobile phones at home in an effort to save money. _____

3. Leaving your mobile phone on in restaurants is rude, but some people do it accidentally. _____

4. When your application is processed, we will let you know; in the meantime, please contact your references. _____

5. Amber is on a leave of absence and plans to return to work in September. _____

Write the correct letter after each of the following numbered items. Then compare your answers with those below.

a. correctly punctuated sentence **c. comma splice**
b. fragment **d. run-on sentence**

6. My parents arrived on Wednesday my sister is expected shortly. _____

7. On the fifth floor is the Customer Service Department. _____

8. If you agree to serve on the task force. _____

9. On Monday my e-mail box is overflowing, on Friday my box is empty. _____

10. Because Justin, who is one of our best employees, was ill last week. _____

1.c 2.a 3.b 4.d 5.a 6.d 7.a 8.b 9.c 10.b

Begin your review by rereading Chapters 1–2. Then check your comprehension of those chapters by writing *T* (true) or *F* (false) in the following blanks. Compare your responses with the key at the end of the book.

1. Because of advances in technology, you can expect to be doing more communicating than ever before in today's workplace. _____

2. Technology and social media have made writing less important in today's workplace. _____

3. When you write and speak on the job, you are representing both yourself and your company. _____

4. Being able to identify parts of speech will help you punctuate sentences properly. _____

5. Every word in the English language can function as only one part of speech. _____

6. Proper nouns are capitalized. _____

7. To be complete, sentences must have subjects and predicates, and they must make sense. _____

8. A complex sentence contains two independent clauses. _____

9. The most common sentence pattern in business writing is inverted order. _____

10. The subject in all commands is understood to be *you*. _____

Read the following sentence carefully. Identify the parts of speech for the words as they are used in this sentence.

Wow! The applicant was very impressive in the interview, and we will hire him.

11. **Wow!**	a. noun	b. interjection	c. pronoun	d. adjective	_____
12. **The**	a. conjunction	b. preposition	c. adjective	d. adverb	_____
13. **applicant**	a. adjective	b. pronoun	c. interjection	d. noun	_____
14. **was**	a. adverb	b. verb	c. conjunction	d. preposition	_____
15. **very**	a. adverb	b. adjective	c. pronoun	d. interjection	_____
16. **impressive**	a. verb	b. adverb	c. adjective	d. noun	_____
17. **in**	a. preposition	b. interjection	c. adverb	d. conjunction	_____
18. **interview**	a. pronoun	b. adjective	c. verb	d. noun	_____
19. **and**	a. adjective	b. interjection	c. conjunction	d. preposition	_____
20. **we**	a. pronoun	b. noun	c. adjective	d. preposition	_____

Choose the correct answer.

21. In the sentence *Excellent communication skills are essential in today's workplace*, the simple subject is *(a) communication, (b) skills, (c) essential, (d) workplace.* _____

22. In the sentence *Here is your order*, the simple subject is *(a) Here, (b) is, (c) your, (d) order.* _____

23. In the sentence *The CEO addressed the enthusiastic crowd*, the simple predicate is *(a) CEO, (b) addressed, (c) enthusiastic, (d) crowd.* _____

24. In the sentence *I feel bad about your accident*, the complement is *(a) I, (b) feel, (c) bad, (d) accident.* _____

25. The sentence *She sent many purchase invoices* represents what sentence pattern? *(a) subject–verb, (b) subject–action verb–object, (c) subject–linking verb–complement, (d) inverted order.* _____

From the following list, select the letter to accurately describe each of the following groups of words. End punctuation has been omitted.

a. phrase **c. dependent clause**
b. independent clause

26. In the spring of last year _____

27. Although he wore sandals, white socks, and a T-shirt with a beer company's logo _____

28. Clara Nabbity volunteers regularly for her local elementary school _____

29. Should have been posting online today _____

30. When the workweek is over _____

From the following list, select the letter to accurately describe each of the following sentences.

a. simple sentence **c. complex sentence**
b. compound sentence **d. compound-complex sentence**

31. Many companies feature profit-sharing plans, but some employees are reluctant to participate. _____

32. General Motors ran three commercials during the Super Bowl; however, not one was devoted to its core brand. _____

33. Although Alan Greenspan no longer heads the Federal Reserve, he is still influential in shaping economic policy. _____

34. Because he is a student, Dongmei works part-time; however, he plans to work full-time over the summer. _____

35. Elizabeth was hired by a local retailer and will start her new job on Monday. _____

From the following list, select the letter to accurately describe each of the following groups of words.

a. complete sentence **c. comma splice**
b. fragment **d. run-on**

36. Armando hates receiving spam, he uses filters to avoid unwanted messages. _____

37. Since the founding of the company. _____

38. Leave at least one blog entry daily to keep the site fresh. _____

39. That company's products are excellent that is why we use them exclusively. _____

40. Brianna loves her job, however, she also enjoys her free time. _____

FAQs About Business English Review

Write the letter of the word or phrase that correctly completes each statement.

41. *(a) Thankyou, (b) Thank-you, (c) Thank you* for covering for me during lunch today. _____

42. Is it *(a) all right, (b) alright* to leave my computer on overnight? _____

43. In this job I learn something new *(a) everyday, (b) every day (c) every-day.* _____

44. Please arrive early at the job *(a) sight, (b) site, (c) cite* tomorrow morning. _____

45. Which of the following is an acronym? *(a) FBI, (b) Dr., (c) scuba* _____

46. A famous economist wrote the *(a) forward, (b) foreword* to the textbook. _____

47. Please send your cover and résumé to me by *(a) email, (b) e-mail, (c) E-mail.* _____

48. I know that *(a) allot, (b) alot, (c) a lot* of messages we receive are spam. _____

49. We had to go *(a) through, (b) thru, (c) threw* security before boarding our flight. _____

50. The new CEO's remarks *(a) peaked, (b) peeked, (c) piqued* the interest of employees. _____

NAME _____

Developing Proofreading Skills

As you complete a set of chapters (a unit), you will find a workshop exercise that introduces various techniques to help you improve your writing skills. This first workshop emphasizes proofreading skills. You will learn about proofreading marks, which are often used by writers to edit printed material. Although editing today is also done digitally, you are well-served to know what these basic manual symbols mean. See the inside back cover of your textbook for a more comprehensive list.

≡ Capitalize	∨ Insert apostrophe	⊙ Insert period
ℛ Delete	∧ Insert comma	/ Lowercase
∧ Insert	⩟ Insert hyphen	◡ Close up space

Example:

Proof reading marks are used by writers an editors too make corrections and revisions in printed copy they use these standard marks for clarity and consistency. If you are revising your own work youll probable use these mark only occasional. In many jobs today however you will be working in a team environment where writing tasks are shared. Thats when its important to able to aply these well known marks correctly.

Practice:

Now it's your turn! Use the proofreading marks above to edit the following e-mail message. You will insert ten proofreading marks.

> Marcus,
>
> Thank-you for letting me know about our up coming meeting. Im sure that it will be productive
>
> and the company will benefit as a result. I have alot of good ideas to share you an the others.
>
> when you have a rough draft of the agenda please send it to me by email

Proofreading Tips

- Use your computer's spell-checker. But don't rely on it totally. It can't tell the difference between *your* and *you're* and many other confusing words.

- Look for grammar and punctuation errors. As you complete this book, you will be more alert to problem areas, such as subject-verb agreement and comma placement.

- Double-check names and numbers. Compare all names and numbers with their sources because inaccuracies are not always visible. Verify the spelling of the names of individuals receiving the message. Most of us dislike when someone misspells our name.

- For long or important documents, always print a copy (preferably double-spaced), set it aside for at least a day, and then proofread when you are fresh.

Writing Application 1.1. Using Figure 1.1 as a model, write a similar introductory personal business letter to your instructor. Explain why you enrolled in this class, evaluate your present communication skills, name your major, describe the career you seek, and briefly tell about your current work (if you are employed) and your favorite activities. Give a printout of the letter to your instructor, or send it by e-mail. Your instructor may ask you to write a first draft quickly, print it, and then use proofreading marks to show corrections before preparing your final copy. If so, double-space the rough draft; single-space the final copy. Turn in both copies.

FIGURE 1.1
Personal Business Letter, Block Style

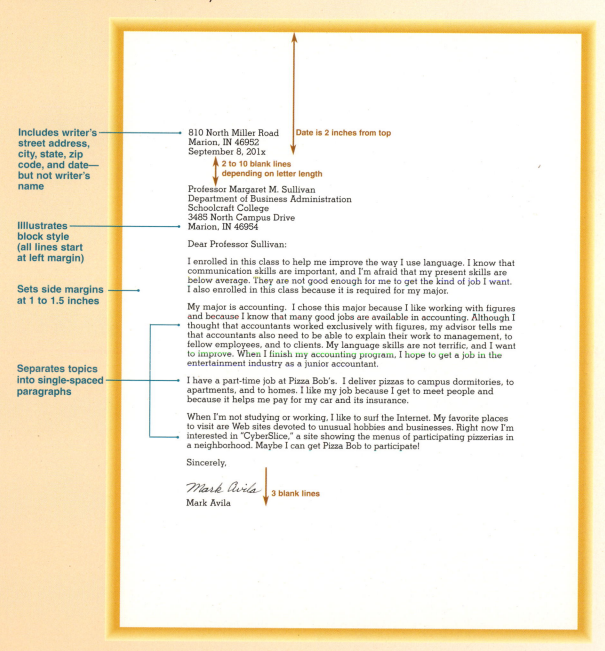

Includes writer's street address, city, state, zip code, and date— but not writer's name

Date is 2 inches from top

810 North Miller Road
Marion, IN 46952
September 8, 201x

2 to 10 blank lines depending on letter length

Professor Margaret M. Sullivan
Department of Business Administration
Schoolcraft College
3485 North Campus Drive
Marion, IN 46954

Illustrates block style (all lines start at left margin)

Dear Professor Sullivan:

I enrolled in this class to help me improve the way I use language. I know that communication skills are important, and I'm afraid that my present skills are below average. They are not good enough for me to get the kind of job I want. I also enrolled in this class because it is required for my major.

Sets side margins at 1 to 1.5 inches

My major is accounting. I chose this major because I like working with figures and because I know that many good jobs are available in accounting. Although I thought that accountants worked exclusively with figures, my advisor tells me that accountants also need to be able to explain their work to management, to fellow employees, and to clients. My language skills are not terrific, and I want to improve. When I finish my accounting program, I hope to get a job in the entertainment industry as a junior accountant.

Separates topics into single-spaced paragraphs

I have a part-time job at Pizza Bob's. I deliver pizzas to campus dormitories, to apartments, and to homes. I like my job because I get to meet people and because it helps me pay for my car and its insurance.

When I'm not studying or working, I like to surf the Internet. My favorite places to visit are Web sites devoted to unusual hobbies and businesses. Right now I'm interested in "CyberSlice," a site showing the menus of participating pizzerias in a neighborhood. Maybe I can get Pizza Bob to participate!

Sincerely,

Mark Avila   3 blank lines
Mark Avila

Knowing the Namers

3 Nouns: Plurals and Possessives

© iStockphoto.com/nyul

"Of all the arts in which the wise excel, nature's chief masterpiece is writing well."

– André Breton,
French writer (1896–1996)

Objectives

When you have completed the materials in this chapter, you will be able to do the following:

LEVEL 1

1. Distinguish between proper and common nouns.
2. Make regular and irregular nouns plural.
3. Spell correctly the plural forms of nouns ending in *y*, *o*, and *f*; proper nouns; surnames; compound nouns; and numerals, letters, degrees, and abbreviations.
4. Follow three steps in applying the apostrophe to show possession.

LEVEL 2

5. Distinguish between descriptive nouns and possessive nouns.
6. Create correct possessive forms of compound nouns, names, and abbreviations while also avoiding awkward possessives.

LEVEL 3

7. Make challenging nouns plural, including foreign nouns and special nouns.
8. Construct correct forms for possessives that involve time, money, incomplete phrases, separate and combined ownership, and academic degrees.

Circle art: © iStockphoto.com/Pavel Khorenyan

Underline any incorrectly spelled noun plurals in the following sentences. Each sentence contains one error. Write the correct spelling in the space provided. Then compare your answers with those below.

1. Three attornies started their own firm. _____

2. Our supervisor sent out two important memoes this morning. _____

3. Both of our CPAs asked for leave of absences in June. _____

4. Based on all the criterion, several diagnoses were given. _____

5. Bill Clinton was president of the United States for most of the 1990's. _____

Underline any incorrect possessive forms in the following sentences. Each sentence contains one error. Write correct version in the space provided.

6. Several companys will take part in community volunteer efforts. _____

7. All students grades will be posted by Friday. _____

8. The Perrys stock portfolio contains a variety of holdings. _____

9. Because of her training, Katherine's salary is greater than Troys. _____

10. Giving two weeks notice is standard when leaving a job. _____

As professional writers such as André Breton know, nouns play significant roles in sentences. Being able to use nouns effectively will make you a better writer. As you will recall from Chapter 1, nouns *name* persons, places, things, qualities, feelings, concepts, activities, and measures. In this chapter you will learn to spell regular and irregular plural nouns. The principal emphasis, however, will be on learning how to use the apostrophe in making nouns possessive. Learning to make nouns possessive can be difficult, but don't give up!

Beginning with this chapter, we present concepts in levels, progressing from basic, frequently used concepts at Level 1 to more complex and less frequently used concepts at Level 3. This unique separation of concepts will help you understand, retain, and apply the information taught in this book.

LEVEL 1

Common and Proper Nouns

As the "namers" in our language, **nouns** perform an important function. They often serve as sentence subjects. In addition, nouns can serve as objects of verbs and objects of prepositions. Although nouns can be grouped into many categories, this chapter focuses on two classes that are important to business writers: common and proper nouns.

Common nouns name *generalized* persons, places, and things. Because they are general, common nouns are not capitalized. **Proper nouns** name *specific* persons, places, and things. They are always capitalized.

Trivia Tidbit

The oldest word in the English language that is still used today is the common noun *town*.

1. attorneys 2. memos 3. leaves of absence 4. criteria or criterions 5. 1990s
6. companies 7. students' 8. Perrys' 9. Troy's 10. weeks'

Common Nouns		
tablet computer	organization	software
magazine	airline	professor

Proper Nouns		
iPad	Phi Beta Lambda	QuickBooks
BusinessWeek	United Airlines	Dr. Virginia Green

Making Nouns Plural: The Basics

Singular nouns name one person, place, or thing. **Plural nouns** name *two* or more.

Plurals of Regular Nouns

Most regular nouns, including both common and proper nouns, form the plural with the addition of *s*.

calendar, calendars	supervisor, supervisors	Monica, Monicas
supplier, suppliers	password, passwords	Miller, the Millers

Plural of Nouns Ending in *s, x, z, ch,* or *sh*

Nouns ending in *s, x, z, ch,* or *sh* form the plural with the addition of *es*.

business, businesses	tax, taxes	Valdez, the Valdezes
hunch, hunches	brush, brushes	BUT: quiz, quizzes

Plural of Irregular Nouns

Irregular nouns form the plural by changing the spelling of the word. Dictionaries show the plural forms of irregular nouns, but you should be familiar with the most common irregular noun plurals, such as the following:

child, children	man, men	tooth, teeth
foot, feet	mouse, mice	woman, women

Making Nouns Plurals: Beyond the Basics

You can greatly improve your ability to make nouns plural by studying the following rules and examples.

Common Nouns Ending in *y*

Common nouns ending in *y* form the plural in two ways.

a. When the letter before *y* is a vowel (*a, e, i, o, u*), form the plural by adding *s* only.

day, days	journey, journeys	attorney, attorneys
delay, delays	monkey, monkeys	valley, valleys

b. When the letter before *y* is a consonant (all letters other than vowels), form the plural by changing the *y* to *i* and adding *es*.

city, cities	library, libraries	quality, qualities
currency, currencies	army, armies	supply, supplies

Common Nouns Ending in *f* or *fe*

Nouns ending in *f* or *fe* follow no standard rules in the formation of plurals. Study the examples shown here, and use a dictionary when in doubt. When dictionaries recognize two plural forms for a word (such as *calves, calfs*), they usually show the preferred form first.

Add *s*	Change to *ves*	Both Forms Recognized
brief, briefs	half, halves	wharfs, wharves
belief, beliefs	knife, knives	scarves, scarfs

Common Nouns Ending in *o*

Nouns ending in *o* may be made plural by adding *s* or *es*.

a. When the letter before *o* is a vowel, form the plural by adding *s* only. In addition, musical terms ending in *o* always form the plural with the addition of *s* only.

kilo, kilos	ratio, ratios	tattoo, tattoos
portfolio, portfolios	studio, studios	soprano, sopranos

b. When the letter before *o* is a consonant, form the plural by adding *s* or *es*. Study the following examples and again use your dictionary whenever in doubt. When dictionaries recognize two plural forms for a word, the preferred one usually appears first.

Add *s*	Add *es*	Both Forms Recognized
photo, photos	potato, potatoes	tornadoes, tornados
logo, logos	hero, heroes	zeros, zeroes

Proper Nouns and Surnames

Most proper nouns form the plural by adding *s* or *es* depending on the ending of the noun. When making proper nouns and **surnames** (last names) plural, don't change the original spelling of the word. Simply add *s* or *es* to the end. Note that when the word *the* appears before a surname, the name is always plural (*the Obamas*).

a. Most proper nouns become plural by adding *s*.

Gardner, the Gardners	Germany, Germanys	Oropeza, the Oropezas
February, Februarys	Copeland, the Copelands	Elizabeth, Elizabeths

b. Proper nouns and surnames that end in *s, x, z, ch,* or *sh* are made plural by adding *es*.

Woods, the Woodses	Lex, Lexes	Rodriguez, the Rodriguezes
Finch, the Finches	Bush, the Bushes	Paris, Parises

Compounds

Compound words and phrases are formed by combining words into single expressions. Compounds may be written as single words, may be hyphenated, or may appear as two words.

a. When written as single words, compound nouns form the plural by appropriate changes in the final element of the word.

database, databases   bookshelf, bookshelves   photocopy, photocopies

b. When written in hyphenated or **open form** (as two or more separate words), compounds form the plural by appropriate changes in the principal (most important) noun.

brother-in-law,   board of directors,   account payable,
brothers-in-law   boards of directors   accounts payable

c. If the compound has no principal noun, the final element is made plural.

start-up,   five-year-old,   no-show,
start-ups   five-year-olds   no-shows

d. Some compound noun plurals have two recognized forms. In the following list, the preferred plural form is shown first.

attorney general: attorneys general, attorney generals

notary public: notaries public, notary publics

teaspoonful: teaspoonfuls, teaspoonsful

Numerals, Alphabet Letters, Isolated Words, and Degrees

Numerals, alphabet letters, isolated words, and degrees are made plural by adding *s*, *es*, or *'s*. The trend is to use *'s* only when necessary for clarity.

a. Numerals and uppercase letters standing alone (with the exception of *A*, *I*, *M*, and *U*) require only *s* in plural formation (no apostrophe).

W-2s and 1040s   the 1800s   three Cs of credit

b. Isolated words used as nouns are made plural with the addition of *s* or *es*, as needed for pronunciation.

ifs, ands, or buts   pros and cons   ins and outs

c. Academic degrees are made plural with the addition of *s* only (no apostrophe). Notice that degrees are written without periods or spaces. You will learn more about degrees and other abbreviations in Chapter 12.

AAs   MBAs   PhDs

d. Isolated (standing alone) lowercase letters and the capital letters *A*, *I*, *M*, and *U* are made plural with *'s* for clarity. Without the apostrophe, these letters might be confused with other words, such as the verb *is* or the abbreviation *Ms*.

A's   M's   p's and q's

Abbreviations

Abbreviations are usually made plural by adding *s* only (no apostrophe) to the singular form.

     dept., depts.   CPA, CPAs   No., Nos.

The singular and plural forms of abbreviations for units of measurement are, however, often identical. Notice that some of these abbreviations end in periods, and others do not.

     oz. (ounce or ounces)   km (kilometer or kilometers)

     ft. (foot or feet)   kW (kilowatt or kilowatts)

Some units of measurement have two plural forms.

     lb. or lbs. (pounds)   qt. or qts. (quarts)   yd. or yds. (yards)

Now complete the reinforcement exercises for Level 1.

• LEVEL 2 •

Showing Possession with Apostrophes

Possession occurs when one noun possesses another. Notice in the following phrases how possessive nouns show ownership, origin, authorship, or measurement:

     Pamela Hawkins's students (Ownership)   F. Scott Fitzgerald's novels (Authorship)

     Florida's beaches (Origin)   two years' time (Measurement)

In expressing possession, speakers and writers have a choice. They may show possession with an apostrophe, or they may use a prepositional phrase with no apostrophe:

     the students of Pamela Hawkins   the novels of F. Scott Fitzgerald

     the beaches of Florida   the time of two years

The use of a prepositional phrase to show ownership is more formal and tends to emphasize the ownership word. The use of the apostrophe to show ownership is more efficient and more natural, especially in conversation. In writing, however, deciding where to place the apostrophe can be perplexing and is probably the most common error in noun usage. Here are three simple but effective steps that will help you write possessives correctly using the apostrophe.

Three Steps in Using the Apostrophe Correctly

1. **Look for possessive construction.** Usually two nouns appear together. The first noun shows ownership of (or a special relationship to) the second noun.

     the woman['s] presentation   the children['s] teacher

     the witness['s] testimony   both investors['] portfolios

Trivia Tidbit

Many languages do not use an apostrophe to show possession. For example, in the French language, possession is shown with prepositional phrases, such as *the fine wines of the vineyard* instead of *the vineyard's fine wines.*

Study Tip

Remember that the apostrophe is used to make nouns possessive, not plural. Do not use an apostrophe to indicate more than one of something.

Study Tip

Whenever you have any doubt about using an apostrophe, always put the expression into an *of* phrase. Doing this will help you immediately recognize the ownership word and see whether it ends in an *s.*

2. **Reverse the nouns.** Use the second noun to begin a prepositional phrase to help you identify the ownership word. The object of the preposition is the ownership word.

presentation of the *woman*   teacher of the *children*

testimony of the *witness*   portfolios of both *investors*

3. **Examine the ownership word.** To determine the correct placement of the apostrophe, you must know whether the ownership word is singular or plural and whether it ends in an *s*.

   a. **If the ownership word does NOT end in *s*, add an apostrophe and *s*, whether the noun is singular or plural.**

      the *woman's* briefcase (Ownership word is singular, does not end in *s*.)

      the *children's* teacher (Ownership word is plural, does not end in *s*.)

   b. **If the ownership word DOES end in *s* and is <u>singular</u>, add an apostrophe and *s*.**

      the *witness's* testimony (Ownership word is singular, ends in *s*.)

   c. **If the ownership word DOES end in *s* and is <u>plural</u>, add an apostrophe only.**

      both *investors'* portfolios (Ownership word is plural, ends in *s*.)

Notice that an apostrophe and *s* is added to make all nouns possessive, unless the noun is plural and ends in *s*. In this case, add an apostrophe only.

In very rare situations you will make singular nouns ending in *s* possessive by adding just an apostrophe, but only when pronunciation of the extra syllable is difficult, as in the following sentence:

Arkansas' economy is strengthening. (An extra *s* would be difficult to pronounce; add an apostrophe only.)

Here is a brief summary showing the four possible scenarios of possession:

	Singular Ownership Word	**Plural Ownership Word**
Does not end in *s*	**Add an apostrophe and *s*** child's room (one child) doctor's office (one doctor)	**Add an apostrophe and *s*** children's games women's clothing
Ends in *s*	**Add an apostrophe and *s*** waitress's tips (one waitress) boss's office (one boss)	**Add an apostrophe only** waitresses' uniforms (more than one waitress) doctors' convention (more than one doctor)

Making Nouns Possessive: Beyond the Basics

The guides for possessive construction presented thus far cover the majority of possessives found in business and professional writing. However, you can greatly improve your skill in using apostrophes by understanding the following additional possessive constructions.

Descriptive Versus Possessive Nouns

When nouns provide description or identification only, the possessive form is NOT used. Writers have the most problems with descriptive nouns ending in *s*, such as *Human Resources* Department. No apostrophe is needed, just as none is necessary in *Legal* Department.

> the electronics industry (Not *electronics' industry*)
>
> United States Coast Guard (Not *United States' Coast Guard*)

Compound Nouns

Make compound nouns possessive by adding an apostrophe or *'s* to the end of the compound word.

> editor in chief's office (Singular)
>
> sisters-in-law's children (Plural, does not end in *s*.)
>
> several start-ups' financial reports (Plural, ends in *s*.)

Names of Organizations

Organizations with possessives in their names may or may not use apostrophes. Follow the style used by the individual organization. Consult the organization's stationery, directory listing, or website if you are unsure.

Organization's Legal Name Contains Apostrophe	Organization's Legal Name Does Not Contain Apostrophe
McDonald's	Starbucks
Noah's Bagels	Sears

Names of People

When making proper names possessive, follow the same rules for making other nouns possessive. Singular names are made possessive by adding an apostrophe and *s* to the end. Plural names will always end in *s*; to make the plural name possessive, simply add an apostrophe.

Singular Name	Singular Possessive	Plural Possessive
Ms. Laham	Ms. Laham's résumé	the Lahams' vacation
Mr. Horowitz	Mr. Horowitz's job	the Horowitzes' business

Notice that you can use the apostrophe and *s* to make singular names possessive, even if the name ends in an *s* or an *s* sound. This **traditional style** is used by many writers, and it is the style we recommend.

Abbreviations

Make abbreviations possessive by following the three steps in using the apostrophe described earlier.

> the FBI's most-wanted list (Singular, does not end in *s*.)
>
> CBS's fall schedule (Singular, ends in *s*.)
>
> both CEOs' signatures (Plural, ends in *s*.)
>
> Levi Strauss & Co.'s jeans (Notice that apostrophe and *s* come after the period.)

Study Tip

To identify descriptive nouns, ask whether ownership is involved. Is *Department* owned by *Human Resources*? Is *industry* possessed by *electronics*? When the answer is no, omit the apostrophe.

Trivia Tidbit

In 1977 Quebec passed Bill 101, which makes French the only official language of Quebec. Part of this rule outlaws apostrophes in company names, unless the company has an internationally registered trademark, such as *McDonald's*.

Study Tip

To avoid an awkward possessive, use an *of* phrase starting with the object owned, such as *advice of my sister's attorney.*

Awkward Possessives

When the addition of an apostrophe results in an awkward construction, show ownership by using a prepositional phrase.

Awkward: my sister's attorney's advice
Improved: advice of my sister's attorney

Now complete the reinforcement exercises for Level 2.

LEVEL 3

Challenging Noun Plurals

Selected nouns borrowed from foreign languages and other special nouns require your attention because their plural forms can be challenging and sometimes confusing.

Nouns from Foreign Languages

Nouns borrowed from other languages may retain a foreign plural. A few, however, have an Americanized plural form, shown in parentheses in the following list. Check your dictionary for the preferred form, which will be listed first.

Study Tip

Language purists contend that the word *data* can only be plural (*the data are*). However, see the FAQs About Business English for another view.

Singular	Plural
alumna (*feminine*)	alumnae (pronounced a-LUM-nee)
alumnus (*masculine*)	alumni (pronounced a-LUM-ni)
analysis	analyses
basis	bases
crisis	crises
criterion	criteria (or criterions)
curriculum	curricula (or curriculums)
datum	data
diagnosis	diagnoses
emphasis	emphases
formula	formulae (or formulas)
hypothesis	hypotheses
matrix	matrices (matrixes)
medium	media (or mediums)
memorandum	memoranda (or memorandums)
parenthesis	parentheses
phenomenon	phenomena (or phenomenons)
stimulus	stimuli

Special Nouns

Some nouns ending in *s* or *es* may normally be *only* singular or *only* plural in meaning. Other special nouns may be considered *either* singular *or* plural in meaning, whether they end in *s* or not. Notice that many of the nouns that are usually singular refer to games, fields of study, or diseases. Many of the nouns that are usually plural refer to clothing and tools. Those nouns that may be singular or plural often refer to animals or nationalities.

Usually Singular	Usually Plural	May Be Singular or Plural
billiards	clothes	Chinese
dominos	earnings	deer
economics	goods	headquarters
mathematics	pliers	offspring
measles	scissors	politics
mumps	thanks	sheep
news	trousers	statistics

Study Tip

You can practice these special nouns by using them with the singular verb *is* or the plural verb *are*. For example, *Mathematics is my favorite subject* (singular); *scissors are useful* (plural).

Challenging Possessive Constructions

A few situations related to possession can be extremely challenging, including showing possession with time and money, incomplete possessives, separate and combined ownership, and academic degrees. This section covers the rules for these challenging situations.

Showing Possession with Time and Money

Pay particular attention to the following possessive constructions, keeping in mind that time and money can show possession. The explanations and hints in parentheses will help you understand and remember these conventional expressions.

> one year's salary (the salary of one year)
>
> five years' experience (the experience of five years)
>
> a dollar's worth (the worth of one single dollar)
>
> ten dollars' worth (the worth of ten dollars)
>
> your money's worth (the worth of your money)
>
> today's weather (the weather of today)
>
> tomorrow's schedule (the schedule of tomorrow)

Incomplete Possessives

When the second noun in a possessive noun construction is unstated, the first noun is nevertheless treated as a possessive. It can help to think about what implied noun is being possessed. The implied noun is shown in brackets in these examples.

> I need to run by the attorney's [office] on the way home to sign the contract.
>
> The team members will meet at Patrick's [home] after the game.

This year's sales are higher than last year's [sales].

Her test scores are higher than other students' [test scores].

Separate or Combined Ownership

When two nouns express **separate ownership**, make both nouns possessive. When two nouns express **combined ownership** (both nouns own an item jointly or together), make only the *second* noun possessive.

Study Tip

Look at the object owned (*rights, business*). If that object is singular, ownership is usually combined.

Separate Ownership

Both landlords' and tenants' rights will be considered during our talks.

Michelle's and Sam's cell phones both rang at the same time.

Combined Ownership

The husband and wife's business is thriving. (The husband and wife own one business.)

Michelle and Sam's apartment is near many restaurants and cafés. (Michelle and Sam live in the same apartment.)

Academic Degrees

When academic degrees are written in a generic sense, they should be written with possessive apostrophes. The apostrophe is necessary even if the word *degree* is implied. You will learn more about academic degrees, including when to capitalize them, in future chapters.

She earned her *associate's* (not *associate*) degree before transferring to a four-year university.

A *bachelor's* (not *bachelor*) degree can open many doors.

Jeff earned his *master's* before taking the certification exam.

But, Earning his *doctoral* degree was the proudest moment of his life. (No apostrophe)

Now complete the reinforcement exercises for Level 3.

Q: I just had an argument with a contractor who is painting our home, including a sign that says *The Burtons*. He wants to make it *The Burton's*. Should I listen to the contractor?

A: Absolutely not! The plurals of nouns and names NEVER require apostrophes. All sign makers should be required to take a course in business English.

Q: One member of our staff consistently corrects our use of the word *data*. He says the word is plural. Is it never singular?

A: The word *data* is plural; the singular form is *datum*. Through frequent usage, however, *data* has recently become a collective noun. Collective nouns may be singular or plural depending on whether they are considered as one unit or as separate units. Therefore, *data* can be considered either singular or plural, depending on how it is used. For example, *These data are much different from those findings* (plural). Or, *This data is conclusive* (singular). It should be noted, however, that veteran copy editors almost always consider data to be plural.

Q: How do I type the names *Macy★s* and *Wal★Mart*—when the stores actually use stars instead of apostrophes? I don't have a star on my keyboard. What if a company writes its name in lowercase, such as *eBay*, and that company name comes at the beginning of a sentence?

A: Some companies (and individuals) seek distinction by displaying their names in lowercase or by including atypical symbols. You are under no obligation to reproduce such idiosyncrasies. We agree with outspoken copy editor Bill Walsh, who considers such usage exhibitionism and illiterate. Use only appropriate punctuation. Change the stars to appropriate punctuation (*Macy's, Wal-Mart*). Capitalize organization names exactly as the legal name is written. However, do capitalize them when they begin sentences.

Q: In preparing an announcement for sales reps, our sales manager wrote about a *two months' training period*. I wanted to make it *a two-month training period*. Who is right?

A: Actually, you both are correct! The expression *two months' training period* is possessive (training period of two months). If the expression is *two-month training period* without an *s* on *month*, the expression is descriptive and no apostrophe is required. Only a slight difference in wording distinguishes a descriptive phrase from a possessive phrase. Sometimes it is hard to tell them apart.

Q: My boss wrote a report with this sentence: *Saleswise, our staff is excellent.* Should I change it?

A: Never change wording without checking with the author. You might point out, however, that the practice of attaching *-wise* to nouns is frowned on by many language experts. Such combinations as *budgetwise, taxwise,* and *productionwise* are considered commercial jargon. Suggest this revision: *On the basis of sales, our staff is excellent.*

Circle art: © iStockphoto.com/Pavel Khorenyan

Q: I work for the Supreme Court in Arizona, and I have a problem with the following sentence involving the restaurant chain Denny's: *The plaintiff was in fact fired ostensibly for violating Denny's alcoholic beverage service policy.* How do I make possessive a proper name that is already possessive?

A: As you suspected, you can't add another apostrophe. In the interests of clarity, we would consider the name descriptive, thus avoiding an additional *'s*. You would write *Denny's alcoholic beverage service policy.* By the same reasoning, you would not add another apostrophe to anything possessed by *McDonald's*.

Q: Why does *Martha's Vineyard* have an apostrophe whereas *Harpers Ferry* doesn't?

A: The federal government maintains a Board on Geographic Names in the United States. This board has a policy that "geographic names in the U.S. should not show ownership of a feature." British maps, says board secretary Roger Payne, are "littered with apostrophes." To avoid such clutter, the board allows no possessive on any federal maps or documents, unless previously dispensated. Only four geographic names have dispensations: *Martha's Vineyard* (Massachusetts), *Carlos Elmer's Joshua View* (Arizona), *Ike's Point* (New Jersey), and *John E.'s Pond* (Rhode Island).

Q: Is there an apostrophe in *Veterans Day*, and if so, where does it go?

A: *Veterans Day* has no apostrophe, but *New Year's Day* does have one. Other holidays that are spelled with an apostrophe are *Valentine's Day, St. Patrick's Day, Mother's Day, Father's Day, President's Day,* and *April Fool's Day.* In addition, if you are referring to one season, you would write *Season's Greetings.*

Q: I just received a Christmas card in the mail that was engraved with this greeting: *The Lopezes' send their holiday greeting's!* It looks wrong to me, but I can't figure out what the error is. Can you help?

A: Wow! This engraved holiday greeting actually has two errors. It should have been engraved like this: *The Lopezes send their holiday greetings.* Both *Lopezes* and *greetings* are plural nouns; they are not possessive. The apostrophe is never used to make nouns plural. Your friends should get their money back from the printers!

Q: Can you tell me which word I should use in this sentence? *A [stationary/stationery] wall will be installed.*

A: In your sentence use *stationary*, which means "not moving" or "permanent" (*she exercises on a stationary bicycle*). *Stationery* means "writing paper" (*his stationery has his address printed on it*). You might be able to remember the word *stationery* by associating *envelopes* with the *e* in *stationery*.

SPOT THE Blooper

Using the skills you are learning in this class, try to identify why the following items are bloopers. Consult your textbook, dictionary, or reference manual as needed. To see if you recognized the blooper, go to **www.cengagebrain.com** and use your access code to see the Spot the Blooper key.

Blooper 1: Official name of a pediatric dentist office in Hyannis, Massachusetts: Kid's Smiles, Inc.

Blooper 2: From the *Democrat and Chronicle* [Rochester, New York]: "Foremans and supervisors will receive training."

Blooper 3: In an advertisement for Accelerated Schools in Colorado's *Rocky Mountain News*: "STUDENT'S DON'T HAVE TO FAIL."

Blooper 4: The *San Jose Mercury News* printed a photo of a plaque located on the Stanford University campus that reads "The Stanford's purchased 'the farm' from the Gordon's in 1876." [Did you spot two bloopers?]

Blooper 5: An article in *The Press* [Atlantic City, New Jersey] said that *American Idol's* Kelli Clarkson "remains the most successful alumnus by far."

Blooper 6: A headline in the *San Francisco Chronicle*: "Numbers put face on a phenomena."

Blooper 7: Father's Day sign at a chocolate shop in San Francisco's North Beach neighborhood: "Dad's Love Candy."

Blooper 8: From the cover of *Florida Today's TV Week*: "Tune in to see who will win this years [Indianapolis 500] trophy."

Blooper 9: From an article in *The Telegraph* [Nashua, New Hampshire]: "According to the state police statement, Platte lived in the basement of his parent's ranch-style home, while his parent's Lawrence and Linda Platte lived on the second floor." [Can you spot two errors?]

Blooper 10: Announcement pasted on top of a Domino's pizza box: "We accept all competitors coupons."

3 Reinforcement Exercises

LEVEL 1

A. Self-Check. Plural Nouns. Choose the correct answer.

Example: Computer *(a) virus, (b) viruses, (c) virus's* can cause a network to crash.   **b**

1. Our state legislators passed several new *(a) tax's, (b) taxs, (c) taxes* to meet the budget deficit.   _____

2. The economic downturn has affected many small *(a) business, (b) business's, (c) businesses.*   _____

3. The condition will not change unless Congress passes a law with *(a) tooths, (b) teeth, (c) teeths* in it.   _____

4. Two *(a) attornies, (b) attorneys, (c) attorney's, (d) attorneys'* were disbarred for unethical behavior.   _____

5. We need to start collecting all outstanding *(a) accounts payable, (b) account payables, (c) account's payables*   _____

6. John Grant filed his two *(a) brieves, (b) brief's, (c) briefs* before the 5 p.m. deadline.   _____

7. Small businesses can afford few administrative *(a) luxurys, (b) luxuries, (c) luxury's.*   _____

8. The *(a) Simmonses, (b) Simmons's, (c) Simmons'* bought a vacation home in Maine.   _____

9. Students had to show their *(a) IDs, (b) ID's* before they were admitted.   _____

10. Four everyday *(a) hero's, (b) heros, (c) heroes* were recognized at the community event.   _____

Check your answers below.

B. Plural Nouns. Choose the correct answer.

Example: The advertising agency submitted several *(a) sketches, (b) sketch's (c) sketchs* of the design.   **a**

11. Many *(a) patches, (b) patch's, (c) patchs* were needed to update the software.   _____

12. The tennis match turned out to be a battle of the *(a) sex's, (b) sexes.*   _____

13. After several *(a) brushes, (b) brush's* with success, Charlie Shi finally reached his goal.   _____

14. Business students were required to take three *(a) quiz's, (b) quizzes, (c) quizes* this morning.   _____

15. Courtney Redis purchased two different *(a) lens, (b) lenses, (c) len's, (d) lens's* for her new camera.   _____

16. People who run their businesses out of coffee shops and *(a) cafés, (b) café's* are called *laptop nomads.*   _____

17. Three *(a) mices, (b) mouses, (c) mice* just ran right through the kitchen!   _____

1.c 2.c 3.b 4.b 5.a 6.c 7.b 8.a 9.a 10.c

18. Several (a) *CEO's,* (b) *CEOs* will run as a team in a 5K race for charity. _____

19. Many (a) *companys,* (b) *company's,* (c) *companies* believe strongly in the importance of being socially responsible. _____

20. We compared the liquidity (a) *ratios,* (b) *ratio's,* (c) *ratioes* of the two companies. _____

21. President Krista Johns wants to hire a manager with contemporary (a) *believes,* (b) *beliefs,* (c) *belief's.* _____

22. Reunification of the two (a) *Germanies,* (b) *Germany's,* (c) *Germanys* occurred in 1990. _____

23. Most (a) *MBA's,* (b) *MBAs* have taken classes in business ethics. _____

24. Do the (a) *Wolf's,* (b) *Wolfs* subscribe to *BusinessWeek*? _____

25. Congress established the Small Business Administration in the (a) *1950s,* (b) *1950's.* _____

26. Computer users must distinguish between zeros and (a) *O's,* (b) *Os.* _____

27. The two (a) *boards of directors,* (b) *boards of director,* (c) *board of directors* voted to begin merger negotiations. _____

28. President Lincoln had four (a) *brother-in-laws,* (b) *brothers-in-laws,* (c) *brothers-in-law* serving in the Confederate Army. _____

29. We didn't expect so many (a) *no-show's,* (b) *no-shows.* _____

30. How many (a) *sopranos,* (b) *sopranoes,* (c) *soprano's* will sing in Friday night's performance? _____

C. Writing Exercise. Plural Nouns. Write plural forms for the nouns listed. Use your dictionary as needed.

31. ATM _____   **41.** blitz _____

32. louse _____   **42.** dept. _____

33. watch _____   **43.** goose _____

34. No. _____   **44.** bias _____

35. franchise _____   **45.** A _____

36. quota _____   **46.** C _____

37. subsidiary _____   **47.** governor-elect _____

38. foot _____   **48.** woman _____

39. balance of trade _____   **49.** logo _____

40. Sanchez _____   **50.** ox _____

D. Writing Exercise. Plural Nouns. Write complete sentences using the plural form of the nouns shown in parentheses.

51. (business) _____

52. (child) _____

53. (Alvarez) _____

54. (standby) _____

55. (do and don't) _____

56. (portfolio) _____

57. (hero) _____

58. (witness) _____

59. (attorney) _____

60. (belief) _____

LEVEL 2

A. Self-Check. Possessive Nouns. Choose the correct answer.

Example: The *(a) FBI's, (b) FBIs, (c) FBIs'* website features photos of wanted criminals.   **a** _____

61. The *(a) United States, (b) United State's, (c) United States'* Marine Corps recruits on college campuses. _____

62. The *(a) Morris, (b) Morris's, (c) Morrises'* vacation home provides a beautiful place to relax. _____

63. Warren *(a) Buffetts, (b) Buffett's* wealth makes him one of America's richest citizens. _____

64. Author Jane *(a) Austen's, (b) Austens* birthplace is located in Hampshire, England. _____

65. The first *(a) runner's-up, (b) runner-ups', (c) runner-up's* prize of $500 went to Shannon Daly. _____

66. The *(a) SECs', (b) SEC's, (c) SECs* ruling in the securities fraud case is expected today. _____

67. Many *(a) company's, (b) companies', (c) companies* employees receive full pay on legal holidays. _____

68. Her *(a) brother's-in-laws, (b) brother-in-laws, (c) brother-in-law's* position was eliminated. _____

69. Where can I find the *(a) editor in chiefs, (b) editor in chief's, (c) editor in chieves* office? _____

70. Our Human *(a) Resources, (b) Resources', (c) Resource's* Department has several job listings. _____

Check your answers below.

B. Writing Exercise. Possessive Nouns. Using apostrophes, change the following prepositional phrases to possessive constructions. Ownership words are italicized.

Example: requirements of the *position*   **the position's requirements** _____

71. signatures of the three *CEOs* _____

72. presentations of the *students* _____

73. college application of the *student* _____

74. luncheon of the *sisters-in-law* _____

75. addresses of *customers* _____

76. website of the *company* _____

61. a   62. c   63. b   64. a   65. c   66. b   67. b   68. c   69. b   70. a

77. merger of the two *companies* _____

78. prices of *competitors* _____

79. offices of several *doctors* _____

80. meeting of *stockholders* _____

C. Possessive Nouns.
Underline the errors in possessive construction in the following sentences. Each sentence contains one error. Write the correct form in the space provided.

Example: Several <u>students</u> scholarship applications were successful.　　　　　**students'**

81. All citizens votes have been counted, and the measure passed. _____

82. My bosses office is always such a mess! _____

83. One witness' testimony convinced the jury to convict. _____

84. Passenger's concerns about cell phone use on planes are justified. _____

85. Some managers are cutting expenses by requiring employee's, customers, and vendors to communicate by e-mail. _____

86. Several organizations websites were recognized for being innovative. _____

87. The profits of all company's are being affected by developing technologies and worldwide competition. _____

88. Many company's products and services are marketed globally. _____

89. Communication skills' are most frequently mentioned by recruiters. _____

90. Success depends on an individuals ability to adapt to change. _____

91. America's first telephone directory was distributed to 50 subscriber's in New Haven, Connecticut, in 1878. _____

92. The United States' Treasury promotes economic growth and stability. _____

93. Web graphic's must be designed with the audience's needs in mind. _____

94. On the second floor is the chief of staffs office. _____

95. The SECs goal is to simplify the language used in financial statements. _____

96. Airline deregulation significantly affected the avionics' industry. _____

97. CBSs fall schedule has not been finalized yet. _____

98. You can download many new's releases promoting software programs. _____

99. Chuck Norris' films are enjoyed by fans of the martial arts. _____

100. Apple Incs. products have revolutionized the way we listen to music. _____

D. Writing Exercise. Possessive Nouns.
Rewrite these sentences to remedy awkward or incorrect possessives.

Example: His company's accountant's suggestions are wise.
　　　　　The suggestions of his company's accountant are wise.
　　　　　(**Hint:** Start your sentence with the word that is owned.)

101. My sister's lawyer's hourly fee is high.

_____

_____

102. Michael Phelps's mother's support was instrumental to the Olympic athlete's success.

_____

_____

103. Stephenie Meyer's latest book's success has been overwhelming.

_____

_____

104. The engineer's assistant's computer held all the necessary equations.

_____

_____

105. My supervisor's friend's motor home is always parked in the company lot.

_____

_____

LEVEL 3

A. Self-Check. Plural and Possessive Nouns. Choose the correct answer.

106. I'd like to give *(a) thanks, (b) thank's* to all of you for your hard work. _____

107. Black holes are but one of the many *(a) phenomenon, (b) phenomena* of astronomy. _____

108. Numerous *(a) crises, (b) crisis, (c) crisises* within education will only be worsened by budget cuts. _____

109. We contacted all *(a) alumnus, (b) alumni* of Clemson University about the reunion. _____

110. Let's plan to meet at *(a) Sophias, (b) Sophia's* before driving to the college. _____

111. *(a) Microsoft's and Mozilla's, (b) Microsoft and Mozilla's* browsers support the latest animation technology. _____

112. *(a) Lisa's and Greg's, (b) Lisa and Greg's* daughter is applying to medical schools. _____

113. This year's new home sales are higher than last *(a) year, (b) year's, (c) years'*. _____

114. Eve plans to earn her *(a) master, (b) masters', (c) master's* degree in engineering. _____

115. George has three *(a) year's, (b) years', (c) years* experience in broadcasting. _____

Check your answers below.

B. Plural Nouns. Select the correct answer. Use your dictionary as needed.

116. Substantial *(a) datum, (b) data, (c) datas* show that online users worry about privacy. _____

117. The private girls' school will honor its illustrious *(a) alumna, (b) alumni, (c) alumnae.* _____

118. Several *(a) species, (b) specie's, (c) specie* are on the verge of extinction. _____

119. Ray Gilmore's proposal contains six *(a) appendixes, (b) appendix.* _____

120. Page references are shown in *(a) parenthesis, (b) parentheses.* _____

121. Susan Lamb requested information about two related *(a) curricula, (b) curriculum.* _____

122. Many of Galileo's *(a) hypothesises, (b) hypothesis, (c) hypotheses* were rejected by his peers. _____

106. a 107. b 108. a 109. b 110. b 111. a 112. b 113. b 114. c 115. b

123. Use *(a) ellipses, (b) ellipsis, (c) ellipsises* to show omitted words in a passage. _____

124. The mathematician studied many *(a) matrix, (b) matrix's, (c) matrices.* _____

125. Dr. Lisa Hudson's master's and doctoral *(a) theses, (b) thesis, (c) thesises* are both available online. _____

C. Possessive Nouns. Underline the errors in possessive construction in the following sentences. Each sentence contains one error. Write the correct form in the space provided.

126. Nick's and Kelly's new home is located in Pacific Heights. _____

127. This company's customer service is superior to that companys. _____

128. At least a dozen buyers and sellers' finances were scrutinized. _____

129. We were all invited to the party at the Thomas. _____

130. Despite a weeks delay, the package finally arrived. _____

131. It took William two years to earn his masters degree. _____

132. A dollars worth of gas won't get you very far. _____

133. After seven years time, the property reverts to state ownership. _____

134. I can find other peoples errors but not my own. _____

135. Attorney's salaries have increased significantly over the last decade. _____

D. Review of Plural and Possessive Nouns. Underline the errors in plural or possessive construction in the following sentences. Each sentence contains one error. Write the correct form in the space provided.

136. The Japanese are renowned for their advances in electronic's and other technologies. _____

137. Many banks have installed multilingual ATM's to serve their customers. _____

138. Her goal is to earn all As this semester. _____

139. The huge number of inquirys resulting from the news announcement overwhelmed their two websites. _____

140. Although many stimulus are being studied, scientists have not yet determined an exact cause of the bacterial mysteries. _____

141. The Ruiz's named three beneficiaries in their insurance policies. _____

142. Despite the new flexible hours for Mondays through Thursdays, all employee's must put in a full workday on Fridays. _____

143. The Williamses discussed all the pro's and cons of the transaction before signing the contract. _____

144. Many companies' investment portfolioes lost millions last year. _____

145. Dylan and his two brother-in-laws opened a business together. _____

146. Brooke's goal is to earn her bachelors degree from Columbia University in New York City. _____

147. We were surprised when Allison married her bosses son. _____

148. The butler stood at the door and called the guests names as they arrived. _____

149. At the CPAs annual conference, we interviewed the graduates of many colleges and universities. _____

150. Ryan decided to follow his father-in-law advice in seeking a job in the aerospace industry. _____

151. Barbara always wants to put her two cents worth in. _____

152. Many employee's are upset about the new policy. _____

153. One waitresses service was outstanding. _____

154. Charlie and Tom's bikes were stolen from their garages last night. _____

E. Writing Exercise. Noun Possessives. Compose original sentences illustrating the possessive forms of the words shown in parentheses.

Example: (two years)   <u>You must have two years' experience to apply for the job.</u>

155. (Leonard) _____

156. (contractor) _____

157. (Milli and Robert) _____

158. (Congress) _____

159. (customers) _____

160. (mother-in-law) _____

F. FAQs About Business English Review. In the space provided, write the correct answer choice.

161. She rides her *(a) stationery, (b) stationary* bike every morning before work. _____

162. Many artists' works are featured on the free e-mail *(a) stationery, (b) stationary* offered with Outlook Express. _____

163. The sign on their Lake Tahoe cabin should say *(a) The Barrett's, (b) The Barretts, (c) The Barretts'*. _____

164. The *(a) datum, (b) datums, (c) data* suggest that red wine can reduce cholesterol levels. _____

165. Which of the following represents better expression?

  a. On the basis of taxes, we are in a good position this year.

  b. Taxwise, we are in a good position this year. _____

166. Which of the following is the correct greeting to print on a holiday card?

  a. Happy Holiday's from the Smith's!

  b. Happy Holidays from the Smith's!

  c. Happy Holidays from the Smiths! _____

167. She plans to apply for a job at *(a) Macy's, (b) Macy*s, (c) Macys*. _____

168. On *(a) Veterans, (b) Veteran's, (c) Veterans'* Day we honor those who served our country. _____

169. The office will be closed on *(a) St. Patricks', (b) St. Patrick's, (c) St. Patricks* Day. _____

170. At all of its restaurants, *(a) Denny's, (b) Dennys', (c) Dennys's* employees are trained to give good service. _____

Chat About It ◀◀

Your instructor may assign any of the following topics for you to discuss in class, in an online chat room, or on an online discussion board. Some of the discussion topics may require outside research. You may also be asked to read and respond to postings made by your classmates.

Discussion Topic 1: Employers look for various traits in job applicants, including *reliability*, *initiative*, and *flexibility*. These words are all nouns that name qualities. Assume you had to tell an employer about your five greatest strengths. What strengths would you name and why? Be sure to express these strengths as nouns.

Discussion Topic 2: Many English nouns are borrowed from other languages, including those listed in Level 3 of this chapter. Select five nouns that do not appear on this list and share the following information with your classmates: the singular form, the plural form (traditional and Americanized forms, if applicable), and the language from which the noun was borrowed.

Discussion Topic 3: Practice making your own name possessive. Write four complete sentences showing your name in these formats: singular, singular possessive, plural, plural possessive. (Remember that you must add the word *the* before your last name to make it plural.)

Share your sentences with your classmates. Be prepared to give them feedback on their sentences.

Discussion Topic 4: The apostrophe is one of the most frequently misused punctuation marks. Find an example of a misused apostrophe in a newspaper or magazine article, on a sign in your neighborhood, or online. Share the error with your classmates. Be sure to explain why the apostrophe has been misused, and provide a corrected version.

Discussion Topic 5: Some individuals believe that the apostrophe should be abolished from the English language. Do a Google search using the search term *abolish apostrophe* to locate various websites and blog entries devoted to this topic. Review several sites and then decide how you feel about this issue. Should we abolish the apostrophe in English? Why or why not? Share your thoughts with your classmates, and be sure to defend your position.

Posttest

Underline any incorrectly spelled nouns. Each sentence contains one error. Write the correct form. Then compare your answers with those below.

1. The Valdez's vacation each year in Cabo San Lucas. _____
2. In the early 2000s many companys were seeking employees with MBAs. _____
3. After several business crises, we hired two attornies. _____
4. How many sister-in-laws does he have? _____
5. We purchased several DVD's for training purposes. _____

Underline any incorrect possessive forms. Write correct versions. Then compare your answers with those below.

6. A major vote will take place at the stockholders meeting. _____
7. Our Human Resource's Department is on the fifth floor. _____
8. This month's sales figures were better than last month. _____
9. In just two years time, your profits will likely double. _____
10. She will earn her bachelors degree next spring. _____

1. Valdezes 2. companies 3. attorneys 4. sisters-in-law 5. DVDs 6. stockholders' 7. Resources 8. last month's 9. years' 10. bachelor's

Pronouns 4

When something has been read without effort, great effort has gone into its writing.

—Enrique Jardiel Poncela, Spanish playwright and novelist

Circle art: © iStockphoto.com/Pavel Khorenyan

© iStockphoto.com/Su Min-Hsuan

Objectives

When you have completed the materials in this chapter, you will be able to do the following:

LEVEL 1
1. Use subjective, objective, and possessive pronouns correctly.
2. Choose the correct pronoun in compound constructions, comparatives, appositives, reflexives, and following linking verbs.

LEVEL 2
3. Make pronoun references clear, and ensure that personal pronouns agree with their antecedents in number and gender.
4. Make personal pronouns agree with subjects joined by *or* or *nor,* indefinite pronouns, collective nouns, company and organization names, and the adjectives *each* and *every.*

LEVEL 3
5. Understand the functions of *who, whom, whoever,* and *whomever,* and follow a five-step procedure in using these words correctly.
6. Use the possessive pronoun *whose* and the contraction *who's* correctly.

Choose the correct pronoun. Then compare your answers with those below.

1. Shauna and (*I, me, myself*) redesigned the company's Facebook page. _____

2. Send the signed contract to Robert or (*she, her*) by November 30. _____

3. (*Us, We*) employees will vote whether to approve the contract. _____

4. No one in the office worked harder on the project than (*her, she*). _____

5. Are you sure it was (*she, her*) who called me this morning? _____

6. A patient must show (*his, their, his or her*) proof of insurance upon arrival. _____

7. The office manager, along with her staff, submitted (*her, their*) time sheet. _____

8. The committee submitted (*its, their*) recommendation to the board. _____

9. (*Who, Whom*) did you select for the management trainee position? _____

10. Do you know (*whose, who's*) briefcase this is? _____

One area of writing that will require great effort is deciding how to use pronouns properly. As you will remember from Chapter 1, **pronouns** are words that substitute for nouns and other pronouns. They enable us to communicate efficiently without awkward repetition. But they can also get us into trouble if the nouns to which they refer—their **antecedents**—are unclear. This chapter shows you how to use pronouns correctly so that you can avoid pronoun–antecedent and other common pronoun problems.

Grammatically, pronouns may be divided into seven types: personal, relative, interrogative, demonstrative, indefinite, reflexive, and reciprocal. Rather than consider all seven pronoun types, this textbook will be concerned only with those pronouns that cause difficulty in use.

LEVEL 1

Guidelines for Using Personal Pronouns

Personal pronouns indicate the person speaking, the person spoken to, or the person or object spoken of. Notice in the following table that personal pronouns change their form (or **case**) depending on who is speaking (called the **person**), how many are speaking (the **number**), and the sex (or **gender**) of the speaker. For example, the third-person feminine singular objective case is

1. I 2. her 3. We 4. she 5. she 6. his or her 7. her 8. its 9. Whom 10. whose

her. Most personal pronoun errors by speakers and writers involve faulty usage of case forms. Study this table to avoid errors in personal pronoun use.

	Subjective Case*		Objective Case		Possessive Case	
	Sing.	Plural	Sing.	Plural	Sing.	Plural
First Person (person speaking)	I	we	me	us	my mine	our ours
Second Person (person spoken to)	you	you	you	you	your yours	your yours
Third Person (person or thing spoken of)	he she it	they	him her it	them	his, her hers, its	their theirs

*Some authorities prefer the term *nominative case.*

Basic Use of the Subjective Case

Subjective-case pronouns are used primarily as the subjects of verbs. Every verb or verb phrase, regardless of its position in a sentence, has at least one subject. If that subject is a pronoun, it must be in the subjective case.

> *They* are going to Barbados for their honeymoon.

> *He* wonders whether *they* will have wireless Internet access at their hotel.

Basic Use of the Objective Case

Objective-case pronouns most commonly are used as objects of verbs or objects of prepositions.

Object of a Verb

As you learned in Chapter 2, objects of action verbs can be direct or indirect. A **direct object** is a noun or pronoun that answers the question *What?* or *Whom?* An **indirect object** is a noun or pronoun that answers the question *To whom?*, *To what?*, *For whom?*, or *For what?* When pronouns act as direct or indirect objects of verbs, they must be in the objective case.

> Please ask *her* when the marketing plan will be delivered. (Direct object)

> Can you meet *them* at the airport at 10 a.m.? (Direct object)

> The attorney sent *them* signed copies of the contract. (Indirect object)

> The network supervisor issued *her* a new password. (Indirect object)

Object of a Preposition

As you learned in Chapter 1, a preposition is a connecting word that joins a noun or pronoun to the sentence. It appears in a position *before* its object. The **object of a preposition** is a noun or pronoun. The objective case is used for pronouns that are objects of prepositions.

> Our CEO has an important announcement for *us.* (Object of the preposition *for*)

> The photographer took a professional photo of *her.* (Object of the preposition *of*)

> Every employee except Weston and *her* [not *she*] will work overtime this weekend. (Object of the preposition *except*)

When the words *except, between, but,* and *like* are used as prepositions, errors in pronoun case are likely to occur. To avoid such errors, isolate the prepositional phrase, and then use an objective-case pronoun as the object of the preposition (*Every employee [but Weston and her] will work overtime this weekend*).

Basic Use of the Possessive Case

Possessive pronouns show ownership. Unlike possessive nouns, possessive pronouns never have apostrophes. Study these five common possessive pronouns: *hers, yours, ours, theirs, its.* Notice the absence of apostrophes.

Do not confuse possessive pronouns with contractions. **Contractions** are shortened (contracted) forms of subjects and verbs, such as *it's* (for *it is* or *it has*), *there's* (for *there is*), *they're* (for *they are*), and *you're* (for *you are*). In these examples the apostrophes indicate omitted letters.

Possessive Pronouns	Contractions
These reserved seats are *theirs.*	*There's* one more project to complete.
To reset your device, press *its* control button.	*It's* easy to operate a smartphone.
Is this credit card *yours*?	*You're* the next speaker.
Hers was the best presentation. (Never *Her's*)	
That vacation home is *ours.* (Never *our's*)	

As you learned in Chapter 2, words such as *my, our, your, his, her, its,* and *their* function as adjectives when they describe nouns (*my career, our retreat, your address, his car, her condo, its trunk, their vacation*). This concept will be further explained in Chapter 7.

Challenges in Using Personal Pronouns

Choosing the correct personal pronouns in compound constructions, comparatives, appositives, reflexives, and following linking verbs requires a good understanding of the following guidelines.

Compound Subjects and Objects

When a pronoun appears in combination with a noun or another pronoun, choosing the proper pronoun case (subjective or objective) can be challenging. Use this technique to help you choose the correct pronoun case: Ignore the extra noun or pronoun and its related conjunction (usually *and*), and consider separately the pronoun in question to determine what the case should be.

~~Stephen and~~ *she* met with the consultant. (Ignore *Stephen and.*) (Compound subject)

~~You and~~ *I* must make our reservations. (Ignore *You and.*) (Compound subject)

Morgan asked ~~you and~~ *me* for advice. (Ignore *you and.*) (Compound object)

Would you like ~~Rasheed and~~ *them* to help you? (Ignore *Rasheed and.*) (Compound object)

Notice in the first sentence, for example, that when *Stephen and* is removed, the pronoun *she* must be selected because it functions as the subject of the verb *met.* In the third sentence, when *you and* is removed, the pronoun *me* must be selected because it functions as the object of the verb *asked.*

Comparatives

In statements of **comparison**, words are often implied but not actually stated. **Comparatives** are often introduced by words such as *than* or *as*. To determine pronoun case in only partially complete comparative statements introduced by *than* or *as*, always mentally finish the comparative by adding the implied missing words.

> Deborah enjoys hiking as much as *he*. (Deborah enjoys hiking as much as *he* [not *him*] enjoys hiking.)

> Nader Sharkes is a better cook than *she*. (. . . better cook than *she* [not *her*] is.)

> Tardiness annoys Judy Sunayama-Foster as much as *me*. (. . . as much as it annoys *me* [not *I*].)

Appositives

Appositives are words or groups of words that explain or rename previously mentioned nouns or pronouns. When a pronoun has an appositive, it takes the same case as the appositive that follows it. To determine more easily what pronoun case to use for a pronoun in combination with an appositive, temporarily ignore the appositive.

> *We* ~~teachers~~ are devoted to our students. (Ignore the appositive *teachers*.)

> Action must be taken by *us* ~~employees~~. (Ignore the appositive *employees*.)

Reflexive Pronouns

Reflexive pronouns that end in *-self* or *-selves* emphasize or reflect on their **antecedents** (the nouns or pronouns previously mentioned). Examples of reflexive pronouns include *myself, yourself, himself, herself, itself, ourselves, yourselves,* and *themselves*.

> *I* prepared the gourmet meal *myself*. (*Myself* reflects on *I*.)

> The president *himself* greeted each voter. (*Himself* emphasizes *president*.)

Errors result when we use reflexive pronouns instead of personal pronouns. If no previously mentioned noun or pronoun is stated in the same sentence, use a personal pronoun instead of a reflexive pronoun.

> Send your request to either James or *me*. (Not *myself*)

> Helen Benjamin and *I* analyzed the research implications. (Not *myself*)

Please note that *hisself, themself,* and *theirselves* are not acceptable words.

Subject Complements

As you have learned, subjective-case pronouns usually function as subjects of verbs. Less frequently, subjective-case pronouns also perform as subject complements. A pronoun that follows a linking verb and renames the subject must be in the subjective case. As you learned in Chapter 1, **linking verbs** express a state of being and generally link to the subject words that describe or rename them. Some linking verbs are *am, is, are, was, were, be, being,* and *been*. Other linking verbs express the senses: *feels, appears, tastes, sounds, seems, looks*.

> It *is she* who will make the hiring decision. (Not *her*)

> I am sure it *was he* who sent the text message. (Not *him*)

> If you *were I*, what would you do? (Not *me*)

Study Tip

Whenever a pronoun follows a linking verb, that pronoun will be in the subjective case.

When a sentence includes a verb phrase, look at the final word of the verb phrase. If it is a linking verb, use a subjective pronoun.

> It *might have been they* who made the suggestion. (Not *them*)

> The driver *could have been he*. (Not *him*)

> If the manager *had been I*, your money would have been refunded. (Not *me*)

In conversation it is common to say, *It is me*, or more likely, *It's me*. Careful speakers and writers, though, normally use subjective-case pronouns after linking verbs. If the resulting constructions sound too formal, revise your sentences appropriately. For example, instead of *It is I who placed the order*, use *I placed the order*. When answering the telephone, careful speakers say, *This is she* or *This is he*.

Now complete the reinforcement exercises for Level 1.

Fundamentals of Pronoun–Antecedent Agreement

When pronouns substitute for nouns, the pronouns must agree with their antecedents in number (singular or plural) and gender (masculine, feminine, or neuter). Here are suggestions for using pronouns effectively.

Making Pronoun References Clear

Do not use a pronoun if your listener or reader might not be able to identify the noun it represents.

Unclear:	When Annette Jenkins followed Dawn O'Malley as president, many of *her* policies were reversed.
Clear:	When Annette Jenkins followed Dawn O'Malley as president, many of O'Malley's policies were reversed.
Unclear:	In that ball park *they* do not allow *you* to smoke in the stands.
Clear:	The ball park management does not allow fans to smoke in the stands. *Or:* Smoking is not allowed in the ball park stands.

Making Pronouns Agree With Their Antecedents in Number

Pronouns must agree in number with the nouns they represent. For example, if a pronoun replaces a singular noun, that pronoun must be singular. If a pronoun replaces a plural noun, that pronoun must be plural.

> *Michelangelo* felt that *he* was a failure. (Singular antecedent and pronoun)

> Great *artists* often doubt *their* success. (Plural antecedent and pronoun)

If a pronoun refers to two nouns joined by *and*, the pronoun must be plural.

> The *managers* and *union representatives* discussed *their* differences.
> (Plural antecedent and pronoun)

Trivia Tidbit

Ships have traditionally been referred to with feminine pronouns, even those that have masculine names.

74   **CHAPTER 4**   PRONOUNS

Circle art: © iStockphoto.com/Pavel Khorenyan

Max and *Sarah* need new passwords issued to *them* immediately.
(Plural antecedent and pronoun)

Pronoun–antecedent agreement can be complicated when words or phrases come between the pronoun and the word to which it refers. Disregard phrases such as those introduced by *as well as, in addition to, together with,* and *along with.* Find the true antecedent and make the pronoun agree with it.

The *president,* together with his cabinet members, is sending *his* personal thanks.
(Singular antecedent and pronoun)

The *cabinet members,* along with the president, are sending *their* personal thanks.
(Plural antecedent and pronoun)

A female *member* of the group of protesting employees demanded that *she* be treated equally. (Singular antecedent and pronoun)

Making Pronouns Agree With Their Antecedents in Gender

Pronouns exhibit one of three *genders*: masculine (male), feminine (female), or neuter (neither masculine nor feminine). Pronouns must agree with their antecedents in gender.

Warren Buffett discussed *his* investment strategies. (Masculine gender)

Kathy Overby prepared for *her* trip to Beirut. (Feminine gender)

The suggestion has *its* strong points. (Neuter gender)

Choosing Alternatives to Common-Gender Antecedents

Occasionally, writers and speakers face a problem in choosing pronouns of appropriate gender. Although first-person (*I*) and second-person (*you*) singular pronouns may be used to refer to either gender, third-person singular pronouns (*he, she*) refer to specific genders. English has no all-purpose third-person singular pronoun to represent indefinite nouns (such as *a student* or *an employee*).

For this reason writers and speakers have in the past used masculine pronouns to refer to nouns that might be either masculine or feminine. For example, in the sentence *An employee has his rights,* the pronoun *his* referred to its antecedent *employee,* which might name either a feminine or masculine person.

Communicators today, however, avoid masculine pronouns (*he, his*) when referring to indefinite nouns that could be masculine or feminine. Critics call these pronouns "sexist" or "gender-biased" because they exclude women. To solve the problem, sensitive communicators rewrite those sentences requiring such pronouns. Although many alternatives exist, here are three options:

Gender-Biased: A *passenger* must show *his* passport before boarding.

Alternative No. 1: *Passengers* must show *their* passports before boarding. (Make the subject plural to avoid the need for a singular pronoun. Remember to make the object [*passports*] plural too.)

Trivia Tidbit

Despite efforts for more than 160 years, no one has yet come up with an acceptable multipurpose, unisex pronoun. Suggested replacements: *ne* (1850), *le* (1884), *se* (1938), *ve* (1970), *e* (1977), *ala* (1988), *pers* (1992), and *wun* (1995). What would you suggest to fill the void in our language?

Alternative No. 2:	A passenger must show *a* passport before boarding. (Use an article [*a*] to replace the pronoun. This alternative, however, is less emphatic.)
Alternative No. 3:	A *passenger* must show *his or her* passport before boarding. (Use both masculine and feminine pronouns [*his or her*]. Because this construction is wordy and clumsy, avoid its frequent use.)
Wrong:	A passenger must show *their* passport before boarding. (Substituting the plural pronoun *their* is incorrect because *their* does not agree with its singular antecedent, *passenger*.)

Special Pronoun–Antecedent Agreement Challenges

The following guidelines will help you avoid errors in pronoun–antecedent agreement in special cases. These special instances include sentences in which the antecedents (a) are joined by *or* or *nor*, (b) are indefinite pronouns, (c) are collective nouns or company names, or (d) are preceded by the words *each* or *every*.

Antecedents Joined by *or* or *nor*

When antecedents are joined by *or* or *nor*, the pronoun should agree with the closer antecedent. The closer antecedent will be the one that comes after the *or* or *nor*. You may be wondering why antecedents joined by *and* are treated differently from antecedents joined by *or* or *nor*. The conjunction *and* joins one plus one to make two antecedents; therefore, use a plural pronoun. The conjunctions *or* and *nor* require a choice between two antecedents. Always match the pronoun to the closer antecedent.

Either Sandra or *Monica* left *her* briefcase in the conference room. (The pronoun *her* agrees with the closer antecedent, Monica.)

Neither the employees nor *Supervisor Ken Riley* expects to see *his* salary increased this year. (The pronoun *his* refers to the closer antecedent, *Ken Riley*.)

Neither Supervisor Ken Riley nor the *employees* expect to see *their* salaries increased this year. (The pronoun *their* refers to the closer antecedent, *employees*. Notice that *salaries* must also be made plural.)

Indefinite Pronouns as Antecedents

Indefinite pronouns are pronouns such as *anyone*, *something*, and *everybody*. These pronouns are indefinite because they refer to no specific person or object. Some indefinite pronouns are always singular; others are always plural.

Always Singular		Always Plural
anybody	neither	both
anyone	nobody	few
anything	no one	many
each	nothing	several
either	somebody	
everybody	someone	
everyone	something	
everything		

When an indefinite pronoun functions as an antecedent of a pronoun, make certain that the pronoun agrees with its antecedent. Do not let a prepositional phrase obscure the true antecedent.

Somebody on the women's softball team left *her* mitt in the locker room. (The antecedent *Somebody* is singular and feminine.)

Everyone in the men's choir made *his* song choice. (The antecedent *Everyone* is singular and masculine.)

Each of the corporations has *its* own Twitter feed. (The antecedent *Each* is singular and neutral.)

Few of our employees have *their* own private parking spaces. (The antecedent *Few* is plural. Notice that *spaces* is also plural.)

Several of our branches list *their* job openings on the company's intranet. (The antecedent *Several* is plural.)

The words *either* and *neither* can be confusing. When these words stand alone and function as sentence subjects, they are always considered singular. When they are joined with *or* or *nor* to form conjunctions, however, they may connect plural subjects. These plural subjects, then, may act as antecedents to plural pronouns.

Either of the women *is* willing to share *her* expertise. (*Either* is a singular pronoun and functions as the subject of the sentence. It controls the singular verb *is*. *Either* is also the antecedent of the pronoun *her*.)

Neither the man *nor* his children left *their* packages on the train. (The conjunction *neither/nor* joins two subjects, *man* and *children*. The pronoun *their* agrees with its plural antecedent, *children*.)

Collective Nouns as Antecedents

Collective nouns refer to a collection of people, animals, or objects. Examples are *jury, faculty, committee, staff, union, team, flock,* and *group*. Such words may be either singular or plural depending on the mode of operation of the collection to which they refer. When a collective noun operates as a unit, it is singular. When the elements of a collective noun operate separately, the collective noun is plural.

Our *committee* released *its* progress report. (*Committee* operates as one unit.)

The *jury* rendered *its* verdict. (*Jury* operates as one unit.)

The *jury* were divided in *their* opinions. (*Jury* operates as individuals.)

However, if you want to use a collective noun in a plural sense, the sentence will seem less awkward if you add a plural noun (*The jury members were divided in their opinions*).

Company and Organization Names as Antecedents

Company and organization names, including names of sports teams and musical groups, are generally considered singular. Unless the actions of the organization are attributed to individual representatives of that organization, pronouns referring to organizations should be singular.

Study Tip

When *either* or *neither* is followed by an *of* phrase, it is functioning as a singular pronoun (for example, *Either of the books is available*).

Trivia Tidbit

In American English, companies and organizations are generally considered to be singular. In British English, companies and organizations are generally considered to be plural.

JetBlue Airways is adding several new cross-country flights to *its* schedule.

The United Nations, in addition to other organizations, is expanding *its* campaign to improve women's rights in African countries.

Downey, Felker & Torres, Inc., plans to move *its* corporate headquarters.

The band Counting Crows got *its* start in Berkeley, California.

The *Green Bay Packers* won *its* fourth Super Bowl in 2011.

The Adjectives *each* and *every*

When the adjective *each* or *every* comes before a compound subject joined by *and*, the compound subject is considered singular.

> *Each* female player and coach is expected to purchase *her* own uniform. (Think *Each single female player and each single coach is expected to purchase her own uniform.*)
>
> *Every* father and son received *his* invitation separately. (Think *Every single father and every single son received his invitation separately.*)

Now complete the reinforcement exercises for Level 2.

LEVEL 3

Advanced Pronoun Use

The use of the pronouns *who* and *whom* and *whoever* and *whomever* presents a continuing dilemma for speakers and writers. In conversation the correct choice of *who* or *whom* or *whoever* or *whomever* is especially difficult because of the mental gymnastics necessary to locate subjects and objects. The following guidelines explain when to use *who* and *whom* and *whoever* and *whomever*.

Another challenge is using the pronoun *whose* correctly. In this section you will learn how to avoid confusing this pronoun with *who's*, which is the contraction for "who is" or "who has."

The Challenge of *who* and *whom*

In conversation, speakers may have difficulty analyzing a sentence quickly enough to use the correct *who* or *whom* form. In writing, however, an author has ample time to scrutinize a sentence and make a correct choice—if the author understands the traditional functions of *who* and *whom*. *Who* is the subjective-case form. Like other subjective-case pronouns, *who* may function as the subject of a verb or as the subject complement of a noun following a linking verb. *Whom* is the objective-case form. It may function as the object of a verb or as the object of a preposition.

> *Who* do you think will win the primary election? (*Who* is the subject of the verb phrase *will win*.)
>
> Allison asked me *who* my boss is. (*Who* is the complement of *boss*.)
>
> *Whom* should we recommend? (*Whom* is the object of the verb phrase *should recommend*.)
>
> Edmund is the one to *whom* I spoke. (*Whom* is the object of the preposition *to*.)

How to Choose Between *who* and *whom*

The choice between *who* and *whom* becomes easier if the sentence in question is approached using the following five steps:

1. Isolate the *who/whom* clause.

2. Invert the clause, if necessary, to restore normal subject–verb–object order.

3. Substitute *he* or *him* for *who* or *whom*. Only one pronoun, *he* or *him*, will correctly complete the clause.

4. Equate the subjective pronoun *he* with *who* and the objective pronoun *him* with *whom*.

5. If the sentence sounds correct with *he*, complete the sentence by replacing *he* with *who*. If the sentence sounds correct with *him*, complete the sentence by replacing *him* with *whom*.

Study the following sentences and notice how the choice of *who* or *whom* is made:

Do you know (who/whom) his supervisor is?

Isolate:	_____ his supervisor is
Invert:	his supervisor is _____ (*or* _____ is his supervisor)
Substitute:	his supervisor is <u>he</u> (*or* <u>he</u> is his supervisor)
Equate:	his supervisor is <u>who</u> (*or* <u>who</u> is his supervisor)
Complete:	Do you know *who* his supervisor is?

Here are the records of the applicant (who/whom) we have selected.

Isolate:	_____ we have selected
Invert:	we have selected _____
Substitute:	we have selected <u>him</u>
Equate:	we have selected <u>whom</u>
Complete:	Here are the records of the applicant *whom* we have selected.

In choosing *who* or *whom*, ignore parenthetical expressions such as *I hope, we think, I believe, they said,* and *you know.*

Edward is the candidate (who/whom) we believe is best.

Isolate:	_____ we believe is best
Ignore:	_____ [we believe] is best
Substitute:	<u>he</u> is best
Equate:	<u>who</u> is best
Complete:	Edward is the candidate *who* we believe is best.

Examples:

Whom do you think we should hire? (Invert: You do think we should call him/*whom*.)

The person to *whom* we gave our evaluation was Elijha. (Invert: The evaluation was given to him/*whom*.)

Do you know *who* the coach is? (Invert: The coach is he/*who*.)

Whom would you like to include in the acknowledgment? (Invert: You would like to include him/*whom* in the acknowledgment.)

Study Tip

Notice that both *him* and *whom* end with the letter *m*. This is an easy way to remember that if a sentence sounds correct with *him*, the pronoun *whom* should be used.

Study Tip

In studying this example, remember that subjective-case pronouns follow linking verbs.

The Use of *whoever* and *whomever*

As with *who* and *whom*, *whoever* is subjective and *whomever* is objective. The selection of the correct form is sometimes complicated when *whoever* or *whomever* appears in a clause. These clauses may act as objects of prepositions, objects of verbs, or subjects of verbs. Within the clauses, however, you must determine how *whoever* or *whomever* is functioning in order to choose the correct form. Study the following examples and explanations.

> Issue a refund to *whoever requests one.* (The clause *whoever requests one* is the object of the preposition *to.* Within the clause itself, *whoever* acts as the subject of *needs* and is therefore in the subjective case. Think: *he requests one.*)
>
> A scholarship will be given to *whoever meets the criteria.* (The clause *whoever meets the criteria* is the object of the preposition *to.* Within the clause, *whoever* acts as the subject of *meets* and is therefore in the subjective case. Think: *he meets the criteria.*)
>
> We will accept the name of *whomever they nominate.* (The clause *whomever they nominate* is the object of the preposition *of.* Within the clause, *whomever* is the object of *they nominate* and is therefore in the objective case. Think: *they nominate him.*)

The Use of *whose*

The pronoun *whose* functions as a possessive pronoun. Like other possessive pronouns, *whose* has no apostrophe. Do not confuse it with the contraction *who's*, which means "who is" or "who has."

> We haven't decided *whose* business plan looks most promising.
>
> *Whose* applications were submitted by the deadline?
>
> Please let me know *who's* on call this evening.
>
> Do you know *who's* already been trained on the new software?

Summary of Pronoun Cases

The following table summarizes the uses of subjective- and objective-case pronouns.

Subjective Case	
Subject of the verb	*They* are managers.
Subject complement	The top applicant is *he.*

Objective Case	
Direct or indirect object of the verb	Give *him* another chance.
Object of a preposition	Send the order to *him.*
Object of an infinitive	Ann hoped to call *us.*

Now complete the reinforcement exercises for Level 3.

Types of Pronouns

For those of you interested in a total view, here is a summary of the seven types of pronouns. This list is presented for your interest alone, not for potential testing.

1. **Personal pronouns** replace nouns or other pronouns. Examples:

   Subjective Case: I, we, you, he, she, it, they

   Objective Case: me, us, you, him, her, it, them

   Possessive Case: my, mine, our, ours, your, yours, his, hers, its, their, theirs

2. **Reflexive pronouns** emphasize or reflect on antecedents. Examples: *myself, yourself, himself, herself, itself, oneself,* and so on.

3. **Indefinite pronouns** replace nouns. Examples: *everyone, anyone, someone, each, everybody, anybody, one, none, some, all,* and so on.

4. **Relative pronouns** join subordinate clauses to antecedents. Examples: *who, whose, whom, which, that, whoever, whomever, whichever, whatever.*

5. **Interrogative pronouns** replace nouns in a question. Examples: *who, whose, whom, which, what.*

6. **Demonstrative pronouns** designate specific persons or things. Examples: *this, these, that, those.*

7. **Reciprocal pronouns** indicate mutual relationship. Examples: *each other, one another.*

Courtesy of Mary Ellen Guffey

Courtesy of Carolyn M. Seefer

Dr. Guffey   Professor Seefer

Q: I often catch myself using the response *me too* when I agree or have taken part in the same activity as someone else. For example, my friend will say, *I love that new sushi restaurant*, and I will respond, *Me too*. Is this a correct use of the pronoun *me*?

A: Although you will hear this response commonly used, grammatically it is incorrect. When you respond with these words, you are really saying, *Me love that new sushi restaurant too*. However, responding with *I too*, which is grammatically correct, would probably sound too stuffy. If you want to respond correctly but naturally, try saying something like *So do I* or *I do too*.

Q: Should a hyphen be used in the word *dissimilar*? How about *undercapitalized*?

A: No. Prefixes such as *dis*, *pre*, *non*, and *un* do not require hyphens. Even when the final letter of the prefix is repeated in the initial letter of the root word, no hyphens are used: *disspirited, preenroll, nonnutritive*. In addition, the prefixes *under* and *over* are not followed by hyphens. These prefixes join the main word: *undercapitalized, underdeveloped, underbudgeted, overbuild, overhang, overjoyed,* and so forth.

Q: I thought I knew the difference between *to* and *too*, but could you provide me with a quick review?

A: *To* may serve as a preposition (*I am going to the store*), and it may also serve as part of an infinitive construction (*to sign his name*). The adverb *too* may be used to mean "also" (*Andrea will attend too*) or "to an excessive extent" (*the letter is too long*).

Q: I just included this sentence in a letter to a customer: *We look forward to having you as apart of our celebration*. Did I do something wrong?

A: Yes, but your error is easy to fix. The word *apart* should be written as two words in your sentence (*a part*). Write *apart* as one word when used as an adverb meaning "at a distance" or "as a separate unit." (*This is my first year living apart from my family*, or, *It is hard to tell their twin daughters apart*.) Write *a part* as two words when you are using the article *a* followed by the noun *part*, as is the case in your sentence (*. . . having you as a part of our celebration*). Here is a trick: If you can remove the *a* and the sentence still makes sense, write *a part* as two words.

Q: Is the word *backup* written as one word or two? Or should I hyphenate it?

A: It depends on how the word is being used. When using *backup* as a noun (*We need a backup in case this plan doesn't work*) or as an adjective (*I keep my backup files on a flash drive*), write it as one word. When using it as a verb, write it as two words (*We recommend that you back up your files every week*). Whether one word or two, don't hyphenate!

Q: I am disgusted with and infuriated at a New York University advertisement I just saw in our newspaper. It says, *It's not just __who__ you know....* Why would a leading institution of learning use such poor grammar?

A: Because it sounds familiar. But familiarity doesn't make it correct. You are right in recognizing that the proper form is *whom* (isolate the clause *you know him* or *whom*). The complete adage—or more appropriately, cliché—correctly stated is: *It's not what you know but __whom__ you know.*

Q: Please help me decide which *maybe* to use in this sentence: *He said that he (maybe, may be) able to help us.*

A: Use the two-word verb *may be.* Don't confuse it with the adverb *maybe,* which means "perhaps" (*Maybe she will call*).

Q: I am totally confused by job titles for women today. What do I call a woman who is a *fireman,* a *policeman,* a *chairman,* or a *spokesman*? And what about the word *mankind*?

A: As more and more women enter nontraditional careers, some previous designations are being replaced by neutral, inclusive titles. Here are some substitutes:

actor	for *actress*
firefighter	for *fireman*
mail carrier	for *mailman*
police officer	for *policeman*
flight attendant	for *steward* or *stewardess*
reporter or journalist	for *newsman*
server	for *waiter* or *waitress*

Words such as *chairman, spokesman,* and *mankind* traditionally have been used to refer to both men and women. Today, though, sensitive writers strive to use more inclusive language. Possible substitutes are *chair, spokesperson,* and *humankind.*

Q: I am confused by indefinite pronouns such as *everyone, anyone, someone,* and so on. Is there a trick I can use to remember whether to write these as one word or two?

A: Yes, indefinite pronouns can be tricky! First of all, *someone* (*we need to hire someone new*) is nearly always written as one word, and *no one* is always written as two (*no one has applied for the position yet*). If the word *of* follows *everyone* or *anyone,* write it as two words (*every one of the suggestions is valid; any one of our employees can answer your question*). If the word *of* does not follow, write these indefinite pronouns as one word (*everyone voted yes; I didn't see anyone at the door*).

Q: I am a woman who will be getting married next year. Do I refer to the man I am marrying as my *fiancé* or *fiancée*? What is the difference?

A: First of all, congratulations on your upcoming marriage! You should refer to the man you are going to marry as your *fiancé,* the word that describes a man who is engaged to be married. He will refer to you as his *fiancée,* which describes a woman engaged to be married.

SPOT THE Blooper

Using the skills you are learning in this class, try to identify why the following items are bloopers. Consult your textbook, dictionary, or reference manual as needed. To see if you recognized the blooper, go to **www.cengagebrain.com** and use your access code to see the Spot the Blooper key.

Blooper 1: AT&T sent this notice to its customers: "AT&T supports the human spirit through it's sponsorship of the US Paralympic Team."

Blooper 2: United States Secretary of Education Arne Duncan said of a friend and mentor, "He gave my sister and I the opportunity to start a great school on the South Side of Chicago."

Blooper 3: In an *Entertainment Weekly* interview, President Barack Obama was asked if he and Michelle argue about anything. He replied, "She likes *American Idol*, her and the girls, in a way that I don't entirely get. I think the girls did vote in last year's contest. I don't know who they voted for, but I recall that a vote was cast." [Did you spot two errors?]

Blooper 4: Senator Charles Schumer in a letter to *The Wall Street Journal*: "Democrats like myself do not oppose all new domestic oil supplies."

Blooper 5: Paris Hilton wore a T-shirt that said "Thats Hot" on the front and "Your Not" on the back.

Blooper 6: J. K. Rowling on her website before the final Harry Potter book was released: "I'd like to ask everyone who calls themselves a Potter fan to help preserve the secrecy of the plot for all those who are looking forward to reading the book at the same time on publication day."

Blooper 7: Billboard for a Ford dealership seen on I-275 in Tampa, Florida: "Who's country are you supporting?"

Blooper 8: Sign in an Office Depot restroom: "Employees must wash your hands."

Blooper 9: From the *FEEA Helping Hand* newsletter under advice for scholarship applicants: "Carefully check your application and essay for spelling and grammar—it counts."

Blooper 10: From a letter to members of the National Council of Teachers of English: "It takes a special person to choose teaching as their life goal."

4 Reinforcement Exercises

LEVEL 1

A. Self-Check. Personal Pronouns. Choose the correct pronoun.

1. I am having lunch today with Bethany Stewart and (*she, her*). _____

2. We are very impressed with (*your, you're*) application. _____

3. Our university business club is having (*its, it's*) annual banquet in May. _____

4. My colleague and (*I, me*) were surprised to learn that the word *ginormous* was added to the dictionary. _____

5. A flexible benefits plan was offered to (*we, us*) employees. _____

6. No one knows technical jargon better than Neal Skapura and (*she, her*). _____

7. Proposals submitted by (*her and me, she and I*) were considered first. _____

8. Your completed application form can be sent to Tom Fritts or (*I, me, myself*). _____

9. The announcement surprised Professor Kiledal as much as (*she, her*). _____

10. If you were (*he, him*), would you send personal e-mail and text messages during work hours? _____

Check your answers below.

B. Subjective and Objective Pronouns. In the spaces provided, write the correct letter to indicate how the italicized pronouns function in these sentences.

a. subject of a verb   **b. object of a verb**   **c. object of a preposition**

Example: Please tell *her* that the refund is being processed.   b

11. Once Edna completes her degree, *she* will look for a full-time position. _____

12. We need more politicians like *her*. _____

13. The office received an announcement that *he* will be the keynote speaker. _____

14. After Jeff finished his presentation, the supervisor praised *him*. _____

15. The agreement between Tom Kayler and *her* will benefit the organization. _____

16. Everyone except *you* approved the terms of the new contract. _____

17. To prepare for their study abroad trip, Antonia and *she* will take a conversational Italian class. _____

18. Please send Allan Lacayo and *me* information about tablet computers. _____

19. When the product was introduced, other salespeople and *they* attended four training sessions. _____

20. Please forward the e-mail message to Jake and *me* immediately. _____

1. her 2. your 3. its 4. I 5. us 6. she 7. her and me 8. me 9. her 10. he

C. Personal Pronouns. Choose the correct pronoun.

21. Just between you and (*I, me*), I think Paul Bernhardt is most qualified. _____

22. Everyone except (*she, her*) took part in the conference call. _____

23. The CEO's announcement surprised him as much as (*I, me*). _____

24. My colleague and (*I, me*) plan to expand our operations overseas. _____

25. Corey has been with the company six months longer than (*I, me*). _____

26. Our CEO said that no other employees were quite like Anastasia and (*he, him*). _____

27. He has no one but (*hisself, himself*) to blame. _____

28. It is interesting that (*us, we*) accountants were audited this year. _____

29. It must have been (*they, them*) who reported the missing funds. _____

30. An argument between Nikki and (*he, himself, him*) caused problems in the office. _____

31. Believe me, no one knows that problem better than (*I, me*). _____

32. News of the merger pleased President Reuben Ellis as much as (*I, me*). _____

33. A proposed annual budget was sent to (*we, us*) homeowners prior to the vote. _____

34. When Gayle answered the telephone, she said, "This is (*she, her*)." _____

35. The committee chair asked Emma and (*I, me*) to serve on a special task force. _____

36. We tried to contact (*he and she, him and her*) in Beijing. _____

37. The student club invited Jeff Bezos and (*she, her*) to speak at a campus event. _____

38. Ratha and Zach were certain it was not (*they, them*) who caused the network to crash. _____

39. When Christopher opened the door, he expected to see you and (*he, him*). _____

40. If the caller is (*he, him*), please get his cell phone number. _____

D. Possessive Pronouns and Contractions. Choose the correct answers.

41. The cheetah is the only cat in the world that cannot retract (*its, it's*) claws. _____

42. Was that great idea (*yours, your's*)? _____

43. The white binder is (*her's, hers*). _____

44. (*There's, Theres, Theirs*) not a lot we can do about the decision. _____

45. The city is proud that (*it's, its*) implemented a disaster preparedness training program. _____

46. (*Your, You're*) going to love our new supervisor. _____

47. Are you sure that this apartment is (*there's, theirs, their's*)? _____

48. (*It's, Its*) been so nice getting to know you. _____

49. (*Your, You're*) new office is on the third floor. _____

50. (*Ours, Our's*) is the third building on the right. _____

E. Review of Personal Pronouns. To make sure you have mastered personal pronouns, read the following sentences and underline any faulty pronoun use. Each sentence contains one error. Write an improved form in the space provided.

51. CEO Gary Kelly and her discussed how to improve public relations at Southwest Airlines after passengers were stranded for hours on the tarmac because of bad weather. _____

52. Please submit your marketing plan to Liz or I by Friday afternoon. _____

53. If neither Matt nor I receive an e-mail confirmation of our itinerary, him and I cannot make the trip. _____

54. E-mail messages intended for she and him were accidently forwarded to the entire department. _____

55. Just between you and I, neither Kris nor he met the monthly quota. _____

56. Because of it's success, our organization's ethics program is being expanded. _____

57. Both owners, Mark Messenger and him, agreed to sign the lease agreement by 5 p.m. _____

58. It's surprising that us renters were not consulted about the roofing project. _____

59. If you were me, would you apply for the promotion? _____

60. All students except Jake and she use tablet computers in class. _____

61. I think that failing to get to meetings on time is rude, and it angers the boss even more than I. _____

62. We are supposed to change our passwords monthly, but some employees don't change their's at all. _____

63. The yellow Toyota Prius in the employee parking lot is her's. _____

64. If you and her are selected for the training program, you will both have your tuition paid. _____

65. If the computer continues to give you trouble, check it's wiring. _____

66. I'm afraid its too late to apply for the scholarship. _____

67. Several year-end bonuses were awarded to we employees. _____

68. Your sure to enjoy our new interactive training program. _____

69. Her boyfriend loves Thai food as much as her. _____

70. Are you sure this lunch bag is your's? _____

F. Writing Exercise. Personal Pronouns. Write complete sentences that use the words shown.

Example: Julie Hall and (pronoun)

    Julie Hall and I agreed to market our invention. _____

71. The two sales reps, Peter and (pronoun)

_____

72. Except for Yumiko and (pronoun)

_____

73. The manager expected Jeff and (pronoun)

_____

74. its

_____

75. ours

_____

A. Self-Check. Pronoun–Antecedent Agreement. Choose the correct answer.

76. The union reached agreement on (a) *their*, (b) *its* new contract
with management.

    _____

77. (a) *They*, (b) *Researchers* reported that women are tested too often for osteoporosis.

    _____

78. Users were upset when Facebook changed (a) *its*, (b) *their* terms of
service agreement.

    _____

79. Either Laurie McDonough or Lorraine Love will present (a) *her*, (b) *their* research
findings at the meeting.

    _____

80. Every man, woman, and child in the club made (a) *his*, (b) *her*, (c) *his or her*,
(d) *their* own contribution to the used clothing drive.

    _____

81. The president asked for budget cuts, and Congress indicated (a) *its*, (b) *their*
willingness to legislate some of them.

    _____

Choose the better of the following sentence pairs.

82. (a) An employee is not required to retire when he reaches the age of sixty-five.

    (b) No employees are required to retire when they reach the age of sixty-five.

    _____

83. (a) Every online sales rep must improve their writing skills to handle chat sessions.

    (b) All online sales reps must improve their writing skills to handle chat sessions.

    _____

84. (a) Anyone in the department can share their suggestions for increasing sales.

    (b) All department members can share their suggestions for increasing sales.

    _____

85. (a) We require that all applicants submit their résumés online at our website.

    (b) We require that each applicant submit their résumé online at our website.

    _____

Check your answers belows.

B. Pronoun–Antecedent Agreement. Choose the correct answers.

86. Some people are afraid of having (a) *his*, (b) *his or her*, (c) *their* identities stolen.

    _____

87. An office manager, as well as other members of management,
must do (a) *his*, (b) *her*, (c) *his or her*, (d) *their* best to exhibit strong ethics.

    _____

88. Both Dr. Awbrey and Dr. Marion submitted (a) *her*, (b) *their* registration forms
for the American Dental Association convention.

    _____

89. Bob Eustes, one of our top chefs, entered (a) *his*, (b) *their* signature dish in
the competition.

    _____

90. In some doctors' offices (a) *you*, (b) *patients* are not allowed to use cell phones.

    _____

76.b 77.b 78.a 79.a 80.c 81.a 82.b 83.b 84.b 85.a

Circle art: © iStockphoto.com/Pavel Khorenyan

91. Neither her dog nor her cat has had (a) *their*, (b) *its* annual shots. _____

92. No one can go home for the evening until the jury announces (a) *its*, (b) *their* verdict. _____

93. Not one of the employees cast (a) *his*, (b) *her*, (c) *his or her*, (d) *their* vote to approve the new union contract. _____

94. Every woman in the martial arts class had to purchase (a) *her*, (b) *their* own safety equipment. _____

95. All employees are expected to display (a) *his*, (b) *her*, (c) *his or her*, (d) *their* photo name tags prominently. _____

Choose the better of the following sentence pairs. Notice that many of these pairs use alternative language to avoid incorrect or gender-biased pronouns.

96. (a) A judge must deliver his jury instructions in plain English.

    (b) A judge must deliver jury instructions in plain English. _____

97. (a) An employee should know what rights they have in the workplace.

    (b) Employees should know what rights they have in the workplace. _____

98. (a) Accountants must always double-check their figures for accuracy.

    (b) An accountant must always double-check his figures for accuracy. _____

99. (a) Before an applicant is hired, he must have his references checked.

    (b) Before applicants are hired, they must have their references checked. _____

100. (a) The Supreme Court will announce its decision in January.

     (b) The Supreme Court will announce their decision in January. _____

101. (a) Neither the glamour nor the excitement of the job had lost its appeal.

     (b) Neither the glamour nor the excitement of the job had lost their appeal. _____

102. (a) Any new subscriber may cancel their subscription within the first 30 days.

     (b) New subscribers may cancel their subscriptions within the first 30 days. _____

103. (a) Every manager should listen to their employees.

     (b) All managers should listen to their employees. _____

104. (a) If any student needs assistance, Kathy Yerkes will help them.

     (b) If any student needs assistance, Kathy Yerkes will help. _____

105. (a) Employees must be told when their annual performance reviews will be held.

     (b) Every employee must be told when their annual performance review will be held. _____

C. **Writing Exercise. Gender Agreement.** Rewrite the following sentences to avoid the use of gender-biased pronouns. Show three versions of each sentence.

106. Every new teacher must have *her* lesson plans approved.

     a. _____

     b. _____

     c. _____

107. Be sure that each new employee has received *his* orientation packet.

a. _____

b. _____

c. _____

108. A doctor must submit *his* insurance paperwork on time.

a. _____

b. _____

c. _____

D. Writing Exercise. Clear Pronoun Reference. Rewrite these sentences to make the pronoun references clear.

109. The article reported that Google had acquired Nijinsky and that it planned to use its travel platform.

_____

_____

110. They make you wear a coat and tie in that restaurant.

_____

111. Mr. Winterstein told Mr. Petrino that he needed to take a vacation.

_____

112. Recruiters like to see job objectives on résumés; however, it may restrict their chances.

_____

_____

113. Ms. Hartman talked with Lisbeth about her telecommuting request, but she needed more information.

_____

_____

LEVEL 3

A. Self-Check. *Who/Whoever* and *Whom/Whomever*. Choose the correct pronoun.

114. (*Who, Whom*) do you think we should promote to the office manager position? _____

115. We are not sure (*who, whom*) discovered the security breach. _____

116. This is the applicant (*who, whom*) impressed the hiring team _____

117. The contract will be awarded to (*whoever, whomever*) submits the lowest bid. _____

118. Madeline Moreno is the investment counselor of (*who, whom*) I spoke. _____

119. When I return the call, for (*who, whom*) should I ask? _____

120. (*Who, Whom*) may I say is calling? _____

121. Will you recommend an electrician (*who, whom*) can rewire our building? _____

122. Do you know (*whose, who's*) been invited to give the keynote address? _____

123. (*Whose, Who's*) car is blocking the entry? _____

Check your answers below.

114. Whom 115. who 116. who 117. whoever 118. whom 119. whom 120. Who 121. who 122. who's 123. Whose

B. *Who/Whoever* **and** *Whom/Whomever*. Choose the correct pronoun.

124. Ingrid, (*who, whom*) left last week, was our most experienced quality assurance inspector. _____

125. Melissa will help (*whoever, whomever*) is next in line. _____

126. He is the vocational counselor (*who, whom*) we believe has the most connections to local employers. _____

127. Mona Nia, (*who, whom*) recently passed the bar exam, immediately hung out her shingle. _____

128. (*Who, Whom*) have you asked to revamp our corporate website? _____

129. For (*who, whom*) does the bell toll? _____

130. I have hotel recommendations for (*whoever, whomever*) plans to travel to Iceland this summer. _____

131. The "Father of Accounting" to (*who, whom*) the professor referred is Luca Pacioli. _____

132. James Franklin is the one (*who, whom*) launched the *New-England Courant* in 1721, which marks the birth of the American newspaper. _____

133. Please tell us the name of (*whoever, whomever*) you recommend for the position. _____

134. Adam Smith, (*who, whom*) is known as the "Father of Capitalism," was born in 1723. _____

135. Do you know (*who, whom*) will be taking your place? _____

136. Please put the call through to (*whoever, whomever*) is in charge of the project. _____

137. I wonder (*who, whom*) the speaker is talking about. _____

138. In making introductions, who should be introduced to (*who, whom*)? _____

139. LinkedIn has an older base of individuals (*who, whom*) use its service than Facebook and Google+. _____

140. Barack Obama sent text messages to millions of supporters to let them know (*who, whom*) he had selected as his running mate. _____

141. Jimmy Carter said, "As a superdelegate, I would not disclose (*who, whom*) I am rooting for, but I leave you to make that guess." _____

142. Female CEOs, (*who, whom*) make roughly 85 percent of what male CEOs make, took their case to the media. _____

143. A University of Illinois sociologist found that those (*who, whom*) have better social skills earn an average $3,200 more yearly than those with poorer social skills. _____

C. *Whose/Who's*. Choose the correct word.

144. (*Whose, Who's*) had a chance to see Steven Spielberg's new film? _____

145. (*Whose, Who's*) movie reviews do you trust the most? _____

146. Rose Kessler was nominated by her students for the "(*Whose, Who's*) Who Among American High School Teachers" list. _____

147. While looking for a volunteer, the office manager asked, "(*Whose, Who's*) it going to be?" _____

148. The committee chair asked, "(*Whose, Who's*) recommendation should we adopt?" _____

149. We are not sure (*whose, who's*) proposal will be adopted. _____

150. It is unclear (*whose, who's*) planning to take part in tomorrow's walkout. _____

151. A State University of New York psychologist found that someone (*whose, who's*) handshake is firm is more likely to be socially dominant. _____

152. (*Whose, Who's*) handshake demonstrated more confidence? _____

153. (*Whose, Who's*) on first? _____

D. Review. Pronouns. To make sure you have mastered chapter concepts in all three levels, read the following sentences and underline any faulty pronoun use. Write an improved form in the space provided. Each sentence contains one error.

154. The Baltimore Orioles announced that their ticket prices would increase by $20 next season. _____

155. The task force submitted their recommendation a week early. _____

156. All Google employees, except for CEO Eric Schmidt, received his or her free LG Android phones at the end of the year. _____

157. Anyone who grew up in the 1970s probably has some vinyl in their music collection. _____

158. Each of the companies calculated their assets and liabilities before the merger. _____

159. *American Demographics* is known for their solid reputation among marketing executives. _____

160. Do you know who you will be voting for in the presidential primary? _____

161. Please direct my inquiry to whomever is in charge of issuing refunds. _____

162. Neither the cabinet members nor President Obama was ready for their decision to be revealed. _____

163. Who would you like to partner with on this project? _____

164. Each of the supermarkets featured their advertisements on Thursday. _____

165. Every one of the girls was pleased with their internship program. _____

166. Whose willing to serve as chair of the committee? _____

167. Our entire staff agreed that their response must be unified. _____

168. The instructor whom won the teaching award is Roni Cook. _____

169. An all-expense-paid trip to Jamaica will be given to whomever wins the sales contest. _____

170. Ford Motor Company reported that their sales increased during the fourth quarter. _____

171. The best CEO demonstrates transparency when communicating with his employees. _____

172. Researchers at Carnegie Mellon found that people are more likely to reveal his or her bad behavior when asked about it casually. _____

173. It's impossible to determine who's presentation was best. _____

E. FAQs About Business English Review. In the space provided, write the correct answer choice.

174. Is the newly hired person any better *(a) than, (b) then* the previous manager? _____

175. This *(a) maybe, (b) may be* our most profitable year yet. _____

176. *(a) Maybe, (b) May be* I will apply for that position after all. _____

177. *(a) Everyone, (b) Every one* of the ideas was discussed thoroughly. _____

178. All *(a) stewards, (b) stewardesses, (c) flight attendants* must pass a rigorous safety training. _____

179. A man engaged to be married is referred to as a *(a) fiancée, (b) fiancé.* _____

180. Because the office buildings are so *(a) dis-similar, (b) dissimilar, (c) dis similar,* we cannot make exact comparisons. _____

181. She hung up after being on hold for *(a) to, (b) too* long. _____

182. Many performers wanted to be *(a) apart, (b) a part* of the inauguration festivities. _____

183. Be sure to *(a) backup, (b) back-up, (c) back up* your files before going home tonight. _____

Chat About It ◀◀

Your instructor may assign any of the following topics for you to discuss in class, in an online chat room, or on an online discussion board. Some of the discussion topics may require outside research. You may also be asked to read and respond to postings made by your classmates.

Discussion Topic 1: People frequently misuse pronouns. For example, they have trouble knowing whether to choose *I* or *me*, *he* or *him*, *she* or *her*, and so on. Why do you think pronouns are so troublesome? After reading Chapter 4, what did you discover about your pronoun use? What types of mistakes have you been making? How will your pronoun use change? Do you think it is important to use pronouns correctly in the workplace? Do you have any tricks for deciding what pronoun to use when writing and speaking? Share your comments, tips, and suggestions with your classmates.

Discussion Topic 2: In this chapter you learned that Birmingham, England, has outlawed apostrophes on street signs. Do some research to find out more about this ban. (**Hint:** Search for the words *Birmingham* and *apostrophes*.) Report your findings, in your own words, to your classmates. Remember to cite your sources by providing the names and website addresses. How do you feel about this ban? Do you think the United States should do the same? Why or why not?

Discussion Topic 3: A magazine ad for Black-Berry wireless devices included the following headline: "Ask Someone Why They Love Their Blackberry." Similarly, a magazine ad for James Hardie International, a manufacturer of building projects, included this heading: "Because no one ever wished they'd spent more time painting their house." Both of these sentences include pronoun–antecedent disagreements, and similar disagreements appear in numerous print ads. Why do you think so many companies make these types of errors? How do errors like this make you feel about a company? What

alternatives could these companies use to avoid these types of errors?

Discussion Topic 4: When George Bush (George W. Bush's father) ran for president against Bill Clinton in 1992, he used trust as a central theme of his campaign. Bumper stickers and posters were made saying "Who Do You Trust?" When he made his nomination acceptance speech at the Republican National Convention in Houston, he included several sentences such as, "Who do you trust to make change work for you?" and "Who do you trust in this election?" In each case, he should have used *whom* instead of *who*. Many years later, when Barack Obama held his first press conference after being elected president in November 2008, he said this in response to a reporter's question: "Well, President Bush graciously invited Michelle and I to meet with him and first lady Laura Bush." Within minutes articles and blog entries began appearing online calling attention to Obama's grammatical error. What error did he make? Why do you think the press was so quick to jump on this grammatical mistake? Do you consider these errors to be important or minor? Why? Does a president have an obligation to use proper grammar? Why or why not? Why do you think these men made these pronoun errors? Do you think they were intentional or accidental?

Discussion Topic 5: Samuel Johnson, who wrote the first true English dictionary, said, "What is written without effort is in general read without pleasure." What do you think he meant by this? What does this mean to you as a business communicator?

Posttest

Choose the correct pronoun. Then compare your answers with those below.

1. Do you know whether the new social media director is (*she*, *her*)? _____

2. (*We*, *Us*) hotel workers plan to negotiate for higher wages. _____

3. The layoff announcement surprised my colleagues as much as (*I*, *me*). _____

4. My staff and (*I*, *me*, *myself*) will be happy to help you. _____

5. Just between you and (*I*, *me*), I am not happy with the contract changes. _____

6. On our college campus, (*they*, *instructors*) serve as advisors for student clubs. _____

7. A rider must show (*his*, *his or her*, *their*) ticket before boarding the train. _____

8. Macy's advertised (*their*, *its*) annual sale in today's newspaper. _____

9. (*Who*, *Whom*) would you like to see as the next department manager? _____

10. (*Whose*, *Who's*) bid is most cost-effective? _____

1. she 2. We 3. me 4. I 5. me 6. instructors 7. his or her 8. its 9. Whom 10. Whose

Begin your review by rereading Chapters 3–4. Then test your comprehension of those chapters by filling in the blanks in the exercises that follow. Compare your responses with the key at the end of the book.

LEVEL 1

1. Several employees' *(a) childs, (b) children, (c) childrens* participated in this year's "Take Your Child to Work Day." _____

2. The Cape Cod National Seashore has some of the most spectacular *(a) beachs, (b) beaches, (c) beach's* on the East Coast. _____

3. The home of the *(a) Ramirezes, (b) Ramirez's, (c) Ramirezes's* is located near the bike path. _____

4. Let's keep this news between you and *(a) me, (b) I.* _____

5. All employees except Ryan and *(a) he, (b) him* agreed to the reorganization. _____

6. Although he hired two *(a) attorneys, (b) attornies, (c) attornies', (d) attorneys'* to represent him, he did not win his case. _____

7. Larry Israel and *(a) she, (b) her* planned the high school reunion. _____

8. Both George W. Bush and Barack Obama served as president during the *(a) 2000s, (b) 2000's, (c) 2000s'.* _____

9. Insincerity irritates Dr. Loranjo as much as *(a) I, (b) me.* _____

10. Please mail the completed application to *(a) I, (b) me, (c) myself.* _____

11. *(a) We, (b) Us* college students take our education seriously. _____

12. Many *(a) CPAs, (b) CPA's, (c) CPAs'* complete tax forms for individuals. _____

13. If I were *(a) her, (b) she,* I would decline the offer. _____

14. *I, he, she, we,* and *they* are *(a) subjective-case, (b) objective-case* pronouns. _____

LEVEL 2

15. We are giving careful consideration to each *(a) company's, (b) companies', (c) companys* stock. _____

16. Ask both of the designers when *(a) she, (b) he, (c) he or she, (d) they* can give us estimates. _____

17. When a customer complains, *(a) he, (b) she, (c) he or she, (d) they* must be taken seriously. _____

18. The committee completed *(a) it's, (b) its, (c) their* work last week. _____

19. Our Human *(a) Resource's, (b) Resources, (c) Resources'* Department posted six new positions. _____

20. We read an announcement that the *(a) Millers, (b) Miller's, (c) Miller, (d) Millers'* son won a scholarship.

21. Your *(a) bosses, (b) boss's, (c) bosses'* signature is required on this expense form.

22. Neither the foreman nor the jury members wanted *(a) his name, (b) their names* to be released by the media.

23. Every clerk and every administrative assistant elected to exercise *(a) his, (b) her, (c) his or her, (d) their* voting rights.

24. Hewlett-Packard was the first company to have *(a) it's, (b) its, (c) their* own personalized postage.

25. Neither the receptionist nor her colleagues submitted *(a) her, (b) their, (c) his or her* applications for the company's tuition reimbursement program on time.

26. Either the board members or CEO Dick Costolo will give *(a) his, (b) their, (c) his or her* approval to allow Twitter to issue additional shares of stock.

27. Everybody attending today's conference must submit *(a) his, (b) her, (c) their, (d) an* expense claim by February 28.

28. Nancy Whitworth consulted her three *(a) sister-in-laws, (b) sister-in-law's, (c) sisters-in-law* before making a decision.

LEVEL 3

29. *(a) Greg and Patricia's, (b) Greg's and Patricia's* new cabin is located on the shores of Lake Ontario.

30. I certainly hope that today's weather is better than *(a) yesterdays, (b) yesterday's, (c) yesterday*.

31. In seven *(a) days, (b) day's, (c) days'* time, Maxwell will retire.

32. Following several financial *(a) crisis, (b) crises, (c) crisises*, the corporation was forced to declare bankruptcy.

33. Economics *(a) is, (b) are* Rachel's favorite academic subject.

34. After raising her children, she went back to college and earned her *(a) bachelors, (b) bachelor's* degree.

35. A *(a) dollars, (b) dollars' (c) dollar's* worth of gas won't get you very far.

36. To *(a) who, (b) whom* did you send your application?

37. *(a) Who, (b) Whom* is available to work overtime this weekend?

38. Give the extra supplies to *(a) whoever, (b) whomever* needs them.

39. *(a) Who, (b) Whom* would you prefer to see in that job?

40. *(a) Whose, (b) Who's* lunch was left in the refrigerator over the weekend?

41. Do you know *(a) whose, (b) who's* going to speak at today's seminar?

42. He dreams of earning his *(a) masters, (b) masters', (c) master's* degree in chemical engineering.

FAQs About Business English Review

43. Professor Kartchner said it was *(a) to, (b) too* early to sign up for these classes. _____

44. He hates to be *(a) apart, (b) a part* from his wife for too long. _____

45. It can be difficult to get medical insurance if you have a *(a) pre-existing, (b) pre existing, (c) preexisting* condition. _____

46. I hope you made a *(a) backup, (b) back-up, (c) back up* copy of your hard drive. _____

47. Much beachfront land is *(a) overdeveloped, (b) over developed, (c) over-developed.* _____

48. You *(a) maybe, (b) may be* our most talented Web designer. _____

49. *(a) Any one, (b) Anyone* of these applicants could do the job. _____

50. A woman engaged to be married is referred to as a *(a) fiancée, (b) fiancé.* _____

Techniques for Effective Sentences

The basic unit in writing is the sentence. Sentences come in a variety of sizes, shapes, and structures. As business and professional communicators, we are most interested in functional sentences that say what we want to say correctly and concisely. In this workshop you will concentrate on two important elements: writing complete sentences and writing concise sentences.

Writing Complete Sentences

To be complete, a sentence must have a subject and a predicate and it must make sense. As you learned in Chapter 2, incomplete sentences are fragments. Let's consider four common fragment errors you will want to avoid.

1. The fragment contains a subject and a predicate, but it begins with a subordinate word (such as *because, as, although, since,* or *if*) and fails to introduce a complete clause. You can correct this problem by joining the fragment to a relevant main clause.

   Fragment: Because world markets and economies are becoming increasingly intermixed.

   Revision: Because world markets and economies are becoming increasingly intermixed, Americans will be doing more business with people from other cultures.

   Fragment: Although Americans tend to get to the point directly.

   Revision: Although Americans tend to get to the point directly, people from some other cultures prefer indirectness.

2. The fragment does not contain a subject and a predicate, but a nearby sentence completes its meaning.

   Fragment: In July and August every year in Europe. That's when many Europeans take vacations.

   Revision: In July and August every year, many Europeans take vacations.

3. The fragment starts with a relative pronoun such as *which, that,* or *who.* Join the fragment to a main clause to form a complete sentence.

   Fragment: Which is a precious item to North Americans and other Westerners.

   Revision: Concise business letters save time, which is a precious item to North Americans and other Westerners.

4. The fragment starts with a noun followed by a *who, that,* or *which* clause. Add a predicate to form a complete sentence.

   Fragment: The visiting Vietnamese executive who was struggling to express his idea in English.

   Revision: The visiting Vietnamese executive who was struggling to express his idea in English appreciated the patience of his listener.

Skill Check 2.1 Eliminating Sentence Fragments

Each of the following consists of a fragment and a sentence, not necessarily in that order. Identify the fragment; then revise the sentence to eliminate the fragment.

Example: Speak in short sentences and use common words. If you want to be understood abroad.

Revision: Speak in short sentences and use common words if you want to be understood abroad.

1. Although you should not raise your voice. You should speak slowly and enunciate clearly.

   _____

2. A glazed expression or wandering eyes. These alert a speaker that the listener is lost.

   _____

3. When speaking with foreign businesspeople, be careful to avoid jargon. Which is special terminology that may confuse listeners.

   _____

   _____

4. Kevin Chambers, who is an international specialist and consultant. He said that we should take the time to learn about others.

   _____

   _____

5. Graciously accept the blame for not making your meaning clear. If a misunderstanding results.

   _____

Skill Check 2.2 Making Sentences Complete

Expand the following fragments into complete sentences. Add your own ideas. Be ready to explain why each fragment is incomplete and what you did to remedy the problem.

Example: If we keep in mind that Americans abroad are often accused of talking too much.

Revision: If we keep in mind that Americans abroad are often accused of talking too much, we will become better listeners.

1. The businessperson who engages a translator for important contracts

   _____

2. Assuming that a nod, a yes, or a smile indicates agreement

   _____

3. If you learn greetings and a few phrases in the language of the country you are visiting

   _____

4. Although global business transactions are often conducted in English

   _____

5. Which is why Americans sometimes put words in the mouths of foreign friends struggling to express an idea

   _____

   _____

Writing Concise Sentences

Businesspeople and professionals value concise, economical writing. Wordy communication wastes the reader's time and sometimes causes confusion. You can make your sentences more concise by avoiding opening fillers, revising wordy phrases, and eliminating redundant words.

Avoiding Opening Fillers

Openers such as *there is, it is, you might be interested to learn that*, and *this is to inform you that* fill in sentences but generally add no meaning. Train yourself to question these constructions. About 75 percent can be eliminated, almost always resulting in more concise sentences.

Wordy: *There are* three students who volunteered to help.

Revised: Three students volunteered to help.

Wordy: *This is to inform you that* our offices will be closed on Monday.

Revised: Our offices will be closed on Monday.

Revising Wordy Phrases

Some of our most common and comfortable phrases are actually full of "word fat." When examined carefully, these phrases can be pared down considerably.

Wordy Phrases	Concise Substitutes
as per your suggestion	as you suggested
at this point in time	now
due to the fact that	because
for the purpose of	to
give consideration to	consider
in all probability	probably
in spite of the fact that	even though
in the amount of	for
in the event that	if
in the near future	soon
in the neighborhood of	about
in view of the fact that	since
with regard to	about

Notice how you can revise wordy sentences to make them more concise:

Wordy: *Due to the fact that* fire damaged our distribution center, we must delay some shipments.

Revised: *Because* fire damaged our distribution center, we must delay some shipments.

Wordy: We expected growth *in the neighborhood of* 25 percent.

Revised: We expected *about* 25 percent growth.

Eliminating Redundant Words

Words that are needlessly repetitive are said to be redundant. Writers must be alert to eliminating redundant words and phrases, such as the following:

advance warning	exactly identical	perfectly clear
alter or change	few in number	personal opinion
assemble together	free and clear	potential opportunity
basic fundamentals	grateful thanks	positively certain
collect together	great majority	proposed plan
consensus of opinion	integral part	reason why
contributing factor	last and final	refer back
dollar amount	midway between	true facts
each and every	new changes	very unique
end result	past history	visible to the eye

Wordy: This paragraph is *exactly identical* to that one.

Revised: This paragraph is *identical* to that one.

Wordy: The *reason why* we are discussing the issue is to reach a *consensus of opinion*.

Revised: The *reason* we are discussing the issue is to reach a *consensus*.

Skill Check 2.3 Writing Concise Sentences

In the space provided, rewrite the following sentences to make them more concise.

1. There is a free booklet that shows all the new changes in employee benefits.

_____

2. In view of the fact that health care benefits are being drastically altered, this is to inform you that an orientation meeting will be scheduled in the near future.

_____

_____

3. The reason why we are attending the protest is to make our opinions perfectly clear.

_____

4. In the event that McDonald's offers new menu items for the purpose of increasing sales, experts think that there is every reason to believe that the effort will be successful.

_____

5. There will be a special showing of the orientation training film scheduled at 10 a.m. due to the fact that there were so few in number who were able to attend the first showing.

_____

6. This is to give you advance warning that we plan to alter or change the procedures for submitting travel expenses in the very near future.

_____

7. I am writing this e-mail message to let you know that each and every employee is invited to attend our holiday banquet.

_____

8. You might be interested to learn that accounting mistakes this past fiscal year were few in number.

_____

9. My personal opinion is that you understand the basic fundamentals of our operations.

_____

10. Please give consideration to the very unique skills I have to offer your organization.

_____

Writing Application 2.1. Assume you are Marcia Murphy and that you received the memo shown in Figure 2.1. Read the memo carefully, and then prepare a memo that responds to it. Show your appreciation to Jason Corzo for his advice. Explain that you are both excited and worried about your new assignment. Use your imagination to tell why. Describe how you expect to prepare for the new assignment. You might say that you plan to start learning the language, to read about the culture, and to talk with colleagues who have worked in Japan. Put this in your own words and elaborate. Make sure that your memo uses complete sentences and concise wording.

FIGURE 2.1

Interoffice Memo

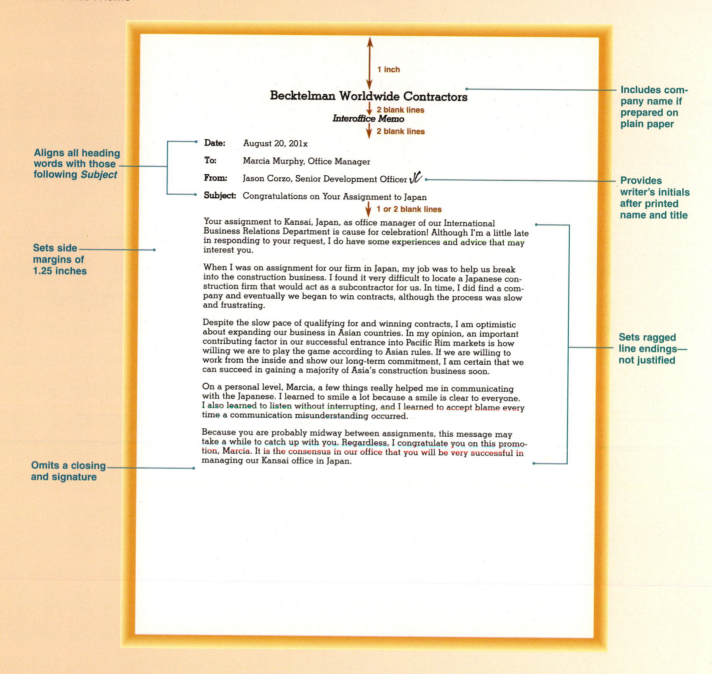

1 inch

Becktelman Worldwide Contractors

2 blank lines

Interoffice Memo

2 blank lines

Date: August 20, 201x

To: Marcia Murphy, Office Manager

From: Jason Corzo, Senior Development Officer *JC*

Subject: Congratulations on Your Assignment to Japan

1 or 2 blank lines

Your assignment to Kansai, Japan, as office manager of our International Business Relations Department is cause for celebration! Although I'm a little late in responding to your request, I do have some experiences and advice that may interest you.

When I was on assignment for our firm in Japan, my job was to help us break into the construction business. I found it very difficult to locate a Japanese construction firm that would act as a subcontractor for us. In time, I did find a company and eventually we began to win contracts, although the process was slow and frustrating.

Despite the slow pace of qualifying for and winning contracts, I am optimistic about expanding our business in Asian countries. In my opinion, an important contributing factor in our successful entrance into Pacific Rim markets is how willing we are to play the game according to Asian rules. If we are willing to work from the inside and show our long-term commitment, I am certain that we can succeed in gaining a majority of Asia's construction business soon.

On a personal level, Marcia, a few things really helped me in communicating with the Japanese. I learned to smile a lot because a smile is clear to everyone. I also learned to listen without interrupting, and I learned to accept blame every time a communication misunderstanding occurred.

Because you are probably midway between assignments, this message may take a while to catch up with you. Regardless, I congratulate you on this promotion, Marcia. It is the consensus in our office that you will be very successful in managing our Kansai office in Japan.

Includes company name if prepared on plain paper

Aligns all heading words with those following *Subject*

Provides writer's initials after printed name and title

Sets side margins of 1.25 inches

Sets ragged line endings—not justified

Omits a closing and signature

Showing the Action

5 Verbs

Uttering a word is like striking a note on the keyboard of the imagination.

– Ludwig Wittgenstein,
Austrian philosopher

Objectives

When you have completed the materials in this chapter, you will be able to do the following:

LEVEL 1

1. Identify transitive, intransitive, linking, and helping verbs.

2. Recognize the functions and uses of active- and passive-voice verbs.

3. Use correctly verbs in the present, past, and future tenses.

LEVEL 2

4. Recognize and use correctly gerunds, infinitives, and participles.

5. Identify and remedy dangling verbal phrases and other misplaced modifiers.

6. Understand and apply the subjunctive mood correctly.

LEVEL 3

7. Write the correct forms of irregular verbs.

8. Recognize verb forms in the progressive and perfect tenses.

Choose the correct answer. Then compare your answers with those below.

1. In the sentence *Robin worked on the report*, the verb *worked* is (a) transitive, (b) intransitive, (c) linking. _____

2. In the sentence *Pete felt bad after hearing the news*, the verb *felt* is (a) transitive, (b) intransitive, (c) linking. _____

3. In the sentence *The meeting was canceled*, the verbal phrase *was canceled* is in the (a) active voice, (b) passive voice, (c) subjunctive mood. _____

4. In the sentence *Dylan wishes he were rich*, the verb is in the (a) active mood, (b) subjunctive mood, (c) imperative mood. _____

5. We appreciate (a) you, (b) your bringing the matter to our attention. _____

6. Walking down the street, (a) our sign is easily seen, (b) customers can easily see our sign. _____

7. If we had (a) gone, (b) went to the training session, we might have learned something. _____

8. All the financial statements are (a) laying, (b) lying on your desk. _____

9. The accountant (a) brought, (b) brung, (c) brang all the reports to the meeting. _____

10. That partially completed building has (a) set, (b) sat there untouched for a year. _____

Verbs are words that energize sentences and delight the imagination. They tell what is happening, what happened, and what will happen. The verb is the most complex part of speech. A complete treatment of its forms and uses would require at least a volume. Our discussion of verbs will be limited to practical applications for businesspeople and professionals. In this chapter you will learn about types of verbs, verb voices, primary verb tenses, and verb moods. You will also learn about verbals, including gerunds, infinitives, and participles. Finally, you will study irregular verbs and the progressive and perfect tenses.

LEVEL 1

Types of Verbs

Verbs express an action, an occurrence, or a state of being.

Rachel <u>creates</u> our online materials. (Action)

Winter holidays <u>end</u> the fall semester. (Occurrence)

Max <u>is</u> the new manager. (State of being)

1.b 2.c 3.b 4.b 5.b 6.b 7.a 8.b 9.a 10.b

Transitive and Intransitive Verbs

Verbs that express action may be divided into two categories: *transitive* and *intransitive*. A verb expressing an action directed toward a person or thing is **transitive**. A transitive verb needs, in addition to its subject, a noun or pronoun to complete its meaning. This noun or pronoun functions as the **direct object** of the transitive verb. Notice in the following sentences that the verbs direct action toward objects.

> Employees made suggestions. (The transitive verb *made* transfers action from the subject to the object *suggestions*.)

> Yesterday the president called her. (The transitive verb *called* transfers action from the subject to the object *her*).

An action verb that does not require an object to complete its action is **intransitive**.

> Meaghan worked in our department last summer. (The intransitive verb *worked* requires no object to complete its action.)

> Stan dreams of opening his own business. (The intransitive verb *dreams* requires no object to complete its action.)

Linking Verbs

Linking verbs *link* to the subject words that rename or describe the subject. A noun, pronoun, or adjective that renames or describes the subject is called a **complement** because it *completes* the meaning of the subject.

> Mohamed is the new researcher. (*Researcher* is a noun complement that completes the meaning of the sentence by renaming *Mohamed*.)

> The caller was she. (*She* is a pronoun complement that completes the meaning of *caller*.)

Many linking verbs are derived from the *to be* verb form: *am, is, are, was, were, be, being, been*. Other words that often serve as linking verbs are *feels, appears, tastes, seems, sounds, looks,* and *smells*. Notice that several of these words describe sense experiences.

> Sam feels bad that her cell phone rang in the meeting. (*Bad* is an adjective complement following the linking verb *feel*. An adjective—not the adverb *badly*—is needed here to describe the senses.)

> Jay looks good in his interview suit. (*Good* is an adjective complement following the linking verb *looks*.)

Helping Verbs

Helping verbs are added to main verbs, which can be action or linking, to form verbal phrases. The primary helping verbs are forms of the verb *to be* (*am, is, are, was, were, be, being, been*), *to have* (*have, had, had*), and *to do* (*do, did, does*). Other helping verbs express necessity or possibility (*can, could, may, might, will, would, shall, should, must, ought to*).

> Alicia is scanning all incoming files for viruses. (The helping verb *is* is added to the main verb *scanning* to form a verbal phrase.)

> Mark can speak Chinese fluently. (The helping verb *can* is added to the main verb *speak* to create a verbal phrase.)

Verb Voices

Transitive verbs fall into two categories depending on the receiver of the action of the verbs.

Active Voice

When the verb expresses an action directed by the subject toward the object of the verb, the verb is in the **active voice**. Verbs in the active voice are direct and forceful; they clearly identify the doer of the action. For these reasons, writing that frequently uses the active voice is vigorous and effective. Writers of business and professional communications strive to use the active voice; in fact, it is called the **voice of business**.

> Angela sent the text message. (The action of the verb is directed to the object, *message*. The doer of the action is clearly identified.)

Passive Voice

When the action in a verb is directed toward the subject, the verb is in the **passive voice**. Because the passive voice can be used to avoid mentioning the performer of the action or to place less emphasis on the doer of the action, the passive voice is sometimes called the **voice of tact**. Although directness in business writing is generally preferable, in certain instances the passive voice is used, such as when indirectness is desired. Study the following examples:

Study Tip

In the passive voice, verbs always require a *helping verb*, such as *is, are, was, were, being, been*.

Active Voice:	Technicians scan our computers for viruses. (The doer of the action is clearly identified.)
Passive Voice:	Our computers are scanned for viruses by technicians. (The doer of the action is subordinated to a *by* phrase. Emphasis is on the action rather than the doer.)
Active Voice:	The accountant made three errors in the report. (The doer of the action is named.)
Passive Voice:	Three errors were made in the report. (The doer is unnamed. When the doer is unimportant or when tact is necessary, the passive voice may be used.)

Primary Tenses

English verbs change **form (inflection)** to indicate four ideas: (a) number (singular or plural); (b) person (first, second, or third); (c) voice (active or passive); and (d) tense (time).

In contrast to languages such as French and German, English verbs today are no longer heavily inflected. That is, our verbs do not change form extensively to indicate number or person. To indicate precise time, however, English uses three rather complex sets of tenses: primary tenses, perfect tenses, and progressive tenses. We will begin our discussion of verbs with the **primary tenses** (also called **simple tenses**). These tenses are used to indicate the present, the past, and the future.

Present Tense

Verbs in the **present tense** express current or habitual action. Present-tense verbs may also be used in constructions showing future action.

> We *celebrate* employees' birthdays once a month. (Current or habitual action)

> Shana *travels* to Miami next week. (Future action)

Past Tense

Verbs in the **past tense** show action that has been completed. Regular verbs form the past tense with the addition of *d* or *ed*.

> Two CPAs *audited* our firm last month.

> The report *focused* on changes in our department.

Future Tense

Verbs in the **future tense** show actions that are expected to occur at a later time. Traditionally, the helper verbs *shall* and *will* have been joined with principal verbs to express future tense. In business and professional writing today, however, the verb *will* is generally used as the helper to express future tense. Careful writers continue to use *shall* in appropriate first-person constructions (*I/We shall attend the meeting*).

> Researchers *will study* the effects of cell phone use on brain cells.

> You *will receive* the contract before June 5.

Summary of Primary Tenses

The following table gives examples of the primary tenses:

	Present Tense		Past Tense		Future Tense	
	Sing.	Plural	Sing.	Plural	Sing.	Plural
First Person	I need	we need	I needed	we needed	I will need	we will need
Second Person	you need	you need	you needed	you needed	you will need	you will need
Third Person	he, she, it needs	they need	he, she, it needed	they needed	he, she, it will need	they will need

Challenges Using Primary Tenses

Most adult speakers of our language have few problems using present, past, and future tenses. A few considerations, however, merit mention.

Using the *-s* Form Verbs

Note that third-person singular verbs require an *-s* ending (*he needs*). Therefore, whenever your subject is singular (other than *I* or *you*), you will add an *s* to the present-tense form of the verb. Add *es* if the verb ends in *s*, *sh*, *ch*, *x*, or *z*.

> She *works* (not *work*) for a large corporation.

> He *teaches* (not *teach*) English to immigrants.

Expressing "Timeless" Facts

Present-tense verbs are used to express "timeless" facts, even if these verbs occur in sentences with other past-tense verbs.

> What *is* (not *was*) the name of the customer who called yesterday?

> Joan Brault's maiden name *is* (not *was*) Haitz.

> What did you say his duties *are* (not *were*)? (Use the present-tense *are* if he continues to perform these duties.)

Spelling Verbs That Change Form

Use a dictionary to verify the spelling of verbs that change form. You must be particularly careful in spelling verbs ending in *y* (*hurry, hurries, hurried*) and verbs for which the final consonant is doubled (*occurred, expelled*).

Now complete the reinforcement exercises for Level 1.

• LEVEL 2 •

Present and Past Participles

To be able to use all the tenses of verbs correctly, you must understand the four principal parts of verbs: present, past, present participle, and past participle. You have already studied the present and past forms. Now, let's consider the participles.

Present Participle

The **present participle** of regular and irregular verbs is formed by adding *ing* to the present tense of the verb. The present participle must be preceded by one or more helping verbs, which are usually forms of the verb *to be* such as *am, is, are, was, were, be,* and *been.*

> Madison *is preparing* for her interview. (Present participle *preparing* plus the helping verb *is*)

> I *am writing* my résumé. (Present participle *writing* plus the helping verb *am*)

Past Participle

The **past participle** of a regular verb is formed by adding a *d* or *ed* to the present tense of the verb. (Irregular verbs form their past participle forms differently.) Like present participles, past participles must combine with one or more helping verbs, which are usually forms of *to have,* such as *has, had,* or *have:*

> Madison *has researched* the company thoroughly. (Past participle *researched* plus the helping verb *has*)

> I *have called* many companies. (Past participle *called* plus the helping verb *have*)

Avoid using participial phrases that sound awkward, such as these:

Awkward: Pam's having been promoted to office manager was cause for celebration.
Better: Pam's promotion to office manager was cause for celebration.

Awkward: Being as you live nearby, should we carpool?
Better: Because you live nearby, should we carpool?

Career Tip

You will win the respect of your colleagues if you avoid using *being, being as,* or *being that* when you mean *since* or *because* (*Being it was hot...*). These substandard usages indicate poor education and can limit a career.

Verbals

As you learned earlier, English is a highly flexible language in which a given word may have more than one grammatical function. **Verbals** are words that function as nouns, adjectives, or adverbs. Three kinds of verbals are gerunds (verbal nouns), infinitives, and participles (verbal adjectives).

Gerunds

A **gerund** is a verb form ending in *ing* that is used as a noun. Gerunds often describe activities.

> *Marketing* our products on the Web is necessary. (The gerund *Marketing* is used as the subject.)

> Travis insisted on *revealing* the code. (The gerund *revealing* is used as the object of a preposition.)

In using gerunds, follow this rule: Make any noun or pronoun modifying a gerund possessive. Because we sometimes fail to recognize gerunds as nouns, we fail to make their modifiers possessive:

> Amelia resented *his calling* during lunch. (The gerund *calling* requires the possessive pronoun *his*, not the objective-case pronoun *him*.)

> The manager appreciated *your working* late. (The gerund *working* requires the possessive pronoun *your*.)

> The staff objects to *Curtis's smoking*. (The staff objects to the smoking, not to Curtis.)

Infinitives

When the present form of a verb is preceded by *to*, the most basic verb form results: the **infinitive**. The sign of the infinitive is the word *to*. In certain expressions infinitives may be misused. Observe the use of the word *to* in the following infinitive phrases. Do not substitute the conjunction *and* for the *to* of the infinitive.

> Try *to call* (not *try and call*) when you arrive.

> Be sure *to* (not *be sure and*) *speak* softly when you use your cell phone in public.

When any word appears between *to* and the verb (*to* carefully *prepare*), an infinitive is said to be split. At one time split infinitives were considered great grammatical sins. Today most authorities agree that infinitives may be split if necessary for clarity and effect. Avoid, however, split infinitives that result in awkward sentences.

> **Awkward:** Neal wanted *to*, if he could find time, *take* the online class.
> **Better:** If he could find time, Neal wanted *to take* the online class.

Avoiding Misplaced Verbal Modifiers

Used correctly, verbal modifiers and phrases add clarity and description to your writing. Used incorrectly, they may seem humorous.

Introductory Verbal Phrases

Introductory verbal phrases must be followed by the words they can logically modify. Such phrases can create confusion or unintended humor when placed incorrectly in a sentence. Consider this sentence: *Sitting in the car, the mountains were breathtaking.* The introductory verbal phrase in this sentence is said to *dangle* because it is not followed immediately by a word it can logically modify. This sentence says the mountains are sitting in the car. The sentence could be improved by adding a logical subject: *Sitting in the car, we saw the breath-taking mountains.*

After reading an introductory verbal phrase, ask the question *Who?* The answer to that question must immediately follow the introductory phrase. For example, *To find a good job, who?* Answer: *To find a good job, Derek wrote to many companies.*

Observe how the following illogical sentences have been improved:

Illogical: Slipping on the stairs, his ankle was injured.
Logical: Slipping on the stairs, *he* injured his ankle.

Illogical: Opening my iPad, his message came up immediately.
Logical: Opening my iPad, *I* saw his message immediately.

Illogical: Skilled with computers, the personnel director hired Liz McGrath.
Logical: Skilled with computers, Liz McGrath was hired by the personnel director.

But: To master a language, listen carefully to native speakers. (In commands the understood subject is *you. To master a language, [you] listen carefully to native speakers.* Therefore, the introductory phrase is correctly followed by the word to which it refers.)

Misplaced Verbal Phrases in Other Positions

In other positions within sentences, verbal phrases must also be placed in logical relation to the words they modify.

Illogical: The missing purchase orders were found by his assistant lying in the top desk drawer.
Logical: His assistant found the missing purchase orders lying in the top desk drawer.

Illogical: Doctors discovered that his wrist had been fractured in five places during surgery.
Logical: During surgery, doctors discovered that his wrist had been fractured in five places.

Verb Moods

Three verb moods enable a speaker or writer to express an attitude toward a subject: (a) The **indicative mood** expresses a fact (*We need the contract*); (b) the **imperative mood** expresses a command (*Send the contract immediately*); (c) the **subjunctive mood** expresses a doubt, a conjecture, or a suggestion (*If the contract were here, we could begin*). The subjunctive mood may cause speakers and writers difficulty and therefore demands special attention.

Subjunctive Mood

Careful speakers and writers use the subjunctive mood in clauses that express a doubt, a conjecture, or a suggestion. Some of those clauses begin with *if* and *wish.*

If and wish Clauses

When a statement that is doubtful or contrary to fact is introduced by *if, as if,* or *wish,* substitute the subjunctive form *were* for the indicative form *was.*

Ann acts as if she *were* the boss. (Ann is *not* the boss.)

Jason wishes he *were* able to program. (Jason is *not* able to program.)

Trivia Tidbit

Although English has more total speakers than any other language (1,143 million), only a small minority (331 million) are native speakers. The others are "lingua franca" speakers who use English as their second or third language.

Career Tip

To be an effective communicator, you will want to use the subjunctive mood correctly. A business or professional person would avoid saying *If I was you,* for example.

But if the statement could possibly be true, use the indicative form.

> If José *was* in the audience, I missed him. (José might have been in the audience.)

That Clauses

When a *that* clause follows a verb expressing a command, recommendation, request, suggestion, or requirement, use the subjunctive verb form *be for to be* verbs.

> The CEO required that all board members *be* (not *are*) present at the meeting.

> Our manager recommends that all reports *be* (not *are*) proofread twice.

Motions

When a meeting motion is stated, a subjunctive verb form should be used in the following *that* clause.

> Manuel moved that a vote *be* (not *is*) taken.

> Sierra seconded the motion that the meeting *be* (not *is*) adjourned.

Now complete the reinforcement exercises for Level 2.

LEVEL 3

Irregular Verbs

Up to this point, we have considered only regular verbs. Regular verbs form the past tense by the addition of *d* or *ed* to the present-tense form. **Irregular verbs**, however, form the past tense by varying the root vowel and, commonly, adding *en* to the past participle. A list of the more frequently used irregular verbs follows. Learn the forms of these verbs by practicing in patterns such as the following:

Present Tense:	Today I <u>drive</u>.
Past Tense:	Yesterday I <u>drove</u>.
Future Tense:	Tomorrow I <u>will drive</u>.
Past Participle:	In the past I <u>have driven</u>.
Present Participle:	Next week I <u>am driving</u>.

Frequently Used Irregular Verbs

Career Tip

In employment interviews, recruiters listen carefully to a candidate's spoken English. One quick way to be eliminated is to substitute a verb past tense for a past participle. INCORRECT: *He come over last night* or *I seen them.*

Present	Past	Past Participle	Present Participle
arise	arose	arisen	arising
be (am, is, are)	was, were	been	being
become	became	become	becoming
begin	began	begun	beginning
bite	bit	bitten	biting
blow	blew	blown	blowing

Present	Past	Past Participle	Present Participle
break	broke	broken	breaking
bring	brought	brought	bringing
build	built	built	building
burst	burst	burst	bursting
buy	bought	bought	buying
catch	caught	caught	catching
choose	chose	chosen	choosing
come	came	come	coming
dig	dug	dug	digging
do	did	done	doing
draw	drew	drawn	drawing
drink	drank	drunk	drinking
drive	drove	driven	driving
eat	ate	eaten	eating
fall	fell	fallen	falling
fight	fought	fought	fighting
fly	flew	flown	flying
forget	forgot	forgotten *or* forgot	forgetting
forgive	forgave	forgiven	forgiving
freeze	froze	frozen	freezing
get	got	gotten *or* got	getting
give	gave	given	giving
go	went	gone	going
grow	grew	grown	growing
hang (an object)	hung	hung	hanging
hang (a person)	hanged	hanged	hanging
hide	hid	hidden *or* hid	hiding
know	knew	known	knowing
lay (to place)	laid	laid	laying
lead	led	led	leading
leave	left	left	leaving
lend	lent	lent	lending
lie (to rest)	lay	lain	lying
lie (to tell a falsehood)	lied	lied	lying
lose	lost	lost	losing
make	made	made	making

Study Tip

When you look up an irregular verb in the dictionary, the dictionary will generally show its tenses in this order: past, past participle, present participle.

Present	Past	Past Participle	Present Participle
pay	paid	paid	paying
prove	proved	proved *or* proven	proving
ride	rode	ridden	riding
ring	rang	rung	ringing
rise (to move up)	rose	risen	rising
run	ran	run	running
see	saw	seen	seeing
set (to place)	set	set	setting
shake	shook	shaken	shaking
shrink	shrank	shrunk	shrinking
sing	sang	sung	singing
sink	sank	sunk	sinking
sit (to rest)	sat	sat	sitting
speak	spoke	spoken	speaking
spring	sprang	sprung	springing
steal	stole	stolen	stealing
strike	struck	struck *or* stricken	striking
swear	swore	sworn	swearing
swim	swam	swum	swimming
take	took	taken	taking
teach	taught	taught	teaching
tear	tore	torn	tearing
throw	threw	thrown	throwing
wake	woke	woken	waking
wear	wore	worn	wearing
write	wrote	written	writing

Three Pairs of Frequently Misused Irregular Verbs

Three pairs of verbs often cause confusion: *lie–lay, sit–set,* and *raise–rise.* The secret to using them correctly lies in (a) recognizing their tense forms and (b) knowing whether they are transitive or intransitive. Recall that transitive verbs require objects; intransitive verbs do not.

Lie–Lay

These two verbs are confusing because the past tense of *lie* is spelled in the same way that the present tense of *lay* is spelled. To be safe, memorize these verb forms:

	Present	Past	Past Participle	Present Participle
Intransitive:	lie (to rest)	lay	lain	lying
Transitive:	lay (to place)	laid (not *layed*)	laid	laying

The verb *lie* is intransitive; therefore, it requires no direct object to complete its meaning.

> I *lie* down for a nap every afternoon. (Present tense. Note that *down* is not a direct object.)

> "*Lie* down," Mark told his dog. (Commands are given in the present tense.)

> Tomorrow I *will lie* down for a nap after lunch. (Future tense)

> Yesterday I *lay* down for a nap. (Past tense)

> Those sheets *have lain* in the copy machine for some time. (Past participle)

> The contract *is lying* on the desk. (Present participle)

The verb *lay* is transitive and must have a direct object to complete its meaning. The objects in the following sentences have been underlined.

> Did you *lay* your <u>cell phone</u> on the conference table? (Present tense)

> *Lay* the <u>report</u> over there. (Command in the present tense)

> We *will lay* new <u>tile</u> in the reception area. (Future tense)

> He *laid* the <u>handouts</u> on the conference table. (Past tense)

> He *has laid* <u>bricks</u> all his life. (Past participle)

> The contractor *is laying* new <u>flooring</u> in the kitchen. (Present participle)

Sit–Set

Less troublesome than *lie–lay,* the combination of *sit–set* is nevertheless perplexing because the sounds of the verbs are similar. The intransitive verb *sit* (past tense, *sat;* past participle, *sat*) means "to rest" and requires no direct object.

> I like to *sit* in the front row in class. (Present tense)

> They *sat* in the theater through the closing credits. (Past tense)

> They *had sat* in the waiting room for two hours before they decided to leave. (Past participle)

The transitive verb *set* (past tense, *set;* past participle, *set*) means "to place" and must have a direct object. The objects in the following sentences have been underlined.

> Letty usually *sets* her coffee <u>mug</u> there. (Present tense)

> The movers *set* the <u>printer</u> on your desk yesterday. (Past tense)

> CEO Harding *had set* the <u>deadline</u> before conferring with his employees. (Past participle)

Study Tip

Whenever you use *lay* in the sense of "placing" something, you must provide a receiver of the action: Try asking yourself "Lay what?" *Please lay the book down (lay what? the book).* If nothing receives the action, you probably want the verb *lie,* which means "resting."

Study Tip

To help you remember that these verbs are intransitive, look at the second letter of each: l*i*e, s*i*t, r*i*se. Associate *i* with intransitive.

Trivia Tidbit

The English word with the most definitions is *set.* This word can be used as a noun, a verb, or an adjective.

Rise–Raise

The intransitive verb *rise* (past tense, *rose;* past participle, *risen*) means "to go up" or "to ascend" and requires no direct object.

> The sun *rises* every morning in the east. (Present tense. *Every morning* is an adverbial phrase, not an object.)
>
> The president *rose* from her chair to greet us. (Past tense)
>
> The room temperature *has risen* steadily since the meeting began. (Past participle)

The transitive verb *raise* (past tense, *raised;* past participle, *raised*) means "to lift up" or "to elevate" and must have a direct object. The objects in the following sentences have been underlined.

> Please *raise* the <u>window</u>. (Present tense)
>
> The nonprofit *raised* needed <u>funds</u> during its annual event. (Past tense)
>
> That restaurant *will raise* <u>prices</u> next month. (Future tense)
>
> Airlines *have raised* <u>fares</u> over the past year. (Past participle)

Progressive and Perfect Tenses

Thus far in this chapter, you have studied the primary tenses and irregular verbs. The remainder of this chapter focuses on two additional sets of verb tenses: the perfect and the progressive. Most native speakers and writers of English have little difficulty controlling these verb forms because they have frequently heard them used correctly. This largely descriptive section is thus presented for those who are not native speakers and for those who are eager to study the entire range of verb tenses.

Progressive Tenses

The **progressive tenses** are used to show continuous or repeated actions. The **present-progressive tense** describes ongoing actions that are happening presently. The **past-progressive tense** describes ongoing actions that occurred in the past, usually as another action was taking place. The **future-progressive tense** describes ongoing actions that will take place in the future. Form the progressive tenses by adding a form of *to be* to the present participle (*-ing*) form of a verb, as you can see in the following table.

Present-Progressive Tense		
First Person	**Second Person**	**Third Person**
I am hearing	you are hearing	he, she, it is hearing
we are hearing		they are hearing
Past-Progressive Tense		
First Person	**Second Person**	**Third Person**
I was hearing	you were hearing	he, she, it was hearing
we were hearing		they were hearing
Future-Perfect Tense		
First Person	**Second Person**	**Third Person**
I will be hearing	you will be hearing	he, she, it will be hearing
we will be hearing		they will be hearing

Examples of Progressive-Tense Verbs in Sentences

We *are importing* many of our products from China. (Present-progressive tense expresses action in progress.)

We *were sitting* down to dinner when we lost power. (Past-progressive tense indicates action that was begun in the past.)

They *will be receiving* the announcement shortly. (Future-progressive tense indicates action in the future.)

Perfect Tenses

The **perfect tenses** are used to show actions that are already completed, or *perfected*. The **present-perfect tense** describes actions that began in the past and have continued to the present. The **past-perfect tense** describes past actions that took place before other past actions. The **future-perfect tense** describes actions that will take place before other future actions. Form progressive tenses by adding a form of *to have* to the past participle form of a verb, as you can see in the following table.

Present-Perfect Tense		
First Person	**Second Person**	**Third Person**
I have heard	you have heard	he, she, it has heard
we have heard		they have heard

Past-Perfect Tense		
First Person	**Second Person**	**Third Person**
I had heard	you had heard	he, she, it had heard
we had heard		they had heard

Future-Perfect Tense		
First Person	**Second Person**	**Third Person**
I will have heard	you will have heard	he, she, it will have heard
we will have heard		they will have heard

Examples of Perfect-Tense Verbs in Sentences

The national debt *has increased* substantially. (Present-perfect tense expresses action just completed, or *perfected*.)

The check *had cleared* the bank before I canceled payment. (Past-perfect tense shows an action finished before another action in the past.)

The polls *will have been closed* two hours when the results are telecast. (Future-perfect tense indicates action that will be completed before another future action.)

Now complete the reinforcement exercises for Level 3.

Courtesy of Mary Ellen Guffey

Courtesy of Carolyn M. Seefer

Dr. Guffey   Professor Seefer

Q: As a command, which is correct: *lay down* or *lie down?*

A: Commands are given in the present tense. You would never tell someone to *Closed the door* because commands are not given in the past tense. To say *Lay down* (which is the past-tense form of *lie*) is the same as saying *Closed the door*. Therefore, use the present tense: *Lie down.*

Q: Is it correct to say, *I messaged you* or *I texted you?* Are these real verbs?

A: English is a flexible and receptive language. It often allows the conversion of nouns into verbs. The practice is called *verbing* (he *cornered* the market, we *tabled* the motion, she *calendared* the date). New uses of words usually become legitimate when the words fill a need and are immediately accepted. Some word uses, though, appear to be mere fads, such as *The homeless child could not language her fears.* Forcing the noun *language* to function as a verb is unnecessary when a good word already exists for the purpose: *express.*

Q: I learned that the verb *set* requires an object. If that is true, how can we say that the sun *sets* in the west?

A: Good question! The verb *set* generally requires an object, but it does have some standardized uses that do not require an object, such as the one you mention. Here's another: *Some concretes set quickly.* We doubt that anyone would be likely to substitute *sit* in either of these unusual situations. While we are on the subject, the verb *sit* also has some exceptions. Although generally the verb *sit* requires no object, *sit* has a few uses that require objects: *Sit yourself down* and *The waiter sat us at Table 1.*

Q: I thought I knew the difference between *principal* and *principle,* but now I'm not so sure. In a report from management, I saw this: *The principal findings of the market research are negative.* I thought *principal* always meant your "pal," the school principal.

A: You're partly right and partly wrong. *Principal* may be used as a noun meaning "chief" or "head person." In addition, it may be used as an adjective to mean "chief" or "main." This is the meaning most people forget, and this is the meaning of the word in your sentence. The word *principle* means a "law" or "rule." Perhaps it is easiest to remember *principle = rule.* All other uses require *principal:* the *principal* of the school, the *principal* of the loan, the *principal* reason.

Q: I saw this in an auction announcement for a Beverly Hills home: *Married to interior decorator Dusty Bartlett, their home saw many of the great Hollywood parties with friends such as Ingrid Bergman and Katharine Hepburn setting by the pool on weekends.* Am I just imagining, or does this sentence say that the home was married to the interior decorator?

A: Amazing, isn't it! But that's what the sentence says. This is a classic dangling modifier. An introductory verbal phrase must be immediately followed by words that the phrase can logically modify. This sentence doesn't give a clue. Did you see another problem? The verb *setting* should be *sitting.*

Circle art: © iStockphoto.com/Pavel Khorenyan

Q: I received a magazine advertisement recently that promised me a *free gift* and a *15 percent off discount* if I subscribed. What's wrong with this wording?

A: You have got a double winner here in the category of redundancies. The word *gift* suggests *free*; therefore, to say *free gift* is like *saying I am studying English English.* It would be better to say *special gift.* In the same way, *15 percent off discount* repeats itself. Omit *off.*

Q: When do you use *may* and when do you use *can*?

A: Traditionally, the verb *may* is used in asking or granting permission (*yes, you may use that desk*). *Can* is used to suggest ability (*you can succeed in business*). In informal writing, however, authorities today generally agree that *can* may be substituted for *may.*

Q: On my computer I am using a program that checks the writer's style. My problem is that it flags every passive-voice verb and tells me to consider using an active-voice verb. Are passive-voice verbs totally forbidden in business and professional writing?

A: Of course not! Computer style-checkers capitalize on language areas that can be detected mechanically, and a passive-voice verb is easily identified by a computer. Although active-voice verbs are considered more forceful, passive-voice verbs have a genuine function in business and professional writing. Because they hide the subject and diffuse attention, passive-voice verbs are useful in sensitive messages where indirect language can develop an impersonal, inconspicuous tone. For example, when a lower-level employee must write a persuasive and somewhat negative message to a manager, passive-voice verbs are quite useful.

Q: What's the correct verb in this sentence? *If I (was or were) manager, things would be much different.*

A: The verb should be *were* because the clause in which it functions is not true. Statements contrary to fact that are introduced by words such as *if* and *wish* require subjunctive-mood verbs.

Q: Even when I use a dictionary, I can't tell the difference between *affect* and *effect*. What should the word be in this sentence? *Changes in personnel (affected/effected) our production this month.*

A: No words generate more confusion than do *affect* and *effect*. In your sentence, use *affected.* Let's see if we can resolve the *affect/effect* dilemma. *Affect* is a verb meaning "to influence" (*smoking affects health; government policies affect citizens*). *Affect* may also mean "to pretend or imitate" (*he affected a British accent*). *Effect* can be a noun or a verb. As a noun, it means "result" (*the effect of the law is slight*). As a verb (and here's the troublesome part) *effect* means "to produce a result" (*small cars effect gasoline savings; GM effected a new pricing policy*).

SPOT THE Blooper

Using the skills you are learning in this class, try to identify why the following items are bloopers. Consult your textbook, dictionary, or reference manual as needed. To see if you recognized the blooper, go to **www.cengagebrain.com** and use your access code to see the Spot the Blooper key.

Blooper 1: A trousers ad in the Lands' End catalog says, "Cargo pockets lay flat, never bulky."

Blooper 2: From the book *A Thousand Days in Venice*: "Plumped and tied up in cotton string, I braised the veal in butter and white wine."

Blooper 3: The manager of the Denver Nuggets quoted in the *Denver Post*: "I appreciate them giving it more time because Melo and us want everybody to know he's innocent." [Did you spot two bloopers?]

Blooper 4: On the Fox Sports website, describing the competition for the Most Valuable Player trophy in the Pro Bowl: "The honor could have went to Terrell Owens, who caught two TD passes."

Blooper 5: A restaurant critic in the *Chicago Tribune* gave a tip regarding a Chinese eatery: "Chose from 47 varieties of dim sum."

Blooper 6: In an *Indianapolis Star* article about a search for Bigfoot by a man identified only as "Tom": "Allegedly covered in hair, standing more than 8 feet tall and reeking of a pungent odor, Tom believes the creature he saw in June to be Bigfoot."

Blooper 7: In a summons from Santa Clara County to potential jurors: "You might not qualify for a jury if you do not read, right, or understand the English language."

Blooper 8: From an advertisement for the Egyptian Tourist Authority appearing in *The Boston Globe*: "I wish I was in Egypt."

Blooper 9: In the *Atlanta Journal-Constitution*: ". . . [a University of Georgia player] apologized for an unspecified 'mistake' that led to him participating in the team's first practice of the season as a reserve."

Blooper 10: From the *Chicago Tribune's* "Redeye": "Trekking through the sand dunes of the Sahara atop a camel wearing vintage Dior and ultrahigh stilettos was just another day on the set for Sara Jessica Parker."

Reinforcement Exercises

A. Self-Check. Verbs. Choose the correct answer.

1. A verb expressing an action toward a person or thing is *(a) transitive, (b) intransitive, (c) subjunctive.* _____

2. An action verb that does not require an object to complete its action is *(a) transitive, (b) intransitive, (c)subjunctive.* _____

3. Mia felt *(a) bad, (b) badly* when she was not hired. _____

4. When a verb directs its action toward an object, the verb is in the *(a) active voice, (b) passive voice.* _____

5. Is the verb in the following sentence *(a) active or (b) passive? Our organization raised funds for scholarships.* _____

6. Is the verbal phrase in the following sentence *(a) active or (b) passive? Additional funds for scholarships were raised by college donors.* _____

7. Is the verb in the following sentence *(a) active or (b) passive? Energy drinks were given away at campus events to promote a brand.* _____

8. She *(a) write, (b) writes* e-mails, tweets, and texts every day. _____

9. The bank *(a) denied, (b) denyed* our loan application. _____

10. What *(a) is, (b) was* the name of eBay's former CEO? _____

Check your answers below.

B. Active and Passive Voice. Indicate whether the verbs in the following sentences are in the (a) active or (b) passive voice.

11. Steelcase Inc. *designed* a special office chair for brainstorming sessions. _____

12. Our company *monitors* the Web activity of all employees. _____

13. The Web activity of all employees *is monitored* by our company. _____

14. New subscribers *were offered* a bonus. _____

15. Bradley *was asked* to give the keynote address. _____

16. Workplaces *celebrate* National Boss's Day on October 16. _____

17. Researchers *found* a correlation between childhood obesity and asthma. _____

18. The White House website *was redesigned* to improve communication. _____

19. Increasingly, businesses *are storing* their data in digital files. _____

20. Security breaches *were disclosed* by T.J. Maxx and Marshalls. _____

1.a 2.b 3.a 4.a 5.a 6.b 7.b 8.b 9.a 10.a

C. Writing Exercise. Active and Passive Voice. Careful writers use the active voice in business and professional communications when they want to identify the "doer" of the action. Rewrite the following sentences changing their passive-voice verbs to active voice. Normally you can change a verb from passive to active voice by making the doer of the action—usually contained in a *by* phrase—the subject of the sentence.

Example: (Passive) Production costs must be reduced by manufacturers.

(Active) Manufacturers must reduce production costs._____

21. Pollution was greatly reduced by General Motors when the company built its new plant. (**Hint:** *Who* greatly reduced pollution? Start your new sentence with that name.)

_____

22. A car with solar panels that will power the air-conditioning system was designed by Toyota.

_____

23. Approximately one billion text messages are sent every day by Filipinos.

_____

24. Massive short-term financing is used by Nike to pay off its production costs during its slow season.

_____

25. Doctors are offered cash rewards by insurance companies for prescribing generic drugs.

_____

Some sentences with passive-voice verbs do not identify the doer of the action. Before these sentences can be converted to active voice, a subject must be provided.

Example: (Passive) New subscribers will be offered a bonus. (By whom?—let's say by *The Wall Street Journal*.)

(Active) *The Wall Street Journal* will offer new subscribers a bonus._____

In each of the following sentences, first answer the question *By whom?* Then rewrite the sentence in the active voice, beginning with your answer as the subject.

26. Net income before taxes must be calculated carefully when you fill out your tax return. (By whom?)

_____

27. The documents were carefully reviewed during the audit. (By whom?)

_____

28. The website was recently redesigned to increase its attractiveness and effectiveness. (By whom?)

_____
_____

29. Only a few of the many errors and changes were detected during the first proofreading. (By whom?)

_____

30. A cell phone tower was constructed in their neighborhood. (By whom?)

_____

D. Writing Exercise. Primary Tenses. In the following sentences, provide three tenses for each verb.

Example: He (arrive) at the office at 7:45 a.m.

Past <u>arrived</u>   Present <u>arrives</u>   Future <u>will arrive</u>

31. Our local bookstore (carry) 27 different cookbooks.

Past _____   Present _____   Future _____

32. A dental clinic (open) in our local supermarket.

Past _____   Present _____   Future _____

33. Our supervisor (copy) us on every e-mail message related to the pending merger.

Past _____   Present _____   Future _____

34. Samantha (hurry) to catch the early train.

Past _____   Present _____   Future _____

35. Jason (try) to improve his writing skills.

Past ____   Present ____   Future ____

36. Judy Reinman (cover) the same material in her class.

Past _____   Present _____   Future _____

37. Courtney (plan) to major in finance.

Past _____   Present _____   Future _____

38. The local community college (invest) in child-care facilities for student parents.

Past _____   Present _____   Future _____

39. Interviewers (prefer) candidates with excellent communication skills.

Past _____   Present _____   Future _____

40. Questionnaires (sample) customers' reactions to our new product.

Past _____   Present _____   Future _____

LEVEL 2

A. Self-Check. Participles, Verbals, and Subjunctive Mood. Choose the correct answer.

41. *(a) Because, (b) Being that* we're friends, we tweet and text every day.   _____

42. We appreciate *(a) you, (b) your* filling in for us at the meeting.   _____

43. The auditor questioned *(a) Rachel's, (b) Rachel* traveling first class.   _____

44. We hope you will *(a) try and, (b) try to* call when you arrive.   _____

45. *(a) Being as, (b) Because* you have the qualifications, you should be hired.   _____

46. Which is more logical? *(a) Driving to the office, an accident occurred.*
(b) Driving to the office, we saw an accident.   _____

47. Which is more logical? *(a) After reading it thoroughly, the proposal was rejected.*
(b) After reading it thoroughly, we rejected the proposal.   _____

48. Which is more logical? *(a) In my office I have the report you wrote. (b) I have the report you wrote in my office.* _____

49. If I *(a) was, (b) were* the manager, I would have acted more ethically. _____

50. Our company requires that all visitors *(a) be given, (b) are* given identification passes. _____

Check your answers below.

B. Gerunds, Infinitives. Choose the correct answer.

51. Eric's hiring depends on *(a) him, (b) his* making a good impression in the interview. _____

52. *(a) You, (b) Your* developing the new ad campaign made a big difference in this year's profits. _____

53. Fellow workers would appreciate *(a) your, (b) you* not smoking on the premises. _____

54. Did the boss recommend *(a) them, (b) their* attending the demonstration? _____

55. *(a) Him, (b) His* being on time for the appointment is very important. _____

56. He has to *(a) as soon as he graduates, find a full-time job, (b) find a full-time job as soon as he graduates.* _____

57. *(a) Be sure to (b) Be sure and* arrive on time. _____

58. *(a) When the occasion was right, she planned to ask her boss for a raise. (b) She planned to, when the occasion was right, ask her boss for a raise.* _____

59. *(a) Being as, (b) Because* you understand the process, please explain it to the staff. _____

60. I think *(a) them, (b) their* being present at the hearing is critical. _____

C. Writing Exercise. Misplaced Verbal Modifiers. The following sentences have illogical introductory verbal phrases. Rewrite each sentence keeping that introductory phrase, but be sure it is followed by a word it can logically modify. You may need to add a subject.

Example: Cycling up Mount Diablo, the summit came into view.

Revision: Cycling up Mount Diablo, we saw the summit come into view. _____

61. Driving to the sales meeting, the radio was tuned to NPR.

_____

62. To be binding, a consideration must support every contract.

_____

63. Scattered all over my desk, my manager was surprised at the many files for our project.

_____

64. Selected as Employee of the Year, the CEO presented an award to Cecile Chang.

_____

65. After breaking into the building, the police heard the alarm set off by the burglars.

_____

The preceding sentences had misplaced introductory verbal phrases. The next sentences have misplaced verbal phrases in other positions. Rewrite these sentences so that the verbal phrases are close to the words they can logically modify.

66. Here are some tips for protecting your car from our insurance company.

_____

67. An investor said that someone stole a coin collection from a safe in his home office, which was valued at $50,000.

_____

68. An autopsy revealed the cause of death to be strangulation by the coroner.

_____

69. His wallet was found by Dave lying under the front seat of his car.

_____

70. Geologists inspected the site where the boulders broke free from a helicopter.

_____

D. Subjunctive Mood. Choose the correct answer.

71. Tony wishes that he *(a) is, (b) was, (c) were* able to retire by age fifty. _____

72. I move that Marcella *(a) is, (b) be, (c) was* appointed chair of our Hiring Committee. _____

73. The CEO recommended that each employee *(a) is, (b) was, (c) be* given one Friday off per month. _____

74. If a better employee benefits program *(a) was, (b) were, (c) is* available, recruiting would be easier. _____

75. A stockholder moved that dividends *(a) be, (b) are, (c) were* declared immediately. _____

76. If he *(a) were, (b) was, (c) be* in my position, he would have made the same decision. _____

77. I wish that our server *(a) were, (b) was, (c) be* working so that I could read my e-mail. _____

78. Our IT manager strongly advised that computer firewalls *(a) are, (b) be, (c) were* installed. _____

79. Stevie said she wished that you *(a) was, (b) were, (c) be* able to join her for lunch today. _____

80. If Tanya Patrick *(a) was, (b) were, (c) be* in the office that day, I did not see her. _____

LEVEL 3

A. Self-Check. Irregular Verbs. Choose the correct answer.

81. Have you *(a) spoke, (b) spoken* with the security officer about the alarm? _____

82. We might have *(a) chose, (b) choose, (c) chosen* a different office if we had known. _____

83. No one has *(a) seen, (b) saw* the design for the new buildings. _____

84. They have *(a) flew, (b) flown* over Kauai's Na Pali Coast in a helicopter. _____

85. Jason and she have *(a) gone, (b) went* camping for years. _____

86. Our e-mail and Web-use policy was *(a) wrote, (b) written* by Leslie Leong. _____

87. This morning's mild earthquake *(a) shaked, (b) shook* the windows in the conference room. _____

88. Over the past year, Dr. Deborah Kerlin has *(a) gave, (b) given* freely of her services. _____

89. How did he *(a) lose, (b) loose* so much weight? _____

90. The cabin's pipes *(a) busted, (b) bust, (c) burst* during the cold snap. _____

Check your answers below.

B. Irregular Verbs. Choose the correct answer.

91. Many pages were *(a) teared, (b) tore, (c) torn* from the old telephone book. _____

92. The world has *(a) shrinked, (b) shrank, (c) shrunk* considerably as a result of new communication technologies. _____

93. Candace *(a) bought, (b) buyed, (c) buy* a Vespa so that she could get around the city more easily. _____

94. Because stock prices had *(a) sank, (b) sunk, (c) sinked* to an all-time low, many investors decided to purchase safe government bonds. _____

95. Blogs have *(a) become, (b) became* an important marketing tool for many businesses. _____

96. Some observers claim that Mark Zuckerburg *(a) stealed, (b) stole, (c) stolen* the idea for Facebook from his classmates. _____

97. After you have *(a) took, (b) taken, (c) tooken* a speech course, you will feel more comfortable. _____

98. We should have *(a) thrown, (b) threw, (c) throwed* out that old printer long ago. _____

99. She *(a) payed, (b) paid* a premium to purchase a copy of the book signed by the author. _____

100. The accounting fraud investigation *(a) leaded, (b) leded, (c) led* to several arrests. _____

101. In the late 1800s, women *(a) fighted, (b) fought* for their right to vote. _____

102. Our landline has *(a) rang, (b) rung, (c) ringed* only twice in the past two days. _____

103. I can't believe that Allison *(a) brought, (b) brang, (c) brung* her dog to work. _____

104. Howling winds *(a) blowed, (b) blew, (c) blewed* all day, making outside work difficult. _____

105. The first pitch of the season was *(a) thrown, (b) threw, (c) throwed* out by the president. _____

106. One witness *(a) sweared, (b) swore, (c) swored* that he had seen the defendant the night of the robbery. _____

107. Having *(a) driven, (b) drove, (c) drived* all night, the trucker was weary. _____

108. A city museum was *(a) builded, (b) built, (c) builted* from donors' funds. _____

109. The museum idea *(a) begin, (b) began, (c) begun* to take hold two years ago. _____

110. If Taylor had *(a) wore, (b) worn, (c) weared* more suitable clothes, she might have been hired. _____

81. b 82. c 83. a 84. b 85. a 86. b 87. b 88. b 89. a 90. c

C. *Lie–Lay.* Choose the correct word for the following sentences using these verbs.

Present	Past	Past Participle	Present Participle
lie (to rest):	lay	lain	lying
lay (to place):	laid	laid	laying

111. Ms. Rivera *(a) layed, (b) laid* her cell phone on the table at the beginning of the meeting.

112. Brandy had to *(a) lay, (b) lie* down until the dizziness passed. _____

113. Please *(a) lay, (b) lie* the foundation for your presentation in your introduction. _____

114. The contracts have been *(a) lying, (b) laying* in her inbox for some time. _____

115. In fact, they had *(a) laid, (b) lain* there for more than a week. _____

116. Newman told his dog to *(a) lay, (b) lie* down. _____

117. Please *(a) lay, (b) lie* your hand on the bible and take the oath. _____

118. Last night she *(a) lay, (b) laid* on the couch for hours watching old movies. _____

119. Some people risk developing skin cancer because they insist on *(a) laying, (b) lying* in the sun. _____

120. Shops in Broadway Plaza are *(a) laying, (b) lying* plans for the holiday season. _____

D. *Sit–Set; Rise–Raise.* Choose the correct answer.

121. Members of the club decided to *(a) raise, (b) rise* funds for Doctors Without Borders. _____

122. Cooper always tries to *(a) sit, (b) set* next to the CEO during meetings. _____

123. Close the windows if you want to *(a) raise, (b) rise* the temperature in the room. _____

124. My temperature *(a) raises, (b) rises* when I exercise vigorously. _____

125. Have you been *(a) sitting, (b) setting* goals for your future? _____

126. Consumer prices are *(a) rising, (b) raising* faster than consumer income. _____

127. Brenda Woodward *(a) raised, (b) rose* the question of retroactive benefits. _____

128. Please *(a) sit, (b) set* your briefcase on the table for inspection. _____

129. Our office building *(a) sits, (b) sets* on the corner of Front and Pine. _____

130. The world literacy rate has *(a) risen, (b) raised* over the past few decades, especially for women. _____

E. Writing Exercise. Irregular Verbs. Compose original sentences using the verbs shown. Add helping verbs as needed.

131. drawn _____

132. lent _____

133. sung _____

134. caught _____

135. blown _____

136. torn _____

137. drank _____

138. forgiven _____

139. driven _____

140. arose _____

F. **FAQs About Business English Review.** Choose the correct answer.

141. When guests arrived, Andrew repeatedly had to tell his dog to *(a) lay, (b) lie* down. _____

142. The *(a) principle, (b) principal* reason for the Google investigation was concern that the way it ordered search results constituted illegal anticompetitive behavior. _____

143. To celebrate the opening of their boutique, owners offered a *(a) gift, (b) free gift* of designer fragrance. _____

144. You definitely *(a) may, (b) can* succeed in that field. _____

145. If I *(a) were, (b) was* in your shoes, I would be thrilled. _____

146. Because Brad has high *(a) principles, (b) principals*, he refused the free trip to Hawaii. _____

147. When stocks are falling, the end *(a) effect, (b) affect* is a *bear*, or downward, market. _____

148. Rising stocks *(a) affect, (b) effect* a market; when stocks are increasing, it is a *bull* market. _____

149. Many students were *(a) effected, (b) affected* when tuition costs rose. _____

150. *(a) While working on the big project, her computer hard drive failed.*
(b) While she was working on the big project, her computer hard drive failed. _____

Chat About It ◀◀

Your instructor may assign any of the following topics for you to discuss in class, in an online chat room, or on an online discussion board. Some of the discussion topics may require outside research. You may also be asked to read and respond to postings made by your classmates.

Discussion Topic 1: As you learned in the FAQs, English is a wonderfully flexible language, and "verbing" is common. Think of three nouns that have been converted to verbs. Write two complete sentences for each word—one showing the word used as a noun and one showing the word used as a verb. Share your six sentences with your classmates. Be prepared to give feedback on your classmates' sentences.

Discussion Topic 2: Think of three things you enjoy doing. Write a complete sentence for each activity, using the activity as a gerund in each sentence. Share your three sentences with your classmates; then read and give feedback on their sentences. Did they use gerunds properly?

Discussion Topic 3: Why do you think the active voice is called the "voice of business"? Why should most writing be done using active-voice verbs? When would passive voice, or the "voice of tact," be more appropriate? Think of two workplace examples in which the passive voice would be preferred, and share these examples with your classmates.

Discussion Topic 4: Prior to studying this chapter, had you ever heard of the subjunctive mood? Had you ever used it when speaking or writing? Now that you have learned about the subjunctive mood, will you start to use it? Why or why not?

Discussion Topic 5: Meg Whitman, former CEO of eBay, said, "When people use your brand name as a verb, that is remarkable." A classic example is the delivery company FedEx, which began its history as Federal Express. Over time the company's name became so synonymous with delivery that people began to use *FedEx* as a verb (*I will FedEx that package to you first thing tomorrow*). To capitalize on this phenomenon, the company officially changed its name to FedEx in 2000. Think of another company's name or brand that is now used as a verb. Share the company or brand name and a brief history with your classmates.

Choose the correct answer. Then compare your answers with those below.

1. In the sentence *She listened carefully to the instructions*, the verb *listened* is *(a) transitive, (b) intransitive, (c) linking.* _____

2. In the sentence *The cookies tasted delicious*, the verb *tasted* is *(a) transitive, (b) linking, (c) helping.* _____

3. In the sentence *An error was made*, the verbal phrase *was made* is in the *(a) active, (b) passive, (c) subjunctive* voice. _____

4. In the sentence *Elizabeth wishes she were CEO*, the verb is in the *(a) active mood, (b) subjunctive mood, (c) imperative mood.* _____

5. Nearly everyone in the office objects to *(a) you, (b) your* smoking in the break room. _____

6. Cooper usually *(a) sits, (b) sets* in the economy section when he travels. _____

7. If Susan had *(a) wrote, (b) written* the report, it would have been perfect. _____

8. Those contracts have been *(a) laying, (b) lying* on the counter for five days. _____

9. The company van was *(a) stolen, (b) stole* from the parking lot. _____

10. After being photocopied, *(a) the contract was delivered, (b) the assistant delivered the contract.* _____

1. b 2. b 3. b 4. b 5. b 6. a 7. b 8. b 9. a 10. a

Subject–Verb Agreement 6

The beautiful part of writing is that you don't have to get it right the first time, unlike, say, a brain surgeon.

– Robert Cormier, writer

Objectives

When you have completed the materials in this chapter, you will be able to do the following:

LEVEL 1
1. Locate the subjects of verbs despite prepositional phrases, intervening elements, and inverted sentence structure.
2. Make verbs agree with subjects joined by *and*, with company and organization names, and with titles.

LEVEL 2
3. Make verbs agree with subjects joined by *or* or *nor*.
4. Select the correct verbs to agree with indefinite pronouns and collective nouns.

LEVEL 3
5. Make verbs agree with *a number/the number*; quantities and measures; fractions, portions, and percentages; and *who* and *that* clauses.
6. Achieve subject–verb agreement with phrases and clauses as subjects and with subject complements.

Pretest

Choose the correct answer. Then compare your answers with those below.

1. There *(a) is, (b) are* four new appointees to the Delaware State Supreme Court. _____
2. The professor and her students *(a) is, (b) are* visiting the Bureau of Engraving and Printing tomorrow. _____
3. McDonald's *(a) has, (b) have* seen an increase in sales in its Middle Eastern locations. _____
4. One of the plant supervisors *(a) plans (b) plan* to design a new safety program. _____
5. The head surgeon, along with her entire operating room team, *(a) was, (b) were* given training on the newest laser technology. _____
6. Neither the supervisor nor members of his team *(a) is, (b) are* satisfied with the level of service. _____
7. Neither the members of his team nor the supervisor *(a) is, (b) are* satisfied with the level of service. _____
8. Everyone *(a) is, (b) are* welcome to attend the grand-opening ceremony. _____
9. The team *(a) has, (b) have* implemented a new quality assurance plan. _____
10. The number of corporate text messages *(a) is, (b) are* increasing daily. _____

Study Tip

This is one of the most important chapters in the book. Nothing reveals a person's education, or lack thereof, so quickly as verbs that don't agree with subjects. Study this chapter carefully to ensure that you sound educated and professional on the job.

Writing isn't brain surgery, but at times it can seem every bit as difficult. Fortunately, you have the opportunity to edit your writing. One important item to test for during editing is subject–verb agreement. Subjects must agree with verbs in number and person. Beginning a sentence with *He don't* damages the credibility and effectiveness of a writer or speaker.

If an error is made in subject–verb agreement, it can generally be attributed to one of three lapses: (a) failure to locate the subject, (b) failure to recognize the number (singular or plural) of the subject after locating it, or (c) failure to recognize the number of the verb. Suggestions for locating the true subject and determining the number of the subject and its verb follow.

LEVEL 1

Locating Subjects

All verbs have subjects. Locating these subjects can be difficult, particularly when (a) a prepositional phrase comes between the verb and its subject, (b) an intervening element separates the subject and verb, (c) sentences begin with *there* or *here*, and (d) sentences are inverted. You practiced locating subjects in Chapter 2, but because this is such an important skill, we provide additional instruction here.

1.b 2.b 3.a 4.a 5.a 6.b 7.a 8.a 9.a 10.a

Prepositional Phrases

Subjects of verbs are never found in prepositional phrases. Therefore, you must learn to ignore such phrases in identifying subjects of verbs. Some of the most common prepositions are *of, to, in, from, for, with, at, on,* and *by*. Notice in these sentences that the italicized prepositional phrases do not contain the subjects of the verbs.

Each *of our representatives* is knowledgeable about the issue. (The verb *is* agrees with its singular subject *Each*.)

It appears that the invoice *for the two shipments* was lost. (The verb *was* agrees with its singular subject *invoice*.)

The online version *of the magazine's college rankings* is available at its website. (The verb *is* agrees with its singular subject *version*.)

Some of the less easily recognized prepositions are *except, but, like,* and *between*. In the following sentences, distinguish the subjects from the italicized prepositional phrases.

All employees *but Bruce* are using the on-site health club regularly. (The verb *are* agrees with its plural subject *employees*.)

Everyone *except the managers* is a member of the union. (The verb *is* agrees with its singular subject *everyone*.)

Intervening Elements

Groups of words introduced by expressions such as *along with, as well as, in addition to, such as, including, together with, plus,* and *other than* do NOT contain sentence subjects.

Her favorite basketball star, *as well as other local sports figures,* is scheduled to attend the fund-raiser.

In this sentence the writer has elected to emphasize the singular subject *star* and to de-emphasize *other local sports figures*. The writer could have given equal weight to these elements by writing *Her favorite basketball star and other local sports figures are scheduled to attend the fund-raiser*. Notice that the number (singular or plural) of the verb changes when both *star* and *figures* are given equal emphasis. Study these additional examples:

Our president, *together with her entire staff of employees,* agrees that the company will rebound. (The singular subject *president* agrees with the singular verb *agrees*.)

Entrepreneurs *such as Debbi Fields* have started companies based on a single idea. (The plural subject *entrepreneurs* agrees with the plural verb *have*.)

Our job application *plus other important employment documents* is available on our website. (The singular subject *application* agrees with the singular verb *is*.)

Sentences Beginning With *there* and *here*

In sentences beginning with *there* or *here*, look for the true subject AFTER the verb. The words *here* and *there* are function words that are not classified as subjects.

Study Tip

One of the most important things to remember is that sentence subjects are *not* found in prepositional phrases. Occasionally a prepositional phrase may help to determine whether an indefinite pronoun, portion, or fraction is singular or plural. But the object of the preposition cannot function as the subject of a verb.

Career Tip

Skillful writers avoid starting sentences or clauses with *there*, a word-wasting filler. Usually sentences can be rewritten without it.

There <u>are</u> several <u>tools</u> you can use to conduct online research. (The plural subject *tools* follows the verb *are*.)

Here <u>is</u> the fuel oil consumption <u>report</u>. (The singular subject *report* follows the verb *is*.)

Be especially careful when using contractions. Remember that *here's* is the contraction for *here is*; therefore, it should be used only with singular subjects. Similarly, *there's* is the contraction for *there is* and should also be used only with singular subjects.

Incorrect:	<u>Here's</u> the <u>items</u> you ordered. (The plural subject *items* does not agree with the verb *is*.)
Correct:	Here <u>are</u> the <u>items</u> you ordered. (The plural subject *items* agrees with the verb *are*.)
Incorrect:	<u>There's</u> three <u>reasons</u> you should hire me for the editor position. (The plural subject *reasons* does not agree with the verb *is*.)
Correct:	There <u>are</u> three <u>reasons</u> you should hire me for the editor position. (The plural subject *reasons* agrees with the verb *are*.)

Inverted Sentence Order

Look for the subject after the verb in inverted sentences and in questions.

Related to everyday business <u>are</u> <u>law</u> and <u>ethics</u>. (Verb precedes plural subject.)

On the president's advisory team <u>are</u> several prominent <u>economists</u>. (Verbal precedes plural subject.)

<u>Have</u> the product <u>specifications</u> <u>been submitted</u>? (Subject separates verbal phrase.)

How important <u>are</u> <u>salary</u>, <u>benefits</u>, and <u>job security</u>? (Verb precedes subjects.)

Basic Rules for Subject–Verb Agreement

Once you have located the sentence subject, decide whether the subject is singular or plural and select a verb that agrees in number. Basic challenges occur when you have compound subjects joined by *and*, when your subject is a company or organization, and when your subject is a title of a publication or song.

Subjects Joined by *and*

When one subject is joined to another by the word *and*, the subject is generally plural and thus requires a plural verb.

<u>Mark Zuckerberg</u> and <u>Jack Dorsey</u> <u>are</u> two influential people in the world of social media.

The proposed <u>law</u> and its <u>amendment</u> <u>are</u> before the legislature.

Subjects joined by *and* are singular and thus take singular verbs in only two cases: (1) when the words are preceded by *each* or *every* and (2) when the words represent a single person or thing.

Each expense claim and purchase order <u>requires</u> a manager's signature. (Think *Each individual expense claim and each individual purchase order requires. . . .*)

Study Tip

To help you select correct verbs, temporarily substitute *it* or *he* for singular subjects or *they* for plural subjects. Then you can more easily make verbs agree with their subjects.

Every man, woman, and child <u>is</u> eligible for a free birthday meal. (Think *Every single man, every single woman, and every single child is. . . .*)

Macaroni and cheese <u>is</u> their daughter's favorite meal. (Words represent one dish.)

His <u>wife and best friend</u> <u>is</u> Christina. (Words represent one person.)

Company and Organization Names

Even though they may appear to be plural, company and organization names, including the names of sports teams and musical groups, are generally considered singular; therefore, they require singular verbs.

<u>General Motors</u> <u>was</u> able to emerge from bankruptcy after a government bailout. (Company)

<u>Richards, Bateman, and Richards, Inc.,</u> <u>is</u> offering the bond issue. (Organization)

The <u>Minnesota Vikings</u> <u>was recognized</u> for strong recruiting. (Sports team)

The <u>White Stripes</u> has just <u>announced</u> its summer concert calendar. (Musical group)

Titles

Titles of publications and of artistic works such as songs are singular; therefore, they require singular verbs.

<u>100 Ways to Make Yourself Indispensable at Work</u> <u>was</u> an instant best seller.

"<u>Tears in Heaven</u>" <u>is</u> one of Eric Clapton's most popular songs.

Now complete the reinforcement exercises for Level 1.

• LEVEL • 2

Special Rules for Subject–Verb Agreement

Making sure your subjects agree with your verbs sometimes requires the application of special rules. This is especially true when dealing with subjects joined by *or* or *nor*, indefinite pronouns as subjects, and collective nouns as subjects.

Subjects Joined by *or* or *nor*

When two or more subjects are joined by *or* or *nor*, the verb should agree with the closer subject (the subject that follows *or* or *nor*).

Neither the webmaster nor the <u>managers</u> <u>know</u> the employees' passwords.

Neither the managers nor the <u>webmaster</u> <u>knows</u> the employees' passwords.

Either Marcia or <u>you</u> <u>are</u> in charge of planning the event.

Either you or <u>Marcia</u> <u>is</u> in charge of planning the event.

Study Tip

Unlike subjects joined by *and*, subjects joined by *or* or *nor* require a choice between Subject No. 1 and Subject No. 2.

Indefinite Pronouns as Subjects

As you learned in Chapter 4, some indefinite pronouns are always singular, whereas other indefinite pronouns are always plural. In addition, some may be singular or plural depending on the words to which they refer.

	Always Singular		Always Plural	Singular or Plural
anyone	everyone	nobody	both	all
anybody	everybody	nothing	few	any
anything	everything	someone	many	more
each	neither	somebody	several	most
either	no one	something		none
every				some

Singular indefinite pronouns require singular verbs. Ignore any prepositional phrases that follow the indefinite pronoun.

Either of the two candidates is acceptable.

Somebody on the task force has to take the minutes.

Each of our employees is eligible for health benefits.

Everybody possesses the ability to succeed.

Plural indefinite pronouns require plural verbs.

Both of the ideas are valid.

Few interviewees send thank-you notes after job interviews.

Many of our politicians are working hard to represent their constituents.

Several websites offer online technical support.

Some indefinite pronouns can be **singular or plural**. These indefinite pronouns, including *all, more, most, some, any,* and *none,* provide one of the few instances in which prepositional phrases become important in determining agreement. Although the prepositional phrase does not contain the subject of the sentence, it does contain the noun to which the indefinite pronoun refers. If that noun is singular, use a singular verb. If the noun is plural, use a plural verb.

Some of the documentary film is controversial. (*Some* is singular because it refers to *film.*)

Some of the managers agree that the company needs reorganizing. (*Some* is plural because it refers to *managers.*)

Most of the work is completed. (*Most* is singular because it refers to *work.*)

Most of the applicants are college graduates. (*Most* is plural because it refers to *graduates.*)

The indefinite pronouns *anyone* and *everyone* are spelled as two words when followed by *of* phrases.

Every one of us should attend the marketing brainstorming session.

Any one of those websites can be used to book air and hotel reservations.

Collective Nouns as Subjects

Collective nouns such as *faculty, committee, team, audience, group, jury, crowd, class, board, flock,* and *council* may be singular or plural depending on how they are used in a sentence. When a collective noun operates as a single unit, its verb should be singular. When the elements of a collective noun operate separately, the verb should be plural.

The team has carefully studied the opponent's videos. (*Team* is operating as a single unit.)

The team were still dressing when the reporter entered the locker room. (*Team* members were acting separately. Although technically correct, the sentence would be less awkward if it read *The team members* were still dressing. . . .)

The city council has unanimously approved the new smart parking meters. (*Council* is operating as a single unit.)

The city council were sharply divided over whether to install smart parking meters. (*Council* members were acting separately. Although technically correct, the sentence would be less awkward if it read *The city council members* were sharply divided. . . .)

Now complete the reinforcement exercises for Level 2.

Trivia Tidbit

In the United States, collective nouns are almost always considered to be singular (*The staff is*...). In Britain, however, collective nouns are usually plural (*The staff are*...).

LEVEL 3

Additional Rules for Subject–Verb Agreement

In some instances it is difficult to know whether a subject is singular or plural. This is especially true when the word *number* is the subject of a sentence; when the subject is a quantity, measure, fraction, or portion; and when the subject is a phrase or clause. *Who* and *that* clauses and subject complements present additional challenges. Here are a few rules to guide you in selecting appropriate verbs for such subjects.

The Distinction Between *the number* and *a number*

When the word *number* is the subject of a sentence, its article (*the* or *a*) becomes significant. *The* is specific and therefore implies **singularity**; *a* is general and therefore implies **plurality**. This means that *the number* is singular and *a number* is plural. Ignore any prepositional phrases that follow.

The number of times you have been late to work is unacceptable. (Singular)

The number of text messages sent by business professionals is growing annually. (Singular)

A number of specials are included on today's menu. (Plural)

A number of stocks are traded daily. (Plural)

Quantities and Measures

When they refer to *total* amounts, quantities and measures are singular. When they refer to individual units that can be counted, quantities and measures are plural.

> Fifty dollars is all you will pay for monthly wireless access. (The quantity is expressed as a total amount.)

> Fifty dollars were laid out on the table during the demonstration. (The quantity is expressed as individual units. Although technically correct, the sentence would be less awkward if it read *Fifty dollar bills* were laid out. . . .)

> Three years is the period of the loan. (The quantity is expressed as a total amount.)

> Three years are needed to completely renovate the property. (The quantity is expressed as individual units.)

Fractions, Portions, and Percentages

Fractions, portions, and percentages may be singular or plural depending on the nouns to which they refer. To determine whether the subject is singular or plural, look at the prepositional phrase that follows.

> One third of the report was filled with errors. (The fraction *one third* is singular because it refers to *report*.)

> Only one third of voters approve of the new federal budget. (The fraction *one third* is plural because it refers to *voters*.)

> A majority of the report discusses how to implement the recommendations. (The subject *majority* is singular because it refers to *report*.)

> A majority of employees agree with the CEO's decision to restructure. (The subject *majority* is plural because it refers to *employees*.)

> A percentage of the budget is allocated to employee benefits. (The subject *percentage* is singular because it refers to *budget*.)

> A percentage of the proceeds go to charity. (The subject *percentage* is plural because it refers to *proceeds*.)

Who and *That* Clauses

Verbs in *who* and *that* clauses (known as **relative pronoun clauses**) must agree in number and person with the nouns to which they refer. In *who* and *that* clauses introduced by *one of*, the verb is usually plural because it refers to a plural noun.

> Jan Jones is *one of* those managers who always get excellent results from their employees. (Read: Of those managers who always get excellent results from their employees, Jan Jones is one. Note that the pronoun *their* also must agree with its antecedent.)

> *To Kill a Mockingbird* is *one of* those books that have an influence on readers of all ages. (Read: Of those books that have an influence on readers of all ages, *To Kill a Mockingbird* is one.)

Study Tip

When the preposition *of* follows a fraction (*three fourths of*…), do not hyphenate the fraction.

Study Tip

For sentences with *one of those who* clauses, begin reading with the word *of*: *Of those people who are late sleepers, John is one.* The verb will always be plural. However, if the sentence is limited by *only one*, the verb is always singular.

In *who* and *that* clauses introduced by *the only one of*, the verb is singular.

Maria is *the only one of* our employees who is certified to give CPR. (The adverb *only* makes the *who* clause singular.)

To Kill a Mockingbird is *the only one of* those books that is read in high school classes today. (The adverb *only* makes the *that* clause singular.)

Verbs must agree in person with the nouns or pronouns to which they refer. Identifying the subject can be even trickier when pronouns are combined with *who* clauses.

It is you who are responsible for contacting the client.

Could it be I who am to blame?

Was it you who were on the phone?

Phrases and Clauses as Subjects

Use a singular verb when the subject of a sentence is a phrase or clause.

Learning about different cultures is fascinating.

That verbs must agree with subjects is accepted.

Subject Complements

In Chapter 5 you learned that linking verbs are followed by complements. Although a complement may differ from the subject in number, the linking verb should always agree with the subject. To avoid awkwardness, reword sentences so that subjects and complements agree in number.

Awkward: The best part of the website is the graphics and video. (Although the singular subject *part* agrees with the singular verb *is*, it sounds awkward because of the plural complement *graphics and video*.)

Better: The best parts of the website are the graphics and video. (The plural subject agrees with the plural complement.)

Awkward: The reason for his bankruptcy was poor management and decision making.

Better: The reasons for his bankruptcy were poor management and decision making.

Now complete the reinforcement exercises for Level 3.

Trivia Tidbit

Each year approximately 10,000 new words are introduced to the English language. Of those, about 1,000 are widely used, and roughly 200 of those words become a part of our permanent vocabulary.

FAQs

About Business English

Dr. Guffey   Professor Seefer

Q: My uncle insists that *none* is singular. My English book says that it can be plural. Who's right?

A: Times are changing. Several years ago *none* was almost always used in a singular sense. Today, through usage, *none* may be singular or plural depending on what you wish to emphasize. For example, *None are more willing than we*. But, *None of the students is* (or *are* if you wish to suggest many students) *failing*.

Q: Is there a difference between the words *premier* and *premiere*? How can I decide which to use?

A: These words are the masculine (*premier*) and feminine (*premiere*) forms of "first" in the French language. However, they have different meanings in English. *Premier* can be used as an adjective meaning "first in position, rank, importance, or time" (*Google is one of the premier Web search tools*). As a noun, *premier* refers to "the prime minister of a parliamentary government" (*The premier spoke to a large crowd*). The word *premiere* can serve as a noun or verb. As a noun, *premiere* means "a first performance or exhibition" (*The Hollywood premiere was an exciting event*). As a verb, *premiere* means "to give a first public performance" (*The film will premiere in New York City*) or "to appear for the first time as a performer" (*Johnny Depp premiered in the film* A Nightmare on Elm Street).

Q: Are there two meanings for the word *discreet*?

A: You are probably confusing the two words *discreet* and *discrete*. *Discreet* means "showing good judgment" and "prudent" (*the witness gave a discreet answer, avoiding gossip and hearsay*). The word *discrete* means "separate" or "noncontinuous" (*Alpha, Inc., has installed discrete computers rather than a network computer system*). You might find it helpful to remember that the *e*'s are separate in *discrete*.

Q: When should I write *cannot* as one word, and when should I write it as two words?

A: The word *cannot* is always written as one word.

Q: I just checked the dictionary and found that *cooperate* is now written as one word. It seems to me that years ago it was *co-operate* or *coöperate*. Has the spelling changed?

A: Yes, it has. And so has the spelling of many other words. As new words become more familiar, their spelling tends to become more simplified. For example, *per cent* and *good will* are now shown by most dictionaries as *percent* and *goodwill*. By the same token, many words formerly hyphenated are now written without hyphens: *strike-over* is now *strikeover*, *to-day* is *today*, *editor-in-chief* is *editor in chief*, *vice-president* is *vice president*, and *passer-by* is now *passerby*. Current dictionaries reflect these changes.

Q: My son is studying a foreign language; and he asked me, an English teacher, why we capitalize the personal pronoun *I* in English when we don't capitalize other pronouns.

A: That's a fascinating topic, and a little research on the Web revealed that linguists ponder the same question. In a linguistic journal, professionals discussed some relevant theories. One linguist thought that perhaps the lowercase *i* was too easily confused with the number *1* or with similar-looking *i*'s, *u*'s, and *v*'s in medieval handwriting. Another attributed the word's capital letter to our egocentric nature. Another suggested that because the pronoun *I* usually appeared as the first word in a sentence, it was capitalized for that reason. In earlier centuries, before the language was standardized, most nouns and pronouns were capitalized haphazardly. One linguist thought that a better question to ask would be why all of the other pronouns lost their capital letters and *I* retained its.

Q: When writing e-mail messages, I often type in all capital letters. My boss just told me that I should stop this practice. Why?

A: Your boss is correct. Typing in all caps is often referred to as *shouting*. Because many people are offended by these types of messages, writing in all caps should be avoided. In addition, messages written in all caps or in all lowercase letters are difficult to read and look unprofessional. On the job, business communicators want their messages to be as professional and as easy to read as possible. Therefore, always use standard upper- and lowercase letters when writing your e-mail messages.

Q: I confuse *i.e.* and *e.g.* What's the difference?

A: The abbreviation *i.e.* stands for the Latin *id est*, meaning "that is" (*The package exceeds the weight limit, i.e., 5 pounds*). The abbreviation *e.g.* stands for the Latin *exempli gratia*, meaning "for the sake of example" or "for example" (*The manufacturer may offer a purchase incentive, e.g., a rebate or discount plan*). Notice the use of a comma after *i.e.* and *e.g.* Also notice that both abbreviations are written using lowercase letters and periods.

Q: I included this sentence in a job acceptance letter to my new employer: *I am anxious to begin my new position with Miller and Associates.* Is this sentence acceptable?

A: Have you mailed this letter yet? If not, you should change *anxious* to *eager* before doing so. *Anxious* is an adjective meaning "worried or apprehensive" (*Maggie is anxious about getting her biopsy results*). *Eager* is an adjective meaning "anticipating with enthusiasm" (*Stan is eager to get started on the new project*). Our guess is that you are eager to begin your new position!

Q: What part of speech is *there* when it begins a sentence, such as *There are two vice presidents*?

A: The word *there* generally is classified as an adverb. But in this position, the word *there* functions as a pronoun. *Merriam-Webster's Collegiate Dictionary* calls *there* a "function" word when it replaces the grammatical sentence subject.

SPOT THE Blooper

Using the skills you are learning in this class, try to identify why the following items are bloopers. Consult your textbook, dictionary, or reference manual as needed. To see if you recognized the blooper, go to **www.cengagebrain.com** and use your access code to see the Spot the Blooper key.

Blooper 1: Article in the *Cape Cod Times*: "None of this is to say hard work, education, and following your dreams and passions isn't the thing to do—for it's own sake." [Did you spot two bloopers?]

Blooper 2: From an article in *The Dupont Current* [Washington, DC]: "Google wants to try out the new fiber-to-home connections in select cities and communities, and many are anxious to serve as test subjects."

Blooper 3: In the University of St. Thomas *Daily Bulletin*: "Tim Scully's Videography class will present its world premier of music videos."

Blooper 4: In an article in *The Times-Union* [Albany, New York], the interim superintendent of schools said: "A large number of students arrives without the basic skills we expect them to have."

Blooper 5: Message printed on a Gap T-shirt: "The Days of This Society Is Numbered."

Blooper 6: Official banner welcoming Super Bowl fans to Tampa: "Welcome to Downtown Tampa: There's so many reasons to like it."

Blooper 7: An article in *The New York Times* reporting that the firing of Merrill Lynch's chair and CEO was partly because of the company's depressed stock price: "Last week, the stock sunk to as low as $59 a share."

Blooper 8: Headline in the *Cincinnati Enquirer*: "Europe lays low, hopes U.S. can mediate with Russia."

Blooper 9: Question asked in *The Hartwell Sun* [Georgia]: "How will possible layoffs effect the Hart County School System?"

Blooper 10: In the program for the Florida Center for the Books theatrical production of *Papa*, a play about Ernest Hemingway: "[the director] received her principle theatrical education at Yale University."

6 Reinforcement Exercises

LEVEL 1

A. Self-Check. Subject–Verb Agreement. Select the correct answer.

1. Speaking today *(a) is, (b) are* two top journalists, Ann Curry and Thomas Friedman. _____

2. The word *tweet*, along with several other words, *(a) was, (b) were* added to the dictionary in 2011. _____

3. Here *(a) is, (b) are* three possibilities for improving employee morale. _____

4. One of the first computer viruses *(a) was, (b) were* the "elk cloner," which was written by a ninth-grade student in 1982. _____

5. Every man, woman, and child in the country *(a) is, (b) are* to be counted in the census. _____

6. There *(a) is, (b) are* many steps Eastman Kodak must take to survive. _____

7. Addressing the conference *(a) is, (b) are* employees of the Federal Reserve. _____

8. Southwest Airlines *(a) is, (b) are* known for a fun culture that motivates employees. _____

9. A set of guidelines for protecting network security *(a) was, (b) were* developed. _____

10. *Freakonomics* by Steven D. Levitt and Stephen J. Dubner *(a) appears, (b) appear* to be one of the best-selling economics books of all time. _____

Check your answers below.

B. Identifying Simple Subjects. In the following groups of words, underline the simple subject(s).

Example: the <u>controller</u> and the <u>treasurer</u> of the county

11. a directory of current employees

12. the network administrator together with her staff

13. other services such as Web hosting and HTML coding

14. the production cost and the markup of each item

15. one of the many reasons for developing excellent communication skills

16. current emphasis on product safety and consumer protection

17. Farkas, Evans, & Everett, Inc., an executive placement service

18. the anger and frustration of passengers

19. the lead actor, as well as those in supporting roles

20. the time and money involved in the project

1.b 2.a 3.b 4.a 5.a 6.b 7.b 8.a 9.a 10.a

C. Subject–Verb Agreement. For each of the following sentences, circle the sentence subject. Next cross out any phrases that separate the verb from its subject. Then choose the correct answer.

Examples: The faculty [advisor,] ~~along with club members,~~ *(a) is, (b) are* here.   **a**

Our [catalog] ~~of wireless devices~~ *(a) is, (b) are* being sent to you.   **a**

21. Compensation, along with benefits and vacation time, *(a) is, (b) are* generally discussed after a job offer is made. _____

22. Now, just in time for the holidays, *(a) comes, (b) come* a variety of products made from recyclable materials. _____

23. The use of smartphones and tablets *(a) is, (b) are* not allowed during meetings. _____

24. A bachelor's degree from an accredited institution and three years of experience, *(a) is, (b) are* required for this position. _____

25. Everyone except temporary workers employed during the last year *(a) has, (b) have* become eligible for retroactive benefits. _____

26. The wingspan on each of Boeing's latest passenger planes *(a) is, (b) are* longer than the Wright brothers' first flight. _____

27. All cooperatives except the Lemon Growing Exchange *(a) has, (b) have* been able to show a profit for participating members. _____

28. Although the economy has been declining, at least one of the major automobile manufacturers *(a) has, (b) have* been able to show a profit. _____

29. Successful entrepreneurs such as Donald Trump *(a) seems, (b) seem* to possess enormous energy and passion. _____

30. The range of prices for these models *(a) makes, (b) make* it difficult to provide complete information online. _____

D. Subject–Verb Agreement. Choose the correct answer.

31. Each bridge and highway overcrossing *(a) was, (b) were* retrofitted for earthquake safety. _____

32. The book *The Investor's Dilemma (a) discusses, (b) discuss* how new technologies cause great firms to fail. _____

33. Bacon and eggs *(a) is, (b) are* the most popular breakfast item on the menu. _____

34. The New Orleans River Kings *(a) was, (b) were* a popular jazz band in the 1920s. _____

35. Here *(a) is, (b) are* a complete menu of dessert selections. _____

36. On the southern shore of Hawaii *(a) is, (b) are* numerous windmill farms. _____

37. Some managers think that grammar and punctuation *(a) doesn't, (b) don't* matter. _____

38. Janet *(a) doesn't, (b) don't* mind working extra hours this weekend. _____

39. Our governor, along with top congressional leaders, *(a) is, (b) are* speaking out against the Supreme Court decision. _____

40. Steve Jobs and Steve Wozniak *(a) was, (b) were* the original founders of Apple Computer. _____

41. British Airways *(a) is, (b) are* refusing to honor the $40 flight to India that was mistakenly advertised online. _____

42. Displayed on my desk *(a) is, (b) are* a photo of my family and a potted plant. _____

43. Rutter, Hobbs, and Davidoff, Inc., a legal firm in Los Angeles, *(a) specializes,* *(b) specialize* in environmental law.

44. Considerable time and effort *(a) was, (b) were* spent on developing the plans.

45. How essential *(a) is, (b) are* experience and education in this field?

46. The Rolling Stones *(a) has, (b) have* been a popular rock band since 1962.

47. Biscuits and gravy *(a) is, (b) are* a popular dish in the South.

48. The New York Knicks *(a) is, (b) are* probably the most experienced team in the NBA.

49. Every online order and return *(a) is, (b) are* processed within one day.

50. Beyoncé's "Single Ladies (Put a Ring on It)" *(a) was, (b) were* recently awarded a Grammy for Song of the Year.

LEVEL 2

A. Self-Check. Subject–Verb Agreement. Choose the correct answer.

51. Everyone except a few voters *(a) agrees, (b) agree* that the president has a difficult job.

52. Either the AMC Pacer or the Yugo *(a) is, (b) are* considered to be the worst car of all time.

53. No one but the Human Resources director and a few managers ever *(a) talks,* *(b) talk* about balancing work and family issues.

54. Each of the research studies *(a) concludes, (b) conclude* that women in their thirties are the most active social media users.

55. Officers and members of the union *(a) has, (b) have* to approve the strike.

56. Every one of the new start-up companies *(a) is, (b) are* seeking venture capital.

57. Neither the employees nor their supervisor *(a) thinks, (b) think* the theft was an inside job.

58. *(a) Everyone, (b) Every one* of the sales reps made quota this month.

59. All that work *(a) is, (b) are* yet to be logged in.

60. Many surgeons, including Dr. Lisa Hudson, *(a) listens, (b) listen* to classical or rock music while operating.

Check your answers below.

B. Subject–Verb Agreement. Choose the correct answer.

61. The Department of Homeland Security *(a) reports, (b) report* that the agency continues to work hard to strengthen the safety, security, and resilience of our nation.

62. Neither Julie Rieman nor Susan Kline *(a) is, (b) are* afraid of hard work.

63. *(a) Everyone, (b) Every one* of the résumés contained grammatical errors.

51. a 52. a 53. a 54. a 55. b 56. a 57. a 58. b 59. a 60. b

64. Several of the proposals *(a) contains, (b) contain* complex formulas. _____

65. Either the owner or her partners *(a) is, (b) are* responsible for the taxes. _____

66. Either the partners or the owner *(a) was, (b) were* contacted by the IRS. _____

67. The group of players, coaches, and fans *(a) plans, (b) plan* to charter a plane. _____

68. The group *(a) is, (b) are* taking their seats on the plane. _____

69. *(a) Is, (b) Are* either of the clients satisfied with our marketing campaign? _____

70. Something about these insurance claims *(a) appears, (b) appear* questionable. _____

71. An online version of *Fortune's* list of the best big companies to work for *(a) is, (b) are* now available. _____

72. The faculty *(a) agrees, (b) agree* that student learning is paramount. _____

73. The faculty *(a) was, (b) were* divided among themselves regarding the tuition hike. _____

74. Many people using Facebook *(a) accesses, (b) access* the application on their smartphones. _____

75. Most of Guy Kawasaki's blog, entitled "How to Change the World," *(a) is, (b) are* dedicated to being a successful entrepreneur. _____

76. *(a) Anyone, (b) Any one* of these messages could be considered spam. _____

77. *(a) Anyone (b) Any one* can see that we need to hire more research assistants. _____

78. Everything about the contract clauses *(a) seems, (b) seem* debatable. _____

79. None of the passengers *(a) is, (b) are* upset with the new regulations. _____

80. None of the contract *(a) deals, (b) deal* with monetary issues. _____

C. Writing Exercise. Subject–Verb Agreement. Use your imagination in expanding the following sentences. When necessary, select the correct verb form first.

81. The staff is _____

_____

82. The staff are _____

_____

83. Our city council (has, have) _____

_____

84. Not one of the plans (was, were) _____

_____

85. Some of the jury members (believe, believes) _____

_____

86. Some of the proposal (need, needs) _____

_____

87. Somebody in the theater filled with patrons (was, were) _____

_____

88. Either Anne or you (is, are) _____

_____

89. Either you or Anne (was, were) _____

_____

90. Everything about the speeches (was, were) _____

_____

A. Self-Check. Subject–Verb Agreement. Choose the correct answer.

91. The number of companies using Google to perform background checks on potential employees *(a) is, (b) are* growing. _____

92. A number of companies *(a) is, (b) are* also using social media sites such as Facebook to investigate applicants. _____

93. Laury Fischer is one of those teachers who *(a) has, (b) have* earned the respect of their students. _____

94. Fifteen feet of rope *(a) is, (b) are* exactly what is needed for the project. _____

95. Didn't you know it is you who *(a) has, (b) have* been selected as Employee of the Year? _____

96. A large percentage of the donation *(a) goes, (b) go* to help homeless families. _____

97. She is the only one of the service reps who *(a) speaks, (b) speak* three languages. _____

98. Whoever is named for the job *(a) has, (b) have* my approval. _____

99. To take online classes while working full-time *(a) is, (b) are* challenging. _____

100. The hardest part of the job *(a) is, (b) are* the bending and lifting. _____

Check your answers below.

B. Subject–Verb Agreement. Choose the correct answer.

101. Two thousand dollars *(a) is, (b) are* required as a down payment on the new Fiat 500. _____

102. One hundred pennies *(a) is, (b) are* needed to make one dollar. _____

103. Our latest advertisements featuring the new Android eco charger *(a) is, (b) are* being broadcast on all major networks. _____

104. Is it Reid Hoffman who *(a) is, (b) are* the founder of LinkedIn? _____

105. Michael Burnside is the only one of the lab assistants who *(a) was, (b) were* able to work effectively with disabled students. _____

106. Michael is one of those lab assistants who *(a) is, (b) are* valued as employees. _____

107. "Moon River" is one of those songs that *(a) continues, (b) continue* to sound fresh year after year. _____

91. a 92. b 93. b 94. a 95. b 96. a 97. a 98. a 99. a 100. a (Better: *The hardest parts of the job are . . .*)

108. Sixty days *(a) is, (b) are* the period of the loan. _____

109. Sixty days *(a) is, (b) are* reserved during the year for staff meetings. _____

110. Located on-site at the Google office complex *(a) is, (b) are* a doctor, oil change and car wash services, dry cleaning, massage therapy, a gym, a hair stylist, and a bike repair shop. _____

111. Only a fraction of the conference delegates *(a) was, (b) were* unable to find accommodations at The Fairmont Heritage Place in Telluride, Colorado. _____

112. Only a fraction of the conference room *(a) was, (b) were* set up by the time the meeting was scheduled to begin. _____

113. Keeping your skills up-to-date *(a) is, (b) are* important in today's economy. _____

114. Over three fourths of the individuals attending the lecture series *(a) is, (b) are* college students. _____

115. Over three fourths of the contract *(a) has, (b) have* been ratified. _____

116. A number of women with MBAs *(a) chooses, (b) choose* to stay home to raise their children. _____

117. The number of women with MDs or law degrees who choose to stay home to raise a family *(a) is, (b) are* much lower. _____

118. Collaborating online with colleagues *(a) is, (b) are* easier than ever before. _____

119. A large percentage of younger employees *(a) is, (b) are* using social media to collaborate and share knowledge in the workplace. _____

120. A large percentage of each day *(a) is, (b) are* spent online. _____

C. Writing Exercise. Subject–Verb Agreement. Some subject–verb constructions are grammatically correct but sound incorrect. Revise the following correct sentences so that they are not only correct but sound so. **Hint:** Make the subject and its complement agree in number.

Example: The best part of my job is meeting people and learning new things.

Revision: The best parts of my job are meeting people and learning new things.

121. The most important trait I have to offer an employer is energy and enthusiasm.

_____

122. The best part of my job is greeting and interacting with customers.

_____

123. The principal task in this law office is briefs and affidavits.

_____

124. The primary reason for his wealth is wise stock and other investment choices.

_____

125. The main objective this fiscal year is to increase sales and decrease expenses.

_____

For further practice in subject–verb agreement, write complete sentences using the following words as subjects.

Example: The number of voters is increasing rapidly as we approach the election date.

126. A number of businesses _____

_____

127. The number of businesses _____

_____

128. Every one of the students _____

_____

129. Some of the employees _____

_____

130. Some of the plan _____

_____

D. Review. Subject–Verb Agreement. To offer extra help in areas that cause hesitation for business and professional writers, this exercise reviews subject–verb agreement. Underline any subject–verb problem and write an improved form(s) in the space provided. Each sentence has one error.

131. *The Four Steps to the Epiphany* have tips for successfully bringing a product to market. _____

132. There's many advantages to earning a college degree. _____

133. Corned beef and cabbage are a traditional Irish dish. _____

134. Persistent inflation and interest rate worries often causes stock prices to drop. _____

135. Was any of the members of Congress in agreement on the act to stop online piracy? _____

136. After several days of deliberation, the jury has announced their verdict. _____

137. Neither the defendant nor the plaintiffs was satisfied with the judgment. _____

138. Are either of the applicants available to interview on Friday? _____

139. Preparing the dinner for the annual fund-raiser is gourmet chefs from around the world. _____

140. Globalization and the changing ethnic composition of the United States is causing many organizations to embrace diversity programs. _____

141. The use of wireless handheld inventory units, virtual shelves, in-store interactive kiosks, and smart registers are changing and improving the retail industry. _____

142. One of the problems, in addition to those already mentioned, seem to be resistance to change. _____

143. Both a written proposal and an oral presentation is required for this project. _____

144. If the level of antioxidants in your diet are low, you may be susceptible to health problems. _____

145. A host of ethical issues surround business including economic justice, marketing irregularities, executive compensation, and whistle-blowing. _____

146. Dell Computers, along with many other technology companies, are outsourcing thousands of customer support jobs to India. _____

147. Any one of the stockholders have the right to delegate his or her proxy. _____

148. Nick is one of those accountants who strives for accurate and objective financial statements. _____

149. Kirsty is the only one of our accountants who have access to all financial data. _____

150. Everyone of the books she read last year discussed business concepts. _____

E. **FAQs About Business English Review.** Choose the correct answer.

151. Horns blow in different keys and tones; *(a) e.g., (b) i.e.,* American car horns beep in the tone of F. _____

152. Mosquito sprays block the mosquito's sensors so that the mosquitoes don't know you are there; *(a) e.g., (b) i.e.,* the sprays hide you. _____

153. Paul is *(a) anxious, (b) eager* for his upcoming vacation to Bermuda. _____

154. Marta is *(a) anxious, (b) eager* about the upcoming exam because she didn't study for it. _____

155. Many websites now promise *(a) discreet, (b) discrete* investigative services to locate old friends, competitive information, and deadbeat spouses. _____

156. The menu was divided into two *(a) discreet, (b) discrete* sections: vegetarian and nonvegetarian. _____

157. Our supervisor wants our *(a) co-operation, (b) co operation, (c) cooperation* in adopting the new policy. _____

158. The *(a) premier, (b) premiere* of the film *The Rock* took place on Alcatraz Island. _____

159. The product's *(a) premier, (b) premiere* selling feature is its lifetime warranty. _____

160. We *(a) cannot, (b) can not* issue a cash refund for these returned items. _____

Chat About It ◀◀

Your instructor may assign any of the following topics for you to discuss in class, in an online chat room, or on an online discussion board. Some of the discussion topics may require outside research. You may also be asked to read and respond to postings made by your classmates.

Discussion Topic 1: A study tip in this chapter said the following: "Nothing reveals a person's education, or lack thereof, so quickly as verbs that don't agree with subjects." Do you agree with this statement? Why or why not?

Discussion Topic 2: What have you learned so far in this class that will help you sound educated and professional on the job? Why do you think it is important to sound this way in the workplace?

Discussion Topic 3: You learned in this chapter that American and British English rules treat collective nouns differently. Americans generally treat collective nouns as singular, whereas the English generally treat collective nouns as plural. What do you think accounts for this difference? What other differences have you noticed between American and British English?

Discussion Topic 4: In this chapter you learned that each year approximately 10,000 new words are introduced to the English language. Of those, about 1,000 are widely used, and roughly 200 of those words become a part of our permanent vocabulary. Why do you think so many words are added that never become a permanent part of our vocabulary?

Discussion Topic 5: American novelist Charlotte Perkins Gilman said, "Life is a verb." What do you think she meant by this? Do you agree? Why or why not? Share your opinions and thoughts with your classmates.

Posttest

Choose the correct answer. Then compare your answers with those below.

1. Appearing next on the program *(a) is, (b) are* Chad Hurley, Steve Chen, and Jawed Karim, the founders of YouTube. _____

2. Banana leaves and coconut husks *(a) is, (b) are* being used as materials in carpets and seat cushions for cars. _____

3. Everyone except the president and other management members *(a) is, (b) are* eligible for early retirement. _____

4. The cost of supplies, along with service and equipment costs, *(a) is, (b) are* a major problem. _____

5. There *(a) is, (b) are* many ways we can use Facebook and Twitter as professional communication tools. _____

6. A number of surprising events *(a) is, (b) are* creating spikes in the stock market. _____

7. Starbucks *(a) has, (b) have* launched the Create Jobs for USA Fund to help employers hire and retain U.S. workers. _____

8. Neither the CFO nor members of his staff *(a) is, (b) are* surprised by the revenue declines. _____

9. The research team *(a) has, (b) have* determined that the No. 1 feature women want in a vehicle is extra storage. _____

10. The number of union strikes in the United States *(a) is, (b) are* decreasing. _____

1.b 2.b 3.a 4.a 5.b 6.b 7.a 8.b 9.a 10.a

SUBJECT–VERB AGREEMENT

Begin your review by rereading Chapters 5–6. Then test your comprehension of those chapters by completing the exercises that follow. Compare your responses with the key at the end of the book.

LEVEL 1

1. The *(a) active voice, (b) passive voice* is known as the "voice of business." _____

2. In the sentence *The contract was approved yesterday*, the verb is in the *(a) active, (b) passive* voice. _____

3. In the sentence *"Freegans" search through dumpsters to find usable items*, the verb is in the *(a) active, (b) passive* voice. _____

4. How important *(a) is, (b) are* seat comfort and legroom on flights? _____

5. In the sentence *The newly laundered sheets smell fresh*, the verb *smell* is *(a) transitive, (b) intransitive, (c) linking, (d) helping*. _____

6. In the sentence *We listened carefully to the professor's lecture*, the verb *listened* is *(a) transitive, (b) intransitive, (c) linking, (d) helping*. _____

7. In the sentence *Tom Langlois is the consultant*, the word *consultant* is *(a) an object, (b) a linking verb, (c) a complement*. _____

8. In the sentence *Maggie issued an ultimatum to her teenager*, the word *issued* is *(a) transitive, (b) intransitive, (c) linking, (d) helping*. _____

9. In the sentence *Women comprise just 33 percent of Silicon Valley's technical workforce*, the verb *comprise* is in the *(a) present tense, (b) past tense, (c) future tense*. _____

10. Wikipedia, along with several other U.S. Internet companies, *(a) was, (b) were* pleased with the results of the fight against the Stop Online Piracy Act. _____

11. In the sentence *The global economy will become strong over the next decade*, the verb *will become* is *(a) present tense, (b) past tense, (c) future tense*. _____

12. Verizon Communications *(a) is, (b) are* one of the best companies to work for according to *Fortune*. _____

13. In the sentence *William Le Baron Jenney designed the world's first skyscraper*, the verb *designed* is in the *(a) present tense, (b) past tense, (c) future tense*. _____

14. There *(a) is, (b) are* many kind words we will be able to say about him at his retirement dinner. _____

15. The tone and wording of a business message *(a) is, (b) are* very important. _____

16. What *(a) is, (b) was* the name of the sales rep who offered the discount? _____

17. *Boomerang: Travels in the New Third World (a) discusses, (b) discuss* countries such as Iceland, Greece, and Ireland that were affected by the recent financial crisis. _____

Circle art: © iStockphoto.com/Pavel Khorenyan

18. Nearly everyone objected to *(a) Sara, (b) Sara's* using her iPhone during the meeting. _____

19. Every employee and supervisor *(a) attends, (b) attend* an ethics workshop every year. _____

20. She suggested that everyone *(a) meets, (b) meet* for dinner after work. _____

21. He acts as if he *(a) was, (b) were* the only employee who had to work overtime. _____

22. The National Transportation Safety Board recommends that cell phones and text messaging *(a) are, (b) be* completely banned while driving. _____

23. Try *(a) to, (b) and* attend tomorrow's workshop about social media marketing strategies. _____

24. In the sentence *Some homeowners are wondering how the bailout will affect them*, the verbal phrase *are wondering* represents a *(a) present participle, (b) past participle*. _____

25. We think that *(a) everyone, (b) every one* of the candidates is qualified for the position. _____

26. The jury *(a) needs, (b) need* more time to make a decision. _____

27. If I *(a) was, (b) were* qualified, I would apply for that position. _____

28. Either the teenager or his parents *(a) is, (b) are* using the car right now. _____

29. Neither the parents nor the teenager *(a) is, (b) are* staying home tonight. _____

30. In the sentence *The deficit has grown over the past decade*, the verbal phrase *has grown* represents a *(a) present participle, (b) past participle*. _____

For each of the following pairs of sentences, select the one that is more logically written.

31. (a) To qualify for a full scholarship, applications must be submitted by January 1.
(b) To qualify for a full scholarship, submit your application by January 1. _____

32. (a) Skilled at troubleshooting Web security problems, Maria Lyan was hired instantly by the personnel manager.
(b) Skilled at troubleshooting Web security problems, the personnel manager hired Maria Lyan instantly. _____

33. (a) The waiter served a bowl of soup to the woman that was steaming hot.
(b) The waiter served a bowl of soup that was steaming hot to the woman. _____

34. Many items that have *(a) laid, (b) lain, (c) lay* on the shelves of antique bookshops for years are quite valuable. _____

35. If you had *(a) gone, (b) went* to the meeting, you would understand why this change is necessary. _____

36. The number of taxpayers who file online *(a) is, (b) are* growing rapidly. _____

37. A large percentage of people *(a) is, (b) are* simplifying their lives. _____

38. It looks as if three fourths of the proposal *(a) has, (b) have* yet to be written. _____

39. She is one of those executives who always *(a) tells, (b) tell* the truth. _____

40. Waiting for miracles to occur *(a) is, (b) are* not the way to be successful in life. _____

Circle art: © iStockphoto.com/Pavel Khorenyan

FAQs About Business English Review

41. We value one trait in our employees above all others, *(a) i.e., (b) e.g.,* integrity. _____

42. State budget cuts will certainly *(a) affect, (b) effect* education adversely. _____

43. The *(a) affects, (b) effects* of the state budget cuts will be felt by all students. _____

44. Chemist Laura Burns announced her *(a) principle, (b) principal* findings in a journal article. _____

45. One important *(a) principle, (b) principal* of accounting is that business and personal assets must be kept separately. _____

46. Typing an e-mail message in all capital letters is known as *(a) preening, (b) shouting, (c) efficiency*. _____

47. Chuck is *(a) eager, (b) anxious* to start his backpacking trip in Europe. _____

48. Many notable celebrities attended the movie *(a) premier, (b) premiere*. _____

49. We trusted that Evelyn would be *(a) discrete, (b) discreet* during the negotiations. _____

50. If everyone will *(a) co-operate, (b) co operate, (c) cooperate*, our meeting might end on time. _____

NAME _____

Techniques for Effective Paragraphs

As you learned in the Writer's Workshop for Unit 2, the basic unit in writing is the sentence. The next unit is the paragraph. Although no rule regulates the length of paragraphs, business writers recognize the value of short paragraphs. Paragraphs with fewer than eight printed lines look inviting and readable, whereas long, solid chunks of print appear formidable. In this workshop you will learn writing techniques for organizing sentences into readable, coherent, and clear paragraphs. The first important technique involves topic sentences.

Organizing Paragraphs Around Topic Sentences

A well-organized paragraph has two important characteristics. First, it covers just one subject. For example, if you are writing about your booth at the Las Vegas technology expo, you wouldn't throw in a sentence about trouble with the IRS. Keep all the sentences in a paragraph related to one topic. Second, a well-organized paragraph begins with a topic sentence that summarizes what the paragraph is about. A topic sentence helps readers by preparing them for what follows.

Consider the following scenario. Assume your company promotes an extensive schedule of team sports for employees after hours. One group enjoys weekend bicycling. You have been assigned the task of writing an e-mail message to the members of this group stating that they must wear helmets when cycling. One paragraph of your message covers statistics about cycling accidents and the incidence of brain injury for unhelmeted riders. Another paragraph discusses the protection offered by helmets:

> *Helmets protect the brain from injury.* They spread the force of a crash from the point of impact to a wider area. When an accident occurs, an unhelmeted head undergoes two collisions. The first occurs when the skull slams into the ground. The second occurs when the brain hits the inside of the skull. A helmet softens the second blow and acts as a shock absorber. Instead of crushing the brain, the impact crushes the foam core of the helmet, often preventing serious brain injury.

Notice how the preceding paragraph focuses on just one topic: how helmets protect the brain from injury. Every sentence relates to that topic. Notice, too, that the first sentence functions as a topic sentence, informing the reader of the subject of the paragraph.

The best way to write a good paragraph is to list all the ideas you may include. Following is a rough draft of ideas for the preceding paragraph. Notice that the fourth item doesn't relate to the topic sentence. By listing the ideas to be included in a paragraph, you can immediately see what belongs—and what doesn't. Once the list is made, you can easily write the topic sentence.

Paragraph Idea List

1. Helmets spread the force of impact.

2. Crashes cause two collisions, the first when the skull hits the ground and the second when the brain hits the skull.

3. The foam core of the helmet absorbs the impact.

4. ~~The federal government has issued biking regulations requiring helmets~~. [Cross out items that don't belong.]

Topic Sentence: Helmets protect the brain from injury.

Skill Check 3.1 Organizing a Paragraph

In a letter to the college president, the athletic director is arguing for a new stadium scoreboard. One paragraph will describe the old scoreboard and why it needs to be replaced. Study the following list of ideas for that paragraph.

1. The old scoreboard was originally constructed in the 1960s.

2. It is now hard to find replacement parts for it when something breaks.

3. The old scoreboard is not energy efficient.

4. Coca-Cola has offered to buy a new sports scoreboard in return for exclusive rights to sell soda on campus.

5. The old scoreboard should be replaced for many reasons.

6. It shows only scores for football games.

7. When we have soccer games or track meets, we are without a functioning scoreboard.
  a. Which sentence should be the topic sentence?   _____
  b. Which sentence(s) should be developed in a different paragraph? _____
  c. Which sentences should follow the topic sentence?   _____

Writing Coherent Paragraphs

Effective paragraphs are coherent; that is, they hold together. **Coherence** is a quality of good writing that doesn't happen accidentally. It is consciously achieved through effective organization and through skillful use of three devices. These writing devices are (a) repetition of key ideas or key words, (b) the use of pronouns that refer clearly to their antecedents, and (c) the use of transitional expressions.

Repetition of Key Ideas or Key Words. Repeating a key word or key thought from a preceding sentence helps guide a reader from one thought to the next. This redundancy is necessary to build cohesiveness into writing. Notice how the word *deal* is repeated in the second sentence.

> For the past six months, college administrators and Coca-Cola have been working on a *deal* in which the college would receive a new sports scoreboard. The *deal* would involve exclusive rights to sell soft drinks on the 12,000-student campus.

Use of Pronouns That Refer Clearly to Their Antecedents. Pronouns such as *this, that, they, these, those,* and *it* help connect thoughts in sentences. However, these pronouns are useful only when their antecedents are clear. Often it is better to make the pronoun into an adjective joined with its antecedent to ensure that the reference is absolutely clear. Notice how the pronoun *this* is clearer when it is joined to its antecedent *contract*.

Confusing: The Coca-Cola offer requires an exclusive contract committing the college for ten years without any provision preventing a price increase. *This* could be very costly to students, staff, and faculty.

Improved: The Coca-Cola offer requires an exclusive contract committing the college for ten years without any provision preventing a price increase. *This contract* could be very costly to students, staff, and faculty.

Avoid vague pronouns, such as *it* in the following example.

Confusing: Both Coca-Cola and PepsiCo offered to serve our campus, and we agreed to allow *it* to submit a bid.

Improved: Both Coca-Cola and PepsiCo offered to serve our campus, and we agreed to allow Coca-Cola to submit a bid.

Use of Transitional Expressions. One of the most effective ways to achieve paragraph coherence is through the use of transitional expressions. These expressions act as road signs. They indicate where the message is headed, and they help the reader anticipate what is coming. Some common transitional expressions follow:

although	furthermore	moreover
as a result	hence	nevertheless
consequently	however	of course
for example	in addition	on the other hand
for this reason	in this way	therefore

Other words that act as connectives are *first, second, finally, after, meanwhile, next, after all, instead, specifically, thus, also, likewise, as,* and *as if.*

The following paragraph achieves coherence through the use of all three techniques. (a) The key idea of *surprising battle* in the first sentence is echoed in the second sentence with repetition of the word *battle* coupled with *unexpected,* a synonym for *surprising.* (b) The use of a pronoun, *This,* in the second sentence connects the second sentence to the first. (c) The transitional words *however* and a*s a result* in following sentences continue to build coherence.

> A *surprising battle* between two global cola giants was recently fought in Venezuela. *This battle* was *unexpected* because Venezuelans had always been loyal Pepsi drinkers. *However,* when the nation's leading bottler sold half of its interest to Coca-Cola, everything changed. *As a result,* Coca-Cola turned the Pepsi-drinking nation of Venezuela into Coke drinkers almost overnight.

Skill Check 3.2 Improving Paragraph Coherence

In the following space or on a separate sheet of paper, use the information from Skill Check 3.1 to write a coherent paragraph about replacing the sports scoreboard. Remember that this paragraph is part of a letter from the athletic director to the college president. Include a topic sentence. Strive to illustrate all three techniques to achieve coherence.

_____

_____

_____

_____

_____

Developing Parallel Construction

Paragraph clarity can be improved by expressing similar ideas with similar grammatical structures. For example, if you are listing three ideas, do not use *ing* words for two of the ideas and a *to* verb with the third idea: *reading, eating, and studying* (not *to study*). Use adjectives with adjectives, verbs with verbs, phrases with phrases, and clauses with clauses. In the following list, use all verbs: *the machine sorted, stamped, and counted* (not *and had a counter*). For phrases, the wording for all parts of the list should be matched; *safety must be improved in the home, in the classroom, and on the job* (not *for office workers*).

Poor: Professor Callahan is energetic, resourceful, and can be relied on.

Improved: Professor Callahan is energetic, resourceful, and reliable. (Matches adjectives.)

Poor: The new shredder helped us save money, reduce pollution, and paper could be recycled.

Improved: The new shredder helped us save money, reduce pollution, and recycle paper. (Matches verb–noun construction.)

Skill Check 3.3 Improving Parallel Construction

Revise each of the following sentences to improve parallel construction.

1. Some airlines offer frequent fliers free upgrades, priority boarding, and they can call special reservation numbers.

   _____

   _____

2. Your job is to research, design, and the implementation of a diversity program.

   _____

3. Few managers are able to write e-mail messages accurately, concisely, and with efficiency.

   _____

4. The new software totals all balances, gives weekly reports, and statements are printed.

   _____

5. Our objectives are to make our stock profitable, to operate efficiently, and developing good employee relations.

   _____

Writing Application 3.1

Revise the following paragraph, which is an announcement to current employees notifying them of new openings within a company. Add a topic sentence, improve the organization, and correct the problems in parallelism. Add transitional expressions if appropriate. **Hint:** Here's a possible topic sentence: *A number of high-level positions are now available to current employees.*

New Positions Available

You may be interested in applying for a new position within the company. The Human Resources Department has a number of jobs available immediately. The positions are at a high level. Current employees may apply immediately for open positions in production, for some in marketing, and jobs in administrative support are also available. To make application, these positions require immediate action. Come to the Human Resources Department. We have a list showing the open positions, what the qualifications are, and job descriptions are shown. Many of the jobs are now open. That's why we are announcing this now. To be hired, an interview must be scheduled within the next two weeks.

Writing Application 3.2

Revise the following poorly written announcement. Add a topic sentence and improve the organization and expression.

Demonstration of New Software on April 18

As you probably already know, this company (Lasertronics) will be installing new computer software shortly. There will be a demonstration on April 18, which is a Tuesday. We felt this was necessary because this new software is so different from our previous software. It will be from 9 to 12 a.m. in the morning. This will show employees how the software programs work. They will learn about the operating system, and this should be helpful to nearly everyone. There will be information about the new word processing program, which should be helpful to administrative assistants and product managers. For all you people who work with payroll, there will be information about the new database program. We can't show everything the software will do at this one demo, but for these three areas there will be some help at the Tuesday demo. Oh yes, Paula Roddy will be presenting the demonstration. She is the representative from Quantum Software.

Writing Application 3.3

Assume you work in the Human Resources Department of Bank of America. You must write an e-mail announcement describing a special program of classes for your employees. Use the following information to write a well-organized paragraph announcement. This information is purposely disorganized; you must decide how to best organize it. Add any information needed for clarity.

Explain that Bank of America will reimburse any employee the full cost of tuition and books if that employee attends classes. Describe the plan. Skyline Community College, in cooperation with Bank of America, will offer a group of courses for college credit at very convenient locations for our employees. Actually, the classes will be offered at your downtown and East Bay branches. Tell employees that they should call Jean Fujimoto at Ext. 660 if they are interested. You'd better mention the tuition: $180 for a semester course. Explain that we (Bank of America) are willing to pay these fees because we value education highly. However, make it clear that employees must receive a grade of C or higher before they are eligible for reimbursement of course and book fees. It might be a good idea to attach a list of the courses and the times that they will be offered. Include a deadline date for calling Jean.

Use the e-mail message in Figure 3.1 as a model as you compose your e-mail announcement. You can refer to an attached list of courses and times, but you do not have to prepare the actual attachment.

FIGURE 3.1

E-Mail Message

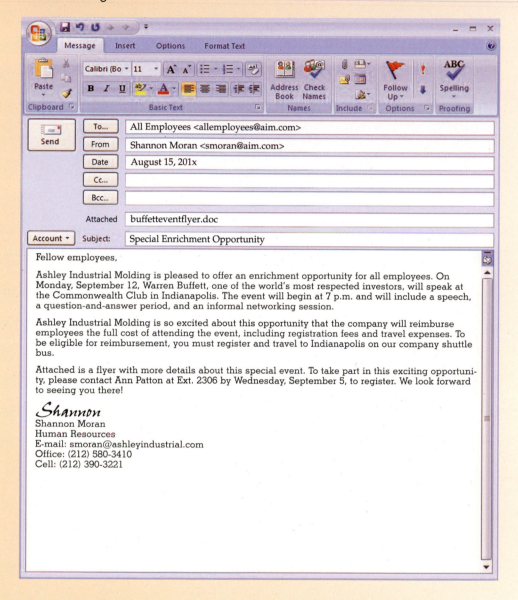

Modifying and Connecting Words

7 Modifiers: Adjectives and Adverbs

© iStockphoto.com/Clerkenwell_Images

A man's character may be learned from the adjectives which he habitually uses in conversation.

—Mark Twain, writer

Objectives

When you have completed the materials in this chapter, you will be able to do the following:

LEVEL 1

1. Decide whether to use adjectives or adverbs in sentences.
2. Form the comparative and superlative degrees of regular and irregular adjectives and adverbs.

LEVEL 2

3. Use articles, demonstrative adjectives, possessive adjectives, compound adjectives, and independent adjectives correctly.
4. Avoid double negatives.

LEVEL 3

5. Master the correct use of commonly confused adjectives and adverbs.
6. Make comparisons within a group, and place adverbs and adjectives close to the words they modify.

Circle art: © iStockphoto.com/Pavel Khorenyan

Pretest

Choose the correct answer. Then compare your answers with those below.

1. Of the two hybrid vehicles, I like this one *(a) better, (b) best.* _____

2. When it is raining, people should drive *(a) carefuller, (b) more carefully.* _____

3. California has the *(a) worse, (b) worst* failure rate for small businesses. _____

4. Tyler and Ann did *(a) a, (b) an* exceptional job in redesigning our website. _____

5. *(a) This, (b) These* sorts of meetings can be very productive. _____

6. We *(a) couldn't, (b) could* hardly believe the news. _____

7. If you did *(a) good, (b) well* in the interview, you will be hired. _____

8. The art world is comparing the *(a) seven-year-old, (b) seven year old* child prodigy to Picasso. _____

9. United Airlines showed off its *(a) newly painted, (b) newly-painted* planes after its merger with Continental. _____

10. Elizabeth took *(a) less, (b) fewer* sick days this year than she did last year. _____

You can use adjectives and adverbs to add character to your writing. Both adjectives and adverbs act as modifiers; that is, they describe or limit other words. Many of the forms and functions of adjectives and adverbs are similar. Because of this similarity, these two parts of speech may be confused. That is why we will treat adjectives and adverbs together in this chapter.

LEVEL 1

Basic Functions of Adjectives and Adverbs

Career Tip

Good writers avoid vague and overworked adverbs and adjectives (such as *interesting, good, nice, great, very, really, so,* and *bad*). You should strive to use precise words that say exactly what you mean.

Adjectives describe or limit nouns and pronouns. As you learned in Chapter 1, adjectives often answer the questions *What kind?, How many?,* or *Which one?* Adjectives in the following sentences are italicized.

Green and *blue* walls in homes and offices are *relaxing.* (Adjectives answer *What kind?*)

Small, independent businesses are becoming *numerous.* (Adjectives answer *What kind?*)

The National Institutes of Health awarded *six government* grants to *the four top* institutions. (Adjectives answer *How many?* and *What kind?*)

This book discusses *economic* theory. (Adjectives answer *Which one?* and *What kind?*)

1.a 2.b 3.b 4.b 5.b 6.b 7.b 8.a 9.a 10.b

Study Tip

Not all words that end in *ly* are adverbs. For example, *costly, friendly, cowardly, lovely, lonely, curly,* and *ugly* are all adjectives.

Adverbs usually describe or limit verbs, adjectives, or other adverbs. Adverbs may also modify pronouns, numerals, phrases, or entire sentences. Many adverbs are formed by adding *ly* to adjectives (*efficient, efficiently*). However, some of the most commonly used adverbs do not end in *ly*, including *here, there, tomorrow, today, always, later, never, now, often, seldom, sometimes, soon, still, when, indeed, much, not, so,* and *too*.

Adverbs often answer the questions *When?, How?, Where?,* or *To what extent?,* as you can see in these examples:

Today we left work *early*. (Adverbs answer *When?* and *How?*)

Please hang your coat *there*. (Adverb answers *Where?*)

Because we drove *so slowly*, we arrived *late*. (Adverbs answer *To what extent?, How?,* and *When?*)

The introductions were made *very quickly*. (Adverbs answer *To what extent?* and *How?*)

Deciding Whether to Use Adjectives or Adverbs

Because they are closely related, adjectives are sometimes confused with adverbs. Here are guidelines that will help you choose the appropriate adjective or adverb.

When to Use Adjectives

Use adjectives to modify or describe nouns and pronouns. Note particularly that adjectives (not adverbs) should follow linking verbs.

The politicians gave *rousing* speeches.

This cheesecake tastes *delicious*. (Not *deliciously*)

I feel *bad* about the loss. (Not *badly*)

She looks *good* in her business suit. (Not *well*)

When to Use Adverbs

Use adverbs to modify or describe verbs, adjectives, or other adverbs. Note that adverbs (not adjectives) should follow action verbs.

The merger went *smoothly*. (Not *smooth*)

Our car runs *more smoothly* after the tune-up. (Not *smoother*)

Listen *carefully* to the directions. (Not *careful*)

A few adverbs have two acceptable forms: *slow, slowly; quick, quickly; deep, deeply; direct, directly;* and *close, closely*.

Drive *slowly*. (Or, less formally, *slow*)

You may contact us *directly*. (Or, less formally, *direct*)

Time passes *quickly*. (Or, less formally, *quick*)

Career Tip

The misuse of *badly* for *bad* is one of the most frequent errors made by educated persons. Following the linking verb *feel*, use the adjective *bad*, not the adverb *badly*.

Comparative and Superlative Forms

Most adjectives and adverbs have three **forms**, or **degrees**: positive, comparative, and superlative. The **positive degree** of an adjective or an adverb is used to merely describe or to limit another word. The **comparative degree** is used to compare two persons or things. The **superlative degree** is used to compare three or more persons or things.

Regular Adjectives and Adverbs

Regular adjectives and **regular adverbs** form their comparative and superlative degrees similarly, which you will see in the following two sections.

Regular Adjectives

The **comparative degree** of most one-syllable and some two-syllable adjectives is formed by adding *r* or *er* (*nicer, quieter*). The **superlative degree** of short adjectives is formed by the addition of *st* or *est* (*warmest*). When a two-syllable adjective ends in *y*, change the *y* to *i* before adding *er* or *est* (*prettier, heaviest*).

Long adjectives and those that are awkward or difficult to pronounce form the comparative and superlative degrees with the addition of *more* and *most* (*more careful, most beautiful*) or *less* and *least* (*less popular, least popular*). The following examples illustrate the comparative and superlative degrees of regular adjectives.

	Positive	Comparative	Superlative
One Syllable:	new	newer	newest
Two Syllable:	quiet	quieter	quietest
Ending in *y*:	happy	happier	happiest
Two Syllable (Awkward):	useful	more/less useful	most/least useful
Three or More Syllables:	advantageous	more/less advantageous	most/least advantageous

The following sentences illustrate degrees of comparison for regular adjectives.

Sales are unusually *high*.	(Positive degree)
Sales are *higher* than ever before.	(Comparative degree)
Sales are the *highest* in years.	(Superlative degree)
The new process is *efficient*.	(Positive degree)
The new process is *more* (or *less*) *efficient* than our previous one.	(Comparative degree)
The new process is the *most* (or *least*) *efficient* one possible.	(Superlative degree)

Regular Adverbs

The **comparative degree** of some short adverbs (nearly all one-syllable) is formed by adding *r* or *er* (*faster*), and the **superlative degree** is formed by adding *st* or *est* (*fastest*). Most adverbs, however, form the comparative and superlative degrees with the addition of *more* and *most* (*more slowly, most beautifully*) or *less* and *least* (*less efficiently, least carefully*).

	Positive	Comparative	Superlative
One Syllable:	fast	faster	fastest
Two or More Syllables:	neatly	more (or less) neatly	most (or least) neatly

The following examples illustrate how the comparative and superlative degrees of regular adverbs are formed.

He drives *carefully*.	(Positive degree)
He drives *more* (or *less*) *carefully* now.	(Comparative degree)
He drives *most* (or *least*) *carefully* at night.	(Superlative degree)

Do not create a double comparative form by using *more* and the suffix *er* together (such as *more neater*) or by using *most* and the suffix *est* together (such as *most fastest*).

Irregular Adjectives and Adverbs

A few adjectives and adverbs form the comparative and superlative degrees irregularly.

		Positive	Comparative	Superlative
Adjectives:		good, well	better	best
		bad	worse	worst
		far	farther, further	farthest, furthest
		little	littler, less	littlest, least
		many, much	more	most
Adverbs:		well	better	best
		much	more	most

Study Tip

The comparative and superlative forms of irregular adjectives and adverbs appear in most dictionaries. The comparative forms of regular adjectives and adverbs do not.

Now complete the reinforcement exercises for Level 1.

LEVEL 2

Modifiers That Deserve Special Attention

A few adjectives and adverbs require special attention because they cause writers and speakers difficulty.

Articles

The **articles** *a*, *an*, and *the* make up a special category of adjectives, and these words must be used carefully. The **definite article** *the* is used to describe a specific person or thing, as in *the film* or *the films*. The definite article *the* can be used with singular or plural nouns.

When describing persons or things in general, use the **indefinite article** *a* or *an*, as in *a film* (meaning *any* film). Indefinite articles are used only with singular nouns. The choice of *a* or *an* is determined by the initial sound of the word modified. *A* is used before consonant sounds; *an* is used before vowel sounds.

Study Tip

The sound, not the spelling, of a word governs the choice between *a* and *an*. When the letter *u* sounds like a *y*, it is treated as a consonant: *a utility*, *a used car*.

Before Vowel Sounds		Before Consonant Sounds	
an operator		a shop	
an executive		a plan	
an hour ⎫	*h* is not voiced;	a hook ⎫	
an honor ⎭	vowel is heard	a hole ⎭	*h* is voiced

MODIFIERS: ADJECTIVES AND ADVERBS

Circle art: © iStockphoto.com/Pavel Khorenyan

Before Vowel Sounds		Before Consonant Sounds	
an office } an onion	o sounds like a vowel	a one-man show } a one-week trip	o sounds like the consonant w
an understudy } an umbrella	u sounds like a vowel	a union } a unit	u sounds like the consonant y
an X-ray } an M.D.	x and m sound like vowels		

Demonstrative Adjectives

Demonstrative adjectives indicate whether a noun is plural or singular and whether it is located nearby or farther away. The demonstrative adjective *this*, and its plural form *these*, indicates something nearby. The demonstrative adjective *that*, and its plural form *those*, indicates something at a distance. Be careful to use the singular forms of these words with singular nouns and the plural forms with plural nouns: *this shoe, that road, these accounts, those records*. Pay special attention to the nouns *kind*, *type*, and *sort*. Match singular adjectives with the singular forms of these nouns and plural adjectives with the plural forms.

Incorrect: Job interviewees should be prepared for *these type* of situational questions.

Correct: Job interviewees should be prepared for *this type* of situational question.

Correct: Job interviewees should be prepared for *these types* of situational questions.

Study Tip

When used with nouns, *this, that, these,* and *those* are adjectives (*This book is fascinating!*). When used alone, these same words are pronouns (*This is fascinating!*).

Possessive Adjectives

As you learned in Chapters 1 and 4, some possessive pronouns serve as **possessive adjectives** when they describe nouns. Examples of these words include *my, our, your, his, her, its*, and *their*. You can tell that a pronoun is functioning as an adjective when it comes before the noun it is describing.

His car is in the shop.

Our restaurant serves the best tiramisu in town.

Please submit *your application* online.

Compound Adjectives

Writers may form their own adjectives by joining two or more words. When these words act as a single modifier preceding a noun, they are temporarily hyphenated. If these same words appear after a noun, they are generally not hyphenated.

Study Tip

Words forming a compound adjective are not in their normal order. Therefore, they need hyphens to "glue" them together.

Words Temporarily Hyphenated Before a Noun	Same Words Not Hyphenated After a Noun
well-trained accountant	accountant who is well trained
never-say-die attitude	attitude of never say die
eight-story building	building of eight stories
state-sponsored program	program that is state sponsored
a case-by-case analysis	analysis that is case by case

Words Temporarily Hyphenated Before a Noun	Same Words Not Hyphenated After a Noun
follow-up appointment	an appointment to follow up
income-related expenses	expenses that are income related
six-year-old child	child who is six years old
home-based business	business that is home based
30-year mortgage	a mortgage of 30 years

Compound adjectives shown in your dictionary with hyphens are considered permanently hyphenated. Regardless of whether the compound adjective appears before or after a noun, it retains the hyphen. Use a current dictionary or reference manual to determine what expressions are always hyphenated. Be sure that you find the dictionary entry that is marked *adjective*. Here are samples:

Permanent Hyphens Before Nouns	Permanent Hyphens After Nouns
on-site day care	day care that is on-site
first-class seats	seats that are first-class
up-to-date information	the information is up-to-date
old-fashioned attitude	attitude that is old-fashioned
short-term goals	goals that are short-term
well-known expert	expert who is well-known
full-time (part-time) employee	employee who is full-time (part-time)

Don't confuse adverbs ending in *ly* with compound adjectives: *newly decorated office* and *highly regarded architect* would not be hyphenated.

As compound adjectives become more familiar, they are often simplified and the hyphen is dropped. Some familiar compounds that are not hyphenated are *high school, charge account, income tax, home office, word processing, health care, human resources, voice mail,* and *data processing.*

Hyphens are used even if part of the compound adjective is implied.

Several *three-* and *four-bedroom* homes are for sale.

High- and *low-priced* homes are selling quickly.

We have openings for *part-* and *full-time* cashiers.

Independent Adjectives

Independent adjectives occur when two or more adjectives appearing before a noun independently modify the noun. Writers must separate independent adjectives with commas. Do not use a comma, however, when the first adjective modifies the combined idea of the second adjective and the noun.

Study Tip

To determine whether successive adjectives are independent, mentally insert the word *and* between them. If the insertion makes sense, the adjectives are probably independent and require a comma.

Two Adjectives Independently Modifying a Noun	First Adjective Modifying a Second Adjective Plus a Noun
professional, motivated employee	efficient administrative assistant
economical, safe vehicle	British racing green Mini Cooper
stimulating, provocative book	assistant deputy director

MODIFIERS: ADJECTIVES AND ADVERBS

Double Negatives

When a negative adverb (*no, not, nothing, scarcely, hardly, barely*) is used in the same sentence with a negative verb (*didn't, don't, won't*), a substandard construction called a **double negative** results. Among professionals, such constructions are considered to be illogical and illiterate. In the following examples, notice that eliminating one negative corrects the double negative.

Trivia Tidbit

At one time in the history of the English language, multiple negatives were used to emphasize an idea. (*Don't never say nothing wicked!*) But in the eighteenth century, grammarians adopted Latin logic and decreed that two negatives created a positive.

Incorrect:	Telling her the truth *won't* do *no* good.
Correct:	Telling her the truth will do no good.
Correct:	Telling her the truth won't do any good.
Incorrect:	We *couldn't hardly* believe the breaking news story.
Correct:	We could hardly believe the breaking news story.
Correct:	We couldn't believe the breaking news story.
Incorrect:	Drivers *can't barely* see in the heavy fog.
Correct:	Drivers can barely see in the heavy fog.
Correct:	Drivers can't see in the heavy fog.
Incorrect:	He *didn't have nothing* to do with it.
Correct:	He had nothing to do with it.
Correct:	He didn't have anything to do with it.

Now complete the reinforcement exercises for Level 2.

LEVEL 3

Adjective and Adverb Challenges

In this section you will learn to use commonly confused adjectives and adverbs correctly. You will also learn how to make comparisons within a group and how to place adjectives and adverbs appropriately in sentences.

Commonly Confused Adjectives and Adverbs

The following adjectives and adverbs cause difficulty for some writers and speakers. With a little study, you can master their correct usage.

almost (adj.—nearly): *Almost* (not *Most*) everyone took the ethics training class.
most (adj.—greatest in amount): *Most* employees make good ethical decisions.

farther (adv.—actual distance): How much *farther* is the airport?
further (adv.—additionally): Let's discuss the issue *further*.

sure (adj.—certain): She is *sure* that she wants this position.
surely (adv.—undoubtedly): He will *surely* be victorious.

later (adv.—after expected time): The contract arrived *later* in the day.
latter (adj.—the second of two things): Of the two options, I prefer the *latter*.

fewer (adj.—refers to countable items): *Fewer* requests for funding were granted this year.
less (adj.—refers to amounts or quantities): *Less* time remains than we anticipated.

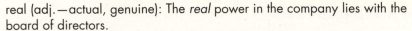

Study Tip

Typically, *well* is an adverb. But Americans use it as an adjective when referring to health (*I feel well*). When referring to good spirits, use *good* (*I feel good*). By the way, the British do not make this distinction.

real (adj.—actual, genuine): The *real* power in the company lies with the board of directors.
really (adv.—actually, truly): Gretchen is *really* eager to take her vacation.

good (adj.—desirable): A number of *good* candidates were interviewed.

well   (adv.—satisfactorily): Brooke did *well* on her performance evaluation.
        (adj.—healthy): Jamal feels *well* enough to return to work.

Comparisons Within a Group

When the word *than* is used to compare a person, place, or thing with other members of a group to which it belongs, be certain to include the words *other* or *else* in the comparison. This inclusion ensures that the person or thing being compared is separated from the group with which it is compared.

Illogical: Rhode Island is smaller than any state in the United States. (This sentence suggests that Rhode Island is smaller than itself.)
Logical: Rhode Island is smaller than any *other* state in the United States.

Illogical: Our team had better results than any team in the company.
Logical: Our team had better results than any *other* team in the company.

Illogical: Alex works harder than anyone in the office.
Logical: Alex works harder than anyone *else* in the office.

Placing Adverbs and Adjectives

The position of an adverb or adjective can seriously affect the meaning of a sentence. Study these examples:

Only Cathi MacPherson can convince the boss. (No one else can convince the boss.)

Cathi MacPherson can *only* convince the boss. (She can't do anything else.)

Cathi MacPherson can convince *only* the boss. (She can't convince anyone else.)

To avoid confusion, adverbs and adjectives should be placed close to the words they modify. In this regard, special attention should be given to the words *only*, *merely*, *first*, and *last*.

Confusing: He *merely* said that the report could be improved.
Clear: He said *merely* that the report could be improved.

Confusing: Seats in the five *first* rows have been reserved.
Clear: Seats in the *first* five rows have been reserved.

Now complete the reinforcement exercises for Level 3.

Trivia Tidbit

The longest word in the English language with no repeated letters is the adjective *uncopyrightable*.

Q: Is it necessary to hyphenate *25 percent* in the phrase *a 25 percent discount*?

A: No. Percents are not treated in the same way that numbers appearing in compound adjectives are treated. Thus, you would not hyphenate *15 percent* in *a 15 percent loan*, but you would hyphenate *15 year* in *a 15-year loan*.

Q: Why does the sign above my grocery store's quick-check stand say *Ten or less items*? Shouldn't it read *Ten or fewer items*?

A: Right you are! *Fewer* refers to numbers or countable items, as in *fewer items*. *Less* refers to amounts or quantities, as in *less food*. Perhaps grocery stores prefer *less* because it has fewer letters.

Q: How many hyphens should I use in this sentence? *The three, four, and five year plans continue to be funded.*

A: Three hyphens are needed: *The three-, four-, and five-year plans continue to be funded.* Hyphenate compound adjectives even when the parts of the compound are separated or suspended.

Q: Why can't I remember how to spell *already*? I want to use it in this sentence: *Your account has already been credited with your payment.*

A: You—and many others—have difficulty with *already* because two different words (and meanings) are expressed by essentially the same sounds. The adverb *already* means "previously" or "before this time," as in your sentence. The two-word combination *all ready* means "all prepared," as in *The club members are all ready to board the bus*. If you can logically insert the word *completely* between *all* and *ready*, you know the two-word combination is needed.

Q: Here are some expressions that cause us trouble in our business letters. We want to hyphenate all of the following. Right? *Well-produced play, awareness-generation film, decision-making tables, one-paragraph note, swearing-in ceremony, point-by-point analysis, commonly-used book.*

A: All your hyphenated forms are correct except the last one; this should be written as *commonly used book*. Don't use a hyphen with an *ly*-ending adverb.

Q: Is this a double negative? *We <u>can't</u> schedule the meeting because we have <u>no</u> room available.*

A: No, this is not regarded as a double negative. In grammar a double negative is created when two negative adverbs modify a verb, such as *can't hardly*, *won't barely*, or *can't help but*. Avoid such constructions.

Q: I can never seem to keep *desert* and *dessert* straight. When do I use each?

A: Yes, these two words can be tricky, especially because *desert* has several different meanings and two different pronunciations. As a noun, *desert* refers to arid land (*they were lost for days in the desert*). As an adjective, *desert* is used to describe something that is desolate or sparsely occupied (*a desert island*). These two forms have the same pronunciation, with the accent on the first syllable. As a verb, *desert* means "to withdraw from or leave" (*the army will desert the village at noon*). The word *dessert* is a noun referring to a sweet course or dish (*my favorite part of the meal is dessert*). Both the verb *desert* and the noun *dessert* have the same pronunciation, with the accent on the second syllable.

Q: Is there a difference between *awhile* and *a while*?

A: Yes. Here's how to decide whether to write this as one word or two. *Awhile* as one word is an adverb meaning "for a period of time" (*we sat awhile to rest our feet*) As two words *a while* is a noun phrase with *a* serving as an article to describe the noun *while* (*I have been searching for a while for the perfect site*). A good trick to remember is that if this word follows the word *for*, write it as two words.

Q: One of my favorite words is *hopefully*, but I understand that it is often used improperly. How should it be used?

A: Language purists insist that the word *hopefully* be used to modify a verb (*We looked at the door hopefully, expecting Mr. Guerrero to return momentarily*). The word *hopefully* should not be used as a substitute for *I hope that* or *We hope that*. Instead of saying *Hopefully, interest rates will decline*, one should say *I hope that interest rates will decline*.

Q: I'm confused. What is the correct spelling: *all together* or *altogether*? I can never remember whether it's one word or two.

A: It depends on how you're using the word. When spelled as one word, *altogether* means "completely or as a whole" (*Altogether we spent $400 on our vacation*). When spelled as two words, *all together* means "gathered in one location or all acting collectively" (*The committee members were all together in one room*).

SPOT THE Blooper

Using the skills you are learning in this class, try to identify why the following items are bloopers. Consult your textbook, dictionary, or reference manual as needed. To see if you recognized the blooper, go to **www.cengagebrain.com** and use your access code to see the Spot the Blooper key.

Blooper 1: Movie review for the film *J. Edgar* in *Rolling Stone*: "Say this for Leonardo DiCaprio: He doesn't scare off easy from acting challenges."

Blooper 2: Title of a biography of Steve Jobs, former founder and CEO of Apple, written for young adults: *Steve Jobs: The Man Who Thought Different.*

Blooper 3: Headline in the Real Estate section of the *San Francisco Chronicle*: "A bit noisy but real nice."

Blooper 4: From a Citibank brochure: "Your Citibank card will only access your checking account for these type purchases." [Did you spot two errors?]

Blooper 5: From a full-page IBM advertisement: "Can you really buy a computer that makes someone feel differently about their job?" [Did you spot two errors?]

Blooper 6: Steve Carell, playing the role of Michael Scott on *The Office*: "I think that I'm approachable as one of the guys, but maybe I need to be approachabler."

Blooper 7: From a radio advertisement for an Internet Service Provider (ISP): "With our Internet service you'll get less annoying pop-up ads."

Blooper 8: Headline from *The Atlanta Journal-Constitution*: "Braves Fans Owe Nothing to No One."

Blooper 9: From a radio commercial for The Club, a device to prevent auto theft: "The Club works where other cheap imitations fail." [Does this statement say that The Club is a cheap imitation?]

Blooper 10: From *The Naples* [Florida] *Daily News*: "We may publish more letters to the editor than any newspaper in America."

7 Reinforcement Exercises

LEVEL 1

A. Self-Check. Adjectives and Adverbs. Choose the correct answer.

1. Gabrielle felt *(a) bad, (b) badly* that she couldn't attend the wedding.   _____

2. This is the *(a) worse, (b) worst* the economy has been since the Great Depression.   _____

3. The company's profits are *(a) worse, (b) worst* this quarter than last quarter.   _____

4. Unless online orders can be processed *(a) more efficient, (b) more efficiently*, we will lose business to our competitors.   _____

5. Try to write *(a) conversational, (b) conversationally* in your business messages.   _____

6. With *(a) more careful, (b) carefuller* planning, the conference will be a success.   _____

7. I can't think of a *(a) better, (b) more better* person for the position.   _____

8. New York City suffered its *(a) coldest, (b) most cold* winter ever in 1934.   _____

9. When giving your presentation, try to speak *(a) natural, (b) naturally*.   _____

10. The outcome of the race between Tony Stewart and Dale Earnhardt, Jr., will determine the *(a) faster, (b) fastest* driver.   _____

Check your answers below.

B. Adjectives and Adverbs. Choose the correct answer.

11. Four of the *(a) worse, (b) worst* business failures in history were Pan Am, DeLorean Motor Company, Commodore Computers, and Pets.com.   _____

12. Politicians have discovered that social media sites work *(a) beautiful, (b) beautifully* for campaigning.   _____

13. Kroger, the largest grocery store chain in America, is the *(a) more, (b) most* generous of all corporate donors.   _____

14. Chad looked *(a) longing, (b) longingly* at the freshly baked cookies.   _____

15. The cookies smelled *(a) delicious, (b) deliciously*.   _____

16. Since we started processing returns online, the process runs *(a) smoother, (b) more smoothly*.   _____

17. Please don't take her comments during the meeting *(a) personal, (b) personally*.   _____

18. Yuki looked *(a) calm, (b) calmly* as she approached the podium.   _____

19. This vendor offers *(a) faster, (b) more fast* delivery.   _____

20. Georgetown was beaten *(a) bad, (b) badly* in the NCAA basketball tournament.   _____

21. Having prepared for months, we won the bid *(a) easy, (b) easily*.   _____

22. To reduce legal costs, they wanted to reach a settlement *(a) quick, (b) quickly*.   _____

23. Reaching a *(a) quick, (b) quickly* settlement could save the firm millions.   _____

1.a 2.b 3.a 4.b 5.b 6.a 7.a 8.a 9.b 10.a

24. Our new ergonomically designed office furniture should keep employees working *(a) comfortable, (b) comfortably*. _____

25. Of the two proposals, this one is *(a) more, (b) most* persuasive. _____

26. If you had been *(a) more observant, (b) observanter*, you would have noticed the speaker's body language. _____

27. Between Tom and Max, Tom's credentials are *(a) stronger, (b) strongest*. _____

28. Sarah is the *(a) friendlyest, (b) friendliest* person in our office. _____

29. San Francisco is *(a) more close, (b) closer* to Hawaii than Los Angeles is. _____

30. Please let employees know if you would like them to dress *(a) nicer, (b) more nicely* for business meetings. _____

C. Writing Exercise. Comparatives and Superlatives. In the space provided, write the correct comparative or superlative form of the adjective shown in parentheses.

Example: Of the two Moroccan restaurants, which is (good)?   better _____

31. Ian is the (intellectual) student in the class. _____

32. She did (good) on the CPA exam than she expected. _____

33. Please send me the (current) figures you can find. _____

34. The newly designed website is (easy) to navigate than the old one. _____

35. Hotel rooms on upper floors are (quiet) than rooms on lower floors. _____

36. Of all the employees, Richard is the (little) talkative. _____

37. This candidate is (professional) than the previous interviewee. _____

38. Have you ever met a (kind) individual than Lynn McDonald? _____

39. This is the (bad) winter we have had in years. _____

40. Which is the (interesting) of the two novels? _____

LEVEL 2

A. Self-Check. Adjective and Adverbs. Choose the correct answer.

41. The witness for the defense seems to be *(a) a, (b) an* honest person. _____

42. Hotel workers are trying to form *(a) a, (b) an* union. _____

43. *(a) This kind, (b) These kinds* of poor financial results worried management. _____

44. We *(a) can, (b) can't* hardly expect employees to feel good about the layoffs. _____

45. We don't have *(a) nothing, (b) anything* we can offer our guests. _____

46. *(a) This type, (b) These types* of computer virus can be difficult to detect. _____

47. A CEO must be concerned with the *(a) day-to-day, (b) day to day* operations of the organization. _____

48. We prefer to meet with you *(a) face-to-face, (b) face to face* to finalize the contract. _____

49. Some small businesses barely exist from *(a) year-to-year, (b) year to year.* _____

50. In the sentence *Her vacation must be postponed*, the word *Her* is a *(a) possessive adjective, (b) possessive pronoun.* _____

Check your answers below.

B. Adjectives and Adverbs. Choose the correct answer.

51. Converting to a cashless system will be *(a) a, (b) an* large undertaking. _____

52. The cattle ranching industry is growing at *(a) a, (b) an* unusually fast pace. _____

53. I *(a) can, (b) can't* hardly believe that more than 3 billion videos are viewed every day on YouTube. _____

54. Our *(a) five-year-old, (b) five year old* vehicle must be traded in for a newer model. _____

55. It is hard to believe that our company is already *(a) five-years-old, (b) five years old.* _____

56. Zappos.com received *(a) a (b) an* A grade for customer service. _____

57. *(a) This kind, (b) These kinds* of rumors can cause stock prices to plunge. _____

58. We can have your order delivered in about *(a) a, (b) an* hour. _____

59. The mortgage company *(a) don't have no, (b) doesn't have any* reason to deny the loan. _____

60. *(a) This type, (b) These types* of errors can be caught by proofreading carefully. _____

61. After paying his taxes, Mark complained that he *(a) has, (b) hasn't* barely a dollar left. _____

62. The wealthy financier left everything to *(a) a, (b) an* heir he had never met. _____

63. Sadie said she couldn't see *(a) no, (b) any* other way to approach the problem. _____

64. The company knew that it couldn't afford to give *(a) nothing, (b) anything* to its favorite charity this year. _____

65. It is wise to keep your résumé and e-portfolio *(a) up-to-date, (b) up to date* at all times. _____

66. We are having difficulty selling our *(a) high priced, (b) high-priced* merchandise. _____

67. Consumers are looking for quality merchandise that is *(a) low priced, (b) low-priced.* _____

68. The rescue squad arrived quickly to help the *(a) dog bite, (b) dog-bite* victim. _____

69. In the sentence *The last piece of pizza is all yours*, the word *yours* is a *(a) possessive adjective, (b) possessive pronoun.* _____

70. In the sentence *Your raise has been approved*, the word *Your* is a *(a) possessive adjective, (b) possessive pronoun.* _____

41. b 42. a 43. b 44. a 45. b 46. a 47. a 48. b 49. b 50. a

C. Articles. Supply the proper article (*a* or *an*) for the following words.

Example: <u>an</u> adjustment

71. ____ budget	76. ____ warehouse	81. ____ insult
72. ____ honor	77. ____ F grade	82. ____ X-ray
73. ____ inventory	78. ____ hour	83. ____ illegible letter
74. ____ usual occurrence	79. ____ idea	84. ____ one-year lease
75. ____ Hawaiian	80. ____ utility	85. ____ eight-year lease

D. Compound Adjectives. In each of the following, choose the correct group of words. Use your dictionary if needed to determine whether compound adjectives have permanent hyphenation.

86. a. state of the art building
    b. state-of-the-art building _____

87. a. well-documented study
    b. well documented study _____

88. a. child who is nine-years-old
    b. child who is nine years old _____

89. a. nine-year-old child
    b. nine year old child _____

90. a. fully certified nurse
    b. fully-certified nurse _____

91. a. salary of $75,000 a year
    b. salary of $75,000-a-year _____

92. a. $75,000 a year salary
    b. $75,000-a-year salary _____

93. a. part-time job
    b. part time job _____

94. a. job that is part-time
    b. job that is part time _____

95. a. on-site health club
    b. on site health club _____

96. a. first-class accommodations
    b. first class accommodations _____

97. a. voice-mail message
    b. voice mail message _____

98. a. high school diploma
    b. high-school diploma _____

99. a. last-minute preparations
    b. last minute preparations _____

100. a. widely-acclaimed cure
     b. widely acclaimed cure _____

101. a. well known writer
     b. well-known writer _____

102. a. writer who is well known
     b. writer who is well-known _____

103. a. health care provider
     b. health-care provider _____

104. a. figures that are up-to-date
     b. figures that are up to date _____

105. a. no fault insurance
     b. no-fault insurance _____

E. Independent Adjectives. Place commas where needed in the following groups of words.

106. lightning blue sports car

107. honest fair assessment

108. concise courteous e-mail message

109. innovative software program

110. direct practical approach

111. snug cheerful apartment

112. imaginative daring filmmaker

113. skilled financial analyst

114. impractical budget item

115. rising stock prices

F. **Writing Exercise. Compound Adjectives.** Compose sentences using the compound adjectives shown. Be sure that compound adjectives precede nouns. Add hyphens as needed.

Example: (up to the minute)

Stay up-to-the-minute by reading our Twitter feed.

116. (health care)

_____

_____

117. (first class)

_____

_____

118. (part time)

_____

_____

119. (two year old)

_____

_____

120. (once in a lifetime)

_____

_____

121. (month by month)

_____

_____

122. (work related)

_____

_____

123. (state of the art)

_____

_____

124. (up to date)

_____

_____

125. (day care)

_____

_____

A. Self-Check. Adjectives and Adverbs. Choose the correct answer.

126. Despite media reports, *(a) most, (b) almost* everyone agreed that politicians work hard for their constituents. _____

127. In comparing online auction fraud and identity theft, the *(a) later, (b) latter* makes up the largest percentage of complaints to the Federal Trade Commission. _____

128. Patricia Franzoia was *(a) real, (b) really* surprised to learn that her performance review would be delivered online. _____

129. Companies have reported *(a) fewer, (b) less* security breaches this year. _____

130. The airport was *(a) farther, (b) further* away than it appeared on our map. _____

131. My business professor Deborah Kitchen is more intelligent than *(a) any teacher, (b) any other teacher* I have ever had. _____

132. We were told to answer the *(a) ten last questions, (b) last ten questions.* _____

133. We are concerned *(a) with only, (b) only with* your welfare and happiness. _____

134. Billy Crystal performed *(a) good, (b) well* as host for the Academy Awards. _____

135. Tourists say that the people in Charleston, South Carolina, are more polite than those in *(a) any city, (b) any other city* in the United States. _____

Check your answers below.

B. Adjectives and Adverbs. Choose the correct answer.

136. Lesley Silverthorn, founder of Angaza Design, feels *(a) good, (b) well* that she was chosen by *Bloomberg BusinessWeek* as one of America's best young entrepreneurs. _____

137. Christopher thought that he did *(a) good, (b) well* in the Duke University Start-Up Challenge. _____

138. Your new interview suit certainly fits you *(a) good, (b) well.* _____

139. Your new interview suit looks very *(a) good, (b) well* on you. _____

140. Apples and brie cheese taste *(a) good, (b) well* on pizza. _____

141. We had *(a) fewer, (b) less* time to conduct the research than expected. _____

142. Rick feels *(a) sure, (b) surely* that part-time salaries will improve. _____

143. You will *(a) sure, (b) surely* be surprised to learn that Warren Buffett doesn't use a cell phone. _____

144. She wanted to debate the question *(a) further, (b) farther.* _____

145. You'll find the café just a little *(a) further, (b) farther* down the street on the left. _____

146. In an effort to reduce expenses, New Tech will offer employees *(a) fewer, (b) less* benefit options next year. _____

147. Lavonda wasn't *(a) real, (b) really* sure she could attend the meeting. _____

148. Lisa Genova's *(a) three last, (b) last three* books have been best sellers. _____

126. b   127. b   128. b   129. a   130. a   131. b   132. b   133. b   134. b   135. b

Circle art: © iStockphoto.com/Pavel Khorenyan

149. Colonel Bauer asserted that the U.S. Army is safer for women than *(a) any other, (b) any* organization in America. _____

150. I *(a) only have, (b) have only* one idea for solving the security problem. _____

151. Of the two independent films we saw this weekend, I prefer the *(a) later, (b) latter*. _____

152. Jacksonville is larger than *(a) any other, (b) any* city in Florida. _____

153. Many items are *(a) only available, (b) available only* on Eddie Bauer's website. _____

154. The *(a) first two, (b) two first* applicants presented excellent résumés. _____

155. *(a) Less, (b) Fewer* money was spent on corporate holiday parties this year. _____

C. Writing Exercise. Commonly Confused Adjectives and Adverbs. Compose sentences using the following words.

156. (farther) _____

_____

157. (further) _____

_____

158. (latter) _____

_____

159. (fewer) _____

_____

160. (less) _____

_____

D. Review. Adjectives and Adverbs. Choose the correct answers.

161. Their daughter, who is *(a) six years old, (b) six-years-old*, already speaks three languages. _____

162. RadioShack was chastised by the media when it announced employee layoffs in *(a) a, (b) an* e-mail message. _____

163. Which of the two Super Bowl ad campaigns do you like *(a) better, (b) best*? _____

164. Many Americans *(a) could, (b) couldn't* barely believe that Hostess Brands, makers of Twinkies and Wonder Bread, filed for bankruptcy. _____

165. Because of excessive costs, designer Donna Karan made *(a) less, (b) fewer* trips to the Far East and Africa in search of "creative inspiration." _____

166. Mr. Wu interviewed a Canadian official and *(a) a, (b) an* European diplomat concerning the proposed two-year trade program. _____

167. Jeff McCormick felt that he had done *(a) good, (b) well* presenting his ideas to the venture capitalists. _____

168. I like this job better than *(a) any other, (b) any* job I have ever had. _____

169. You shouldn't have spoken so *(a) rude, (b) rudely* during the meeting. _____

170. Julie Perzel's only task was to make a *(a) point by point, (b) point-by-point* comparison of the programs. _____

E. FAQs About Business English Review. Choose the correct answer.

171. If you purchase the Ultrabook today, we will give you a *(a) 20 percent, (b) 20-percent* discount. _____

172. We have an *(a) all together, (b) altogether* different situation here. _____

173. Do you prefer a *(a) 24, 36, or 48 month, (b) 24-, 36-, or 48-month* loan? _____

174. Justin was *(a) all ready, (b) already* to purchase a new car when his loan fell through. _____

175. He had *(a) all ready, (b) already* selected the model and all of its accessories. _____

176. I believe we should offer this discount *(a) awhile, (b) a while* longer. _____

177. After using our wireless service for *(a) awhile, (b) a while*, you will begin to appreciate our quality. _____

178. My favorite *(a) desert, (b) dessert* is anything made with chocolate. _____

179. She promised to never *(a) desert, (b) dessert* us. _____

180. Driving across a *(a) desert, (b) dessert* can be dangerous. _____

Chat About It ◀◀

Your instructor may assign any of the following topics for you to discuss in class, in an online chat room, or on an online discussion board. Some of the discussion topics may require outside research. You may also be asked to read and respond to postings made by your classmates.

Discussion Topic 1: Assume you are asked the following question during a job interview: *What is your greatest strength?* How would you answer? Come up with ONE adjective that describes your greatest strength (e.g., *dependable, flexible, conscientious*) and write a success story that proves you have this strength. Then share your success story with your classmates, beginning with this statement: *My greatest strength is that I am _____. For example. . . .*

Discussion Topic 2: Think of your favorite published piece; it might be a novel, poem, song, essay, or article. Now, find a paragraph, passage, or stanza that is highly descriptive. The piece you select should make excellent use of adjectives and adverbs. Share your selection with your classmates. Be sure to tell them the name of the author and the title of the publication. Also tell them why you selected this piece of work.

Discussion Topic 3: Mark Twain once said the following: "Substitute 'damn' every time you're inclined to write 'very'; your editor will delete it and the writing will be just as it should be." What does he mean by this? How can you apply this technique to your own writing? Should all adverbs such as *very* be avoided when writing? Why or why not?

Discussion Topic 4: Thousands of adjectives exist in the English language that can be used to describe someone's personality. What TEN adjectives would you use to best describe yourself? Share these adjectives with your classmates.

Discussion Topic 5: Assume that you are selling an item on eBay. Choose the item; then write a one-paragraph description for it that will make it sound attractive. Be sure to use appropriate modifiers. Share your description with your classmates.

Choose the correct answer. Then compare your answers with those below.

1. Delta Airlines is looking for ways to help its boarding process go *(a) smoother, (b) more smoothly*. _____

2. Steve feels *(a) badly, (b) bad* about having to reduce employee benefits. _____

3. *(a) This kind, (b) These kinds* of employees help make a company successful. _____

4. Gelato has *(a) fewer, (b) less* calories than ice cream. _____

5. It would be *(a) a, (b) an* honor to meet Michael Lewis, the author of *The Blind Side*. _____

6. The employees of REI in Portland felt *(a) good, (b) well* when their building received LEED certification. _____

7. Cassie completed a *(a) page by page, (b) page-by-page* review of the document. _____

8. Visitors were impressed with the *(a) completely-renovated, (b) completely renovated* building. _____

9. We must travel a little *(a) farther, (b) further* before stopping for the night. _____

10. We *(a) could, (b) couldn't* hardly believe the change in her personality. _____

1.b 2.b 3.b 4.a 5.b 6.a 7.b 8.b 9.a 10.a

Circle art: © iStockphoto.com/Pavel Khorenyan

Prepositions 8

This is the sort of English up with which I will not put.

— Winston Churchill, prime minister, United Kingdom (1940–1945, 1951–1955)

Objectives

When you have completed the materials in this chapter, you will be able to do the following:

LEVEL 1
1. Use objective-case pronouns as objects of prepositions.
2. Avoid using prepositions in place of verbs and adverbs.

LEVEL 2
3. Use challenging prepositions correctly.
4. Retain necessary prepositions, omit unnecessary ones, and construct formal sentences that avoid terminal prepositions.

LEVEL 3
5. Recognize idioms and idiomatic constructions, and use idioms involving prepositions correctly.

Pretest

Choose the correct word to complete the sentence.
Then compare your answers with those below.

1. Innovators like Steve Jobs and *(a) she, (b) her* are admired. _____

2. Please send your suggestions to the office manager or *(a) I, (b) me.* _____

3. Alyssa was honored to sit *(a) beside, (b) besides* the CEO at the banquet. _____

4. Lydia is frustrated because she receives *(a) to, (b) too* many text messages from her colleagues. _____

5. She feels *(a) as if, (b) like* these numerous text messages are affecting her productivity. _____

6. Divide the profits evenly *(a) between, (b) among* the three partners. _____

7. Please turn your form *(a) in to, (b) into* your supervisor by Friday. _____

8. Do you plan *(a) on taking, (b) to take* a two-week vacation this summer? _____

9. Management and workers alike agreed *(a) to, (b) with* the contract. _____

10. This plan is different *(a) from, (b) than* the one I suggested. _____

Legend has it that Winston Churchill made his oft-repeated quotation after an editor rearranged one of his sentences to avoid having it end with a preposition. Whether this story is true has long been debated, but it does illustrate how grammar rules can change over time. At one time it was considered unacceptable to end sentences with prepositions; however, this rule has changed, as you will learn later in this chapter.

Prepositions are connecting words. They show the relationship of a noun or pronoun to other words in a sentence. This chapter reviews the use of objective-case pronouns following prepositions. It also focuses on common problems that communicators have with troublesome prepositions. Finally, it presents many idiomatic expressions in our language that require specific prepositions to sound correct.

LEVEL 1

Common Uses of Prepositions

This list contains the most commonly used prepositions. Notice that prepositions may consist of one word or more than one word.

about	behind	except	on account of
above	below	for	opposite

1. b 2. b 3. a 4. b 5. a 6. b 7. a 8. b 9. a 10. a

according to	beneath	from	outside
across	beside	in/into	over
after	besides	in addition to	through
against	between	in spite of	to
along	beyond	inside	toward
along with	but	like	under
alongside	by	near	until
among	despite	of	up
around	down	off	upon
at	due to	on	with
before	during	onto	within/without

A preposition often appears in a **prepositional phrase**, which consists of the preposition followed by the object of the preposition. The **object of a preposition** is a noun or pronoun. As you learned in Chapter 1, prepositions in phrases show a relationship between the object of the preposition and another word (or words) in the sentence. In the following sentences, prepositional phrases are italicized. Notice that a sentence can contain more than one prepositional phrase.

> Some *of our greatest innovations* were launched *during difficult economic times.*

> Many *of the most important ideas in business* were developed *over the past 100 years.*

> The assembly line, created *in 1910 by Henry Ford,* had a positive effect *on productivity.*

Study Tip

Two of the most commonly used prepositions are *of* and *for.* Remember that any nouns or pronouns following these or other prepositions in prepositional phrases serve as objects. Objects of prepositions cannot be subjects of sentences.

Objective Case Following Prepositions

As you learned in Chapter 4, pronouns that are objects of prepositions in prepositional phrases must be in the objective case. Objective-case pronouns include *me, us, you, him, her, it,* and *them.*

> We received feedback *from him* and *her* about their stay in our hotel.

> The disagreement is with the distributor, not *with you* and *me.*

> Please send a welcome packet *to them.*

Less frequently used prepositions are *like, between, except,* and *but* (meaning "except"). These prepositions may lead to confusion in determining pronoun case. Consider the following examples.

> Just *between you and me,* I think Alfred Hitchcock should have won an Oscar in his lifetime. (Not *between you and I*)

> Volunteers *like Alyson and him* are rare. (Not *like Alyson and he*)

> New product suggestions were made by everyone *but them.* (Not *but they*)

Typical Problems With Prepositions

In even the most casual speech or writing, the following misuses of prepositions should be avoided.

Of for have

The verbal phrases *should have*, *would have*, and *could have* should never be written as *should of*, *would of*, or *could of*. The word *of* is a preposition and does not appear in verbal phrases.

> Gina *should have* cited her sources in her business report. (Not *should of*)

> I *would have* covered for you if I had been available. (Not *would of*)

> Mallory *could have* done better in the interview, but she wasn't prepared. (Not *could of*)

Off for from

The preposition *from* should never be replaced by *off* or *off of*.

> Kenneth had to borrow a highlighter pen *from* Jeff. (Not *off of*)

> Fiona said she got the information *from* you. (Not *off* or *off of*)

To for too

The preposition *to* means "in a direction toward." Do not use the word *to* in place of the adverb *too*, which means "additionally," "also," or "excessively." The word *to* may also be part of an infinitive construction.

> The 1965 Voting Rights Act is a monument *to* civil rights. (*To* meaning "in a direction toward")

> Profits were *too* small to declare dividends. (*Too* meaning "excessively")

> I plan to try the new Burmese restaurant *too*. (*Too* meaning "also")

> She is learning *to* program in C++ and Java. (*To* as part of the infinitive *to program*)

Now complete the reinforcement exercises for Level 1.

LEVEL 2

Challenges With Prepositions

Prepositions can present many challenges for business communicators. Some prepositions may be confused with other words. In addition, writers may find it difficult to determine whether a preposition is necessary in a sentence or whether it is acceptable to end a sentence with a preposition.

Commonly Confused Prepositions

Use special caution with the following prepositions.

Among, between

Among means "in or through the midst of" or "surrounded by." It is usually used to speak of three or more persons or things; *between* means "shared by" and is usually used for two persons or things.

> A merger agreement was made *between* United Airlines and Continental Airlines.

> Try to divide the work evenly *among* the four interns.

Beside, besides

Beside means "next to"; *besides* means "in addition to."

> The woman sitting *beside* me on the plane was Meg Whitman, CEO of Hewlett-Packard.

> *Besides* a résumé, you should bring a list of your references to the interview.

Except

The preposition *except*, meaning "excluding" or "but," is sometimes confused with the verb *accept*, which means "to receive."

> Everyone *except* Paula and him attended the training session.

> Jake was excited to *accept* the job offer from Berkeley Research Group.

In, into, in to

In indicates a position or location. *Into* can mean several things, including (a) entering something, (b) changing form, or (c) making contact. Some constructions may employ *in* as an adverb preceding an infinitive:

> The FCIC public hearing was held *in* the Russell Senate Office Building. (Preposition *in* indicates location.)

> We will move *into* our new facilities on May 1. (Preposition *into* indicates entering something.)

> Their son has grown *into* a fine young man. (Preposition *into* indicates changing form.)

> I ran *into* Mico on the way to the seminar. (Preposition *into* indicates making contact with someone.)

> They went *in* to see the manager. (Adverb *in* precedes the infinitive *to see*.)

Like

The preposition *like* should be used to introduce a noun or pronoun. Do not use *like* to introduce a clause (a group of words with a subject and a predicate). To introduce clauses, use *as*, *as if*, or *as though*.

> She looks a lot *like* the actress Minka Kelly. (*Like* used as a preposition to introduce the object *Minka Kelly*.)

> He looks *as if* (not *like*) he is prepared. (Do not use *like* to introduce the clause *he is prepared*.)

> As (not *Like*) I said in my e-mail message, the production deadline has changed. (Do not use *like* to introduce the clause *I said in my e-mail message*.)

Necessary Prepositions

Don't omit those prepositions necessary to clarify a relationship. Be particularly careful when two prepositions modify a single object.

> Our appreciation *for* and interest *in* your ideas remain strong. (Do not omit *for*.)

> What type *of* commitment are you looking for? (Do not omit *of*.)

> Bernice Dandridge is unsure *of* how to secure financing for her business. (Do not omit *of*.)

> Benefits for exempt employees seem to be higher than *for* nonexempt employees. (Do not omit *for*.)

> When did you graduate *from* high school? (Do not omit *from*.)

Trivia Tidbit

Prepositions are especially challenging when one is learning a new language. For example, in English we live "*on* a street." In other languages, such as Italian, we live "*in* a street."

Study Tip

Look at the word(s) following *like*. If many words follow, chances are they function as a clause; use *as*, *as if*, or *as though* instead of *like*.

Unnecessary Prepositions

Omit unnecessary prepositions that clutter sentences.

Leave the shipment *outside* the door. (Better than *outside of*)

Both candidates are qualified. (Better than *both of the candidates*)

I am not sure when the diversity training is scheduled. (Better than *is scheduled for*)

Where is the meeting? (Better than *meeting at*)

She could not help laughing. (Better than *help from laughing*)

Keep the paper near the printer. (Better than *near to*)

My supervisor's office is opposite mine. (Better than *opposite to* or *opposite of*)

He met with the new manager at lunch. (Better than *met up with*)

Did I wake you? (Better than *Did I wake you up?*)

Ending a Sentence With a Preposition

In the past, language authorities warned against ending a sentence (or a clause) with a preposition. In formal writing today, some careful authors continue to avoid ending sentences with prepositions. In conversation and informal writing, however, terminal prepositions are acceptable.

Informal: What professional organization is he a member *of*?
Formal: *Of* what professional organization is he a member?

Informal: What is this tool used *for*?
Formal: *For* what is this tool used?

Informal: We missed the television news program he appeared on.
Formal: We missed the television news program on which he appeared.

Informal: When you called, whom did you speak to?
Formal: When you called, *to* whom did you speak?

Now complete the reinforcement exercises for Level 2.

LEVEL 3

Idiomatic Use of Prepositions

Every language has **idioms**, which are word combinations that are unique to that language. These combinations have developed over time through usage and often cannot be explained rationally. A native speaker usually is unaware of idiom usage until a violation jars his or her ear, such as "He is capable *from* (rather than *of*) violence."

The following list shows words that require specific prepositions to denote precise meanings. This group is just a sampling of the large number of English

Circle art: © iStockphoto.com/Pavel Khorenyan

idioms. Consult a dictionary when you are unsure of the correct preposition to use with a particular word.

acquainted with	Are you *acquainted with* my new colleague?
addicted to	Candace is *addicted to* chocolate.
adept in	Are you *adept in* negotiation tactics?
adhere to	All employees must *adhere to* certain Web-use policies.
agree on (or upon) (mutual ideas)	Our team members *agree on* (or *upon*) nearly everything.
agree to (a proposal or to undertake an action)	Did they *agree to* reduced benefits? We *agree to* supporting our CEO.
agree with (a person or his or her idea)	I *agree with* you on this issue. We *agree with* her suggestion.
all of (when followed by a pronoun)	All *of* us contributed. (For efficiency omit *of* when *all* is followed by a noun, as *All members contributed.*)
angry about (a situation or condition)	Employees are *angry about* the reduction in benefits.
angry at (a thing)	Troy is *angry at* his car for breaking down this morning.
angry with (a person)	Are you *angry with* me for being late?
appreciation for	She has an *appreciation for* organic products.
both of (when followed by a pronoun)	Both *of them* were hired. (For efficiency omit *of* when *both* is followed by a noun, as *Both candidates were hired.*)
buy from	You may *buy from* any one of our approved vendors.
capable of	She is *capable of* remarkable accomplishments.
center on (not *around*)	His campaign speech *centered on* the economy.
comply with	We must *comply with* governmental regulations.
conform to	Your products do not *conform to* our specifications.
contrast with	The angles *contrast with* the curves in that logotype.
convenient to (a location)	The office building is *convenient to* public transportation.
convenient for (a person)	We make returns *convenient for* our customers.
correspond to (a thing)	A company's success *corresponds to* its leadership.
correspond with (a person in writing)	We *correspond with* our clients regularly.
differ from (things)	Debit cards *differ from* credit cards.
differ with (person)	I *differ with* you in small points only.
different from (not *than*)	This product is *different from* the one I ordered.
disagree with	Do you *disagree with* him?

expert in	Dr. Rand is an *expert in* electronics.
guard against	We must *guard against* complacency.
identical with (or *to*)	Our strategy is *identical with* (or *to*) our competitor's.
independent of (not *from*)	Living alone, the young man was *independent of* his parents.
infer from	I *infer from* your remark that you are dissatisfied.
interest in	Matt has a great *interest in* the bond market.
negligent of	Mike was *negligent of* the important duties of his position.
oblivious of (or *to*)	He is often *oblivious of* (or *to*) what goes on around him.
plan to (not *on*)	We *plan to* expand our target market.
prefer to	Do you *prefer to* work a four-day week?
reason with	We tried to *reason with* the unhappy customer.
reconcile with (match)	Checkbook figures must be *reconciled with* bank figures.
reconcile to (accept)	He has never become *reconciled to* retirement.
respect for	He has great *respect for* his hardworking colleagues.
responsible for	William is *responsible for* locking the building.
retroactive to (not *from*)	The salary increase is *retroactive to* last July 1.
sensitive to	He is unusually *sensitive to* his employees' needs.
similar to	Your proposal topic is *similar to* mine.
speak/talk to (tell something)	I must *speak/talk to* her about her tardiness.
speak/talk with (discuss with)	I enjoyed *speaking/talking with* you yesterday at lunch.
standing in (not *on*) line	How long have you been *standing in* line?

Now complete the reinforcement exercises for Level 3.

Trivia Tidbit

An idiom can also be a phrase in which the words together have a different meaning from the dictionary definitions of the individual words, such as *ace in the hole*, *face value*, *seed money*, and *melting pot*. What do these idioms mean?

Courtesy of Mary Ellen Guffey

Courtesy of Carolyn M. Seefer

Dr. Guffey   Professor Seefer

Q: Can you help me? I just wrote this sentence: *She is suppose to place the order tomorrow.* Is there something wrong with it?

A: Yes, you should have used *supposed* instead of *suppose*. The verb *suppose* means to "lay down tentatively," or "to hold as an opinion" (*We suppose you might get a raise*). The adjective *supposed* means "something intended" (*I was supposed to call my mom today*). Here is a trick: If the word *to* follows this word, use *supposed*.

Q: What's wrong with saying *Lisa graduated college last year*?

A: The preposition *from* must be inserted for syntactical fluency. Two constructions are permissible: *Lisa graduated from college* or *Lisa was graduated from college*. The first version is more popular; the second is preferred by traditional grammarians.

Q: I'm writing a sentence that reads *Please proceed to the podium.* . . . Is this correct, or should I use *precede* instead of *proceed*?

A: You're correct to use *proceed*, which means "to go forward or continue," in this sentence. The word *precede* means "to go before" (*A discussion will precede the final vote*).

Q: I was always taught that you should never end a sentence with a preposition. But sometimes following this rule sounds so stuffy and unnatural, such as saying *From where are you?* instead of *Where are you from?* Is it ever acceptable to end a sentence with a preposition?

A: In the past, language authorities warned against ending a sentence (or a clause) with a preposition. In formal writing today some careful authors continue to avoid terminal prepositions. In conversation and informal writing, however, terminal prepositions are acceptable.

Q: Can you tell me what sounds strange in this sentence and why? *The building looks like it was redesigned.*

A: The word *like* should not be used as a conjunction, as has been done in your sentence. Substitute *as if* (*the building looks as if it was redesigned*).

Q: Should *sometime* be one or two words in the following sentence? *Can you come over (some time) soon?*

A: In this sentence you should use the one-word form. *Sometime* means "an indefinite time" (*the convention is sometime in December*). The two-word combination means "a period of time" (*we have some time to spare*).

Circle-art · © iStockphoto.com/Pavel Khorenyan

Q: I saw this printed recently: *Some of the personal functions being reviewed are job descriptions, job specifications, and job evaluation.* Is *personal* used correctly here?

A: Indeed not! The word *personal* means "private" or "individual" (*your personal letters are being forwarded to you*). The word *personnel* refers to employees (*all company personnel are cordially invited*). The sentence you quote requires *personnel*.

Q: Is there any difference between *proved* and *proven*?

A: As a past participle, the verb form *proved* is preferred (*he has proved his point*). However, the word *proven* is preferred as an adjective form (*that company has a proven record*). *Proven* is also commonly used in the expression *not proven*.

Q: How should I write *industry wide*? It's not in my dictionary.

A: A word with the suffix *wide* is usually written solid: *industrywide, nationwide, countrywide, statewide, worldwide*.

Q: Should the word *onto* be written as one word or two in this sentence? *I think we're really onto something.*

A: You are correct to write *onto* as one word in this sentence. As one word, *onto* is a preposition meaning "in or into a state of awareness about" or "to a position on" (*He turned onto Main Street*). Write *on to* as two words when neither of these definitions apply (*I moved on to the next chapter of my book. I passed the information on to my colleague*). Here is another trick to help you decide: if you can remove the word *on* and the sentence still makes sense, write *on to* as two words.

Q: Everyone says "consensus of opinion." Yet, I understand that there is some objection to this expression.

A: Yes, the expression is widely used. However, because *consensus* means "collective opinion," the addition of the word *opinion* results in a redundancy.

SPOT THE Blooper

Using the skills you are learning in this class, try to identify why the following items are bloopers. Consult your textbook, dictionary, or reference manual as needed. To see if you recognized the blooper, go to **www.cengagebrain.com** and use your access code to see the Spot the Blooper key.

Blooper 1: In a *Washington Post* article, President Obama discussed why he was happy that his oldest daughter Malia had braces put on: "...which is good because, you know, she looks like a kid. She was getting, you know, she was starting to look to old."

Blooper 2: In a *Sacramento Bee* article about the growing popularity of social networking: "It seems, all of a sudden, like everyone is on Facebook."

Blooper 3: Bill Maher to John Kerry on Maher's MSNBC show: "You could of went to New Hampshire and killed two birds with one stone." [Did you notice two bloopers?]

Blooper 4: From a national ad for Amtrak: "We plan your vacation. You plan on having a great time."

Blooper 5: From a job applicant's résumé: "Education: Bachelor of engineering. Passed out in top 2 percent."

Blooper 6: From *The Atlanta Journal-Constitution*: A teacher accused of stealing drugs "resigned from his two-year job at Lanier Middle School before turning himself into authorities."

Blooper 7: Sign at an Arby's restaurant in West St. Paul, Minnesota: "We now except checks!"

Blooper 8: Newspaper headline in Thatcham, Berkshire, England: "Newbury Bride To Be Found Dead."

Blooper 9: From a newspaper ad urging readers to call the Literacy Hot Line: "If you or someone you know wants to improve their reading skills, call the Literacy Hot Line."

Blooper 10: From a job applicant's cover letter: "I would be prepared to meet with you at your earliest convenience to discuss what I can do to your company."

NAME _____

A. Self-Check. Prepositions. Choose the correct answer.

1. Bill and Melinda Gates *(a) could of, (b) could have* kept their fortune, but they chose to use it to fight extreme poverty and poor health in developing countries. _____

2. In addition to several others, Warren Buffett and Martha Choe serve on the board of the Bill & Melinda Gates Foundation *(a) to, (b) too.* _____

3. Everyone seems to have a LinkedIn account but *(a) I, (b) me.* _____

4. All residents in our neighborhood except *(a) they, (b) them* have installed security systems. _____

5. Many believe that corporate annual reports are *(a) too, (b) to* cryptic to understand. _____

6. We were able to get her Twitter account name *(a) off of, (b) from* Jacqueline. _____

7. Will invitations be sent to Sharif and *(a) her, (b) she*? _____

8. Government has *(a) to, (b) too* consider the effects of a tax increase. _____

9. With more experience, Roeena *(a) would of, (b) would have* qualified for the position. _____

10. Let's keep this news between you and *(a) I, (b) me.* _____

Check your answers below.

B. Prepositions. Choose the correct answer.

11. It is *(a) to, (b) too* soon to tell whether touch computing will completely replace keyboards. _____

12. Ursula Burns, CEO of Xerox, spoke with reporters and *(a) I, (b) me* about what it is like to be the first African-American woman to head a major U.S. corporation. _____

13. *(a) To, (b) Too* save money, many people are taking *staycations*, which means they are staying home instead of traveling. _____

14. Suggestions from everyone but *(a) they, (b) them* have been received. _____

15. Everyone in the office except *(a) her, (b) she* uses an iPad. _____

16. Our supervisor *(a) would of, (b) would have* published our performance reviews online if he had his choice. _____

17. I am going to try to get the price quote *(a) off of, (b) from* Richard. _____

18. You should make an appointment with Dr. Rosen or *(a) she, (b) her.* _____

19. Our union said that management's offer was "too little and *(a) too, (b) to* late." _____

20. Many small business owners think that the federal budget *(a) should have, (b) should of* included more tax breaks. _____

1.b 2.b 3.b 4.b 5.a 6.b 7.a 8.a 9.b 10.b

21. *(a) To, (b) Too* many people have lost money in the stock market. _____

22. Just between you and *(a) me, (b) I*, the difference between a job and a career is the difference between 40 and 60 hours a week. _____

23. You *(a) could of, (b) could have* gotten that promotion if you had worked a little harder. _____

24. Our manager, together with Tanya and *(a) he, (b) him*, helped to close the sale. _____

25. Last year we tried to order supplies *(a) from, (b) off of* them too. _____

26. You can always rely on coworkers like Arthur and *(a) she, (b) her* when you need extra help to meet a deadline. _____

27. Everyone except him and *(a) I, (b) me* received the announcement too late to respond. _____

28. To make sure your message gets through, you must use contact information *(a) off of, (b) from* their website. _____

29. Women were first given the right *(a) to, (b) too* vote in the Pitcairn Islands in 1838. _____

30. In 1920 women in the United States were finally given the right to vote *(a) to, (b) too*. _____

LEVEL 2

A. Self-Check. Prepositions. Choose the correct answer.

31. Voice control, which allows you to send text messages and search the Web using just your voice, is making its way *(a) in, (b) into* corporate offices. _____

32. Who *(a) beside, (b) besides* you uses Siri on an iPhone? _____

33. Overhead expenses will be divided equally *(a) between, (b) among* the six departments. _____

34. We engrave identification serial numbers *(a) inside, (b) inside of* all new equipment. _____

35. The office *(a) besides, (b) beside* ours has become a victim of cybercrime. _____

36. It looks *(a) like, (b) as if* China will continue to block sites such as Facebook, Twitter, and YouTube. _____

37. Have you decided whether you will *(a) except, (b) accept* the position? _____

38. With his increased salary and new title, Tony feels *(a) like, (b) as* a king. _____

39. Differences *(a) between, (b) among* the two brothers affected their management styles. _____

40. When Tropical Storm Irene hit our small town in Vermont, the doors and shutters blew *(a) off, (b) off of* several buildings. _____

Check your answers below.

31. b 32. b 33. b 34. a 35. b 36. b 37. b 38. a 39. a 40. a

Circle art: © iStockphoto.com/Pavel Khorenyan

PREPOSITIONS

B. Writing Exercise. Necessary and Unnecessary Prepositions. Rewrite the following sentences to omit unnecessary prepositions and include necessary ones.

Examples: What type network security is needed?
<u>What type of network security is needed?</u>
Where are you traveling to this summer?
<u>Where are you traveling this summer?</u>

41. Where should I send the signed contract to?

_____

42. A new café is opening opposite to the park.

_____

43. Special printing jobs must be done outside of the office.

_____

44. Charles had great respect and interest in the stock market.

_____

45. Who can tell me what time the appointment is scheduled for?

_____

46. What style clothes is recommended for the formal dinner?

_____

47. Leah couldn't help from laughing when Noah spilled his latte as he walked into the conference room.

_____

48. Where shall we move the extra desks and chairs to?

_____

49. Lee Montgomery graduated college with a degree in graphic design.

_____

50. What type return policy does Zappos.com have?

_____

51. Please write up her performance appraisal quickly.

_____

52. Our appreciation and interest in the program remain strong.

_____

53. When did you graduate college?

_____

54. Where do you live at?

_____

55. I didn't mean to wake you up.

_____

C. Prepositions. Choose the correct answer.

56. *(a) Between, (b) Among* Marriott and Omni, which hotel provides the most in-room amenities? _____

57. All sites *(a) accept, (b) except* ours offer real-time technical support. _____

58. She hopes to go *(a) in to, (b) into* the civil engineering field. _____

59. The police chief likes to park *(a) near to, (b) near* the station. _____

60. Relief funds were divided *(a) among, (b) between* all flood victims. _____

61. *(a) As, (b) Like* we mentioned yesterday, Friday will be a half day. _____

62. The new systems analyst will move into the office *(a) beside, (b) besides* mine. _____

63. He ran *(a) in to, (b) into* an old college buddy at the airport. _____

64. Your interior design plans look just *(a) like, (b) as* mine. _____

65. Honda's new advertising campaign featuring Ferris Bueller looks *(a) like, (b) as if* it will be quite successful. _____

66. Has anyone been *(a) in to, (b) into* see me this morning? _____

67. You are going to have to *(a) accept, (b) except* the changes. _____

68. Employees are required to turn expense reports *(a) in to, (b) into* their supervisors within one week. _____

69. If he *(a) accepts, (b) excepts* the position, he will have to move to Sioux Falls, South Dakota. _____

70. *(a) Beside, (b) Besides* Zoe Stone and Jason Scogna, whom have you invited? _____

71. It looks *(a) like, (b) as if* RIM's new CEO, Thorsten Heins, will have many challenges ahead of him. _____

72. James Johnson, former CEO of Fannie Mae, has turned *(a) in to, (b) into* an important political leader. _____

73. She *(a) met up with, (b) met with* her new boss this morning. _____

74. Richard Branson, founder of Virgin Atlantic Airways, never *(a) graduated from, (b) graduated* high school. _____

75. Her political views are *(a) opposite from, (b) opposite* mine. _____

D. Writing Exercise. The following sentences end in prepositions. Rewrite them to avoid terminal prepositions.

Example: Here is the information you asked about.

Here is the information about which you asked. _____

76. Whom did you send payment to?

_____

77. Please locate the file you put the contract in.

_____

78. What positions did you apply for?

_____

79. We have a number of loyal members we can rely upon.

_____

80. What company did you purchase these supplies from?

_____

A. Self-Check. Idiomatic Expressions. Choose the correct answer.

81. In a televised address, the president will speak *(a) to, (b) with* the nation at 6 p.m. _____

82. The president's address will center *(a) on, (b) around* education and the economy. _____

83. Some people are exceptionally adept *(a) at, (b) in* expressing their ideas clearly. _____

84. Public companies must comply *(a) with, (b) to* Sarbanes-Oxley requirements. _____

85. Many people plan *(a) to simplify, (b) on simplifying* their lives. _____

86. Donald Trump's management philosophy is quite different *(a) than, (b) from* mine. _____

87. Are you angry *(a) with, (b) at* me for disagreeing with you during the meeting? _____

88. How can they reconcile this new business venture *(a) to, (b) with* their recent bankruptcy? _____

89. Jordan is an expert *(a) at, (b) in* data communications. _____

90. Citizens must adhere *(a) to, (b) with* all local, state, and federal laws. _____

Check your answers below.

B. Idiomatic Expressions. Choose the correct answer.

91. Jack Welch's work ethic is similar *(a) with, (b) to* mine. _____

92. Julia is addicted *(a) with, (b) to* updating her status on Facebook. _____

93. I differ *(a) with, (b) from* you about how to improve our country's educational system. _____

94. Our new office building is convenient *(a) to, (b) with* many restaurants and cafés. _____

95. We will make the salary increase retroactive *(a) from, (b) to* January 1. _____

96. I am very sensitive *(a) to, (b) with* your feelings. _____

97. How does common stock differ *(a) with, (b) from* preferred stock? _____

98. It was a pleasure talking *(a) to, (b) with* you yesterday during the interview. _____

99. Samsung plans *(a) on developing, (b) to develop* phones with flexible screens. _____

100. Customers were upset after standing *(a) in, (b) on* line for an hour. _____

101. Have you become acquainted *(a) with, (b) to* the new intern yet? _____

102. The film version of *Fever Pitch* is much different *(a) than, (b) from* Nick Hornby's book. _____

103. Your success on the job will correspond *(a) to, (b) with* your ability to adapt to change. _____

104. The light background on the Web page contrasts *(a) to, (b) with* the font color. _____

105. A firewall will help guard *(a) against, (b) from* unauthorized access to our intranet. _____

106. We infer *(a) from, (b) about* your statement that you will be running for city supervisor. _____

107. Discussion during today's meeting will center *(a) around, (b) on* how to increase our market share. _____

81. a 82. a 83. b 84. a 85. a 86. b 87. a 88. b 89. b 90. a

108. Christina has a great appreciation *(a) for, (b) in* contemporary art.   _____

109. Employees reached their decision independent *(a) from, (b) of* the influence of union organizers.   _____

110. Liz has an interest *(a) in, (b) for* increasing recycling in the workplace.   _____

C. Writing Exercise. Idiomatic Expressions. Write complete sentences using the expressions shown in parentheses.

111. (oblivious to)

_____

112. (reconcile with)

_____

113. (reconciled to)

_____

114. (plan to)

_____

115. (different from)

_____

D. FAQs About Business English Review. In the space provided, write the correct answer choice.

116. Jonathan said that he hopes to *(a) graduate from, (b) graduate* college within two years.   _____

117. Liliana will take her vacation *(a) some time, (b) sometime* in July.   _____

118. All *(a) personal, (b) personnel* matters are now handled by our Human Resources Department.   _____

119. Employees are not allowed to send *(a) personal, (b) personnel* e-mail messages during work hours.   _____

120. If you have *(a) some time, (b) sometime* to spare on Saturday, please drop by to help us.   _____

121. New *(a) industry wide, (b) industry-wide, (c) industrywide* standards should make it easier to distribute our products internationally.   _____

122. She moved *(a) on to, (b) onto* the next step in the process.   _____

123. To reach our offices, turn left *(a) on to, (b) onto* Market Street.   _____

124. AAA has a *(a) proved, (b) proven* record of providing excellent customer service.   _____

125. We are *(a) suppose, (b) supposed* to earn a bonus at the end of the year.   _____

Chat About It ◂◂

Your instructor may assign any of the following topics for you to discuss in class, in an online chat room, or on an online discussion board. Some of the discussion topics may require outside research. You may also be asked to read and respond to postings made by your classmates.

Discussion Topic 1: The opening quote to this chapter, widely attributed to Winston Churchill, states, "This is the sort of English up with which I will not put." In this quote he is mocking the traditional rule that says a sentence should not end with a preposition. As you learned, this traditional rule has changed, and in most cases it is acceptable to end a sentence with a preposition. Why do you think grammar rules change over time? How can you keep up with current rules?

Discussion Topic 2: A U.S. gymnast said the following during an Associated Press interview: "All the girls were like, 'You can do it, it's fine.' I was like, 'C'mon, guys. I'm fine.' I'm like, 'OK, I've done this routine so many times.'" Do you or does anyone you know use the word *like* in this way? Why do you think this use is so common today? Is this type of language appropriate in the workplace? Explain.

Discussion Topic 3: You learned in this chapter that idioms are word combinations that are unique to a language. Some idioms involve prepositions, such as *angry with* and *different from*. Other idioms are common expressions such as *above board* and *loose cannon*. Perform an Internet search for other English-language idioms that you find interesting, and share ten idiomatic expressions with your classmates. Also share your thoughts about whether idiomatic expressions in the latter category should be used in business writing. Why or why not?

Discussion Topic 4: In this chapter you were introduced to some English idiomatic expressions such as *seed money* and *melting pot*. Choose another language and do Internet research to find five idiomatic expressions from that language. Share them with your classmates.

Discussion Topic 5: Marilyn vos Savant, an American writer and magazine columnist, said, "Although spoken English doesn't obey the rules of written language, a person who doesn't know the rules thoroughly is at a great disadvantage." What do you think she means by this? Do you agree with this statement? Why or why not?

Posttest

Choose the correct answer. Then compare your answers with those below.

1. Between you and *(a) I, (b) me*, what do you think he'll do after he retires? _____

2. No one *(a) except, (b) accept* our entry-level bookkeeper was willing to report the accounting discrepancies. _____

3. Please turn your uniform *(a) into, (b) in to* your supervisor on your last day. _____

4. Her presentation is still three minutes *(a) too, (b) to* long. _____

5. It looks *(a) like, (b) as if* we will be able to avoid layoffs. _____

6. Is it necessary for all documents to comply *(a) to, (b) with* the new guidelines? _____

7. Dividends will be distributed *(a) between, (b) among* preferred stockholders only. _____

8. *(a) Beside, (b) Besides* Jeffrey, who is able to work Saturday? _____

9. Borders Books *(a) could of, (b) could have* survived with better management. _____

10. Employees have respect *(a) for, (b) in* leaders who exhibit ethical behavior. _____

Conjunctions 9

© Helder Almeida/Shutterstock.com

Circle art: © iStockphoto.com/Pavel Khorenyan

The American constitutions were to liberty, what a grammar is to language: they define its parts of speech, and practically construct them into syntax.

—Thomas Paine,
British revolutionary and intellectual

Objectives

When you have completed the materials in this chapter, you will be able to do the following:

LEVEL 1

1. Punctuate compound sentences using coordinating conjunctions such as *and, or, nor,* and *but.*

2. Punctuate compound sentences using conjunctive adverbs such as *therefore, however,* and *consequently.*

LEVEL 2

3. Join unequal sentence elements using subordinating conjunctions such as *although, because, if, since,* and *when.*

4. Punctuate introductory dependent, terminal dependent, parenthetical, essential, and nonessential clauses.

LEVEL 3

5. Recognize correlative conjunctions such as *either . . . or, not only . . . but also,* and *neither . . . nor.*

6. Add variety to sentences by using more complex sentence patterns.

In each pair of sentences, choose the one that is punctuated or written properly. Then compare your answers with those below.

1. (a) Download the driver and install it
   (b) Download the driver, and install it. _____

2. (a) Luke Wilkinson prefers to remain in Atlanta but Reece Soltani is considering the Knoxville area.
   (b) Luke Wilkinson prefers to remain in Atlanta, but Reece Soltani is considering the Knoxville area. _____

3. (a) Michael Paez attended the Phi Beta Lambda competition in Orlando and brought home several medals.
   (b) Michael Paez attended the Phi Beta Lambda competition in Orlando, and brought home several medals. _____

4. (a) All employees must be able to communicate effectively; therefore, we evaluate communication skills during employment interviews.
   (b) All employees must be able to communicate effectively, therefore, we evaluate communication skills during employment interviews. _____

5. (a) Performance reviews, therefore, will include discussion of employees' communication skills.
   (b) Performance reviews; therefore, will include discussion of employees' communication skills. _____

6. (a) When you receive the quote, be sure to have our legal counsel review it.
   (b) When you receive the quote be sure to have our legal counsel review it. _____

7. (a) Please let me know, when you receive confirmation.
   (b) Please let me know when you receive confirmation. _____

8. (a) Sherilyn said that Travis Garcia who works in our Finance Department will be leaving next month.
   (b) Sherilyn said that Travis Garcia, who works in our Finance Department, will be leaving next month. _____

9. (a) Employees who work in our Finance Department are eligible for bonuses.
   (b) Employees, who work in our Finance Department, are eligible for bonuses. _____

10. (a) Not only is this wireless service more reliable but it also is cheaper than the others.
    (b) This wireless service is not only more reliable but also cheaper than the others. _____

Study Tip

Understanding the differences among different types of conjunctions will help you use proper sentence structure and punctuate correctly.

This chapter covers an important part of speech: conjunctions. **Conjunctions** are connecting words. They may be separated into two major groups: those that join grammatically equal words or word groups and those that join grammatically unequal words or word groups. Recognizing conjunctions and understanding their patterns of usage will, among other things, enable you to use commas and semicolons more appropriately.

1.a 2.b 3.a 4.a 5.a 6.a 7.b 8.b 9.a 10.b

Coordinating Conjunctions

Coordinating conjunctions connect words, phrases, and clauses of equal grammatical value or rank. The most common coordinating conjunctions are *and*, *or*, *but*, and *nor*. Notice in these sentences that coordinating conjunctions join grammatically equal elements.

> Important leadership traits include *vision, integrity,* and *self-confidence.* (Here the word *and* joins equal words.)
>
> Open your mind *to new challenges* and *to new ideas.* (Here *and* joins equal phrases.)
>
> You will find job listings *on our website* or *on our Facebook page.* (Here *or* joins equal phrases.)
>
> *Gasoline prices are falling,* but *college tuition costs are rising.* (Here *but* joins equal clauses.)

Three other coordinating conjunctions should also be mentioned: *yet*, *for*, and *so*. The words *yet* and *for* may function as coordinating conjunctions, although they are infrequently used as such.

> We use e-mail extensively, *yet* we still prefer personal contact with our customers.
>
> The weary traveler was gaunt and ill, *for* his journey had been long and arduous.

The word *so* is sometimes informally used as a coordinating conjunction. In more formal contexts, the conjunctive adverbs *therefore* and *consequently* should be substituted for the conjunction *so*. You will study conjunctive adverbs later in this chapter.

> **Informal:** The plane leaves at 2:15, *so* you still have time to get to the airport.
>
> **Improved:** The plane leaves at 2:15; *therefore,* you still have time to get to the airport.

To avoid using *so* as a conjunction, try starting your sentence with *because* or *although*.

> **Informal:** Texting while driving can be dangerous, *so* some states have made this practice illegal.
>
> **Improved:** *Because* texting while driving can be dangerous, some states have made this practice illegal.

Punctuating Compound Sentences Using Coordinating Conjunctions

As you learned in Chapter 2, a **simple sentence** has one **independent clause**, that is, a clause that can stand alone. A **compound sentence** has two or more independent clauses. When coordinating conjunctions (*and, or, but, nor, for, yet,* and *so*) join independent clauses in compound sentences, place a comma before the coordinating conjunction.

> We can handle our payroll processing internally, *or* we can outsource it to a reputable firm. (Use a comma before *or* to join two independent clauses.)
>
> You can place your orders online, *and* you can track your shipments with ease. (Use a comma before *and* to join two independent clauses.)

Study Tip

An easy way to remember the seven coordinating conjunctions is to think of the acronym *FANBOYS*. Each letter stands for one of the coordinating conjunctions: *for, and, nor, but, or, yet,* and *so.*

Analyze all your possible property risks, *and* protect yourself with our comprehensive homeowners' insurance. (Use a comma before *and* to join two independent clauses; the subject of each clause is understood to be *you*.)

However, when the coordinating conjunction *and* is used to connect short compound sentences, you may omit the comma. Consider a sentence short when the entire sentence contains up to 13 words.

Virginia received a text message *and* she responded immediately.

I submitted my vacation request *and* my supervisor approved it.

Do not use commas when coordinating conjunctions join compound verbs, objects, or phrases.

You can place your orders online *and* track your shipments with ease. (No comma needed because *and* joins the compound verbs of a single independent clause.)

Our CEO said that employees should not have to choose between working overtime *and* spending time with their families. (No comma needed because *and* joins the compound objects of a prepositional phrase.)

Stockholders are expected to attend the meeting *or* to send their proxies. (No comma needed because *or* joins two infinitive phrases.)

Conjunctive Adverbs

Conjunctive adverbs may also be used to connect equal sentence elements. Because conjunctive adverbs are used to effect a transition from one thought to another and because they may consist of more than one word, they have also been called **transitional expressions** or **transitional conjunctions**. The most common conjunctive adverbs follow:

accordingly	however	nevertheless
also	in fact	on the contrary
anyway	in other words	on the other hand
consequently	in the meantime	otherwise
for example	indeed	that is
for instance	likewise	then
furthermore	moreover	therefore
hence	namely	thus

In the following compound sentences, observe that conjunctive adverbs join clauses of equal grammatical value. Note that semicolons (NOT commas) are used before conjunctive adverbs that join independent clauses. Commas should immediately follow conjunctive adverbs of two or more syllables. Note also that the word following a semicolon is not capitalized—unless, of course, it is a proper noun.

Some companies oppose employee use of social media in the workplace; *however*, other companies find that it encourages team collaboration and knowledge sharing.

Samantha is working hard to become a forensic accountant; *nevertheless*, she did not pass her CFE exam the first time.

Equipment expenditures are great this quarter; *on the other hand*, new equipment will reduce labor costs.

Generally, no comma is used after one-syllable conjunctive adverbs such as *hence, thus,* and *then* (unless a strong pause is desired).

"Typo squatters" buy domain names spelled similarly to those of real companies; thus these squatters take advantage of people with poor keyboarding skills.

The first entertainment on planes began in 1928 when Transcontinental began distributing playing cards; *then* TWA installed radios in 1939.

Distinguishing Conjunctive Adverbs From Parenthetical Adverbs

Many words that function as conjunctive adverbs may also serve as parenthetical adverbs. **Parenthetical adverbs,** such as *however, therefore,* and *consequently,* are used to effect transitions from one thought to another in independent clauses. Use semicolons *only* with conjunctive adverbs that join two independent clauses. Use commas to set off parenthetical adverbs that interrupt the flow of one independent clause. Notice the differences in these examples:

We believe, *however,* that tablet computer sales will continue to grow. (An adverb is used parenthetically.)

We agree that tablets are convenient; *however,* some people prefer laptops. (A conjunctive adverb joins two clauses.)

The Federal Reserve System, *therefore,* is a vital force in maintaining a sound banking system and a stable economy. (An adverb is used parenthetically.)

The Federal Reserve System is a vital force in maintaining a sound banking system; *therefore,* it is instrumental in creating a stable economy. (A conjunctive adverb joins two clauses.)

Now complete the reinforcement exercises for Level 1.

Study Tip

Use a semicolon ONLY when you are joining two complete sentences.

LEVEL 2

Subordinating Conjunctions

To join unequal sentence elements, such as independent and dependent clauses, use **subordinating conjunctions.** As you learned in Chapter 2, **dependent clauses** depend on independent clauses for their meaning. Dependent clauses are often introduced by subordinating conjunctions such as *if, when, because,* and *as.* A list of the most common subordinating conjunctions follows:

after	because	provided	until
although	before	since	when
as	even though	so that	where
as if	if	that	whether
as though	in order that	unless	while

You should become familiar with this list of conjunctions. However, don't feel that you need to memorize it. Generally, you can recognize a subordinating conjunction by the way it limits, or subordinates, the clause it introduces. In the

Study Tip

Some experts refer to subordinating conjunctions as "dependent conjunctions." This term may help you remember that these conjunctions make clauses dependent on independent clauses for their meaning.

clause *because he wants to go to graduate school*, the subordinating conjunction *because* limits the meaning of the clause it introduces. The clause is incomplete and could not stand alone as a sentence.

Punctuating Sentences With Dependent Clauses

Business and professional writers are especially concerned with clarity and accuracy. A misplaced or omitted punctuation mark can confuse a reader by altering the meaning of a sentence. The following guidelines for using commas help ensure clarity and consistency in writing. Some professional writers, however, take liberties with accepted conventions of punctuation, particularly in regard to comma usage. These experienced writers may omit a comma when they feel that such an omission will not affect the reader's understanding of a sentence. Beginning writers, though, are well advised to first develop skill in punctuating sentences by following traditional guidelines.

Introductory Dependent Clauses

Use a comma after a dependent (subordinate) clause that precedes an independent clause.

> *Even though* Philo Farnsworth invented the television in 1927, he was never able to personally introduce it to consumers.

> *If* you want to see where the first television image was transmitted, go to the corner of Green and Sansome Streets in San Francisco.

> *Because* Philo Farnsworth invented the first television, he is known as "The Genius of Green Street."

Use a comma after an introductory dependent clause even though the subject and verb may not be stated.

> *As* [it was] expected, many businesses now offer Foursquare discounts.

> *If* [it is] possible, please send a replacement immediately.

> *When* [they are] printed, your brochures will be distributed.

Terminal Dependent Clauses

Generally, a dependent clause introduced by a subordinating conjunction does not require a comma when the dependent clause is **terminal**, meaning that it falls at the end of a sentence.

> Please call me *if* you have any questions.

> We must book the conference room *before* we send out invitations.

> Many people are experiencing negative equity *because* their homes are worth less than what they owe on their mortgage loans.

If, however, the dependent clause at the end of a sentence interrupts the flow of the sentence, provides nonessential information, or sounds as if it were an afterthought, a comma should be used.

> I am sure I paid the bill, *although* I cannot find my receipt.
> (Dependent clause adds unnecessary information.)

> We will ship the goods within the week, *if* that is satisfactory with you.
> (Dependent clause sounds like an afterthought.)

Parenthetical Clauses

A **parenthetical clause** adds additional information to a sentence. Within sentences, dependent parenthetical clauses that interrupt the flow and are unnecessary for the grammatical completeness of the sentence are set off by commas.

> The motion, *unless* you want further discussion, will be tabled until our next meeting.

> At our next meeting, *provided* we have a quorum, the motion will be reconsidered.

Relative Clauses

The **relative pronouns** *who*, *whom*, *whose*, *which*, and *that* function as conjunctions when they introduce dependent clauses. Here is how to use relative pronouns correctly:

Relative Pronoun	Used to Refer to	Used to Introduce
who, whom, whose	Persons	Essential and nonessential clauses
that	Animals and things	Essential clauses
which	Animals and things	Nonessential clauses

The tricky part is deciding whether a clause is essential or nonessential. In some cases, only the writer knows whether a clause is intended to be essential or nonessential.

An **essential (restrictive) clause** is needed to identify the noun to which it refers; therefore, no commas should separate this clause from its antecedent.

> Any citizen *who wants to vote in November* must register by October. (The relative pronoun *who* refers to a person [*citizen*] and it introduces an essential clause. The dependent clause is essential because it is needed to identify which citizens must register soon. No commas are needed.)

> Students *whose GPAs are above 3.0* qualify for the scholarship. (The relative pronoun *whose* refers to people [*Students*], and it introduces an essential clause. The dependent clause is essential because it is needed to identify which students qualify for the scholarship. No commas are needed.)

> A company *that* (not *who* or *which*) values its employees is likely to succeed. (The relative pronoun *that* refers to a thing [*company*], and it introduces an essential clause. The dependent clause is essential because it is needed to identify which company is likely to succeed. No commas are needed.)

A **nonessential (nonrestrictive) clause** contains information that the reader does not need to know. The main clause is understandable without this extra information. Careful writers use *which* (not *that*) to introduce nonessential clauses. If the clause is nonessential, it should be set off from the rest of the sentence by commas. Notice that *two* commas are used to set off internal nonessential dependent clauses.

> Heather Bresch, *who* is CEO of Mylan Pharmaceuticals, is the youngest female CEO of a Fortune 500 company. (The relative pronoun *who* introduces a nonessential clause that is set off by commas. The antecedent of the dependent clause, *Heather Bresch*, is clearly identified.)

> Bruce R. Bent, *whose* career was in finance, launched the first U.S. money market fund in 1970. (The relative pronoun *whose* introduces a nonessential clause that is set off by commas. The antecedent of the dependent clause, *Bruce R. Bent*, is clearly identified.)

Study Tip

Careful writers use the word *that* for essential clauses and the word *which* for nonessential clauses. Remember that dependent clauses introduced by *which* require commas.

Software giant Microsoft, *which* is headquartered in Redmond, has many other offices in the state of Washington. (The relative pronoun *which* introduces a nonessential clause that is set off by commas. The antecedent of the dependent clause, *Microsoft,* is clearly identified.)

Punctuation Review

The following three common sentence patterns are very important for you to study and understand. Notice particularly how the sentences are punctuated.

Independent clause, + { and / or / nor / but } + Independent clause. (Comma used when a coordinating conjunction joins independent clauses.)

Independent clause; + { therefore, / consequently, / however, / nevertheless, } + Independent clause. (Semicolon used when a conjunctive adverb joins independent clauses.)

{ Because / If / As / When } Dependent clause, + Independent clause. (Comma used after a dependent clause introduced by a subordinate conjunction.)

Independent clause + { because / if / as / when } + Dependent clause. (No comma used with terminal dependent clauses.)

Now complete the reinforcement exercises for Level 2.

LEVEL 3

Correlative Conjunctions

Correlative conjunctions, like coordinating conjunctions and conjunctive adverbs, join grammatically equal sentence elements. Correlative conjunctions are always used in pairs: *both . . . and, not only . . . but (also), either . . . or,* and *neither . . . nor.* When greater emphasis is desired, these paired conjunctions are used instead of coordinating conjunctions. Notice the difference in these examples when correlative conjunctions are used:

Zappos offers excellent customer service *and* a lenient return policy.

Zappos offers *not only* excellent customer service *but also* a lenient return policy. (More emphatic)

Your best choice for an executive MBA program is Carnegie Mellon *or* Villanova.

Your best choice for an executive MBA program is *either* Carnegie Mellon *or* Villanova. (More emphatic)

Study Tip

When using correlative conjunctions, concentrate on the words immediately following each conjunction. These words must be arranged in the same grammatical construction.

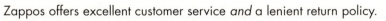

In using correlative conjunctions, place them so that the words, phrases, or clauses being joined are parallel in construction.

Not Parallel: *Either* Gretchen was flying to Boston *or* to Providence.
Parallel: Gretchen was flying *either* to Boston *or* to Providence.

Not Parallel: I *neither* have the time *nor* the energy for this.
Parallel: I have *neither* the time *nor* the energy for this.

Not Parallel: He was *not only* talented, *but* he was *also* intelligent.
Parallel: He was *not only* talented *but also* intelligent.

Sentence Variety

To make messages more interesting, good writers strive for variety in sentence structure. Notice the monotony and choppiness of a paragraph made up entirely of simple sentences:

> Leila Peters founded her own dessert business. She specialized in molded containers made of French chocolate. Her 350 designs were unique. She copyrighted them. Another chocolatier copied her spiral chocolate seashell. Leila sued. She won.

Compare the following version of this paragraph, which uses dependent clauses and other structures to achieve greater sentence variety:

> Leila Peters, who founded her own dessert business, specialized in molded containers made of French chocolate. Because her 350 designs were unique, she copyrighted them. When another chocolatier copied her spiral chocolate seashell, Leila sued and won.

Recognizing the kinds of sentence structures available to writers and speakers is an important step in achieving effective expression. Here is a review of four kinds of sentences you studied in Chapter 2.

Trivia Tidbit

The average American has a vocabulary of about 10,000 words. Compare this vocabulary to William Shakespeare's, whom many consider to be the greatest writer in the English language. He had a vocabulary of roughly 29,000 words.

Kind of Sentence	Minimum Requirement	Example
Simple	One independent clause	Leila Peters founded her own dessert business.
Compound	Two independent clauses	Leila founded her own dessert business, and she specialized in molded containers of French chocolate.
Complex	One independent clause and one dependent clause	Since Leila Peters founded her own dessert business, she has specialized in molded containers of French chocolate.
Compound complex	Two independent clauses and one dependent clause	Leila's chocolate designs were copyrighted; therefore, when another chocolatier copied one, she sued and won.

Developing the ability to use a variety of sentence structures to facilitate effective communication takes practice and writing experience.

Now complete the reinforcement exercises for Level 3.

Courtesy of Mary Ellen Guffey

Courtesy of Carolyn M. Seefer

Dr. Guffey   Professor Seefer

Q: I'm trying to figure out if this sentence is correct: *Her negative comment during today's meeting didn't phase me.* Is *phase* the right word to use here?

A: You should have used *faze* in this sentence instead of *phase*. The verb *faze* means "to disturb, disconcert, or daunt" (*You can't let his critical remarks faze you*). The word *phase* is generally used as a noun meaning "a particular part in a course, development, or cycle" (*Their child is going through a difficult phase*). *Phase* can also function as a verb meaning "to adjust or to introduce in stages" (*We will phase in the new process slowly*).

Q: I don't seem to be able to hear the difference between *than* and *then*. Can you explain it to me?

A: The conjunction *than* is used to make comparisons (*Elaine is taller than her husband Bob*). The adverb *then* means "at that time" (*We must complete this task; then we will take our break*) or "as a consequence" (*If all the angles of the triangle are equal, then it must be equilateral as well*).

Q: I seem to get the words *since* and *sense* mixed up. When do I use each?

A: These two words are often confused because they sound similar. *Since* is a conjunction that means "from a definite past time until now" or "because" (*Since I started this course, I've learned a lot about English grammar* or *Since you won't need the car on Friday night, can I borrow it?*). *Sense* is a noun meaning "the faculty of perceiving by means of sense organs" or "conscious awareness." *Sense* can also be a verb meaning "to perceive." (*Her sense of smell is very acute* or *I sense that you're upset with me.*) How can you keep these words straight? Look at the role the word plays in the sentence. Is it a connector word? If so, use *since*. Is it showing action? If so, use *sense*. Is it serving as a subject or object in the sentence? If so, use *sense*.

Q: A friend of mine gets upset when I say something like, *I was so surprised by her remark.* She thinks I'm misusing *so*. Am I?

A: Your friend is right, if we are talking about formal expression. The intensifier *so* requires a clause to complete its meaning. For example, *I was so surprised by her remark that I immediately protested.* When one hears *so* as a modifier without a qualifying clause, the sentence sounds incomplete. *He was so funny.* So funny that what? *He was so funny that he became a stand-up comedian.*

Q: I don't think I'll ever understand when to use *that* and when to use *which*. Any advice for keeping them straight?

A: The problem usually is the substitution of *which* for *that*. Whenever you're tempted to use *which*, remember that it requires a comma. Think *which + comma*. If the sentence doesn't sound right with a comma, then you know you need *that*. One eminent language specialist, William Strunk, advised careful writers to go *which*-hunting and remove all defining *whiches*. Examples: *The contract that we sent in June was just returned* (defines which one). *The Wilson contract, which we sent in June, was just returned* (adds a fact about the only contract in question).

Circle art: © iStockphoto.com/Pavel Khorenyan

Q: Can the word *that* be omitted from sentences? For example, *She said (that) she would come.*

A: The relative pronoun *that* is frequently omitted in conversation and casual writing. For absolute clarity, however, skilled writers include it.

Q: I'm not sure which word to use in this sentence: *They have used all (they're, their, there) resources in combating the disease.*

A: Use *their*, which is the possessive form of *they*. The adverb *there* means "at that place" or "at that point" (*We have been there before*). *There* is also used as an expletive or filler preceding a linking verb (*There are numerous explanations*). *They're* is a contraction of *they* and *are* (*They're coming this afternoon*).

Q: Can you help me with the words *averse* and *adverse*? I have never been able to straighten them out in my mind.

A: *Averse* is an adjective meaning "disinclined" and generally is used with the preposition *to* (*The little boy was averse to bathing*). *Adverse* is also an adjective, but it means "hostile" or "unfavorable" (*Adverse economic conditions halted the company's growth*). In distinguishing between these two similar words, it might help you to know that the word *averse* is usually used to describe animate (living) objects.

Q: Should *rewrite* and *reread* be hyphenated?

A: No. It is not necessary to use a hyphen after the prefix *re* unless the resulting word may be confused with another word (*to re-mark the sales ticket, to re-cover the chair, to re-create the crime scene*).

Q: I plan to use this sentence in a letter I am writing to my references: *You will be receiving a call from one of my perspective employers.* Is this correct?

A: Before you send the letter, change *perspective* to *prospective*. *Perspective* is a noun that means "a mental picture or outlook" (*She has a new perspective of the company after reading the article*). *Prospective* is an adjective that means "likely to become" (*We have a prospective buyer for the building*).

SPOT THE Blooper

Using the skills you are learning in this class, try to identify why the following items are bloopers. Consult your textbook, dictionary, or reference manual as needed. To see if you recognized the blooper, go to **www.cengagebrain.com** and use your access code to see the Spot the Blooper key.

Blooper 1: The aviation magazine *Air Classics* referred to baseball as "America's national past time."

Blooper 2: From a set of bylaws: "Each condominium unit may have a reasonable number of household pets. Which at the desecration of the Association do not create a nuisance to other owners." [Did you spot two bloopers?]

Blooper 3: Sign on a snack cart in New York City, located near the carriage-ride terminal in Central Park: "Filly Cheese Steak."

Blooper 4: In a newsletter of the Friends of Music at Guilford [Vermont]: "The lunch was delicious and folks munched away merrily on folding chairs."

Blooper 5: Professionally made sign attached to an overhead bin on an Alaska Airlines plane: "THIS BINS FOR YOU."

Blooper 6: From a New York sport columnist: "While checking my bags at the counter, Magic Johnson arrived in a stretch limo."

Blooper 7: From the *Patriot-Ledger* [Quincy, Massachusetts]: "Clemens is able to come off the disabled list Sunday, but tests by Dr. Arthur Pappas led to the conclusion that Clemens' groin is still too weak to pitch in a game."

Blooper 8: Advice from a Canadian telephone company booklet: "Hang up if the caller doesn't say anything, or if the caller doesn't identify themself to your satisfaction." [Did you spot two bloopers?]

Blooper 9: From *The Atlanta Journal-Constitution*: "A Clayton County man, whom authorities say stole two cars, opened fire on several people and led police on a chase."

Blooper 10: From an article in London's *Sunday Mail* about soccer great David Beckham, in which he discusses being baffled by his seven-year-old son's math homework: "It's done totally differently to what I was teached at school."

Reinforcement Exercises

LEVEL 1

A. Self-Check. Coordinating Conjunctions. Select *a*, *b*, or *c* to identify the following sentences.

    a. A comma correctly punctuates a compound sentence.

    b. The sentence is not compound; thus the comma should be omitted.

    c. Although the sentence is compound, the clauses are too short to require a comma.

Example: In 1908 the Model T went into production in Detroit, and Robert Peary also began his conquest of the North Pole.   a

1. Glide Memorial Church in San Francisco auctioned off a lunch with Warren Buffett, and the winning bid was $2,626,411.   _____

2. A New York restaurant received so many complaints about cell phone users that it set up a cell phone lounge, and banished their use elsewhere.   _____

3. Update your résumé, and upload it to our site.   _____

4. The wealth gap between younger and older Americans is at an all-time high, and young adults are now left with record housing and college debts.   _____

5. Albert Einstein was four years old before he could speak, and seven years old before he could read.   _____

In each pair of sentences, select the one that is punctuated or written properly.

6. (a) Mother Teresa was best known for her work in Calcutta; however, she also founded facilities for the poor in the United States.
  (b) Mother Teresa was best known for her work in Calcutta, however, she also founded facilities for the poor in the United States.   _____

7. (a) Kenisha read that the best time to ask for a raise is 9 a.m. or 1 p.m. midweek, thus, she made an appointment to see her boss.
  (b) Kenisha read that the best time to ask for a raise is 9 a.m. or 1 p.m. midweek; thus, she made an appointment to see her boss.
  (c) Kenisha read that the best time to ask for a raise is 9 a.m. or 1 p.m. midweek; thus she made an appointment to see her boss.   _____

8. (a) She was disappointed; however, when her boss was unavailable until Friday.
  (b) She was disappointed, however, when her boss was unavailable until Friday.   _____

9. (a) Women live an average of seven years longer than men, consequently, three in four women are single when they die.
  (b) Women live an average of seven years longer than men; consequently, three in four women are single when they die.   _____

10. (a) Women must, consequently, plan carefully for retirement.
  (b) Women must; consequently, plan carefully for retirement.   _____

Check your answers below.

1.a 2.b 3.c 4.a 5.b 6.a 7.c 8.b 9.b 10.a

B. Coordinating Conjunctions. In each pair of sentences, select the one that is punctuated properly.

11. (a) Eastman Kodak created the first digital camera in 1975 but didn't bring it to market for fear of taking away from its film business.
(b) Eastman Kodak created the first digital camera in 1975, but didn't bring it to market for fear of taking away from its film business. _____

12. (a) Eastman Kodak created the first digital camera in 1975 but the company didn't bring it to market for fear of taking away from its film business.
(b) Eastman Kodak created the first digital camera in 1975, but the company didn't bring it to market for fear of taking away from its film business. _____

13. (a) Amazon.com's products are numerous, and its prices are low.
(b) Amazon.com's products are numerous and its prices are low. _____

14. (a) The city of Harrisburg has declared bankruptcy yet it remains optimistic that it will bounce back.
(b) The city of Harrisburg has declared bankruptcy, yet it remains optimistic that it will bounce back. _____

15. (a) The city of Harrisburg has declared bankruptcy yet remains optimistic that it will bounce back.
(b) The city of Harrisburg has declared bankruptcy, yet remains optimistic that it will bounce back. _____

16. (a) You can send me a text message when you get the results, or you can e-mail me.
(b) You can send me a text message when you get the results or you can e-mail me. _____

17. (a) Research the target company, then prepare success stories.
(b) Research the target company; then prepare success stories. _____

18. (a) Some companies require employees to carry wireless devices with location-tracking software; however, many employees find this practice intrusive.
(b) Some companies require employees to carry wireless devices with location-tracking software, however, many employees find this practice intrusive. _____

19. (a) The companies; however, say that they have the right to monitor their employees' whereabouts.
(b) The companies, however, say that they have the right to monitor their employees' whereabouts. _____

20. (a) Many patients seek luxury amenities in hospitals, in fact, some even demand gourmet meals and flat-screen TVs.
(b) Many patients seek luxury amenities in hospitals; in fact, some even demand gourmet meals and flat-screen TVs. _____

C. Writing Exercise. Coordinating Conjunctions. In the following sentences, insert all necessary commas and semicolons. If no additional punctuation is needed, write *Correct*.

Examples: Antonio came to work ten minutes late on Monday‸and he was absent on Tuesday and Friday.
Some loans must be secured‸therefore‸the borrower must supply collateral.

21. Most people never thought it could happen but the IBM computer Watson beat both human competitors on the television game show *Jeopardy*.

22. IBM researchers have found that the same particles used to create silicon chips can be used to heal wounds and can even help fight cancer.

23. Several companies have been forced to lay off employees yet they are retaining their older, more experienced workers.

24. Periods of stock market growth are called *bull markets* and periods of stock market decline are known as *bear markets*.

25. Please choose your vacation dates and let me know immediately.

CONJUNCTIONS

26. Many people fear becoming victims of identity theft however identity theft rarely results in actual financial loss for consumers.

27. Some people are surprised to learn however that most identity theft occurs through "dumpster diving."

28. Pharmaceutical companies are faced nevertheless with unusually expensive research and development costs.

29. Charity fraud has become a huge problem thus it is wise for donors to scrutinize each charity to be sure that it is legitimate.

30. The Equal Pay for Equal Work Act was passed in 1963 consequently women's wages became more equitable.

D. Writing Exercise. Using Coordinating Conjunctions. Write sentences using the conjunctions as described. Be sure to punctuate each sentence correctly.

31. Write a complete sentence using the coordinating conjunction *and* between two independent clauses.

_____

_____

32. Write a complete sentence using the coordinating conjunction *and* separating equal words.

_____

_____

33. Write a complete sentence using the coordinating conjunction *or* between two phrases.

_____

_____

34. Write a complete sentence using the coordinating conjunction *but* between two independent clauses.

_____

_____

35. Write a complete sentence using the coordinating conjunction *yet* between two independent clauses.

_____

_____

36. Write a complete sentence using the conjunctive adverb *consequently* between two independent clauses.

_____

_____

37. Write a complete sentence using *consequently* as a parenthetical adverb.

_____

_____

38. Write a complete sentence using the conjunctive adverb *then* between two independent clauses.

_____

_____

39. Write a complete sentence using the conjunctive adverb *however* between two independent clauses.

_____

_____

40. Write a complete sentence using *however* as a parenthetical adverb.

_____

_____

LEVEL 2

A. Self-Check. Punctuating Sentences With Dependent Clauses. In each of the following pairs, select the properly punctuated sentence.

41. (a) Before you interview for a position you should research the company.
 (b) Before you interview for a position, you should research the company. _____

42. (a) You should research a company, before you interview for a position.
 (b) You should research a company before you interview for a position. _____

43. (a) Procter and Gamble, which made a fortune with Ivory soap, discovered the formula by accident.
 (b) Procter and Gamble which made a fortune with Ivory soap discovered the formula by accident. _____

44. (a) The company, that made a fortune with Ivory soap, discovered the formula by accident.
 (b) The company that made a fortune with Ivory soap discovered the formula by accident. _____

45. (a) As predicted Facebook had one of the most historic IPOs in history.
 (b) As predicted, Facebook had one of the most historic IPOs in history. _____

46. (a) A magazine that features the 100 best places to work is now on the newsstands.
 (b) A magazine, that features the 100 best places to work, is now on the newsstands. _____

47. (a) Victoria Lintelman, who was the top salesperson in the country, received a Porsche convertible as a bonus.
 (b) Victoria Lintelman who was the top salesperson in the country, received a Porsche convertible as a bonus. _____

48. (a) Any salesperson who sells more than the weekly quota will receive a bonus.
 (b) Any salesperson, who sells more than the weekly quota, will receive a bonus. _____

49. (a) Please contact me immediately if you would like to apply for the position.
 (b) Please contact me immediately, if you would like to apply for the position. _____

50. (a) If you would like to apply for the position please contact me immediately.
 (b) If you would like to apply for the position, please contact me immediately. _____

Check your answers below.

41. b 42. b 43. a 44. b 45. b 46. a 47. a 48. a 49. a 50. b

B. Relative Clauses. Choose the correct answer. Remember that the relative pronoun *which* should be used only to introduce nonessential clauses and, as such, requires commas. Also remember that *who*, *whom*, and *whose* are used to refer to people. *That* and *which* refer to animals or things.

51. Companies *(a) who, (b) that, (c) which* offer benefits attract numerous job applicants. _____

52. Google, *(a) who, (b) that, (c) which* offers excellent benefits, attracts numerous job applicants. _____

53. We are looking for individuals *(a) who, (b) that, (c) whom* are certified management accountants. _____

54. The homeowners' association must come up with a solution *(a) which, (b) that* will satisfy all residents. _____

55. Are you the one *(a) who, (b) that, (c) which* processes expense claims? _____

56. The IRS, *(a) who, (b) that, (c) which* audits only 1.5 percent of all income tax returns, is choked with paperwork. _____

57. Enterprise Rent-a-Car is known as an organization *(a) who, (b) that, (c) which* emphasizes outstanding customer service. _____

58. Employers are looking for workers *(a) who, (b) that, (c) whom* demonstrate self-confidence, professionalism, and excellent communication skills. _____

59. Interviewees *(a) who, (b) that, (c) which* demonstrate self-confidence and professionalism are more likely to be hired. _____

60. A book *(a) that, (b) which* has greatly influenced the business world is *Servant Leadership* by Robert Greenleaf. _____

C. Conjunctions. In three lists under the following headings, sort these words: *and, however, if, but, yet, moreover, although, nor, because, consequently, or, thus, since, then, when.*

Coordinating Conjunctions	Conjunctive Adverbs	Subordinating Conjunctions
_____	_____	_____
_____	_____	_____
_____	_____	_____
_____	_____	_____
_____	_____	_____

D. Punctuating Sentences With Dependent Clauses. In each pair of sentences, select the one that is punctuated or written properly.

61. (a) Because President Franklin D. Roosevelt passed a series of securities laws in the 1930s, he helped create the Securities and Exchange Commission (SEC) to enforce them.
(b) Because President Franklin D. Roosevelt passed a series of securities laws in the 1930s he helped create the Securities and Exchange Commission (SEC) to enforce them. _____

62. (a) When completed the San Francisco-Oakland Bay Bridge will be the largest self-anchored suspension bridge in the world.
(b) When completed, the San Francisco-Oakland Bay Bridge will be the largest self-anchored suspension bridge in the world. _____

Circle art: © iStockphoto.com/Pavel Khorenyan

63. (a) Philip Knight who was the cofounder and former CEO of Nike was tattooed with the company's "swoosh" logo.
    (b) Philip Knight, who was the cofounder and former CEO of Nike, was tattooed with the company's "swoosh" logo.
    _____

64. (a) The man who was the cofounder and former CEO of Nike was tattooed with the company's "swoosh" logo.
    (b) The man, who was the cofounder and former CEO of Nike, was tattooed with the company's "swoosh" logo.
    _____

65. (a) If you have any questions about our proposal, please e-mail them to Kris Bertrand.
    (b) If you have any questions about our proposal please e-mail them to Kris Bertrand.
    _____

66. (a) Please e-mail Kris Bertrand, if you have any questions.
    (b) Please e-mail Kris Bertrand if you have any questions.
    _____

67. (a) We were notified that the network would be down for six hours, although we were not told why.
    (b) We were notified that the network would be down for six hours; although we were not told why.
    _____

68. (a) The warranty that you refer to in your recent message covers only merchandise brought to our shop for repair.
    (b) The warranty, that you refer to in your recent message, covers only merchandise brought to our shop for repair.
    _____

69. (a) Your home warranty which covers earthquake damage expires in two years.
    (b) Your home warranty, which covers earthquake damage, expires in two years.
    _____

70. (a) John Halamka, who serves as Harvard Medical School's chief information officer, was among the first to have a radio-frequency chip put into his arm to help doctors locate his medical records in an emergency.
    (b) John Halamka who serves as Harvard Medical School's chief information officer was among the first to have a radio-frequency chip put into his arm to help doctors locate his medical records in an emergency.
    _____

71. (a) The person, who serves as Harvard Medical School's chief information officer, was among the first to have a radio-frequency chip put into his arm to help doctors locate his medical records in an emergency.
    (b) The person who serves as Harvard Medical School's chief information officer was among the first to have a radio-frequency chip put into his arm to help doctors locate his medical records in an emergency.
    _____

72. (a) A flight attendant who joined our crew only two months ago was chosen to fly to Germany to help bring our troops home.
    (b) A flight attendant, who joined our crew only two months ago, was chosen to fly to Germany to help bring our troops home.
    _____

73. (a) Jenny Lambert who joined our crew only two months ago was chosen to fly to Germany to help bring our troops home.
    (b) Jenny Lambert, who joined our crew only two months ago, was chosen to fly to Germany to help bring our troops home.
    _____

74. (a) Zone Improvement Program codes, which are better known as zip codes, are designed to expedite the sorting and delivery of mail.
    (b) Zone Improvement Program codes which are better known as zip codes are designed to expedite the sorting and delivery of mail.
    _____

75. (a) If needed, I can cover your Friday night shift for you.
    (b) If needed I can cover your Friday night shift for you.
    _____

76. (a) Marketers, who develop advertising targeted at heavy users, are attempting to build brand loyalty.
   (b) Marketers who develop advertising targeted at heavy users are attempting to build brand loyalty. _____

77. (a) Because the economy dipped rents have decreased in many housing markets.
   (b) Because the economy dipped, rents have decreased in many housing markets. _____

78. (a) Rents have decreased in many housing markets because of the recession.
   (b) Rents have decreased in many housing markets, because of the recession. _____

79. (a) Companies that retain experienced workers are generally more successful.
   (b) Companies which retain experienced workers are generally more successful. _____

80. (a) We are looking for an accountant that demonstrates highly ethical behavior.
   (b) We are looking for an accountant who demonstrates highly ethical behavior. _____

E. Writing Exercise. Subordinating Conjunctions and Relative Pronouns. Write sentences using the conjunctions and relative pronouns as described. Be sure to punctuate each sentence correctly.

81. A sentence using the subordinating conjunction *if* in an introductory dependent clause.

_____

_____

82. A sentence using the subordinating conjunction *if* in a terminal dependent clause.

_____

_____

83. A sentence using the subordinating conjunction *because* in an introductory dependent clause.

_____

_____

84. A sentence using the subordinating conjunction *because* in a terminal dependent clause.

_____

_____

85. A sentence using the subordinating conjunction *although* in an introductory dependent clause.

_____

_____

86. A sentence using the subordinating conjunction *after* in an introductory dependent clause.

_____

_____

87. A sentence using the relative pronoun *who* to introduce an essential clause.

_____

_____

88. A sentence using the relative pronoun *who* to introduce a nonessential clause.

_____

_____

89. A sentence using the relative pronoun *that* to introduce an essential clause.

_____

90. A sentence using the relative pronoun *which* to introduce a nonessential clause.

_____

_____

LEVEL 3

A. Self-Check. Correlative Conjunctions and Sentence Types. Select the more effective version of each of the following pairs of sentences. Write its letter in the space provided.

91. (a) Either she will work for her father or start her own business.
(b) She will either work for her father or start her own business. _____

92. (a) Lisa Gores did not enjoy the new Steven Spielberg film, and neither did James O'Keefe.
(b) Neither Lisa Gores nor James O'Keefe enjoyed the new Steven Spielberg film. _____

93. (a) Our investing objectives are both to get a decent return and to protect our assets.
(b) Our investing objectives are both to get a decent return and protecting our assets. _____

94. (a) Be sure to either book first- or business-class seats.
(b) Be sure to book either first- or business-class seats. _____

95. (a) The new network is not only faster but also more efficient.
(b) Not only is the new network faster, but it is also more efficient. _____

Indicate the structure of the following sentences by writing the appropriate letter in the spaces provided.

a. simple sentence	**c. complex sentence**
b. compound sentence	**d. compound-complex sentence**

Example: Because some business owners want to avoid Sarbanes-Oxley requirements, they are securing funding using creative methods. _____c_____

96. Sending telegrams was a popular way to communicate for over 100 years, but Western Union discontinued the service in 2006. _____

97. Netscape's initial public offering (IPO) in 1995 was the catalyst for the Internet stock explosion of the late 1990s. _____

98. Because the needs of today's luxury travelers are changing, Ritz-Carlton is retraining its employees. _____

99. Apple released its first computer in 1977, and it revolutionized the music industry when it released the iPod in 2001. _____

100. Gary was offered a sales position in Grand Rapids; therefore, he eagerly made plans to travel to Michigan, where he looked forward to continuing his sales career. _____

Check your answers below.

91. b   92. b   93. a   94. b   95. a   96. b   97. a   98. c   99. d   100. d

CONJUNCTIONS

B. Correlative Conjunctions. Which sentence in each sentence pair below is more effective?

101. (a) The pilot has decades of experience not only flying planes but also teaching others how to fly them more safely.
    (b) The pilot not only has decades of experience flying planes but teaches others how to fly them more safely. _____

102. (a) Citigroup would neither admit responsibility nor deny guilt during the SEC hearing.
    (b) Neither would Citigroup admit responsibility nor was it willing to deny guilt during the SEC hearing. _____

103. (a) The company will either relocate to Nevada or Arizona.
    (b) The company will relocate to either Nevada or Arizona. _____

104. (a) Either bankruptcy can be declared by the debtor or it can be requested by the creditors.
    (b) Bankruptcy can be either declared by the debtor or requested by the creditors. _____

105. (a) Our travel counselor will both plan your trip and make your reservations.
    (b) Our travel counselor will both plan your trip and reservations will be made. _____

106. (a) Either send the proposal to Angelica Cabunoc or to me.
    (b) Send the proposal either to Angelica Cabunoc or to me. _____

107. (a) Not only do companies use Facebook as a marketing tool, but they also use Facebook for getting customer feedback.
    (b) Companies use Facebook not only as a marketing tool but also to get customer feedback. _____

108. (a) Neither the employees nor the managers were happy with the proposed cutbacks in benefits.
    (b) Neither the employees were happy with the proposed cutbacks in benefits, and nor were the managers. _____

109. (a) Our customer service rep will process your return, and she will ship out replacements too.
    (b) Our customer service rep will both process your return and ship out replacements. _____

110. (a) FotoNation not only patented red-eye detection for cameras but also software that detects smiles.
    (b) FotoNation patented not only red-eye detection for cameras but also software that detects smiles. _____

C. Writing Exercise. Coordinating and Correlative Conjunctions. Rewrite the following sentences to make them more effective.

111. Either stocks can be purchased online or they can be purchased from a broker.

_____

_____

112. Neither the staff was happy with the proposed reductions in class offerings, and nor were the students.

_____

_____

113. Not only does the Small Business Administration (SBA) provide training, but it also guarantees loans.

_____

_____

114. Cell phone users are often guilty of rude behavior, so many restaurants have imposed bans.

_____

_____

115. Old computer hardware creates hazardous dump sites, so many communities offer e-waste recycling programs.

_____

_____

_____

D. Writing Exercise. Sentence Variety. Rewrite the following groups of simple sentences into _one_ sentence for each group. Add coordinating conjunctions, conjunctive adverbs, and subordinating conjunctions as needed to create more effective complex, compound, and compound-complex sentences.

Example: LivingSocial needed a sales rep. It advertised online. It finally hired a recent graduate. The graduate had excellent skills.

After advertising for sales rep online, LivingSocial finally hired a recent graduate

who had excellent skills.

116. Rusty was recently hired as a transportation engineer. She will work for Werner Enterprises. Werner Enterprises is located in Omaha, Nebraska.

_____

_____

117. Marlon Lodge is a British linguist and musician. He taught English to German employees of HSBC. He discovered that his students caught on more quickly when he set new vocabulary to music.

_____

_____

118. Cows will respond to beeps. Some Japanese ranchers learned of this phenomenon and equipped their cattle with pagers. Now they herd cattle with beepers. These ranchers need fewer workers as a result.

_____

_____

119. Skilled writers save time for themselves. They also save it for their readers. They organize their ideas into logical patterns. They do this before sitting down at their computers.

_____

_____

120. Nancy Burnett is a single parent. She has merchandising experience. Nancy started a mall-based chain of stores. These stores sell fashionable, durable clothing for children.

_____

_____

E. FAQs About Business English Review. In the space provided, write the correct answer choice.

121. Do you know whether *(a) their, (b) they're, (c) there* planning to attend Friday's financial planning symposium? _____

122. Please wait right over *(a) their, (b) they're, (c) there* until your table is ready. _____

123. *(a) Their, (b) They're, (c) There* car broke down on the way to the airport. _____

124. Because of *(a) adverse, (b) averse* weather conditions, several airlines had to delay flights. _____

125. Management is *(a) adverse, (b) averse* to any decrease in employee health benefits. _____

126. We will need to *(a) re-write, (b) rewrite* the entire contract. _____

127. Because of his position, he has an excellent *(a) perspective, (b) prospective* on the problem. _____

128. I sent my résumé to a *(a) perspective, (b) prospective* employer. _____

129. Is the newly hired person any better *(a) than, (b) then* the previous manager? _____

130. If all parties agree, *(a) than, (b) then* the contract should be approved. _____

Chat About It ◀◀

Your instructor may assign any of the following topics for you to discuss in class, in an online chat room, or on an online discussion board. Some of the discussion topics may require outside research. You may also be asked to read and respond to postings made by your classmates.

Discussion Topic 1: How does the coordinating conjunction *but* affect you psychologically? Consider these two sentences: *Your interview went well, but we would like to invite you to come back* versus *Your interview went well, and we would like to invite you to come back.* How does the conjunction change the meaning in these two sentences? When you hear the word *but*, do you feel that bad news is coming? What can you do in your own communication to avoid the *"but* syndrome"?

Discussion Topic 2: Chapter 9 concludes our discussion of the parts of speech. What are the most important things that you have learned about the parts of speech in Chapters 1 through 9? Write four complete sentences that describe what you have learned. Each sentence should contain a different type of conjunction: coordinating conjunction, conjunctive adverb, subordinating

conjunction, and correlative conjunction. Share your sentences with your classmates.

Discussion Topic 3: E-mail is used extensively to communicate in the business world; therefore, it is important to use this communication tool effectively and professionally. What is the most important advice you have for using e-mail in the workplace? Share your advice with your classmates. Be as detailed as possible.

Discussion Topic 4: Explain how you think being able to identify the eight parts of speech will help you on the job, in school, and in your personal life.

Discussion Topic 5: The American writer Wallace Stegner said, "Hard writing makes easy reading." What does he mean by this? Do you agree? How can you apply this quote to your business writing? Explain.

In each pair of sentences, choose the one that is punctuated or written properly. Then compare your answers with those below.

1. (a) Customers voiced their outrage over Bank of America's debit card fees, therefore, the bank stopped the unpopular practice.
   (b) Customers voiced their outrage over Bank of America's debit card fees; therefore, the bank stopped the unpopular practice. _____

2. (a) Judy spoke with the customer, and Benjamin processed the return.
   (b) Judy spoke with the customer and Benjamin processed the return. _____

3. (a) Congress is not sure, however, whether the bill will pass.
   (b) Congress is not sure; however, whether the bill will pass. _____

4. (a) Try text messaging if your organization requires real-time communication.
   (b) Try text messaging, if your organization requires real-time communication. _____

5. (a) If your organization requires real-time communication try text messaging.
   (b) If your organization requires real-time communication, try text messaging. _____

6. (a) We are posting the job announcement online, and we are also asking for employee referrals.
   (b) We are posting the job announcement online and we are also asking for employee referrals. _____

7. (a) The iPhone app demonstration by Paul Iatomasi who represents Mindfire Solutions will be Friday.
   (b) The iPhone app demonstration by Paul Iatomasi, who represents Mindfire Solutions, will be Friday. _____

8. (a) The individual who represents Mindfire Solutions will give the iPhone app demonstration on Friday.
   (b) The individual, who represents Mindfire Solutions, will give the iPhone app demonstration on Friday. _____

Select the sentence that is more effective.

9. (a) Neither can we ship the printer nor the computer until April 1.
   (b) We can ship neither the printer nor the computer until April 1. _____

10. (a) Malware not only includes viruses but also spyware.
    (b) Malware includes not only viruses but also spyware. _____

1.b 2.b 3.a 4.a 5.b 6.a 7.b 8.a 9.b 10.b

Begin your review by rereading Chapters 7–9. Then test your comprehension with the following exercises. Compare your responses with the key at the end of the book.

LEVEL 1

1. I have never seen a *(a) worst, (b) worse* film adaptation of a novel.   _____

2. In comparing the three wireless providers, we decided that Verizon is *(a) best, (b) better* for our company.   _____

3. Many people think that Apple *(a) should have, (b) should of* advertised during the Super Bowl.   _____

4. Rooms at the Ritz are *(a) to, (b) too* expensive.   _____

5. We are fortunate to have exceptional employees like Selena and *(a) him, (b) he*.   _____

6. Josh feels *(a) bad, (b) badly* about his performance during the job interview.   _____

7. Our department runs *(a) smoother, (b) more smoother, (c) more smoothly* after the reorganization.   _____

8. Can I borrow some change for the vending machine *(a) from, (b) off of* you?   _____

9. Just between you and *(a) I, (b) me*, I'm afraid that Sal is going to be let go.   _____

10. (a) Gina first took a job in Honolulu and later decided to move to San Diego.
    (b) Gina first took a job in Honolulu, and later decided to move to San Diego.   _____

11. (a) Cheng Saechao might be assigned to work in our legal office or he might be assigned to our administrative headquarters.
    (b) Cheng Saechao might be assigned to work in our legal office, or he might be assigned to our administrative headquarters.   _____

12. (a) Amy's day spa was a huge success, consequently, she is opening a second location.
    (b) Amy's day spa was a huge success; consequently, she is opening a second location.   _____

13. (a) Kristin wrote a chronological résumé, but Cameron preferred a functional strategy for his résumé.
    (b) Kristin wrote a chronological résumé but Cameron preferred a functional strategy for his résumé.   _____

LEVEL 2

14. If you need *(a) a, (b) an* example of her work, take a look at her e-portfolio.   _____

15. *(a) This, (b) These* kinds of actions are unacceptable in the workplace.   _____

16. We will hear grade appeals on a *(a) case by case, (b) case-by-case* basis.   _____

17. The company is *(a) four years old, (b) four-years old.* _____

18. No one *(a) accept, (b) except* the CEO can sign off on the financial statements. _____

19. Power in our government is balanced *(a) among, (b) between* its three branches. _____

20. You must turn your paperwork *(a) into, (b) in to* me by Friday. _____

21. Does anyone *(a) beside, (b) besides* you support this mayoral candidate? _____

22. The plan *(a) that, (b) which* we adopted will save the company thousands of dollars annually. _____

23. (a) Alice Waters, who owns Chez Panisse in Berkeley, is a champion of locally grown organic food.
    (b) Alice Waters who owns Chez Panisse in Berkeley is a champion of locally grown organic food. _____

24. (a) Before posting her résumé online Holly made sure it was flawless.
    (b) Before posting her résumé online, Holly made sure it was flawless. _____

25. (a) We are looking for an affordable, efficient heating system.
    (b) We are looking for an affordable efficient heating system. _____

26. (a) Send all checks to Gretchen Scotvold, who is in charge of contributions.
    (b) Send all checks to Gretchen Scotvold who is in charge of contributions. _____

LEVEL 3

27. Morgan had a *(a) real, (b) really* productive morning. _____

28. Esteban, who wants to earn his MBA, performed *(a) good, (b) well* on the GMAT. _____

29. Let's discuss these ideas *(a) further, (b) farther* over lunch. _____

30. If you have *(a) less, (b) fewer* than ten items, you may use the quick-check lane. _____

31. Boston is larger than *(a) any other city, (b) any city* in Massachusetts. _____

32. Examine carefully the *(a) 50 first, (b) first 50* pages of the prospectus. _____

33. IndiGo, India's second-largest airline, *(a) plans to fly, (b) plans on flying* to Singapore, Bangkok, and Dubai. _____

34. The approved contract is not very different *(a) than, (b) from* the first version. _____

35. We asked that our salary increase be retroactive *(a) to, (b) from* the first of the year. _____

36. Andrew Mason's speech to Groupon employees will center *(a) on, (b) around* future plans for the company. _____

37. It was a pleasure speaking *(a) to, (b) with* you over lunch today. _____

38. (a) You can either be transferred to Seattle or to Portland.
    (b) You can be transferred either to Seattle or to Portland. _____

39. (a) He is not only qualified but also fully certified.
    (b) He is not only qualified but he is also fully certified too. _____

Circle art: © iStockphoto.com/Pavel Khorenyan

FAQs About Business English Review

40. She has *(a) all ready, (b) already* applied for the promotion. _____

41. *(a) Adverse, (b) Averse* working conditions caused many employees to resign. _____

42. When you visit New York, be sure to spend *(a) sometime, (b) some time* at the Metropolitan Museum of Art. _____

43. All *(a) personnel, (b) personal* matters are now handled in our Human Resources Department. _____

44. Facebook *(a) maybe, (b) may be* facing some tough competition from Google+. _____

45. I feel as if our supervisor will *(a) dessert, (b) desert* us if things go badly. _____

46. As a single mom, she has a unique *(a) perspective, (b) prospective* on the situation. _____

47. I would like my item to *(a) proceed, (b) precede* yours on the agenda. _____

48. I passed the information *(a) onto, (b) on to* my supervisor. _____

49. The senator called for a *(a) nation-wide, (b) nation wide, (c) nationwide* ban on phosphates. _____

50. This document must be *(a) rewritten, (b) re-written*. _____

NAME _____

E-Mail Messages and Memos

E-mail messages and memos are vital forms of internal communication for companies today. Organizations are downsizing, flattening chains of command, forming work teams, and empowering rank-and-file employees. Given more power in making decisions, employees find that they need more information. They must collect, exchange, and evaluate information about the products and services they offer. Management also needs input from employees to respond rapidly to local and global market actions. This growing demand for information results in an increasing use of memos and especially e-mail. That is why anyone entering a business or profession today should know how to write effective and professional e-mail messages and memos.

Characteristics of E-Mail Messages and Memos

E-mail messages and memos have a number of characteristics in common:

- They begin with the headings *To, From, Date,* and *Subject.*
- They generally cover just one topic.
- They are informal.
- They are concise.

E-mail messages and memos use efficient standard formats, such as you see in Figure 4.1. So that they can be acted on separately, e-mail messages and memos should discuss only one topic. Let's say you send your supervisor an e-mail message requesting a copier repair. You also add a comment about an article you want to appear in the company newsletter. The supervisor may act on one item and overlook the other. He might also want to forward your request for a copier repair directly to the operations manager, but he has to edit or rekey the message because of the second topic. Thus, e-mail messages and memos are most helpful when they cover just one subject.

Because they replace conversation, these messages tend to be informal. They may include first-person pronouns, such as *I* and *me,* as well as occasional contractions, such as *can't* or *haven't.* The tone, however, should not become unprofessional or overly familiar. Moreover, e-mail messages and memos should not be wordy. Concise messages save time and often are more easily understood than longer messages.

Writing Plan

For most informational and procedural messages, follow a **direct writing plan** that reveals the most important information first. Here are specific tips for writing the subject line, first sentence, body, and closing of e-mail messages and memos.

Subject Line. In the subject line, summarize the message. Although brief, a subject line must make sense and should capture the reader's interest. Instead of *Meeting,* for example, try *Meeting to Discuss Hiring Two New Employees.* A subject line is like a newspaper headline. It should snag attention, create a clear picture, and present an accurate summary. It should not be a complete sentence and should rarely occupy more than one line. When writing a subject line, capitalize the first letter of all major words to make the subject line look important and professional.

FIGURE 4.1

Comparing E-Mail Messages and Memos

E-mail

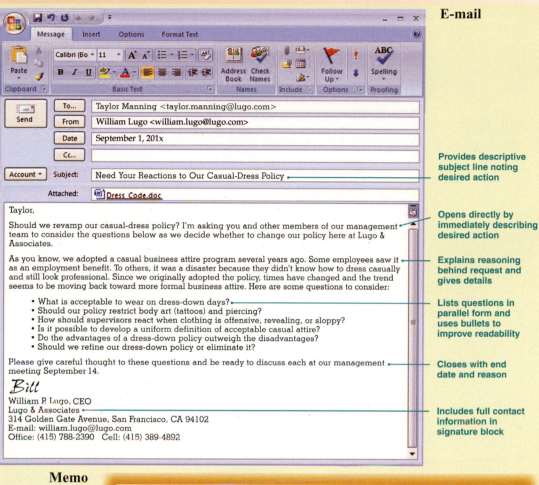

- Provides descriptive subject line noting desired action
- Opens directly by immediately describing desired action
- Explains reasoning behind request and gives details
- Lists questions in parallel form and uses bullets to improve readability
- Closes with end date and reason
- Includes full contact information in signature block

Memo

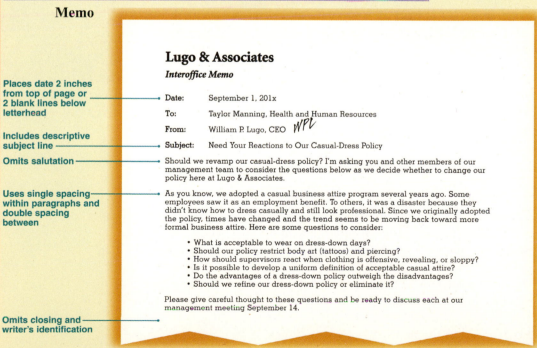

- Places date 2 inches from top of page or 2 blank lines below letterhead
- Includes descriptive subject line
- Omits salutation
- Uses single spacing within paragraphs and double spacing between
- Omits closing and writer's identification

Circle art: © iStockphoto.com/Pavel Khorenyan

First Sentence. Although an explanation occasionally may precede the main idea, the first sentence usually tells the primary idea of the message. For example, an appropriate first sentence in an e-mail message announcing a new vacation procedure follows:

> Here are new guidelines for employees taking two- or three-week vacations between June and September.

The opening of the message may issue a polite command (*Please answer the following questions about . . .*), make a request (*Please begin research on a summer internship program*), or ask a question (*Can your department complete the printing of a . . .?*). Try not to begin with a lengthy explanation. Get to the point as quickly as possible.

Skill Check 4.1 Openings for E-Mail Messages and Memos

Which subject line is better for an e-mail or memo? Circle its letter.

1. a. SUBJECT: Inventory

    b. SUBJECT: Annual Pharmacy Inventory Scheduled for June 2

2. a. SUBJECT: This E-Mail Message Announces Revised Procedures for Applying for Dental Benefits

    b. SUBJECT: Revised Procedures for Dental Benefits Applications

Which opening sentence is better for an e-mail or memo?

3. a. Employees interested in learning about new communication technologies are invited to a workshop on January 31.

    b. For some time now we have been thinking about the possibility of holding a workshop about new communication technologies for some of our employees.

4. a. We have noticed recently a gradual but steady decline in the number of customers purchasing items from our website.

    b. Please conduct a study and make recommendations regarding the gradual but steady decline of online customer purchases.

5. Write a subject line for a memo that describes the possibility of a new sports scoreboard sponsored by Coca-Cola, a topic to be discussed at the next management council meeting.

    _____

    _____

6. Write a subject line for an e-mail or memo announcing a demonstration of new smartphone apps for all employees to be given November 16.

    _____

    _____

Body of Message. Provide details of the message in the body. If you are asking for information, arrange your questions in a logical order. If you are providing information, group similar information together. Think about using side headings in bold print, such as the one at the beginning of this paragraph. They help readers understand, locate, and reference information quickly. You can also improve the readability of any message by listing items with numbers or bullets. Compare the two sets of instructions that follow:

Hard to Read

The instructions for operating our copy machine include inserting your meter in the slot, loading paper in the upper tray, and then copies are fed through the feed chute.

Improved

Here are instructions for using the copy machine:
- Insert your meter in the slot.
- Load paper in the upper tray.
- Feed copies through the feed chute.

Notice that all the items in the preceding bulleted list are parallel in construction. That means that each item uses the same grammatical form. All begin with verbs. This kind of balanced writing helps readers anticipate and understand information more readily.

Skill Check 4.2 Listing Information

In the space provided, revise the following paragraph so that it includes an introductory sentence and a list of four items.

> We are trying to improve budget planning, and we would also like to control costs. To accomplish these goals, we must change our procedures for submitting requests in the future for outside printing jobs. The new procedures include first determining your exact printing specifications for a particular job. Then we want you to obtain two estimates for the job. These estimates should be submitted in writing to Kelly. Finally, you may place the outside print order—but only after receiving approval.

_____

_____

_____

_____

_____

Closing an E-Mail Message or Memo. E-mail messages and memos frequently end with (a) a request for action, (b) a summary of the message, or (c) a closing thought. If action on the part of the reader is sought, be sure to spell out that action clearly. A vague request such as *Drop by to see this customer sometime* is ineffective because the reader may not understand exactly what is to be done. A better request might be worded as follows: *Please make an appointment to see Rebecca Miller before June 2 so that we can complete the contract by June 15.* Notice that an **end date** is given. This technique, particularly when coupled with a valid reason, is effective in prompting people to act.

Another way to close an internal message is by summarizing its major points. A closing summary is helpful if the message is complicated. When no action request is made and a closing summary is unnecessary, the writer may prefer to end the memo with a simple closing thought, such as *I appreciate your assistance, What do you think of this proposal?*, or *Call me if I may answer questions*. Avoid tired, mechanical phrases such as *Please don't hesitate to call on me*, or *Thank you in advance for your cooperation*. If you wish to express these thoughts, find a fresh way to say them.

Figure 4.1 shows how the four parts of a writing plan (subject line, first sentence, body, closing) combine to create a readable, efficient e-mail message. For more information on memo and e-mail formats, see Appendix C.

Special Tips for Sending E-Mail Message

Instead of using paper to send memos, businesspeople more typically use e-mail to send messages. To make the best use of e-mail, implement the following suggestions:

- **Get the address right.** E-mail addresses are sometimes complex, often illogical, and always unforgiving. Omit one character or misread the letter *l* for the number *1*, and your message bounces. Solution: Use your electronic address book for people you write to frequently. And double-check every address that you key in manually. Also be sure that you don't reply to a group of receivers when you intend to answer only one.

- **Keep lines, paragraphs, and messages short.** Try to keep your lines under 65 characters in length and your paragraphs no longer than eight lines. Above all, keep your message short. If it requires more than three screens, consider sending it in hard-copy form.

- **Care about correctness.** Senders and receivers of e-mail tend to be casual about spelling, grammar, and usage. However, people are still judged by their writing; and you never know how far your message will travel. Remember that any message you send will be representing both you and your organization; therefore, it must be correct and professional. Read and edit any message before hitting the **Send** button!

- **Don't send anything you wouldn't want published.** Because e-mail seems like a telephone call or a person-to-person conversation, writers sometimes send sensitive, confidential, inflammatory, or potentially embarrassing messages. Beware! E-mail creates a permanent record that often does not go away even when deleted. And every message is a corporate communication that can be used against you or your employer. Don't write anything that you wouldn't want your boss, your family, or a judge to read.

- **Test your message for tone before sending it.** Try reading your message out loud before sending it to make sure that your tone is professional and positive. Messages that sound angry, sarcastic, or frustrated can damage you and your organization.

- **Include your name and contact information at the bottom of your messages.** Many people have a prepared signature block that can be inserted into messages so that their contact information appears with every message.

Special Tips for Replying to E-Mail Messages

Before replying to an e-mail message, think about some of the suggestions provided here. You can save yourself time and heartache by developing good reply procedures.

- **Scan all messages in your inbox before replying to each individually.** Because subsequent messages often affect the way you respond, read them all first (especially all those from the same individual).

- **Don't automatically return the sender's message**. When replying, cut and paste the relevant parts. Avoid irritating your recipients by returning the entire "thread" (sequence of messages) on a topic.

- **Revise the subject line if the topic changes**. When replying or continuing an e-mail exchange, revise the subject line as the topic changes.

- **Never respond when you are angry.** Always allow some time to cool off before shooting off a response to an upsetting message. You often come up with different and better alternatives after thinking about what was said. If possible, iron out differences in person.

Finally, remember that office computers are meant for work-related communication. Unless your company specifically allows it, never use your employer's computers for personal messages, personal shopping, or entertainment. Assume that all e-mail is monitored. Employers legally have the right to eavesdrop on employee e-mail messages, and many do.

Writing Application 4.1

Revise the following poorly written message. It suffers from wordiness, indirectness, and confusing instructions. Include a numbered list in your revision, and be sure to improve the subject line. Prepare this as an e-mail message or as an internal memo. See the Instructor's Manual for suggested solutions.

TO:	All Staff Members
FROM:	Roy Minami, Manager
DATE:	July 11, 201x
SUBJECT:	COPIER RULES

Some of you missed the demonstration of the operation of our new Turbo X copier last week. I thought you might appreciate receiving this list of suggestions from the salesperson when she gave the demonstration. This list might also be helpful to other employees who saw the demo but didn't take notes and perhaps can't remember all these pointers. It's sometimes hard to remember how to operate a machine when you do it infrequently. Here's what she told us to do. There are two paper loading trays. Load 8 ½ × 11-inch or 8 ½ × 14-inch paper in the two loading trays. The paper should curve upward in the tray. You should take your copy and feed it into the machine face up. However, if you have small sheets or book pages or cut-and-pasted copy, lift the copier door and place your copy facedown on the glass.

Before you begin, select the number of copies to be made by pressing the touch selector panel. Don't push too hard. If copies become jammed, open the front door and see where the paper got stuck in the feed path. Remove jammed paper. Oh yes, your meter must be inserted before the machine will operate. We urge you, of course, to make only as many copies as you really need. Keep this list to use again.

Don't hesitate to call on me if you need a private demonstration.

Writing Application 4.2

As the manager of Reprographic Services, write an e-mail message to Kevin Suzuki, manager, Technical Services. You are very worried that one of the computers of your operators may be infected with a virus. The computer belongs to Jackie Jimenez. Jackie says that each time she opens a previously stored document in her Word program, the contents of the document are immediately deleted. Fortunately, because Jackie has backup files, she hasn't lost anything yet. But obviously she can't go on using this computer. You plan to assign Jackie some temporary tasks for the rest of the day; however, she must have her computer up and running by tomorrow. You want a technician to inspect her machine before 5 p.m. today. You know that Kevin likes to learn as much about a computer problem as possible before he sends a technician, so include sufficient details to help him identify the problem.

Writing Application 4.3

As the manager of the Customer Services Division, Milwaukee Breweries, write an e-mail message to Melissa Miller, supervisor, Customer Services. Ask Melissa to draft a form letter that can be sent to groups requesting plant tours. In your e-mail message, explain that the brewery has always encouraged tour groups to see your home plant brewery. However, you cannot sponsor tours at this time because of extensive remodeling. You are also installing a new computer-controlled bottling system. Tours are expected to resume in September. You need a form letter that can be sent to all groups but that can be personalized for individual responses. You want the letter draft by Monday, April 6. The letter should build good customer relations, a primary goal of your tour policy. The letter might enclose a free product coupon and a brochure picturing your operations. Tell Melissa to add any information that she feels would improve the letter.

Punctuating Sentences

10 Commas

© iStockphoto.com/Courtney Keating

Think of punctuation marks as the traffic signs of writing. Just as traffic signs guide drivers, so punctuation marks guide readers and writers.

—Marie Rackham,
retired English teacher

Circle art: © iStockphoto.com/Pavel Kharenyan

Objectives

When you have completed the materials in this chapter, you will be able to do the following:

LEVEL 1
1. Use commas correctly in series, direct address, and parenthetical expressions.
2. Use commas correctly in punctuating dates, time zones, addresses, geographical items, and appositives.

LEVEL 2
3. Use commas correctly in punctuating independent adjectives and with the adverb *too*.
4. Use commas correctly in punctuating verbal phrases; prepositional phrases; and independent, introductory, terminal, and nonessential clauses.

LEVEL 3
5. Use commas correctly in punctuating degrees, abbreviations, and numerals.
6. Use commas correctly to indicate omitted words and contrasting statements, for clarity, and with short quotations.

Pretest

Insert appropriate commas in the following sentences. Then compare your answers with those below.

1. Jollibee Foods will expand its operations to Vietnam Hong Kong and China this year.

2. Bill Cosby PhD is a popular American comedian and actor.

3. After a long search Kathy Sarnie found a charming historic apartment in downtown Providence.

4. Your interview Ms. Twarog will take place on Wednesday August 20 at 10 a.m.

5. Zappos ships its shoes from Shepherdsville Kentucky to U.S. addresses only.

6. The attorney had reason to believe by the way that the judge was not impartial and might even be biased against this case.

7. The construction of the U.S. interstate highway system began in 1956 and it has given birth to many new industries.

8. Although tired employees preferred the evening not the morning in-service training programs.

9. Patricia T. O'Conner said "When a tiny word gives you a big headache it's probably a pronoun."

10. Thomas Edison the inventor of the electric light and the phonograph has 1093 patents to his name.

When you talk with a friend, you are probably unaware of the "invisible" commas, periods, and other punctuation marks that you are using. In conversation your pauses and voice inflections punctuate your thoughts and clarify your meaning. In writing, however, you must use a conventional set of symbols, punctuation marks, to help your reader understand your meaning, just as traffic signs help to guide drivers.

Over the years we have gradually developed a standardized pattern of usage for all punctuation marks. This usage has been codified (set down) in rules that are observed by writers who wish to make their writing as precise as possible. As noted earlier, some professional writers may deviate from conventional punctuation practices. In addition, some organizations, particularly newspapers and publishing houses, maintain their own style manuals to establish a consistent "in-house" style.

The punctuation guidelines presented in this book represent a consensus about punctuation styles that are acceptable in business and professional writing. Following these guidelines will enable you to write with clarity, consistency, and accuracy.

Trivia Tidbit

Some writers in other languages envy English. Our systematic use of commas and other punctuation marks makes it easy to signal pauses, to emphasize ideas, and to enhance readability.

1. Vietnam, Hong Kong,   2. Cosby, PhD,   3. search, charming,   4. interview, Twarog, Wednesday, August 20,   5. Shepherdsville, Kentucky,   6. believe, way,   7. 1956,   8. tired, evening, morning,   9. said, headache,   10. Edison, phonograph, 1,093

Basic Guidelines for Using Commas

The most used and misused punctuation mark, the **comma**, indicates a pause in the flow of a sentence. *Not all sentence pauses, however, require commas.* It is important for you to learn the standard rules for the use of commas so that you will not be tempted to clutter your sentences with needless, distracting commas. Here are the guidelines for basic comma usage.

Series

Commas are used to separate three or more equally ranked elements (words, phrases, or short clauses) in a series. Remember to place a comma (called a **serial comma**) before the final conjunction in a series. A comma before the conjunction ensures the separation of the last two items. Some writers omit the comma before the conjunction in a series. Business writers, however, are encouraged to use this comma to ensure clarity and ease of reading. No commas are used when conjunctions join all the items in a series.

> Our favorite beachside restaurant is open only in June, July, and August. (Series of words. Notice that a comma precedes *and*; this comma is called a serial comma.)

> Wireless technology enables you to respond to customers' requests, change sales forecasts, and manage suppliers while you are away from the office. (Series of phrases)

> Caroline Geishecker is the owner, Rich Koury is the marketing manager, and Amy Fierro is the executive assistant. (Series of clauses)

> We need wireless access to e-mail and websites and the company intranet. (No commas needed when conjunctions are repeated.)

Direct Address

Direct address occurs when a person is being addressed or spoken to directly, rather than being spoken about. Words and phrases of direct address, including names, affiliations, and titles, are set off with commas.

> *Britt*, do you have our new client's e-mail address? (At the beginning of the sentence)

> Are you, *members of the class of 2014*, ready to go out and take on the world? (In the middle of the sentence)

> We are happy to confirm your dinner reservation, *sir*. (At the end of the sentence)

Parenthetical Expressions

Parenthetical words, phrases, and clauses may be used to create transitions between thoughts. These expressions interrupt the flow of a sentence and are unessential to its grammatical completeness. These commonly used expressions, some of which are listed here, are considered nonessential because they do not specifically answer questions such as *When?*, *Where?*, *Why?*, or *How?* Set off these expressions with commas when they are used parenthetically.

Study Tip

As you begin to learn about commas, try to name a rule or guideline for every comma you insert. For example, *comma/series, comma/parenthetical*, and so forth.

Trivia Tidbit

Serial commas have actually played roles in court cases. For example, the will of a deceased man left everything to *John, Phil and Mary*. John's attorneys argued that John received half and Phil and Mary had to share the other half. What do you think?

after all	in conclusion	no doubt
as a matter of fact	incidentally	of course
as a result	in fact	on the other hand
at the same time	in general	otherwise
by the way	in my opinion	that is
consequently	in other words	then
finally	in summary	therefore
for example	in the first place	too
fortunately	in the meantime	under the circumstances
furthermore	needless to say	unfortunately
however	nevertheless	without a doubt
in addition	no	yes

Yes, I will be voting in the presidential primary. (At the beginning of the sentence)

We know, *without a doubt*, that our customer service is outstanding. (In the middle of the sentence)

You have checked your résumé for accuracy, *no doubt*. (At the end of the sentence)

The words in question are set off by commas only when they are used parenthetically and actually interrupt the flow of a sentence.

However the vote goes, we will abide by the result. (No comma is needed after *however*.)

We have *no doubt* that you will be able to fulfill the duties of this position. (No commas are needed to set off *no doubt*.)

Dates and Time Zones

Commas are used to set off elements of dates and time zones in sentences.

Dates

Dates can be made up of various elements, including weekday, calendar date, and year. When dates contain more than one element, the second and succeeding elements are normally set off by commas. Study the following examples:

On March 2 we opened for business. (No comma needed for one element.)

On March 2, 2012, we opened for business. (Two commas set off the second element.)

On Friday, March 2, 2012, Yelp started selling its stock to the public. (Commas set off the second and third elements.)

In March 2012 investors saw the stock price increase substantially. (Commas are not used with the month and year only.)

Time Zones

Commas also set off time zones used with clock times.

Our flight leaves Raleigh at 6:55 a.m., EST, and arrives in Omaha at 1:05 p.m., CST.

He placed his online bid at 6:38 p.m., PST, which was two minutes before the auction closed.

Study Tip

How important are commas? Notice how commas change the meaning of this sentence. Version 1: *The actress Judi Dench says Meryl Streep is the best actress in films.* Version 2: *The actress Judi Dench, says Meryl Streep, is the best actress in films.*

Study Tip

Phrases are essential (no commas) when they answer the questions *When?, Where?, Why?,* or *How?*

Study Tip

In separating dates and years, many writers remember the initial comma but forget the final one (*On July 1, 2014, the new fiscal year begins*).

Study Tip

When separating cities and states, remember to include the comma after the state if the sentence continues (*My friend from Milwaukee, Wisconsin, called*).

Addresses and Geographical Items

When dates, addresses, and geographical items contain more than one element, the second and following elements should be set off by commas.

Addresses

When addresses are written in sentence form, separate the parts of the address with commas. Do not, however, place a comma between the city and zip code.

> Please send a copy of your passport to Edward Piegza, Classic Journeys, 7855 Ivanhoe Avenue, Suite 220, La Jolla, California 92037, before your trip. (Commas are used between all elements except the state and zip code, which are considered a single unit.)

Geographical Items

Use commas to set off a state when it follows the name of a city. Commas are also used to set off the name of a country when it follows the name of a city.

> The Smith family moved from Peachtree City, Georgia, to Grand Rapids, Michigan. (Two commas set off the state unless it appears at the end of the sentence.)

> The 19-hour flight from Shanghai, China, to Newark, New Jersey, is the longest scheduled nonstop flight in the world. (Two commas set off the country unless it appears at the end of the sentence.)

Appositives

You will recall that **appositives** rename, describe, or explain preceding nouns or pronouns. An appositive that provides information not essential to the identification of its antecedent should be set off by commas.

> Nicole Dawes, *the AT&T U-verse representative*, is here. (The appositive adds nonessential information; commas set it off.)

> You may pick up your order from the location closest to your home, *our Barnstable branch*

When an appositive is needed to identify the noun or pronoun referred to earlier in the sentence, do not set it off with commas.

> The AT&T U-verse sales representative *Nicole Dawes* is here to see you. (The appositive is needed to identify which sales representative has arrived; therefore, no commas are used.)

> The book *Socialnomics* explains how social media has transformed the way we live and do business. (The appositive is needed to identify the specific book; therefore, no commas are used.)

Closely related one-word appositives do not require commas.

> My supervisor *Doug* sometimes uses my computer.

Now complete the reinforcement exercises for Level 1.

LEVEL 2

Special Guidelines for Using Commas

Now that you are familiar with the basic uses of the comma, we will cover some special guidelines for comma use.

Circle art: © iStockphoto .com/Pavel Khorenyan

Independent Adjectives

Use a comma to separate two or more adjectives that equally modify or describe a noun (see Chapter 7).

> Online customers can conduct *secure, real-time* banking transactions.

> We are looking for an *industrious, ambitious* person to hire.

Study Tip

When trying to decide whether to place a comma between adjectives, read the sentence with the conjunction *and* between the conjunctions. If the sentence makes sense, place a comma between the adjectives.

With the Adverb *too*

When the adverb *too* is used to mean "also," omit the preceding comma when *too* appears at the end of a clause or sentence. When *too* appears elsewhere in a sentence, set it off with two commas.

> If you believe in this cause *too,* consider making a donation. (End of a clause)

> Many celebrities support our cause *too.* (End of a sentence)

> You, *too,* can really make a difference for children with autism. (Elsewhere in a sentence)

When the adverb *too* is used to mean "excessively," don't set it off with commas.

> Some people share *too* much information on social media sites.

Introductory Verbal Phrases

Verbal phrases (see Chapter 5) that precede main clauses should be followed by commas. Prepositional phrases containing verb forms are also followed by commas.

> *To apply for the scholarship,* you must have three letters of recommendation. (Infinitive verbal phrase)

> *Working overtime,* we completed the project before the deadline. (Participial verbal phrase with a verb form ending in *ing*)

> *Intrigued by the idea,* Emily researched study abroad opportunities. (Participial verbal phrase with a verb form ending in *ed*)

> *By enrolling early,* you will receive our special discount. (Prepositional phrase with a verb form)

Prepositional Phrases

One or more introductory prepositional phrases (see Chapter 8) totaling four or more words should be followed by a comma.

> *On the first Tuesday of each month,* museum admission is free.

> *During the winter months,* sales of firewood usually increase.

Introductory prepositional phrases of fewer than four words require *no* commas.

> *In 2012* the Golden Gate Bridge celebrated its seventy-fifth anniversary.

> *On November 30* we expect a major announcement.

Prepositional phrases in other positions do not require commas when they are essential and do not interrupt the flow of the sentence.

> The research development team *in our Chicago office* has discovered a new diabetes drug. (No commas are needed around the prepositional phrase because it answers the question *Where?* and does not interrupt the flow of the sentence.)

The announcement *about our fall promotion* will be made next week. (No commas are needed because the prepositional phrase answers the question *Which one?* and does not interrupt the flow of the sentence.)

Independent Clauses

When a coordinating conjunction (see Chapter 9) joins independent clauses, use a comma before the coordinating conjunction. When using the coordinating conjunction *and*, you can omit the comma when the entire sentence is short (up to 13 words).

> Microsoft is aggressively pursuing the smartphone market, but it's having a hard time catching up with Google and Apple.

> Joshua ordered pasta and Isabella ordered lobster. (No comma is needed because the entire sentence is short.)

Introductory Clauses

Dependent clauses that precede independent clauses are followed by commas. Remember that dependent clauses usually begin with subordinating conjunctions (see Chapter 9).

> *When you have finished*, please turn out the lights and lock the door.

> *If you have any questions*, please call me at Ext. 2306.

> *Because we rely on e-mail and texting*, we have cut back on voice mail.

Terminal Dependent Clauses

Whether to use a comma to separate a dependent clause at the end of a sentence depends on whether the added information is essential. Generally, terminal dependent clauses add information that answers questions such as *When?*, *Why?*, and *How?* Such information is essential; thus no comma is necessary. Only when a terminal clause adds unnecessary information or an afterthought should a comma be used.

> Please turn out the lights and lock the door *when you have finished*. (No comma is needed because the terminal clause provides essential information and answers the question *When?*)

> Please call me at Ext. 2306 *if you have any questions*. (No comma is needed because the terminal clause provides essential information and answers the question *Why?*)

> We have cut back on voice mail *because we rely on e-mail and texting*. (No comma is needed because the terminal clause provides essential information and answers the question *Why?*)

> I plan to leave at 3:30, *although I could stay if you need me*. (A comma is needed because the terminal clause provides additional unnecessary information.)

Nonessential Clauses

Use commas to set off **nonessential clauses**. These types of clauses are used parenthetically or supply information unneeded for the grammatical completeness of a sentence.

> Workplace accidents, *as you will surely agree*, must be avoided if at all possible. (Commas are needed because the italicized clause adds unnecessary information.)

> We received a phone call from Senator John McCain, *who will be speaking to our organization next week*. (Commas are necessary because the italicized clause adds unnecessary information.)

The culprit behind the spam, *which advertised everything from cable de-scramblers to herbal remedies,* was finally apprehended. (Commas are necessary because the italicized clause adds unneeded information. The relative pronoun *which* is a clue that the clause is unnecessary.)

Do NOT use commas to set off clauses that contain essential information. You might want to review this topic in Chapter 9.

An entrepreneur *who plans to open a small business* should use the re-sources provided by the Small Business Administration. (No commas are necessary because the italicized clause is essential; it tells what entrepre-neur should use the resources.)

An organization *that offers a strong compensation package* will have no trouble recruiting job applicants. (No commas are necessary because the italicized clause is essential; it tells what organization will have no trouble recruiting job applicants.)

Now complete the reinforcement exercises for Level 2.

LEVEL 3

Additional Guidelines for Using Commas

The following guidelines for comma use include suggestions for punctuating degrees, abbreviations, numerals, omitted words, contrasting statements, and short quotations.

Degrees and Abbreviations

The abbreviations *Jr.* and *Sr.* and Roman numerals added to a person's name are not set off by commas unless the person chooses to include them. When in doubt, ask the person or look at his or her business card.

Attorney Harry Connick Sr. is the father of singer Harry Connick Jr.

Stafford Elahi III received his master's degree last year.

Degrees, personal titles, and professional designations following individu-als' names are set off by commas.

Norman Rosen, MD, uses telemedicine connections to keep in touch with his patients.

Cathy Formusa, PhD, believes in using holistic methods in her practice.

Lisa Godbey Wood, Esq., was the first female federal judge in the state of Georgia.

Company abbreviations such as *Inc.* and *Ltd.* are set off by commas only if the company's legal name includes the commas.

Despair, Inc., provides motivational products and posters for pessimists and underachievers. (The company's legal name includes a comma.)

Lucasfilm Ltd. is probably best known for its *Star Wars* films. (The legal name does not include a comma.)

Study Tip

In the United States, the term *Esq.* may be used as a courtesy title by attorneys addressing each other. If used, no other title is written (*Don Smith, Esq.*).

Trivia Tidbit

A variety of abbrevia-tions are used in company names in the United States to designate the type of business. For example, *Inc.* ("incorporated") identifies a corporation; *Ltd.* ("limited") identifies a limited liability company; *LLP* identifies a limited liability partnership; and *PC* identifies a profes-sional corporation.

Numerals

Unrelated figures appearing side by side should be separated by commas.

> By 2016, 350 million businesspeople will be using smartphones in the workplace.

> On page 10, two illustrations show the wiring diagram.

Numbers of more than three digits require commas when expressed in U.S. format.

1,760	47,950	6,500,000

However, calendar years and zip codes are written without commas within the numerals.

Calendar Years:	1776	1945	2015
Zip Codes:	02116	45327	90265

Telephone and fax numbers, house numbers, decimals, page numbers, serial numbers, metric numbers, social security numbers, policy numbers, and contract numbers are also written without commas within the numerals.

Telephone/Fax Number:	(415) 937-5594
House Number:	5411 Redfield Circle
Decimal Number:	.98651, .0050
Page Number:	Page 1036
Serial Number:	36-5710-1693285763
Contract Number:	No. 359063420

Omitted Words

A comma is used to show the omission of words that are understood.

> Last summer our firm hired 12 interns; this summer, only 3 interns.
> (A comma shows the omission of *we hired* after *summer*.)

Contrasting Statements

Commas are used to set off contrasting or opposing expressions. These expressions are often introduced by such words as *not*, *never*, *but*, and *yet*.

> We chose Franchino's, not L'Osteria del Forno, to host our study abroad reunion. (Two commas set off a contrasting statement that appears in the middle of a sentence.)

> The riskier the investment, the greater the potential return. (One comma sets off a contrasting statement that appears at the end of a sentence.)

> The more he protests, the less we believe him. (One comma sets off a contrasting statement that appears at the end of a sentence.)

Clarity

Commas are used to separate words repeated for emphasis and words that may be misread if not separated.

> It will be a very, very long time before Miguel is able to return to the Philippines.

> Whoever goes, goes at his or her own expense.

No matter what, you know you have our support.

In business, time is money.

Short Quotations

A comma is used to separate a short quotation from the rest of a sentence. If the quotation is divided into two parts, two commas are used.

Study Tip

Here's a good rule to follow in relation to the comma: *When in doubt, leave it out!*

Alice Beasley said, "The first product to use a bar code was Wrigley's gum."

"The first product to use a bar code," said Alice Beasley, "was Wrigley's gum."

Now complete the reinforcement exercises for Level 3.

Dr. Guffey   Professor Seefer

Q: I remember when company names with *Inc.* and *Ltd.* always had commas around these abbreviations. Has this changed?

A: Today's practice is to use commas only if the official company name includes the commas. For example, the following company names are written without commas: Gap Inc., Apple Inc., Pfizer Inc., Caterpillar Inc. However, other companies include the commas: Canon U.S.A., Inc.; Motorola, Inc.; Novell, Inc.; Cisco Systems, Inc. One way to check on the official name is to search for the company's website and look at it there.

Q: When the company name *Sun Microsystems, Inc.,* appears in the middle of a sentence, is there a comma following *Inc.*?

A: Current authorities recommend the following practice in punctuating *Inc.*: If the legal company name includes a comma preceding *Inc.,* then a comma should follow *Inc.* if it is used in the middle of a sentence (*We learned that Sun Microsystems, Inc., has an education software program*).

Q: My boss always leaves out the comma before the word *and* when it precedes the final word in a series of words. Should the comma be used?

A: Although some writers omit that comma, which is called a serial comma, careful writers favor its use so that the last two items in the series cannot be misread as one item. For example, *The departments participating are Engineering, Accounting, Marketing, and Advertising*. Without that final comma, the last two items might be confused as one item.

Q: I thought the past tense of *spell* is *spelled*. One of my colleagues, however, uses the past tense *spelt*. Are both forms acceptable?

A: Your colleague is probably from Great Britain, where the past tense of *spell* is indeed *spelt*. However, the American past-tense form is *spelled*, just as you thought. In fact, many words are spelled differently in American and British English. For example, in the United States, we spell *organization* with a *z*; in Great Britain this word is spelled *organisation*. When writing for American audiences, always use the American spelling of words.

Q: Are these three words interchangeable: *assure, ensure,* and *insure*?

A: Good question! Although all three words mean "to make secure or certain," they are not interchangeable. *Assure* refers to persons and may suggest setting someone's mind at rest (*let me assure you that we are making every effort to locate it*). *Ensure* means "to make sure, certain, or safe" (*the company has ensured the safety of all workers*). The word *insure* means "to protect or indemnify against loss" (*the building and its contents are insured*).

Q: It seems to me that the word *explanation* should be spelled as *explain* is spelled. Isn't this unusual?

A: Many words derived from root words change their grammatical form and spelling. Consider these: *disaster, disastrous; maintain, maintenance; repeat, repetition; despair, desperate, desperation; pronounce, pronunciation.*

Q: Is *appraise* used correctly in this sentence? *We will appraise stockholders of the potential loss.*

A: No, it's not. Your sentence requires *apprise*, which means "to inform or notify." The word *appraise* means "to estimate" (*He will appraise your home before you set its selling price*).

Q: The following three sentences appeared in an assignment my daughter received from her fifth-grade teacher: *It's going to be interesting! For each state list it's geographical region. On your map identify each state and note its' capital.* I always have trouble myself with *its* and *it's*, but it seems as if something is wrong here.

A: You're right! Even teachers have trouble with *its* and *it's*. In the first sentence, *it's*, a contraction for *it is*, has been used correctly (*It is going to be interesting!*). In the last two sentences, the teacher should have used the possessive form of *it*, which is *its*, to show possession. In fact, the word *its'* does not exist. Now your only decision is whether you should point out these errors to your daughter's teacher!

Q: I've been told that I should spell *judgment* without the *e* after *g*. Why, then, do I sometimes see this word spelled *judgement*? Are both spellings acceptable?

A: Most dictionaries will give both the preferred and any alternate spellings of a word. The preferred spelling will always be listed first. Although *judgement* is included in many dictionaries as an alternate spelling, it should not be used in business or any other type of writing because most people would identify it as being misspelled. If you use this spelling in Word, it will be flagged as being misspelled. In addition, if you look this word up in any law dictionary using this spelling, you won't find it because *judgment* is the only accepted spelling in the legal field.

Q: I just moved to the United States from Croatia. Did I *emigrate* or *immigrate*?

A: To *emigrate* means "to move from a country," so you emigrated from Croatia. To *immigrate* means "to move to a country," so you immigrated to the United States.

SPOT THE Blooper

Using the skills you are learning in this class, try to identify why the following items are bloopers. Consult your textbook, dictionary, or reference manual as needed. To see if you recognized the blooper, go to **www.cengagebrain.com** and use your access code to see the Spot the Blooper key.

Blooper 1: From an online article posted on the *Inquirer Technology* website: "[Angelina] Jolie raised eyebrows, and probably temperatures, by exposing a thigh in a gown with a full-length slit while presenting one of the award's at Sunday's nights Oscars show in Hollywood." [Did you spot three bloopers?]

Blooper 2: From the *San Francisco Chronicle*: "And the online discussions started on the outside website will by default simultaneously appear on the comment maker's Facebook wall, although he or she can chose to not post it."

Blooper 3: Sentence printed in a British newspaper: "The defendant said his barrister had a history of drug abuse." [How could two commas have changed the meaning of this sentence?]

Blooper 4: A large portable sign located near Soperton, Georgia: "We sell crack and shell pecans."[How would the addition of commas change the meaning of this sentence?]

Blooper 5: Poster for a university departmental event: "Door prizes will include lab equipment, books written by members of the biology department and a fruitcake."

Blooper 6: Sign outside a restaurant in Grenada, Mississippi: "LETS EAT SENIOR CITIZENS." [Did you spot two bloopers?]

Blooper 7: From *The Union-Leader* [Manchester, New Hampshire]: "Prince Louis Ferdinand of Prussia, a grandson of Germany's last emperor who worked in a Detroit auto plant in the 1930s and later opposed Nazi dictator Adolf Hitler, has died at age 86." [Could a comma help clarify who worked in the auto plant?]

Blooper 8: From the *Pacifica Tribune* [Pacifica, California]: "The land was eventually sold to Andy Oddstad who built homes and also became the site of Linda Mar Shopping Center."

Blooper 9: Banner at an educational task force meeting in Raleigh, North Carolina: "Excellance in Secondary Education."

Blooper 10: Photo caption in the *Cherokee Ledger-News* [Woodstock, Georgia]: "Gordon Wilson points out places where his unit operated during World War II in his Woodstock home."

10

Reinforcement Exercises

LEVEL 1

A. Self-Check. Commas. Insert necessary commas. In the space provided, indicate briefly the reason for each comma (or its absence). For example, write *series, parenthetical, direct address, date, address, essential appositive,* and so forth. Write *C* if the sentence is correct.

Example: Do you think, in the meantime, that we should contact those who have already sent in their requests?   parenthetical _____

1. Webvan Pets.com and Kozmo.com were the three biggest dot-com failures.   _____

2. Hong Kong is on the other hand one of the most densely populated areas in the world.   _____

3. Tuesday September 11 2001 is a day that many Americans will never forget.   _____

4. Herb Kelleher grew up in Haddon Heights New Jersey before he moved to Dallas Texas to start Southwest Airlines in 1971.   _____

5. Clarence Darrow the famous trial lawyer defended John Scopes in the evolution trial.   _____

6. The famous journalist H. L. Mencken covered the Scopes Trial.   _____

7. The plane landed safely in Oklahoma City at 7:13 p.m. CST in the middle of an ice storm.   _____

8. Your refund Mr. Rossi was issued yesterday.   _____

9. We have no doubt that such practices are widespread.   _____

10. Please send the order to Alison Spence 34 Wildwood Drive Chatham Massachusetts 02633.   _____

Check your answers below.

B. Commas. Insert necessary commas. In the space provided, indicate briefly the reason for each comma (or its absence). For example, write *series, parenthetical, direct address, date, address, essential appositive,* and so forth. Write *C* if the sentence is correct.

11. Bronte Tennyson Athens Florence London Paris and Tarzan are all towns in the state of Texas.   _____

12. The first ball dropped in Times Square in New York City on January 1 1908 at 12 a.m. EST.   _____

13. On May 14 1908 Charles Furnas became the first airplane passenger in the United States.   _____

14. The American explorer Admiral Robert Peary set out from New York City for the North Pole in July 1908.   _____

1. Webvan, Pets.com, (series)   2. Hong Kong is, hand, (parenthetical)   3. Tuesday, September 11, 2001, (date)   4. Haddon Heights, New Jersey, Dallas, Texas, (geographical items)   5. Darrow, lawyer, (nonessential appositive)   6. C (essential appositive)   7. 7:13 p.m., CST, (time zone)   8. refund, Mr. Rossi, (direct address)   9. C (not parenthetical)   10. Spence, Drive, Chatham, (address)

15. Everything that happened in 1908 was bigger better faster and stranger than anything that had happened before. _____

16. Some people say consequently that modern life in the United States began in 1908. _____

17. Please tell us Mr. Trump what it's like to produce and star in *The Celebrity Apprentice*. _____

18. *The Celebrity Apprentice* has had a variety of famous contestants including Trace Adkins Herschel Walker Joan Rivers and Cheryl Tiegs. _____

19. As a matter of fact these celebrity contestants compete to raise money for their favorite charities. _____

20. Sam Walton the founder of Wal-Mart started out running a small store in Arkansas. _____

21. Wal-Mart opened its first store in Moscow on January 11 2012 in a highly populated area. _____

22. This store in Russia opened of course 20 years after Sam Walton's death. _____

23. Nevertheless his family has continued to run the business with great success. _____

24. Popular places for destination weddings include Hawaii Mexico and the Caribbean because of their warm weather. _____

25. My sister Susan and her husband Gary traveled to Aruba in the Caribbean for the wedding of friends. _____

26. Applications for *The Amazing Race* should be sent to the Casting Department 200 North Continental Boulevard El Segundo CA 90245 by the deadline. _____

27. Strict rules are needed however to make sure that companies don't start charging for access to public information. _____

28. In February 1935 Parker Brothers started selling the board game *Monopoly*. _____

29. Charles B. Darrow who was a heater salesman in Pennsylvania was the first to patent the board game *Monopoly*. _____

30. The National Monopoly Championship will be aired on ESPN at 8 p.m. EST. _____

C. **Commas.** Insert necessary commas. In the space provided for each sentence, write the number of commas that you inserted. If the sentence is correct, write *C*. Be prepared to explain each comma.

31. I hope Donna that you will accept the position in Marrakesh Morocco as soon as possible. _____

32. We have no doubt that you will accept our offer by Friday April 9. _____

33. Your new position of course will require that you learn the Arabic language. _____

34. In the meantime you can learn about Moroccan greetings customs and food by reading business travel guides. _____

35. Mitchell Alicia and Rebecca arrived in Dubai on November 2. _____

36. Mitchell a journalist for a U.S. newspaper was assigned to cover a story in Dubai. _____

37. His wife Alicia was happy to come along on the trip. _____

38. Dubai has banned dancing loud music kissing holding hands and hugging in public. _____

39. You can also get in trouble in Dubai for wearing skimpy clothing or swearing or displaying rude gestures. _____

40. The author Mark Twain was born in the town of Florida Missouri on Sunday November 30 1835 and was raised in Hannibal. _____

41. Mark Twain was a printer's apprentice a licensed riverboat pilot and a newspaper reporter. _____

42. Damon Washington the chief security officer responded to a disturbance that awoke nearly everyone in the building at 1:30 a.m. PST. _____

43. Send your application to Cathy Verrett 1110 Houston Street Laredo Texas 78040 before September 30. _____

44. Incidentally we have shipped your wood sample to our designers in Reno Nevada and Little Rock Arkansas for their inspection. _____

45. Members may choose from many martial arts dance yoga and sports conditioning classes offered at Club One Fitness Centers. _____

46. Western Air Express a former U.S. airline served the first food on planes in 1928. _____

47. Our 2014 records Mr. and Mrs. Henshaw show that you owe additional taxes for 2011 2012 and 2013. _____

48. Most people by the way don't like the idea of passengers using cell phones while flying on planes. _____

49. The Small Business Administration which celebrated its sixtieth anniversary in 2013 helps entrepreneurs start manage and finance small companies. _____

50. The famous investor Warren Buffett agreed to give $37 billion to charity. _____

LEVEL 2

A. Self-Check. Commas. Insert necessary commas. In the space provided, indicate briefly the reason for each comma (or its absence). For example, write *independent adjectives*, *the adverb* too, *introductory verbal phrase, independent clauses*, and so forth. Write *C* if the sentence is correct.

Example: Nadia read several enlightening? business-relatedarticles.   independent adjectives

51. To succeed in life find a career that you are passionate about. _____

52. If you want to make money too get the education and experience you need. _____

53. At the end of each fiscal year we prepare our financial statements. _____

54. In March we will launch a satellite office in Denver. _____

55. It takes 43 facial muscles to frown but it takes only 17 muscles to smile. _____

56. You may be the victim of malware if your computer seems to be working more slowly lately. _____

57. The work in this office is strictly confidential as I am sure you are well aware. _____

58. The person who designed your website is talented. _____

59. Dr. Marialice Kern who studies how exercise can be used to control diabetes will speak at the conference in Cambridge. _____

60. We expect honest thorough answers during the interview process. _____

Check your answers below.

B. Commas. Insert necessary commas. In the space provided, indicate briefly the reason for each comma (or its absence). For example, write *independent adjectives*, *the adverb* too, *introductory verbal phrase*, *independent clauses*, and so forth. Write *C* if the sentence is correct.

61. Texas A&M will join the Southeastern Conference too. _____

62. In 1927 Herbert Hoover placed the first videoconference call from Washington to the president of AT&T in New York. _____

63. The "picturephone" was demonstrated at the 1964 World's Fair but the device never became popular with consumers. _____

64. PictureTel a subsidiary of IBM released the first PC-based videoconferencing system in 1991. _____

65. In 2001 doctors conducted the first transatlantic telesurgery. _____

66. Today's voters are looking for honest hardworking candidates. _____

67. Agreeing to serve as our leader Michelle Brock worked with students and faculty to devise an online learning program. _____

68. If I were you I would invest in gold. _____

69. When you look up the meaning of "ecotourism" in an online dictionary you learn that it is the practice of touring natural habitats in a manner meant to minimize ecological impact. _____

70. Dan Bricklin who created the first spreadsheet also developed a multiuser wiki spreadsheet program. _____

71. The man who created the first spreadsheet also developed a multiuser wiki spreadsheet program. _____

72. Because today's college graduates owe an average of $30,000 each in student loans some refer to these graduates as "Generation Broke." _____

73. Many of these college graduates are moving back home because they can't afford to live on their own. _____

74. Only college graduates will be considered and only those with technical skills will be hired. _____

75. Any increase in salaries as you might have expected is presently impossible because of declining profits. _____

76. For a period of at least six months we cannot increase salaries. _____

77. In 2011 the word *cyberbullying* was officially added to the *Oxford English Dictionary*. _____

78. The sportswriter charged that professional football players are overpaid overprivileged athletes. _____

51. life, (introductory verbal phrase) 52. too, (introductory clause) 53. year, (long introductory prep. phrase) 54. C (short prepositional phrase) 55. frown, (independent clauses) 56. C (terminal dependent clause) 57. confidential, (unnecessary terminal clause) 58. C (essential clause) 59. Kern, diabetes, (nonessential clause) 60. honest, (independent adjectives)

Circle art: © iStockphoto.com/Pavel Khorenyan

79. Ben Cohen the cofounder of Ben & Jerry's visited Google headquarters to sign copies of his book for employees. _____

80. You too can attend one of Google's weekly book-signing events. _____

C. **Commas.** Insert necessary commas. For each sentence write, in the space provided the number of commas that you inserted. If the sentence is correct, write *C*. Be prepared to explain each comma.

81. Employees too agreed with management's plan for restructuring the company. _____

82. ATMs around the world hand out an estimated $26 billion daily which might surprise some people. _____

83. The first ATM was placed outside a bank in Enfield a north London suburb in June 1967. _____

84. If scientists are correct the earth's surface is composed of a number of shifting plates that move a few inches each year. _____

85. Our current carbon monoxide detectors in view of the new law that went into effect July 1 need to be updated. _____

86. The happy carefree students celebrated the completion of their examinations although many were stressed about their final grades. _____

87. Agreeing to serve as our chair Patrick Leong made valuable contributions to our committee. _____

88. She wants a peppy sporty Fiat 500 for her fiftieth birthday. _____

89. By the spring of next year we plan to move into our new facilities. _____

90. Antonio Perez who is chief executive officer of Eastman Kodak said that Kodak needs to focus on its printer business if it hopes to come out of bankruptcy. _____

91. Some companies make excellent use of social media but others haven't figured out how to use these tools to their advantage. _____

92. In 2011 more than 300 billion e-mail spam messages were sent each day. _____

93. Although it costs about $3.5 billion for a 30-second commercial many companies see the value in advertising during the Super Bowl. _____

94. They do not at this time see any reason for discontinuing this efficient profitable practice. _____

95. When you make a comment on Facebook remember that your employer may see it. _____

96. As Professor Churchill predicted the resourceful well-trained graduate was hired immediately. _____

97. We hope that the new year will be prosperous for you and that we may have many more opportunities to serve you. _____

98. Rutherford Hayes who went to Harvard Law School was the first U.S. president with a law degree. _____

99. Many teenage accidents are related to speeding and the impact of teen-related car crashes amounts to $40 billion annually. _____

100. Safeco a Seattle-based insurance company introduced Teensurance which uses a device under the dashboard that alerts parents by e-mail if their child is speeding. _____

A. Self-Check. Commas. Insert necessary commas. In the space provided, indicate briefly the reason for each comma (or its absence). For example, write *omitted words*, *contrasting statement*, *clarity*, *short quotation*, and so forth.

101. "As a small businessperson" said John Greenleaf Whittier "you have no greater leverage than the truth." _____

102. What it is is a matter of integrity. _____

103. Most employees arrived to work at 7 a.m.; the rest at 8 a.m. _____

104. Ruth Sison PhD specializes in information management. _____

105. In April 2012 34 heads of state and government met in Cartagena Colombia for the Summit of the Americas. _____

106. Bank of America announced that it will cut over 30000 jobs this year. _____

107. We were expecting Ms. Vanore not Mr. Kivel to conduct the audit. _____

108. "Effort only fully releases its reward after a person refuses to quit" said Napoleon Hill. _____

109. In the spring we will open a branch in Auburn; in the fall in Macon. _____

110. The octogenarians had known each other for a long long time. _____

Check your answers below.

B. Commas. Insert necessary commas. In the space provided, indicate briefly the reason for each comma (or its absence). For example, write *omitted words*, *contrasting statement*, *clarity*, *short quotation*, and so forth.

111. "If you listen to your fears" said Robert H. Schuller "you will die never knowing what a great person you might have been." _____

112. You will find the index starting on page 1135 of the textbook. _____

113. It is good to be confident not arrogant. _____

114. "All lasting business is built on friendship" said Alfred A. Montapert. _____

115. In February 2009 7500 people in Australia were left homeless because of brushfires. _____

116. On January 1 your Policy No. 8643219 will expire. _____

117. Claudia Operto LVN and Shaun Parrisher RN work at John Muir Medical Center. _____

118. On paper diets often sound deceptively simple. _____

119. The better we treat our customers the more loyal they will be to our company. _____

120. Major responsibility for the loan lies with the signer; secondary responsibility with the cosigner. _____

101. businessperson," Whittier, (short quotation) 102. is, (clarity) 103. rest, (omitted words) 104. Sison, PhD, (abbreviation) 105. 2012, (adjacent numerals); Cartagena, Colombia, (geographical items) 106. 30,000 (numeral) 107. Vanore, Kivel, (contrasting statement) 108. quit," (short quotation) 109. fall, (omitted words) 110. long, (clarity) [**Note:** Do not use a comma after a short introductory prepositional phrase.]

121. We are looking for stable not risky stocks in which to invest. _____

122. Motion-picture producer Samuel Goldwyn said "A verbal contract isn't worth the paper it's written on." _____

123. In short employees must be more considerate of others. _____

124. Donna Meyer PhD and Victor Massaglia MD spoke at the opening session. _____

125. In 2011 11500000 Toyota vehicles were recalled worldwide. _____

126. It was Toyota not Ford Motor Co. that had the most recalls. _____

127. General Motors Corp. recalled 455901 vehicles in 2011; Ford Motor Co. 3.2 million. _____

128. What it was was an international power struggle. _____

129. "A successful life is one that is lived through understanding and pursuing one's own path" said Chin-Ning Chu "not chasing after the dreams of others." _____

130. The White House is located at 1600 Pennsylvania Avenue. _____

C. **Writing Exercise. Comma Rules.** Select five comma rules that you think are most important. Name each rule; then write an original sentence illustrating that rule.

	Comma Rule	Sentence Illustration
131.	_____	_____
132.	_____	_____
133.	_____	_____
134.	_____	_____
135.	_____	_____

D. **Review. Commas.** To make sure you have mastered the use of commas, try your skill on these challenging sentences that cover all levels. Insert needed commas and write the number that you added in the space provided. Write *C* if the sentence is correct. Be prepared to discuss the rule for each comma you add.

136. Do you think Dr. Bloch that I should try to lose some weight? _____

137. The flight to Washington DC will depart at 7:51 a.m. PST. _____

138. You can cancel your reservation by writing to Norwegian Cruise Lines 7665 Corporate Center Drive Miami Florida 33126. _____

139. On October 24 1901 Annie Taylor at the age of 64 became the first person to go over Niagara Falls in a barrel. _____

140. John D. Rockefeller who founded Standard Oil was known as a driven determined and philanthropic man. _____

141. Rockefeller by the way was born in Richford New York in July 1839. _____

142. Elizabeth Witts who was our first team leader moved to Philadelphia Pennsylvania. _____

143. The person who became our next team leader was from Columbia South Carolina. _____

144. At a recent meeting of our team we decided that members should at their convenience complete an online training module. _____

145. Although *National Geographic* prints only about 30 photographs for each article the photographer takes about 14000 images. _____

146. If you work in an office with open cubicles it is rude to listen to Web radio any kind of streaming audio or your iPod without headphones. _____

147. Renouncing her wealthy social background Florence Nightingale became a nurse and is considered the founder of modern nursing. _____

148. The Glass-Steagall Act of 1933 banned banks from investing in stocks but was repealed in 1999. _____

149. Although bored employees managed to stay awake during the CEO's speech. _____

150. Whatever it is it is not very amusing. _____

151. Our yearly budget was over $2000000 for equipment supplies and utilities. _____

152. Cooperation not competition is what is needed at this time. _____

153. "There is no such thing" said Tom Peters "as a minor lapse in integrity." _____

154. My cousin Rich lives in Slingerlands New York. _____

155. In June 2012 an extra leap second was added to the end of the year. _____

E. FAQs About Business English Review. In the space provided, write the correct answer choice.

156. The Millers could not *(a) ensure, (b) insure, (c) assure* their home because they live directly on an earthquake fault. _____

157. Mrs. Miller tried to *(a) ensure, (b) insure, (c) assure* the insurance agent that their house was stable and secure. _____

158. To *(a) ensure, (b) insure, (c) assure* your timely arrival, please leave an hour early. _____

159. A realtor should *(a) apprise, (b) appraise* your property before you list it for sale. _____

160. Our insurance agent *(a) apprises, (b) appraises* all clients of the limitations of home ownership policies. _____

161. She *(a) spelt, (b) spelled* the word incorrectly. _____

162. *(a) It's, (b) Its', (c) Its* been a pleasure working with you on this project. _____

163. The paralegal prepared a summary *(a) judgment, (b) judgement* for the legal case against a major corporation. _____

164. Be sure to use correct *(a) pronounciation, (b) pronunciation* during your job interview. _____

165. Drazan *(a) emigrated, (b) immigrated* from his homeland of Croatia in 2008. _____

Chat About It ◀◀

Your instructor may assign any of the following topics for you to discuss in class, in an online chat room, or on an online discussion board. Some of the discussion topics may require outside research. You may also be asked to read and respond to postings made by your classmates.

Discussion Topic 1: As you learned in this chapter, punctuation in written documents sometimes plays a role in court cases. The punctuation used helps the court interpret the meanings of these documents. Do research to find an example of a court case that involved punctuation. Share your findings with the class.

Discussion Topic 2: Patricia T. O'Conner wrote a book called *Woe Is I: The Grammarphobe's Guide to Better English in Plain English*. Find a copy of the book at your college or local library and select one chapter to read. Summarize the chapter and share your summary with your classmates. Include personal comments about what you read.

Discussion Topic 3: The actor Matthew McConaughey said, "Life is a series of commas, not periods." What do you think he meant

by this? Share your interpretation with your classmates.

Discussion Topic 4: In this chapter you learned that various abbreviations such as *Inc.* and *Ltd.* are used to identify businesses in the United States. Different such abbreviations are used throughout the world. Choose a country and find out what company abbreviations are used. Share your findings with your class.

Discussion Topic 5: In the beginning of this chapter, you read this quote by Marie Rackham: "Think of punctuation marks as the traffic signs of writing. Just as traffic signs guide drivers, so punctuation marks guide readers and writers." Do you agree with this analogy? Share your thoughts about punctuation with your classmates. What analogy would you use to describe punctuation?

Insert appropriate commas in the following sentences. Write *C* if the sentence is correct. Then compare your answers with those below.

1. Successful entrepreneurs must have vision energy and self-confidence.

2. Fortunately America tends to survive economic downturns which gives us all hope.

3. Rick Skrenta who created the first computer virus wrote the malicious code in 1982 as a harmless prank.

4. In 1999 we experienced the first computer virus that was spread over e-mail.

5. Please let us know Ms. Bacastow what we can do to ensure a pleasant smooth transition.

6. The manager thinks on the other hand that all service calls must receive prior authorization and that current service contracts must be honored.

7. Deborah Dash PhD and Tim Murphy CPA have been asked to speak at our Tampa Florida conference.

8. When trained all employees in this company should be able to offer logical effective advice to customers.

9. To meet the deadline make sure your application fee is received by January 25 2015 at 5 p.m. PST.

10. Francesca attended an eye-gazing party in Los Angeles and within two minutes she had met her soul mate.

1. vision, energy, 2. Fortunately, downturns, 3. Skrenta, virus, 4. C 5. know, Ms. Bacastow, pleasant, 6. thinks, hand, 7. Dash, PhD, Murphy, CPA, Tampa, Florida, 8. trained, logical, 9. deadline, January 25, 2012, 5 p.m., 10. Angeles,

270 **CHAPTER 10** COMMAS

Semicolons and Colons **11**

> But the thermals that benignly waft our sentences to new altitudes—that allow us to coast on air, and loop-the-loop, suspending the laws of gravity—well, they are the colons and semicolons.
>
> —Lynne Truss, *Eats, Shoots & Leaves*

Circle art: © iStockphoto.com/Pavel Khorenyan

© Dmitriy Shironosov/Shutterstock.com

Objectives

When you have completed the materials in this chapter, you will be able to do the following:

LEVEL 1

1. Use semicolons correctly in punctuating compound sentences.
2. Use semicolons when necessary to separate items in a series.

LEVEL 2

3. Learn the proper and improper use of colons to introduce listed items.
4. Correctly use colons to introduce quotations and explanatory sentences.

LEVEL 3

5. Distinguish between the use of commas and semicolons preceding expressions such as *namely*, *that is*, and *for instance*.
6. Use colons appropriately in business letter salutations, website addresses, time, and publication titles; and be able to capitalize words following colons when necessary.

271

Pretest

Insert commas, semicolons, and colons to punctuate the following sentences correctly. Then compare your answers with those below.

1. Facebook got a head start in the social networking world consequently many experts don't think Google+ can compete.

2. Sony Betamax was one of the most famous failures in history Microsoft's Windows Vista was another well-known disappointment.

3. We are not sure however that any business failure can match the Ford Edsel.

4. Three of the world's most innovative companies are Salesforce.com Amazon.com and Apple.

5. Apple earns most of its revenue from iPads iPods and iPhones.

6. The following experts were invited to speak Janet Black College of San Mateo Lanny Hertzberg Cosumnes River College and Bob Duxbury Santa Rosa Junior College.

7. Although the committee had many cities from which to choose it decided to focus on resort locations namely Las Vegas Scottsdale and Honolulu.

8. Gilbert Amelio said "Developing excellent communication skills is absolutely essential to effective leadership. The leader must be able to share knowledge and ideas to transmit a sense of urgency and enthusiasm to others. If a leader can't get a message across clearly and motivate others to act on it, then having a message doesn't even matter."

9. John Moe has one major career goal he wants to become CEO of a large corporation.

10. The meeting will begin promptly at 230 p.m.

Study Tip

Semicolons and colons are timing signals. They make readers pause. Used skillfully, these punctuation marks alert readers to slow down and look for a special relationship to follow.

This chapter introduces semicolons and colons, which can be two powerful punctuation marks in business writing. Skilled writers use semicolons and colons to signal readers about the ideas that follow. You can improve your writing and look more professional if you know how to use semicolons and colons correctly. In this chapter you will learn basic uses and advanced applications of these two important punctuation marks.

1. world; consequently, 2. history; 3. sure, however, 4. Salesforce.com, Amazon.com, 5. iPads, iPods, 6. speak: Black, Mateo; Hertzberg, College; Duxbury, 7. choose, locations; namely, Las Vegas, Scottsdale, 8. said: 9. goal: 10. 2:30

Basic Uses of the Semicolon

Semicolons tell readers that two closely related ideas should be thought of together. The semicolon is a stronger punctuation mark than the comma, which signifies a pause; however, the semicolon is not as strong as the period, which signifies a complete stop. Understanding the use of semicolons will help you avoid fundamental writing errors, such as the comma splice and the run-on sentence. The most basic use of the semicolon occurs in compound sentences. Many business and professional communicators use a comma when they should be using a semicolon. Study the following examples to make sure you don't make this error.

Independent Clauses Separated by Conjunctive Adverbs

Semicolons are used primarily when two independent clauses are separated by a conjunctive adverb or a transitional expression. Common conjunctive adverbs include *therefore*, *however*, *consequently*, and *then*. You studied this basic semicolon use in Chapter 9. Here are some review examples:

> Kevin Powell wanted to improve his presentation skills; *consequently*, he joined Toastmasters International. (A semicolon separates two independent clauses joined by the conjunctive adverb *consequently*.)

> Kevin learned a lot from his Toastmasters experience; *therefore*, he started a student chapter on campus. (A semicolon separates two independent clauses joined by the conjunctive adverb *therefore*.)

> Toastmasters International was founded in 1924; *thus* it has many years of experience as the world's premier public speaking organization. (A semicolon separates two independent clauses joined by the conjunctive adverb *thus*.)

Remember that words functioning as conjunctive adverbs may also serve as parenthetical adverbs. As you learned in Chapter 9, use semicolons only with conjunctive adverbs that join two independent clauses. Use commas to set off parenthetical adverbs that interrupt the flow of an independent clause.

> We are sure, consequently, that strong leaders need strong communication skills.

> We hope, therefore, that you will consider taking a business communications class.

Independent Clauses Without Coordinating Conjunctions or Conjunctive Adverbs

Two or more closely related independent clauses not separated by a conjunctive adverb or a coordinating conjunction (*and*, *or*, *nor*, *but*, *so*, *yet*, *for*) require a semicolon.

> Sales meetings during prosperous times were lavish productions that focused on entertainment; meetings today focus on training and decision making.

> Not all job openings are found posted online or in job databases; the "hidden" job market accounts for more than half of all available positions.

Study Tip

Remember that a comma is used only after a two-syllable conjunctive adverb. And don't capitalize the word following a semicolon unless it is a proper noun.

Study Tip

Notice that when a semicolon is used in this way, the clause on either side is independent; that is, it can stand on its own as a sentence.

Circle art: © iStockphoto.com/Pavel Khorenyan

Series Containing Internal Commas or Complete Thoughts

Semicolons are used to separate items in a series when one or more of the items in the series contain internal commas. Using a semicolon in this way will make your sentences clearer to your readers.

> The three cities with the largest populations are Tokyo, Japan; Seóul, South Korea; and Mexico City, Mexico.

> According to *Harvard Business Review*, the three best-performing CEOs in the world are Yun Jong-Yong, Samsung Electronics; Alexey B. Miller, Gazprom; and John T. Chambers, Cisco Systems.

Semicolons are also used to separate three or more independent clauses that appear in a series and contain internal commas.

> The first step consists of surveying all available information related to the company objective so that an understanding of all problems can be reached; the second step involves interviewing consumers, wholesalers, and retailers; and the third step consists of developing a research design in which the actual methods and procedures to be used are indicated.

A series of short independent clauses, however, may be separated by commas.

> Facebook was founded in 2004, it opened to the public in 2006, and it started selling its stock in 2012.

> Now complete the reinforcement exercises for Level 1.

LEVEL 2

Basic Uses of the Colon

Although it has a variety of functions, the **colon** is most often used to introduce lists, quotations, and explanatory sentences.

Formally Listed Items

Use a colon after an independent clause that introduces one item, two items, or a list of items. A list may be shown vertically or horizontally in sentence form and is usually introduced by such words as *the following*, *as follows*, *these*, or *thus*. A colon is also used when words like these are implied but not stated.

> The best leaders possess *one* important trait: integrity. (An independent clause introduces a single item.)

> Text messages are now used to deliver *the following* types of information: medical, financial, educational, and political. (A formal list with an introductory expression stated)

> Several of the world's tallest buildings are located in Dubai: Burj Khalifa, 23 Marina, Elite Residence, and Emirates Park Towers. (A formal list with an introductory expression only implied)

> *These* are some of the financial services the Federal Reserve provides to member banks:
> 1. Collecting checks, payments, and other credit instruments
> 2. Transferring funds electronically
> 3. Distributing and receiving cash and coins (A formal list shown vertically)

Do not use a colon in a sentence unless the list is introduced by an independent clause. Lists often function as sentence complements or objects. When this is the case and the statement introducing the list is incomplete, no colon should be used. It might be easiest to remember that lists introduced by verbs or prepositions require no colons (because the introductory statement is incomplete). Therefore, generally do not place a colon after a verb or a preposition.

> The four countries with the highest literacy rates in the world are Cuba, Georgia, Estonia, and Latvia. (No colon is used because the introductory statement is not complete; the list is introduced by the verb *are*.)

> Three requirements for this position are a master's degree, computer knowledge, and five years' experience in systems analysis. (No colon is used because the introductory statement is not complete; the list is introduced by a *to be* verb and functions as a complement to the sentence.)

> Awards of merit were presented to Professor Laham, Mr. Langlois, and Dr. Pieroni. (No colon is used because the introductory statement is not an independent clause; the list functions as an object of the preposition *to*.)

Do not use a colon when an intervening sentence falls between the introductory statement and the list.

> According to a recent survey, these are the best companies to work for. The survey was conducted by *Fortune*.

> Google   Boston Consulting Group
> SAS Institute   Wegmans Food Markets

Long Quotations

Use a colon to introduce long one-sentence quotations and quotations of two or more sentences. Remember to enclose the quotation in quotation marks.

> Oprah Winfrey said: "Do the one thing you think you cannot do. Fail at it. Try again. Do better the second time. The only people who never tumble are those who never mount the high wire. This is your moment. Own it."

Longer quotations that will take up more than three lines are placed in a separate paragraph without quotation marks. Indent the left and right margins to set the quote apart from its introductory sentence and any sentence that follows.

> Patricia T. O'Connor, author and former editor at *The New York Times Book Review*, explains why grammar is so difficult for many people:

>> We all come from the factory wired for language. By the time we know what it is, we've got it. Toddlers don't think about language; they just talk. Grammar is a later addition, an ever-evolving set of rules for using words in ways that we can all agree upon. But the laws of grammar come and go. English today isn't what it was a hundred years ago, and it's not what it will be a hundred years from now.

Incomplete quotations not interrupting the flow of a sentence require no colon, no comma, and no initial capital letter.

> Those who are successful in life tend to say "yes I can" in any type of situation.

Explanatory Sentences

Use a colon to separate two independent clauses if the second clause explains, illustrates, or supplements the first.

> The company's new directors faced a perplexing dilemma: they had to choose between declaring bankruptcy and investing more funds to recoup previous losses. (The second clause explains what the "perplexing dilemma" is.)

> To succeed in this job, you must remember one thing: you are here to serve the customer. (The second clause explains what the "one thing" is.)

Now complete the reinforcement exercises for Level 2.

LEVEL 3

Special Uses of Semicolons

You have just studied the basic uses of semicolons. Occasionally, though, semicolons are used in circumstances demanding special attention.

Introductory Expressions Such as *namely*, *for instance*, and *that is*

When introductory expressions (such as *for example*, *for instance*, *that is*, and *namely*) immediately follow independent clauses, they may be preceded by either commas or semicolons. Generally, if the words following the introductory expression form a series or an independent clause, use a semicolon before the introductory expression and a comma after.

> Google offers unique on-site benefits to its employees; *for instance*, hair stylists, meals prepared by gourmet chefs, massage therapy, oil changes, car wash services, bike repair, and an outdoor volleyball court. (A semicolon is used because *for instance* introduces a series.)

> Several books give tips to business owners about how to use social media effectively; *for example*, Dave Kerpen's *Likeable Social Media* is an excellent resource. (A semicolon is used because *for example* introduces an independent clause.)

If the list or explanation that follows the introductory expression is not a series or an independent clause, use commas before and after the introductory expression.

> We are proposing many new additions to the health care package, *for example*, holistic medicine and chiropractic benefits. (A comma is used because *for example* introduces neither a series nor an independent clause.)

> We value one trait in our employees above all others, i.e., integrity. (A comma is used because *i.e.* introduces neither a series nor an independent clause.)

These same introductory expressions may introduce parenthetical words within sentences. Commas usually punctuate individual items introduced parenthetically within sentences. If the introductory expression introduces several items punctuated by internal commas, then use dashes or parentheses. Dashes and parentheses will be treated in detail in Chapter 12.

Trivia Tidbit

The first printed semicolon appeared in the work of Aldus Manutius in 1494. Manutius was a famous Italian printer and publisher.

Study Tip

Some of these introductory expressions have abbreviations. Instead of *for example*, you can use the abbreviation *e.g.* Instead of *that is*, you can use the abbreviation *i.e.* Instead of *namely*, you can use the abbreviation *viz.* Punctuate these abbreviations in the same way you would the full word.

Study Tip

A series consists of three or more items.

Circle art: © iStockphoto.com/Pavel Khorenyan

The biggest health problem facing employees, *namely*, work-related stress, costs a large employer about $3.5 million annually. (Commas are used because the introductory expression *namely* introduces a single item.)

Basic employee rights—*for instance*, minimum wage, overtime, and child labor protection—were first mandated in 1938 with the passage of the Fair Labor Standards Act. (Dashes are used because the introductory expression *for instance* introduces several items punctuated with internal commas.)

Special Uses of Colons

Colons also have other uses that are common in business writing.

Business Letter Salutations

Colons are placed after the salutation of a business letter when mixed punctuation is used.

> Dear Dr. Washburn: Dear Human Resources: Dear Anita:

Website Addresses

Colons are used after the "http" part of website addresses.

> http://www.meguffey.com   http://www.whitehouse.gov

Time

In expressions of time, use a colon to separate hours from minutes.

> 10:45 a.m.   4:45 p.m.   18:30 (24-hour clock)

Publication Titles

Place a colon between titles and subtitles of books, articles, and other publications.

> *Small Town Rules: How Big Brands and Small Businesses Can Prosper in a Connected Economy* (Book title)

> "Wall Street to Lawmakers: Here's How to Fix the Deficit" (Article title)

Capitalization Following Colons

When a colon is used to introduce a series in sentence format, do not capitalize the first word after the colon unless it is a proper noun.

> The six Cs of effective business communication are the following: clarity, courtesy, conciseness, completeness, correctness, and confidence.

> These companies are among the most admired according to *Fortune*: Apple, Google, Amazon.com, and Coca-Cola.

When a colon is used to introduce a series in a vertical list, capitalize the first letter of each item in the list.

> To be legally enforceable, a contract must include at least three elements:
> 1. Mutual assent of competent parties
> 2. A consideration
> 3. A lawful purpose

Do not capitalize the first letter of an independent clause following a colon if that clause explains or supplements the first one (unless, of course, the first word is a proper noun).

Study Tip

When using mixed punctuation in a business letter, place a colon after the salutation and a comma after the complimentary close. When using open punctuation, omit the semicolon and comma.

Study Tip

Use end punctuation in a vertical list only when the items are complete sentences.

Special Olympics has one overriding mission: through the power of sport, Special Olympics strives to create a better world by fostering the acceptance and inclusion of all people.

Safe drivers have a specific feature to anticipate: most new cars will have voice-control features that will help drivers contact emergency numbers in case of a crash.

Capitalize the first letter of an independent clause following a colon if that clause states a formal rule or principle as a complete sentence.

Ancient Greece's Golden Rule should still be followed today: Do not do to others what would anger you if done to you by others.

Capitalize the first letter of a quotation that follows a colon.

Samuel Smiles, a Scottish author and reformer, once said: "Lost wealth may be replaced by industry, lost knowledge by study, lost health by temperance or medicine, but lost time is gone forever."

A Final Word

Semicolons are excellent punctuation marks when used carefully and knowingly. After reading this chapter, though, some students are guilty of semicolon overkill. They begin to string together two—and sometimes even three—independent clauses with semicolons. Remember to use semicolons in compound sentences *only* when two ideas are better presented together.

Now complete the reinforcement exercises for Level 3.

Q: My partner and I are preparing an announcement describing our new online business. We don't agree on how to punctuate this sentence: *We offer a wide array of network services; such as design, support, troubleshooting, and consulting, etc.*

A: First, drop the semicolon before *such as*. No comma or semicolon is necessary before a list introduced by *such as*. Second, do not use *etc.* at the end of a series. If you have other services to offer, name them. Tacking on *etc.* suggests that you have more items but for some reason you are not listing them.

Q: When I list items vertically, should I use a comma or semicolon after each item? Should a period be used after the final item? For example,

Please inspect the following rooms and equipment:
1. *The control room*
2. *The power transformer and its standby*
3. *The auxiliary switchover equipment*

A: Do not use commas or semicolons after items listed vertically, and do not use a period after the last item in such a list. However, if the listed items are complete sentences, periods should be used after each item.

Q: How can I keep the words *advice* and *advise* straight? I can never decide which one to use.

A: It's best to remember that *advice* is a noun meaning "a suggestion or recommendation" *(She went to her CPA for tax advice)*. The word *advise* is a verb meaning "to counsel or recommend" *(Her attorney advised her to open an IRA)*.

Q: Which word should I use in this sentence? *Our department will (disburse or disperse) the funds shortly.*

A: Use *disburse*. *Disperse* means "to scatter" *(Police dispersed the unruly crowd)* or "to distribute" *(Information will be dispersed to all divisions)*. *Disburse* means "to pay out." Perhaps this memory device will help you keep them straight: associate the *b* in *disburse* with *bank* *(Banks disburse money)*.

Q: I can never keep the words *capital* and *capitol* straight. Which one would I use in the sentence *He invested $150,000 of his own (capital, capitol) in his new business?*

A: This sentence requires the noun *capital*, which means "the wealth of an individual or firm." The noun *capital* also refers to a city serving as the seat of government *(Montpelier is the capital of Vermont.)*. As an adjective, *capital* describes (a) an uppercase letter *(capital letter)*, (b) something punishable by death *(capital punishment)*, or (c) something excellent *(a capital idea)*. The noun *capitol* is used to describe a building used by the U.S. Congress (always capitalized) or a building where a state legislature meets (capitalized only to describe the full building name). *They visited the United States Capitol on their recent trip to Washington, DC. They had visited their state capitol building many times before their trip.*

Q: A memo from our vice president said, *The new benefits package is equally as good as the previous package.* Is *equally as* correct English?

A: Writers should use *equally* or *as* but not both together. *The new benefits package is as good as the previous package* OR *The new benefits package equals the previous package* OR *The new benefits package and the previous package are equally good.*

Q: The other day I said, *Do you think he meant to infer that employees might be laid off?* A coworker corrected me. What's wrong with what I said?

A: You should have used *imply* in your sentence. The word *imply* means "to suggest without stating." the word *infer* means to reach a conclusion *(From the survey results, we inferred that customers want live online customer support).*

Q: I work in an office where we frequently send letters and e-mail messages addressed to people on a first-name basis. Should I use a comma or a colon after a salutation like *Dear Antonio*?

A: The content of the letter, not the salutation (greeting), determines the punctuation after the salutation. If the letter is a business letter, always use a colon. If the letter is personal, a comma may be used, although a colon would also be appropriate. In an e-mail message, either a comma or a colon is appropriate depending on the formality of the message; however, commas are becoming more common.

Q: Should I space once or twice after a colon?

A: You can space once or twice after a colon that introduces a list, a long quotation, or an explanatory sentence. Spacing twice after a colon increases clarity in business documents. Do not space after a colon used in time, and space just once after a colon used in a publication title.

Q: I've just signed a contract to rent an apartment. Am I the *lessee* or the *lessor*?

A: You are the *lessee*, and your landlord is the *lessor*.

SPOT THE Blooper

Using the skills you are learning in this class, try to identify why the following items are bloopers. Consult your textbook, dictionary, or reference manual as needed. To see if you recognized the blooper, go to **www.cengagebrain.com** and use your access code to see the Spot the Blooper key.

Blooper 1: Radio traffic report following an Ohio storm: "All of the interstates and roads that were closed this morning are now reopen thanks to the black ice."

Blooper 2: Article about a proposed ban on plastic bags: "The intent was never to nickel or dime anybody. But if it takes 10 cents to remind somebody that their habits are in their control, I think that's something we're willing to consider doing." [Did you notice two errors?]

Blooper 3: Advertisement for a car wash: "We do not scratch your paint finish with machinery, we do it by hand." [Did you notice two errors?]

Blooper 4: From a bad-news letter to a client: "We apologize for any incontinence this delay has caused."

Blooper 5: From the website for the National Steinbeck Center, announcing the annual Steinbeck Festival: "The focus this year will be on the many awards Steinbeck received during his career and the affect awards and fame have on a writer's literary career and personal life."

Blooper 6: From *The Wall Street Journal:* "The casino has hired a former French waiter to ride a three-wheeled bicycle through the lobby with fresh bread baked by French bakers in the bike basket."

Blooper 7: Story on radio station KCBS about a ship that ran into the San Francisco Bay Bridge: "Pilot pleaded guilty to dumping oil and killing birds in a San Francisco courtroom."

Blooper 8: Statement by Lawrence Bunin, general manager of the SAT college entrance exams: "Less kids are taking the SAT, threatening the viability of the program itself."

Blooper 9: Billboard for McDonald's: "Get your 4 dollar's worth."

Blooper 10: Sign in a public park: "Dog's allowed on leash's with scooper's." [Did you notice three errors?]

11

Reinforcement Exercises

LEVEL 1

A. Self-Check. Commas and Semicolons. For each of the following sentences, underline any errors in punctuation. Then in the space provided, write the correct punctuation mark plus the word preceding it. Write *C* if the sentence is correct.

Example: The price of gas has been steadily increasing, therefore, people are starting to use public transportation more.

increasing;

1. Woodrow Wilson is the only U.S. president who had a PhD, he earned his degree at Johns Hopkins in 1886.

   _____

2. Texting is a leap backward in the science of communication, in fact, it is similar to Morse Code.

   _____

3. Super Bowl ads have become more interactive, many companies now persuade viewers to go to Twitter to tweet about their ads.

   _____

4. Investors' expectations were high consequently, competitive bidding for the new IPO was brisk.

   _____

5. E-business has always been a risky undertaking, online companies seem to disappear as quickly as they appear.

   _____

6. According to the *Fortune* "Global 500" list, the four biggest companies in the world are Wal-Mart Stores, United States; Royal Dutch Shell, Netherlands; Exxon Mobil, United States; and BP, Great Britain.

   _____

7. The United States has the most companies on the list; and Japan and China come in second and third.

   _____

8. Fannie Mae is the fastest-growing organization on the list, Freddie Mac is the third fastest-growing organization.

   _____

9. One of the hottest areas is mobile communications, a number of companies offer chipsets and software to manage the downloading of music, videos, and apps to tablet computers and smartphones.

   _____

10. Consumers are also looking for compact sources of power, thus some companies are offering such products as paper-thin batteries for compact devices.

    _____

Check your answers below.

B. Commas and Semicolons. Add any necessary commas or semicolons to the following sentences. (Do not add periods.) In the spaces provided, write the number of punctuation marks you inserted. Write *C* if a sentence is correct as written.

Example: No one likes to lose a job, however, unemployment benefits in some countries make it less painful.

2

11. Norway has a low unemployment rate, consequently, the country is able to offer the highest unemployment benefits in the world.

    _____

1. PhD; 2. communication; 3. interactive; 4. high; 5. undertaking; 6. C 7. list, 8. list, 9. communications; 10. power;

Circle art: © iStockphoto.com/Pavel Khorenyan

12. Lindsay arrived she greeted the receptionist and she waited for her interview to begin.

13. German shoppers generally bring their own plastic or cloth bags for groceries therefore they were unaccustomed to Wal-Mart's bagging techniques.

14. Greenland is the largest island in the world it is about ten times the size of Great Britain.

15. The five cities expected to bid on the 2022 Winter Olympics are Toulouse France Munich Germany Oslo Norway Geneva Switzerland and Reno Nevada USA.

16. The city to host the 2020 Summer Olympics will be announced soon the 2020 Summer Paralympics will be held in the same city.

17. The shortest recorded reign of any monarch was that of Louis XIX of France it lasted only 15 minutes.

18. General Motors wants to maintain its status as the world's largest automaker hence the company sells such varied brands as Chevrolet, Buick, Cadillac, GMC, and Opel.

19. Anthony identified the problem William offered suggestions and Charlene critiqued each idea.

20. Web advertising attempts to reach large international audiences television advertising is aimed at national or local audiences.

21. San Luis Obispo, California, was chosen as the city where people would most like to live Milton, Massachusetts, came in second.

22. Computer hackers can easily decode short passwords thus passwords should be at least six characters long and be a mix of letters and numerals.

23. We have hired "white hat" hackers their job is to test how well our computer systems withstand assaults by real hackers.

24. Smart companies assume their computer networks will be broken into consequently they develop computer-use policies to limit the damage.

25. Among the oddly named towns in the United States are Boring, Maryland; Truth or Consequences, New Mexico; Rough and Ready, California; and Slap Out, Alabama.

26. Recent speakers at the Commonwealth Club include Dan Akerson CEO General Motors Ed Lee Mayor San Francisco and Rachel Maddow host *The Rachel Maddow Show*.

27. Consumers expect anytime anywhere access to businesses therefore around-the clock customer service access is growing.

28. Women now earn the majority of bachelor's degrees in business, biological sciences, social sciences and history in addition women outpace men in degrees in education and psychology.

29. If you want to tie all actions at a cash register to an individual install fingerprint scanners as a result you will experience fewer instances of theft.

30. Some of the most popular products sold on Amazon.com, along with the companies that market them, include the Lumix camera Panasonic the Kindle Fire Amazon and TurboTax Intuit.

A. Self-Check. Colons. For each of the following sentences, underline any errors in punctuation. Then in the space provided, write the correct punctuation plus the preceding word. If a colon should be omitted, write *Omit colon*. Write *C* if the sentence is correct.

Example: Business model patents were awarded to: Netflix, TiVo, and Priceline.   Omit colon

31. In order to be awarded a business model patent, the idea must be: concrete, useful, new, and unique. _____

32. *Fortune* selected the following companies as the world's most socially responsible: Statoil, Grupo Ferrovial, Walt Disney Company, Edison, and ENI. _____

33. Other socially responsible companies include the following: Please check the *Fortune* website for the complete list.
    Whole Foods Market   Nestle   Weyerhauser _____

34. Two of the top ten socially responsible companies in the world are based in one city; Milan. _____

35. Mary Kay Ash said; "We must have a theme, a goal, a purpose in our lives. If you don't know where you're aiming, you don't have a goal. My goal is to live my life in such a way that when I die, someone can say, she cared." _____

36. Five of the worst computer passwords are: your first name, your last name, the Enter key, *Password*, and the name of a sports team. _____

37. We have asked for quotes from three local restaurants: Circa at Dupont, Old Ebbitt Grill, and Ben's Chili Bowl. _____

38. The computer virus scheduled to hit September 9 was called: "Hellgate." _____

39. The most commonly observed holidays in the United States are the following: New Year's Day, Memorial Day, Independence Day, Labor Day, Veterans Day, Thanksgiving, and Christmas. _____

40. Shane proposed a solution to our day-care problem: open a home office and share child-care duties. _____

Check your answers below.

B. Commas and Colons. For the following sentences, add any necessary but missing punctuation marks. For each sentence indicate in the space provided the number of additions you have made. Mark *C* if the sentence is correct as it stands.

Example: According to the Federal Trade Commission (FTC) the following are the top consumer complaint categories identity theft debt collection sweepstakes and catalog sales.   5

41. Barack Obama broadcast his reelection campaign simultaneously on Facebook, Twitter, and YouTube. _____

42. Political expert David Lombardo said: "In recent years, politicians have begun using Facebook by creating candidate pages, inviting people to events, and encouraging constituents to 'like' them. Now the ante has been raised, as Facebook allows cheap and very targeted advertisements." _____

31. Omit colon 32. C 33. following: 34. city: 35. said: 36. Omit colon 37. C 38. Omit colon 39. C 40. C

43. Brent Wilkes, a candidate for mayor of Saratoga, cited one important reason for using Facebook advertisements during his campaign the ads are seen only by the demographic he wants.

44. Three similar types of tropical storms with different names are cyclones typhoons and hurricanes.

45. American Apparel, maker of trendy clothing, unveiled its latest, hippest retail outlet a computer-generated boutique operating as a simulation game.

46. Polygraph examinations generally consist of four elements a preexamination interview, a demonstration, questioning of the examinee, and a postexamination interview.

47. Babe Ruth, renowned former American League baseball player, once said "The way a team plays as a whole determines its success. You may have the greatest bunch of individual stars in the world, but if they don't play together, the club won't be worth a dime."

48. Experts suggest the following tips for choosing a business name
     1. Avoid generic names.
     2. Keep it brief.
     3. Don't be too narrow or too literal.

49. Each balance sheet is a statement of assets liabilities and owner's equity.

50. In addition to its Web-search tool, Google offers many other services including the following Chrome iGoogle Google Play Gmail Panoramio and Google Earth.

51. Google has also acquired these popular online products YouTube Blogger and Picasa.

52. For graduation you must complete courses in mathematics, accounting, English, management, and business communication.

53. The law of supply and demand can function only under the following condition: producers must know what consumers want.

54. Professor Marilyn Simonson asked that research reports contain the following sections introduction body summary and bibliography.

55. Additional costs in selling the house are title examination, title insurance, transfer tax, preparation of documents, and closing fee.

56. Ben Bernanke said "Over the years, the U.S. economy has shown a remarkable ability to absorb shocks of all kinds, to recover, and to continue to grow. Flexible and efficient markets for labor and capital, an entrepreneurial tradition, and a general willingness to tolerate and even embrace technological and economic change all contribute to this resiliency."

57. Of all the discoveries and inventions in human history, the four greatest are said to be these speech, fire, agriculture, and the wheel.

58. Ritz-Carlton employees follow these four rules build strong relationships with guests, create memorable experiences for guests, seek opportunities to innovate, and continuously learn and grow.

59. Many young employees today are making one big mistake they are sharing too much information about their personal lives online.

60. BJ Fogg, director of Stanford University's Persuasive Technology Lab, said "Finding the right balance will take time, if it is ever achieved. Unlike face-to-face conversations, there's really no good way yet for people to let one another know that they are being too revealing."

C. Writing Exercise. Semicolons and Colons. Write original sentences to illustrate the following. For example: *I generally use the Internet for e-mail; however, I plan to get better at using it for research.*

61. (Semicolon with conjunctive adverb) _____

_____

62. (Semicolon without coordinating conjunction or conjunctive adverb) _____

_____

63. (Semicolon with series containing internal commas) _____

_____

64. (Colon with listed items) _____

_____

65. (Colon with an explanatory sentence) _____

_____

LEVEL 3

A. Self-Check. Commas, Semicolons, and Colons. Insert necessary punctuation. In the space provided, write the number of punctuation marks that you inserted. Write *C* if the sentence is correct.

66. *Newsweek* has identified the greenest companies in the United States; namely, IBM, Hewlett-Packard, Spring Nextel, Baxter, and Dell. _____

67. Many airlines, including Delta and American, now charge for items like checked bags, premium seats, and food; Spirit Airlines, which is trying to reduce its expenses, even charges for carry-on bags. _____

68. Many new compound words have been added to the dictionary; for example, *fist bump*, *social media*, *helicopter parent*, and *boomerang child*. _____

69. The meeting started promptly at 1:15 p.m. and ended at 3:45 p.m. _____

70. "Smart kitchens" are now offered in many new homes for example some smart kitchens come with refrigerators that can reorder ice cream when you're running low. _____

71. All employees are urged to observe the following rule: When faced with an ethical dilemma, talk with someone you trust. _____

72. The writer of a research report should include a variety of references; for example, websites, books, periodicals, government publications, and newspapers. _____

73. A must-read book for businesspeople is *The Power of Habit Why We Do What We Do in Life and Business*. _____

74. You may pay your invoice using any of the following methods: credit card, check, or online payment. _____

75. For the opening session of the East Bay Women's Leadership Conference, the keynote speaker will be Gloria Steinem, American feminist and journalist; the afternoon keynote speaker will be Alice Waters, American chef and owner of Chez Panisse. _____

Check your answers below.

66. C   67. C   68. C   69. C   70. 2   71. C   72. C   73. 1   74. C   75. C

B. Commas, Semicolons, and Colons. For the following sentences, add necessary punctuation. For each sentence indicate the number of additions you made.

Example: If she can get her boss's approval, Laura Spinella will fly to Knoxville on Tuesday; if not, she will leave on Thursday.

_____3_____

76. We are looking for many traits in our new sales associate, for example, good communication skills, outgoing personality, and patience.

_____

77. Because of her computer expertise, Wendy O'Leary was chosen as our network administrator; because of his people skills, Greg Spangler was chosen as trainer.

_____

78. The book group will discuss Michael Lewis's *The Big Short: Inside the Doomsday Machine* at next week's meeting.

_____

79. Companies that plan to expand in China should be aware of several important factors, for example, regulatory environment, cultural differences, and technologies in use.

_____

80. Large and small companies have an important reason for expanding in China; that is, by 2025 China is predicted to become the world's largest economy.

_____

81. Three times have been designated for the interviews: Monday at 6:30 p.m., Wednesday at 3:30 p.m., and Friday at 10 a.m.

_____

82. An author, composer, or photographer may protect his or her product with a government-approved monopoly, namely a copyright.

_____

83. The U.S. Justice Department is planning to sue Apple Inc. and five U.S. publishers for colluding to raise the price of e-books; however, none of the parties will comment on the issue.

_____

84. Invitations were sent to Hiroyuki Yanagi, CEO, Yamaha Corporation; Keith Wandell, CEO, Harley Davidson; and John Bingham, CEO, Piaggio America.

_____

85. AT&T plans to provide the following to low-income families: computer equipment, Internet access, and training.

_____

C. FAQs About Business English Review. In the space provided, write the correct answer choice.

86. We admired the architecture on the *(a) capital, (b) capitol* building in Jefferson City, Missouri.

_____

87. Austin is the *(a) capital, (b) capitol* of Texas.

_____

88. We will invest in *(a) capital, (b) capitol* so that we can expand our business.

_____

89. Reimbursements will be *(a) disbursed, (b) dispersed* to employees on Friday.

_____

90. Some cities use fogging machines to *(a) disburse, (b) disperse* mosquito-control pesticides.

_____

91. We *(a) inferred, (b) implied* from the latest research that customers prefer a natural sweetener in their beverages.

_____

92. Did her comment *(a) infer, (b) imply* that she is looking for another job?

_____

93. Each month Brandi must write a rent check to her *(a) lessor, (b) lessee*.

_____

94. Andrew's counselor gave him good *(a) advice, (b) advise* about what courses to take.

_____

95. Our network administrator will *(a) advice, (b) advise* you about how often to change your password.

_____

Chat About It ◀◀

Your instructor may assign any of the following topics for you to discuss in class, in an online chat room, or on an online discussion board. Some of the discussion topics may require outside research. You may also be asked to read and respond to postings made by your classmates.

Discussion Topic 1: Do you use semicolons when writing? Why or why not? Do you think your habits will change now that you have studied this chapter? Explain.

Discussion Topic 2: Lewis Thomas wrote about the semicolon in *The Medusa and the Snail*:

> The semicolon tells you that there is still some question about the preceding full sentence; something that needs to be added. The period tells you that that is that; if you didn't get all the meaning you wanted or expected, anyway you got all the writer intended to parcel out and now you have to move along. But with the semicolon there you get a pleasant feeling of expectancy; there is more to come; read on; it will get clearer.

Is this how the semicolon makes you feel when you see it in print? How do you think a semicolon differs from a comma or a period in the way it makes a reader feel?

Discussion Topic 3: Search an online bookseller or your local bookshop to find an interesting book that uses a colon in its title. Share the title, author, and a brief summary of the book with your classmates. The summary should be in your own words.

Discussion Topic 4: In this chapter you learned that business letter salutations (*Dear Ms. Lawrence*) are followed by colons (when using mixed punctuation), not commas. Commas are used in salutations in personal correspondence and in most e-mail messages. Why do you think there are differences in punctuation for salutations depending on whether the letter is professional or personal? And why do you think punctuation after salutations is different for business letters and e-mail messages?

Discussion Topic 5: In the beginning of this chapter, you read this quote by Lynne Truss: "But the thermals that benignly waft our sentences to new altitudes—that allow us to coast on air, and loop-the-loop, suspending the laws of gravity—well, they are the colons and semicolons." What do you think she means by this? Share your interpretation of this quote with your classmates.

Posttest

Add appropriate semicolons, colons, and commas. Write *C* if the sentence is correct. Then compare your answers with those below.

1. Nostalgia sells in uncertain times that is why companies like Dunkin' Donuts and Nationwide Insurance are resurrecting old advertising campaigns.

2. Other companies that are reviving old advertising campaigns are Bumble Bee Foods, Eight O'Clock Coffee, and Carl's Jr.

3. Nick Hahn, managing consultant, said "Placing the product in the past is comforting to consumers. It grounds them in a time when things were better."

4. Dunkin' Donuts recently tried pushing coffee drinks and bagels now it is returning its focus to donuts.

5. Companies must have one goal when using nostalgia in advertising campaigns they must evoke a brand's heritage in a contemporary way.

6. Gas prices are rising dramatically therefore more people are walking and riding their bikes to work.

7. The following instructors have been chosen to represent their schools at the professional meeting Jessica Stoudenmire El Camino College Sandra Farrar Louisiana Technical College and Sandra Ostheimer Southwest Wisconsin Technical College.

8. All morning sessions begin at 930 a.m. all afternoon sessions begin at 1 45 p.m.

9. Macworld Expo which is one of the most high-profile technology conferences in the world features hundreds of exhibitors for example, Western Digital, iKlear, Seagate Technology, and OtterBox.

10. Have you read Robert K. Greenleaf's book *Servant Leadership A Journey Into the Nature of Legitimate Power and Greatness*?

1. times; 2. C 3. said: 4. bagels; 5. campaigns: 6. dramatically; therefore, 7. meeting: Stoudenmire, El Camino College; Farrar, Louisiana Technical College; Ostheimer, 8. 9:30 a.m.; 1:45 9. Expo, world, exhibitors; 10. *Leadership:*

Other Punctuation   12

© Corbis RF/Alamy

Punctuation isn't some subtle, arcane concept that's difficult to manage and probably won't make much of a difference one way or another. It's not subtle, it's not difficult, and it can make all the difference in the world.

—Patricia T. O'Conner, *Woe Is I*

Circle art: © iStockphoto.com/Pavel Khorenyan

Objectives

When you have completed the materials in this chapter, you will be able to do the following:

291

Pretest

Use proofreading marks to insert appropriate punctuation in the following sentences. See the inside back cover for a list of proofreading marks. Then compare your answers with those below.

1. Would you please let me know your thoughts about my proposal

2. Wow   What an entertainer

3. Three industries   renewable energy biotechnology and environmental consulting   are experiencing the most growth

4. Please invite Grace Hill PhD and J W Francini

5. Dr Victoria Wims Ms Jennifer Lambert and Mr Zachary Norman have been appointed to the SEC

6. The chapter titled Taking the Mystery Out of Futures was the best one in the book *Market Wizards: Interviews With Top Traders* by Jack D Schwager

7 I wonder whether all candidates for the CEO position completed MBA degrees

8. Did Ted Turner say You should set goals beyond your reach so you always have something to live for

9. My ex boss may reconsider and hire me back

10. The 50s brought us the Beat Generation the first credit card and Elvis Presley

As you have already learned, punctuation really can make all the difference in your writing. This chapter continues our discussion of punctuation by teaching you how to use periods, question marks, and exclamation marks correctly. It also includes suggestions for punctuating with hyphens, dashes, parentheses, quotation marks, brackets, italics, and apostrophes.

LEVEL 1

Uses for the Period

The period can be used to punctuate sentences, abbreviations, initials, and numerals. Guidelines for each use are covered in this section.

To Punctuate Statements, Commands, and Indirect Questions

Use a period at the end of a statement, a command, or an indirect question.

> In 1809 Mary Kies became the first woman to be issued a U.S. patent. (Statement)
>
> Please turn in your expense report before 5 p.m. (Command)
>
> Our union president asked whether we had voted yet. (Indirect question)

Study Tip

If the last word in a sentence is an abbreviation that ends with a period, do not add an extra period to end the sentence. Only one period is necessary.

1. proposal. 2. Wow! entertainer! 3. industries—renewable energy, biotechnology, environmental consulting—growth. 4. Grace Hill, PhD, J. W. Francini. 5. Dr. Victoria Wims, Ms. Jennifer Lambert, Mr. SEC. 6. "Taking the Mystery Out of Futures" D. Schwager. 7. degrees. 8. say, "You for?" 9. ex-boss back. 10. '50s Beat Generation, credit card, Presley.

Circle art: © iStockphoto.com/Pavel Khorenyan

To Punctuate Polite Requests

Use a period, not a question mark, to punctuate a polite request, suggestion, or command. A **polite request** is a command or suggestion phrased as a request. Such a request asks the reader to perform a specific action instead of responding with a *yes* or *no*.

> Will you be sure to tell the customer that her return will be processed soon. (Polite request)

> May I suggest that you prepare an e-portfolio to showcase your work. (Polite suggestion)

> Could you please refrain from texting during the meeting. (Polite command)

If you are uncomfortable using a period at the end of a polite request, rephrase the sentence so that it is a statement:

> Be sure to tell the customer that her return will be processed soon. (Polite request rephrased as a statement)

> You should prepare an e-portfolio to showcase your work. (Polite request rephrased as a statement)

> Please refrain from texting during the meeting. (Polite request rephrased as a statement)

To Punctuate Abbreviations

Abbreviations are shortened versions of words. Because of their inconsistencies, abbreviations present problems to writers. The following suggestions will help you organize certain groups of abbreviations and provide many models. In studying these models, note the spacing, capitalization, and use of periods. For a more thorough list of acceptable abbreviations, consult an up-to-date reference manual or dictionary.

Lowercase Abbreviations

Use periods after most abbreviations beginning with lowercase letters. Notice that the internal periods are not followed by spaces.

a.m. (ante meridiem)	i.e. (that is)	etc. (et cetera)
p.m. (post meridiem)	e.g. (for example)	ft. (foot or feet)
misc. (miscellaneous)	yd. (yard or yards)	in. (inch or inches)

Exceptions: mph (miles per hour), mpg (miles per gallon), wpm (words per minute), rpm (rotations per minute), mm (millimeter), and kg (kilogram).

Upper- and Lowercase Abbreviations

Use periods for most abbreviations containing capital and lowercase letters.

Dr. (Doctor)	Esq. (Esquire)	Mr. (Mister)
Ms. (blend of Miss and Mrs.)	No. (number)	Sat. (Saturday)

Exceptions: Academic degrees such as AA (associate of arts), BS (bachelor of science), MBA (master of business administration), PhD (doctor of philosophy), and EdD (doctor of education).

Uppercase Abbreviations

Use all capital letters without periods or internal spaces for the abbreviations of many business and nonprofit organizations, educational institutions, government agencies, radio and television stations, professional organizations, sports

Trivia Tidbit

Did you ever wonder what the dot over the lowercase letters *i* and *j* is called? This dot is called a *tittle*.

Study Tip

Use abbreviations only when you know that your reader will understand what they stand for. If necessary, define an abbreviation the first time you use it in a document.

Study Tip

Many shortened versions of words are not abbreviations and, therefore, should not be followed by a period. Examples include *alum, chemo, demo, expo, fax, info, lab, memo, prep, repo, sync,* and *vet.*

associations, job titles, professional designations, stock symbols, airport codes, and business and technology terms.

NYSE (New York Stock Exchange)	ARF (Animal Rescue Foundation)
UGA (University of Georgia)	RIT (Rochester Institute of Technology)
DOL (Department of Labor)	SBA (Small Business Administration)
NPR (National Public Radio)	PBS (Public Broadcasting Service)
ABA (American Bar Association)	IIA (Institute of Internal Auditors)
MLB (Major League Baseball)	NCAA (National Collegiate Athletic Association)
CEO (chief executive officer)	CFO (chief financial officer)
RN (registered nurse)	CPA (certified public accountant)
GOOG (Google NASDAQ stock symbol)	LUV (Southwest Airlines NYSE stock symbol)
MCO (Orlando International airport code)	CNX (Chiang Mai International airport code)
VAT (value-added tax)	IPO (initial public offering)
LLC (limited-liability company)	GPS (global positioning system)

Exceptions: Periods and spaces are included when initials are used for a person's first and middle names (*Mr. J. A. Jones*). In addition, some abbreviations have two forms (*c.o.d., COD* [collect on delivery], *f.o.b., FOB* [free on board]).

Geographic Abbreviations

Use all capital letters without periods or internal spaces for the abbreviations of geographical areas, two-letter state abbreviations, and Canadian province abbreviations. For a complete list of two-letter state and Canadian province abbreviations, consult Figure C.5 in Appendix C.

USA (United States of America)	UK (United Kingdom)
AR (Arkansas)	AK (Alaska)
NS (Nova Scotia)	NL (Newfoundland)

Exception: In business writing use periods when using the abbreviation for *United States* as an adjective (*U.S. Postal Service, U.S. currency*).

To Punctuate Numerals

For a monetary sum, use a period (decimal point) to separate dollars from cents.

Payments of $13.92 and $28.67 were made from our petty cash fund.

Use a period (decimal point) to mark a decimal fraction.

Approximately 67.8 percent of eligible voters voted in Tuesday's election.

Spacing After Periods

When typewriters and printers used monospaced fonts, typists were taught to leave two spaces after a period at the end of a sentence. Two spaces provided a strong visual break so that the end of the sentence was apparent. With modern proportional fonts, however, this added visual break is unnecessary. Most typists leave only one space after terminal periods today. A two-space break is equally acceptable when used consistently throughout or when misreading may occur. For example, when abbreviations appear at the end of one sentence and the beginning of the next, two spaces prevent confusion. (*Your appointment is at 2 p.m. Dr. Awbrey will see you then.*) The same spacing guidelines you use for periods apply to other end punctuation (question marks and exclamation marks), which will be discussed in the next two sections.

Uses for the Question Mark

The question mark punctuates direct questions and questions added to statements.

To Punctuate Direct Questions

Use a question mark at the end of a direct question. A **direct question** requires an answer.

> When will the CEO make her decision about layoffs?

> Has the music industry been successful in stopping illegal file sharers?

To Punctuate Questions Added to Statements

Place a question mark after a question that is added to the end of a statement. Use a comma to separate the statement from the question.

> We have a productive team, don't we?

> He's the best one for the position, don't you think?

To Indicate Doubt

A question mark within parentheses may be used to indicate a degree of doubt about some aspect of a statement. Include a space before the opening parenthesis; also include a space after the closing parenthesis if the question mark appears in the middle of a sentence.

> Facebook finally went public (2012?) after years of speculation.

> Mark Zuckerberg created Facebook during his sophomore year at Harvard (2004?).

Uses for the Exclamation Mark

Because the exclamation mark expresses strong emotion, business and professional writers use it sparingly.

Trivia Tidbit

American author F. Scott Fitzgerald once said, "Cut out all the exclamation points. An exclamation point is like laughing at your own joke."

To Express Strong Emotion

After a word, phrase, clause, or sentence expressing strong emotion, use an exclamation mark.

> Wow! I honestly didn't think she had it in her.

> How incredible! Our sales increased almost 50 percent this quarter.

> What a work of art!

Do not use an exclamation mark after mild interjections, such as *oh* and *well*.

> Oh, now I see what you mean.

> Well, I guess we have to tell him about the error we found.

Now complete the reinforcement exercises for Level 1.

Uses for the Hyphen

Hyphens are used to form compound words, words with prefixes, and compound numbers. The hyphen can also be used to divide a word over two lines.

To Form Compound Words

Use the hyphen to form compound nouns, verbs, and adjectives.

> Our company is moving to a new *high-rise* in San Francisco's Financial District. (Compound noun)
>
> I didn't mean to *second-guess* you during today's meeting. (Compound verb)
>
> She is hoping to get a *full-time* job. (Compound adjective with permanent hyphenation)
>
> We offer a *money-back* guarantee. (Compound adjective with temporary hyphenation)
>
> Depending on how long they've been with the company, employees are given *two-* or *four-week* vacations. (Compound adjective with common ending *week*)

To Form Words With Prefixes

Use hyphens in words with prefixes such as *ex, self,* or *quasi.*

> The keynote speaker was *ex-President* Clinton.
>
> Employers are impressed by applicants who exhibit strong *self-esteem.*
>
> Anna is our *quasi-official* leader.

Do not hyphenate most words that begin with prefixes such as *anti, bi, co, extra, inter, micro, mini, multi, mid, non, over, under, post, pre, re, semi,* or *un* unless the unhyphenated word could be confused with another word. Also use a hyphen when the prefix is added to a word that starts with a capital (*anti-American, non-European*).

> It is *unnerving* that so many local schools are *underfunded.*
>
> My *coworkers* have *rewritten* the brochure about our *multiuse* facilities.
>
> More *nondiscriminatory* laws should be passed.
>
> When her employment contract expires, Brenda plans to *re-sign.* (Hyphenate to avoid confusing with *resign.*)

When writing family titles, hyphenate words that contain *ex, great,* or *in-law.* Do not hyphenate words that contain *step, half,* or *grand.*

> Her *ex-husband* still keeps in touch with her *grandparents.*
>
> Your *mother-in-law* looks just like her *great-aunt.*
>
> Is he your *stepbrother* or your *half brother*?

To Form Compound Numbers

Use the hyphen in compound numbers between twenty-one and ninety-nine when written in word form. Number expression will be covered in detail in Chapter 14.

> *Fifty-three* applicants applied for the position online.

Study Tip

Compound words can be written as solid words (*stockbroker*), written as separate words (*child care*), or hyphenated (*air-conditioning*). In addition, these style rules change regularly. To decide how to write a compound word, consult an up-to-date dictionary or reference manual.

Study Tip

As you learned in Chapter 7, do not hyphenate compound adjectives that come after the nouns they are describing unless they have permanent hyphenation.

To Divide a Word Over Two Lines

Use a hyphen when you must divide a word over two lines. However, because divided words can be confusing, use this technique sparingly.

> We hope to get a response by late tomorrow from Steven Lawrence, super-intendent of the Mt. Diablo School District.

Uses for the Dash

Do not confuse the hyphen with the dash. The dash is sometimes used in place of a comma, semicolon, colon, or parentheses to show greater emphasis. As an emphatic punctuation mark, however, the dash loses effectiveness when it is overused. With a word processor, you create a dash by typing two hyphens with no space before, between, or after the hyphens. In printed or desktop-published material, a dash appears as a solid line that is longer than a hyphen (an *em* dash). Most word processors will automatically convert two hyphens to an *em* dash. Study the following suggestions for and illustrations of appropriate uses of the dash.

To Set Off Parenthetical Elements and Appositives

Within a sentence, parenthetical elements and appositives are usually set off by commas. If, however, the parenthetical element or appositive itself contains internal commas, use dashes (or parentheses) to set it off.

> Sources of raw materials—farming, mining, fishing, and forestry—are all dependent on energy.

> Four research assistants—Debbie Vanore, Richard Earl, Shama Khan, and Ryan Quinlan—received end-of-year bonuses for outstanding service.

You can place any parenthetical element between dashes instead of commas. However, remember that doing so will emphasize the parenthetical element.

> All employees—and that includes Ann Patterson—must work overtime this weekend.

To Indicate an Interruption or Afterthought

An interruption or abrupt change of thought or afterthought may be separated from the rest of a sentence by a dash. However, sentences with abrupt changes of thought or with appended afterthoughts can usually be improved through rewriting.

> We will refund your full purchase price—no questions asked—if you are not completely satisfied. (Interruption of thought)

> Let's meet Friday to discuss your idea—no, let's make it Thursday instead. (Abrupt change of thought)

To Set Off a Summarizing Statement

Use a dash (not a colon) to separate an introductory list from a summarizing statement.

> Flexibility, initiative, intelligence—these are the qualities we seek in all employees.

> Facebook, Twitter, YouTube, Pinterest—these are some of the most frequently used social media tools.

Study Tip

The dash tends to be overused in writing today. To make your writing look more professional, use the dash only when necessary, and never use more than two dashes in a sentence.

Study Tip

Don't confuse a hyphen with a dash. These two punctuation marks serve different purposes.

To Attribute a Quotation

Place a dash between a quotation and its source. When using a dash this way, the attribution usually appears on a separate line, aligned at the right with the quote.

> Your work is going to fill a large part of your life, and the only way to be truly satisfied is to do what you believe is great work. And the only way to do great work is to love what you do. If you haven't found it yet, keep looking.
>
> —Steve Jobs

Uses for Parentheses

Parentheses are generally used in pairs. Parentheses can be used to enclose a complete sentence or to enclose a word or expression within a sentence. This section covers guidelines for using parentheses correctly.

To Set Off Nonessential Sentence Elements

Generally, nonessential sentence elements may be punctuated as follows: (a) with commas, to make the lightest possible break in the normal flow of a sentence; (b) with dashes, to emphasize the enclosed material; and (c) with parentheses, to de-emphasize the enclosed material.

> Figure 17, which appears on page 9, clearly illustrates the process. (Normal punctuation)
>
> Figure 17—which appears on page 9—clearly illustrates the process. (Dashes emphasize the enclosed material.)
>
> Figure 17 (which appears on page 9) clearly illustrates the process. (Parentheses de-emphasize the enclosed material.)

Explanations, references, and directions are often enclosed in parentheses.

> Our café's current hours (7 a.m. to 3 p.m.) will be extended soon (to 6 p.m.).
>
> A small apartment in Tokyo, Japan, rents for about 208,860 yen ($2,500) per month.
>
> Our management team (see their résumés in Appendix A) is highly skilled.

To Show Numerals and Enclose Enumerated Items

In legal documents and contracts, numerals may appear in both word and figure form. Parentheses enclose the figures. However, business writers are encouraged not to use this wordy technique for most messages.

> Your contract states that the final installment payment is due in sixty (60) days.

When using numbers or letters to enumerate lists within sentences, enclose the numbers or letters in parentheses. Use letters for items that have no particular order. Use numbers for items that suggest a sequence.

> The Transportation Security Administration (TSA) has offered several tips for getting through airport security more quickly, including (a) packing coats and jackets in checked luggage, (b) wearing shoes that are easy to remove, and (c) having boarding passes and IDs ready.
>
> To pay your bill online, (1) log onto our secure website, (2) click the **Pay Bill** link, (3) select the bill you want to pay, (4) input the amount you want to pay, (5) select the date on which you want to make payment, (6) click the **Pay** button, and (7) click the **Confirm** button.

Punctuating Around Parentheses

If the material enclosed by parentheses is embedded within another sentence, a question mark or exclamation mark may be used where normally expected. Do not, however, use a period after a statement embedded within another sentence.

> We uploaded several files to Dropbox (have you tried it?) last night.

> Testimonials (see example on page 11) personalize financial reports.

If the material enclosed by parentheses is not embedded in another sentence, use whatever punctuation is required.

> Report writers must document all references. (See Appendix A for a guide to current documentation formats.)

In sentences involving expressions within parentheses, a comma, semicolon, or colon that would normally occupy the position occupied by the second parenthesis is then placed after that parenthesis.

> When we finalize the contract (on March 3), we can begin the remodel. (Comma follows the closing parenthesis.)

> Your tax return was received before the deadline (April 15); however, you did not report all income. (Semicolon follows the closing parenthesis.)

Now complete the reinforcement exercises for Level 2.

LEVEL 3

Uses for Quotation Marks

Guidelines for using quotation marks to enclose direct quotations, in quotations within quotations, and for literary titles are covered in this section. You will also learn how to place other punctuation in relation to quotation marks.

To Enclose Direct Quotations

Double quotation marks are used to enclose direct quotations. Unless the exact words of a writer or speaker are being repeated, however, do not use quotation marks.

> "A little knowledge that acts is worth infinitely more than much knowledge that is idle," said Kahlil Gibran. (Direct quotation enclosed)

> Hillary Clinton said that voting is every citizen's most precious right. (Indirect quotation requires no quotation marks.)

Capitalize only the first word of a direct quotation.

> "The human race has only one really effective weapon," said Mark Twain, "and that is laughter." (Do not capitalize *and*.)

Single quotation marks (apostrophes on most keyboards) are used to enclose quoted passages cited within quoted passages.

> Delores Tomlin remarked, "In business writing I totally agree with Aristotle, who said, 'A good style must, first of all, be clear.'" (Single quotation marks within double quotation marks)

Study Tip

Be careful that you don't overuse quotation marks. Enclose words in quotation marks only when you have a valid reason for doing so.

To Enclose Titles

Quotation marks are used to enclose the titles of subdivisions of literary and artistic works, such as magazine and newspaper articles, short stories, chapters of books, episodes of television shows, poems, lectures, paintings, sculptures, and songs. However, italics (or underscores) are used to enclose the titles of complete works, such as the names of books, magazines, pamphlets, movies, television series, music albums, and newspapers (see next section).

> I loved the *Wall Street Journal* article titled "Why Does 'Everybody' Now Put 'Everything' in Quotation Marks?"

> In the episode of *The Office* titled "Diversity Day," the boss, played by Steve Carell, managed to offend everyone.

Punctuating Around Quotation Marks

Periods and commas are always placed inside closing quotation marks, whether single or double.

> Katie Wheeler remarked, "I can't believe that during the meeting Allison said, 'I'm fed up with everything.'"

> The article is titled "Work Wear," but I don't have a copy.

Semicolons and colons are, on the other hand, always placed outside closing quotation marks.

> Our contract stipulated that "both parties must accept arbitration as binding"; therefore, the decision reached by the arbitrators is final.

> Three dates have been scheduled for the seminar called "Protecting Customers' Identities": April 1, May 3, and June 5.

Question marks and exclamation marks may go inside or outside closing quotation marks, as determined by the form of the quotation.

> Chris Stefanetti asked, "Have you heard my latest recording?" (Quotation is a question.)

> "The next time we catch you texting during the meeting," fumed the CEO, "we will ask you to leave!" (Quotation is an exclamation.)

> Do you know who it was who said, "You've got to love what you do to really make things happen"? (Incorporating sentence asks a question; the quotation does not.)

> When did the supervisor say, "Who is able to work overtime this weekend?" (Both the incorporating sentence and the quotation are questions. Use only one question mark inside the quotation marks.)

Uses for Italics

Guidelines for using italics to distinguish titles and special words are covered in this section.

To Distinguish Titles

Italics are normally used for titles of books, magazines, pamphlets, newspapers, movies, television shows, music albums, plays, musicals, and other complete published or artistic works that contain subdivisions.

> *The Idea Factory*, a book about the invention of the transistor, was favorably reviewed in *The Wall Street Journal*. (Book title, newspaper title)

Trivia Tidbit

Keeping periods and commas inside quotation marks is an American style that stems from the days of hot type. Periods and commas tended to break off at the ends of lines. Printers set them inside to make sturdier lines. Once established, this practice continued in the United States—but not in Britain.

Trivia Tidbit

Italic type was invented in the 15th century in Italy for use in courts.

The Hunger Games was one of the most popular movies of 2012 according to an article in *Entertainment Weekly*. (Movie title, magazine title)

Taylor Swift performed a song from *Speak Now* on *Saturday Night Live*. (Album title, television show title)

For Short Expressions, Words Being Defined, and Special Words

Jargon, slang, words used in a special sense such as humor or irony, and words following *stamped* or *marked* are usually italicized, although some writers enclose these words in quotation marks. Both techniques are shown here.

Computer criminals are often called *hackers* (OR "hackers"). (Jargon)

My teenager said that the film *The Hunger Games* is *sick* (OR "sick"). (Slang)

Orrin claimed he was *too ill* (OR "too ill") to come to work yesterday. (Irony)

The package was stamped *Fragile*. (OR . . . was stamped "Fragile.") (Words following *stamped*)

Quotation marks are used to enclose specific definitions of words or expressions. The word or expression being defined is italicized. Words and expressions used in a special sense can also be italicized.

The term *tweet* refers to "a post made on the microblogging site Twitter."

Accountants use the term *gross margin* to indicate "the difference between production costs and sales revenue."

In addition, words under discussion in a sentence and words used as nouns are italicized.

Do you think she should have used the phrase *in the interest of justice* in her message? (Words under discussion)

Two of the most frequently misspelled words are *definitely* and *privilege*. (Words used as nouns)

Uses for Brackets

Within quotations, brackets are used by writers to enclose their own inserted remarks. Such remarks may be corrective, illustrative, or explanatory. Brackets are also used within quotations to enclose the word *sic*, which means "thus" or "so." This Latin form is used to emphasize the fact that an error obvious to all actually appears thus in the quoted material.

"A nautical mile," reported Chris Day, "is equal to 6,080 feet [1,853.184 meters]."

"The company's reorganization program," wrote President Theodore Bailey, "will have its greatest affect [sic] on our immediate sales."

Uses for the Apostrophe

As you have already learned, the apostrophe is used to form possessives and contractions. The apostrophe can also be used to take the place of omitted letters and as a symbol for *feet*. The guidelines for these uses are covered in this section.

Trivia Tidbit

What we call *parentheses* in the United States are called *round brackets* in Great Britain.

Trivia Tidbit

Some last names, such as *O'Malley* and *D'Angelo*, contain apostrophes. Most last names with apostrophes have Irish, French, Italian, and African roots.

To Form Noun Possessives

In Chapter 3 you learned that the apostrophe can be used to make common and proper nouns possessive. Do not use the apostrophe to make nouns plural.

> *Today's* college students face many challenges. (Notice that no apostrophes are used with the plural words *students* and *challenges*.)

> The *companies'* attorneys are evaluating the merger agreement. (Notice that *companies'* is a plural word showing possession, whereas *attorneys* is merely plural.)

To Form Contractions

Chapter 4 illustrated how to use the apostrophe to form contractions, which are shortened forms of subjects and verbs. Don't confuse contractions with pronouns.

> *It's* too early to determine whether *we'll* make a profit this year. (*It's* represents *it is; we'll* represents *we will.*)

> *You're* invited to attend a special presale next week. (*You're* represents *you are.*)

> *I've* learned that *there's* a new restaurant opening next door. (*I've* represents *I have; there's* represents *there is.*)

> *You'd* be happier if you *didn't* complain so much. (*You'd* represents *You would; didn't* represents *did not.*)

To Take the Place of Omitted Letters or Figures

The apostrophe can be used to take the place of omitted letters or figures. This is especially common when expressing a year.

> Music, films, and fashions of the *'70s* are suddenly popular again.

> Job prospects for the class of *'15* look promising.

> He stops by *Dunkin' Donuts* on his way to work every morning.

To Serve as the Symbol for *feet*

In technical documents the apostrophe can be used as the symbol for *feet.* (A quotation mark is used as the symbol for inches.)

> The conference room is 14' × 16'. (14 feet by 16 feet)

> Many people are surprised to learn that Tom Cruise is only 5' 7" because he has such screen presence. (5 feet 7 inches)

Now complete the reinforcement exercises for Level 3.

Dr. Guffey   Professor Seefer

Q: Is there some rule about putting periods in organization names that are abbreviated? For example, does *IBM* have periods?

A: When the names of well-known business, educational, governmental, labor, and other organizations or agencies are abbreviated, periods are normally not used to separate the letters. Thus, no periods would appear in IBM, FBI, UCLA, AFL-CIO, YWCA, or AMA. The names of radio and television stations and networks are also written without periods: Station WJR, KNX-FM, PBS, WABC-TV. In addition, geographical abbreviations generally do not require periods: USA, UK, ROC. Finally, the two-letter state abbreviations recommended by the U.S. Postal Service require no periods: NY, OH, CA, MI, NJ, OR, MA, and so on.

Q: What is the order of college degrees, and which ones are capitalized?

A: Two kinds of undergraduate degrees are commonly awarded: the associate's degree, a two-year degree; and the bachelor's degree, a four-year degree. A variety of graduate degrees exist. The most frequently awarded are the master's degree and the doctorate. Notice that these words (*associate's*, *bachelor's*, and *master's*) are written using the possessive case. In addition, Merriam-Webster dictionaries do not capitalize the names of degrees: *associate of arts degree, bachelor of science, master of arts, doctor of philosophy*. However, when used with an individual's name, the abbreviations for degrees are capitalized and written without periods: *Craig Bjurstrom, MA; Rhianna Landini, PhD*.

Q: I never know how to write *part time*. Is it always hyphenated?

A: The dictionary shows all of its uses to be hyphenated. *She was a part-time employee* (used as an adjective). *He worked part-time* (used as an adverb). The adjective *full-time* also has permanent hyphenation.

Q: Does *Ms.* have a period after it? Should I use this title for all women in business today?

A: *Ms.* is probably a blend of *Miss* and *Mrs.* It is written with a period following it. Some women in business prefer to use *Ms.*, presumably because it is a title equal to *Mr.* Neither title reveals one's marital status. It is always wise, if possible, to determine the preference of the individual. However, when in doubt, use the personal title *Ms.* in business correspondence.

Q: I have a phone extension at work, and I often want to tell people to call me at this extension. Can I abbreviate the word *extension*? If so, what is the proper abbreviation?

A: The abbreviation for *extension* is *Ext.* Notice that the abbreviation is capitalized and ends with a period. When you use this abbreviation in conjunction with a phone number, place a comma before and after. (*To reserve your spot, please call me at 685-1230, Ext. 2306, before November 30.*)

Q: We are having an argument in our office about abbreviations. Can *department* be abbreviated *dep't*? How about *manufacturing* as *mf'g*?

A: In informal writing or when space is limited, words may be contracted or abbreviated. If a conventional abbreviation for a word exists, use it instead of a contracted form. Abbreviations are simpler to write and easier to read. For example, use *dept.* instead of *dep't*; use *natl.* instead of *nat'l*; use *cont.* instead of *cont'd*. Other accepted abbreviations are *ins.* for *insurance; mfg.* for *manufacturing; mgr.* for *manager;* and *mdse.* for *merchandise.* Notice that all abbreviations made up of lowercase letters end with periods.

Q: Where should the word *sic* be placed when it is used?

A: *Sic* means "thus" or "so stated," and it is properly placed immediately following the word or phrase to which it refers. For example, *The kidnappers placed a newspaper advertisement that read "Call Monna [sic] Lisa." Sic* is used within a quotation to indicate that a quoted word or phrase, though inaccurately spelled or used, appeared thus in the original. *Sic* is italicized and placed within brackets.

Q: I've looked in the dictionary but I'm still unsure about whether to hyphenate *copilot.*

A: The hyphen is no longer used in most words beginning with the prefix *co (coauthor, cocounsel, codesign, cofeature, cohead, copilot, costar, cowrite*). Only a few words retain the hyphen (*co-official, co-owner, co-organizer*). Check your dictionary for usage. In reading your dictionary, notice that centered periods are used to indicate syllables (*co•work•er*); hyphens are used to show hyphenated syllables (*co-own*).

Q: I sometimes see three periods in a row in documents I'm reading and in book and film reviews. Does this use of periods have a name? When is this type of punctuation used?

A: A series of three periods, with spaces before, between, and after each period, is called an *ellipsis* (. . .). Ellipses are usually used to show that information has been left out of quoted material. (*Roger Ebert's review of* Chicago *includes these words: "By filming it in its own spirit, by making it frankly a stagy song-and-dance revue . . . the movie is big, brassy fun."*) The ellipsis shows that this is not Roger Ebert's complete quote and that words have been omitted between *revue* and *the.*

Q: Should I use *complimentary* or *complementary* to describe free tickets?

A: Use *complimentary*, which can mean "containing a compliment, favorable, or free" (*the dinner came with complimentary wine; he made a complimentary remark*). *Complementary* means "completing or making perfect." (*The online edition of* The Wall Street Journal *is the perfect complement to your print subscription. The complementary colors enhanced the room.*) An easy way to remember *compliment* is by thinking "*I* like to receive a compl*i*ment."

SPOT THE Blooper

Using the skills you are learning in this class, try to identify why the following items are bloopers. Consult your textbook, dictionary, or reference manual as needed. To see if you recognized the blooper, go to **www.cengagebrain.com** and use your access code to see the Spot the Blooper key.

Blooper 1: A woman picketing Coca-Cola's annual stockholders' meeting holds a sign that says "Coca-Cola Leave's a Bad Taste for Working Families."

Blooper 2: In a margin ad on Facebook: "Take advantage of dumb sellers mistakes now! Thousands of items are listed on eBay with titles containing speling mistake's." [Did you spot three errors?]

Blooper 3: From *Titanic: The Artifact Exhibit*: "The iceberg's stone-hard spur punctures Titanic's hull in six of it's forward compartments."

Blooper 4: Ad for Saks Fifth Avenue published in *The New York Times* that features a T-shirt with this slogan: "Saks is a girls best friend."

Blooper 5: A gardening article about the dwarf amaryllis, published in *Florida Today*: "They are an ideal compliment to the larger blooming amaryllis or can be stunning as a mass planting of their own."

Blooper 6: At the bottom of all four pages of the menu at PizzaGram Plus in Guilderland, New York: "Our food is cooked to order. We appreciate your patients."

Blooper 7: A sign at a cafeteria salad bar in Atlanta: "These item's are sold by weight."

Blooper 8: Street sign located in neighborhoods throughout Cape Cod: "Slow Children At Play." [How could punctuation change the meaning of this sign?]

Blooper 9: Sign in a high school in California intended to honor its mascot: "We are the Scots who could be prouder." [Could proper punctuation have changed this message?]

Blooper 10: From a sales brochure for New Life Health Center: "We have every day low prices on hundreds of products. Here's a few to peak your interest!" [Can you spot three errors?]

12

Reinforcement Exercises

A. Self-Check. End Punctuation. In the spaces provided after each sentence, indicate whether a period, question mark, or exclamation mark is needed as end punctuation. Write the correct end punctuation mark in the space provided. If no additional punctuation is required, write *C*.

Example: Could you please drop by my office after lunch   .

1. Will you be sure to sign this form by Friday   _____

2. What an incredible idea   _____

3. The company banquet is on May 9, isn't it   _____

4. Has anyone checked the UPS website to see whether our package was delivered   _____

5. The NYSE stock symbol for Harley-Davidson, Inc., is HOG   _____

6. Wow! How motivating   _____

7. Warren asked whether our company will start using the digital marketing services offered by Ciber, Inc   _____

8. Did Tracy sign out with security when she left at 5 p.m.   _____

9. I wonder whether he has checked with the three credit reporting bureaus to find out whether his credit card has been used fraudulently   _____

10. Dr. Helen C. Haitz and Emile Brault, PhD, will appear on TV at 2 p.m., EST.   _____

Check your answers below.

B. Periods, Question Marks, and Exclamation Marks. Write the letter of the correctly punctuated sentence.

11. a. The C.P.A. exam will take place on Saturday at 8 am.
    b. The CPA exam will take place on Saturday at 8 a.m.
    c. The CPA exam will take place on Saturday at 8 AM.   _____

12. a. Can you please forward the e-mail message to me?
    b. Can you, please, forward the e-mail message to me?
    c. Can you please forward the e-mail message to me.   _____

13. a. Gretchen asked whether Google's original name was Googol.
    b. Gretchen asked whether Google's original name was Googol?
    c. Gretchen asked, whether Google's original name was Googol.   _____

14. a. Did our CFO interview Ms. E. W. Rasheen for the C.P.A. position?
    b. Did our C.F.O. interview Ms. E. W. Rasheen for the C.P.A. position?
    c. Did our CFO interview Ms. E. W. Rasheen for the CPA position?   _____

15. a. Many more MBA programs are available in the USA than in the UK.
    b. Many more M.B.A. programs are available in the U.S.A. than in the U.K.
    c. Many more M.B.A. programs are available in the USA than in the UK.   _____

1. Friday. 2. idea! 3. it? 4. delivered? 5. HOG. 6. motivating! 7. Inc. 8. 5 p.m.? 9. fraudulently. 10. C.

16. a. Advertisements will air on the following radio stations: KFOG, KGO, and KCSM.
    b. Advertisements will air on the following radio stations: K.F.O.G., K.G.O., and K.C.S.M.
    c. Advertisements will air on the following radio stations; KFOG, KGO, and KCSM.

    _____

17. a. The No. 1 official at the E.P.A. has a B.S. in biology from Capital University.
    b. The No. 1 official at the EPA has a BS in biology from Capital University.
    c. The No 1 official at the EPA has a B.S. in biology from Capital University.

    _____

18. a. The recipient's address is 5 Sierra Drive, Rochester, N.Y. 14616.
    b. The recipient's address is 5 Sierra Drive, Rochester, NY 14616.
    c. The recipient's address is 5 Sierra Drive, Rochester, Ny. 14616.

    _____

19. a. Elizabeth wonders whether organic produce is worth the extra cost?
    b. Elizabeth wonders whether organic produce is worth the extra cost.
    c. Elizabeth wonders, whether organic produce is worth the extra cost?

    _____

20. a. Have you ever wondered why GEEK is the stock symbol for Internet America, Inc.?
    b. Have you ever wondered why GEEK is the stock symbol for Internet America, Inc.
    c. Have you ever wondered why G.E.E.K. is the stock symbol for Internet America, Inc.?

    _____

C. **Punctuation.** Write the letter of the correctly punctuated sentence in the space provided. Use a dictionary or reference manual as needed.

21. a. Will you please meet Susan B. Smith, PhD, at F.H.A. headquarters in Washington, DC?
    b. Will you please meet Susan B. Smith, Ph.D., at FHA headquarters in Washington, DC.
    c. Will you please meet Susan B. Smith, PhD, at FHA headquarters in Washington, DC.

    _____

22. a. Dr. Jacqueline A. Young will travel from the U.S.A. to the U.K. in 2016.
    b. Dr. Jacqueline A. Young will travel from the USA to the UK in 2016.
    c. Dr Jacqueline A Young will travel from the USA to the UK in 2016.

    _____

23. a. You did change your PIN as the bank requested, didn't you?
    b. You did change your P.I.N. as the bank requested, didn't you?
    c. You did change your PIN as the bank requested, didn't you.

    _____

24. a. Reece Soltani, M.B.A., was recognized for her work with the S.E.C.
    b. Reece Soltani, M.B.A., was recognized for her work with the SEC.
    c. Reece Soltani, MBA, was recognized for her work with the SEC.

    _____

25. a. What a dilemma the latest S.E.C. regulations have created!
    b. What a dilemma the latest SEC regulations have created?
    c. What a dilemma the latest SEC regulations have created!

    _____

26. a. Deliver the signed contracts to Ms. C. M. Gigliotti before 6 p.m., EST.
    b. Deliver the signed contracts to Ms C. M. Gigliotti before 6 pm EST.
    c. Deliver the signed contracts to Ms. C. M. Gigliotti before 6 PM, EST.

    _____

27. a. Dan wondered whether he had earned enough units for his AA degree?
    b. Dan wondered whether he had earned enough units for his A.A .degree?
    c. Dan wondered whether he had earned enough units for his AA degree.

    _____

28. a. After completing his B.A. degree at U.S.C., Ben Lindsay transferred to U.G.A. and began working on his M.F.A.
  b. After completing his BA degree at USC, Ben Lindsay transferred to UGA and began working on his MFA.
  c. After completing his B.A. degree at USC Ben Lindsay transferred to UGA and began working on his M.F.A.

_____

29. a. Ms. J. S. Novak gave a rousing lecture about the passage of NAFTA.
  b. Ms J. S. Novak gave a rousing lecture about the passage of NAFTA
  c. Ms. J. S. Novak gave a rousing lecture about the passage of N.A.F.T.A.

_____

30. a. Has the erroneous charge of $45.95 been removed from my account?
  b. Has the erroneous charge of $45.95 been removed from my account.
  c. Has the erroneous charge of $45,95 been removed from my account!

_____

LEVEL 2

A. Self-Check. Punctuation. Write the letter of the correctly punctuated sentence in the space provided. Use a dictionary or reference manual as needed.

31. a. Twenty four DVC business students will compete in the Phi Beta Lambda (PBL) state leadership conference.
  b. Twenty-four DVC business students will compete in the Phi Beta Lambda (PBL) state leadership conference.
  c. Twenty four D.V.C. business students will compete in the Phi Beta Lambda (P.B.L.) state leadership conference.

_____

32. a. Many of my coworkers are bilingual, and some can even speak three languages.
  b. Many of my co-workers are bi-lingual, and some can even speak three languages.
  c. Many of my coworkers are bi-lingual, and some can even speak three languages.

_____

33. a. Paul Pogranichny scored a perfect 800 (can you believe it) on the GMAT.
  b. Paul Pogranichny scored a perfect 800 (can you believe it?) on the GMAT.
  c. Paul Pogranichny scored a perfect 800 (can you believe it) on the G.M.A.T.?

_____

34. a. Mission statement, management bios, product description, operating budget: these should all appear in a company's business plan.
  b. Mission statement, management bios, product description, operating budget— these should all appear in a company's business plan.
  c. Mission statement, management bios, product description, operating budget; these should all appear in a company's business plan.

_____

35. a. "Leadership is doing what is right when no one is watching."—George Van Valkenburg
  b. "Leadership is doing what is right when no one is watching," George Van Valkenburg
  c. "Leadership is doing what is right when no one is watching": George Van Valkenburg

_____

36. (Emphasize the parenthetical element.)
  a. Currently our basic operating costs: rent, utilities, and salaries, are 18 percent higher than last year.
  b. Currently our basic operating costs (rent, utilities, and salaries) are 18 percent higher than last year.
  c. Currently our basic operating costs—rent, utilities, and salaries—are 18 percent higher than last year.

_____

37. a. Our operating revenue for 2014 (see Appendix A) exceeded our expectations.
    b. Our operating revenue for 2014, see Appendix A, exceeded our expectations.
    c. Our operating revenue for 2014: see Appendix A, exceeded our expectations. _____

38. a. We have only one day left this month for a reservation (May 27); however, the month of June is completely free.
    b. We have only one day left this month for a reservation; (May 27) however, the month of June is completely free.
    c. We have only one day left this month for a reservation (May 27;) however, the month of June is completely free. _____

39. (Emphasize.)
    a. Sales, sales, and more sales: that's what we need to succeed.
    b. Sales, sales, and more sales—that's what we need to succeed.
    c. Sales, sales, and more sales; that's what we need to succeed. _____

40. (De-emphasize.)
    a. Three categories of apps—games, weather, and social media—are most popular for downloading to smartphones.
    b. Three categories of apps, games, weather, and social media, are most popular for downloading to smartphones.
    c. Three categories of apps (games, weather, and social media) are most popular for downloading to smartphones. _____

Check your answers below.

B. Hyphenation. Select the correctly hyphenated word from each of the following pairs. Write its letter in the space provided. Use a current dictionary or reference manual if needed to determine whether a word should be hyphenated.

41. a. ex wife
    b. ex-wife _____

42. a. self-help
    b. self help _____

43. a. quasi public
    b. quasi-public _____

44. a. stepson
    b. step-son _____

45. a. great-grandmother
    b. great grandmother _____

46. a. half sister
    b. half-sister _____

47. a. anti-trust
    b. antitrust _____

48. a. extracurricular
    b. extra-curricular _____

49. a. interdenominational
    b. inter-denominational _____

50. a. multitalented
    b. multi-talented _____

51. a. semimonthly
    b. semi-monthly _____

52. a. bi-annual
    b. biannual _____

53. a. pre-existing
    b. preexisting _____

54. a. reread
    b. re-read _____

55. a. co-author
    b. coauthor _____

56. a. coorganizer
    b. co-organizer _____

57. a. under-utilized
    b. underutilized _____

58. a. noncontinuous
    b. non-continuous _____

59. a. non-Catholic
    b. nonCatholic _____

60. a. post-industrial
    b. postindustrial _____

31.b 32.a 33.b 34.b 35.a 36.c 37.a 38.a 39.b 40.c

C. Dashes and Parentheses. Insert dashes or parentheses in the following sentences. In the space provided after each sentence, write the number of punctuation marks you inserted. Count each parenthesis and each dash as a single mark.

Example: (Emphasize.) A CNBC analyst found that three S&P corporations—Diamond Offshore, Priceline.com, and Altera Corporation—keep large amounts of cash on their balance sheets.   2

61. (De-emphasize.) The cast of the Tony-award-winning production of *The Book of Mormon* have you seen the reviews? will offer free performances this summer. _____

62. "Those who insert themselves into as many channels as possible look set to capture the most value. They'll be the richest, the most successful, the most connected, capable, and influential among us. We're all publishers now, and the more we publish, the more valuable connections we'll make." Pete Cashmore, founder of Mashable _____

63. Social networking, gaming, microblogging, and livecasting these are just some of the many social media categories. _____

64. (De-emphasize.) Four companies Facebook, Google, Twitter, and LinkedIn are all preparing for intense competition in the social media sector. _____

65. (Emphasize.) Three of the biggest problems with social media privacy, overuse, and etiquette will be discussed at the Social Media Strategies Summit in Chicago. _____

66. HopStop, Google Sky Map, Doodledroid, Flixster these are just some of the many apps available for the Android smartphone. _____

67. (De-emphasize.) As soon as you are able to make an appointment try to do so before December 30, we will process your passport application. _____

68. Funds for the project will be released on the following dates see Section 12.3 of the original grant: January 1, March 14, and June 30. _____

69. (De-emphasize.) Editors of *Condé Nast Traveler* selected four cities Paris, Vienna, Oaxaca, and Los Angeles as the top cities in the world for tourists. _____

70. Your iPhone warranty contract will expire in sixty 60 days. _____

D. Writing Exercise. Commas, Dashes, and Parentheses. Using three different forms of punctuation, correctly punctuate the following sentence. In the space provided, explain how the three methods you have employed differ.

71. Numerous appeals all of which came from concerned parents prompted us to rethink the school closure.

72. Numerous appeals all of which came from concerned parents prompted us to rethink the school closure.

73. Numerous appeals all of which came from concerned parents prompted us to rethink the school closure.

Explanation: _____

_____

A. Self-Check. Punctuation. Indicate whether the following statements are true (*T*) or false (*F*).

74. Double quotation marks are used to enclose the exact words of a writer or speaker. _____

75. Names of books, magazines, television series, movies, and newspapers should be enclosed in quotation marks. _____

76. Periods and commas are always placed before closing quotation marks. _____

77. Brackets are used by writers to enclose their own remarks inserted into a quotation. _____

78. A quotation within a quotation is shown with single quotation marks. _____

79. Semicolons and colons are always placed after closing quotation marks. _____

80. Titles of articles, book chapters, poems, and songs should be italicized. _____

81. If both a quotation and its introductory sentence are questions, use a question mark before the closing quotation marks. _____

82. The word *sic* is used to show that a quotation is free of errors. _____

83. Use the apostrophe to take the place of omitted letters or figures. _____

Check your answers below.

B. Insert all necessary punctuation in the following sentences. Be especially alert for direct quotations.

Example: The term *cloud computing* means "to store, manage, and process data on the network of remote servers hosted on the Web."

84. The graduating class of 04 held its ten year reunion at a dude ranch

85. (De-emphasize.) Three American products Subway, the Ford Fiesta, and Google are extremely popular in the UK

86. Icelands favorite American products include Subway and Winston cigarettes

87. Debbi Fields, CEO of Mrs. Fields Cookies, said You do not have to be superhuman to do what you believe in

88. Whether you think you can or think you can't, said Henry Ford, you're right

89. The word *tethering* is a technology term that means to share the Internet connection of an Internet-capable smartphone or tablet computer with other devices

90. Kym Anderson's chapter titled Subsidies and Trade Barriers appears in the book *How to Spend $50 Billion to Make the World a Better Place*

91. Did the Roman philosopher Seneca really say Luck is what happens when preparation meets opportunity

92. In his speech the software billionaire said Our goal is to link the world irregardless [*sic*] of national boundaries and restrictions

93. Oprah Winfrey said that the best jobs are those we'd do even if we didn't get paid

94. Garth says he plans to do a lot of chillaxing during his vacation*

95. The postal worker said Shall I stamp your package *Fragile*

* "Chillaxing" could also be shown in italics.

74. T 75. F 76. T 77. T 78. T 79. T 80. F 81. T 82. F 83. T

96. Did you see the article titled Tax Bracket Magic in *Forbes*

97. The French expression *répondez s'il vous plaît* means respond if you please

98. Would you please send a current catalog to WellPoint, Inc

99. (Direct quotation.) "The man who does not read good books said Mark Twain has no advantage over the man who cannot read them

100. (Emphasize.) Three of the top contractors Kayler Construction, The Shaw Group, and Flatiron Construction Corporation submitted bids

101. In *BusinessWeek* I saw an article titled Can Speech Recognition Software Work in Mandarin

102. (De-emphasize.) Albert Einstein once said that only two things the universe and human stupidity are infinite

103. (Emphasize.) Albert Einstein once said that only two things the universe and human stupidity are infinite

C. **Writing Exercise. Using Punctuation Marks.** On a separate sheet, write a paragraph describing your ideal job. Try to include as many of the punctuation marks you have studied as possible. Include commas, semicolons, colons, periods, question marks, exclamation marks, hyphens, dashes, parentheses, quotation marks, italics, apostrophes, and possibly even brackets. Include a quotation from your boss. Make up the name of a book or article that you could publish about this job.

D. **FAQs About Business English Review.** In the space provided, write the correct answer choice.

104. Please call me at *(a) ext., (b) Ext., (c) Ext 359* if you have any questions. _____

105. Which informal sentence uses abbreviations correctly?
     a. *IndustryWeek* just selected Western Digital as the top mfg. firm.
     b. *IndustryWeek* just selected Western Digital as the top mf'g. firm. _____

106. One of the best ways to motivate employees is to *(a) compliment, (b) complement* their work. _____

107. White wine is the perfect *(a) compliment, (b) complement* to Thai food. _____

108. Companies often make acquisitions in order to acquire *(a) complimentary, (b) complementary* products. _____

109. Your comments about your neighbor's garden were very *(a) complimentary, (b) complementary.* _____

110. He gets along well with his *(a) co-workers, (b) co workers, (c) coworkers.* _____

111. This document outlines our *(a) co-ownership, (b) coownership, (c) co ownership* agreement. _____

112. She is looking for a *(a) part time, (b) part-time* job for the summer. _____

113. It's a pleasure to meet you, *(a) Ms., (b) Ms* Leonesio. _____

Chat About It ◀◀

Your instructor may assign any of the following topics for you to discuss in class, in an online chat room, or on an online discussion board. Some of the discussion topics may require outside research. You may also be asked to read and respond to postings made by your classmates.

Discussion Topic 1: You learned many punctuation rules in Chapters 10, 11, and 12. What tips and tricks do you have for remembering these rules? Share your techniques with your classmates.

Discussion Topic 2: One of the most misused punctuation marks is the quotation mark. For example, a restaurant in Walnut Creek, California, had a sign that read *Our customers are "special."* Stop-n-Shop advertised *"All Natural" Jumbo Sea Scallops.* And a sign in a New York health club locker room said *Thank you for keeping your "health" club as clean as possible.* What do these misused quotation marks communicate to readers? Why do you think this misuse occurs so often? Share your thoughts with your classmates. If possible, find an example of misused quotation marks to include.

Discussion Topic 3: Do you or does someone you know have a name that contains an apostrophe (*O'Leary, D'Artagnans*), a hyphen (*Al-Kurd, Boutros-Ghali*), or a space (*von Trapp, van der Heiden*)? Names like these can cause problems when using a computer to make appointments,

book reservations, or fill out an online form. Why? Because many computer programs don't know how to handle names that contain punctuation or spaces. Some programs block names like these; others mistake the punctuation for programming code; and some simply drop a portion of the name or close up the space. If you have a name like this, have you ever experienced problems? Share your experiences with your classmates. If you had a name like this, what would you do? Share your ideas.

Discussion Topic 4: Does proper punctuation matter in business? Should you use proper punctuation in all documents or just formal documents? What about using proper punctuation in e-mail messages? Share your opinions with your classmates.

Discussion Topic 5: Yes, there really is a National Punctuation Day! It takes place every year in September. Visit the site **http://www.nationalpunctuationday.com** and explore its contents. Share at least three interesting items you found on the site with your classmates.

Posttest

Use proofreading marks to insert necessary punctuation. Then compare your answers with those below.

1. The CFO wondered whether the decline in GDP would affect his company's stock price

2. You can have unlimited messaging for just $4999 a month

3. Ex president Jimmy Carter builds houses for Habitat for Humanity

4. Will you please send me a copy of the article titled Great Music Needs No Apology

5. When did you receive this message marked Confidential

6. The only guests who have not sent RSVPs are Ms Mendoza Mrs Gold and Mr Sims

7. Paying bills, making purchases, surfing the Web these are just some of the things people do with their smartphones

8. Did Dr Simanek say "I'd like to put you on an exercise program"

9. (De-emphasize.) Of the four best places to retire as selected by *U.S. News & World Report* Flagstaff, Boone, Traverse City, and Walnut Creek two are located in western states

10. (Emphasize.) The three most powerful women in business Irene Rosenfeld, Indra Nooyi, and Patricia Woertz all have business degrees from prestigious universities

1. price.   2. $49.99 month.   3. ex-president Humanity.   4. "Great Music Needs No Apology."   5. "Confidential"? OR *Confidential*?   6. Ms. Mendoza, Mrs. Gold, and Mr. Sims.   7. Web— smartphones.   8. Dr. say, "I'd program"?   9. (Flagstaff, Boone, Traverse City, and Walnut Creek), states.   10. —Irene Rosenfeld, Indra Nooyi, and Patricia Woertz— universities.

Begin your review by rereading Chapters 10–12. Then test your comprehension of those chapters by completing the exercises that follow. Compare your responses with the key at the end of the book.

LEVEL 1

Insert necessary punctuation in the following sentences. In the space at the right, indicate the number of punctuation marks you inserted. Write *C* if the sentence is correct.

1. Because employers want to hire the right people many conduct Web searches and check Facebook pages to discover more about candidates. _____

2. However employers conduct these Web searches they may find information that will eliminate a candidate. _____

3. Professor how can I clean up my "digital dirt" before I look for a job _____

4. A workshop will be held on Monday May 2 to teach students how to maintain a positive online presence. _____

5. Using a technology called "telesensing" smartphones can be used to take someone's pulse check on sick relatives and warn police about criminals hiding behind walls. _____

6. Tod Sizer a researcher at Bell Labs is developing ways to read GPS signals bounced off the body. _____

7. A jogger who has a smartphone with a telesensing chip will be able to monitor heart and respiration rates. _____

8. Nearby mobile phones however can cause interference with telesensing. _____

Select a, b, or c to indicate the correctly punctuated sentence.

9. a. The first multilevel garage was built in Chicago in 1910 the first parking meter was patented in 1935.
b. The first multilevel garage was built in Chicago in 1910, the first parking meter was patented in 1935.
c. The first multilevel garage was built in Chicago in 1910; the first parking meter was patented in 1935. _____

10. a. Cashless parking meters have been installed in Washington, DC, Atlanta, Georgia, and Somerville, Massachusetts.
b. Cashless parking meters have been installed in Washington, DC; Atlanta, Georgia; and Somerville, Massachusetts.
c. Cashless parking meters have been installed in: Washington, DC; Atlanta, Georgia; and Somerville, Massachusetts. _____

11.
a. San Francisco experiences severe parking problems; therefore, it is the first city to use sensors to alter meter prices depending on the number of available spaces.

b. San Francisco experiences severe parking problems, therefore, it is the first city to use sensors to alter meter prices depending on the number of available spaces.

c. San Francisco experiences severe parking problems; therefore it is the first city to use sensors to alter meter prices depending on the number of available spaces. _____

12.
a. Would you please upload the tax file to the IRS website.

b. Would you please upload the tax file to the I.R.S. website.

c. Would you please upload the tax file to the IRS website? _____

13.
a. We are astonished needless to say about the misstatement of financial data.

b. We are astonished, needless to say, about the misstatement of financial data.

c. We are astonished, needless to say; about the misstatement of financial data. _____

14.
a. She said she held AA and BS degrees didn't she?

b. She said she held A.A. and B.S. degrees, didn't she?

c. She said she held AA and BS degrees, didn't she? _____

• LEVEL 2 •

Select a, b, or c to indicate the correctly punctuated sentence.

15.
a. Wow! A total of 89.9 percent of the voters approved!

b. Wow, a total of 89 point 9 percent of the voters approved!

c. Wow. A total of 89.9 percent of the voters approved! _____

16.
a. Rent.com reported that the best three cities for newlyweds are: Austin, Texas, Raleigh/Durham, North Carolina, and Dallas, Texas.

b. Rent.com reported that the best three cities for newlyweds are: Austin, Texas; Raleigh/Durham, North Carolina; and Dallas, Texas.

c. Rent.com reported that the best three cities for newlyweds are Austin, Texas; Raleigh/Durham, North Carolina; and Dallas, Texas. _____

17.
a. In addition, the list included the following cities: Kansas City, Houston, and Denver.

b. In addition, the list included the following cities, Kansas City, Houston, and Denver.

c. In addition, the list included the following cities; Kansas City, Houston, and Denver. _____

18.
a. Meg Whitman said, "When people use your brand name as a verb, that is remarkable."

b. Meg Whitman said: "When people use your brand name as a verb, that is remarkable."

c. Meg Whitman said; "When people use your brand name as a verb, that is remarkable." _____

19.
a. Three of the best U.S. cities for single women: Boston, Austin, and Phoenix, are also state capitals.

b. Three of the best U.S. cities for single women—Boston, Austin, and Phoenix—are also state capitals.

c. Three of the best U.S. cities for single women, Boston, Austin, and Phoenix, are also state capitals. _____

20. a. Wal-Mart, Royal Dutch Shell, Exxon Mobile, BP, and Sinopec Group—these are the five largest companies in the world.

    b. Wal-Mart, Royal Dutch Shell, Exxon Mobil, BP, and Sinopec Group: these are the five largest companies in the world.

    c. Wal-Mart, Royal Dutch Shell, Exxon Mobil, BP, and Sinopec Group, these are the five largest companies in the world.

                                       _____

21. (Emphasize.)

    a. Three companies, Apple, Google, and Amazon.com, were ranked by *Forbes* as having the best reputations in the world.

    b. Three companies: Apple, Google, and Amazon.com, were ranked by *Forbes* as having the best reputations in the world.

    c. Three companies—Apple, Google, and Amazon.com—were ranked by *Forbes* as having the best reputations in the world.

                                       _____

22. a. Three of the largest U.S. charities are the Alzheimer's Association, the American Cancer Society, and the American Diabetes Association.

    b. Three of the largest U.S. charities are: the Alzheimer's Association, the American Cancer Society, and the American Diabetes Association.

    c. Three of the largest U.S. charities are—the Alzheimer's Association, the American Cancer Society, and the American Diabetes Association.

                                       _____

23. (De-emphasize.)

    a. A pilot project—refer to page 6 of the report—may help us justify the new system.

    b. A pilot project, refer to page 6 of the report, may help us justify the new system.

    c. A pilot project (refer to page 6 of the report) may help us justify the new system.

                                       _____

24. a. In 2012, Virgin Galactic, the first carrier to offer commercial space flights, made its maiden voyage.

    b. In 2012 Virgin Galactic, the first carrier to offer commercial space flights, made its maiden voyage.

    c. In 2012, Virgin Galactic, the first carrier to offer commercial space flights; made its maiden voyage.

                                       _____

25. a. If you would like to go to space on SpaceShipTwo, contact Virgin Galactic directly.

    b. If you would like to go to space on SpaceShipTwo contact Virgin Galactic directly.

    c. If you would like to go to space on SpaceShipTwo; contact Virgin Galactic, directly.

                                       _____

26. a. SpaceShipTwo is a beautiful futuristic piece of machinery.

    b. SpaceShipTwo is a beautiful, futuristic piece of machinery.

    c. SpaceShipTwo, is a beautiful futuristic piece of machinery.

                                       _____

27. a. Many celebrities plan to fly to space with Richard Branson, too.

    b. Many celebrities plan to fly to space with Richard Branson; too.

    c. Many celebrities plan to fly to space with Richard Branson too.

                                       _____

28. a. I work hard to increase the self-esteem of my coworkers.

    b. I work hard to increase the self-esteem of my co-workers.

    c. I work hard to increase the selfesteem of my coworkers.

                                       _____

Select a, b, or c to indicate the correctly punctuated sentence.

29.
  a. Incidentally *telematics* enables a car to wirelessly exchange data with external sources such as smartphones, MP3 players, and navigation systems.
  b. Incidentally—*telematics* enables a car to wirelessly exchange data with external sources such as smartphones, MP3 players, and navigation systems.
  c. Incidentally, *telematics* enables a car to wirelessly exchange data with external sources such as smartphones, MP3 players, and navigation systems. _____

30.
  a. Our goal is to encourage, not hamper, honesty and integrity.
  b. Our goal is to encourage—not hamper, honesty and integrity.
  c. Our goal is to encourage, not hamper honesty and integrity. _____

31.
  a. One American company is going to try to sell Mexican food in Mexico, namely Taco Bell.
  b. One American company is going to try to sell Mexican food in Mexico, namely, Taco Bell.
  c. One American company is going to try to sell Mexican food in Mexico: namely, Taco Bell. _____

32.
  a. Four companies offer the best opportunities for new college graduates, namely, Enterprise Rent-a-Car, Teach for America, Verizon Wireless, and Hertz Automotive Rental.
  b. Four companies offer the best opportunities for new college graduates; namely, Enterprise Rent-a-Car, Teach for America, Verizon Wireless, and Hertz Automotive Rental.
  c. Four companies offer the best opportunities for new college graduates; namely Enterprise Rent-a-Car, Teach for America, Verizon Wireless, and Hertz Automotive Rental. _____

33.
  a. The computer was producing "garbage," that is, the screen showed gibberish.
  b. The computer was producing "garbage"; that is, the screen showed gibberish.
  c. The computer was producing "garbage;" that is, the screen showed gibberish. _____

34.
  a. Boston is often called "Beantown" and "The Hub of the Universe".
  b. Boston is often called 'Beantown' and 'The Hub of the Universe.'
  c. Boston is often called "Beantown" and "The Hub of the Universe." _____

35.
  a. The Economist, a British magazine, featured an article called "China and Nepal: Calling the Shots."
  b. *The Economist*, a British magazine, featured an article called "China and Nepal: Calling the Shots."
  c. "The Economist," a British magazine, featured an article called *China and Nepal: Calling the Shots*. _____

36.
  a. "It has been my observation, said Henry Ford, that most people get ahead during the time that others waste time."
  b. "It has been my observation," said Henry Ford, "That most people get ahead during the time that others waste time."
  c. "It has been my observation," said Henry Ford, "that most people get ahead during the time that others waste time." _____

37. a. Who was it who said, "If I'm going to do something, I do it spectacularly or I don't do it at all."?
b. Who was it who said, "If I'm going to do something, I do it spectacularly or I don't do it at all?"
c. Who was it who said, "If I'm going to do something, I do it spectacularly or I don't do it at all"?

_____

38. a. Did the office manager really say, "Stamp this package *Fragile*?"
b. Did the office manager really say, "Stamp this package *Fragile*"?
c. Did the office manager really say, "Stamp this package *Fragile*?

_____

39. a. Rudy Giuliani said, "When you confront a problem, you begin to solve it."
b. Rudy Giuliani said; "When you confront a problem, you begin to solve it."
c. Rudy Giuliani said, "When you confront a problem you begin to solve it".

_____

40. a. The graduating class of 13' faced bleak job prospects.
b. The graduating class of 13 faced bleak job prospects.
c. The graduating class of '13 faced bleak job prospects.

_____

FAQs About Business English Review

Write the letter of the word or phrase that correctly completes each sentence.

41. Every measure has been taken to *(a) insure, (b) ensure* your safety.

_____

42. Because few stockholders were *(a) appraised, (b) apprised* of the CEO's total salary package, no complaints were heard.

_____

43. Lucia feels fortunate because she enjoys working with her *(a) coworkers, (b) co-workers, (c) co workers*.

_____

44. Do you think Lucas meant to *(a) infer, (b) imply* that he is planning to resign?

_____

45. We offer *(a) complimentary, (b) complementary* shipping for all purchases.

_____

46. Paul invested $20,000 as *(a) capitol, (b) capital* to start a new business.

_____

47. Cheyenne is the *(a) capital, (b) capitol* of Wyoming.

_____

48. All rebates will be *(a) dispersed, (b) disbursed* next month.

_____

49. John Muir, who founded the Sierra Club, *(a) emigrated, (b) immigrated* from Sweden when he was eleven years old.

_____

50. Janice was late giving her rent check to her *(a) lessee, (b) lessor*.

_____

Professional Business Letters

Business letters are important forms of external communication. That is, they deliver information to individuals outside an organization. Although e-mail has become incredibly successful for both internal and external communication, many important messages still require written letters. Business letters are necessary when a permanent record is required, when formality is significant, and when a message is sensitive and requires an organized, well-considered presentation. Business letters may request information, respond to requests, make claims, seek adjustments, order goods and services, sell goods and services, recommend individuals, develop goodwill, apply for jobs, or achieve many other goals. All business and professional people have to write business letters of various kinds, but a majority of those letters will be informational.

Characteristics of Business Letters

Writers of good business letters—whether the messages are informational, persuasive, or negative—are guided by the six Cs: conciseness, clarity, correctness, courtesy, completeness, and confidence. In earlier Writer's Workshops, you learned techniques for making your writing concise and clear. You have also studied many guidelines for correct grammar and usage throughout this textbook. At this point we will review some of these techniques briefly as they relate to business letters.

Conciseness. Concise letters save the reader's time by presenting information directly. You can make your letters concise by avoiding these writing faults: (a) wordy phrases (such as *in addition to the above* and *in view of the fact that*), (b) excessive use of expletives (such as *There are four reasons that explain . . .* or *It is a good plan*), (c) long lead-ins (such as *This message is to inform you that* or *I am writing this letter to*), (d) needless adverbs (such as *very, definitely, quite, extremely,* and *really*), and (e) old-fashioned expressions (such as *attached please find* and *pursuant to your request*).

Clarity. Business letters are clear when they are logically organized and when they present enough information for the reader to understand what the writer intended. Informational letters are usually organized directly with the main idea first. Clarity can be enhanced by including all the necessary information. Some authorities estimate that one third of all business letters are written to clarify previous correspondence. To ensure that your letters are clear, put yourself in the reader's position and analyze what you have written. What questions may the reader ask? Does your information proceed logically from one point to another? Are your sentences and paragraphs coherent?

Correctness. Two aspects of correctness are accuracy of facts and accuracy of form. In regard to facts, good writers prepare to write by gathering relevant information. They collect supporting documents (previous letters, memos, e-mail messages, and reports), they make inquiries, they jot down facts, and they outline the message. Correct letters require thorough preparation. In the same manner, correct letters require careful proofreading and attention to form. Typographical errors, spelling irregularities, and grammatical faults distract the reader and damage the credibility of the writer. Correct business letters also follow one of the conventional formats, such as block or modified block, shown in Appendix C.

Courtesy. You develop courtesy in business letters by putting yourself in the place of the reader. Imagine how you would like to be treated, and show the same consideration and respect for the individual receiving your message. The ideas you express and the words used to convey those ideas create an impression on the reader. Be alert to words that may create a negative feeling such as *you claim, unfortunately, you neglected, you forgot*, and *your complaint*.

Completeness. To be complete, a letter should answer all questions your reader might have. When formulating your message, consider the *who, what, when, where, why*, and *how*. The goal in writing complete letters is to avoid unnecessary follow-up. You don't want to waste your reader's time or your own.

Confidence. Employers want employees who are confident in themselves and in what they do. Therefore, avoid using words that make you sound weak such as *I think, I feel*, and *I believe*. Just come right out and say it with confidence!

Skill Check 5.1 Reviewing the Six Cs

1. Which of the following is *most* concise?
   a. Due to the fact that we had a warehouse fire, your shipment is delayed.
   b. This is to inform you that your shipment will be delayed.
   c. Because of a warehouse fire, your shipment is delayed.
   d. There was a warehouse fire, which explains why your shipment is delayed. _____

2. Which of the following is clear and logical?
   a. If the strike is not settled quickly, it may last a while.
   b. Flying over the rain forests of Indonesia, the trees form a solid and menacing green carpet.
   c. This is not to suggest that Salt Lake, Denver, and Houston are not the most affordable areas for housing.
   d. Prince Charles complained that the citizens of Britain speak and write their language poorly. _____

3. Which of the following is grammatically correct?
   a. We hope that you and he will be in town for our next seminar.
   b. A host of ethical issues involve business, including e-mail privacy, whistleblowing, and mission statements.
   c. We must develop a policy on returning merchandise. So that they know about it before they are made.
   d. Jeffrey has 20 years experience in the technology industry. _____

4. Which of the following is *most* courteous?
   a. During your interview, I informed you that if we were not successful in finding a suitable candidate, I would contact you.
   b. We appreciate receiving your letter describing your treatment by our store security personnel.
   c. In your letter of June 1, you claim that you were harassed by our store security personnel.
   d. Unfortunately, we are unable to complete your entire order because you neglected to provide a shirt size. _____

5. Which of the following sounds *most* conversational?
   a. Attached herewith is the form you requested.
   b. Pursuant to your request, we are forwarding the form you requested.
   c. Under separate cover we are sending the form you requested.
   d. You will receive the form you requested in a separate mailing.

   _____

6. Which of the following sounds *most* confident?
   a. I hope to hear from you soon about the available position.
   b. Our committee thinks that this is the best way to handle the problem.
   c. I look forward to speaking with you about my proposal.
   d. We believe that our product will best meet your needs.

   _____

Writing Plan

Most business letters have three parts: opening, body, and closing. This three-part writing plan will help you organize the majority of your business messages quickly and effectively.

Opening. The opening of a business letter may include a subject line that refers to previous correspondence or summarizes the content of the message. If you decide to include a subject line, it should make sense but should not be a complete sentence; it is not followed by a period.

The first sentence of a business letter that requests or delivers information should begin directly with the main idea. If you are asking for information, use one of two approaches. Ask the most important question first, such as *Do you have a two-bedroom cottage on Devil's Lake available for the week of July 8–15?* A second approach involves beginning with a summary statement, such as *Please answer the following questions regarding. . . .* If the letter delivers information, begin with the most important information first, such as *Yes, we have a two-bedroom cottage on Devil's Lake available for. . . .* or *Here is the information you requested regarding. . . .* Most informational business letters should NOT begin with an explanation of why the letter is being written.

Body. The body of the letter provides explanations and additional information to clarify the first sentence. Use a separate paragraph for each new idea, being careful to strive for concise writing. If the message lends itself to enumeration, express the items in a bulleted or numbered list. Be certain, of course, to construct the list so that each item is parallel.

Think about the individual reading your message. Will that person understand what you are saying? Have you included enough information? What may seem clear to you may not be so evident to your reader. In responding to requests, don't hesitate to include more information than was requested—if you feel it would be helpful. Maintain a friendly, conversational, and positive tone.

Closing. Business letters that demand action should conclude with a specific request, including end dating if appropriate. That is, tell the reader when you would like the request complied with, and, if possible, provide a reason (for example, *Please send me this information by June 1 so that I can arrange my vacation*).

Letters that provide information may end with a summary statement or a pleasant, forward-looking thought (for example, *We are happy to provide this information to help you plan your summer vacation*). Business organizations may also use the closing to promote products or services. Avoid ending your letters with mechanical phrases such as *If I can be of further service, don't hesitate to call on me*, or *Thanks for any information you can provide.* Find a fresh way to express your desire to be of service or to show appreciation.

Figure 5.1 illustrates the application of the writing plan to an information request. Notice that the subject line summarizes the main topic of the letter, while the first paragraph provides more information about the reason for writing. The body of the letter explains the main idea and includes a list of questions so that the reader can see quickly what information is being requested. The closing includes an end date with a reason.

FIGURE 5.1
Information Request

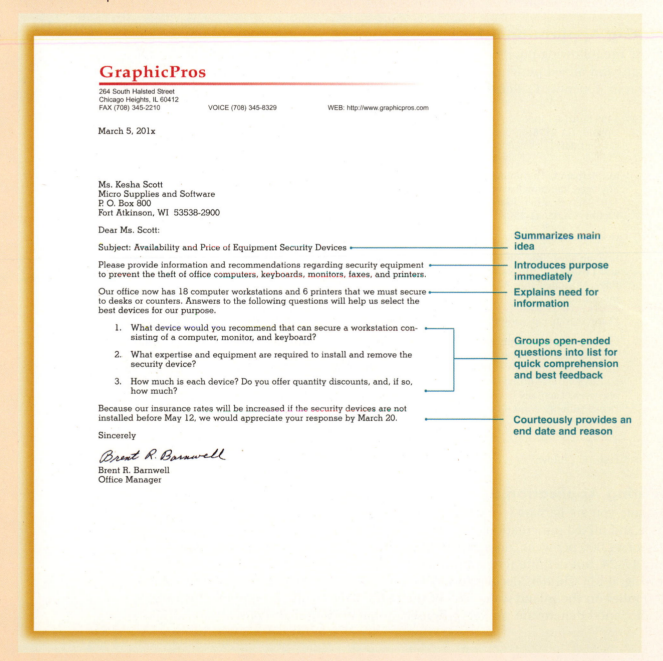

Skill Check 5.2 Reviewing the Writing Plan

In the space provided, write *a*, *b*, or *c* to identify the letter part where each of the following might logically be found.

a. Opening   **b. Body**   **c. Closing**

1. Explanation and details

2. Subject line that summarizes main idea

3. End date with reason

4. Numbered or bulleted list

5. Main idea

6. Summary statement or forward-looking thought

Writing Application 5.1

Revise the following poorly written letter. Use block style (every line starts at the left margin) and mixed punctuation. This is a personal business letter; follow the format shown in Appendix C. Remember that the following letter is poorly written. Improve it!

1435 Sunrise Circle
Upland, CA 91786
Current date

Ms. Barbara L. Hernandez
Manager, Rainbow Resort
1102 West Brannan Island Road
Isleton, CA 95641-1102

Dear Ms. Hernandez:

I saw an advertisement recently in *Sunset* magazine where Rainbow Resort rents houseboats. My family and I (there are three kids and my wife and me) would like to take a vacation on a houseboat from July 17 through July 24 in the California Delta area. We have never done this before, but it sounds interesting.

Please send me any information you may have. I will have to make my vacation plans soon.

I have no idea how much this might cost. If we rent a houseboat, we want to know do you provide bedding, dishes, pots and pans, and the like? I am wondering about navigating a houseboat. Will we have to take a course or training on how to operate it? It may be too difficult for us to operate. How far can we travel in the Delta area in one of your houseboats? What if we decide to stay on more than one week? I actually have two weeks of vacation, but we may want to travel in our RV part of the time. Does insurance come with the rental fee? Our kids want to know if it has TV.

Yours,

Leslie E. Childers

Writing Application 5.2

Assume you are Barbara Hernandez. Write a response to Mr. Childers's letter. Use block style and mixed punctuation. Tell Mr. Childers that the rental fee, which is $175 per day or $1,000 per week, does include insurance. You have a houseboat available for July 17–24, but definite reservations must be made for that time and for the week following, if Mr. Childers decides to stay two weeks. Your houseboats can travel about 100 miles on the inland waterways of the Delta. Rainbow Resort provides bedding, dishes, and kitchenware. Yes, each houseboat has a TV. You also provide an AM/FM radio and a DVD player. Your houseboats accommodate four to ten people, and you require a deposit of $500 for a one-week reservation. Reservations must be received by June 1 to ensure a July vacation. Your houseboats are easy to operate. No special training is required, but you do give each operator about 30 minutes of instruction. Send Mr. Childers a brochure describing Rainbow Resort and the memorable holiday he and his family can enjoy. The scenery and attractions are good.

Writing Application 5.3

Write a personal business letter in response to the following problem. For your home office you ordered a VoIP phone system called the Plantronics Calisto Pro Series DECT 6.0. This hands-free system comes with a Bluetooth headset that allows you to answer your landline, mobile, and VoIP phone calls with one device. It had many other attractive features, and you were eager to try it. When the system arrived, however, you followed all installation instructions and discovered that an irritating static sound interfered with every telephone call you made or received. You don't know what is causing the static, but the product description promised the following: "Thanks to the system's superior noise-canceling Bluetooth headset with extended mouthpiece, you will always sound professional. The Calisto Pro phone operates on DECT 6.0 frequency, which means that call clarity is not affected by Wi-Fi networks or home appliances, such as microwaves, and you can roam up to 300 feet from the base without suffering any degradation in sound quality."

Because you need a clear signal for your business, you returned the VoIP phone system January 15 by UPS Next Business Day shipping service to ElectroWare, Inc., the Web-based supplier from whom you purchased the system. You still have a copy of the invoice, which states that merchandise may be returned for any reason within 30 days after purchase. You also have the UPS receipt proving that you returned it. However, your Visa statement (No. 5390-3390-2219-0002) has not shown a credit for the return. Your last two statements show no credit for $249.95. You are wondering what happened. Did ElectroWare receive the returned VoIP phone system? Why hasn't your account been credited? If ElectroWare did not receive the shipment, you want UPS to trace it. Write to ElectroWare, Inc., 22121 Crystal Creek Boulevard, Bothell, Washington 98201-2212. You have complied with their instructions regarding returning merchandise, and you want them to credit your account. You do not want another VoIP phone system from ElectroWare. Be sure to open your letter with a direct request for the action you want taken.

Writing With Style

13 Capitalization

There is no rule on how to write. Sometimes it comes easily and perfectly; sometimes it's like drilling rock and then blasting it out with charges.

—Ernest Hemingway,
American writer

Objectives

When you have completed the materials in this chapter, you will be able to do the following:

LEVEL 1

1. Properly capitalize sentence beginnings, the pronoun *I*, proper nouns, and proper adjectives.
2. Determine when to capitalize geographic locations, organization names, academic courses and degrees, and seasons.

LEVEL 2

3. Understand how to capitalize business correspondence components and personal titles.
4. Correctly capitalize numbered and lettered items; points of the compass; departments, divisions, offices, agencies, and committees; government terms; product names; and published and artistic titles.

LEVEL 3

5. Capitalize beginning words; laws, bills, acts, treaties, and amendments; celestial bodies; ethnic, cultural, language, and religious references; and words following *marked* and *stamped*.
6. Apply special rules in capitalizing personal titles and terms.

Use proofreading marks to show any letters that should be capitalized in the following sentences. See the inside back cover for a list of proofreading marks. Then compare your answers with those below.

1. Have you read the swedish version of the book *the girl with the dragon tattoo* that i sent you?

2. Subject: task force meeting on thursday, september 20

3. the week before mother's day is the busiest time for the united states postal service.

4. The securities and exchange commission will meet at trump tower in new york city on april 29 to discuss requirements for using plain english in proxy statements.

5. Last spring father traveled to new england to visit his mother in providence, rhode island.

6. After receiving a bachelor's degree from the university of north dakota, cerise became director of the merchant services department in the corporate offices of bank of america.

7. Our company president and vice president met with several supervisors on the west coast to discuss how to develop apps for facebook.

8. The internal revenue service requires corporations to complete form 1120 before the april 15 deadline.

9. Jim Baldwin will fly to the east coast on united airlines so that he can run in the boston marathon.

10. Tennessee is called the volunteer state because of the record number of volunteers the state provided during the war of 1812 and the mexican war.

One difficult aspect of writing is learning the rules that will help you write with style. In this chapter you will learn the rules of capitalization. Rules governing capitalization reflect conventional practices; that is, they have been established by custom and usage. By following these conventions, a writer tells a reader, among other things, what words are important. In earlier times writers capitalized most nouns and many adjectives at will; few conventions of capitalization or punctuation were consistently observed. Today most capitalization follows definite rules that are fully accepted and practiced at all times. Dictionaries are helpful in determining capitalization practices, but they do not show all capitalized words. To develop skill in controlling capitals, study the rules and examples in this chapter.

Study Tip

Many people overcapitalize. Remember that capitalization is used to show that a word is important or should be emphasized. If you overcapitalize, you are taking away from the words that are truly important.

1. Swedish   *The Girl With the Dragon Tattoo*   I   2. Task Force Meeting   Thursday   September   3. The   Mother's Day   United States Postal Service   4. Securities and Exchange Commission   Trump Tower   New York City   April   English   5. Father   New England   Providence   Rhode Island   6. University of North Dakota   Cerise   Merchant Services Department   Bank of America   7. West Coast   Facebook   8. Internal Revenue Service   Form   9. East Coast   United Airlines   Boston Marathon   10. Volunteer State   War   Mexican War

Basic Rules of Capitalization

Some of the basic rules of capitalization involve the first word in a sentence, the pronoun *I*, proper nouns and adjectives, geographic locations, organization names, academic courses and degrees, and seasons.

Beginning of a Sentence

Capitalize the first letter of a word beginning a sentence.

> Some companies, including Atomic Object, hold meetings at which everyone is required to stand up.

> The object of stand-up meetings is to keep employees more focused and energized.

The Pronoun *I*

Capitalize the pronoun *I*, no matter where it appears or how it is used in a sentence.

> If *I* were you, *I'd* accept the position.

> If you give me a chance, *I'm* sure *I* could change your mind.

Proper Nouns

Capitalize proper nouns, including the *specific* names of persons, places, schools, streets, parks, buildings, holidays, events, months, days, nicknames, agreements, websites, software programs, apps, games, historical periods, and so forth. Do NOT capitalize common nouns that make *general* references.

Proper Nouns	Common Nouns
Sandra Day O'Connor	the first female Supreme Court judge
Mexico, Canada	neighboring countries of the United States
Ohio State University, Northgate High School	a university and a high school
Abbey Road, Baker Street	famous streets in London
Fenway Park, Wrigley Field	legendary baseball parks
Chrysler Building, Empire State Building	famous buildings in New York City
New Year's Day, Memorial Day	two holidays
Super Bowl, World Series, World Cup	well-known sporting events
October, November, December	last three months of the year
Saturday, Sunday	weekend days
the Windy City, the Sunflower State	city and state nicknames
European Union	an agreement among several countries
Facebook.com, YouTube.com, Pinterest.com	popular social media websites
PowerPoint, QuickBooks, Photoshop	software programs
Instagram, Flixster, WorldMate	popular mobile apps
Words With Friends, Angry Birds	well-known mobile games

Trivia Tidbit

Some languages don't have capital letters, including Hebrew, Arabic, Korean, Thai, Japanese, and Chinese.

Trivia Tidbit

English is the only language in which the first-person singular pronoun (*I*) is capitalized. For example, in Italian (*io*) and French (*je*), the first-person pronoun is capitalized only if it appears at the beginning of a sentence. In some languages, such as German, the second-person pronoun *you* is capitalized.

Career Tip

Many large companies publish style manuals showing their preferred capitalization and the spelling of frequently used terms. One of the first tasks of a new employee is becoming familiar with the company style manual.

Trivia Tidbit

Months and days of the week are not capitalized in all languages. These are some of the languages that do not capitalize months or days: Dutch, Finnish, French, Hungarian, Italian, Polish, Russian, Spanish, Swedish, and Vietnamese.

Great Depression, Digital Age	periods of time
U.S. Postal Service, Internal Revenue Service	government entities
Redwood Room, Clift Hotel	a room in the hotel
Golden Gate Bridge, Brooklyn Bridge	bridges over bodies of water
Supreme Court, Senate	components of government

Proper Adjectives

Capitalize most adjectives that are derived from proper nouns.

American politics	Swiss watch
Renaissance art	British rock
Freudian slip	Jamaican dollar
Keynesian economics	Internet access

Study Tip

Most proper nouns retain their capital letters when they become adjectives—for example, French toast, Russian roulette, Persian cat, Spanish moss, Italian marble, and Swedish massage.

Do not capitalize those adjectives originally derived from proper nouns that have become common adjectives (without capitals) through usage. Consult your dictionary when in doubt.

congressional aides	venetian blinds
french fries	china dishes
chauvinist	diesel engine
monarch butterfly	arabic numerals

Geographic Locations

Capitalize the names of *specific* places such as continents, countries, states, cities, counties, mountains, valleys, lakes, rivers, seas, oceans, geographic regions, and neighborhoods. Capitalize *county* and *state* when they follow proper nouns.

North America, Africa, Asia	Lake Ontario, Lake Tahoe
Canada, Morocco, Beijing	Snake River, Amazon River
Idaho, Nebraska, New York State	Sea of Cortez, Baltic Sea
Boise, Lincoln, Rochester	Atlantic Ocean, Pacific Ocean
Barnstable County, Monroe County	Pacific Northwest, Florida Keys
Mount Fuji, Rocky Mountains	European Community (EC)
Yosemite Valley, Shenandoah Valley	Upper West Side, Chinatown, Silicon Valley

Do not capitalize the words *city*, *state*, or *county* when they precede geographic locations unless they are part of the official geographical name or unless they are used by a governing body as part of an official name.

I spent two weeks in the city of Miami (*City* is not part of the geographical name.)

In the *City of Industry* is a McDonald's restaurant that is used strictly for filming movies and commercials. (*City* is part of the geographical name.)

Laura plans to attend college in the *state* of Iowa. (*State* is used generically.)

The website for the *State* of Nebraska lists statewide job openings. (*State* is used by a governing body as part of its official name.)

Organization Names

Capitalize the principal words in the names of all business, civic, educational, government, labor, military, philanthropic, political, professional, religious, sports, and social organizations. Capitalize *the* only when it is part of an organization's official name (such as *The Coca-Cola Company* and *The World Bank*). In organization names, articles (*a, an, the*), short conjunctions (*and, but, or, nor*), prepositions that have two or three letters (*of, in, on, for, to*), the word *to* in infinitives, and the word *as* are not capitalized unless they are the first or last word in the organization name.

Boston Consulting Group	Chamber of Commerce
Gonzaga University	Department of Homeland Security
United Farm Workers of America	United States Coast Guard
Animal Rescue Foundation	Green Party
American Dental Association	Knights of Columbus
National Basketball Association	Alpha Omicron Pi

Generally, do NOT capitalize *committee, company, association, board*, and other shortened name forms when they are used to replace full organization names. If these shortened names, however, are preceded by the word *the* and are used in formal or legal documents (contracts, bylaws, minutes), they may be capitalized.

Does the company offer on-site child care? (Informal document)

The Treasurer of the *Association* is herein authorized to disburse funds. (Formal document)

Academic Courses and Degrees

Capitalize the names of numbered courses and specific course titles. Do not capitalize the names of academic subject areas unless they contain a proper noun.

Marina took Accounting 181, English 122, and Marketing 265 last semester.

Marina excelled in her accounting, English, and business marketing courses last semester.

All finance majors must take business English and business law courses.

Capitalize abbreviations of academic degrees whether they stand alone or follow individuals' names. Do not capitalize general references to degrees unless they are used after and in conjunction with an individual's name.

Julie Perzel earned AA, BA, and MS degrees before her thirtieth birthday. (Associate of Arts, Bachelor of Arts, and Master of Science degrees)

Patrick Couglin, JD, gave his opening statement in court this morning. (Juris Doctor)

Matthew hopes to earn bachelor's and master's degrees in business administration. (General reference to degrees and major)

Elizabeth Wyman, Doctor of Engineering, served as a consultant on the project. (Degree used in conjunction with a name)

Study Tip

Course titles with numbers are capitalized (*Marketing 101*) because they refer to specific courses. Those without numbers usually are not capitalized (*marketing*).

Seasons

Do not capitalize seasons unless they are combined with a year.

> Our annual sales meeting is held each fall.
>
> Lynn Spiesel will begin working on her master's degree during the Fall 2016 semester.
>
> Now complete the reinforcement exercises for Level 1.

Special Rules of Capitalization

You have learned the basic rules of capitalization. We will now cover some special rules that involve capitalization in business correspondence; titles of people; numbered and lettered items; the points of a compass; departments, divisions, offices, agencies, and committees; government terms; product names; and titles of literary and artistic works.

Business Correspondence Components

Capitalize the first word of certain business correspondence components that are included in letters, memos, and e-mail messages. In subject lines do NOT capitalize articles (*a, an, the*), conjunctions (*and, but, or, nor*), and prepositions with three or fewer letters (*in, to, by, for*) unless they appear at the beginning or end of the subject line.

> **SUBJECT:** Monthly Marketing Meeting on March 19 (Capitalize the first letter of all primary words in a subject line to make it look important and professional.)
>
> Dear Mr. Robinson: (Capitalize the first word and any nouns in a **salutation**.)
>
> Sincerely yours, (Capitalize the first word of a **complimentary close**.)

Study Tip

Capitalize only the first word in a salutation (*My dear Ms. Jones*) or in a complimentary close (*Very truly yours*).

Titles of People

Many rules exist for capitalizing personal and professional titles of people.

Titles Preceding Names

Capitalize courtesy titles (such as *Mr., Mrs., Ms., Miss,* and *Dr.*) when they precede names. Also capitalize titles representing a person's profession, company position, military rank, religious station, political office, family relationship, or nobility when the title precedes the name and replaces a courtesy title.

> The hotel staff welcomed *Mr.* and *Mrs.* Gary Smith. (Courtesy titles)
>
> Speakers included *Professor* Franco Guidone and *Dr.* Janet Black. (Professional titles)
>
> Sales figures were submitted by *Budget Director* Magee and *Vice President* Anderson. (Company titles)
>
> Will *Major General* Donald M. Franklin assume command? (Military title)

Career Tip

"Choose a job you love, and you will never have to work a day in your life."
—Confucius

Circle art: © iStockphoto.com/Pavel Khorenyan

Discussing the issue are *Rabbi* Isaac Elchanan, *Archbishop* Jean-Pierre Ricard, and *Reverend* Cecil Williams. (Religious titles)

We expect *President* Barack Obama to meet with *Prime Minister* David Cameron. (Political titles)

Only *Aunt* Brenda and *Uncle* Skip have been to Antarctica. (Family relationships)

Onlookers waited for *Prince* Charles and *Queen* Elizabeth to arrive. (Nobility)

Titles Followed by Appositives

Do not capitalize a person's title—professional, business, military, religious, political, family, or one related to nobility—when the title is followed by the person's name and the name is being used as an appositive. You will recall that **appositives** rename or explain previously mentioned nouns or pronouns.

Only one *professor*, Marcella Kelly, was available to serve as club advisor.

University employees asked their *president*, Peter Garcia, to help raise funds.

Reva Hillman discovered that her *uncle*, Paul M. Hillman, had named her as his heir.

Titles or Offices Following Names

Do not capitalize titles or offices following names unless they appear in a displayed list.

Darren Schwartz, *senior vice president* of Groupon, met with Mary Williams, *director* of Research and Development, to discuss possibilities for new smartphone apps.

After repeated customer requests, Kay Carver, *manager* of Straits Cafe, announced extended hours.

Barack Obama, *president* of the United States, conferred with Hillary Clinton, *secretary of state*.

John Roberts, *chief justice* of the U.S. Supreme Court, promised a ruling in October.

The following employees will represent Cisco Systems at this year's Emerging Technology Conference (ETech):

Blair Christie, Chief Marketing Officer

Rebecca Jacoby, Chief Information Officer

Bob Friday, Chief Technology Officer

Titles or Offices Replacing Names

Generally, do not capitalize a title or office that replaces a person's name. However, if using a title in direct address (speaking directly to a person), capitalize the title if it replaces the name.

Neither the *president* nor the *general counsel* of the company could be reached for comment.

An ambitious marketing plan was developed by the *director of marketing* and the *sales manager*.

The *president* conferred with the *joint chiefs of staff* and the *secretary of defense*.

At the reception the *mayor* of Provincetown spoke with the *governor* of West Virginia.

What do you think I can do, *Professor*, to improve my grade? (Direct address)

Titles in Business Correspondence

Capitalize titles in addresses and closing lines of business correspondence.

Ms. Chrisanne Knox
Director of Marketing and Communications
Diablo Valley College
321 Golf Club Road
Pleasant Hill, CA 94523

Very sincerely yours,

Stephen Finton
Comptroller

Family Titles

Do not capitalize family titles used with possessive pronouns or possessive nouns.

We are meeting my *aunt* and *uncle* for lunch at L'Osteria del Forno.

Did you hear that his *father* met Adam's *cousin* at the sales conference?

But do capitalize titles of close relatives when they are used without pronouns.

We are meeting *Aunt Susan* and *Uncle Gary* for lunch at L'Osteria del Forno.

What do you think about my decision, *Dad*?

Numbered and Lettered Items

Capitalize nouns followed by numbers or letters except in *page, paragraph, line, size, verse,* and *vitamin* references.

Virgin Atlantic Flight 7401 to Sydney will depart from Gate E64.

Take Exit 12 off State Highway 5 and follow the signs to Building I-63-B.

Volume II, Appendix A, contains a copy of Medicare Form 72T. Instructions are on page 6, line 12.

Taking vitamin C daily can help protect against immune system deficiencies and cardiovascular disease.

Points of the Compass

Capitalize *north, south, east, west,* and other points of a compass when they represent *specific* regions.

the Middle East, the Far East	the Midwest, the Southeast
the East Coast, the West Coast	the Pacific Northwest
Northern and Southern Hemispheres	Easterners, Southerners
Northern California, Southern California	North Georgia, South Georgia

Do not capitalize the points of the compass when they are used in directions or in general references.

To find the conference facility, drive *north* on Highway 13 and turn *east* on Grizzly Peak Road.

Mickey Todd will cover the territory consisting of all states *south* of the Mason-Dixon Line.

The *southern* part of California is prone to wildfires.

Study Tip

A clue to the capitalization of a region is the use of *the* preceding it: *the East Coast, the West, the Pacific Northwest.*

Departments, Divisions, Offices, Agencies, and Committees

Capitalize the principal words in the official names of divisions, departments, offices, government agencies, and committees. Also capitalize the main words in the names of schools or colleges within universities. When a department or division is referred to by its function because the official name is unknown, do not capitalize this reference. Outside your organization capitalize only *specific* department, division, or committee names.

> Miguel Zuliani works with the International Division of Apple. (Specific company division)
>
> Contact our Customer Service Department about making a return. (Specific company department)
>
> The Office of Thrift Supervision regulates the savings and loan industry. (Specific office)
>
> The nation's unemployment rate is calculated by the Bureau of Labor Statistics. (Specific government agency)
>
> Phil Angelides chaired the Financial Crisis Inquiry Commission. (Specific committee)
>
> The Wharton School of Business at the University of Pennsylvania is always listed as having one of the country's best MBA programs. (School within a university)
>
> I will be sending my résumé to the human resources departments of several companies. (Unofficial or unknown department name)
>
> A steering committee has not yet been named. (Unofficial or unknown name)

Government Terms

Do not capitalize the words *federal, government, nation,* or *state* unless they are part of a specific title.

> Neither the state government nor the federal government would fund the proposal.
>
> The Bureau of Consumer Financial Protection helps consumers make smarter financial decisions.
>
> The president should do everything possible to uphold our nation's values.

Product Names

Capitalize product names only when they represent specific brand names or trademarks of products. Except in advertising, common names following manufacturers' names are not capitalized. Also note that all words capitalized in the following list are protected trademarks and should, therefore, not be used generically.

Coca-Cola	ChapStick lip balm	Band-Aid
Kleenex tissues	Dumpster waste receptacle	Saran Wrap
Jet Ski	Post-It notes	Scotch tape
Gap jeans	Styrofoam cup	Starbucks coffee
Xerox copier	Apple computer	Chrysler Jeep
Q-tip swab	Ace bandage	Excel spreadsheet

Trivia Tidbit

Would you capitalize *aspirin, bikini, corn flakes, crock pot, dry ice, escalator, granola, margarine, pilates, raisin bran, tabloid, videotape,* or *zipper*? All were once trademarks that have slipped into common use. Because companies have huge investments in their trademarks, they spend millions each year protecting them; the Web has made this an even more difficult task.

Study Tip

The legal names of many companies and products are written with an unconventional style called *intercaps*. Examples include *iPad, QuickBooks, PowerPoint, YouTube,* and *BlackBerry*. When writing a company or product name, always use the company's preferred style.

Trivia Tidbit

One of the most widely publicized legal battles over trademark protection involved Parker Brothers. It threatened to sue an economics professor at San Francisco State University for naming his new board game "Anti-Monopoly." After nine years of litigation, courts stripped "Monopoly" of trademark protection, thus making the name generic.

Published and Artistic Titles

Capitalize the main words in the titles of books, magazines, newspapers, articles, movies, plays, albums, songs, poems, websites, and reports. Do NOT capitalize articles (*a, an, the*), conjunctions (*and, but, or, nor*), and prepositions with three or fewer letters (*in, to, by, for*) unless they begin or end the title. The word *to* in infinitives (*to run, to say, to write*) and the word *as* are also not capitalized unless they appear as the first word of a title or subtitle.

Remember that the titles of published works that contain subdivisions (such as books, magazines, pamphlets, newspapers, TV series, plays, albums, and musicals) are italicized or underscored. Titles of literary or artistic works without subdivisions (such as chapters, newspaper articles, magazine articles, songs, poems, and episodes in a TV series) are placed in quotation marks.

> Michael Miller's *B2B Digital Marketing: Using the Web to Directly Market to Businesses* (Book)
>
> "The Dangers of a Messy Desk" appearing in *Forbes* (Article in magazine)
>
> "Investing in Real Life" appearing in *The Wall Street Journal* (Article in a newspaper)
>
> *The Amazing Race* (TV series)
>
> *Life Is Beautiful* (Movie)
>
> Bob Dylan's "When the Ship Comes In" on *The Times They Are A-Changin'* (Song and album)
>
> "Personal Branding," a link at Quintessential Careers (Link at a website)

Now complete the reinforcement exercises for Level 2.

LEVEL 3

Additional Rules of Capitalization

Business writers should be aware of additional ways professionals use capitalization in their writing.

Beginning Words

In addition to capitalizing the first word of a complete sentence, capitalize the first words in quoted sentences, independent phrases, enumerated items, and formal rules or principles following colons.

> Bill Gates said, "Your most unhappy customers are your greatest source of learning." (Quoted sentence)
>
> No, not at the present time. (Independent phrase)
>
> Follow these steps to apply for a student visa:
>
> 1. Complete the visa application for the appropriate country.
> 2. Gather the required information and arrange to pay the application fee.
> 3. Submit your application in person prior to traveling to the country. (Enumerated items)
>
> Our office manager repeated his favorite rule: Treat the customer as you would like to be treated. (Rule following colon)

Laws, Bills, Acts, Treaties, and Amendments

Capitalize the official names of government laws, bills, acts, treaties, and amendments. Do not capitalize generic references to legislation.

> The Patient Protection and Affordable Health Care Act is a principal part of health care reform legislation.

> The Stolen Valor Act makes it a misdemeanor to falsely represent oneself as having received a military medal of distinction.

> The first ten amendments to the U.S. Constitution make up the Bill of Rights.

Celestial Bodies

Capitalize the names of **celestial bodies** including planets, planet satellites, stars, constellations, and asteroids. Do not capitalize the terms *earth, sun,* or *moon* unless they are used as the names of specific bodies in the solar system.

> Why on earth didn't you apply sunscreen in this bright sun?

> The planets closest to the Sun are Mercury, Mars, and Earth.

Trivia Tidbit

Language references are not capitalized in all languages. For example, here are just a few of the languages that do not capitalize language names: Bosnian, Catalan, Danish, Finnish, French, Icelandic, Italian, Latvian, Portuguese, and Serbian.

Ethnic, Cultural, Language, and Religious References

Terms that relate to a particular culture, language, race, or religion are capitalized.

> In Hawaii, Asian and Western cultures merge.

> Both English and Hebrew are spoken by Jews in Israel.

> Native Americans and Latinos turned out to support their candidates.

Hyphenate terms such as *African-American* and *French-Canadian* when they are used as adjectives (*African-American community* or *French-Canadian citizens*). Do not hyphenate these terms when they are nouns.

> Asian-American communities can be found in almost every major U.S. city.

> Many Asian Americans place great value on higher education.

Words Following *marked* and *stamped*

Capitalize words that follow the words *marked* and *stamped.*

> Although the package was stamped *Fragile* (or "Fragile"), the postal carrier threw it into the back of the truck.

> The check came back marked *Insufficient Funds* (or "Insufficient Funds").

Special Uses of Personal Titles and Terms

Generally, titles are capitalized according to the specifications set forth earlier. However, when a title of an official appears in that organization's minutes, bylaws, or other official documents, it is capitalized.

> The Controller will have authority over departmental budgets. (Title appearing in bylaws)

> By vote of the stockholders, the President is empowered to declare a stock dividend. (Title appearing in an annual report)

When the terms *ex, elect, late,* and *former* are used with capitalized titles, they are not capitalized.

We went to hear ex-President Bush and Mayor-elect Lee speak at the symposium.

The late President Reagan has been honored with a library and museum in Simi Valley, California.

We just learned that former President Clinton will speak on campus next month.

Now complete the reinforcement exercises for Level 3.

Dr. Guffey   Professor Seefer

Q: Today everyone seems to use the word *google* as a generic verb (*You should google your name to see what comes up*). Should this word be capitalized when it's used as a verb?

A: The general rule is to capitalize *Google* when referring to the company name or website and to use a lowercase letter when using it as verb (*google*). However, be very careful when using a company name in this way. Google is extremely protective of its name and has even written cease-and-desist letters to people who use *google* as a generic term.

Q: I don't know how to describe the copies made from our copy machine. Should I call them *Xerox* copies or something else?

A: They are *Xerox* copies only if made on a Xerox copier. Copies made on other machines may be called *xerographic* copies, *machine* copies, *photocopies,* or *copies*.

Q: Lately I've noticed odd capitalization in some company and product names. For example, is the online auction site written as *EBay, eBay,* or *Ebay*? How can I ever keep these company names straight?

A: The correct way to write this company name is *eBay*. And you're absolutely right that it can be difficult to keep company and product names straight when they use unusual capitalization, which is known as *intercaps* or *BiCaps*. Other examples include YouTube, JetBlue Airways, PowerPoint, QuickBooks, iPhone, iPod, iPad, BlackBerry, TurboCAD, ConocoPhillips, DuPont, FedEx, ExxonMobil, FreeWave Technologies, PayPal, iRobot, MasterCard, NetZero, PeopleSoft, i-flex Solutions, PepsiCo, SkyWest Airlines, TheStreet.com, MySpace, and UTStarcom. To make things even more confusing, just because a company or product sounds like two separate words, don't assume that each word is capitalized. For example, in the names of these products and companies, only the first letter is capitalized: Photoshop, Lucasfilm, Amtrak, Autodesk, Citigroup, Ecolab, Facebook, Kmart Corporation, Craigslist, and Sun Microsystems. To ensure that you are writing product and company names correctly, check the official website for the company or product.

Q: I'm having trouble not capitalizing *president* when it refers to the president of the United States. It used to be capitalized. Why isn't it now?

A: For some time the trend has been away from "upstyle" capitalization. Fewer words are capitalized. Our two principal authorities (*Merriam-Webster's Collegiate Dictionary* and *The Chicago Manual of Style*) both recommend lowercase for *president of the United States.* In addition, many publications, including *The New York Times,* capitalize the word *president* only when it's used as a title with a last name (*President Obama*). However, other authorities maintain that the term should always be capitalized because of high regard for the office.

Q: In the doctor's office where I work, I see the word *medicine* capitalized, as in *the field of Medicine*. Is this correct?

A: No. General references should not be capitalized. If it were part of a title, as in the Northwestern College of *Medicine*, it would be capitalized.

Q: I'm writing a paper for my biology class on *in vitro fertilization*. Since this is a medical term, shouldn't I capitalize it?

A: Don't capitalize medical procedures or diseases unless they are named after individuals (*Tourette's syndrome*). *In vitro* means "outside the living body." Specialists in the field use the abbreviation *IVF* after the first introduction of the term.

Q: I work for a state agency, and I'm not sure what to capitalize or hyphenate in this sentence: *State agencies must make forms available to non-English-speaking applicants*.

A: Words with the prefix *non* are usually not hyphenated (*nonexistent, nontoxic*). But when *non* is joined to a word that must be capitalized, it is followed by a hyphen. Because the word *speaking* combines with *English* to form a single-unit adjective, it should be hyphenated. Thus, the expression should be typed *non-English-speaking applicants*.

Q: How do you spell *marshal*, as used in *the Grand Marshal of the Rose Parade*?

A: The preferred spelling is with a single *l*: *marshal*. In addition to describing an individual who directs a ceremony, the noun *marshal* refers to a high military officer or a city law officer who carries out court orders (*the marshal served papers on the defendant*). As a verb, *marshal* means "to bring together" or "to order in an effective way" (*the attorney marshaled convincing arguments*). The similar-sounding word *martial* is an adjective and means "warlike" or "military" (*martial law was declared after the riot*). You'll probably need a dictionary to keep those words straight!

Q: My boss has just placed me in charge of editing a new company newsletter, which will be published bimonthly. I hate to admit it, but I was afraid to ask my boss what *bimonthly* means. Does this mean that the newsletter will come out twice a month? That's a lot of work!

A: You can relax! *Bimonthly* means that your company newsletter will be published every other month. If your boss had said the newsletter would be published *semimonthly*, you would have been editing two newsletters every month. The same applies to the words *biweekly* (every other week) and *semiweekly* (twice a week).

Q: Is the word *make up* written as one word or two? Is it hyphenated?

A: It depends on how you're using the word. If you're using it as a noun, write it as one word. (*She applied her makeup carefully before her date. The makeup of this task force includes individuals from all departments. Because Raul missed the test, he must take a makeup.*) If you're using the word as an adjective, also write it as one word. (*Raul did well on his makeup exam.*) However, if you're using it as a verb, write it as two words. (*Raul will make up the work he missed last week.*) This word is never hyphenated.

SPOT THE Blooper

Using the skills you are learning in this class, try to identify why the following items are bloopers. Consult your textbook, dictionary, or reference manual as needed. To see if you recognized the blooper, go to **www.cengagebrain.com** and use your access code to see the Spot the Blooper key.

Blooper 1: On AOL's website, reporting on the royal wedding in London: "Walking hand in hand, William and Kate left Buckingham Palace, where they stayed the night, in a helicopter."

Blooper 2: Front of a menu at Lonely Beach Restaurant in Thailand: "Welcome to a 'clean' western Restaurant." [Did you spot two errors? In addition, how do the quotation marks affect the message?]

Blooper 3: On the front of a T-shirt sold by American Eagle: "Love the one your with."

Blooper 4: From an advertisement in *The New Yorker*: "Safer than any car Volvo's ever built."

Blooper 5: From a Wendy's International poster: "Be Cool in School! Good Grades Has Its Rewards!"

Blooper 6: Billboard outside a Niagara Falls fast-food restaurant: "We have men in black toys." [Would capital letters have changed the meaning of this sentence?]

Blooper 7: From the *Minnesota Daily*: "The *Daily* is having it's annual Spring Awards Banquet, in order to attend you must purchase tickets through our web link." [Did you spot three errors?]

Blooper 8: ABC News anchor Charlie Gibson: "What makes a presidential candidate lose their cool?"

Blooper 9: From an Associated Press (AP) article: "It would take a person spending $1 million per day, everyday, the next 169 years to spend as much money as AIG lost during the fourth quarter, which lasted just 92 days."

Blooper 10: Headline in *The Washington Times*: "Threat of espionage hinder Paris air show."

13

Reinforcement Exercises

LEVEL 1

A. Self-Check. Capitalization. In the following sentences, use standard proofreading marks to correct errors you find in capitalization. Use three short lines (see the example below) under a lowercase letter to indicate that it is to be changed to a capital letter. Draw a diagonal (/) through a capital letter you wish to change to a lowercase letter. Indicate at the right the total number of changes you have made in each sentence.

Example: The Bandit Henry McCarthy was also known as Billy the kid.   2

1. The Makers of the popular mobile game angry birds plan to open Theme Parks in europe, china, and the united states.   _____

2. Born in houston, michael dell, CEO of dell computers, grew up in the State of texas.   _____

3. Starbucks ensures high standards by training its Baristas in Coffee preparation techniques and Customer Service.   _____

4. In the Fall i plan to begin my Master's Degree in Finance at the massachusetts institute of technology.   _____

5. Facebook's acquisition of instagram was one of the largest in internet history.   _____

6. Tourists who visit grimsey island, located off iceland's northern coast, can walk across the arctic circle there.   _____

7. Regulations of the sarbanes-oxley act of 2002 resulted in costly expenses for our Company.   _____

8. Salt lake city, in the State of Utah, was founded by Brigham Young and a small Party of Mormons in 1847.   _____

9. To this day, AT&T remains a dominant force in the Telecommunications industry.   _____

10. The boston marathon is an annual Sporting Event hosted by the City of Boston, Massachusetts, on patriot's day, the third Monday of April.   _____

Check your answers below.

B. Capitalization. Use proofreading marks to correct any capitalization errors in these sentences. Indicate the total number of changes at the right. If no changes are needed, write *0*.

11. The Actor Alec Baldwin was kicked off an American Airlines Flight for refusing to stop playing words with friends on his Smartphone.   _____

12. Do you think i should prepare the outline for today's Meeting using Arabic or Roman numerals?   _____

13. The Abejuela Family visited rhode island during the Summer and soon learned why it is known as the ocean state.

_____

14. Cathy Paulsen took a Sabbatical during the Months of april and may, but she hopes to return to her Job by Summer.

_____

15. Our Company encourages Employees to earn Associate's and Bachelor's Degrees at nearby Colleges and Universities.

_____

16. Nontraditional Students face the challenge of juggling full-time jobs while working on their Degrees.

_____

17. The Post Office doesn't deliver mail to Steven Stark's home in the City of Santa Maria, California, anymore.

_____

18. Steven Stark, who owns an internet company, now gets all his mail delivered Online.

_____

19. A company in beaverton, oregon, called earth class mail has developed Technology that makes digital mail possible.

_____

20. People who receive digital mail worry about Mail Fraud and Identity Theft.

_____

21. The united states postal service says it is losing a lot of Business because of the increasing popularity of Digital Mail.

_____

22. All company representatives gathered in kansas city in the chouteau room of the hyatt regency crown center for the annual Spring sales meeting.

_____

23. Work schedules will have to be adjusted in september for labor day.

_____

24. Last Fall Tish Young took out a policy with the prudential life insurance company. (The word *the* is part of the company name.)

_____

25. The green bay packers won the first super bowl in 1967.

_____

26. Professor Solis used the socratic method of questioning students to elicit answers about Business Law.

_____

27. After driving through New York state, we stayed in New York city and visited the Empire State building.

_____

28. Bob Mensch completed the requirements for a Master's Degree at ucla.

_____

29. The Nonprofit organization kiva.com gives individuals the opportunity to make business loans to people in Developing Countries.

_____

30. The most popular snacks eaten during the super bowl are Chicken Wings, Tortilla Chips, Pizza, and Pretzels.

_____

LEVEL 2

A. **Self-Check. Capitalization.** Use proofreading marks to correct errors you find in capitalization. Indicate at the right the total number of changes you make. If no changes are needed, write *0*.

Example: Project manager Karen O'Brien was promoted to Vice President.   3

31. Kevin Systrom, Founder and CEO of instagram, a photo-sharing App, also served as an Associate in google's Corporate Development Department.

_____

32. Martin Cooper, a General Manager at Motorola, created the first true Cell Phone.

_____

33. General manager Cooper made his first call to his Rivals in AT&T's research and development department. (Assume this is the official name of this department.)

_____

34. Additional information on the features of our new Security Software is available on Page 41 in appendix B. _____

35. Both my Mother and my Sister purchased iPad Tablet Computers as christmas gifts to themselves. _____

36. The Fishing Industry in the Pacific northwest is reeling from the impact of recent Federal regulations. _____

37. Our business manager and our executive vice president recently attended an e-business seminar in southern California. _____

38. My Professor recommended that I read the article titled "Best And Worst Jobs Of 2015." _____

39. Please send the order to Ms. Milagros Ojermark, manager, customer services, Atlas Fitness Equipment inc., 213 Summit Drive, Spokane, Washington 99201. _____

40. SUBJECT: new payroll processing procedure _____

Check your answers below.

B. Capitalization. Use proofreading marks to correct capitalization errors in the following sentences. Indicate the number of changes you make for each sentence.

41. A team of Physicists in california is using google's collection of scanned books to track the Evolution of Language. _____

42. All Government Agencies must make their Websites accessible to the Blind. _____

43. U.S. district judge Marilyn Hall Patel authorized a Class-Action Lawsuit against Target corporation for failure to make its site accessible. _____

44. Health minister Anbumani Ramadoss is proud that India was the first Country to ban images of smoking in all tv shows and new films. _____

45. My uncle Louie recently purchased a ford focus to use for his trip to the east coast this Fall. _____

46. Because brazil, australia, and argentina are located in the southern hemisphere, their Summers and Winters are the opposite of ours. _____

47. When the president, the secretary of state, and the secretary of labor traveled to minnesota, stringent security measures were put into place. _____

48. To locate the exact amount of Federal funding, look on Line 7, Page 6 of supplement no. 4. _____

49. Tony Fadell, one of the Developers of the iPod, hurried to gate A84 to catch flight 250 to west Virginia. _____

50. My Supervisor recommended that I read the book *Marketing In The Age Of Google*. _____

51. Google was originally named googol; however, an Angel Investor made a check out to "Google, inc.," and this typo became the Company's name. _____

52. Send all inquiries in writing to Do Won Chang, CEO, Forever 21, 2001 south Alameda street, los angeles, california 90058. _____

53. SUBJECT: your report needed by friday _____

54. Veterans Day is a Federal Holiday; therefore, Banks will be closed. _____

55. Franklin became an Assistant to the Administrator of the Governor Bacon Health center, which is operated by the department of health and social services in Delaware. _____

56. Many Cybercriminals use a fraudulent scheme known as "Phishing" to obtain personal information from Victims. _____

57. For lunch Hamed ordered a big mac, French fries, and a coca-cola. _____

58. A midwesterner who enjoys sunshine, Mr. Larsson travels South each Winter to vacation in Florida. _____

59. Illy, a company founded in the Northern part of Italy during World war I, produces coffee made from pure arabica beans. _____

60. Please contact our customer service department to discuss a refund for your Acer Tablet Computer. _____

LEVEL 3

A. Self-Check. Capitalization. Use standard proofreading marks to indicate necessary changes in capitalization. Write the total number of changes at the right.

Example: Even though mercury is closest to the sun, venus, is the hottest planet.   _3_

61. Even though the E-mail message was marked "confidential," the Vice President forwarded it to her entire Staff. _____

62. His guiding principle for running his company is this: demand the very best from everyone. _____

63. In South America most Brazilians speak portuguese, most Surinamese speak dutch, and most Guyanese speak english. _____

64. The Late President Franklin D. Roosevelt, who served in Office during the great depression, is remembered for passing the new deal, a legislative package that helped the american economy recover. _____

65. Malcolm Forbes once said, "failure is success if we learn from it." _____

66. The most common lies job seekers make on their Résumés are the following:
  1. inflated job titles
  2. false employment dates
  3. fake academic credentials _____

67. How on Earth do these job seekers think they will get away with it? _____

68. Money traders watched carefully the relation of the american dollar to the kuwaiti dinar, the swiss franc, and the british pound. _____

69. The library of congress featured a collection of asian-american writers. _____

70. Our Organization's bylaws state the following: "The Secretary of the Association will submit an agenda two weeks before each meeting." _____

Check your answers below.

61. (5) e-mail "Confidential" vice president staff   62. (1) Demand   63. (3) Portuguese Dutch English   64. (7) late office Great Depression New Deal American   65. (1) Failure   66. (4) résumés   Inflated False Fake   67. (1) earth   68. (4) American Kuwaiti Swiss British   69. (4) Library Congress   70. (1) organization's Asian-American

B. Capitalization. Use proofreading marks to indicate necessary changes in capitalization. Write the number of changes at the right.

71. A new Employee of Goldman Sachs was surprised to read this rule in the employee handbook: "it is the policy of the firm to make no comment on rumors whatsoever, even to deny rumors you believe to be untrue." _____

72. Long considered the ninth Planet, pluto lost this classification in 2006. _____

73. As the Sun beat down on the crowd, Eric Schmidt, Former Chief Executive and current Chairman of google, delivered the Graduation Address to the Students of UC berkeley. _____

74. Would you like more coffee? no, I'm fine for now. _____

75. The fair labor standards act, which was passed in 1938, established the Country's first Minimum Wage. _____

76. Terry noticed that the english spoken by asians in hong kong sounded more british than american. _____

77. Our accounting department should mark this Invoice "paid." _____

78. The Minutes of our last meeting contained the following statement: "the vice president acted on behalf of the president, who was attending a conference in the far east." _____

79. Our Office Manager always uses "Best Regards" as his complimentary close. _____

80. Labor specialists predict that these career fields will offer strong job growth through 2020:
    1. sales and marketing
    2. engineering
    3. computer systems
    4. accounting and finance
    5. renewable energy
    6. health care
    7. security
    8. service industries _____

C. Review. Capitalization. Select *a* or *b* to indicate correct capitalization. Assume that each group of words is part of a complete sentence.

81. a. my occupational therapist   b. my Occupational Therapist _____

82. a. the Golden Gate bridge   b. the Golden Gate Bridge _____

83. a. awarded a Master's degree   b. awarded a master's degree _____

84. a. courses in Italian and art history   b. courses in italian and art history _____

85. a. the Venetian Room at the Fairmont Hotel   b. the venetian room at the fairmont hotel _____

86. a. French fries and a pepsi-cola   b. french fries and a Pepsi-Cola _____

87. a. a message marked "private"   b. a message marked "Private" _____

88. a. a winter ski trip   b. a Winter ski trip _____

89. a. the mayor's speech   b. the Mayor's speech _____

90. a. a Television show on PBS   b. a television show on PBS _____

91. a. she and i will attend   b. she and I will attend _____

92. a. Euclid Avenue in Cleveland   b. Euclid avenue in Cleveland _____

93. a. on a Friday in July	b. on a friday in july	_____
94. a. conduct a google search	b. conduct a Google search	_____

95. a. SUBJECT: 2014 Annual Report
    Available
	b. SUBJECT: 2014 annual report
	    available
		_____

96. a. a british rock band	b. a British rock band	_____
97. a. talking with my Mom and Dad	b. talking with my mom and dad	_____
98. a. visiting the City of Seattle	b. visiting the city of Seattle	_____
99. a. in the eastern part of town	b. in the Eastern part of town	_____
100. a. Samsung Smartphone	b. Samsung smartphone	_____

D. Writing Exercise. Using Capitalization. On a separate sheet, write one or two paragraphs summarizing an article from a local newspaper. Choose an article with as many capital letters as possible. Apply the rules of capitalization you learned in this chapter.

E. FAQs About Business English Review. In the space provided, write the correct answer choice.

101. Please make a *(a) xerox, (b) photocopy* of the contract to send to Washington. _____

102. We have special tutoring available for any *(a) nonEnglish-speaking,*
(b) non-English-speaking students. _____

103. He plans to pursue a career in the field of *(a) economics, (b) Economics.* _____

104. Many people get a *(a) Flu, (b) flu* shot each year. _____

105. The fire *(a) marshal, (b) martial* suspected that arson was involved in the fire. _____

106. To prevent looting after the earthquake, officials declared *(a) marshal,*
(b) martial law. _____

107. Our e-mail newsletter is sent to customers *(a) bimonthly, (b) semimonthly* on the
15th and the last day of the month. _____

108. Employees are paid *(a) biweekly, (b) semiweekly*, which means they get 26 paychecks
a year. _____

109. Because you were out last week, you need to *(a) make up, (b) makeup, (c) make-up*
18 hours of work. _____

110. The film *Iron Lady* won an Oscar for best *(a) make-up, (b) makeup, (c) make up.* _____

Chat About It ◀◀

Your instructor may assign any of the following topics for you to discuss in class, in an online chat room, or on an online discussion board. Some of the discussion topics may require outside research. You may also be asked to read and respond to postings made by your classmates.

Discussion Topic 1: In this chapter you learned that the first-person singular pronoun *I* is capitalized; however, in other languages such as French and Italian, this same pronoun is not capitalized. Why do you think we capitalize this pronoun in English? Try doing research to find an answer. Share your thoughts and findings with your classmates.

Discussion Topic 2: The word *capitalize* comes from *capital*, meaning "head." The word *capital*, in all its uses (capital of a state or country, capital punishment, capitalism, capital letter), is associated with some sort of importance. Why do you think some words are capitalized in English and others are not? What do capitalized words communicate in our writing? Why do you think it is important to follow standard capitalization rules? Share your thoughts with your classmates.

Discussion Topic 3: Choose a language other than English and conduct research to find out what capitalization rules are used. What words are commonly capitalized? What pronouns are capitalized, if any? Does the language use capital letters at all? Share your findings with your classmates.

Discussion Topic 4: Many countries, especially in Europe, have a system similar to U.S. trademarks based on **geographical indications (GIs)**. Certain products can be identified only if they originate from a particular area. For example, Gorgonzola cheese, Kalamata olives, and Champagne can be labeled as such only if they come from the designated region of Italy, Greece, or France. Choose a specific country and do research on its use of geographical indications. What specific products are covered by GIs in this country? Share your findings with your classmates.

Discussion Topic 5: In this chapter you learned that some company and product names contain unconventional capitalization known as *intercaps* or *BiCaps*; for example, *iPad, LinkedIn, eBay, PeopleSoft, PowerPoint,* and *QuickBooks*. If you were writing to these companies or writing about these products, would it be important to get the capitalization right? Why or why not? What if you were including these software packages on a résumé? Would it matter whether you capitalized them properly? Share your opinions with your classmates.

Posttest

Use proofreading marks to correct errors you find in capitalization. Then compare your answers with those below.

1. Do you think i should try to earn a PhD Degree?

2. SUBJECT: employee retreat this friday

3. I really enjoyed the book *Making Ideas Happen: Overcoming The Obstacles Between Vision And Reality*.

4. My Neighbor is trying to become fluent in arabic before her trip this Summer to the Northern part of Africa.

5. The fair housing act, which was passed in 1968, protects Buyers and Renters from Seller or Landlord discrimination.

6. The Wedding will take place in the monomoy room of the chatham bars inn next saturday.

7. Applicants must have a Master's Degree to be considered for the Controller position.

8. My Cousin attended an online Training Session on Waze, a GPS navigation App that he plans to use on his Smartphone.

9. Charles Darwin, the english Naturalist and Writer, once said, "in the long history of humankind, those who learned to collaborate and improvise most effectively have prevailed."

10. At a town hall meeting in Georgia, president Obama said he was embarrassed that he didn't speak a Foreign language.

1. I degree 2. Employee Retreat This Friday 3. the and 4. neighbor Arabic summer northern 5. Fair Housing Act buyers renters seller landlord 6. wedding Monomoy Room Chatham Bars Inn Saturday 7. master's degree controller 8. cousin training session app smartphone 9. English naturalist writer In 10. President foreign

Numbers 14

Not everything that can be counted counts, and not everything that counts can be counted.

—Albert Einstein,
theoretical physicist

Objectives

When you have completed the materials in this chapter, you will be able to do the following:

LEVEL 1
1. Correctly choose between figure and word forms to express general numbers, numbers beginning sentences, and numbers that require hyphens and commas.
2. Express money, dates, clock time, addresses, telephone and fax numbers, and company names appropriately.

LEVEL 2
3. Use the correct form in writing related numbers, consecutive numbers, periods of time, ages, anniversaries, and round numbers.
4. Use the correct form in expressing numbers used with words, abbreviations, and symbols.

LEVEL 3
5. Express correctly weights, measurements, fractions, percentages, and decimals.
6. Use the correct form in expressing grades, scores, voting results, and ordinals.

Circle art: © iStockphoto.com/Pavel Khorenyan

© GlowImages/Alamy

Pretest

Underline any incorrect expression of numbers, and write an improved form in the blank provided (for example, *$10* rather than *ten dollars*). Then compare your answers with those below.

1. High Tech Solutions paid 14000 employees an extra $2500 in bonuses on December thirty-first.

_____

2. 1/5 of the world's mobile smartphone users actively use location-based services such as Foursquare to share their current whereabouts.

_____

3. In addition, 62% of smartphone users plan to use location-based services in the future.

_____

4. Please plan to attend the 1st informational meeting on May 21st at eleven a.m. to learn how our company can use location-based service to promote our products.

_____

5. When Mallory reached 17 years of age, she applied to 3 colleges in 2 states.

_____

6. Please take twenty-two dollars and fifty cents to pick up 50 forty-five-cent stamps at the post office.

_____

7. Of the forty-seven students who took the notary public class on September 22nd, only three scored lower than seventy on the final exam.

_____

8. The art treasure measures only nine inches by twelve inches, but it is said to be worth nearly two million dollars.

_____

9. His childhood home is located at 1 Broad Street in Potsdam, New York.

_____

10. By 2020 nearly 65% of Americans expect to make payments using their smartphones, which means that approximately 211,000,000 people will be carrying "mobile wallets."

_____

Just as capitalization is governed by convention, so is the expression of numbers. Usage and custom determine whether numbers are to be expressed in the form of a figure (for example, *5*) or in the form of a word (for example, *five*). Numbers expressed as figures are shorter and more easily comprehended, yet numbers used as words are necessary in certain instances. The following guidelines are observed in expressing numbers that appear in written *sentences*. Numbers that appear in business documents such as invoices, statements, and purchase orders are always expressed as figures.

LEVEL 1

Basic Guidelines for Expressing Numbers

In this level you will learn the general rules for expressing numbers. You will also learn how to correctly express items that appear frequently in business correspondence, including monetary amounts, dates, clock time, addresses, telephone and fax numbers, and company names.

10. 65 percent 211 million 9. One
two 6. $22.50 fifty 45-cent 7. 47 September 22 8. 9 by 12 inches $2 million 9. One
1. 14,000 $2,500 December 31 2. One fifth 3. 62 percent 4. first May 21 11 a.m. 5. seventeen three

Circle art: © iStockphoto.com/Pavel Khorenyan

General Rules

Writing Numbers in Word or Figure Form

The numbers *one* through *ten* are generally written as words. Numbers above *ten* are written as figures.

> Our local health club has *eight* workout rooms and *three* whirlpool tubs.

> Of the *32* IPOs backed by private-equity firms, only *13* resulted in a positive return to investors.

Study Tip

To remember it better, some people call this the "Rule of Ten": Words for one through ten; figures for 11 and above.

Numbers That Begin Sentences

Numbers that begin sentences are written as words. If a number involves more than two words, however, the sentence should be rewritten so that the number no longer falls at the beginning.

> *Twelve* well-known companies now function completely online without physical office locations.

> A total of *113* complaints related to social media will be reviewed by the National Labor Relations Board. (Not *One hundred thirteen* complaints will be reviewed.)

Placing Commas in Numbers

When expressing numbers in figure form, separate groups of three digits by commas to improve clarity. This rule does not apply, however, when writing some numbers, including years, house numbers, telephone and fax numbers, zip codes, account numbers, and page numbers.

> In 1984 Motorola sold the first cell phone for *$3,995*, which is about *$9,237* in today's dollars.

> Today you can download over *500,000* apps for an iPhone or iPad, many at no cost.

Trivia Tidbit

The dollar sign ($) first appeared in business correspondence among the British, Americans, Canadians, and Mexicans in the 1770s.

Hyphenating Numbers

Compound numbers from *21* through *99* are hyphenated when they are written in word form.

> *Seventy-four* people applied for the business intelligence analyst position.

> *Fifty-six* stocks performed below expectations last month.

Money

Sums of money $1 or greater are expressed as figures. If a sum is a whole dollar amount, most writers omit the decimal and zeros (even if the amount appears with fractional dollar amounts). Always include commas in monetary figures $1,000 or greater. Use the dollar sign ($) instead of the word *dollars*, and do not add a space between the currency symbol and the figure.

> Most airlines now charge between *$15* and *$30* to check a bag.

> This statement shows purchases of *$7.13*, *$10*, *$43.50*, *$90*, and *$262.78*.

> A ticket for a first-class parlor suite on the *Titanic* cost *$4,350* (about *$100,034* today).

Study Tip

When spelling out amounts of money (for example, on a check), remember that the word *and* is used to indicate the position of the decimal point. Therefore, *$245.98* would be written as *Two Hundred Forty-Five and 98/100 Dollars* (not *Two Hundred and Forty-Five and 98/100 Dollars*).

Sums less than $1 are written as figures that are followed by the word *cents*. If they are part of related sums greater than $1, use a dollar sign and a decimal instead of the word *cents* and do not space between the dollar sign and the decimal point. However, if a sentence contains unrelated amounts of money, treat each amount separately.

> It costs about *11.2 cents* to produce one nickel and about *2.4 cents* to produce one penny.

> Our monthly petty cash statement showed purchases of *$7.13*, *$.99*, *$2.80*, *$1*, and *$.40*. (Related numbers)

> For every *$10* you spend in our restaurant, we will donate *50 cents* to Special Olympics. (Unrelated numbers)

Many companies conduct business globally, which requires making transactions in various currencies. When amounts of money from different countries are used in the same sentence, table, or list, place the appropriate currency abbreviation or symbol before the numerical amount.

> The US$10,000 item will cost £6,298 in Great Britain. (U.S. dollars and British pounds)

> The Thomases will take the following amounts of money with them on their trip to Asia:
> US$1,000 (U.S. dollars)
> ¥81,000 (Japanese yen)
> CNY¥6,300 (Chinese yuan)
> HKD$7,700 (Hong Kong dollars)

Dates

Study Tip

Be mindful of the differences between *spoken* numbers in dates and *written* ones. Although we say, "October first," we write *October 1*.

In dates, numbers that appear after the name of the month are written in **cardinal figures** (*1, 2, 3*, etc.). Those that stand alone or appear before the name of a month are written in **ordinal figures** (*1st, 2nd, 3rd*, etc.).

> The Buttonwood Agreement created the New York Stock Exchange on *May 17, 1792*.

> On the *8th* of June and again on the *23rd*, Seattle experienced record rainfall.

Most American communicators express dates in the following form: month, day, year. A comma is used to separate the day and the year. An alternative form, used primarily in military and international correspondence, uses this order without a comma: day, month, year. Some business organizations, especially those doing business globally, prefer the international date style for its clarity.

Career Tip

As American companies become more global, many are adopting the international date style.

> On *March 13, 2012*, Encyclopedia Britannica announced that it would stop printing books. (General date format)

> An international antismoking treaty took effect on *24 February 2005*. (Military and international date format)

Clock Time

Study Tip

Recall that the abbreviations *a.m.* and *p.m.* are written with lowercase letters and periods.

Figures are used when clock time is expressed with *a.m., p.m., noon,* or *midnight*. Omit the colon and zeros with even clock hours (those without minutes), even if they appear with times that contain hours and minutes.

> The first shift starts at *8 a.m.*; the second, at *3:30 p.m.*

> The silent auction opens at *6:30 p.m.*, and bids may be placed until *12 midnight*.

As an alternative, even clock hours can be used with the word *o'clock*. When using this format, either figures or words may be used. Note that phrases such as *in the afternoon* or *in the morning* may follow clock time expressed with *o'clock* but not with time expressed with *a.m.* and *p.m.*

> Department mail is usually distributed at *ten* (or *10*) *o'clock* in the morning.

> The freeway is backed up as early as *three* (or *3*) *o'clock* in the afternoon on weekdays.

In the United States we use a 12-hour clock to express most time, which requires the use of *a.m.* or *p.m.* for clarity. However, much of the world uses a 24-hour clock format, which is known as **international time**. In the United States, we use this 24-hour clock in the military and in other applications such as international flight schedules and online auctions.

> Your Jet Airways flight leaves Newark, New Jersey, at *18:30* and arrives in Moscow, Russia, at *15:25* the next day. (Military and international time format; 18:30 is equivalent to 6:30 p.m., and 15:25 is equivalent to 3:25 p.m.)

Addresses

Except for the number *One*, house numbers are expressed as figures. Apartment numbers, suite numbers, box numbers, and route numbers are also written in figure form. Do not use commas to separate digits in house numbers.

5 Sierra Drive	27321 Van Nuys Boulevard
One Peachtree Plaza, Suite 900	1762 Cone Street, Apt. 2B
P.O. Box 8935	Rural Route 19

Street names that are numbered *ten* or below are written as ordinal words (*First, Second, Third*). In street names involving numbers greater than *ten*, the numeral portion is written in ordinal figure form (*11th, 22nd, 33rd, 41st*).

201 Third Street	1190 54th Street
2320 West 22nd Street	3261 South 103rd Avenue

Study Tip

Ordinal figures are formed by adding *st, nd, rd,* or *th* to the figure.

Telephone and Fax Numbers

Telephone and fax numbers are expressed with figures. When used, the area code is placed in parentheses before the telephone number. Be sure to include a space after the closing parenthesis. As an alternate form, you may separate the area code from the telephone number with a hyphen. A third format that has gained acceptance is to separate the parts of the number with periods. When you include an extension, separate it from the phone number with a comma.

> Please call us at *555-1101* to confirm your reservation for tomorrow evening.

> You may reach me at *(801) 643-3267, Ext. 244*, after 9:30 a.m.

> Call our toll-free number at *800-340-3281* so that we can assist you with your stock trades.

> Please fax your order to 415.937.5594.

Company Names

Some company and product names contain numbers. Always write these names using the organization's preferred style—even if they seem to defy conventional punctuation. Look how many of the following names should be hyphenated but aren't!

7-Eleven	7 For All Mankind	After Eight thin mints
Saks Fifth Avenue	Five Guys	Product 19 cereal
Motel 6	Chanel No. 5 perfume	9Lives cat food
24 Hour Fitness	One A Day vitamins	V8 juice

Now complete the reinforcement exercises for Level 1.

LEVEL 2

Special Guidelines for Expressing Numbers

Special guidelines exist for expressing related and consecutive numbers. In this level you will also learn how to use numbers to express periods of time; ages and anniversaries; round numbers; and numbers used with words, abbreviations, and symbols.

Related Numbers

Related numbers are those used similarly in the same document. They should be expressed as the largest number is expressed. Therefore, if the largest number is greater than *ten*, all the numbers should be expressed as figures.

> Only *3* orders out of *798* could not be filled on time.

> Of the *98* e-mail messages Casey received today, *19* were marked "Urgent" and *7* were marked "Confidential."

> We ordered *15* pizzas, *12* salads, and *4* cakes for the employee luncheon. (Note that items appearing in a series are always considered to be related.)

Unrelated numbers within the same reference are written as words or figures according to the general guidelines presented earlier in this chapter.

> *Twenty-three* contract changes will be discussed by *89* employees working in *eight* departments.

> During the *four* peak traffic hours, *three* bridges carry at least *20,000* cars.

Consecutive Numbers

Consecutive numbers occur when two numbers appear one after the other, both modifying a following noun (such as *ten 45-cent stamps*). Express the first number in words and the second in figures. If, however, the first number cannot be expressed in *one or two words*, place it in figures also (*120 45-cent* stamps). Do not use commas to separate the figures.

> Our department purchased *nine 32GB* Samsung Galaxy Tabs to be used by our marketing team. (Use word form for the first number and figure form for the second.)

> Historians divided the era into *four 25-year* periods. (Use word form for the first number and figure form for the second.)

Career Tip

If your company has a style manual, check it for number preferences. Larger companies may prescribe the figure or word form they prefer for often-used numbers.

Study Tip

Remember that numbers included in a series (three or more items) are ALWAYS considered related.

Study Tip

With consecutive numbers, remember that the second number is ALWAYS a figure. The first number is usually a word, unless it requires three or more words (*120 5-year-old* children.)

— Circle art: © iStockphoto.com/Pavel Khorenyan

Did you request *twenty 60-watt* CFL bulbs? (Use word form for the first number and figure form for the second.)

We will need at least *150 60-watt* CFL bulbs. (Use figure form for the first number because it requires more than two words.)

Periods of Time

Periods of time (seconds, minutes, hours, days, weeks, months, and years) are treated as any other general number. That is, numbers ten and below are written in word form. Numbers above ten are written in figure form.

A customer can finalize an order on our website within *two* to *three* minutes.

After a *183*-day strike, workers returned to their jobs.

Congress has regulated the federal minimum wage for over *75* years.

Figures are used to achieve special emphasis in expressing business concepts such as discount rates, interest rates, contracts, warranty periods, credit terms, loan periods, and payment terms.

Pay your invoice within *15 days* and receive a *2 percent* discount.

Your loan must be repaid within *90 days* in accordance with its terms.

Higher interest rates are offered on *6-* to *9-month* certificates of deposit.

Study Tip

Figures are easier to understand and remember than words are. That's why business terms, even for numbers under ten, are generally written as figures.

Ages and Anniversaries

Ages and anniversaries that can be expressed in one or two words are generally written in word form. Those that require more than two words are written in figures. Figures are also used when an age (a) appears immediately after a person's name; (b) is expressed in exact years, months, and sometimes days; or (c) is used in a legal or technical sense.

When she was *eighty-eight*, Doris Lessing was awarded the Nobel Peace Prize. (Use word form for age expressed in two or fewer words.)

For her *fortieth* birthday, Jennifer traveled by herself to Italy.

January 14, 2015, marked the *twenty-fifth* anniversary of the premiere of *The Simpsons* on FOX. (Use word form for an anniversary expressed in two or fewer words.)

Katharine Ralph, *63*, plans to retire in two years. (Use figure form for age appearing immediately after a name.)

The child was adopted when he was *3 years 8 months and 24 days* old. (Use figure form for age expressed in terms of exact years and months. Notice that commas are not used to separate age expressions.)

Although the legal voting age is *18*, young people must be *21* to purchase alcohol. (Use figure form for age used in a legal sense.)

Round Numbers

Round numbers are approximations. They may be expressed in word or figure form, although figure form is shorter and easier to comprehend.

Approximately *200* (or *two hundred*) people showed up for the grand opening.

We have received about *20* (or *twenty*) reservations for the wine tasting.

For ease of reading, round numbers in the millions or billions should be expressed with a combination of figures and words. If *one million* is used as an approximation, use all word form; otherwise, write this number using figures and words (*1 million*). Use a combination of figures and words for all other numbers.

The U.S. national debt is expected to be more than *$20 trillion* by 2020.

The world population is approximately *7.2 billion*, and the U.S. Census Bureau expects this figure to grow to around *9.2 billion* by 2050.

Facebook now has more than *1 billion* users, up from *900 million* in 2012.

Numbers Used With Words, Abbreviations, and Symbols

Numbers used with words are expressed as figures. Remember to apply the capitalization rules that you learned in Chapter 13. Notice, too, that no commas are used in serial, account, and policy numbers.

page 59	Policy 04-168315	Area Code 508
Room 318	Volume 5	Highway 101
Option 2	Form 1040	Public Law 96-221

Numbers used with abbreviations are also expressed as figures.

Apt. 34-B	Serial No. 265188440	FY2016
Ext. 3206	Account No. 08166-05741	Social Security No. 535-52-2016

The word *number* is capitalized and abbreviated when it precedes a number. However, if the word *number* begins a sentence, do not abbreviate it.

Stieg Larsson, author of *The Girl With the Dragon Tattoo*, became a *No. 1* best-selling author after his death.

Please pay these invoices: *Nos. 4857, 4858,* and *4859.*

Number 348 submitted the winning bid.

Symbols (such as #, %, ¢) are usually avoided in contextual business writing (sentences). In other business documents where space is limited, however, symbols are frequently used. Numbers appearing with symbols are expressed as figures.

67%	99¢	#2 can	2/10, n/60

Now complete the reinforcement exercises for Level 2.

LEVEL 3

Study Tip

When writing temperatures, specify whether the temperature is Fahrenheit or Celsius. Notice that these two common temperature measurement scales are capitalized.

Additional Guidelines for Expressing Numbers

The following guidelines will help you use appropriate forms for weights and measurements; fractions; percentages and decimals; grades, scores, and voting results; and ordinals.

Weights and Measurements

Weights and measurements, including temperatures, are expressed as figures. When one weight or measure consists of several words treated as a single unit (*3 feet 4 inches*), do not use a comma to separate the units.

My new iPhone measures only *4.5 by 2.31 by 0.37 inches* and weighs just *4.9 ounces*.

Your nonstop flight from Detroit to San Antonio will take *3 hours 9 minutes*.

The truck required *21 gallons* of gasoline and *2 quarts* of oil to travel *250 miles*.

The highest temperature ever recorded was *136 degrees Fahrenheit* in 1922 in El Azizia, Libya.

In messages that contain sentences, spell out nouns following numerals in weights and measurements (*21 gallons* instead of *21 gal.*). In business forms or in statistical presentations, however, you may abbreviate weights and measurements.

8′ × 10′	#10	7 oz.	3,500 sq. ft.	2 lb.	12 qt.

Study Tip

Use figures to express metric measurements. When including metric measurements in a sentence, spell out the units of measure (*5 kilometers, 1.75 liters*).

Fractions

Fractions often appear in business documents. The type of fraction determines whether to write it in words or figures.

Simple Fractions

Simple fractions are fractions in which both the numerator and denominator are whole numbers. If the simple fraction can be expressed in two words, use word form. If a fraction functions as a noun, no hyphen is used. If it functions as an adjective, a hyphen separates its parts.

> Linguists predict that as many as *one half* of the world's 6,800 languages could disappear over the next century. (The fraction is used as a noun. Notice that the preposition *of* follows the fraction.)

> A *two-thirds* majority is needed to pass the school bond measure. (The fraction is used as an adjective.)

Long or awkward fractions appearing in sentences may be written either as figures or as a combination of figures and words.

> Scientists have determined that the polio virus measures *1 millionth* of an inch. (A combination of words and figures is easier to comprehend.)

> Flight records revealed that the emergency system was activated *13/200* of a second after the pilot was notified. (Figure form is easier to comprehend.)

Study Tip

A fraction immediately followed by an *of* phrase usually functions as a noun (*one third of the cars*). Therefore, it is not hyphenated.

Mixed Fractions

Mixed fractions, which are whole numbers combined with fractions, are always expressed with figures.

> Her carry-on bag measures *21¼ inches* by *13½ inches* by *8¾ inches*.

Use the special character set of your word processing program to insert fractions that are written in figures. Fractions written in figures that are not found in special character sets of word processing programs are formed by using the diagonal to separate the two parts. When fractions that are constructed with diagonals appear with key fractions, be consistent by using the diagonal construction for all the fractions involved.

> The shelves were supposed to be *36 5/8 inches* wide, not *26 3/8 inches*. (Notice that fractions that must be constructed with diagonals are separated from their related whole numbers.)

Study Tip

Do not add endings such as *ths* or *nds* to fractions that are expressed as figures (*4/300*, NOT *4/300ths*).

Percentages and Decimals

Percentages are expressed with figures followed by the word *percent*. The percent sign (%) is used only on business forms or in statistical presentations.

> The highest U.S. unemployment rate was *23.6 percent* in 1932; the lowest unemployment rate was *1.2 percent* in 1944.

> Of all Facebook users between the ages of eighteen and thirty-four, *28 percent* check their page before even getting out of bed in the morning.

Decimals are expressed with figures. If a decimal does not contain a whole number before the decimal point, a zero should be placed before the decimal. Notice that commas are not used in the decimal portion of a number, no matter how many digits it has.

> Lance Armstrong had the highest average speed in the Tour de France when he maintained an average speed of *25.883* miles per hour in 2005. (The decimal contains a whole number.)

> The smallest winged insect is the Tanzanian parasitic wasp, which has a wingspan of *0.2* millimeters. (Place a zero before a decimal that does not contain a whole number.)

> She purchased a gold nugget from Idaho that weighs *0.045* gram. (Place a zero before a decimal that does not contain a whole number.)

Grades, Scores, and Voting Results

Always use figures to express academic grades, scores on tests or of sporting events, and voting results.

> Melinda scored a *98* on her final exam, giving her an overall average of *94.5* in her management class.

> The highest scoring game in baseball history occurred in 1922 when the Chicago Cubs beat the Philadelphia Phillies *26* to *23*.

> A *5*-to-*4* Supreme Court decision said that the government cannot ban political spending by corporations.

Ordinals

Ordinal numbers are used to show the position in an ordered sequence. Although ordinal numbers are generally expressed in word form (*first, second, third*), three exceptions should be noted: (a) figure form is used for dates appearing before a month or appearing alone; (b) figure form is used for street names involving numbers greater than *ten*; and (c) figure form is used when the ordinal would require more than two words.

Most Ordinals

> The Caldecott Medal, which is awarded to distinguished children's books, recently celebrated its *seventy-fifth anniversary*.

> Before the *eighteenth century*, spelling was not standardized.

> Of the 221 cities analyzed worldwide, Vienna, Austria, ranks *first* in quality of living.

> Richard L. Hanna represents the *Twenty-fourth Congressional District* in New York.

Dates

Please respond by the *20th of July* so that I can make our reservation. (Date appears before the month.)

Paychecks are issued on the *1st* and the *15th* of each month. (Dates appear alone.)

Streets

Forbes magazine ranked *Fifth Avenue* in New York City as the most expensive street in the world. (Street name involves a number between *one* and *ten*.)

Our headquarters will move to 3589 *23rd Street* on the *6th* of September. (Street name involves a number greater than *ten*.)

Larger ordinals

Citigroup's announcement was the *251st* public notification of a data breach this year. (Ordinal requires more than two words.)

Howard Schultz, CEO of Starbucks, ranks *331st* on *Forbes'* list of the 400 richest Americans.

Some word processing programs automatically set ordinal suffixes (*st, nd, rd, th*) superscript. If you dislike this program feature, you may turn it off.

Now complete the reinforcement exercises for Level 3.

Q: I know the abbreviation for *pound* is *lb.*, but that doesn't make sense to me because none of the letters match. Why do we use this abbreviation?

A: The abbreviation *lb.* actually stands for the Latin word *libra*, which refers to the basic unit of Roman weight, from which our present-day pound derives.

Q: I recently saw the following format used by a business to publish its telephone number on its stationery and business cards: 212.582.0903. Is it now an option to use periods in telephone numbers?

A: Yes, this is now an acceptable option for writing telephone and fax numbers that perhaps reflects European influences. To some, the style is upscale and chic; to others, it's just confusing. Telephone and fax numbers written in the traditional formats are most readily recognized. That's why it's probably safer to stick with hyphens or parentheses: 212-582-0903 or (212) 582-0903.

Q: My manager is preparing an advertisement for a charity event. She has written this: *Donors who give $100 dollars or more receive plaques.* I know this is not right, but I can't exactly put my finger on the problem.

A: The problem is in *$100 dollars.* That is like saying *dollars dollars.* Drop the word *dollars* and use only the dollar sign: *Donors who give $100 or more. . . .*

Q: I recently received an invitation to my high school reunion that used the apostrophe like this: *the class of '04.* Is this a correct use of the apostrophe?

A: Yes. In addition to forming noun possession and contractions, the apostrophe has several other uses. It can be used to take the place of omitted letters or figures. This is especially common when expressing a year or a decade. (*Most people were caught off-guard by the stock market crash of '29. The '60s were a time of protest and change.*)

Q: A fellow team member wants to show dollar amounts in two forms, such as the following: *The consultant charges two hundred dollars ($200) an hour.* I think this is overkill. Do we have to show figures in two forms?

A: In formal legal documents, amounts of money may be expressed in words followed by figures in parentheses. However, business writers do not follow this practice because it is unnecessary, wordy, and pretentious. In fact, some readers are insulted because the practice suggests they are not bright enough to comprehend just one set of figures.

Q: Should I put quotation marks around figures to emphasize them? For example, *Your account has a balance of "$2,136.18."*

A: Certainly not! Quotation marks are properly used to indicate an exact quotation, or they may be used to enclose the definition of a word. They should not be used as a mechanical device for added emphasis.

Q: Are roman numerals still used? If so, how?

A: Yes, roman numerals are still used in a number of situations: some historical events (*World War II*); some entertainment and sporting events (*Super Bowl XLVI, Games of the XXXI Olympiad*); main topics in outlines; dates (*MMX* for the year 2010); literary items (*Volume IV, p. viii*); laws (*Title IV*); names of monarchs and popes (*Queen Elizabeth II, Pope Benedict XVI*); sequels to movies and video games (*Rocky IV, Street Fighter III*); and legal names (*Thomas Cruise Mapother IV*, which is Tom Cruise's legal name).

Q: How should I spell the word *lose* in this sentence: *The employee tripped over a* (*lose* or *loose*) *cord?*

A: In your sentence use the adjective *loose*, which means "not fastened," "not tight," or "having freedom of movement." Perhaps you can remember it by thinking of the common expression *loose change*, which suggests unattached, free coins jingling in your pocket. If you *lose* (*mislay*) some of those coins, you have less money and fewer *o's*.

Q: I'm having trouble telling the difference between these two words: *aid* and *aide*. Can they be used interchangeably?

A: Absolutely not! The word *aid* is a verb meaning "to help or assist" (*Ben & Jerry's aids many environmental organizations*). *Aid* is also a noun meaning "assistance" (*The United States plans to send foreign aid to several African countries*). The word *aide* is also a noun but refers to "a person who acts as an assistant" (*The student aide assisted her professor with grading*).

Q: Why should I worry about learning all of these grammar, punctuation, and mechanics rules? Most people I know don't know the rules and make mistakes all the time. Isn't making mistakes okay, as long as I get my point across?

A: It does seem as though fewer and fewer people understand and apply the proper rules of grammar, punctuation, and mechanics. However, that doesn't make learning them any less important. You see, the way you speak and write directly reflects your professionalism, your education, and your credibility in the workplace. In addition, the way you write and speak affects the way customers and clients view your organization. If you make mistakes, people may think that you are sloppy, uneducated, or not very bright. They may also choose not to do business with such a careless, unprofessional organization. Using proper grammar also allows you to get your point across more clearly, and it shows you have respect for those you are communicating with. It is for these reasons that those who communicate correctly and professionally are the ones who are most successful in today's competitive work environment. The time and effort you put into learning the rules will pay off in the long run. We promise!

SPOT THE Blooper

Using the skills you are learning in this class, try to identify why the following items are bloopers. Consult your textbook, dictionary, or reference manual as needed. To see if you recognized the blooper, go to **www.cengagebrain.com** and use your access code to see the Spot the Blooper key.

Blooper 1: On a sign in front of a Days Inn in Las Vegas: "Welcome! Free Wife!"

Blooper 2: Sign in the parking lot of a shopping center in Chatham, Massachusetts: "Parking for Post Office Plaza Patron's Only. Violators will be towed at owners expense." [Did you spot two errors?]

Blooper 3: Beautifully engraved wooden sign in front of the Glen Ellen Inn in Glen Ellen, Sonoma Valley, California: "Oysters & Martini's."

Blooper 4: Sign outlining the lost coat tag policy at Hong Kong, a Faneuil Hall bar in Boston: "If you loose or can not produce your coat check tag, you must way until the close of business, to claim your belongings." [Did you spot four errors?]

Blooper 5: An advertisement for the Fireside Inn in Portland, Maine: "Our menus appeal to a wide set of tastes and we are extremely proud of our staff. Please browse them at your leisure."

Blooper 6: Sign in front of a restaurant: "Open seven days a week and weekends."

Blooper 7: *The Times Union* [Albany, New York] featured an advertisement with the following 2-inch headline: "On Thursday morning, I found the car of my dreams in my pajamas."

Blooper 8: A column in *The Charlotte Observer* mentioned the wealth of Sam Walton's widow and daughter: "Forbes estimates that each are worth $16 billion."

Blooper 9: Large banner displayed prominently behind Hillary Clinton as she spoke during a gathering of Silicon Valley CEOs about the importance in today's economy of training skilled workers: "New Jobs for Tommorrow."

Blooper 10: Print ad for Stella Artois lager: "Perfection Has It's Price."

14 Reinforcement Exercises

LEVEL 1

A. Self-Check. Number Expression. Choose the correct answer.

1. All *(a) eighteen, (b) 18* attendees agreed that the ethics workshop was beneficial. _____

2. *(a) 23, (b) Twenty three (c) Twenty-three* call centers in India announced that they will be switching from customer service to mortgage processing. _____

3. On the *(a) 9th, (b) ninth* of April, Maryland became the first state to pass legislation that will make it illegal for employers to ask employees and job applicants for their social media user names and passwords. _____

4. U.S. Census forms are available in *(a) 6, (b) six* languages. _____

5. The U.S. Census Bureau spends about *(a) $1.00, (b) $1* per person on paid advertising to persuade citizens to take part in the census. _____

6. The new Emporis buildings are located at *(a) Three, (b) 3* Peachtree Pointe in Atlanta. _____

7. Financial institutions are clustered on *(a) Seventh, (b) 7th* Avenue in New York City. _____

8. Send the letter to *(a) 320 27th Street, (b) 320 27* Street. _____

9. Organizers expect *(a) 59000, (b) 59,000* to attend the Natural Products Expo in Anaheim. _____

10. We plan to meet again at *(a) 11:00 a.m., (b) 11 a.m.* Friday. _____

Check your answers below.

B. Number Expression. Assume that the following phrases appear within sentences (unless otherwise noted) in business correspondence. Write the preferred forms in the spaces provided. If a phrase is correct as shown, write *C*.

Example: 1135 54 Street   1135 54th Street

11. seventeen new status updates _____

12. on Sixth Street _____

13. charged $.15 per copy _____

14. received 9 text messages _____

15. on December nineteenth _____

16. located on 5th Avenue _____

17. charges of $3.68, 79 cents, and $40.00 _____

18. on the ninth of May _____

19. meeting at 8:00 a.m. _____

20. arrived at 10 p.m. in the evening _____

1.b 2.c 3.a 4.b 5.b 6.b 7.a 8.a 9.b 10.b

21. a total of fifty-seven orders _____

22. on October 31st _____

23. moved to 12655 32nd Street _____

24. costs $79 dollars _____

25. (Beginning of sentence) 27 interviewees _____

26. 1319 people visited _____

27. the address is 7 Hampton Square _____

28. the address is 1 Hampton Square _____

29. has eighty-one rooms _____

30. (International style) at 6 p.m. _____

31. (International style) on April 15, 2015 _____

32. located at 2742 8th Street _____

33. at six thirty p.m. _____

34. call (800)123-4567 _____

35. for one hundred dollars _____

36. costs exactly 90¢ _____

37. at 18307 Eleventh Street _____

38. call 800/598-3459 _____

39. all 50 states _____

40. bought 2 lattes _____

C. Writing Exercise. Number Expression. Rewrite these sentences correcting any errors you note.

41. 259 identity theft complaints were filed with the FTC on November 2nd alone.

_____

42. Please call me at 925/685/1230 Ext. 2306.

_____

43. On November 15th Ivan submitted the following petty cash disbursements: $2.80, 95 cents, $5.00, and 25 cents.

_____

44. Erika Rothschild moved from 1,716 Sunset Drive to 1 Bellingham Court.

_____

45. 24 different wireless packages are available from our 3 local dealers.

_____

46. On the 18 of August, I sent you 3 e-mail messages about restricting personal Web use.

_____

47. Although McDonald's advertised a sandwich that cost only ninety-nine cents, most customers found that lunch cost between three dollars and three dollars and ninety-nine cents.

_____

_____

48. Regular work breaks are scheduled at 10:00 a.m. in the morning and again at 3:30 p.m. in the afternoon.

_____

49. We want to continue operations through the thirtieth, but we may be forced to close by the twenty-second.

_____

50. The United States experienced 20000 job cuts between April first and April thirtieth.

_____

LEVEL 2

A. Self-Check. Number Expression. Choose the correct answer.

51. Gillian Martin prepared *(a) 2 40-page, (b) two 40-page* business proposals.   _____

52. People have been receiving spam in their e-mail boxes for over *(a) thirty-five, (b) 35* years.   _____

53. Your flight to Honolulu will depart from *(a) Gate Seven, (b) Gate 7.*   _____

54. Of the 235 e-mail messages sent, only *(a) 7, (b) seven* bounced back.   _____

55. Although he is only *(a) 25, (b) twenty-five*, Mohammad Sigari owns his own restaurant in Monterey.   _____

56. AIG lost *(a) $62 billion, (b) $62,000,000,000* in just 92 days.   _____

57. Have you completed your IRS Form *(a) Ten Forty, (b) 1040?*   _____

58. The *(a) 100th, (b) one hundredth* anniversary of the sinking of the Titanic was observed in 2012.   _____

59. Your short-term loan covers a period of *(a) 60, (b) sixty* days.   _____

60. The serial number on my tablet computer is *(a) 85056170, (b) 85,056,170.*   _____

Check your answers below.

B. Number Expression. For the following sentences, underline any numbers or words that are expressed inappropriately and write the correct forms in the spaces provided. If a sentence is correct as written, write *C*.

Example: The documentation group has prepared <u>4 twenty-page</u> reports.   four 20-page

61. Of the 3,022 paintings in the Louvre's permanent collection, one painting, the Mona Lisa, is the most popular.   _____

62. No. 3 on the agenda will take about forty-five minutes to discuss.   _____

63. Our board of directors is composed of 15 members, of whom three are accountants, four are marketing specialists, and eight are in the finance industry.   _____

64. We plan to order five twelve-month data plans for our employees.   _____

65. After a period of sixteen years, ownership reverts to the state. _[handwritten: 16]_ _____

66. In 2006 Facebook had approximately 12,000,000 users; today it has over 1,000,000,000. _[handwritten: million / billion]_ _____

67. The following policy Nos. are listed for Lisa Orta: No. 1355801 and No. 1355802. _[handwritten: C]_ _____

68. Model 8,400 costs $10,000 and can be leased for $275 a month. _____

69. More than 10,000,000 people have downloaded the Instagram app for their Android smartphones. _[handwritten: 10 million]_ _____

70. Of the 385 manuscript pages, ten pages require minor revisions and eight pages demand heavy revision. _[handwritten: 10 ... 8]_ _____

71. John Bologni, forty-one, and Sarah Flores, thirty-three, were recognized for their philanthropic work in the community. _[handwritten: C]_ _____

72. On page forty-four of Volume two, you will see that absenteeism costs American corporations $74,000,000,000 annually. _[handwritten: 2 / billion]_ _____

73. Warranties on all plasma HDTVs are limited to ninety days. _[handwritten: C]_ _____

74. They can't believe that the amateur video they made in their backyard has received eight hundred thousand views on YouTube. _[handwritten: 800,000]_ _____

75. Only two of the 78 staff members took a sick day last month. _[handwritten: Seventy-eight]_ _____

76. Rich Snyder became president of In-N-Out Burger when he was just 24 years old. _[handwritten: Twenty-four]_ _____

77. When the child was two years six months old, his parents established a trust fund for $1.6 million. _[handwritten: 2 ... 6]_ _____

78. Bill Gates' mansion on Lake Washington features a wall of twenty-four video screens, parking for twenty cars, and a reception hall for one hundred people. _[handwritten: 100]_ _____

79. Taking 7 years to construct, the 40,000-square-foot home reportedly cost more than fifty million dollars. _[handwritten: 50]_ _____

80. Ford Motor Company sold more than 17,000,000 Model Ts between 1908 and 1927, making it the best-selling car in history. _[handwritten: million]_ _____

C. **Number Expression.** Assume that the following phrases appear in business or professional correspondence. Write the preferred forms in the spaces provided. If a phrase is correct as shown, write *C*.

81. sold for $3,600,000 _____

82. one hundred four six-page essays _____

83. a law that is one year two months and five days old _____

84. nine offices with eleven computers and fifteen desks _____

85. three seventy-five pound weights _____

86. loan period of ninety days _____

87. Joan Brault, seventy-six, and and Frank Brault, seventy-four _____

88. Account No. 362,486,012 _____

89. four point nine billion dollars _____

90. Highway Six _____

91. you are Number 25 _____

92. sixty-three job applicants _____

93. about three hundred voters _____

94. four point four million people _____

95. Section three point two _____

96. 9 three-bedroom apartments _____

97. warranty period of two years _____

98. insurance for 15 computers, 12 printers,
and 3 scanners _____

99. selected Numbers 305 and 409 _____

100. took out a nine-month CD _____

LEVEL 3

A. Self-Check. Number Expression. Choose the correct answer.

101. More than *(a) one half, (b) one-half, (c) 1/2* of drivers are driving less to keep gas costs down. _____

102. Those over age thirty make up about *(a) 30 percent, (b) thirty percent* of Facebook users, making it the fastest-growing demographic. _____

103. The size of carry-on baggage on Delta flights should not exceed *(a) 22″ × 14″ × 9″, (b) 22 by 14 by 9* inches. _____

104. Most airlines do not allow carry-on baggage that weighs more than *(a) 40, (b) forty* pounds. _____

105. First Federal Bank ranks *(a) 103rd, (b) one hundred third* in terms of capital investments. _____

106. Surprising pollsters, Senator Williams received a *(a) two-thirds, (b) two thirds* majority. _____

107. The highest score in an NBA basketball game occurred in 1983 when the Detroit Pistons beat the Denver Nuggets by a score of *(a) 186 to 184, (b) one hundred eighty six to one hundred eighty four.* _____

108. Maintenance costs are only *(a) 0.5, (b) .5* percent above last year's. _____

109. Hurricane Katrina spawned a "Tiny House Movement," with many people now living in cottages that are less than *(a) five hundred eighty, (b) 580* square feet. _____

110. Did you know that many office buildings have no *(a) 13th, (b) thirteenth* floor? _____

Check your answers below.

101. a   102. b   103. a   104. a   105. a   106. a   107. a   108. a   109. b   110. a

B. Writing Exercise. Using Numbers. Rewrite the following sentences with special attention to appropriate number usage.

111. Formula Rossa, which claims to be the world's fastest roller coaster, reaches speeds of one hundred fifty miles per hour in just four point nine seconds.

_____

_____

112. When the ride first opened on November 4th, 2010, nearly 1/3 of the visitors to Ferrari World in Abu Dhabi lined up for a high-speed joyride on four sixteen-passenger rail cars.

_____

_____

113. Engineers with Intamin used precise instruments to ensure that Formula Rossa's one point four miles of steel track were within 0.05 inches of specifications.

_____

_____

114. To ride Formula Rossa, you must be at least fifty-one inches but less than 6' 5" tall.

_____

115. A ride on the Formula Rossa roller coaster, which lasts one minute thirty-two seconds and climbs to one hundred seventy four feet, lets riders experience the feeling of traveling at one point seven g-forces.

_____

_____

116. Located in Abu Dhabi, Ferrari World is situated under a two million one hundred fifty-two thousand seven hundred eighty-two square foot roof, making it the largest indoor amusement park in the world.

_____

_____

117. Washington, DC, occupies 68 point 3 square miles; and its population is about 618 thousand.

_____

118. Although Washington, DC, has a population of 617996, its population during the week grows to approximately 1,000,000 because of commuters.

_____

119. African Americans make up approximately fifty point seven percent of the population in Washington, DC.

_____

120. Even though 1/2 of Washington, DC, residents have at least a 4-year college degree, 1/3 of all residents are functionally illiterate.

_____

_____

C. Writing Exercise. Using Numbers. In your local newspaper, find ten sentences with numbers. Write those sentences on a separate sheet. After each one, explain what rule the number style represents. Strive to find examples illustrating a variety of rules.

D. FAQs About Business English Review. In the space provided, write the correct answer choice.

121. Your contribution of *(a) $100 dollars, (b) 100 dollars, (c) $100* to the Animal Rescue Foundation is greatly appreciated. _____

122. Kiva.org *(a) aids, (b) aides* entrepreneurs in developing countries by offering them microloans. _____

123. The United States sent foreign *(a) aide, (b) aid* to tsunami victims in Japan. _____

124. Lyle is training to become an *(a) aide, (b) aid* in a psychiatric facility. _____

125. Investors were afraid that they would *(a) loose, (b) lose* money on junk bonds. _____

126. Sharon hunted for *(a) loose, (b) lose* change for the parking meter. _____

127. Your final payment of *(a) $1,895, (b) "$1,895"* is due by January 31. _____

128. The *(a) Class of 08, (b) Class of '08* is planning a reunion for this summer. _____

129. The decade of the *(a) 70's, (b) 70s, (c) '70s* brought us disco music and urban cowboys. _____

130. The abbreviation for *pound* is *(a) pd., (b) lb.* _____

Chat About It ◀◀

Your instructor may assign any of the following topics for you to discuss in class, in an online chat room, or on an online discussion board. Some of the discussion topics may require outside research. You may also be asked to read and respond to postings made by your classmates.

Discussion Topic 1: Many errors have been made in business because people didn't proofread numbers carefully enough. For example, Royal Caribbean Cruise Line listed a $1,399 cabin online for $139. Starwood Hotels left a zero off a price, thereby offering a $850 bungalow for just $85. United Airlines accidentally listed a $2,500 ticket for just 25 cents. And Texas Women's University transposed two numbers in a phone number; instead of reaching the TWU Admissions Department, students called a sex hotline instead! Why do you think it is important to proofread numbers carefully for accuracy? Why do you think errors like these are made? Share your thoughts with your classmates. If you have any related personal experiences, share those too.

Discussion Topic 2: The currency of the United States is the dollar, represented by the dollar sign ($). Other countries use different currencies represented by different symbols. Choose a country and do research to determine the name of the country's currency and its currency symbol. Report your findings to your classmates.

Discussion Topic 3: In this chapter you learned that the United States uses date and time

formats that are different from those used in much of the rest of the world. Choose a country and research its accepted date and time formats. Share your findings with your classmates. In addition, discuss what problems can result from the use of different date and time formats around the world.

Discussion Topic 4: In his book *On Writing*, the author Stephen King wrote, "One of the really bad things you can do to your writing is to dress up the vocabulary, looking for long words because you're maybe a little bit ashamed of your short ones." What do you think Stephen King means by this? How can you apply this advice to your own professional writing? Share your thoughts with your classmates.

Discussion Topic 5: The American writer Mark Twain once said, "I have always tried hard and faithfully to improve my English and never to degrade it. I always try to use the best English to describe what I think and what I feel, or what I don't feel and don't think." Why do you think Mark Twain believed so strongly in using English properly? Do you agree? How has this class changed the way you will use English in your personal and professional lives? Share your thoughts with your classmates.

Underline numbers that are expressed inappropriately. Write corrected forms in the spaces provided. Then compare your answers with those below.

1. 98 restaurants took part in San Francisco's Dine About Town event for charity.

   _____

2. We can offer you unlimited data for just $40 dollars a month.

   _____

3. The mystery author Cara Black tries to post at least 4 140-character updates on Twitter every day.

   _____

4. If you save only five hundred dollars annually, you will have fifty-four thousand dollars after twenty-five years if it earns an average of 10% interest.

   _____

5. Approximately 7,500,000 people in the United States control about 11 trillion dollars in assets.

   _____

6. By the March 31st application deadline, we received sixty-seven applications for a job that pays $11.00 an hour.

   _____

7. Please call our office, located at 3549 6th Avenue, at 585/663-0785, to schedule an appointment.

   _____

8. Flight thirty-seven will depart from Gate five at 5:00 p.m.

   _____

9. On the sixth of May, 13500 technology experts will attend a convention in Las Vegas.

   _____

10. The coldest temperature ever recorded was minus eighty-nine point two degrees Celsius in 1983 in Antarctica.

    _____

1. Ninety-eight   2. $40   3. four 140-character   25   10 percent   4. $500 $54,000   5. 7.5 million $11 trillion   6. March 31   67   7. 3549 Sixth Avenue   (585) 663-0785   8. Flight 37   Gate 5   5 p.m.   9. 6th   13,500   10. –89.2 degrees

Begin your review by rereading Chapters 13–14. Then test your comprehension of those chapters by completing the exercises that follow. Compare your responses with the key at the end of the book.

LEVEL 1

Select the letter of the group of words that is more acceptably expressed.

1. a. courses in Marketing, French, and Psychology | b. courses in marketing, French, and psychology | _____
2. a. living in Solano county | b. living in Solano County | _____
3. a. the State of West Virginia | b. the state of West Virginia | _____
4. a. a fall promotional event | b. a Fall promotional event | _____
5. a. French Fries | b. french fries | _____
6. a. the 12th of February | b. the twelfth of February | _____
7. a. eighty-four dollars | b. $84 | _____
8. a. on 18th Avenue | b. on Eighteenth Avenue | _____
9. a. on July 4th | b. on July 4 | _____
10. a. may i join you? | b. May I join you? | _____
11. a. 35 Graduate Students | b. 35 graduate students | _____
12. a. sold for $100 | b. sold for $100 dollars | _____
13. a. e-mail message to the president | b. E-mail message to the President | _____
14. a. i plan to attend | b. I plan to attend | _____
15. a. 300000 homes in the Suburbs | b. 300,000 homes in the suburbs | _____

LEVEL 2

Select the letter of the group of words that is more acceptably expressed.

16. a. my Grandma and Grandpa | b. my grandma and grandpa | _____
17. a. travel west on Highway 66 | b. travel West on Highway 66 | _____
18. a. our manager, Jan Jones | b. our Manager, Jan Jones | _____
19. a. our Human Resources Department | b. our human resources department | _____
20. a. a message from Alyssa Mendes, Sales Manager | b. a message from Alyssa Mendes, sales manager | _____

21. a. a message from Sales Manager Mendes b. a message from sales manager Mendes _____

22. a. for the past four years b. for the past 4 years _____

23. a. 4 twenty-story buildings b. four 20-story buildings _____

24. a. nine legal assistants assigned to 14 cases b. 9 legal assistants assigned to 14 cases _____

25. a. SUBJECT: Payroll Data Due Today b. SUBJECT: payroll data due today _____

26. a. cost three dollars and forty five cents b. cost $3.45 _____

27. a. traveled south on Highway 1 b. traveled South on Highway 1 _____

28. a. my Father recommended a good Book b. my father recommended a good book _____

29. a. Oscar Wilde said, "some cause happiness wherever they go; others whenever they go." b. Oscar Wilde said, "Some cause happiness wherever they go; others whenever they go." _____

LEVEL 3

Select the correct group of words and write its letter in the space provided.

30. a. a world of possibilities b. a World of possibilities _____

31. a. Governor-Elect Brown b. Governor-elect Brown _____

32. a. an e-mail marked "urgent" b. an e-mail marked "Urgent" _____

33. a. 1/3 of voters b. one third of voters _____

34. a. less than 0.3 percent b. less than .3 percent _____

35. a. 89 degrees Fahrenheit b. eighty-nine degrees fahrenheit _____

36. a. 80% of the votes b. 80 percent of the votes _____

37. a. federal reserve act of 1913 b. Federal Reserve Act of 1913 _____

38. a. a final score of 97 b. a final score of ninety-seven _____

39. a. italian and greek cultures b. Italian and Greek cultures _____

40. a. 3rd place b. third place _____

FAQs About Business English Review

Write the letter of the word or phrase that correctly completes each sentence.

41. The *(a) President, (b) president* of the United States rode in his motorcade through our small town. _____

42. Our newsletter comes out *(a) bimonthly, (b) semimonthly* on the 1st and the 15th of each month. _____

43. The Red Cross immediately sent *(a) aid, (b) aide* following the hurricane. _____

44. The *(a) mashal, (b) martial* escorted the defendant into the courtroom. _____

45. Ramona doesn't want to *(a) loose, (b) lose* her opportunity to travel abroad. _____

46. I'm really happy with the *(a) make-up, (b) makeup, (c) make up* of our task force. _____

47. This scholarship is open to *(a) nonEnglish-speaking (b) non-English-speaking* students. _____

48. On Friday Bob is scheduled to have a *(a) biopsy, (b) Biopsy*. _____

49. Colette dreams of pursuing a career in the field of *(a) medicine, (b) Medicine*. _____

50. Donors who give *(a) $50 dollars, (b) $50, (c) 50 dollars* or more will be recognized at the awards ceremony. _____

Short Reports

Reports are a fact of life in the business world today. They are important because they convey needed information, and they help decision makers solve problems. Organizing information into a meaningful report is an important skill you will want to acquire if your field is business.

Characteristics of Reports

As an introduction to report writing, this workshop focuses on the most important characteristics of reports. You will learn valuable tips about the format, data, headings, and writing plan for short business reports and internal proposals.

Format. How should a business report look? Three formats are commonly used. *Letter format* is appropriate for short reports prepared by one organization for another. A letter report, as illustrated in Figure 6.1, is like a letter except that it is more carefully organized. It includes side headings and lists where appropriate. *Memo format* is common for reports written within an organization. These internal reports look like memos—with the addition of side headings. *Report format* is used for longer, more formal reports. Printed on plain paper (instead of letterhead or memo forms), these reports begin with a title followed by carefully displayed headings and subheadings.

Data. Where do you find the data for a business report? Many business reports begin with personal observation and experience. If you were writing a report on implementing flextime for employees, you might begin by observing current work schedules and asking what schedules employees prefer. Other sources of data for business reports include company records, surveys, questionnaires, and interviews. If you want to see how others have solved a problem or collect background data on a topic, you can consult magazines, journals, and books. Much information is available electronically through online library indexes or from searching databases and the Web.

Headings. Good headings in a report highlight major ideas and categories. They guide the reader through a report. In longer reports they divide the text into inviting chunks, and they provide resting places for the eyes. Short reports often use **functional headings** (such as *Problem, Summary,* and *Recommendations*). Longer reports may employ **talking headings** (such as *Short-Term Parking Solutions*) because they provide more information to the reader. Whether your headings are functional or talking, be sure they are clear and parallel. For example, use *Visible Costs* and *Invisible Costs* rather than *Visible Costs* and *Costs That Don't Show.* Don't enclose headings in quotation marks, and avoid using headings as antecedents for pronouns. For example, if your heading is *Laser Printers*, don't begin the next sentence with *These produce high-quality output. . . .*

Skill Check 6.1 Reviewing the Characteristics of Short Reports

Select a letter to indicate the best format for the report described.

a. Memo format   **b. Letter format**   **c. Report format**

1. A short report to a company from an outside consultant   _____

2. A short report from a product manager to her boss   _____

3. A long report describing a company's diversity program   _____

4. If you were writing a report to persuade management to purchase more computers, the best way to begin collecting data would be to
   a. observe current use
   b. consult books and journals
   c. search the Web   _____

5. Which combination of report headings is best?
   a. Delivery Costs, Suppliers
   b. Reduction of Delivery Costs, Recommendations
   c. "Delivery Costs," "Supply Costs"
   d. Reducing Delivery Costs, Finding New Suppliers   _____

Writing Plan for a Short Report

Short reports often have three parts: introduction, findings, and recommendations. If the report is purely informational, a summary may be made instead of recommendations.

Introduction. The introduction of a report may also be called *Background*. In this section you explain why you are writing. You may also (a) describe what methods and sources you used to gather information and why they are credible, (b) provide any special background information that may be necessary, and (c) offer a preview of your findings.

Findings. The findings section may also be called *Observations, Facts, Results,* or *Discussion*. Important points to consider in this section are organization and display. You may wish to organize the findings (a) chronologically (for example, to describe the history of a problem), (b) alphabetically (if you were, for example, evaluating candidates for a position), (c) topically (for example, discussing sales by regions), or (d) from most to least important (such as listing criteria for evaluating equipment). To display the findings effectively, you could (a) use side headings, (b) number each finding, (c) underline or boldface the keywords, or (d) merely indent the paragraphs.

Summary or Recommendations. Some reports just offer information. Such reports may conclude with an impartial summary. Other reports are more analytical, and they generally conclude with recommendations. These recommendations tell readers how to solve the problem and may even suggest ways to implement the necessary actions. To display recommendations, number each one and place it on a separate line.

Notice that the letter report in Figure 6.1 includes an introduction, findings and analyses, and recommendations.

Writing Plan for an Internal Proposal

Both managers and employees must occasionally write reports that justify or recommend something such as buying equipment, changing a procedure, hiring an employee, consolidating departments, or investing funds. Here is a writing plan for an internal proposal that recommends a course of action.

Circle art: © iStockphoto.com/Pavel Khorenyan

FIGURE 6.1
Short Report—Letter Format

Liberty Environmental, Inc.

2593 North Globe Road
Arlington, VA 22207   (804) 356-1094   www.lei.com

October 9, 201x

Ms. Sharon J. Goode
Richmond Realty, Inc.
3390 Chesterfield Avenue
Richmond, VA 22368

Dear Ms. Goode:

At the request of Richmond Realty, I have completed a preliminary investigation of its
Mountain Park property listing regarding the possibility of environmental liabilities. The
following findings and recommendations are based on my physical inspection of the site,
official records, and interviews of officials and persons knowledgeable about the site.

Findings and Analyses

My preliminary assessment of the Mountain Park listing and its immediate vicinity revealed
rooms with damaged floor tiles on the first and second floors of 2539 Mountain View
Drive. Apparently, in recent remodeling efforts, these tiles had been cracked and broken.
Examination of the ceiling and attic revealed possible contamination from asbestos.

Located on the property is Mountain Technology, a possible hazardous waste generator.
Although I could not examine its interior, this company has the potential for producing
hazardous material contamination.

Recommendations

To reduce its potential environmental liability, Richmond Realty should take the following
steps in regard to its Mountain Park listing:

• Conduct an immediate asbestos survey at the site, including inspection of ceiling
  insulation material, floor tiles, and insulation around a gas-fired heater vent pipe at
  2539 Mountain View Drive.

• Prepare an environmental audit of the generators of hazardous waste currently operating at the site, including Mountain Technology.

• Obtain lids for the dumpsters situated in the parking areas and ensure that the lids
  are kept closed.

If you would like to discuss the findings or recommendations in this report, please call
me and I will be glad to answer your questions.

Sincerely,

Scott R. Evans

Scott R. Evans

Explains purpose, outlines sources of information, and previews findings

Describes findings and explains their significance

Concludes with recommendations for solving the problem

Uses bulleted list to improve readability and comprehension

Begins each recommendation with a verb for consistency

Introduction. In the introduction, identify the problem briefly. Use specific examples,
supporting statistics, and authoritative quotes to lend credibility to the seriousness of
the problem. If you think your audience will be receptive, announce your recommendation, solution, or action immediately and concisely. If you think your audience will
need to be persuaded or educated, do not announce your solution until after you have
explained its advantages.

Body. In writing the body of an internal proposal, you may want to include all or some
of the following elements. Explain more fully the benefits of the recommendations

or steps to be taken to solve the problem. Include a discussion of pros, cons, and costs. If appropriate, describe the factual and ethical negative consequences of the current situation. For example, if your internal proposal recommends purchasing new equipment, explain how much time, effort, money, and morale are being lost by continuing to use outdated equipment that needs constant repairs. Quantification through accurate facts and examples builds credibility and persuasive appeal. Explain the benefits of your proposal. A bulleted list improves readability and emphasis. Anticipate objections to your proposal and discuss ways to counter those objections. The body should also provide a plan and schedule for implementing your proposal. If many people will be implementing the proposal, prepare a staffing section. Describe who will be doing what. You may also describe alternative solutions and show how they will not work as well as your proposal.

Conclusion. In the conclusion summarize your recommendation. Describe the specific action to be taken. Ask for authorization to proceed. To motivate the reader, you might include a date for the action to take place and a reason for the deadline.

An internal proposal is generally formatted as a memo such as the one shown in Figure 6.2. In this memo report, the writer expects the reader to be receptive to the recommendation of pilot testing smart tires. Thus, the proposal begins directly with the recommendations announced immediately. The body discusses how the recommendation would work, and it itemizes benefits. It anticipates objections and counters them. The closing summarizes what action is to be taken and presents a deadline.

Writing Application 6.1

Organize the following information into a short letter report. As Cynthia M. Chavez, president, Chavez and Associates, you have been hired as a consultant to advise the St. Petersburg, Florida, City Council. The City Council has asked you and your associates to investigate a problem with Pinellas Park Beachway.

In 1979 St. Petersburg constructed a 12-foot pathway, now called the Pinellas Park Beachway. It was meant originally for bicycle riders. Now, more than three decades later, it has become very popular for joggers, walkers, bikers, in-line skaters, skateboarders, sightseers, and people walking their dogs. In fact, it has become so popular that it is dangerous. Last year the St. Petersburg Police Department reported an amazing 65 collisions in the area. And this doesn't count the close calls and minor accidents that no one reported. The City Council wants your organization to identify the problem and come up with some workable recommendations for improving safety.

As you look into the matter, you immediately decide that the council is right. A problem definitely exists! In addition to the many pedestrians and riders, you see that families with rented pedal-powered surreys clog the beachway. Sometimes they even operate these vehicles on the wrong side. Your investigation further reveals that bicyclists with rental bikes do not always have bells to alert walkers. And poor lighting makes nighttime use extremely dangerous. You have noticed that conditions seem to be worst on Sundays. This congestion results from nearby art and crafts fairs and sales, attracting even more people to the crowded area.

Your investigation confirms that the beachway is dangerous. But what to do about it? In a brainstorming session, your associates make a number of suggestions for reducing the dangers to users. By the way, the council is particularly interested in lessening the threat of liability to the city. One of your associates thinks that the

FIGURE 6.2

Internal Proposal—Memo Format

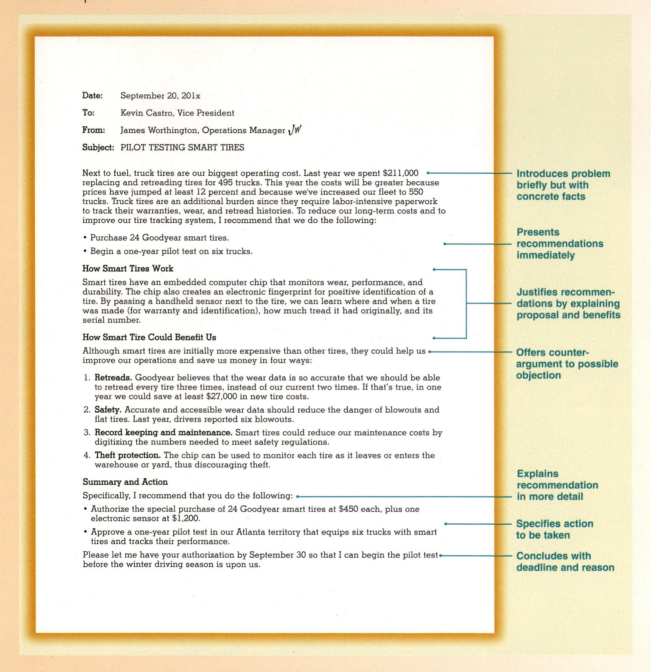

Date: September 20, 201x

To: Kevin Castro, Vice President

From: James Worthington, Operations Manager JW

Subject: PILOT TESTING SMART TIRES

Next to fuel, truck tires are our biggest operating cost. Last year we spent $211,000 replacing and retreading tires for 495 trucks. This year the costs will be greater because prices have jumped at least 12 percent and because we've increased our fleet to 550 trucks. Truck tires are an additional burden since they require labor-intensive paperwork to track their warranties, wear, and retread histories. To reduce our long-term costs and to improve our tire tracking system, I recommend that we do the following:

Introduces problem briefly but with concrete facts

- Purchase 24 Goodyear smart tires.
- Begin a one-year pilot test on six trucks.

Presents recommendations immediately

How Smart Tires Work

Smart tires have an embedded computer chip that monitors wear, performance, and durability. The chip also creates an electronic fingerprint for positive identification of a tire. By passing a handheld sensor next to the tire, we can learn where and when a tire was made (for warranty and identification), how much tread it had originally, and its serial number.

Justifies recommendations by explaining proposal and benefits

How Smart Tire Could Benefit Us

Although smart tires are initially more expensive than other tires, they could help us improve our operations and save us money in four ways:

Offers counter-argument to possible objection

1. **Retreads.** Goodyear believes that the wear data is so accurate that we should be able to retread every tire three times, instead of our current two times. If that's true, in one year we could save at least $27,000 in new tire costs.
2. **Safety.** Accurate and accessible wear data should reduce the danger of blowouts and flat tires. Last year, drivers reported six blowouts.
3. **Record keeping and maintenance.** Smart tires could reduce our maintenance costs by digitizing the numbers needed to meet safety regulations.
4. **Theft protection.** The chip can be used to monitor each tire as it leaves or enters the warehouse or yard, thus discouraging theft.

Summary and Action

Specifically, I recommend that you do the following:

Explains recommendation in more detail

- Authorize the special purchase of 24 Goodyear smart tires at $450 each, plus one electronic sensor at $1,200.
- Approve a one-year pilot test in our Atlanta territory that equips six trucks with smart tires and tracks their performance.

Specifies action to be taken

Please let me have your authorization by September 30 so that I can begin the pilot test before the winter driving season is upon us.

Concludes with deadline and reason

beachway should be made 15 or more feet wide. Another suggests that the beachway be lighted at night. Someone thinks that a new path should be built on the beach side of the existing beachway; this path would be for pedestrians only. Educating users about safety rules and etiquette would certainly be wise for everyone. One suggestion involves better striping or applying colors to designate different uses for the beachway. And why not require that all rental bicycles be equipped with bells? One of the best recommendations involved hiring uniformed "beach hosts" who would monitor the beachway, give advice, offer directions, and generally patrol the area.

In a short report, outline the problem and list your recommendations. Naturally, you would be happy to discuss your findings and recommendations with the St. Petersburg City Council.

Writing Application 6.2

Assume that your office needs a piece of equipment such as a copy machine, a fax machine, a scanner, tablet computers, smartphones, an all-in-one printer, or the like. Do the research necessary to write a convincing internal proposal to your boss. Because you feel that your boss will be receptive to your request, you can use the direct approach.

Developing Spelling Skills

Is English Spelling So Difficult?

No one would dispute the complaint that many English words are difficult to spell. Why is spelling in our language so perplexing? For one thing, our language has borrowed many of its words from other languages. English has a Germanic base on which a superstructure of words borrowed from French, Latin, Greek, and other languages of the world has been erected. For this reason, its words are not always formed by regular patterns of letter combinations. In addition, spelling is made difficult because the pronunciation of English words is constantly changing. Today's spelling was standardized nearly 300 years ago, but many words are pronounced differently today than they were then. Therefore, pronunciation often provides little help in spelling. Consider, for example, the words *sew* and *dough*.

What Can Be Done to Improve One's Spelling?

Spelling is a skill that can be developed, just as arithmetic, keyboarding, and other skills can be developed. Because the ability to spell is a prerequisite for success in business and in most other activities, effort expended to acquire this skill is effort well spent.

Three traditional approaches to improving spelling have met with varying degrees of success.

1. Rules or Guidelines

The spelling of English words is consistent enough to justify the formulation of a few spelling rules, perhaps more appropriately called **guidelines** since the generalizations in question are not invariably applicable. Such guidelines are, in other words, helpful but not infallible.

2. Mnemonics

Another approach to improving one's ability to spell involves the use of mnemonics or memory devices. For example, the word *principle* might be associated with the word *rule* , to form in the mind of the speller a link between the meaning and the spelling of *principle*. To spell *capitol,* one might think of the *dome* of the capitol building and focus on the *o*'s in both words. The use of mnemonics can be an effective device for the improvement of spelling only if the speller makes a real effort to develop the necessary memory hooks.

3. Rote Learning

A third approach to the improvement of spelling centers on memorization. The word is studied by the speller until it can be readily reproduced in the mind's eye.

The 1-2-3 Spelling Plan

Proficiency in spelling is not attained without concentrated effort. Here's a plan to follow in mastering the 400 commonly misspelled words included in this appendix. For each word, try this 1-2-3 approach.

1. Is a spelling guideline applicable? If so, select the appropriate guideline and study the word in relation to that guideline.

2. If no guideline applies, can a memory device be created to aid in the recall of the word?

3. If neither a guideline nor a memory device will work, the word must be memorized. Look at the word carefully. Pronounce it. Write it or repeat it until you can visualize all its letters in your mind's eye.

Before you try the 1-2-3 plan, become familiar with the six spelling guidelines that follow. These spelling guidelines are not intended to represent all the possible spelling rules appearing in the various available spelling books. These six guidelines are, however, among the most effective and helpful of the recognized spelling rules.

Guideline 1: Words Containing *ie* or *ei*

Although there are exceptions to it, the following familiar rhyme can be helpful.

(a) Write *i* before *e*
(b) Except after *c*,
(c) Or when sounded like *a*
As in *neighbor* and *weigh*.

Study these words illustrating the three parts of the rhyme.

(a) *i* Before *e*		(b) Except After *c*	(c) or When Sounded Like *a*
achieve	grief	ceiling	beige
belief	ingredient	conceive	eight
believe	mischief	deceive	freight
brief	niece	perceive	heir
cashier	piece	receipt	neighbor
chief	shield	receive	reign
convenient	sufficient		their
field	view		vein
friend	yield		weight

Exceptions: These exceptional *ei* and *ie* words must be learned by rote or with the use of a mnemonic device.

caffeine	height	seize
either	leisure	sheik
financier	neither	sleight
foreigner	protein	weird

Guideline 2: Words Ending in *e*

For most words ending in an *e*, the final *e* is dropped when the word is joined to a suffix beginning with a vowel (such as *ing, able,* or *al*). The final *e* is retained when a suffix beginning with a consonant (such as *ment, less, ly,* or *ful*) is joined to such a word.

Final e Dropped	Final e Retained
believe, believing	arrange, arrangement
care, caring	require, requirement
hope, hoping	hope, hopeless
receive, receiving	care, careless
desire, desirable	like, likely
cure, curable	approximate, approximately
move, movable	definite, definitely
value, valuable	sincere, sincerely
disperse, dispersal	use, useful
arrive, arrival	hope, hopeful

Exceptions: The few exceptions to this spelling guideline are among the most frequently misspelled words. As such, they deserve special attention. Notice that they all involve a dropped final *e*.

acknowledgment	ninth
argument	truly
judgment	wholly

Guideline 3: Words Ending in *ce* or *ge*

When *able* or *ous* is added to words ending in *ce* or *ge,* the final *e* is retained if the *c* or *g* is pronounced softly (as in *change* or *peace*).

advantage, advantageous	change, changeable
courage, courageous	service, serviceable
outrage, outrageous	manage, manageable

Guideline 4: Words Ending in *y*

Words ending in a *y* that are preceded by a consonant normally change the *y* to *i* before all suffixes except those beginning with an *i*.

Change y to i Because y Is Preceded by a Consonant	Do Not Change y to i Because y Is Preceded by a Vowel
accompany, accompaniment	employ, employer
study, studied, studious	annoy, annoying, annoyance
duty, dutiful	stay, staying, stayed
industry, industrious	attorney, attorneys
carry, carriage	valley, valleys
apply, appliance	

Change y to i Because y Is Preceded by a Consonant	Do Not Change y to i When Adding ing
try, tried	accompany, accompanying
empty, emptiness	apply, applying
forty, fortieth	study, studying

secretary, secretaries	satisfy, satisfying
company, companies	try, trying
hurry, hurries	

Exceptions: day, daily; dry, dried; mislay, mislaid; pay, paid; shy, shyly; gay, gaily.

Guideline 5: Doubling a Final Consonant

If one-syllable or two-syllable words accented on the second syllable end in a single consonant preceded by a single vowel, the final consonant is doubled before the addition of a suffix beginning with a vowel.

Although complex, this spelling guideline is extremely useful and therefore well worth mastering. Many spelling errors can be avoided by applying this guideline.

One-Syllable Words	Two-Syllable Words
can, canned	acquit, acquitting, acquittal
drop, dropped	admit, admitted, admitting
fit, fitted	begin, beginner, beginning
get, getting	commit, committed, committing
man, manned	control, controller, controlling
plan, planned	defer, deferred (but deference*)
run, running	excel, excelled, excelling
shut, shutting	occur, occurrence, occurring
slip, slipped	prefer, preferring (but preference*)
swim, swimming	recur, recurred, recurrence
ton, tonnage	refer, referring (but reference*)

Here is a summary of conditions necessary for application of this guideline.

1. The word must end in a single consonant.
2. The final consonant must be preceded by a single vowel.
3. The word must be accented on the second syllable (if it has two syllables).

Words derived from *cancel, offer, differ, equal, suffer,* and *benefit* are not governed by this guideline because they are accented on the first syllable.

Guideline 6: Prefixes and Suffixes

For words in which the letter that ends the prefix is the same as the letter that begins the main word (such as in *dissimilar*), both letters must be included. For words in which a suffix begins with the same letter that ends the main word (such as in *coolly*), both letters must also be included.

Prefix	Main Word	Main Word	Suffix
dis	satisfied	accidental	ly
ir	responsible	incidental	ly
il	literate	clean	ness
mis	spell	cool	ly
mis	state	even	ness
un	necessary	mean	ness

*Because the accent shifts to the first syllable, the final consonant is not doubled.

On the other hand, do not supply additional letters when adding prefixes to main words.

Prefix	Main Word
dis	appoint (*not* dissappoint)
dis	appearance
mis	take

Perhaps the most important guideline one can follow in spelling correctly is to use the dictionary whenever in doubt.

400 Most Frequently Misspelled Words* (Divided into 20 Lists of 20 Words Each)

List 1

1. absence
2. acceptance
3. accessible
4. accidentally
5. accommodate
6. accompaniment
7. accurately
8. accustom
9. achievement
10. acknowledgment
11. acquaintance
12. acquire
13. across
14. actually
15. adequately
16. admitted
17. adolescence
18. advantageous
19. advertising
20. advice, advise

List 2

21. afraid
22. against
23. aggressive
24. all right
25. almost
26. alphabetical
27. already, all ready
28. although
29. amateur
30. among
31. amount
32. analysis
33. analyze
34. angel, angle
35. annoyance
36. annual
37. answer
38. apologized
39. apparent
40. appliance

List 3

41. applying
42. approaches
43. appropriate
44. approximately
45. arguing
46. argument
47. arrangement
48. article
49. athlete
50. attack
51. attendance, -attendants
52. attitude
53. attorneys
54. auxiliary
55. basically
56. beautiful
57. before
58. beginning
59. believing
60. benefited

*Compiled from lists of words most frequently misspelled by students and businesspeople.

List 4

61. biggest
62. breath, breathe
63. brief
64. business
65. calendar
66. capital, capitol
67. career
68. careless
69. carrying
70. cashier
71. ceiling
72. certain
73. challenge
74. changeable
75. chief
76. choose, chose
77. cloths, clothes
78. column
79. coming
80. committee

List 5

81. companies
82. competition
83. completely
84. conceive
85. conscience
86. conscientious
87. conscious
88. considerably
89. consistent
90. continuous
91. controlling
92. controversial
93. convenience
94. council, counsel
95. cylinder
96. daily
97. deceive
98. decision
99. define, definitely
100. dependent

List 6

101. description
102. desirable
103. destroy
104. development
105. difference
106. dining
107. disappearance
108. disappoint
109. disastrous
110. discipline
111. discussion
112. disease
113. dissatisfied
114. distinction
115. divide
116. doesn't
117. dominant
118. dropped
119. due
120. during

List 7

121. efficient
122. eligible
123. embarrass
124. encourage
125. enough
126. environment
127. equipped
128. especially
129. exaggerate
130. excellence
131. except, accept
132. exercise
133. existence
134. experience
135. explanation
136. extremely
137. familiar
138. families
139. fascinate
140. favorite

List 8

141. February
142. fictitious
143. field
144. finally
145. financially
146. foreigner
147. fortieth
148. forty, fourth, forth
149. forward, foreword
150. freight
151. friend
152. fulfill
153. fundamentally
154. further, farther
155. generally
156. government
157. governor
158. grammar
159. grateful
160. guard

List 9

161. happiness
162. hear, here
163. height
164. heroes
165. hopeless
166. hoping
167. huge
168. humorous
169. hungry
170. ignorance
171. imaginary
172. imagine
173. immediately
174. immense
175. importance
176. incidentally
177. independent, independently
178. indispensable
179. industrious
180. inevitable

List 10

181. influential
182. ingredient
183. initiative
184. intelligence
185. interest
186. interference
187. interpretation
188. interrupt
189. involve
190. irrelevant
191. irresponsible
192. island
193. jealous
194. judgment
195. kindergarten
196. knowledge
197. laboratory
198. laborer
199. laid
200. led, lead

List 11

201. leisurely
202. library
203. license
204. likely
205. literature
206. lives
207. loneliness
208. loose, lose
209. losing
210. luxury
211. magazine
212. magnificence
213. maintenance
214. manageable
215. maneuver
216. manner
217. manufacturer
218. marriage
219. mathematics
220. meant

List 12

221. mechanics
222. medicine
223. medieval
224. mere
225. miniature
226. minutes
227. mischief
228. misspell
229. mistake
230. muscle
231. mysterious
232. naturally
233. necessary
234. neighbor
235. neither
236. nervous
237. nickel
238. niece
239. ninety
240. ninth

List 13

241. noticeable
242. numerous
243. obstacle
244. occasionally
245. occurrence
246. off
247. offered
248. official
249. omitted, omit
250. operate
251. opinion
252. opportunity
253. opposite
254. organization
255. origin
256. original
257. paid
258. pamphlet
259. parallel
260. particular

List 14

261. passed, past
262. pastime
263. peaceable
264. peculiar
265. perceive
266. performance
267. permanent
268. permitted
269. persistent
270. personal, personnel
271. persuading
272. phase, faze
273. philosophy
274. physical
275. piece
276. planned
277. pleasant
278. poison
279. political
280. possession

List 15

281. possible
282. practical
283. precede
284. preferred
285. prejudice
286. preparation
287. prevalent
288. principal, principle
289. privilege
290. probably
291. proceed
292. professor
293. prominent
294. proving
295. psychology
296. pursuing
297. quantity
298. quiet, quite
299. really
300. receipt

List 16

301. receiving, receive
302. recognize
303. recommend
304. reference
305. refer, referring
306. regard
307. relative
308. relieving
309. religious
310. reminiscent
311. repetition
312. representative
313. requirement
314. resistance
315. responsible
316. restaurant
317. rhythm
318. ridiculous
319. sacrifice
320. safety

List 17

321. satisfying
322. scenery
323. schedule
324. science
325. secretaries
326. seize
327. sense, since
328. sentence
329. separate, separately
330. sergeant
331. serviceable
332. several
333. shining
334. shoulder
335. significance
336. similar
337. simply
338. sincerely
339. site, cite, sight
340. source

List 18

341. speak, speech
342. specimen
343. stationary, stationery
344. stopped
345. stories
346. straight, strait
347. strenuous
348. stretch
349. strict
350. studying
351. substantial
352. subtle
353. succeed
354. success
355. sufficient
356. summary
357. suppose
358. surprise
359. suspense
360. swimming

List 19

361. syllable
362. symbol
363. symmetrical
364. synonymous
365. technique
366. temperament
367. temperature
368. tendency
369. than, then
370. their, there, they're
371. themselves
372. theories
373. therefore
374. thorough
375. though
376. through
377. together
378. tomorrow
379. tragedies
380. transferred

List 20

381. tremendous	388. useful	395. weather, whether
382. tried	389. using	396. weird
383. truly	390. vacuum	397. were, where
384. undoubtedly	391. valuable	398. wholly, holy
385. unnecessary	392. varies	399. writing
386. until	393. vegetable	400. yield
387. unusual	394. view	

Developing Vocabulary Skills

If you understand the meanings of many words, you can be said to have a "good vocabulary." Words are the basis of thought. We think with words, we understand with words, and we communicate with words.

A large working vocabulary is a significant asset. It allows us to use precise words that say exactly what we intend. In addition, we understand more effectively what we hear and read. A large vocabulary also enables us to score well on employment and intelligence tests. Lewis M. Terman, who developed the Stanford-Binet IQ tests, believes that vocabulary is the best single indicator of intelligence.

In the business world, where precise communication is extremely important, surveys show a definite correlation between vocabulary size and job performance. Skilled workers, in the majority of cases, have larger vocabularies than unskilled workers. Supervisors know the meanings of more words than the workers they direct, and executives have larger vocabularies than employees working for them.

Having a good vocabulary at our command doesn't necessarily ensure our success in life, but it certainly gives us an advantage. Improving your vocabulary will help you expand your options in an increasingly complex world.

Vocabulary can be acquired in three ways: accidentally, incidentally, and intentionally. Setting out intentionally to expand your word power is, of course, the most efficient vocabulary-building method. One of the best means of increasing your vocabulary involves using 3-by-5 cards. When you encounter an unfamiliar word, write it on a card and put the definition of the word on the reverse side. Just five to ten minutes of practice each day with such cards can significantly increase your vocabulary.

Your campaign to increase your vocabulary can begin with the 18 lists of selected business terms and words of general interest included in this appendix. You may already know partial definitions for some of these words. Take this opportunity to develop more precise definitions for them. Follow these steps in using the word lists:

1. Record the word on a 3-by-5 card.

2. Look up the word in your dictionary. Compare the dictionary definitions of the word with the definition alternatives shown after the word in your copy of *Business English*. Select the correct definition, and write its letter in the space provided in your textbook. (The definitions provided in your textbook are quite concise but should help you remember the word's most common meaning.)

3. On the reverse side of your card, write the phonetic spelling of the word and the word's part of speech. Then write its definition using as much of the dictionary definition as you find helpful. Try also to add a phrase or sentence illustrating the word.

4. Study your 3-by-5 cards often.

5. Try to find ways to use your vocabulary words in your speech and writing.

List 1

1. adjacent = (a) previous, (b) similar, (c) overdue, (d) nearby _____
2. ambivalence = having (a) uncertainty, (b) ambition, (c) compassion, (d) intelligence _____
3. belligerent = (a) overweight, (b) quarrelsome, (c) likable, (d) believable _____
4. contingent = (a) conditional, (b) allowable, (c) hopeless, (d) impractical _____
5. decadent = in a state of (a) repair, (b) happiness, (c) decline, (d) extreme patriotism _____
6. entitlement = (a) label, (b) tax refund, (c) screen credit, (d) legal right _____
7. equivalent = (a) subsequent, (b) identical, (c) self-controlled, (d) plentiful _____
8. paramount = (a) foremost, (b) high mountain, (c) film company, (d) insignificant _____
9. plausible = (a) quiet, (b) acceptable, (c) notorious, (d) negative _____
10. unilateral = (a) powerful, (b) harmonious, (c) one-sided, (d) indelible _____

List 2

1. affluent = (a) rich, (b) slippery, (c) persistent, (d) rebellious _____
2. autocrat = one who (a) owns many cars, (b) is self-centered, (c) has power, (d) collects signatures _____
3. benevolent = for the purpose of (a) religion, (b) doing good, (c) healing, (d) violence _____
4. entrepreneur = (a) business owner, (b) traveler, (c) salesperson, (d) gambler _____
5. impertinent = (a) stationary, (b) bound to happen, (c) obsolete, (d) rude and irreverent _____
6. imprudent = (a) unwise, (b) crude, (c) vulnerable, (d) lifeless _____
7. mediator = one who seeks (a) overseas trade, (b) profits, (c) safe investment, (d) peaceful settlement _____
8. preponderance = (a) thoughtful, (b) exclusive right, (c) majority, (d) forethought _____
9. recipient = (a) receiver, (b) respondent, (c) voter, (d) giver _____
10. reprehensible = (a) obedient, (b) independent, (c) blameworthy, (d) following _____

List 3

1. affable = (a) cheap, (b) pleasant, (c) strange, (d) competent _____
2. consensus = (a) population count, (b) attendance, (c) tabulation, (d) agreement _____
3. criterion = (a) standard, (b) command, (c) pardon, (d) law _____
4. diligent = (a) gentle, (b) industrious, (c) prominent, (d) intelligent _____
5. hydraulic = operated by means of (a) air, (b) gasoline, (c) liquid, (d) mechanical parts _____

6. hypothesis = (a) triangle, (b) promulgate, (c) highest point, (d) theory _____

7. phenomenon = (a) imagination, (b) rare event, (c) appointment, (d) clever saying _____

8. reticent = (a) silent, (b) strong-willed, (c) inflexible, (d) disagreeable _____

9. sanctuary = a place of (a) healing, (b) refuge, (c) rest, (d) learning _____

10. stimulus = something that causes (a) response, (b) light, (c) pain, (d) movement _____

List 4

1. beneficiary = one who (a) receives a license, (b) creates goodwill, (c) receives proceeds, (d) makes friends _____

2. constrain = (a) restrict, (b) filter, (c) use, (d) inform _____

3. corroborate = (a) contradict, (b) recall, (c) erode, (d) confirm _____

4. dun (n) = a demand for (a) legal action, (b) payment, (c) credit information, (d) dividends _____

5. equitable = (a) fair, (b) profitable, (c) similar, (d) clear _____

6. fluctuate = (a) rinse out, (b) magnetic field, (c) pricing schedule, (d) swing back and forth _____

7. indolent = (a) self-indulgent, (b) lazy, (c) pampered, (d) uncertain _____

8. nullify = (a) disappear, (b) imitate, (c) invalidate, (d) enhance _____

9. obsolete = (a) ugly, (b) outmoded, (c) audible, (d) scant _____

10. stabilize = to make (a) pleasant, (b) congenial, (c) traditional, (d) firm _____

List 5

1. arbitrate = (a) decide, (b) construct, (c) conquer, (d) ratify _____

2. coalition = (a) deliberation, (b) allegiance, (c) adherence, (d) alliance _____

3. collate = (a) assemble, (b) denounce, (c) supersede, (d) uninformed _____

4. conglomerate = combination of (a) executives, (b) companies, (c) investments, (d) countries _____

5. franchise = (a) fictitious reason, (b) right, (c) obligation, (d) official announcement _____

6. logistics = (a) speculations, (b) analytic philosophy, (c) reasonable outcome, (d) details of operation _____

7. proxy = authority to (a) act for another, (b) write checks, (c) submit nominations, (d) explain _____

8. subsidiary = (a) below expectations, (b) country dominated by another, (c) company controlled by another, (d) depressed financial condition _____

9. termination = (a) end, (b) inception, (c) identification, (d) evasive action _____

10. virtually = (a) absolutely, (b) precisely, (c) almost entirely, (d) strictly _____

List 6

1. affiliate	= (a) trust, (b) attract, (c) effect, (d) join	_____
2. alter	= (a) table for religious ceremony, (b) solitary, (c) attribute, (d) modify	_____
3. boisterous	= (a) vociferous, (b) masculine, (c) cheerful, (d) brusque	_____
4. configuration	= (a) stratagem, (b) foreign currency, (c) form, (d) comprehension	_____
5. conveyance	= (a) vehicle, (b) transformation, (c) baggage, (d) consortium	_____
6. infringe	= (a) ravel, (b) decorative border, (c) encroach, (d) frivolous	_____
7. jurisdiction	= (a) science of law, (b) enunciation, (c) justice, (d) authority	_____
8. nonpartisan	= (a) unbiased, (b) antisocial, (c) ineffective, (d) untenable	_____
9. parity	= (a) price index, (b) justice under law, (c) plenitude, (d) equality of purchasing power	_____
10. usury	= (a) method of operation, (b) implementation, (c) illegal interest, (d) customary	_____

List 7

1. anonymous	= (a) multiplex, (b) powerless, (c) vexing, (d) nameless	_____
2. cartel	= (a) combination to fix prices, (b) ammunition belt, (c) partnership to promote competition, (d) placard	_____
3. conjecture	= (a) coagulation, (b) gesticulation, (c) guesswork, (d) connection	_____
4. disparity	= (a) unlikeness, (b) separation, (c) lacking emotion, (d) repudiation	_____
5. environment	= (a) urban area, (b) zenith, (c) surroundings, (d) latitude	_____
6. impetus	= (a) oversight, (b) stimulus, (c) hindrance, (d) imminent	_____
7. portfolio	= a list of (a) books, (b) security analysts, (c) corporations, (d) investments	_____
8. quiescent	= (a) presumptuous, (b) latent, (c) immoderate, (d) volatile	_____
9. surrogate	= (a) substitute, (b) accused, (c) authenticate, (d) suspend	_____
10. tariff	= (a) marsupial, (b) announcement, (c) ship, (d) duty	_____

List 8

1. accrue	= (a) conform, (b) accumulate, (c) diminish, (d) multiply	_____
2. amortize	= (a) pay off, (b) reduce, (c) romance, (d) kill	_____
3. commensurate	= (a) infinitesimal, (b) erroneous, (c) reliable, (d) proportional	_____
4. consortium	= (a) configuration, (b) partnership or association, (c) royal offspring, (d) rental property	_____
5. discernible	= (a) perceptive, (b) pretentious, (c) recognizable, (d) dissident	_____
6. frugal	= (a) thrifty, (b) wasteful, (c) judicious, (d) profligate	_____
7. pecuniary	= (a) rudimentary, (b) eccentric, (c) financial, (d) distinctive	_____
8. retract	= (a) disavow, (b) reorganize, (c) reciprocate, (d) hide	_____

9. scrutinize   = (a) cheerfully admit, (b) baffle, (c) persist, (d) examine carefully   _____

10. tenacious   = (a) falling apart, (b) holding on, (c) immobile, (d) chagrined   _____

List 9

1. amiable   = (a) contumacious, (b) impetuous, (c) feasible, (d) congenial   _____

2. credible   = (a) plausible, (b) deceitful, (c) religious, (d) tolerant   _____

3. defendant   = one who (a) sues, (b) answers suit, (c) judges, (d) protects   _____

4. dissipate   = (a) accumulate, (b) partition, (c) liquify, (d) scatter or waste   _____

5. incentive   = (a) impediment, (b) support, (c) motive, (d) remuneration   _____

6. innocuous   = (a) harmless, (b) injection, (c) facetious, (d) frightening   _____

7. oust   = (a) install, (b) instigate, (c) shout, (d) expel   _____

8. pittance   = (a) tiny amount, (b) tithe, (c) abyss, (d) pestilence   _____

9. plaintiff   = one who (a) defends, (b) is sad, (c) sues, (d) responds   _____

10. superfluous   = (a) extraordinary, (b) very slippery, (c) shallow, (d) oversupplied   _____

List 10

1. adroit   = (a) ideal, (b) resilient, (c) witty, (d) skillful   _____

2. derogatory   = (a) minimal, (b) degrading, (c) originating from, (d) devious   _____

3. escrow   = (a) international treaty, (b) public registration, (c) licensed by state, (d) type of deposit   _____

4. facsimile   = (a) principle, (b) prototype, (c) exact copy, (d) counterfeit   _____

5. inordinate   = (a) unwholesome, (b) excessive, (c) unimportant, (d) treacherous   _____

6. logical   = (a) reasoned, (b) irrelevant, (c) lofty, (d) intricate   _____

7. malfeasance   = (a) prevaricate, (b) injurious, (c) superstitious, (d) misconduct   _____

8. noxious   = (a) pernicious, (b) unusual, (c) pleasant, (d) inconsequential   _____

9. résumé   = (a) budget report, (b) minutes of meeting, (c) photo album, (d) summary of qualifications   _____

10. spasmodic   = (a) paralyzing, (b) intermittent or fitful, (c) internal, (d) painful   _____

List 11

1. animosity   = (a) happiness, (b) deep sadness, (c) hatred, (d) study of animals   _____

2. caveat   = (a) headwear, (b) warning, (c) neckwear, (d) prerogative   _____

3. conscientious   = (a) meticulous, (b) productive, (c) cognizant, (d) sophisticated   _____

4. cosmopolitan   = (a) provincial, (b) multicolored, (c) heavenly, (d) worldly   _____

5. decipher   = (a) preclude, (b) decode, (c) demise, (d) reproach   _____

6. euphemism   = (a) religious discourse, (b) facial expression, (c) figurative speech, (d) inoffensive term   _____

7. fraudulent   = (a) loquacious, (b) candid, (c) deceitful, (d) despotic   _____

8. peripheral   = (a) supplementary, (b) imaginary, (c) visionary, (d) supernatural   _____

9. pungent = (a) knowledgeable, (b) wise religious man, (c) acrid, (d) vulnerable _____

10. requisite = (a) essential, (b) demand, (c) skillful, (d) discreet _____

List 12

1. ad valorem = (a) esteemed, (b) genuine, (c) recompense, (d) proportional _____

2. carte blanche = (a) white carriage, (b) credit terms, (c) full permission, (d) geographical expression _____

3. de facto = (a) prejudicial, (b) actual, (c) valid, (d) unlawful _____

4. esprit de corps = (a) group enthusiasm, (b) strong coffee, (c) central authority, (d) government overturn _____

5. modus operandi = (a) method of procedure, (b) practical compromise, (c) business transaction, (d) flexible arbitration _____

6. per capita = per unit of (a) income, (b) population, (c) birth, (d) household _____

7. per diem = (a) daily, (b) weekly, (c) yearly, (d) taxable _____

8. prima facie = (a) self-taught, (b) apparent, (c) principal, (d) artificial effect _____

9. status quo = (a) haughty demeanor, (b) steadfast opinion, (c) position of importance, (d) existing condition _____

10. tort = (a) rich cake, (b) extended dream, (c) wrongful act, (d) lawful remedy _____

List 13

1. acquit = (a) discharge, (b) pursue, (c) interfere, (d) impede _____

2. annuity = (a) yearly report, (b) insurance premium, (c) tuition refund, (d) annual payment _____

3. complacent = (a) appealing, (b) self-satisfied, (c) sympathetic, (d) scrupulous _____

4. contraband = (a) discrepancy, (b) opposing opinion, (c) smuggled goods, (d) ammunition _____

5. insolvent = (a) uncleanable, (b) unexplainable, (c) bankrupt, (d) unjustifiable _____

6. malicious = marked by (a) good humor, (b) ill will, (c) great pleasure, (d) injurious tumor _____

7. negligent = (a) careless, (b) fraudulent, (c) unlawful, (d) weak _____

8. nominal = (a) enumerated, (b) beneficial, (c) extravagant, (d) insignificant _____

9. rescind = (a) consign, (b) oppose, (c) repeal, (d) censure _____

10. stringent = (a) rigid, (b) expedient, (c) compliant, (d) resilient _____

List 14

1. affirm = (a) business organization, (b) validate, (c) elevate, (d) encircle _____

2. exonerate = (a) commend, (b) declare blameless, (c) banish, (d) emigrate _____

3. expedite = (a) elucidate, (b) get rid of, (c) amplify, (d) rush _____

4. hamper (v) = (a) impede, (b) delineate, (c) release, (d) assuage _____

5. implement (v) = (a) suppress, (b) ameliorate, (c) carry out, (d) attribute _____

6. induce = (a) teach, (b) construe, (c) persuade, (d) copy _____

7. obliterate = (a) obstruct, (b) prevent, (c) minimize, (d) erase _____

8. quandary = a state of (a) doubt, (b) certainty, (c) depression, (d) apprehension _____

9. surmount = (a) hike, (b) overcome, (c) interpret, (d) specify _____

10. veracity = (a) truthfulness, (b) swiftness, (c) efficiency, (d) persistence _____

List 15

1. aggregate = constituting a (a) hostile crowd, (b) word combination, (c) total group, (d) sticky mass _____

2. ambiguous = (a) peripatetic, (b) uncertain, (c) enterprising, (d) deceptive _____

3. amend = (a) alter, (b) pray, (c) praise, (d) utter _____

4. apportion = (a) sanction, (b) ratify, (c) estimate, (d) divide _____

5. collaborate = (a) scrutinize, (b) cooperate, (c) surrender, (d) accumulate _____

6. ingenuity = (a) innocence, (b) torpor, (c) cleverness, (d) self-composure _____

7. irretrievable = not capable of being (a) sold, (b) identified, (c) explained, (d) recovered _____

8. lenient = (a) liberal, (b) crooked, (c) benevolent, (d) explicit _____

9. retrench = (a) dig repeatedly, (b) curtail, (c) reiterate, (d) enlighten _____

10. trivial = (a) composed of three parts, (b) momentous, (c) paltry, (d) economical _____

List 16

1. audit = (a) examine, (b) speak, (c) exchange, (d) expunge _____

2. arrears = (a) old-fashioned, (b) gratuity, (c) overdue debt, (d) option _____

3. curtail = (a) obstruct, (b) restore, (c) rejuvenate, (d) shorten _____

4. encumber = (a) grow, (b) substantiate, (c) burden, (d) illustrate _____

5. exemplify = (a) segregate, (b) divulge, (c) illustrate, (d) condone _____

6. extension = (a) unusual request, (b) prolonged journey, (c) haphazard results, (d) extra time _____

7. fortuitous = (a) accidental, (b) courageous, (c) radical, (d) assiduous _____

8. innovation = (a) reorganization, (b) occupancy, (c) introduction, (d) solution _____

9. syndicate = (a) union of writers, (b) council of lawmakers, (c) group of symptoms, (d) association of people _____

10. venture = (a) speculative business transaction, (b) unsecured loan, (c) stock split, (d) gambling debt _____

List 17

1. acquiesce = (a) gain possession of, (b) confront, (c) implore, (d) comply _____

2. enumerate = (a) articulate, (b) list, (c) enunciate, (d) see clearly _____

3. erratic = (a) pleasurable, (b) wandering, (c) exotic, (d) serene _____

4. expedient = serving to promote (a) fellowship, (b) one's self-interests, (c) good of others, (d) speedy delivery _____

5. feasible = (a) auspicious, (b) profuse, (c) reasonable, (d) extraneous _____

6. literal = (a) exact, (b) devout, (c) apropos, (d) noticeable _____

7. lucrative = (a) providential, (b) swift, (c) pleasant, (d) profitable _____

8. negotiable = (a) essential, (b) adequate, (c) open to discussion, (d) economical _____

9. nonchalant = (a) dull, (b) cool, (c) unintelligent, (d) sagacious _____

10. reconcile = (a) resolve differences, (b) calculate, (c) modify, (d) remunerate _____

List 18

1. apprehensive = (a) knowledgeable, (b) fearful, (c) reticent, (d) autonomous _____

2. circumspect = (a) cautious, (b) uncertain, (c) cooperative, (d) frugal _____

3. collateral = (a) revenue, (b) secret agreement, (c) book value, (d) security for a loan _____

4. insinuation = (a) disagreeable proposal, (b) indirect suggestion, (c) elucidating glimpse, (d) flagrant insult _____

5. liaison = (a) legal obligation, (b) treaty, (c) connection between groups, (d) quarantine _____

6. procrastinate = (a) predict, (b) reproduce, (c) postpone, (d) advance _____

7. ratification = the act of (a) confirming, (b) reviewing, (c) evaluating, (d) inscribing _____

8. renovate = (a) renegotiate, (b) restore, (c) supply, (d) deliver _____

9. saturate = to fill (a) slowly, (b) dangerously, (c) as expected, (d) to excess _____

10. vendor = (a) seller, (b) manufacturer, (c) tradesman, (d) coin collector _____

Document Format Guide

Business communicators produce numerous documents that have standardized formats. Becoming familiar with these formats is important because business documents actually carry two kinds of messages. Verbal messages are conveyed by the words chosen to express the writer's ideas. Nonverbal messages are conveyed largely by the appearance of a document and its adherence to recognized formats. To ensure that your documents carry favorable nonverbal messages about you and your organization, you will want to give special attention to the appearance and formatting of your e-mails, letters, envelopes, memos, and résumés.

E-Mail Messages

E-mail is an appropriate channel for *short* messages. E-mail messages should not replace business letters or memos that are lengthy, require permanent records, or transmit confidential or sensitive information. This section describes formats and usage. The following suggestions, illustrated here in Figure C.1 and also in Figure 4.1 in the Writer's Workshop on page xxx, may guide you in setting up the parts of any e-mail. Always check, however, with your organization so that you can follow its practices.

To Line

Include the receiver's e-mail address after *To*. If the receiver's address is recorded in your address book, you just have to click it. Be sure to enter all addresses very carefully since one mistyped letter prevents delivery.

From Line

Most mail programs automatically include your name and e-mail address after *From*.

Cc and *Bcc*

Insert the e-mail address of anyone who is to receive a copy of the message. *Cc* stands for carbon copy or courtesy copy. Don't be tempted, though, to send needless copies just because it is easy. *Bcc* stands for blind carbon copy. Some writers use *bcc* to send a copy of the message without the addressee's knowledge. Writers also use the *bcc* line for mailing lists. When a message is sent to a number of people and their e-mail addresses should not be revealed, the *bcc* line works well to conceal the names and addresses of all receivers.

Subject

Identify the subject of the e-mail with a brief but descriptive summary of the topic. Be sure to include enough information to be clear and compelling. Capitalize the initial letters of main words. Main words are all words except (a) the articles *a, an,* and *the*; (b) prepositions containing two or three letters (such as *at, to, on, by, for*); (c) the word *to* in an infinitive (*to work, to write*); and (d) the word *as*—unless any of these words are the first or last word in the subject line.

Salutation

Include a brief greeting, if you like. Some writers use a salutation such as *Dear Erica* followed by a comma or a colon. Others are more informal with *Hi, Erica; Hello, Erica; Good morning;* or *Greetings.*

FIGURE C.1

E-Mail

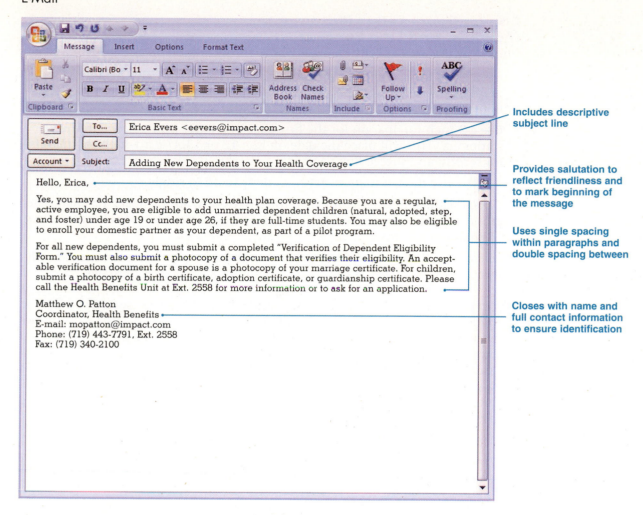

Includes descriptive subject line

Provides salutation to reflect friendliness and to mark beginning of the message

Uses single spacing within paragraphs and double spacing between

Closes with name and full contact information to ensure identification

Message
Cover just one topic in your message, and try to keep your total message under three screens in length. Single-space and be sure to use both upper- and lowercase letters. Double-space between paragraphs.

Closing
Conclude an e-mail, if you like, with *Cheers, Best wishes,* or *Warm regards,* followed by your name and complete contact information. Some people omit their e-mail address because they think it is provided automatically. However, programs and routers do not always transmit the address. Therefore, always include it along with other identifying information in the closing.

Attachment
Use the attachment window or button to select the path and file name of any file you wish to send with your e-mail. You can also attach a Web page to your message.

Business Letters
Business communicators write business letters primarily to correspond with people outside the organization. Letters may go to customers, vendors, other

DOCUMENT FORMAT GUIDE

APPENDIX C   **405**

businesses, and the government. The following information will help you format your letters following conventional guidelines.

Conventional Letter Placement, Margins, and Line Spacing

The following are conventional guidelines for setting up business documents:

- For a clean look, choose a sans serif font such as Arial, Calibri, Tahoma, or Verdana. For a more traditional look, choose a serif font such as Times New Roman. Use a 10-point, 11-point, or 12-point size.

- Use a 2-inch top margin for the first page of a letter printed on letterhead stationery. This will place the date on line 12 or 13. Use a 1-inch top margin for second and succeeding pages.

- Justify only the left margin. Set the line spacing to single.

- Choose side margins according to the length of your letter. Set 1.5-inch margins for short letters (under 200 words) and 1-inch margins for longer letters (200 or more words).

- Leave from 2 to 10 blank lines following the date to balance the message on the page. You can make this adjustment after keying your message.

Formatting Letters With Microsoft Word 2007 and 2010

If you are working with Microsoft Word 2007 or 2010, the default margins are set at 1 inch and the default font is set at 11-point Calibri. The default setting for line spacing is 1.15, and the paragraph default is 10 points of blank space following each paragraph or each tap of the **Enter** key. Many letter writers find this extra space excessive, especially after parts of the letter that are normally single-spaced. The model documents in this book show conventional single-spacing with one blank line between paragraphs.

To format your documents with conventional spacing and yet retain a clean look, we recommend that you change the Microsoft defaults to the following: Arial font set for 11 points, line spacing at 1.0, and spacing before and after paragraphs at 0.

Spacing and Punctuation

For some time typists left two spaces after end punctuation (periods, question marks, and so forth). This practice was necessary, it was thought, because typewriters did not have proportional spacing and sentences were easier to read when two spaces separated them. Professional typesetters, however, never followed this practice because they used proportional spacing, and readability was not a problem. Influenced by the look of typeset publications, many writers now leave only one space after end punctuation. As a practical matter, however, it is not wrong to use two spaces.

Business Letter Parts

Professional-looking business letters are arranged in a conventional sequence with standard parts. Following is a discussion of how to use these letter parts properly. Figure C.2 illustrates the parts of a block style letter. See the Unit 5 Writer's Workshop on page xxx for an additional discussion of letter content and parts.

Letterhead

Most business organizations use 8½ × 11-inch paper printed with a letterhead displaying their official name, street address, Web address, e-mail address, and telephone and fax numbers. The letterhead may also include a logo and an advertising message.

FIGURE C.2
Block and Modified Block Letter Styles

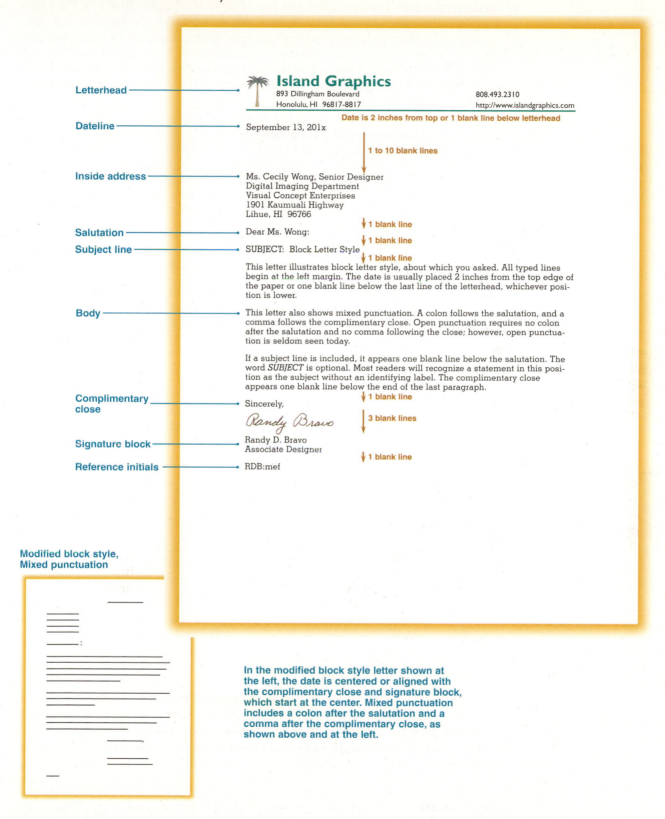

Letterhead

Island Graphics
893 Dillingham Boulevard
Honolulu, HI 96817-8817

808.493.2310
http://www.islandgraphics.com

Dateline

Date is 2 inches from top or 1 blank line below letterhead

September 13, 201x

↓ *1 to 10 blank lines*

Inside address

Ms. Cecily Wong, Senior Designer
Digital Imaging Department
Visual Concept Enterprises
1901 Kaumuali Highway
Lihue, HI 96766

↓ *1 blank line*

Salutation

Dear Ms. Wong:

↓ *1 blank line*

Subject line

SUBJECT: Block Letter Style

↓ *1 blank line*

This letter illustrates block letter style, about which you asked. All typed lines begin at the left margin. The date is usually placed 2 inches from the top edge of the paper or one blank line below the last line of the letterhead, whichever position is lower.

Body

This letter also shows mixed punctuation. A colon follows the salutation, and a comma follows the complimentary close. Open punctuation requires no colon after the salutation and no comma following the close; however, open punctuation is seldom seen today.

If a subject line is included, it appears one blank line below the salutation. The word *SUBJECT* is optional. Most readers will recognize a statement in this position as the subject without an identifying label. The complimentary close appears one blank line below the end of the last paragraph.

↓ *1 blank line*

Complimentary close

Sincerely,

↓ *3 blank lines*

Randy Bravo

Signature block

Randy D. Bravo
Associate Designer

↓ *1 blank line*

Reference initials

RDB:mef

**Modified block style,
Mixed punctuation**

In the modified block style letter shown at the left, the date is centered or aligned with the complimentary close and signature block, which start at the center. Mixed punctuation includes a colon after the salutation and a comma after the complimentary close, as shown above and at the left.

Dateline

On letterhead paper you should place the date one blank line below the last line of the letterhead or 2 inches from the top edge of the paper (line 13). On plain paper place the date immediately below your return address. Because the date goes on line 13, start the return address an appropriate number of lines above it. The most common dateline format is as follows: *June 9, 2014*. Don't use *th* (or *rd*, *nd*, or *st*) when the date is written this way. For European or military correspondence, use the following dateline format: *9 June 2014*. Notice that no commas are used.

Addressee and Delivery Notations

Delivery notations such as *VIA U.S. MAIL AND E-MAIL, FAX TRANSMISSION, FEDEX, MESSENGER DELIVERY, CONFIDENTIAL,* or *CERTIFIED MAIL* are typed in all capital letters between the dateline and the inside address.

Inside Address

Type the inside address—that is, the address of the organization or person receiving the letter—single-spaced, starting at the left margin. The number of lines between the dateline and the inside address depends on the size of the letter body, the type size (point or pitch size), and the length of the typing lines. Generally, one to nine blank lines are appropriate.

Be careful to duplicate the exact wording and spelling of the recipient's name and address on your documents. Usually, you can copy this information from the letterhead of the correspondence you are answering. If, for example, you are responding to *Jackson & Perkins Company*, do not address your letter to *Jackson and Perkins Corp.*

Always be sure to include a courtesy title such as *Mr., Ms., Mrs., Dr.,* or *Professor* before a person's name in the inside address—for both the letter and the envelope. Although many women in business today favor *Ms.,* you should use whatever title the addressee prefers.

In general, avoid abbreviations such as *Ave.* or *Co.* unless they appear in the printed letterhead of the document being answered.

Attention Line

An attention line allows you to send your message officially to an organization but to direct it to a specific individual, officer, or department. However, if you know an individual's complete name, it is always better to use it as the first line of the inside address and avoid an attention line. Two common formats for attention lines follow:

The MultiMedia Company
931 Calkins Avenue
Rochester, NY 14301

The MultiMedia Company
Attention: Marketing Director
931 Calkins Avenue
Rochester, NY 14301

ATTENTION MARKETING DIRECTOR

Attention lines may be typed in all caps or with upper- and lowercase letters. The colon following *Attention* is optional. Notice that an attention line may be placed one blank line below the address block or printed as the second line of the inside address. Use the latter format so that you may copy the address block to the envelope and the attention line will not interfere with the last-line placement of the zip code. Mail can be sorted more easily when the zip code appears in the last line of a typed address. Whenever possible, use a person's name as the first line of an address instead of putting that name in an attention line.

Salutation

For most letter styles, place the letter greeting, or salutation, one blank line below the last line of the inside address or the attention line (if used). If the letter is addressed to an individual, use that person's courtesy title and last name (*Dear Mr. Lanham*). Even if you are on a first-name basis (*Dear Leslie*), be sure to add a colon (not a comma or a semicolon) after the salutation. Do not use an individual's full name in the salutation (not *Dear Mr. Leslie Lanham*) unless you are unsure of gender (*Dear Leslie Lanham*).

For letters with attention lines or those addressed to organizations, the selection of an appropriate salutation has become more difficult. Because no universally acceptable salutation has emerged as yet, you could use *Ladies and Gentlemen* or *Gentlemen and Ladies*.

Subject and Reference Lines

Although experts suggest placing the subject line one blank line below the salutation, many businesses actually place it above the salutation. Use whatever style your organization prefers. Reference lines often show policy or file numbers; they generally appear one blank line above the salutation. Use initial capital letters for the main words or all capital letters.

Body

Most business letters and memorandums are single-spaced, with double-spacing between paragraphs. Very short messages may be double-spaced with indented paragraphs.

Complimentary Close

Typed one blank line below the last line of the letter, the complimentary close may be formal (*Very truly yours*) or informal (*Sincerely* or *Cordially*).

Signature Block

In most letter styles, the writer's typed name and optional identification appear three or four blank lines below the complimentary close. The combination of name, title, and organization information should be arranged to achieve a balanced look. The name and title may appear on the same line or on separate lines, depending on the length of each. Use commas to separate categories within the same line, but not to conclude a line.

Sincerely yours,	Cordially yours,
Jeremy M. Wood	*Casandra Baker-Murillo*
Jeremy M. Wood, Manager	Casandra Baker-Murillo
Technical Sales and Services	Executive Vice President

Some organizations include their names in the signature block. In such cases the organization name appears in all caps one blank line below the complimentary close, as shown here:

Cordially,

LIPTON COMPUTER SERVICES

Shelina A. Simpson

Shelina A. Simpson
Executive Assistant

Reference Initials

If used, the initials of the typist and writer are typed one blank line below the writer's name and title. Generally, the writer's initials are capitalized and the typist's are lowercased, but this format varies.

Enclosure Notation

When an enclosure or attachment accompanies a document, a notation to that effect appears one blank line below the reference initials. This notation reminds the typist to insert the enclosure in the envelope, and it reminds the recipient to look for the enclosure or attachment. The notation may be spelled out (*Enclosure, Attachment*), or it may be abbreviated (*Enc., Att.*). It may indicate the number of enclosures or attachments, and it may also identify a specific enclosure (*Enclosure: Form 1099*).

Copy Notation

If you make copies of correspondence for other individuals, you may use *cc* to indicate courtesy copy, *pc* to indicate photocopy, or merely *c* for any kind of copy. A colon following the initial(s) is optional.

Second-Page Heading

When a letter extends beyond one page, use plain paper of the same quality and color as the first page. Identify the second and succeeding pages with a heading consisting of the name of the addressee, the page number, and the date. Use the following format or the one shown in Figure C.3:

Ms. Sara Hendricks 2 May 3, 2014

Both headings appear six blank lines (1 inch) from the top edge of the paper followed by two blank lines to separate them from the continuing text. Avoid using a second page if you have only one line or the complimentary close and signature block to fill that page.

Plain-Paper Return Address

If you prepare a personal or business letter on plain paper, place your address immediately above the date. Do not include your name; you will type (and sign) your name at the end of your letter. If your return address contains two lines, begin typing so that the date appears 2 inches from the top. Avoid abbreviations except for a two-letter state abbreviation. Shown here is a return address in block style beginning at the left margin.

580 East Leffels Street
Springfield, OH 45501
December 14, 201x

Ms. Ellen Siemens
Escrow Department
TransOhio First Federal
1220 Wooster Boulevard
Columbus, OH 43218-2900

Dear Ms. Siemens:

For letters in the modified block style, start the return address at the center to align with the complimentary close.

Letter and Punctuation Styles

Most business letters today are prepared in either block or modified block style, and they generally use mixed punctuation.

Block Style

In the block style, shown in Figure C.2, all lines begin at the left margin. This style is a favorite because it is easy to format.

FIGURE C.3

Second-Page Heading

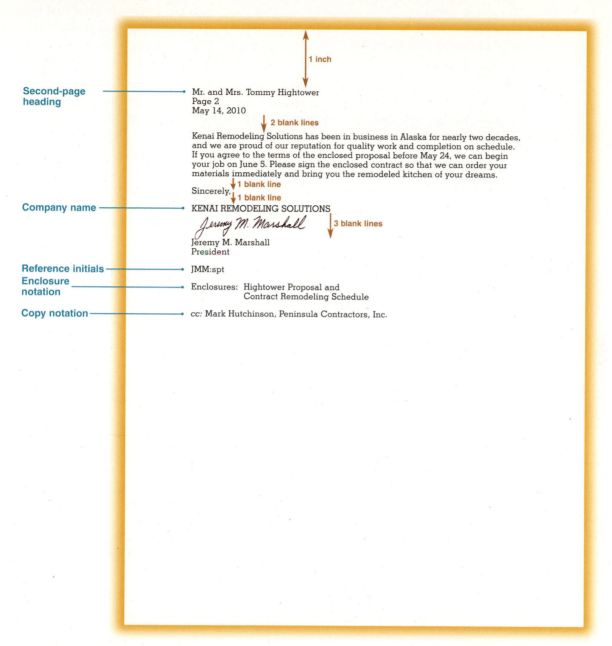

Modified Block Style

The modified block style differs from block style in that the date and closing lines appear in the center, as shown at the bottom of Figure C.2. The date may be (a) centered, (b) begun at the center of the page (to align with the closing lines), or (c) backspaced from the right margin. The signature block—including the complimentary close, writer's name and title, or organization identification— begins at the center. The first line of each paragraph may begin at the left margin or may be indented five or ten spaces. All other lines begin at the left margin.

Mixed Punctuation Style

Most businesses today use mixed punctuation, shown in Figure C.2. It requires a colon after the salutation and a comma after the complimentary close. Even when the salutation is a first name, a colon is appropriate.

Envelopes

An envelope should be of the same quality and color of stationery as the letter it carries. Because the envelope introduces your message and makes the first impression, you need to be especially careful in addressing it. Moreover, how you fold the letter is important.

Return Address

The return address is usually printed in the upper left corner of an envelope, as shown in Figure C.4. In large companies some form of identification (the writer's initials, name, or location) may be typed above the company name and address. This identification helps return the letter to the sender in case of nondelivery.

On an envelope without a printed return address, single-space the return address in the upper left corner. Beginning on line 3 on the fourth space (½ inch) from the left edge, type the writer's name, title, company, and mailing address. On a word processor, select the appropriate envelope size and make adjustments to approximate this return address location.

Mailing Address

On legal-sized No. 10 envelopes (4⅛ × 9½ inches), begin the address on line 13 about 4¼ inches from the left edge, as shown in Figure C.4. For small envelopes (3⅝ × 6½ inches), begin typing on line 12 about 2½ inches from the left edge. On a word processor, select the correct envelope size and check to be sure your address falls in the desired location.

In the past the U.S. Postal Service recommended that addresses be typed in all caps without any punctuation. This Postal Service style, shown in the small envelope in Figure C.4, was originally developed to facilitate scanning by optical character readers. Today's OCRs, however, are so sophisticated that

FIGURE C.4

Envelope Formats

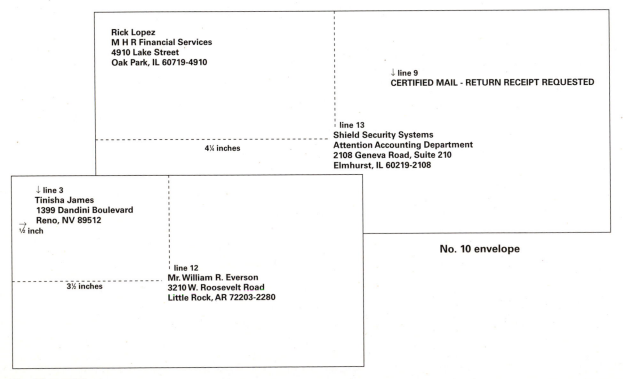

Rick Lopez
M H R Financial Services
4910 Lake Street
Oak Park, IL 60719-4910

↓ line 9
CERTIFIED MAIL - RETURN RECEIPT REQUESTED

line 13
Shield Security Systems
Attention Accounting Department
2108 Geneva Road, Suite 210
Elmhurst, IL 60219-2108

4¼ inches

No. 10 envelope

↓ line 3
Tinisha James
1399 Dandini Boulevard
Reno, NV 89512
½ inch

line 12
Mr. William R. Everson
3210 W. Roosevelt Road
Little Rock, AR 72203-2280

3½ inches

No. 6¾ envelope

they scan upper- and lowercase letters easily. Many companies today do not follow the Postal Service format because they prefer to use the same format for the envelope as for the inside address. If the same format is used, writers can take advantage of word processing programs to copy the inside address to the envelope, thus saving keystrokes and reducing errors. Having the same format on both the inside address and the envelope also looks more professional and consistent. For those reasons you may choose to use the familiar upper- and lowercase combination format. But you will want to check with your organization to learn its preference.

In addressing your envelopes for delivery in this country or in Canada, use the two-letter state and province abbreviations shown in Figure C.5. Notice that these abbreviations are in capital letters without periods.

FIGURE C.5

Abbreviations of States, Territories, and Provinces

State or Territory	Two-Letter Abbreviation	State or Territory	Two-Letter Abbreviation
Alabama	AL	North Dakota	ND
Alaska	AK	Ohio	OH
Arizona	AZ	Oklahoma	OK
Arkansas	AR	Oregon	OR
California	CA	Pennsylvania	PA
Canal Zone	CZ	Puerto Rico	PR
Colorado	CO	Rhode Island	RI
Connecticut	CT	South Carolina	SC
Delaware	DE	South Dakota	SD
District of Columbia	DC	Tennessee	TN
Florida	FL	Texas	TX
Georgia	GA	Utah	UT
Guam	GU	Vermont	VT
Hawaii	HI	Virgin Islands	VI
Idaho	ID	Virginia	VA
Illinois	IL	Washington	WA
Indiana	IN	West Virginia	WV
Iowa	IA	Wisconsin	WI
Kansas	KS	Wyoming	WY
Kentucky	KY		
Louisiana	LA		
Maine	ME	**Canadian Province**	**Two-Letter Abbreviation**
Maryland	MD		
Massachusetts	MA	Alberta	AB
Michigan	MI	British Columbia	BC
Minnesota	MN	Labrador	LB
Mississippi	MS	Manitoba	MB
Missouri	MO	New Brunswick	NB
Montana	MT	Newfoundland	NF
Nebraska	NE	Northwest Territories	NT
Nevada	NV	Nova Scotia	NS
New Hampshire	NH	Ontario	ON
New Jersey	NJ	Prince Edward Island	PE
New Mexico	NM	Quebec	PQ
New York	NY	Saskatchewan	SK
North Carolina	NC	Yukon Territory	YT

Folding

The way a letter is folded and inserted into an envelope sends additional non-verbal messages about a writer's professionalism and carefulness. Most business-people follow the procedures shown here, which produce the least number of creases to distract readers.

For large No. 10 envelopes, begin with the letter face up. Fold slightly less than one third of the sheet toward the top, as shown in the following diagram. Then fold down the top third to within ⅓ inch of the bottom fold. Insert the letter into the envelope with the last fold toward the bottom of the envelope.

For small No. 6¾ envelopes, begin by folding the bottom up to within ⅓ inch of the top edge. Then fold the right third over to the left. Fold the left third to within ⅓ inch of the last fold. Insert the last fold into the envelope first.

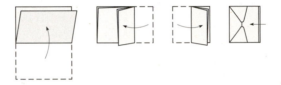

Memorandums

Memorandums deliver messages within organizations, although e-mail is quickly replacing the use of printed memos. Some offices use memo forms imprinted with the organization name and, optionally, the department or division names. The design and arrangement of memo forms vary; however, they usually include the basic elements of *TO, FROM, DATE,* and *SUBJECT.* Large organizations may include other identifying headings, such as *FILE NUMBER, FLOOR, EXTENSION, LOCATION,* and *DISTRIBUTION.*

Because of the difficulty of aligning computer printers with preprinted forms, many business writers use a standardized memo template (sometimes called a "wizard"). This template automatically provides attractive headings with appropriate spacing and formatting. Other writers store their own preferred memo formats.

If no printed or stored computer forms are available, memos may be keyed on company letterhead or plain paper, as shown in Figure C.6. On a full sheet of paper, leave a 1.5-inch top margin. Double-space and type in all caps the guide words *TO:, FROM:, DATE:,* and *SUBJECT.* Align all the fill-in information two spaces after the longest guide word (*SUBJECT:*). Leave two blank lines after the last line of the heading, and begin typing the body of the memo. Like business letters, memos are single-spaced.

Memos are generally formatted with side margins of 1 to 1.25 inches, or they may conform to the printed memo form. For more information about memos and to see a comparison of e-mail and memo formats, see the Writer's Workshop following Chapter 9 on page 240.

FIGURE C.6
Memo on Plain Paper

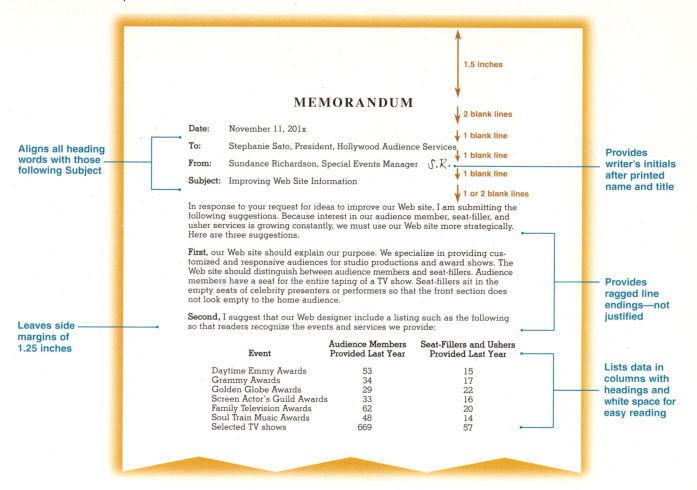

Aligns all heading words with those following Subject

Leaves side margins of 1.25 inches

1.5 inches

2 blank lines

1 blank line

1 blank line

1 blank line

1 or 2 blank lines

Provides writer's initials after printed name and title

Provides ragged line endings—not justified

Lists data in columns with headings and white space for easy reading

MEMORANDUM

Date:	November 11, 201x
To:	Stephanie Sato, President, Hollywood Audience Services
From:	Sundance Richardson, Special Events Manager *S.R.*
Subject:	Improving Web Site Information

In response to your request for ideas to improve our Web site, I am submitting the following suggestions. Because interest in our audience member, seat-filler, and usher services is growing constantly, we must use our Web site more strategically. Here are three suggestions.

First, our Web site should explain our purpose. We specialize in providing customized and responsive audiences for studio productions and award shows. The Web site should distinguish between audience members and seat-fillers. Audience members have a seat for the entire taping of a TV show. Seat-fillers sit in the empty seats of celebrity presenters or performers so that the front section does not look empty to the home audience.

Second, I suggest that our Web designer include a listing such as the following so that readers recognize the events and services we provide:

Event	Audience Members Provided Last Year	Seat-Fillers and Ushers Provided Last Year
Daytime Emmy Awards	53	15
Grammy Awards	34	17
Golden Globe Awards	29	22
Screen Actor's Guild Awards	33	16
Family Television Awards	62	20
Soul Train Music Awards	48	14
Selected TV shows	669	57

Résumés

A résumé is a carefully prepared document that summarizes your education, experience, and other qualifications for a job. The goal of a résumé is obtaining an interview. The résumé format most preferred by recruiters is the chronological résumé, shown in Figure C.7. It focuses on experience and arranges jobs in reverse chronological order. A functional résumé focuses on a candidate's skills rather than on past employment. Résumés have various formats and organization plans, but most include a main heading, career objective, summary of qualifications, education, work experience, capabilities and skills, and awards.

Main Heading

Whether chronological or functional, your résumé should always begin with your name. Add your middle initial for an even more professional look. Following your name, list your contact information, including your complete address, area code and phone number, and e-mail address. Be sure your e-mail address sounds professional.

Career Objective

Include a well-written career objective that is customized for each position you seek. Change the objective for different applications—for example, to apply for an advertised position in an attorney's office: *Career Objective: To obtain a position as an administrative assistant in an attorney's office.*

FIGURE C.7

Chronological Résumé

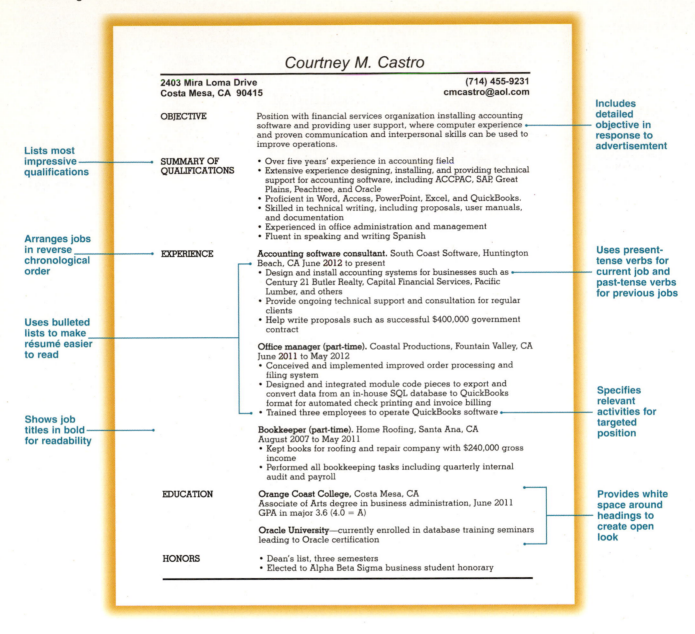

Lists most impressive qualifications

Arranges jobs in reverse chronological order

Uses bulleted lists to make résumé easier to read

Shows job titles in bold for readability

Includes detailed objective in response to advertisemtent

Uses present-tense verbs for current job and past-tense verbs for previous jobs

Specifies relevant activities for targeted position

Provides white space around headings to create open look

Courtney M. Castro

2403 Mira Loma Drive
Costa Mesa, CA 90415

(714) 455-9231
cmcastro@aol.com

OBJECTIVE — Position with financial services organization installing accounting software and providing user support, where computer experience and proven communication and interpersonal skills can be used to improve operations.

SUMMARY OF QUALIFICATIONS
- Over five years' experience in accounting field
- Extensive experience designing, installing, and providing technical support for accounting software, including ACCPAC, SAP, Great Plains, Peachtree, and Oracle
- Proficient in Word, Access, PowerPoint, Excel, and QuickBooks.
- Skilled in technical writing, including proposals, user manuals, and documentation
- Experienced in office administration and management
- Fluent in speaking and writing Spanish

EXPERIENCE — **Accounting software consultant.** South Coast Software, Huntington Beach, CA June 2012 to present
- Design and install accounting systems for businesses such as Century 21 Butler Realty, Capital Financial Services, Pacific Lumber, and others
- Provide ongoing technical support and consultation for regular clients
- Help write proposals such as successful $400,000 government contract

Office manager (part-time). Coastal Productions, Fountain Valley, CA June 2011 to May 2012
- Conceived and implemented improved order processing and filing system
- Designed and integrated module code pieces to export and convert data from an in-house SQL database to QuickBooks format for automated check printing and invoice billing
- Trained three employees to operate QuickBooks software

Bookkeeper (part-time). Home Roofing, Santa Ana, CA August 2007 to May 2011
- Kept books for roofing and repair company with $240,000 gross income
- Performed all bookkeeping tasks including quarterly internal audit and payroll

EDUCATION — **Orange Coast College,** Costa Mesa, CA
Associate of Arts degree in business administration, June 2011
GPA in major 3.6 (4.0 = A)

Oracle University—currently enrolled in database training seminars leading to Oracle certification

HONORS
- Dean's list, three semesters
- Elected to Alpha Beta Sigma business student honorary

Summary of Qualifications

At the top of a résumé, the summary of qualifications lists the skills and experience most appealing to the hiring company. It should include three to eight bulleted statements that prove you are the ideal candidate for the position. Consider your experience, your education, your unique skills, awards you have won, certifications, and any other accomplishments that you want to highlight.

Education

Include your education next—if it is more noteworthy than your work experience. Include the name and location of schools, dates of attendance, major fields of study, and degrees received. Once you have attended college, don't bother to list high school information. Grade point averages are important to potential employers. One way to enhance your GPA is to calculate it in your major courses only. Do not list all the courses you have taken. Refer to specific courses only if you can relate them to the position sought.

Work Experience

When your work experience is significant and relevant to the position sought, this information should appear before education. List your employment in reverse chronological order, with the most recent employment first. Include only those jobs you think will help you win the targeted position. Include (a) employer's name, city, and state; (b) dates of employment (month and year); (c) most important job title; and (d) significant duties, activities, accomplishments, and promotions. In a bulleted list, describe your employment achievements concisely but concretely.

Capabilities and Skills

Recruiters want to know specifically what you can do for their companies. List your special skills, such as your ability to use software programs, office equipment, and communication technology tools. If you speak a foreign language or use sign language, include it on your résumé. Describe proficiencies you have acquired through training and experience. If you are preparing a functional résumé, you will place more focus on skills than on any other section.

Awards, Honors, and Activities

If you have three or more awards or honors, highlight them by listing them under a separate heading. If not, put them in the education or work experience section. Include awards, scholarships, (financial and other), fellowships, dean's list, honors, recognition, commendations, and certificates.

Personal Data

Today's résumés generally omit personal data, such as birth date, marital status, height, weight, national origin, health, and religious affiliation. Such information doesn't relate to genuine occupational qualifications, and recruiters are legally barred from asking for such information. Some job seekers do, however, include hobbies or interests (such as skiing or photography) that might grab the recruiter's attention or serve as conversation starters.

References

Most applicants do not list references on their résumés. They take up valuable space and are not normally instrumental in securing an interview. You should, however, have them listed on a separate sheet and be ready to distribute them when asked.

SELF-HELP EXERCISES

1 Self-Help Exercises
Parts of Speech

Nearly every student who takes this English course says, "I wish I had more exercises to try my skills on." Because of the many requests, we provide this set of self-help exercises for extra reinforcement. Immediate feedback is an important ingredient in successful learning. Therefore, a key to these exercises begins on page 483. Don't check the key, of course, until you have completed each exercise.

Worksheet 1

A. This exercise is designed to help you develop a better understanding of the parts of speech. Using Chapter 1, write a brief definition or description of the eight parts of speech listed here. Then list three examples of each part of speech.

		Brief Definition	**Three Examples**		
1.	noun	Names person, place, thing, quality, feeling, concept, activity, measure	Anthony	paper	truth
2.	pronoun	_____	_____	_____	_____
3.	verb	_____	_____	_____	_____
4.	adjective	_____	_____	_____	_____
5.	adverb	_____	_____	_____	_____
6.	preposition	_____	_____	_____	_____
7.	conjunction	_____	_____	_____	_____
8.	interjection	_____	_____	_____	_____

B. Fill in the parts of speech for all the words in these sentences. Use a dictionary if necessary.

We sent a text message to Julia, but she was very busy.

1. We _____
2. sent _____
3. a _____
4. text _____

5. message _____
6. to _____
7. Julia _____
8. but _____

9. she _____
10. was _____
11. very _____
12. busy _____

Gosh, the computer and printer processed this lengthy report in 20 seconds.

13. Gosh _____
14. the _____
15. computer _____
16. and _____

17. printer _____
18. processed _____
19. this _____
20. lengthy _____

21. report _____
22. in _____
23. 20 _____
24. seconds _____

We arrived promptly, but the committee meeting started late.

25. We _____
26. arrived _____
27. promptly _____

28. but _____
29. the _____
30. committee _____

31. meeting _____
32. started _____
33. late _____

Worksheet 2

Fill in the parts of speech for all the words in these sentences. Use a dictionary if necessary.

I sold property in Hyannis, but one transaction may not clear escrow.

1. I _____

2. sold _____

3. property _____

4. in _____

5. Hyannis _____

6. but _____

7. one _____

8. transaction _____

9. may _____

10. not _____

11. clear _____

12. escrow _____

Oh, did Louis really think he could change that method of operation?

13. Oh _____

14. did _____

15. Louis _____

16. really _____

17. think _____

18. he _____

19. could _____

20. change _____

21. that _____

22. method _____

23. of _____

24. operation _____

The old accounting system was neither accurate nor efficient, but one company had used it faithfully for the past 40 years.

25. The _____

26. old _____

27. accounting _____

28. system _____

29. was _____

30. neither _____

31. accurate _____

32. nor _____

33. efficient _____

34. but _____

35. one _____

36. company _____

37. had _____

38. used _____

39. it _____

40. faithfully _____

41. for _____

42. the _____

43. past _____

44. 40 _____

45. years _____

Candace quietly slipped into an empty seat during the long marketing presentation.

46. Candace _____

47. quietly _____

48. slipped _____

49. into _____

50. an _____

51. empty _____

52. seat _____

53. during _____

54. the _____

55. long _____

56. marketing _____

57. presentation _____

Social media has completely changed the way we communicate with our customers.

58. media _____

59. has _____

60. completely _____

61. changed _____

62. the _____

63. way _____

64. we _____

65. communicate _____

66. with _____

67. our _____

68. customers _____

2 Self-Help Exercises

Sentences: Elements, Varieties, Patterns, Types, Faults

Worksheet 1

Locating Subjects and Verbs

Action verbs tell what the subject is doing or what is being done to the subject. For each of the following sentences, locate the action verb and underline it twice. Then locate the subject of the verb and underline it once. To locate the subject, use the verb preceded by *Who?* or *What?* In the example the verb is *answered*. To help you find the subject, ask, *Who answered?*

Example: A group of applicants answered the advertisement.

1. The applicant with the best qualifications received the first interview.
2. In the afternoon session, the speaker made a dynamic presentation.
3. During the sales campaign, our telephones rang constantly.
4. In the winter we will hire four new employees for this department.
5. Our management team built a strong program of sales and service.
6. The most successful salespeople received trips to Hawaii.
7. In the meantime, our human resources manager will send you an application form.
8. Last week we released our new line of upscale, stylish smartphones.
9. One of the vice presidents was given a promotion recently.
10. Today's technology requires managers to think with new clarity and precision.
11. The file with all the customers' names and addresses was accurate.
12. One of our top salespeople sold $2 million worth of life insurance.
13. A list of restaurants with low-priced meals is available in the lobby.
14. Everything except labor and parts is covered by your warranty.
15. A committee consisting of 11 employees plus the manager was appointed to investigate.

Linking verbs (such as *am, is, are, was, were, be, being,* and *been*) often join to the sentence words that describe or rename the subject. In the following sentences, underline the linking verbs twice and the subjects once.

Example: E. J. Todd was president of the organization last year.
In the morning the air is cool.

16. Mr. Thomas is the office manager for Ryerson Metals Corporation.
17. The new wireless devices are very dependable.
18. Ms. Seymour is the person for the job.
19. Mr. Torres has been our supervisor for nine years.
20. Our new offices are much brighter than our previous ones.

Worksheet 2

Sentence Variety

From the following list, select the letter that accurately describes what type each sentence is.

a. simple   c. complex
b. compound   d. compound-complex

1. Raul applied with five companies, but he interviewed with only two. _____

2. Raul applied with five companies but interviewed with only two. _____

3. Although Raul applied with five companies, he interviewed with only two. _____

4. Raul, who is applying for jobs, sent résumés to five companies; however, he interviewed with only two. _____

5. He brought a list of references, a notebook, and a nice pen to the interview. _____

6. If he is invited to a second interview, he will contact his references. _____

7. Raul answered all of the questions confidently; therefore, he feels as if he did well during the interview. _____

8. When answering the questions, Raul used proper grammar and an enthusiastic tone. _____

9. He focused on his most impressive traits, told success stories, and kept his answers focused on the needs of the employer. _____

10. Because he was properly prepared, both employers were extremely impressed. _____

Sentence Patterns

Finish the following sentences in the patterns indicated.

SUBJECT–VERB

Example: GPS devices navigate.

11. Stockholders _____.   14. The security alarm _____.

12. Stock prices _____.   15. In 1945 World War II _____.

13. Employees _____.   16. Last year's sales _____.

SUBJECT–ACTION VERB–OBJECT

Example: The sales director made a decision.

17. Our salesperson sold a _____.   20. I telephoned _____.

18. The network was infected with a ____. 21. Someone locked _____.

19. Ricky mailed the _____.   22. The clerk filed all the _____.

SUBJECT–LINKING VERB–COMPLEMENT

Examples: She is very <u>friendly</u>.

Eric could have been the <u>manager</u>.

23. Sales have been _____.   **26.** I am _____

24. Susan is the new _____.   **27.** The writer could have been _____

25. Last year the owner was _____.   **28.** The caller was _____

Compose original sentences in the following patterns.

29. (Subject–verb) _____

30. (Subject–action verb–object) _____

31. (Subject–linking verb–adjective complement) _____

32. (Subject–linking verb–noun or pronoun complement) _____

33. (Inverted order) _____

Worksheet 3

Sentence Types

From the following list, select the letter that accurately describes each of the following groups of words. Add end punctuation marks to all complete sentences.

a. fragment   d. question
b. statement   e. exclamation
c. command

1. The management of a multinational corporation with branch offices in several cities _____

2. Send me a brochure describing your latest workout equipment _____

3. Will you be working next weekend or during the week _____

4. The work schedule is usually posted late in the week _____

5. What an amazing presentation _____

6. If you have an opportunity to be promoted to a managerial position _____

7. For a generous return on your funds, invest in second trust deeds _____

8. In all levels of business, communication skills and initiative are extremely important in achieving success _____

9. Because it is difficult to improve your language skills on your own _____

Sentence Faults

From the following list, select the letter that accurately describes each of the following groups of words.

a. correctly punctuated sentence   c. comma splice
b. fragment   d. run-on sentence

10. I will have the answer soon, first I must make a telephone call. _____

11. If you consider all the pros and cons before you make a decision. _____

12. We have no idea what to order only Ms. Sanchez can do that. _____

13. Your entire department is entitled to overtime compensation. _____

14. You check the current address list, and I will check the old one. _____

15. You check the current address list, I will check the old one. _____

16. You check the current address list I will check the old one. _____

17. Although we have complete confidence in our products and prices. _____

18. When you return from the conference, please submit a brief report describing the information you learned. _____

19. We must focus our charitable contributions on areas that directly relate to our business, therefore, we are unable to send a check this year. _____

20. If you agree that this memo accurately reflects our conversation. _____

3 Self-Help Exercises
Nouns: Plurals and Possessives

LEVEL 1

Worksheet 1

Write the preferred plural forms of the nouns shown below. Use a dictionary if necessary.

1. giraffe
2. foot
3. switch
4. Bush
5. box
6. language
7. fax
8. sandwich
9. income tax
10. child
11. success
12. value
13. dress
14. branch
15. recommendation
16. woman
17. mismatch
18. taxi
19. loaf (of bread)
20. annex
21. belief
22. Ross
23. storm
24. ranch
25. Jones
26. Chavez
27. letter
28. business
29. computer
30. wish

Worksheet 2

Write the preferred plural forms of the nouns shown below. Use a dictionary if necessary.

1. wharf _____
2. chief of police _____
3. 1960 _____
4. Wolf _____
5. embargo _____
6. LVN _____
7. size 10 _____
8. amt. _____
9. faculty _____
10. by-product _____
11. entry _____
12. looker-on _____
13. company _____
14. knife _____
15. court-martial _____
16. A _____
17. Sherman _____
18. memo _____
19. valley _____
20. zero _____
21. life _____
22. yr. _____
23. Murphy _____
24. runner-up _____
25. oz. _____
26. journey _____
27. MBA _____
28. wolf _____
29. Kelly _____
30. minority _____

Worksheet 1

Before you begin this exercise, review the three-step plan for placing apostrophes:

1. Look for possessive construction. (Usually two nouns appear together.)

2. Reverse the nouns. (Use a prepositional phrase, such as *employees of the company*.)

3. Examine ownership word. (Does it end in an *s* sound?)
   a. If the ownership word does NOT end in an *s* sound, add an apostrophe and *s*.
   b. If the ownership word DOES end in *s* and is <u>singular</u>, add an apostrophe and *s*.
   c. If the ownership word DOES end in *s* and is <u>plural</u>, add an apostrophe only.

Using apostrophes, change the following prepositional phrases to possessive constructions.

Example: home of the couple   the couple's home _____

1. passwords of all employees
2. office of this company
3. uniforms of the women
4. signature of an employee
5. e-mail message of the supervisor
6. opinions of all members
7. landing of the pilot
8. agreement of both partners
9. notebook of Jeffrey
10. strengths of the department
11. grades of the students
12. customs of those people
13. presentation of a student
14. credit from the bank
15. savings of citizens
16. mountains of Canada
17. requirements of the employer
18. résumés of all candidates
19. policies of the government
20. fees of both attorneys

Worksheet 2

Write the correct possessive form of the word in parentheses in the space provided.

1. He managed to get the (author) signature on the title page of the book. _____

2. Several (drivers) inquiries prompted the posting of a better sign. _____

3. We found the (carpenter) tools after he left the building. _____

4. The electronics store installed a hidden video camera to observe a suspected (thief) activities. _____

5. The (company) ethics statement is posted on its website. _____

6. Several (employees) passwords must be reset. _____

7. Only the (CEO) car may be parked in the special zone. _____

8. Most (readers) letters supported the magazine's editorial position. _____

9. Where is the (caller) message? _____

10. All (authors) rights are protected by copyright law. _____

Correct any errors in the following sentences by underlining the errors and writing the correct forms in the spaces provided. Each sentence contains one error.

11. Like its clothing, the Gaps corporate offices are simple, clean, and comfortable. _____

12. The names of these customers' are not alphabetized. _____

13. Some of the countrys biggest corporations are being investigated. _____

14. All employee's suggestions are confidential. _____

15. Your organizations voice mail system is excellent. _____

16. The vice presidents resignation left a vital position unfilled. _____

17. Are you researching your familys genealogy? _____

18. My attorneys name is William Glass. _____

19. Several employee's plan to take Friday off. _____

20. Not a single farmers crop was undamaged by the storm. _____

21. A citizens committee was formed to address parking problems. _____

22. Several company's relocated to our city last year. _____

23. Each customers complimentary game tickets were mailed today. _____

24. Childrens clothing is on the first floor. _____

25. The announcement of new benefits for employees was made in the supervisors memo, which she sent out yesterday. _____

Worksheet 3

Correct any errors in the following sentences by underlining the errors and writing the correct forms in the spaces provided. Each sentence contains one error.

1. The document required the notary publics signature and his seal. _____

2. Lee Ross office is on the south side of the campus. _____

3. At least one companies' records are computerized. _____

4. My uncle's lawyer's suggestions in this matter were excellent. _____

5. The editor's in chief office is on the fifth floor. _____

6. Beth Browns home is farther away than anyone else's. _____

7. All RN's uniforms must now be identical. _____

8. The president's assistant's telephone number has been changed. _____

9. Have you called the new sales' representative? _____

10. My brother's-in-law beard is neat and well trimmed. _____

11. We spent our vacation enjoying New Englands' historical towns. _____

12. Major changes are forecast for the electronics' industry. _____

13. The bank is reconsidering the Rodriguez's loan application. _____

14. I have no idea where Weses car is parked. _____

15. The Los Angeles' symphony orchestra planned an evening of Beethoven. _____

16. Did you hear that the Horowitz's are moving? _____

17. Have you visited the Morris's vacation home? _____

18. The two architects licenses were issued together. _____

19. Who is James partner for the team project? _____

20. All FBI agent's must pass rigorous security investigations. _____

21. Professor Braults lecture was well organized and informative. _____

22. The Caldwell's are building a new patio in their backyard. _____

23. Visitors at Graceland swore they saw Elvis ghost. _____

24. Fans of the Dallas's Cowboys cheered their team. _____

25. Security checked all of the reporters ID badges carefully. _____

Worksheet 1

Write the preferred plural forms of the nouns shown below. Use a dictionary if necessary.

1. datum _____
2. thesis _____
3. bacterium _____
4. Chinese _____
5. parenthesis _____
6. headquarters _____
7. alumna _____
8. millennium _____
9. genus _____
10. news _____
11. sheep _____
12. alumnus _____
13. larva _____
14. basis _____
15. memorandum _____

Select the correct word in parentheses.

16. The goods produced in that factory (is, are) recyclable. _____

17. Mathematics (is, are) her favorite subject. _____

18. Several (formula, formulas) seem sound. _____

19. Four separate (analysis, analyses) were conducted. _____

20. In the business curriculum, economics (is, are) covered. _____

Worksheet 2

Correct any errors in the following sentences by underlining the errors and writing the correct forms in the spaces provided. Each sentence contains one error.

1. Clark's and Clark's reference manual is outstanding. _____

2. We borrowed my aunt's and uncle's motor home for the weekend. _____

3. Workers said they expected to be paid for an honest days work. _____

4. Robin's and John's new car came with a five-year warranty. _____

5. Diana's and Jason's marriage license was lost. _____

6. He earned his associates degree last spring. _____

7. Our sales this year are greater than last years. _____

8. The union meeting will be held at Larrys. _____

9. I'm going over to Jennifers to pick her up. _____

10. Debbie and Julie's iPods have similar song lists. _____

11. During lunch Juan stopped at the stationers for supplies. _____

12. She will earn her bachelors degree from UCLA. _____

13. This month's expenses are somewhat less than last months. _____

14. Applicants will have at least a years wait for an apartment. _____

15. The days news is summarized every hour on WABC. _____

16. This account has been credited with four months interest. _____

17. One day Stan hopes to earn his masters degree. _____

18. In three years time, the software paid for itself. _____

19. One years interest on the account amounted to $120. _____

20. I see that (someone else) books got wet also. _____

21. Both (class) test results were misplaced. _____

22. The other three (boss) desks are rather neat. _____

23. A dollars worth of gas should get us home. _____

24. Tomorrows meeting has been canceled. _____

25. I hope that tomorrow's sales are as strong as todays. _____

4 Self-Help Exercises
Pronouns

LEVEL 1

Worksheet 1

List seven pronouns that could be used as <u>subjects</u> of verbs.

1. _____   3. _____   5. _____   7. _____

2. _____   4. _____   6. _____

List seven pronouns that could be used as <u>objects</u> of verbs or <u>objects</u> of prepositions.

8. _____   10. _____   12. _____   14. _____

9. _____   11. _____   13. _____

Personal Pronouns as Subjects

Select the correct pronoun to complete each of the following sentences. All the omitted pronouns function as subjects of verbs.

15. Ms. Georges and (I, me) submitted purchase requisitions.   _____

16. In the afternoon training session, the manager and (she, her) will make
    presentations.   _____

17. Will you and (he, him) be going to the sales meeting?   _____

18. Mr. North and (they, them) expect to see you Saturday.   _____

19. It is difficult to explain why Matt and (her, she) decided to move.   _____

20. Of all the applicants, only (we, us) agreed to be tested now.   _____

21. Ramon and (she, her) deserve raises because of their hard work.   _____

22. After Ms. Cortez and (he, him) had returned, customers were handled more rapidly. _____

23. Only you and (her, she) will participate in the demonstration.   _____

24. After the spring sales campaign ends, the marketing manager and (he, him) will
    be promoted.   _____

25. Because we are most familiar with the project, you and (I, me) must complete
    the report.   _____

Worksheet 2

Personal Pronouns as Objects

Select the correct pronoun to complete each of the following sentences. All the omitted pronouns function as objects of verbs or prepositions. Prepositions have been underlined to help you identify them.

1. Just <u>between</u> you and (I, me), our branch won the sales trophy. _____

2. Michelle said that she had seen you and (he, him) at the airport. _____

3. We hope to show (they, them) the billing procedure this afternoon. _____

4. Everybody <u>but</u> (I, me) is ready to leave. _____

5. Have you talked <u>with</u> Brad and (her, she) about this change? _____

6. We need more workers <u>like</u> Maria and (him, he) to finish the job. _____

7. All supervisors <u>except</u> Ms. Young and (her, she) approved the plan. _____

8. This insurance program provides you and (they, them) with equal benefits. _____

9. Terms of the settlement were satisfactory <u>to</u> (we, us). _____

10. Every operator <u>but</u> Maddie and (I, me) had an opportunity for overtime. _____

Possessive-Case Pronouns

Remember that possessive-case pronouns (*yours, his, hers, its, whose,* and *theirs*) do not contain apostrophes. Do not confuse these pronouns with the following contractions: *it's* (it is), *there's* (there is), *who's* (who is), and *you're* (you are). In the following sentences, select the correct word.

11. Do you think (its, it's) necessary for us to sign in? _____

12. Is (theirs, their's) the white house at the end of the street? _____

13. The contract and all (its, it's) provisions must be examined. _____

14. (There's, Theirs) a set of guidelines for us to follow. _____

15. Jack's car and (hers, her's) are the only ones left in the lot. _____

16. The check is good only if (its, it's) signed. _____

17. I was told that Sue's and (yours, your's) were the best departments. _____

18. (Who's, Whose) umbrella is that lying in the corner? _____

19. Most car registrations were sent April 1, but (our's, ours) was delayed. _____

20. (You're, Your) taking Courtney's place, aren't you? _____

Worksheet 3

Select the correct pronoun to complete these sentences.

1. Do you expect Mr. Jefferson and (they, them) to meet you? _____
2. No one could regret the error more than (I, me, myself). _____
3. These photocopies were prepared by Charles and (she, her). _____
4. (We, Us) policyholders are entitled to group discounts. _____
5. Procrastination disturbs Steven as much as (I, me, myself). _____
6. For the summer only, Universal Parcel is hiring James and (I, me, myself). _____
7. Have you corresponded with the authors, Dr. Lee and (she, her)? _____
8. On that project no one works as hard as (he, him, himself). _____
9. Everyone but Mr. Foster and (he, him) can help customers if necessary. _____
10. Do you know whether Gary and (I, me, myself) signed it? _____
11. Only Erik (himself, hisself) knows what is best for him. _____
12. We asked two women, Denise and (she, her), to come along. _____
13. The proceeds are to be divided among Mr. Shelby, Ms. Huerra, and (she, her). _____
14. Ms. Greerson thinks that Mr. Cardillo is a better salesperson than (she, her). _____
15. All property claims must be submitted to my lawyer or (I, me, myself) before April 15. _____
16. The new contract was acceptable to both management and (us, we). _____
17. When reconciling bank statements, no one is more accurate than (she, her). _____
18. The best time for you and (he, him) to enroll is in January. _____
19. The president and (I, me, myself) will inspect the facility. _____
20. Everyone except Kevin and (I, me, myself) was able to join the program. _____
21. Send an application to Human Resources or (I, me, myself) immediately. _____
22. (She and I, Her and me, Her and I) are among the best-qualified candidates. _____
23. Have you invited Jon and (she, her, herself) to our picnic? _____
24. Most of the e-mail messages sent to (us, we) employees are considered spam. _____
25. Only Rasheed and (I, me, myself) were given cell phones by the company. _____
26. It must have been (her, she) who called this morning. _____
27. I certainly would not like to be (he, him). _____
28. Do you think that it was (they, them) who complained? _____
29. Terralyn answered the telephone by saying, "This is (her, she)." _____
30. Are you sure it was (I, me) who was called to the phone? _____

Pronouns must agree with the words for which they substitute. Don't let words and phrases that come between a pronoun and its antecedent confuse you.

Examples: Every one of the women had *her* forms ready. (Not *their*)
Our supervisor Bob, along with four assistants, offered *his* support. (Not *their*)

Select the correct word(s) to complete these sentences.

1. Ms. Kennedy, in addition to many other members of the staff, sent (her, their) best wishes. _____

2. Every employee must have (his, her, his or her, their) physical examination completed by December 31. _____

3. After a job well done, everyone appreciates (his, her, his or her, their) share of credit. _____

4. Several office workers, along with the manager, announced (his or her, their) intention to vote for the settlement. _____

5. Individuals like Mr. Herndon can always be depended on to do (her, his, his or her, their) best in all assignments. _____

6. If a policyholder has a legitimate claim, (he, she, he or she, they) should contact us immediately. _____

7. Every one of the employees brought (her or his lunch, their lunches) to the outdoor event. _____

8. When a customer walks into our store, treat (him, her, him or her, them) as you would an honored guest in your home. _____

9. Carolyn Davis, along with several other company representatives, volunteered to demonstrate (her, his, his or her, their) equipment. _____

10. A few of the members of the touring group, in addition to their guide, wanted (his or her picture, their pictures) taken. _____

11. Any female member of the project could arrange (her, their) own accommodations if desired. _____

12. Every player on the men's ball team complained about (his, their) uniform. _____

Rewrite this sentence to avoid the use of gender-biased pronoun. Show three versions.

Every employee must obtain his parking permit in the supervisor's office.

13. _____

14. _____

15. _____

Worksheet 2

Underline any pronoun–antecedent errors in the following sentences. Then write a corrected form in the space provided.

1. Last Friday either Ms. Monahan or Ms. Chavez left their computer on. _____

2. The Federal Drug Administration has not yet granted it's approval for the drug. _____

3. Every clerk, every manager, and every executive will be expected to do their part in making the carpooling program a success. _____

4. Somebody left his cell phone in the tray at the airport security check. _____

5. Neither one of the men wanted to have their remarks quoted. _____

6. Every one of the delegates to the women's conference was wearing their name tag. _____

7. The vice president and the marketing director had already made his reservations. _____

8. Each of the pieces of equipment came with their own software. _____

9. The firm of Higgins, Thomas & Keene, Inc., is moving their offices to Warner Plaza. _____

10. Every manager expects the employees who report to them to be willing to earn their salaries. _____

11. Neither of the women had their driver's license in the car. _____

12. We hoped that someone in the office could find their copy of the program. _____

13. Either the first telephone caller or the second one did not leave their number. _____

14. If everybody will please take their seats, we can get started. _____

15. The faculty agreed to publicize their position on budget cuts. _____

16. We saw that HomeCo reduced their prices on lawn mowers. _____

17. Few of the color printers had the sale price marked on it. _____

18. Every one of the male employees agreed to be more careful in protecting their computer password. _____

19. Each bridesmaid will pay for their own gown. _____

20. All managers and employees know that she or he must boost productivity. _____

Worksheet 1

In selecting *who* or *whom* to complete the following sentences, follow these five steps:

1. Isolate the *who/whom* clause.

   Example: We do not know (*who, whom*) the contract names.

2. Invert to normal subject–verb order.

   Example: the contract names (*who, whom*)

3. Substitute the *who* or *whom* with *he* or *him*. Only one pronoun, *he* or *him,* will correctly complete the clause.

   Example: the contract names *him*

4. Equate the subjective pronoun *he* with *who* and the objective pronoun *him* with *whom*.

5. If the sentence sounds correct with *he*, complete the sentence by replacing *he* with *who*. If the sentence sounds correct with *him*, complete the sentence by replacing *him* with *whom*.

   Example: *whom* the contract names

   Complete sentence: We do not know *whom* the contract names.

   Example: We do not know (*who, whom*) the contract names.   whom _____

1. (Who, Whom) will you invite to your party? _____
2. Rick Nash is the employee (who, whom) the CEO asked to present to the board. _____
3. Do you know (who, whom) will be taking your place? _____
4. To (who, whom) did she refer in her letter? _____
5. Did Mr. Glade say (who, whom) he wanted to see? _____
6. Dr. Truong is a man (who, whom) everyone respects. _____
7. (Who, Whom) was president of your organization last year? _____
8. (Who, Whom) do you want to work with? _____
9. (Who, Whom) has the best chance to be elected? _____
10. I know of no one else (who, whom) plays so well. _____

In choosing *who* or *whom* to complete these sentences, ignore parenthetical phrases such as *I think*, *we know*, *you feel*, and *I believe*.

11. Julie is a person (who, whom) I know will be successful on the job. _____
12. The human resources director hired an individual (who, whom) he thought would be the best performer. _____
13. Is Ms. Hastings the dealer (who, whom) you think I should call? _____
14. Major Kirby, (who, whom) I think will be elected, is running in the next election. _____
15. (Who, Whom) do you believe will be given the job? _____

Worksheet 2

In the following sentences, selecting *who*, *whom*, *whoever*, or *whomever* first requires isolating the clause within which the pronoun appears. Then, *within the clause*, determine whether a nominative-case (*who*, *whoever*) or objective-case (*whom*, *whomever*) pronoun is required.

> **Example:** Give the package to (whoever, whomever) opens the door.
> (*He* or *she* opens the door = *whoever* opens the door.)   **whoever**

1. A bonus will be given to (whoever, whomever) brings in the most new clients. _____

2. Discuss the problem with (whoever, whomever) is in charge of the program. _____

3. We will interview (whoever, whomever) you recommend. _____

4. You may give the tickets to (whoever, whomever) you wish. _____

5. Johnson said to give the parking pass to (whoever, whomever) asked for it. _____

6. The committee members have promised to cooperate with (whoever, whomever) is selected to chair the committee. _____

7. Please call (whoever, whomever) you believe can repair the machine. _____

8. (Whoever, Whomever) is nominated for the position must be approved by the full membership. _____

9. Reservations have been made for (whoever, whomever) requested them in advance. _____

10. (Whoever, Whomever) is chosen to lead the delegation will command attention at the caucus. _____

In choosing *who* or *whom* to complete these sentences, be especially alert to pronouns following the linking verbs. Remember that the nominative *who* is required as a subject complement.

> **Example:** Was it (who, whom) I thought it was? (It was *he* = *who*.)

11. (Who, Whom) is the customer who wanted a replacement? _____

12. The visitor who asked for me was (who, whom)? _____

13. Was the new CEO (who, whom) we thought it would be? _____

14. The winner will be (whoever, whomever) is the top salesperson. _____

15. For (who, whom) was this new printer ordered? _____

Worksheet 3

In the following sentences, select the correct word.

1. (Who, Whom) did you call for assistance? _____

2. Mr. Lincoln, (who, whom) we thought would never be hired, did well in his first assignment. _____

3. By (who, whom) are you currently employed? _____

4. You should hire (whoever, whomever) you feel has the best qualifications. _____

5. Did the caller say (who, whom) he wanted to see? _____

6. The man (who, whom) I saw yesterday walked by today. _____

7. (Whoever, Whomever) is first on the list will be called next. _____

8. The sales rep sent notices to customers (who, whom) she felt should be notified. _____

9. Is the manager (who, whom) we thought it would be? _____

10. The manager praised the clerk (who, whom) worked late. _____

11. She is the one (who, whom) Kevin helped yesterday. _____

12. Many of us thought Mr. Alison was a nice person with (who, whom) to work. _____

13. (Who, Whom) is Stacy often mistaken to be? _____

14. (Who, Whom) did you say to call for reservations? _____

15. Please make an appointment with (whoever, whomever) you consider to be the best internist. _____

16. Here is a list of satisfied customers (who, whom) you may wish to contact. _____

17. (Whoever, Whomever) is suggested by Mr. Arthur must be interviewed. _____

18. The candidate (who, whom) the party supports will win. _____

19. Marcia is one on (who, whom) I have come to depend. _____

20. For (who, whom) are these contracts? _____

21. Do you know (whose, who's) jacket this is? _____

22. Do you know (whose, who's) working overtime tonight? _____

23. We're not sure (whose, who's) signed up for Friday's seminar. _____

24. It doesn't matter (whose, who's) comments those are. _____

25. You'll never guess (whose, who's) running for president! _____

Worksheet 4

Pronoun Review

Select the correct word to complete the following sentences.

1. Only the president and (he, him) can grant leaves of absence. _____

2. If you were (she, her), would you take the job? _____

3. The body of the manuscript is followed by (its, it's) endnotes. _____

4. Our staff agreed that you and (she, her) should represent us. _____

5. How can you believe (us, we) to be guilty? _____

6. I'm not sure (theirs, there's) enough time left. _____

7. Everyone thought the new manager would be (he, him). _____

8. My friend and (I, me) looked for jobs together. _____

9. This matter will be kept strictly between you and (I, me). _____

10. Good employees like you and (she, her) are always on time. _____

11. Judge Waxman is fully supported by (we, us) consumers. _____

12. We agree that (your, you're) the best person for the job. _____

13. Send the announcement to Ms. Nguyen and (she, her) today. _____

14. All employees except Kim and (he, him) will be evaluated. _____

15. Many locker combinations are listed, but (your's, yours) is missing. _____

16. Apparently the message was intended for you and (I, me, myself). _____

17. Was it (he, him, himself) who sent the mystery text message? _____

18. The bank is closed, but (it's, its) ATM is open. _____

19. Please submit the report to (him or me, he or I) before May 1. _____

20. (There's, Theirs) only one path for us to follow. _____

21. For you and (he, him), I would suggest careers in marketing. _____

22. These personnel changes affect you and (I, me, myself) directly. _____

23. My friend and (I, me, myself) are thinking of a trip to Hawaii. _____

24. Only two branches plan to expand (they're, their) display rooms. _____

25. The operator thought it was (she, her) calling for assistance. _____

26. Because you are a member of the audit review team, you have a better overall picture of the operations than (I, me, myself). _____

27. Though you may not agree with our decision, I hope you'll support Todd and (I, me) in our effort to get the job done. _____

28. Some of the recent decisions made by (us, we) supervisors will be reviewed by the management council when it meets in January. _____

29. I wonder if it was (she, her) who was reprimanded for excessive e-mail use. _____

30. Do you think (theirs, their's, there's) any real reason to change our computer passwords every month? _____

NAME _____

5 Self-Help Exercises
Verbs

LEVEL 1

Worksheet 1

Fill in the answers to the following questions with information found in your text.

1. What kind of action verbs direct action toward a person or thing (transitive or intransitive)? _____

2. What kind of action verbs do not require an object to complete their action (transitive or intransitive)? _____

3. What kind of verbs link to the subject words that rename or describe the subject (action, linking, or helping)? _____

4. What do we call the nouns, pronouns, and adjectives used with linking verbs that complete the meaning of a sentence by renaming or describing the subject? _____

5. What kind of verb is added to a main verb, which can be action or linking, to form a verb phrase? _____

In each of the following sentences, indicate whether the underlined verb is transitive (*T*), intransitive (*I*), or linking (*L*). In addition, if the verb is transitive, write its object. If the verb is linking, write its complement. The first two sentences are followed by explanations to assist you.

6. Jeff <u>ran</u> along the dirt path back to his home. (The verb *ran* is intransitive. It has no object to complete its meaning. The phrase *along the dirt path* tells where Jeff ran; it does not receive the action of the verb.) _____

7. It <u>might have been</u> Jessica who called yesterday. (The verb phrase ends with the linking verb *been*. The complement is *Jessica*, which renames the subject *it*.) _____

8. Juan <u>input</u> the addresses of our most recent customers. _____

9. Customers <u>crowded</u> into the store at the beginning of the sale. _____

10. Sherry <u>was</u> a consultant on the software conversion project. _____

11. Levi Strauss first <u>sold</u> pants to miners in San Francisco in the 1800s. _____

12. The bank <u>faxed</u> you the loan application. _____

13. Chocolate fudge ice cream <u>tastes</u> better than chocolate mint. _____

14. Do you think it <u>was</u> he who suggested the improvement? _____

15. We <u>walked</u> around the shopping mall on our lunch hour. _____

16. Our company recruiter <u>asks</u> the same questions of every candidate. _____

17. Many corporations <u>give</u> gifts to important foreign clients. _____

18. All employees <u>listened</u> intently as the CEO discussed annual profits. _____

19. Ellen <u>feels</u> justified in asking for a raise. _____

20. Customers <u>have</u> high expectations from most advertised products. _____

Worksheet 2

Transitive verbs that direct action toward an object are in the active voice. Transitive verbs that direct action toward a subject are in the passive voice. Writing that incorporates active-voice verbs is more vigorous and more efficient than writing that contains many passive-voice verbs. To convert a passive-voice verb to the active voice, look for the doer of the action. (Generally the doer of the action is contained in a *by* phrase.) In the active voice, the agent becomes the subject.

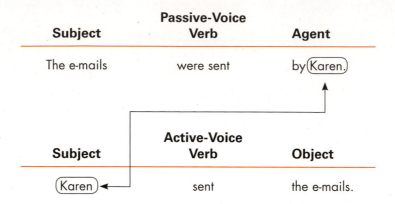

For each of the following sentences, underline the doer of the action. Write that word in the space provided. Then rewrite the sentence changing the passive-voice verbs to active voice. Your rewritten version should begin with the word (and its modifiers) that you identified as the doer of the action.

1. The text message was not received by Mark until Monday morning. _____

_____

_____

2. Our order was shipped last week by Dell. _____

_____

_____

3. Withdrawals must be authorized by Sherri Bradford beginning next week. _____

_____

_____

4. Wyatt was asked by Mr. Stern to be responsible for turning out the lights at the end of the day. _____

_____

_____

5. Employees who travel a great deal were forced by management to surrender their frequent-flyer mileage awards. _____

_____

_____

Worksheet 3

Some sentences with passive-voice verbs do not identify the doer of the action. Before these sentences can be converted, a subject must be provided. Use your imagination to supply subjects.

Passive: Interest will be paid on all deposits. (*By whom?* By First Federal.)

Active: First Federal will pay interest on all deposits.

By whom?

1. Our departmental report must be completed before 5 p.m. _____

   _____

   _____

2. Checks were written on an account with insufficient funds. _____

   _____

   _____

3. Decisions are made in the courts that affect the daily lives of all Americans. _____

   _____

   _____

4. Employees working with computers were warned to change their passwords frequently. _____

   _____

   _____

5. Our accounting records were scrutinized during the audit. _____

   _____

   _____

Worksheet 4

Select the correct verb.

1. Did you tell me that the caller's name (is, was) Scott? _____

2. A bad accident (occured, occurred) late last evening. _____

3. Mr. Anderson says that the car you are driving (is, was) red. _____

4. Are you sure that her maiden name (is, was) Spitnale? _____

5. We were taught that an ounce of prevention (is, was) worth a pound of cure. _____

In the space provided, write the verb form indicated in parentheses.

Example: Joan (carry) a heavy workload every day. (present tense) carries _____

6. The software company (plan) to expand its markets abroad. (present tense) _____

7. A Kentucky Fried Chicken franchise (sell) American-style fast food in Japan. (future tense) _____

8. The giant Mitsubishi conglomerate (supply) the Colonel with chicken in Japan. (past tense) _____

9. The marketing director (study) possible sales sites in foreign countries. (present tense) _____

10. We (analyze) such factors as real estate, construction costs, and local attitudes toward fast food. (future tense) _____

11. Management (apply) a complex formula to forecast the profitability of the new business. (past tense) _____

12. We (consider) the vast differences between the two cultures. (past tense) _____

13. A local franchise (vary) the side dishes to accommodate cultural preferences. (present tense) _____

14. Kentucky Fried Chicken (insist) on retaining its original recipe in foreign stores. (present tense) _____

15. Kentucky Fried Chicken products (appeal) to the average customer in Japan. (future tense) _____

16. Doing business in Japan (require) an appreciation of rituals and formalities. (present tense) _____

17. In East Asia the presentation of business cards (demand) special attention to ceremony. (future tense) _____

18. Western businesspeople (try) to observe local customs. (past tense) _____

Worksheet 1

A verb form ending in *ing* and used as a noun is a gerund.

> *Passing* the examination is important. (Gerund used as a subject.)

A noun or pronoun modifying a gerund should be possessive.

> *Your* passing the examination is important.

Don't confuse verbals acting as nouns with those acting as adjectives.

> The man *passing* the test received his license. (*Passing* functions as an adjective describing *man*.)

> The man's *passing* the test is important. (Verbal noun *passing* functions as the subject of the verb *is*.)

In the following sentences, underline any gerunds and write their modifiers in the space provided. If a sentence contains no gerund, write *None*.

Example: It is your <u>smoking</u> that disturbs the others.   your _____

1. This job offer is contingent on your passing our physical examination. _____

2. Our office certainly did not approve of his investing in high-risk securities. _____

3. It was Mr. Cortina's gambling that caused him to lose his job. _____

Some of the remaining sentences contain gerunds. If any error appears in the modifier, underline the error and write the correct form in the space provided. If the sentence is correct, write *C*.

Example: Jamie Salazar was instrumental in <u>us</u> acquiring the Collins' account.   our _____

4. The individual receiving the award could not be present to accept it. _____

5. Do you think you criticizing the manager had anything to do with your transfer? _____

6. We deeply appreciate you calling us to give us this news at this time. _____

7. An employee taking a message must write clearly. _____

8. Ms. Fackler said that me working overtime was unnecessary this weekend. _____

Worksheet 2

From the sets of sentences that follow, select the sentence that is the more logically stated. Write its letter in the space provided.

1. a. Try and come to lunch with us on Friday.
   b. Try to come to lunch with us on Friday.   _____

2. a. To get to the meeting quickly, a shortcut was taken by Mike.
   b. To get to the meeting quickly, Mike took a shortcut.   _____

3. a. When investing money in the stock market, one must expect risks.
   b. When investing money in the stock market, risks must be expected.   _____

4. a. After filling out an application, the human resources manager gave me an interview.
   b. After filling out an application, I was given an interview by the human resources manager.   _____

5. a. Driving erratically down the street, the driver was stopped by the officer.
   b. Driving erratically down the street, the officer stopped the driver.   _____

Check your answers to the preceding five questions. Using the better sentence versions as models, rewrite the following sentences to make them logical. Add words as necessary, but retain the verbal expressions as sentence openers.

6. Completing the examination in only 20 minutes, a perfect score was earned by Maria.

   _____

   _____

   _____

7. To locate the members' names and addresses, the current directory was used.

   _____

   _____

   _____

8. Driving through the desert, the highway seemed endless.

   _____

   _____

   _____

9. Addressing an audience for the first time, my knees shook and my voice wavered.

   _____

   _____

   _____

Worksheet 3

Write the correct answers in the spaces provided.

1. If I (was, were) you, I would complete my degree first. _____

2. If Mr. Greer (was, were) in the office yesterday, he did not sign the checks. _____

3. One of the stockholders moved that a committee (be, is) constituted to study the problem immediately. _____

4. If the manager were here, he (will, would) sign the work order and we could proceed. _____

5. Government officials recommend that all homes (are, be) stocked with an emergency supply of food and water. _____

6. Dr. Washington suggested that the patient (rest, rests) for the next two days. _____

7. Angela wished that she (was, were) able to fly to Phoenix to visit her sister. _____

8. Under the circumstances, even if the voter registration drive (was, were) successful, we might lose the election. _____

9. After consulting management, our manager suggested that all employees (are, be) given three-week vacations. _____

10. It has been moved and seconded that the meeting (is, be) adjourned. _____

Worksheet 1

Select the correct verb.

1. If her smartphone had (rang, rung), she would have heard it. _____

2. Ice (froze, freezed) in the pipes last night. _____

3. Before leaving on her vacation, Ms. Stanton (hid, hide) her silver and other valuables. _____

4. Have you (chose, chosen) a location for the new equipment? _____

5. Three new homes were recently (builded, built) on Fairfax Avenue. _____

6. He had already (drank, drunk) two bottles of water when he asked for more. _____

7. We (hung, hanged) a new painting in the reception area. _____

8. Are you sure you have (gave, given) him the correct combination? _____

9. Andre and the others had (went, gone) on the hike earlier. _____

10. The smaller dog was (bit, bitten) by a larger neighborhood dog. _____

Underline any errors in the following sentences. Write the correct form in the space provided. Do not add helping verbs, and do not delete any helping verbs that already appear in these sentences.

Example: After we <u>run</u> out of food, we had to return to camp headquarters. ran

11. We had ate a small snack before we ordered dinner. _____

12. The TV commercial was sang by an actress whose lips did not match the sound track. _____

13. I can't believe he sweared during the meeting. _____

14. Hundreds of mushrooms sprung up after the rain. _____

15. Many people were shook by the minor earthquake yesterday. _____

16. Tracy had wore her stylish new boots only twice. _____

17. Fortunately, he had wrote most of his report before his computer crashed. _____

18. Their car was stole from its parking place overnight. _____

19. Because of a threatening storm, she should have took a cab. _____

20. If we had went to the movie premiere, we would have seen the stars. _____

Worksheet 2

Lie–Lay

Use the following chart to help you select the correct form of *lie* or *lay* in these sentences.

Present	Past	Past Participle	Present Participle
lie (rest)	lay (rested)	lain (have, has, or had rested)	lying (resting)
lay (place)	laid (placed)	laid (have, has, or had placed)	laying (placing)

Example: This afternoon I must (rest) down before dinner.   lie _____

1. I am sure that I (placed) the book on the desk yesterday.   _____

2. Andrea angrily told her dog to (rest) down.   _____

3. This month's bills have been (resting) in the drawer for weeks.   _____

4. Kim has (placed) her books on the desk near the entrance.   _____

5. The worker was (placing) concrete blocks for the foundation.   _____

6. This evening I must (rest) down before we leave.   _____

7. Yesterday I (rested) in my room, worrying about today's exam.   _____

8. (Place) the papers in a stack over there.   _____

9. That old candy has (rested) on the shelf for several weeks.   _____

10. Let the fabric (rest) there for several hours until it dries.   _____

Now try these sentences to test your skill in using the forms of *lie* and *lay*.

11. Will you be able to (lie, lay) down before dinner?   _____

12. How long have these papers been (laying, lying) here?   _____

13. Please tell your very friendly dog to (lay, lie) down.   _____

14. Will the mason (lay, lie) bricks over the concrete patio?   _____

15. The contract has (laid, lain) on his desk for over two weeks.   _____

16. Yesterday I (laid, lay) down in the afternoon.   _____

17. Mothers complain about clothes that are left (laying, lying) around.   _____

18. Returned books (lie, lay) in a pile at the library until the staff can return them to the stacks.   _____

19. I'm sure I (laid, layed, lied) my keys on this counter.   _____

20. When you were (lying, laying) the groceries down, did you see my keys?   _____

Worksheet 3

Use Chapter 5 to look up the verb tenses required in the following sentences.

Example: By June 1 you (work) here one full year. (future perfect)   <u>will have worked</u>

1. McDonald's (open) many restaurants in foreign countries. (present perfect) _____

2. McDonald's (plan) to launch a franchise program. (present progressive) _____

3. We (call) for service at least three times before a technician arrived. (past perfect) _____

4. She (work) on that project for the past six months. (present perfect) _____

5. We (see) the very first screening of the documentary. (past progressive) _____

6. The mayor (sign) the proclamation at this afternoon's public ceremony. (future progressive) _____

7. The bulldozer working on street repairs (broke) the water main. (past perfect) _____

8. I (see) two good movies recently. (present perfect) _____

9. We (consider) the installation of a new e-mail system. (present progressive) _____

10. Americans across the country (hear) the president's message in four time zones. (past progressive) _____

The next sentences review Level 3.

11. The alarm had (rang, rung) three times before we responded. _____

12. Yesterday we (drank, drunk) many glasses of water because of the heat. _____

13. You must (chose, choose) a new Internet service provider. _____

14. The car has been (drove, driven) many miles. _____

15. Steve claims he (saw, seen) the report yesterday. _____

16. If Rasheed had (went, gone) earlier, he would have told us. _____

17. Daphne said she (seen, saw) an accident on her way to work. _____

18. The tour guide checked to see whether everyone had (ate, eaten) before we left the lunch stop. _____

19. Rodney had (wrote, written) four e-mail messages before he realized they were not being received. _____

20. The price of our stocks (raised, rose) again yesterday. _____

21. Witnesses had (swear, swore, sworn) to tell the truth during the trial. _____

22. Stock prices (sank, sunk) so low that investors were sitting on their cash. _____

23. Because it was washed in hot water, the cashmere sweater (shrank, shrunk). _____

24. If we had (began, begun) the report earlier, we could have met the deadline. _____

25. Employees had been (forbade, forbidden) to use company computers for social networking, games, or shopping. _____

6 Self-Help Exercises
Subject–Verb Agreement

LEVEL 1

Worksheet 1

For each of the following sentences, cross out any phrase that comes between a verb and its subject. Then select the correct verb and write it in the space provided.

Example: One ~~of the most interesting books on all the lists~~ (is, are) *Becoming a Millionaire at 21.*   is _____

1. Many websites on the government's prohibited list (provide, provides) games or amusement that employees may not access. _____

2. The supervisor, together with two technicians, (is, are) working on the faulty circuit. _____

3. This company's supply of raw materials (come, comes) from South America. _____

4. A good many workers in addition to Jennifer (think, thinks) the work shifts should be rearranged. _____

5. Everyone except you and John (is, are) to repeat the test. _____

6. The table as well as two chairs (was, were) damaged. _____

7. A list with all the customers' names and addresses (is, are) being sent. _____

8. Other equipment such as our terminals and printers (need, needs) to be reevaluated. _____

9. One of the online shopping sites (has, have) a section devoted to clearance items. _____

10. Several copies of the report (is, are) being prepared for distribution. _____

11. The furniture, as well as all the equipment including computers, (is, are) for sale. _____

12. Effects of the disease (is, are) not known immediately. _____

13. Three salespeople, in addition to their district sales manager, (has, have) voiced the same suggestion. _____

14. Profits from his home business (is, are) surprising. _____

15. Every one of the potential businesses that you mention (sounds, sound) good. _____

16. A shipment of 8,000 drill sets (was, were) sent to four warehouses. _____

17. Everyone except the evening employees (is, are) coming. _____

18. We learned that two subsidiaries of the corporation (is, are) successful. _____

19. Officials in several levels of government (has, have) to be consulted. _____

20. A letter together with several enclosures (was, were) mailed yesterday. _____

Worksheet 2

For each of the following sentences, underline the subject. Then select the correct verb and write it in the space provided.

Example: Here (is, are) a <u>copy</u> of the findings for your files.   is

Suggestion: If you know that a subject is singular, temporarily substitute *he*, *she*, or *it* to help you select the proper verb. If you know that a subject is plural, temporarily substitute *they* for the subject.

1. The flow of industrial goods (travel, travels) through different distribution channels from the flow of consumer goods. _____

2. Here (is, are) the newspaper and magazines you ordered. _____

3. Coleman, Harris & Juarez, Inc., one of the leading management consultant firms, (is, are) able to accept our business. _____

4. The books on the open shelves of our company's library (is, are) available to all employees. _____

5. There (appear, appears) to be significant points omitted from the report. _____

6. The various stages in the life cycle of a product (is, are) instrumental in determining profits for that product. _____

7. No one except the Cunninghams (was, were) able to volunteer. _____

8. A member of the organization of painters and plasterers (is, are) unhappy about the recent settlement. _____

9. The size and design of its container (is, are) influential in the appeal of a product. _____

10. Just one governmental unit from the local, state, or national levels (is, are) all we need to initiate the project. _____

11. American Airlines (has, have) improved service while cutting costs. _____

12. Only two seasons of the year (provide, provides) weather that is suitable for gliding. _____

13. (Has, Have) the moving van of the Wongs arrived yet? _____

14. At present the condition of the company's finances (is, are) extremely strong as a result of the recent bond sale. _____

15. Incoming luggage from three flights (is, are) now being sorted. _____

16. The salary of Maria Chavez, along with the earnings of several other employees, (has, have) been increased. _____

17. One of the best designs (appear, appears) to have been submitted by your student. _____

18. Trying to improve relations between doctors and patients, the American Medical Association, along with several dozen medical societies, (is, are) helping doctors embrace online consultations. _____

19. Certainly the ease and convenience of shopping at any hour of the day or night— and getting fast delivery without ever leaving home—(is, are) very appealing. _____

20. Aggressiveness and delinquency in boys (is, are) linked to high levels of lead in their bones, according to a recent study. _____

For each of the following sentences, underline the subject. Then select the correct word and write it in the space provided.

1. Most of the salary compensation to which he referred (is, are) beyond basic pay schedules. _____

2. The Committee on Youth Activities (has, have) enlisted the aid of several well-known athletes. _____

3. Each of the young men and women (deserve, deserves) an opportunity to participate in local athletics. _____

4. Either your company or one of your two competitors (is, are) going to win the government contract. _____

5. All the work for our Special Products Division (is, are) yet to be assigned. _____

6. Either of the two small businesses (is, are) able to secure a loan. _____

7. City council members (was, were) sharply divided along partisan lines. _____

8. Neither the packing list nor the two invoices (mention, mentions) the missing ottoman. _____

9. Every one of your suggestions (merit, merits) consideration. _____

10. Our survey shows that (everyone, every one) of the owner-managed businesses was turning a profit. _____

11. Either Steven or you (is, are) expected to return the call. _____

12. Each of the machines (has, have) capabilities that are suitable for our needs. _____

13. Ms. Roberts said that most of the credit for our increased sales (belong, belongs) to you. _____

14. First on the program (is, are) the group of Indo-European folk dancers. _____

15. Some of the enthusiasm (is, are) due to the coming holiday. _____

16. After 10 p.m. the staff (has, have) to use the front entrance only. _____

17. (Was, Were) any of the supervisors absent after the holiday? _____

18. The union (has, have) made an agreement with management. _____

19. We were informed that neither management nor the employees (has, have) special privileges. _____

20. Most of the work that was delivered to us four days ago (is, are) completed. _____

In the following sentences, select the correct word.

1. Reed says that 75 feet of plastic pipe (has, have) been ordered.

2. The number of women in the labor force (is, are) steadily increasing.

3. Phillip said that he is one of those individuals who (enjoy, enjoys) a real challenge.

4. Over two thirds of the stock issue (was, were) sold immediately after it was released.

5. Gerald is the only one of the four applicants who (was, were) prepared to complete the application form during the interview.

6. That most offices are closed on weekends (is, are) a factor that totally escaped Mr. Brotherton.

7. The majority of the employees (favor, favors) the reorganization plan.

8. Telephones (is, are) one item that we must install immediately.

9. At least four fifths of the women in the audience (is, are) willing to participate in the show.

10. How could it be I who (am, is) responsible, when I had no knowledge of the agreement until yesterday?

11. Let it be recorded that on the second vote the number of members in favor of the proposal (is, are) less than on the first vote.

12. Only half of the box of highlighters (is, are) left in the supply cabinet.

13. Are you one of those people who (like, likes) to sleep late?

14. I'm sure that it is you who (is, are) next on the list.

15. It looks as if 20 inches of extra cord (is, are) what we need.

16. Our office manager reports that a number of printers (need, needs) repair.

17. At least one third of the desserts purchased for the party (was, were) uneaten.

18. Hiking in Europe and sailing to Scandinavia (is, are) what I plan for my future vacations.

19. Sherry Lansing is one of our e-mail users who (complain, complains) about the system.

20. Whoever submitted an application earliest (has, have) the right to be interviewed first.

7 Self-Help Exercises
Modifiers: Adjectives and Adverbs

LEVEL 1

Write the correct comparative or superlative form of the adjective shown in parentheses.

Example: Carmen is (neat) than her sister.   neater

1. We hope that the new procedures prove to be (effective) than previous procedures.   _____

2. Of all the suggestions made, Mr. Bradley's suggestion is the (bad).   _____

3. Mrs. Schrillo's daughter is certainly (friendly) than she is.   _____

4. Of the three individuals who volunteered, Ted is the one about whom I am (less) certain.   _____

5. I don't believe I've ever seen a (beautiful) sunset than this one.   _____

6. We make many printers, but the Model SX6 is the (fast).   _____

7. No restaurant makes (good) hamburgers than Clown Alley.   _____

8. Located next to the airport, Westchester is probably the (noisy) area in the city.   _____

9. The suburbs provide (quiet) surroundings than the city.   _____

10. Of all the applications we have received, this one seems the (sincere).   _____

11. For this job we need the (skilled) employee in the department.   _____

12. I'm afraid Andrea has the (less) chance of being selected in the lottery.   _____

13. No one works (slow) than Bob.   _____

14. DataSource is (likely) to be awarded the contract than CompuPro.   _____

15. This is probably the (unusual) request I've ever received.   _____

16. Juan has had (few) citations than any other driver.   _____

17. The office is certainly looking (good) today than yesterday.   _____

18. Everyone watching the video thought that Thomas looked (credible) than any other actor.   _____

19. It was the (bad) accident I've ever seen.   _____

20. Sharon's report had the (less) errors of all those submitted.   _____

If the underlined word or words in the following sentences are correctly expressed, write *C*. If they are incorrect, write a corrected form in the space provided.

Example: Because <u>less</u> people made contributions, we failed to reach our goal. fewer

1. He played his streaming music so <u>loud</u> that we couldn't work. _____

2. We have decided to increase our <u>point-of-purchase</u> advertising. _____

3. It is <u>a</u> honor to speak to your organization this afternoon. _____

4. Talking with her <u>won't</u> do <u>no</u> good. _____

5. The machine is running <u>quieter</u> since we installed a hood. _____

6. Todd and I felt <u>badly</u> about Kurt's accident. _____

7. The general manager should not become involved in this <u>conflict of interest</u> issue. _____

8. Ms. Edelstein was dressed <u>neatly</u> for the interview. _____

9. At present we're searching for a source of <u>inexpensive, accessible</u> raw materials. _____

10. Rex has been a member of <u>an</u> union for many years. _____

11. <u>These sort</u> of employees can make a company successful. _____

12. Most candidates completed the examinations <u>satisfactory</u>. _____

13. We are conducting the campaign from <u>house-to-house</u>. _____

14. We <u>couldn't hardly</u> imagine the time that went into the project. _____

15. She can't wait to take <u>a</u> one-week vacation. _____

16. The children were playing <u>quiet</u> when the guests arrived. _____

17. He <u>didn't</u> say <u>nothing</u> during the meeting. _____

18. You are a preferred <u>charge-account</u> customer at our store. _____

19. We expect a signed contract in the <u>not too distant</u> future. _____

20. Our customer mailing list is completely <u>up to date</u>. _____

In the following sentences, select the correct word(s).

1. Only the (a) two last, (b) last two speakers made relevant comments. _____

2. Craig is more stubborn than (a) anyone else, (b) anyone I know. _____

3. (a) Ms. Smith reports that she has only one volunteer.
(b) Ms. Smith only reports that she has one volunteer. _____

4. Applications will be given to the (a) first five, (b) five first job candidates. _____

5. Los Angeles is larger than (a) any other city, (b) any city in California. _____

For each of the following sentences, underline any errors in the use of adjectives and adverbs. Then write the correct form. Mark *C* if the sentence is correct as written.

6. Unfortunately, we've had less applications this year than ever before. _____

7. We employees are real concerned about the new parking fee. _____

8. You can sure depend on my help whenever you need it. _____

9. He can be counted on to paint the room as neat as a professional would do the job. _____

10. The uniform you are required to wear certainly fits you good. _____

11. Because we have less work to do this week, we should finish soon. _____

12. The recently-enacted law has received great support. _____

13. Apparently we have picked the worse time of the year to list an office for rent. _____

14. Although it is a honorary position, the chairmanship is important. _____

15. We hadn't hardly reached shelter when it began to rain. _____

16. The Andersons made a round the world tour last year. _____

17. Because of their many kindnesses to us, I feel badly that we cannot reciprocate in some way. _____

18. If less people were involved, the new procedures could have been implemented earlier. _____

19. Festival promoters rented a 840-acre farm in Ulster County. _____

20. How much further must we drive tonight before stopping? _____

21. Less employment opportunities exist in that field; therefore, I'm transferring to a different major. _____

22. My organization has selected the later of the two proposals you submitted. _____

23. Sam said he was sure he did good on his examination. _____

24. In order to farther her career, she is taking business classes. _____

25. Sam did a good job on his examination. _____

8 Self-Help Exercises
Prepositions

LEVEL 1

Underline any errors in the following sentences. Then write the correct form. If the sentence is correct as written, write *C*.

1. You should of seen the looks on their faces! _____

2. No one except Mr. Levine and he had access to the company records. _____

3. I read the book and plan to attend the lecture too. _____

4. Just between you and I, this engine has never run more smoothly. _____

5. Some of the business textbooks were borrowed off of Jeffrey. _____

6. If you address your inquiry too our Customer Relations Department, you will surely receive a response. _____

7. The director of human resources, along with the office manager and she, is planning to improve our hiring procedures. _____

8. We could of done something about the error if we had known earlier. _____

9. Because we are receiving to many spam messages, we are adding filters. _____

10. All salespeople except Ms. Berk and he were reassigned. _____

11. Did you obtain your copy of the team proposal off him? _____

12. Please get your passes from either Ms. Bowman or he. _____

13. See whether you can get some change for the machine off of her. _____

14. Both the project coordinator and he should have verified the totals before submitting the bid. _____

15. The commission for the sale has to be divided between Ms. Carpenter and he. _____

16. Because to few spaces are available, additional parking must be found on nearby streets. _____

17. If you and he could of come yesterday, we might have been able to help you. _____

18. So that we may better evaluate your application, please supply references too. _____

19. You could of had complimentary tickets if you had called her. _____

20. The marketing manager assigned too many customers to Ann and I. _____

For each of the following sentences, underline any errors in the use of prepositions. Then write a correct form. Mark *C* if the sentence is correct as written.

1. We think that beside salary, the major issue is working conditions. _____

2. Your support and participation in this new ethics program are greatly appreciated. _____

3. The warranty period was over with two months ago. _____

4. Please come into see me when you are ready for employment. _____

5. Just inside of the office entrance is the receptionist. _____

6. The senior Mr. Wiggins left $3 million to be divided between three heirs. _____

7. Will you be able to deliver the goods like you said you would? _____

8. For most of us, very few opportunities like this ever arise. _____

9. Exactly what type software did you have in mind? _____

10. Some of the trucks were moved in to the garage at dusk. _____

11. When can we accept delivery of the electrical components ordered from Hellman, Inc.? _____

12. Because of your concern and involvement in our community action campaign, we have received thousands of dollars in contributions. _____

13. I know the time and date of our next committee meeting, but I do not know where it is at. _____

14. If you were willing to accept further responsibility, I would assign you the committee chairmanship. _____

15. Joanna could not help from laughing when she saw her e-mail. _____

16. Please hurry up so that we may submit our proposal quickly. _____

17. What style furniture is most functional for the waiting room? _____

18. After going into meet the supervisor, Carla was hired. _____

19. All parking lots opposite to the corporate headquarters will be cleaned. _____

20. Immediately after Kathy graduated high school, she started college. _____

In the following sentences, select the correct word.

1. Halle found that her voice was rising as she became more and more angry (a) at, (b) with the caller. _____

2. We know of no one who is more expert (a) in, (b) with communication technology than Dr. France. _____

3. Our specifications must comply (a) with, (b) to those in the request for proposal (RFP). _____

4. After corresponding (a) to, (b) with their home office, I was able to clear up the error in my account. _____

5. The houses in that subdivision are identical (a) to, (b) with each other. _____

6. If you (a) plan to attend, (b) plan on attending the summer session, you'd better register immediately. _____

7. A few of the provisions are retroactive (a) for, (b) to January 1. _____

8. Jeff talked (a) to, (b) with his boss about the company's future plans. _____

9. His keynote presentation will center (a) on, (b) around being successful in today's global marketplace. _____

10. She made every effort to reason (a) to, (b) with the unhappy customer. _____

11. Apparently the letters on the screen do not sufficiently contrast (a) with, (b) to the background. _____

12. The courses, faculty, and students in this school are certainly different (a) from, (b) than those at other schools. _____

13. Do you dare to disagree (a) to, (b) with him? _____

14. Being the leader of a business team is similar (a) with, (b) to coaching a sports team. _____

15. I am angry (a) at, (b) with the recommendation that we share offices. _____

16. The president insisted that he was completely independent (a) of, (b) from his campaign contributors. _____

17. He went on working oblivious (a) from, (b) to the surrounding chaos. _____

18. The figures on the balance sheet could not be reconciled (a) to, (b) with the actual account totals. _____

19. A number of individuals agreed (a) to, (b) with the plan. _____

20. Our office is convenient (a) to, (b) for many cafés and restaurants. _____

9 Self-Help Exercises
Conjunctions

Worksheet 1

Name four coordinating conjunctions:

1. _____   2. _____   3. _____   4. _____

When coordinating conjunctions connect independent clauses (groups of words that could stand alone as sentences), the conjunctions are preceded by commas. The two independent clauses form a compound sentence.

> **Compound Sentence:** We hope to increase sales in the South, *but* we need additional sales personnel.

Use a comma only if the sentence is compound. When the words preceding or following the coordinating conjunction do not form an independent clause, no comma is used.

> **Simple Sentence:** The bank will include the check with your monthly statement *or* will send the check to you immediately.

In the following sentences, selected coordinating conjunctions have been underlined. Mark *a* or *b* for each sentence.

a. No punctuation needed   **b. Insert a comma before the underlined conjunction**

5. Marc Green is a specialist in network administration <u>and</u> he will be responsible for advising and assisting all our divisions.   _____

6. Marc Green is a specialist in network administration <u>and</u> will be responsible for advising and assisting all our divisions.   _____

7. This is an orientation session designed for all new employees <u>but</u> topics of interest for all employees will also be discussed.   _____

8. I have studied the plan you are developing <u>and</u> feel that it has real merit.   _____

9. We seek the reaction of the council <u>and</u> of others who have studied the plan.   _____

10. Our executive vice president will make the presentation in New York <u>or</u> he will unveil the plan in London.   _____

Worksheet 2

1. Name five conjunctive adverbs:

   1. _____   3. _____   5. _____

   2. _____   4. _____

2. When a conjunctive adverb joins independent clauses, what punctuation mark precedes the conjunctive adverb?   _____

3. Many words that serve as conjunctive adverbs can also function as parenthetical adverbs. When used parenthetically, adverbs are set off by what punctuation marks?   _____

In the following sentences, words acting as conjunctive or parenthetical adverbs are underlined. Add necessary commas and semicolons to punctuate the sentences.

4. The company is planning <u>nevertheless</u> to proceed with its expansion.

5. Tour prices are contingent on double occupancy <u>that is</u> two people must share accommodations.

6. This organization <u>on the other hand</u> is quite small in the industry.

7. Our group will travel first to New York for the first product presentation <u>then</u> we will proceed to Paris for additional presentations.

8. Today's job market is very competitive <u>however</u> recent graduates can find jobs if they are well trained and persistent.

9. Most recruiters prefer chronological résumés <u>consequently</u> we advise our graduates to follow the traditional résumé format.

10. Human resource professionals spend little time reading a cover letter <u>therefore</u> it is wise to keep your letter short.

Worksheet 1

1. Name five subordinating conjunctions:

   1. _____   **3.** _____   **5.** _____

   2. _____   **4.** _____

Use *T* or *F* to indicate whether the following statements are true or false.

2. A phrase is a group of related words *without* a subject and a verb.   _____

3. A clause is a group of related words containing a subject and a verb.   _____

4. An independent clause has a subject and a verb and makes sense by itself.   _____

5. A dependent clause contains a subject and a verb but depends for its meaning on another clause.   _____

6. Conjunctions such as *because*, *if*, and *when* are used preceding independent clauses.   _____

Indicate whether the following groups of words are phrases (*P*), independent clauses (*I*), or dependent clauses (*D*). Capitalization and end punctuation have been omitted.

Example: he stood in a very long line   I _____

7. in the past year   _____

8. although she came to every meeting   _____

9. she came to every meeting   _____

10. during the period from spring to fall   _____

11. if sales continue to climb as they have for the past four months   _____

12. the director asked for additional personnel   _____

13. as soon as we can increase our production   _____

14. we can increase our production   _____

15. because your organization has financial strength   _____

16. in the future   _____

17. when he returns to the office   _____

18. fill out and mail the enclosed card   _____

19. we are reworking our original plans   _____

20. because your old résumé listed your work history and then went on to describe previous jobs in grim and boring detail disregarding their current relevance   _____

Worksheet 2

Add necessary commas to the following sentences. If a sentence requires no punctuation, write *C* next to it.

1. If you follow my suggestions you will help to improve the efficiency of our department.

2. You will help to improve the efficiency of our department if you follow my suggestions.

3. When completed the renovation should make the seventh floor much more attractive.

4. Let's discuss the problem when Ms. Gardner returns.

5. Drivers who park their cars in the restricted area are in danger of being ticketed.

6. Our latest company safety booklet which was submitted over six weeks ago is finally ready for distribution.

7. As you may know we have paid dividends regularly for over 70 years.

8. These payments provided there is no interruption in profits should continue for many years to come.

9. If necessary you may charge this purchase to your credit card.

10. Any employee who wishes to participate may contact our Human Resources Department.

11. James Gilroy who volunteered to head the program will be organizing our campaign.

12. I assure you that you will hear from Ms. Higgins as soon as she returns.

13. Before you send in the order may I see the catalog?

14. May I see the catalog before you send in the order?

15. We will submit the proposal within four working days if that schedule meets with your approval.

Worksheet 3

Use the information provided within parentheses to construct dependent clauses for the following sentences. Add subordinating conjunctions such as *who*, *which*, *although*, and *since*. The dependent clauses can appear at the beginning, in the middle, or at the end of the sentences.

Example: Dr. Cushman recently moved his practice to Miami Beach. (Dr. Cushman specializes in pediatrics.)

Dr. Cushman, who specializes in pediatrics, recently moved his practice to Miami Beach.

1. The original agreement was drawn between Mr. Hightower and Columbia Communications. (The agreement was never properly signed.)

   _____

   _____

2. Thank you for informing us that your credit card is missing. (This credit card has an expiration date of April 30.)

   _____

   _____

Combine the following clauses into single sentences.

3. (Your account is four months past due.) We will be forced to take legal action. We must hear from you within seven days.

   _____

   _____

4. Sally Horton won an award as this month's outstanding employee. (She works in the Quality Control Department.) Ms. Horton is an assistant to the manager in that department.

   _____

   _____

5. We are sending you four poster advertisements. They will appear in advertisements in magazines in April. (April marks the beginning of a national campaign featuring our sports clothes.)

   _____

   _____

The correlative conjunctions *both . . . and, either . . . or, neither . . . nor*, and *not only . . . but (also)* should be used in parallel constructions. That is, the words these conjunctions join should be similarly patterned. Compare the words that *follow* the conjunctions. For example, if a verb follows *either*, a verb should follow *or*. If the active voice is used with *neither*, then the active voice should be used with *nor*. Study the following examples.

Not Parallel:	*Either* Vicki is typing the Collins' report *or* proofreading it. (The subject follows *either* and a verb follows *or*.)
Parallel:	Vicki is *either* typing the Collins' report *or* proofreading it. (Both conjunctions are followed by verbs.)
Not Parallel:	*Neither* have I pumped the gas *nor* was the oil checked. (An active-voice construction follows *neither* while a passive-voice construction follows *nor*.)
Parallel:	I have *neither* pumped the gas *nor* checked the oil. (Both conjunctions are followed by verbs.)

In the following, write the letters of the sentences that are constructed in parallel form.

1. a. We have neither the energy to pursue this litigation nor do we have the finances.
   b. We have neither the energy nor the finances to pursue this litigation. _____

2. a. You may either write a research report or a book report can be written.
   b. You may either write a research report or make a book report. _____

3. a. He is not only clever but also witty.
   b. Not only is he clever but he is also witty. _____

4. a. The website contains both information and it has an application form.
   b. The website contains both information and an application form. _____

Revise the following sentences so that the correlative conjunctions are used in parallel construction.

5. Either you can e-mail him your response or you can send him a text message.

_____

_____

6. Our goals are both to educate motorists and also lives may be saved.

_____

_____

7. Neither does Tony have a job offer nor does he even have an interview lined up.

_____

_____

8. We knew either that we had to raise more money or begin selling stock.

_____

_____

9. Not only are businesses looking for employees who can work in teams but also can learn effectively in teams.

_____

_____

10 Self-Help Exercises
Commas

Add necessary commas to the following sentences. For each sentence indicate the number of commas you added. If a sentence is correct, write *C*.

1. Your organization's use of cross-functional teams Mr. Wilson explains why your company is able to develop so many innovative products. _____

2. By the way do all of your teams work well together and collaborate effectively? _____

3. To be most successful however all teams require training coaching and other support. _____

4. Our team leader is from Ames Iowa but is now working in Des Moines. _____

5. Developing effective collaborative teams on the other hand is not always possible. _____

6. The CEO's son Mark will be joining our team for the summer. _____

7. Send the shipment to MicroTech Systems 750 Grant Road Tucson Arizona 85703 as soon as possible. _____

8. It appears sir that an error has been made in your billing. _____

9. You have until Friday April 30 to make complete payment on your past-due account. _____

10. Mr. Franklin T. Molloy who is an advertising executive has been elected chairman of the council. _____

11. Anyone who is interested in applying for the job should see Ms. Sheridan. _____

12. The bidding closes at 10 p.m. EST. _____

13. You will in addition receive a free brochure outlining our wireless devices. _____

14. Our latest wireless technology provides support for high-traffic areas such as airports shopping centers and college campuses. _____

15. All things considered the company will be obligated to pay only those expenses directly related to the installation. _____

16. Only Mr. Hudson who is a specialist in information systems is qualified to write that report. _____

17. You can avoid patent trademark and copyright problems by working with an attorney. _____

18. We are convinced incidentally that our attorney's fees are most reasonable. _____

19. Mr. Van Alstyne developed the policy Ms. Thorson worked on the budget and Mr. Seibert handled compensation issues. _____

20. Sasha will travel to Italy Greece and Croatia next summer. _____

Add necessary commas to the following sentences. For each sentence indicate the number of commas you added. If a sentence is correct, write *C*.

1. We must find a practical, permanent solution to our Web access problems. _____

2. For a period of six months it will be necessary to reduce all expenditures. _____

3. Melissa Meyers speaking on behalf of all classified employees gave a welcoming address. _____

4. We held a marketing meeting last week and we included representatives from all divisions. _____

5. I am looking forward to getting together with you when you are in Rochester. _____

6. We do appreciate, as I have told you often, your continuing efforts to increase our sales. _____

7. Consumer patterns for the past five years are being studied carefully by our marketing experts. _____

8. For some time we have been studying the growth in the number of working women and minorities. _____

9. After you have examined my calculations please send the report to Bill Thompson. _____

10. Please send the report to Bill Thompson after you have examined my calculations. _____

11. Would you please after examining my calculations send the report to Bill Thompson. _____

12. Our human resources director is looking for intelligent, articulate young people who desire an opportunity to grow with a start-up company. _____

13. Call me as soon as you return or send me an e-mail message within the next week. _____

14. Beginning on the 15th of June Dell is slashing prices on laptop computers. _____

15. In 2015 we will unveil our most innovative hybrid vehicle. _____

16. I would like to attend the training seminar too. _____

17. On October 25 the president and I visited Sandra Goodell who is president of Sandra Goodell Public Relations. _____

18. You may submit a report describing when where and how we should proceed. _____

19. To begin the purchase process we will need your request by Thursday, June 1, at the latest. _____

20. Any student who has not signed up for a team by this time must see the instructor. _____

Add necessary commas to the following sentences. For each sentence indicate the number of commas you added. If a sentence is correct, write *C*.

1. Michael Ferrari PhD has written another book on consumer buying. _____

2. In 2012 our company expanded its marketing to include the United Kingdom. _____

3. By 2013 12 of our competitors were also selling in Great Britain. _____

4. In 2012 our staff numbered 87; in 2013 103. _____

5. It was in Taiwan not in mainland China where the lightest racing bike in the world was made. _____

6. Long before our president conducted his own research into marketing trends among youthful consumers. (Tricky!) _____

7. "We prefer not to include your name" said the auditor "when we publish the list of inactive accounts." _____

8. You may sign your name at the bottom of this sheet and return it to us as acknowledgment of this letter. _____

9. The provisions of your Policy No. 85000611 should be reviewed every five years. _____

10. Irving Feinstein MD will be the speaker at our next meeting. _____

11. Dr. Feinstein received both a BA and an MBA from Northwestern University. _____

12. Ever since we have been very careful to count the number of boxes in each shipment. _____

13. In his lecture Dr. Hawkins said "One species of catfish reproduces by hatching eggs in its mouth and growing them to about three inches before releasing them." _____

14. Did you say it was Mr. Samuels not Ms. Lambert who made the sale? _____

15. Ten computers were sold in January; nine in February. _____

16. Our figures show that 17365000 separate rental units were occupied in September. _____

17. "The function of a supervisor" remarked Sid Stern "is to analyze results not to try to control how the job is done." _____

18. By the way it was the president not the vice president who ordered the cutback. _____

19. "A diamond" said the therapist "is a chunk of coal that made good under pressure." _____

20. Whoever signs signs at her own risk. _____

11 Self-Help Exercises
Semicolons and Colons

LEVEL 1

Punctuate the following groups of words as single sentences. Add commas and semicolons. Do not add words or periods to create new sentences.

Example: Come in to see our new branch office, meet our friendly tellers and manager.

1. Our principal function is to help management make profits; however, we can offer advice on staffing problems as well.

2. Delegates came from as far as Dallas, Texas, Seattle, Washington, and Miami, Florida.

3. Jerry looked up names, Andrea addressed envelopes, and Janelle stuffed the envelopes.

4. Thank you for your order; it will be filled immediately.

5. Employees often complain about lack of parking space; on the other hand, little interest was shown in a proposed carpooling program.

6. Computers are remarkable; however, they are only as accurate as the people who program them.

7. This sale is not open to the general public; we are opening the store to preferred customers only.

8. Some of the employees being promoted are Jill Roberts, secretary, Legal Department; Lea Lim, clerk, Human Resources; and Mark Cameron, dispatcher, Transportation Department.

9. We will be happy to cooperate with you and your lawyers in settling the estate; however, several matters must be reviewed.

10. In the morning I am free at 10 a.m.; in the afternoon I have already scheduled an appointment.

11. The book was recently selected for a national award; thus, its sales are soaring.

12. Look over our online catalog, make your selections, and click to submit your order.

13. We hope that we will not have to sell the property, but that may be our only option.

14. We are convinced, therefore, that you are the right person for the job.

15. We do not sell airline seats; we sell customer service.

16. Our convention committee is considering the Hyatt Regency Hotel, Columbus, Ohio, Plaza of the Americas Hotel, Dallas, Texas, and the Brown Palace Hotel, Denver, Colorado.

17. As requested, the committee will meet Thursday, May 4; however, it is unable to meet Friday, May 5.

18. Market research involves the systematic gathering, recording, and analyzing of data.

Add colons, semicolons, or commas to the following sentences. Do not add words or periods. Write *C* after the sentence if it is correct.

1. Three phases of our business operation must be scrutinized, purchasing, production, and shipping.

2. The candidates being considered for supervisor are Ned Bingham, Sean Davis, and Anna Donato.

3. George Steinbrenner, New York Yankees owner, said "I want this team to win. I'm obsessed with winning, with discipline, with achieving. That's what this country's all about."

4. Following are four dates reserved for counseling. Sign up soon.

   September 28   January 4
   September 30   January 6

5. At its next meeting, the board of directors must make a critical decision should the chief executive officer be retained or replaced?

6. This year's seminar has been organized to give delegates an opportunity to exchange ideas, plans, techniques, and goals.

7. The three Cs of credit are the following character, capacity, and capital.

8. Our Boston tour package included visits to these interesting historical sites the House of Seven Gables, Bunker Hill, the Boston Tea Party Ship and Museum, and Paul Revere's home.

9. I recommend that you take at least three courses to develop your language arts skills Essentials of College English 105, Business Communication 201, and Managerial Communication 305.

10. The speaker said that membership is voluntary but that contributions would be greatly appreciated.

11. Several of the tax specialists on the panel were concerned with the same thought government spending continues to rise while taxes are being reduced.

12. To determine an individual's FICO credit rating, companies use the following factors payment history, outstanding debt, credit history, inquiries and new accounts, and types of credit in use.

13. Scholarships will be awarded to Jill Hofer Jeremy Stone and Carolina Garay.

14. Our favorite Colorado resort is noted for fly fishing, mountain biking, tennis and hiking.

15. Our favorite Colorado resort is noted for the following fly fishing, mountain biking, and hiking.

Add colons, semicolons, or commas as needed. If a word following a colon should not be capitalized, use a proofreading mark (/) to indicate lowercase. Show words to be capitalized with (≡). Mark *C* if a sentence is correct as it stands.

1. There are three primary ways to make a credit check namely by e-mail, by U.S. mail, or by telephone.

2. Please order the following supplies Cartridges, paper, and labels.

3. Although we are expanding our services we continue to do business according to our original philosophy that is we want to provide you with flexible and professional investment services on a highly personal basis.

4. Employees who conduct Web research are taught this rule Evaluate the validity of all data found on the Web.

5. Dr. Ruglio's plane departed at 2 15 and should arrive at 6 45.

6. Many college professors don't allow students to use http://www.wikipedia.org for research.

7. Three of our top executives are being transferred to the Milwaukee office namely Mr. Thomas, Mr. Estrada, and Mrs. Stranahan.

8. On our list of recommended reading is *Investment an Introduction to Analysis*.

9. Dear Mr. Roberts (mixed punctuation)

10. Our airline is improving service in several vital areas for example baggage handling, food service, and weather forecasts.

11. Julie Schumacher was hired by a brokerage house and given the title of "registered representative" that is she is able to buy and sell securities.

12. Professor Wilson listed five types of advertising Product, institutional, national, local, and corrective.

13. We considered only one location for our fall convention namely San Francisco.

14. Many important questions are yet to be asked concerning our program for instance how can we meet our competitor's low prices in the Southwest?

15. If possible, call him as soon as you return to the office however I doubt that he is still at his desk.

12 Self-Help Exercises
Other Punctuation

Add any necessary punctuation, including end punctuation, to the following sentences. If a sentence is correct, write *C*.

1. Will you please e-mail this form to the IRS as soon as possible.

2. You did say the meeting is at 10 am didn't you?

3. Mr Kephart is a CPA working for Berman, Inc

4. Do you know whether Donald L Cullens Jr applied for the job

5. Help The door is jammed

6. Will you please Ms. Juarez visit our website and register for your gift

7. What a day this has been

8. Although most candidates had AA degrees two applicants had BA degrees

9. Our CEO and CFO normally make all budget decisions

10. Cynthia asked whether invitations had been sent to Miss Tan Mr Roe and Ms Rich

11. All calls made before 9 am EST are billed at a reduced rate

12. Alan Bennett MD and Gina Caracas PhD were our keynote speakers

13. How many FAQs (frequently asked questions) do you think we should post at our website

14. We're expanding marketing efforts in China France and the UK

15. Surprisingly, the CPU of this computer is made entirely of parts from the USA

16. Please send the package to Laurie Adamski 5 Sierra Drive Rochester NY 14616.

17. Would you please check Policy No 44657001 to see whether it includes $50000 comprehensive coverage

18. Did you say the order was received at 5 pm PST

19. Wow How much was the lottery prize

20. After Mike completed his MA he was hired to develop scripts for movie DVDs

Write *T* (true) or *F* (false) after the following statements.

1. In typewritten or simple word processing–generated material, a dash is formed by typing two successive underscores. _____

2. Parentheses are often used to enclose explanations, references, and directions. _____

3. Dashes must be avoided in business writing since they have no legitimate uses. _____

4. Hyphens can be used to form compound words and compound numbers. _____

5. If a comma falls at the same point where words enclosed by parentheses appear, the comma should follow the final parenthesis. _____

Write the letter of the correctly punctuated sentence in the space provided.

6. a. Twenty seven couples will attend the marriage retreat.
   b. Twenty-seven couples will attend the marriage retreat.
   c. Twentyseven couples will attend the marriage retreat. _____

7. (De-emphasize)
   a. Directions for assembly, see page 15, are quite simple.
   b. Directions for assembly—see page 15—are quite simple.
   c. Directions for assembly (see page 15) are quite simple. _____

8. a. Eat, sleep, and read: that's what I plan to do on my vacation.
   b. Eat, sleep, and read—that's what I plan to do on my vacation.
   c. Eat, sleep, and read, that's what I plan to do on my vacation. _____

9. a. To file a complaint with the Better Business Bureau (BBB), call during normal business hours.
   b. To file a complaint with the Better Business Bureau, (BBB) call during normal business hours.
   c. To file a complaint with the Better Business Bureau (BBB) call during normal business hours. _____

10. (Normal emphasis)
    a. Sharon Hunt (who is an excellent manager) may be promoted.
    b. Sharon Hunt, who is an excellent manager, may be promoted.
    c. Sharon Hunt—who is an excellent manager—may be promoted. _____

11. a. "What is needed for learning is a humble mind." (Confucius)
    b. "What is needed for learning is a humble mind.": Confucius
    c. "What is needed for learning is a humble mind."—Confucius _____

12. a. You missed the due date (July 1;) however, your payment is welcome.
    b. You missed the due date; (July 1) however, your payment is welcome.
    c. You missed the due date (July 1); however, your payment is welcome. _____

13. (De-emphasize)
    a. Only one person knows my password—Denise Powell, and I have confidence in her.
    b. Only one person knows my password (Denise Powell), and I have confidence in her.
    c. Only one person knows my password; Denise Powell, and I have confidence in her. _____

14. (Emphasize)
    a. Our current mortgage rates: see page 10 of the enclosed booklet—are the lowest in years.
    b. Our current mortgage rates (see page 10 of the enclosed booklet) are the lowest in years.
    c. Our current mortgage rates—see page 10 of the enclosed booklet—are the lowest in years. _____

Write *T* (true) or *F* (false) for each of the following statements.

1. When the exact words of a speaker are repeated, double quotation marks are used to enclose the words. _____

2. To indicate a quotation within another quotation, single quotation marks (apostrophes on most keyboards) are used. _____

3. When a word is defined, its definition should be underscored. _____

4. The titles of books, magazines, newspapers, and other complete works published separately are italicized. _____

5. The titles of chapters of books and magazine articles may be underscored or enclosed in quotation marks. _____

6. In the United States, periods and commas are always placed inside closing quotation marks. _____

7. Brackets are used when a writer inserts his or her own remarks inside a quotation. _____

8. The Latin word *sic* may be used to call attention to an error in quoted material. _____

9. Semicolons and colons are always placed outside closing quotation marks. _____

10. Use the apostrophe to make nouns plural. _____

Write the letter of the correctly punctuated statement.

11. a. "Jobs," said Mr. Steele, "will be scarce this summer."
b. "Jobs, said Mr. Steele, will be scarce this summer."
c. "Jobs", said Mr. Steele, "will be scarce this summer." _____

12. a. The manager said, "This file was clearly marked Confidential."
b. The manager said, "This file was clearly marked 'Confidential'."
c. The manager said, "This file was clearly marked 'Confidential.'" _____

13. a. *Chattel* is defined as a "piece of movable property."
b. "Chattel" is defined as a *piece of movable property*.
c. "Chattel" is defined as a "piece of movable property." _____

14. a. Do you know who it was who said, "Forewarned is forearmed."
b. Do you know who it was who said, "Forewarned is forearmed"?
c. Do you know who it was who said, "Forewarned is forearmed."? _____

15. a. "We warn all e-mail users to avoid messages that are 'flaming,'" said the CEO.
b. "We warn all e-mail users to avoid messages that are "flaming," said the CEO.
c. "We warn all e-mail users to avoid messages that are 'flaming'", said the CEO. _____

Complete Punctuation Review

Insert all necessary punctuation in the following sentences. Correct any incorrect punctuation. Do not break any sentences into two sentences.

1. Did you see the article titled Soaring Salaries of CEOs that appeared in The New York Times

2. This years budget costs are much higher than last years, therefore I will approve overtime only on a case by case basis.

3. The S.E.C. has three new members Dr. Carla Chang Professor Mark Rousso and Robert Price Esq

4. Needless to say all contract bids must be received before 5 pm EST

5. We formerly depended on fixed-rate not variable rate mortgages.

6. The following representatives have been invited Christine Lenski DataCom Industries, Mark Grant LaserPro, Inc., and Ivan Weiner Image Builders.

7. Last year we moved corporate headquarters to Orlando Florida but maintained production facilities in Atlanta.

8. (Quotation) Did Dr. Tran say We will have no class Friday.

9. Graduation ceremonies for B.A. candidates are at 11 am, graduation ceremonies for M.B.A. candidates are at 2 pm.

10. As we previously discussed the reorganization will take effect on Monday August 8.

11. We feel however that the cars electrical system should be fully warranted for five years.

12. Will you please send copies of our annual report to Anna Golan and DB Rusterholz?

13. Although he had prepared carefully Mitchell feared that his presentation would bomb.

14. In the event of inclement weather we will close the base and notify the following radio stations KJOW KLOB and KOB-TV.

15. (Emphasize) Three excellent employees Gregorio Morales, Dawna Capps, and DaVonne Williams will be honored at a ceremony Friday June 5.

16. (Quotation) "Your attitude not your aptitude will determine your altitude, said Zig Ziglar.

17. By May 15 our goal is to sell 15 cars, by June 15 20 additional cars.

18. The full impact of the EPA ruling is being studied you will receive information as it becomes available.

19. If the fax arrives before 9 pm we can still meet our June 1 deadline.

20. Send the contract to Ms Courtney Worthy Administrative Assistant Globex Industries 7600 Normandale Boulevard Milwaukee WI 53202 as soon as possible.

21. (De-emphasize) Please return the amended budget proposal see page 2 for a summary of the report to the presidents office by Friday March 4.

22. Prospective entrepreneurs were told to read a *Success* magazine article titled A Venture Expert's Advice.

23. Larry Zuckerman our former manager now has a similar position with IBM.

24. If you really want to lose weight you need give up only three things, namely breakfast, lunch, and dinner.

25. As expected this years expenses have been heavy consequently we may have to freeze hiring for the next six months.

13 Self-Help Exercises
Capitalization

LEVEL 1

Write the letter of the group of words that is correctly capitalized.

1. (a) a case of german measles   (b) a case of German measles   _____

2. (a) in the field of marketing   (b) in the field of Marketing   _____

3. (a) the Hancock Building   (b) the Hancock building   _____

4. (a) for all Catholics, Protestants, and Muslims   (b) for all catholics, protestants, and muslims   _____

5. (a) an order for china and crystal   (b) an order for China and crystal   _____

6. (a) both Master's and doctoral degrees   (b) both master's and doctoral degrees   _____

7. (a) the state of Oklahoma   (b) the State of Oklahoma   _____

8. (a) a class in conversational French   (b) a class in Conversational French   _____

9. (a) a memo from our Sacramento Office   (b) a memo from our Sacramento office   _____

10. (a) a British rock album   (b) a british rock album   _____

11. (a) playing angry birds   (b) playing Angry Birds   _____

12. (a) traffic in the big apple   (b) traffic in the Big Apple   _____

13. (a) the King Edward room   (b) the King Edward Room   _____

14. (a) a picnic on Memorial Day   (b) a picnic on Memorial day   _____

15. (a) the waters of Delaware bay   (b) the waters of Delaware Bay   _____

Use proofreading marks to capitalize (≡) or to show lowercase (/) letters in the following sentences.

16. Bob's Chevron Station is located on Speedway Avenue in the next County.

17. Many employees of the Meredith Corporation plan to participate in the Company's profit-sharing plan.

18. Investigators from the securities and exchange commission insisted on seeing all E-Mail messages.

19. During the Winter i will enroll in management, english composition, and accounting.

20. The American Association Of Nurses will open its annual meeting in the Pacific ballroom of the Regency hotel in San Francisco.

21. Our persian cat and russian wolfhound cohabit quite peacefully.

22. Last Summer my family and i visited the grand canyon in arizona.

23. The two companies signed a Contract last april.

24. Interior designers recommended italian marble for the entry and spanish tiles for the patio.

25. A limousine will take guests from kansas city international airport directly to the alameda plaza hotel.

Write the letter of the group of words that is correctly capitalized.

1. (a) my uncle and my aunt   (b) my Uncle and my Aunt   _____

2. (a) Very sincerely yours,   (b) Very Sincerely Yours,   _____

3. (a) Send it to Vice President Lee   (b) Send it to vice president Lee   _____

4. (a) Volume II, Page 37   (b) Volume II, page 37   _____

5. (a) located in the western part of Indiana   (b) located in the Western part of Indiana   _____

6. (a) stored in building 44   (b) stored in Building 44   _____

7. (a) within our Human Resources Department   (b) within our human resources department   _____

8. (a) the Federal Communications Commission   (b) the federal communications commission   _____

9. (a) in appendix III   (b) in Appendix III   _____

10. (a) heading South on Highway 5   (b) heading south on Highway 5   _____

11. (a) the book *Ethics and Business*   (b) the book *Ethics And Business*   _____

12. (a) both federal and state laws   (b) both Federal and State laws   _____

13. (a) Q-tips and kleenexes   (b) Q-Tips and Kleenexes   _____

14. (a) orders from Sales Director Ali   (b) orders from sales director Ali   _____

15. (a) a trip to the east coast   (b) a trip to the East Coast   _____

Use proofreading marks to capitalize (≡) or to show lowercase letters (/) in the following sentences.

16. We received a directive from Ruth Jones, the Supervisor of our Administrative Services Division.

17. The President of our Company gave an address entitled "Leadership: What Effective Managers do and how They do it."

18. Gina Schmidt, customer service representative, attended a convention on the east coast.

19. To reach my home, proceed north on highway 10 until you reach exit 7.

20. Mayor Bruno visited the governor in an attempt to increase the city's share of State funding.

21. The best article is "Does your training measure up?" by Leslie Brokaw.

22. John put on his ray-ban sunglasses and took off in his jeep.

23. Sue's Mother and Father were scheduled to leave on flight 37 from gate 6 at phoenix sky harbor international airport.

24. Subject: task force meeting this friday

25. Taxicab, Bus, and Limousine service is available from the airport to the ritz-carlton hotel.

Write the letter of the group of words that is correctly capitalized.

1. (a) photographs sent from Venus to Earth
   (b) photographs sent from Venus to earth
   _____

2. (a) a room marked "private"
   (b) a room marked "Private"
   _____

3. (a) the Egyptian Room and the Sahara Room
   (b) the Egyptian room and the Sahara room
   _____

4. (a) the finest production on earth
   (b) the finest production on Earth
   _____

5. (a) from Senator-Elect Ross
   (b) from Senator-elect Ross
   _____

6. (a) speaks German and French
   (b) speaks german and french
   _____

7. (a) some asian cultures
   (b) some Asian cultures
   _____

8. (a) an envelope stamped confidential
   (b) an envelope stamped "Confidential"
   _____

9. (a) our sales director, Joe Hines
   (b) our Sales Director, Joe Hines
   _____

10. (a) to ex-President Clinton
    (b) to Ex-President Clinton
    _____

Use proofreading marks to capitalize (≡) or to show lowercase (/) letters in the following sentences.

11. The returned check was stamped "Insufficient funds."

12. A paddleboat traveled south down the Mississippi river.

13. No one recognized ex-senator Thurston when he toured the Napa valley.

14. We wonder, professor, if the gravity of Mars might be similar to that of earth.

15. The Organization's bylaws state: "On the third monday of every month, the Club's Treasurer will prepare the financial report."

16. The President of our Company has traveled to Pacific Rim Countries to expand foreign markets.

17. The homestead act was passed in 1862 to encourage Westward Expansion.

18. British english is the Dialect taught in most countries where english is not a native language.

19. In malaysia we soon learned that muslims do not eat pork and that buddhists and hindus do not eat beef.

20. Although he was known as a "banker's banker," Mr. Lee specialized in Mortgage Financing.

14 Self-Help Exercises
Numbers

LEVEL 1

In the space provided, write the letter of the correctly expressed group of words.

1. (a) for 24 employees   (b) for twenty-four employees   _____

2. (a) only 9 days left   (b) only nine days left   _____

3. (a) twenty-five dollars   (b) $25   _____

4. (a) on the thirtieth of May   (b) on the 30th of May   _____

5. (a) it cost 20 cents   (b) it cost twenty cents   _____

6. (a) (military style) 5 April 2012   (b) April 5, 2012   _____

7. (a) $2.05, 85¢, and $5.00   (b) $2.05, $.85, and $5   _____

8. (a) we started at 9 a.m.   (b) we started at nine a.m.   _____

9. (a) 2 Highland Avenue   (b) Two Highland Avenue   _____

10. (a) 226 Sixth Street   (b) 226 6th Street   _____

Underline any errors in the expression of numbers in the following sentences. Write the correct forms.

11. 194 businesses were sent the ethics survey on December 1st.   _____

12. 2 companies have moved their corporate offices to twenty-fifth avenue.   _____

13. Three of the least expensive items were priced at $5.00, $3.29, and 99 cents.   _____

14. If your payment of $100.00 is received before the 2 of the month, you will receive a discount.   _____

15. On February 1st the guidelines for all fifteen departments went into effect.   _____

16. Our office, formerly located at Two Ford Place, is now located at One Kent Avenue.   _____

17. Please call me at 815 611-9292, Ext. Three, before 4 p.m.   _____

18. On May 15th 2 performances will be given: one at two p.m. and another at eight p.m.   _____

19. 3 of our employees start at 8:00 a.m., and 5 start at 8:30 a.m.   _____

20. If reservations are made before the fifteenth of the month, the fare will be 204 dollars.   _____

21. Grossmont College offers a fifteen-hour training course that costs one hundred twenty-five dollars.   _____

22. Classes meet Monday through Thursday from 11:45 a.m. until one p.m.   _____

23. The Werners moved from 1,762 Milburn Avenue to 140 East 14 Street.   _____

24. Lisa had only $.25 left after she purchased supplies for forty-four dollars.   _____

25. On the third of January and again on the 18th, our copy machine needed service.   _____

Write the letter of the correctly expressed group of words.

1. (a) for 82 students in 3 classes   (b) for 82 students in three classes   _____

2. (a) an interest period of ninety days   (b) an interest period of 90 days   _____

3. (a) over the past thirty years   (b) over the past 30 years   _____

4. (a) two 35-day contracts   (b) 2 35-day contracts   _____

5. (a) he is 45 years old   (b) he is forty-five years old   _____

6. (a) line three   (b) line 3   _____

7. (a) nearly 2.6 billion units   (b) nearly 2,600,000,000 units   _____

8. (a) fifteen 50-page pamphlets   (b) 15 fifty-page pamphlets   _____

9. (a) Lois Lamb, 65, and John Lamb, 66   (b) Lois Lamb, sixty-five, and John Lamb, sixty-six   _____

10. (a) the child is 2 years 4 months old   (b) the child is two years four months old   _____

Underline any errors in the expression of numbers in the following sentences. Write the corrected form.

11. We have received fifty reservations over the past 14 days.   _____

12. Tour guests will be transported in three thirty-five-passenger air-conditioned motor coaches throughout the fifteen-day excursion.   _____

13. 53 of the corporations had operating budgets that exceeded one million dollars.   _____

14. Only 10 telephones are available for the forty-eight employees in 5 offices.   _____

15. Chapter eight in Volume two provides at least three references to pumps.   _____

16. About 100 chairs are stored in Room Four, and another eight chairs are in Room 14.   _____

17. We ordered two thirty-inch desks and three chairs.   _____

18. Of the twenty requests we received, five were acted on immediately and three had to be tabled.   _____

19. The 2 loans must be repaid within 90 days.   _____

20. When she was only 24 years old, Mrs. Markham supervised more than 120 employees.   _____

21. Only two of the 125 mailed surveys were undeliverable.   _____

22. Frank Morris, sixty-four, plans to retire in one year.   _____

23. Linda Hannan and her fifteen-person company signed a three million dollar contract.   _____

24. She purchased new equipment to beam fifty-two World Cup games from nine locations to forty million avid soccer fans in Pacific Rim countries.   _____

25. The thirty-year mortgage carries an interest rate of eight percent.   _____

Assume that all of the following phrases appear in complete sentences. Write the letter of the phrase that is appropriately expressed.

1. (a) the tank holds just 9 gallons   (b) the tank holds just nine gallons   _____

2. (a) only a three percent gain   (b) only a 3 percent gain   _____

3. (a) 4/5 of the voters   (b) four fifths of the voters   _____

4. (a) a final score of two to three   (b) a final score of 2 to 3   _____

5. (a) a one-half share   (b) a one half share   _____

6. (a) a decline of .5 percent   (b) a decline of 0.5 percent   _____

7. (a) he placed 3rd in the state   (b) he placed third in the state   _____

8. (a) in the nineteenth century   (b) in the 19th century   _____

9. (a) a 5-pound box of candy   (b) a five-pound box of candy   _____

10. (a) at least 95% of the stockholders   (b) at least 95 percent of the stockholders   _____

Underline any errors in the expression of numbers. Write the corrected form.

11. A No. Ten envelope actually measures four and a half by nine and a half inches. _____

12. The two candidates in the 33d Congressional District waged hard-hitting campaigns. _____

13. Tests show that the driver responded in less than seven two hundredths of a second. _____

14. Great strides in communication technology have been made in the 21st century. _____

15. The desk top measured thirty and three-fourths inches by sixty and a half inches. _____

16. Payment must be received by the thirtieth to qualify for a three percent discount. _____

17. Our office was moved about fifty blocks from 7th Street to 58th Street. _____

18. Temperatures in Phoenix were over one hundred degrees for 8 consecutive days. _____

19. The notebook computer weighs just seven point nine four pounds and is fifteen and a half inches wide. _____

20. Appropriation measures must be passed by a 2/3 majority. _____

21. She ordered a nine by twelve rug to cover two-thirds of the floor. _____

22. After completing Form Ten Forty, the accountant submitted his bill for 800 dollars. _____

23. By the year 2,014, the number of employees over the age of 55 will increase by 52%. _____

24. Nine different airlines carry over one hundred thousand passengers daily. _____

25. The company car was filled with fifteen gallons of gasoline and one quart of oil. _____

Chapter 1 Self-Help Answers

Worksheet 1

A. *Answers will vary.* **2.** Substitutes for a noun *he she it* **3.** Shows action, occurrence, or state of being *jumps works is* **4.** Describes nouns or pronouns *tall soft five* **5.** Modifies verbs, adjectives, or other adverbs *hurriedly very nicely* **6.** Joins nouns and pronouns to other words in a sentence *to for at* **7.** Connects words or groups of words *and but or* **8.** Shows strong feelings *Wow! Gosh! No!*

B. 1. pronoun **2.** verb **3.** adjective (article) **4.** adjective **5.** noun **6.** preposition **7.** noun **8.** conjunction **9.** pronoun **10.** verb **11.** adverb **12.** adjective **13.** interjection **14.** adjective (article) **15.** noun **16.** conjunction **17.** noun **18.** verb **19.** adjective **20.** adjective **21.** noun **22.** preposition **23.** adjective **24.** noun **25.** pronoun **26.** verb **27.** adverb **28.** conjunction **29.** adjective (article) **30.** adjective **31.** noun **32.** verb **33.** adverb

Worksheet 2

1. pronoun **2.** verb **3.** noun **4.** preposition **5.** noun **6.** conjunction **7.** adjective **8.** noun **9.** verb **10.** adverb **11.** verb **12.** noun **13.** interjection **14.** verb **15.** noun **16.** adverb **17.** verb **18.** pronoun **19.** verb **20.** verb **21.** adjective **22.** noun **23.** preposition **24.** noun **25.** adjective (article) **26.** adjective **27.** adjective **28.** noun **29.** verb **30.** conjunction **31.** adjective **32.** conjunction **33.** adjective **34.** conjunction **35.** adjective **36.** noun **37.** verb **38.** verb **39.** pronoun **40.** adverb **41.** preposition **42.** adjective (article) **43.** adjective **44.** adjective **45.** noun **46.** noun **47.** adverb **48.** verb **49.** preposition **50.** adjective (article) **51.** adjective **52.** noun **53.** preposition **54.** adjective (article) **55.** adjective **56.** adjective **57.** noun **58.** noun **59.** verb **60.** adverb **61.** verb **62.** adjective (article) **63.** noun **64.** pronoun **65.** verb **66.** preposition **67.** adjective **68.** noun

Chapter 2 Self-Help Answers

Worksheet 1

Locating Subjects and Verbs: 1. (S) applicant (V) received **2.** (S) speaker (V) made **3.** (S) telephones (V) rang **4.** (S) we (V) will hire **5.** (S) team (V) built **6.** (S) salespeople (V) received **7.** (S) manager (V) will send. **8.** (S) we (V) released **9.** (S) one (V) was given **10.** (S) technology (V) requires **11.** (S) file (V) was **12.** (S) One (V) sold **13.** (S) list (V) is **14.** (S) Everything (V) is covered **15.** (S) committee (V) was appointed **16.** (S) Mr. Thomas (V) is **17.** (S) devices (v) are **18.** (S) Ms. Seymour (V) is **19.** (S) Mr. Torres (V) has been **20.** (S) offices (V) are

Worksheet 2

Sentence Variety: 1. b **2.** a **3.** c **4.** d **5.** a **6.** c **7.** b **8.** c **9.** a **10.** c **Sentence Patterns:** *Answers will vary.* **11.** voted **12.** fell **13.** arrived **14.** rang **15.** ended **16.** dropped **17.** policy **18.** virus **19.** package **20.** him **21.** the door **22.** documents **23.** good **24.** manager

25. Mr. Jones **26.** Mary **27.** Mr. Smith **28.** John **29–33.** *Answers will vary.*

Worksheet 3

Sentence Types: 1. a **2.** c (period) **3.** d (question mark) **4.** b (period) **5.** e (exclamation mark) **6.** a **7.** c (period) **8.** b (period) **9.** a **Sentence Faults: 10.** c **11.** b **12.** d **13.** a **14.** a **15.** c **16.** d **17.** b **18.** a **19.** c **20.** b

Chapter 3 Self-Help Answers

Level 1

Worksheet 1

1. giraffes **2.** feet **3.** switches **4.** the Bushes **5.** boxes **6.** languages **7.** faxes **8.** sandwiches **9.** income taxes **10.** children **11.** successes **12.** values **13.** dresses **14.** branches **15.** recommendations **16.** women **17.** mismatches **18.** taxis **19.** loaves **20.** annexes **21.** beliefs **22.** the Rosses **23.** storms **24.** ranches **25.** The Joneses **26.** the Chavezes **27.** letters **28.** businesses **29.** computers **30.** wishes

Worksheet 2

1. wharves **2.** chiefs of police **3.** 1960s **4.** the Wolfs **5.** embargoes **6.** LVNs **7.** size 10s **8.** amts. **9.** faculties **10.** by-products **11.** entries **12.** lookers-on **13.** companies **14.** knives **15.** courts-martial **16.** A's **17.** the Shermans **18.** memos **19.** valleys **20.** zeros **21.** lives **22.** yrs. **23.** the Murphys **24.** runners-up **25.** oz. **26.** journeys **27.** MBAs **28.** wolves **29.** the Kellys **30.** minorities

Level 2

Worksheet 1

1. all employees' passwords **2.** this company's office **3.** the women's uniforms **4.** an employee's signature **5.** the supervisor's e-mail message **6.** all members' opinions **7.** the pilot's landing **8.** both partners' agreement **9.** Jeffrey's notebook **10.** the department's strengths **11.** the students' grades **12.** those people's customs **13.** a student's presentation **14.** the bank's credit **15.** citizens' savings **16.** Canada's mountains **17.** the employer's requirements **18.** all candidates' résumés **19.** the government's policies **20.** both attorneys' fees

Worksheet 2

1. author's **2.** drivers' **3.** carpenter's **4.** thief's **5.** company's **6.** employees' **7.** CEO's **8.** readers' **9.** caller's **10.** authors' **11.** Gap's **12.** customers **13.** country's **14.** employees' **15.** organization's **16.** president's **17.** family's **18.** attorney's **19.** employees **20.** farmer's **21.** citizens' **22.** companies **23.** customer's **24.** Children's **25.** supervisor's

Worksheet 3

1. public's **2.** Ross's **3.** company's **4.** the suggestions of my uncle's lawyer **5.** editor in chief's **6.** Brown's **7.** RNs'

8. telephone number of the president's assistant 9. sales
10. brother-in-law's 11. England's 12. electronics 13. the
Rodriguezes' 14. Wes's 15. Angeles 16. the Horowitzes
17. the Morrises' 18. architects' 19. James's 20. agents
21. Brault's 22. the Caldwells 23. Elvis's 24. Dallas
25. reporters'

Level 3

Worksheet 1

1. data 2. theses 3. bacteria 4. Chinese 5. parentheses
6. headquarters 7. alumnae 8. millennia 9. genera 10. news
11. sheep 12. alumni 13. larvae 14. bases 15. memoranda
or memorandums 16. are 17. is 18. formulas 19. analyses
20. is

Worksheet 2

1. Clark and Clark's 2. aunt and uncle's 3. day's 4. Robin and
John's 5. Diana and Jason's 6. associate's 7. last year's
8. Larry's 9. Jennifer's 10. Debbie's and Julie's 11. stationer's
12. bachelor's 13. last month's 14. year's 15. day's
16. months' 17. master's 18. years' 19. year's 20. else's
21. classes' 22. bosses' 23. dollar's 24. Tomorrow's
25. today's

Chapter 4 Self-Help Answers

Level 1

Worksheet 1

1–14. *Order of answers may vary.* **1–7.** I, you, he, she, it,
we, they **8–14.** me, you, him, her, it, us, them **15.** I **16.** she
17. he **18.** they **19.** she **20.** we **21.** she **22.** he **23.** she
24. he **25.** I

Worksheet 2

1. me 2. him 3. them 4. me 5. her 6. him 7. her 8. them
9. us 10. me 11. it's 12. theirs 13. its 14. There's 15. hers
16. it's 17. yours 18. Whose 19. ours 20. You're

Worksheet 3

1. them 2. I 3. her 4. We 5. me 6. me 7. her 8. he 9. him
10. I 11. himself 12. her 13. her 14. she 15. me 16. us
17. she 18. him 19. I 20. me 21. me 22. She and I
23. her 24. us 25. I 26. she 27. he 28. they 29. she 30. I

Level 2

Worksheet 1

1. her 2. his or her 3. his or her 4. their 5. their 6. he
or she 7. his or her lunch 8. him or her 9. her 10. their
pictures 11. her 12. his 13-15. *Order of answers may vary.*
Every employee must obtain his or her parking permit in the
supervisor's office. Every employee must obtain a parking permit
in the supervisor's office. All employees must obtain their parking
permits in the supervisor's office.

Worksheet 2

1. *her* instead of *their* 2. *its* instead of *it's* 3. *his or her* instead
of *their* 4. *his or her* instead of *his* 5. *his* instead of *their*
6. *her or a* instead of *their* 7. *their* instead of *his* 8. *its* instead
of *their* 9. *its* instead of *their* 10. *him or her* instead of *them*
11. *her* instead of *their* 12. *his or her* instead of *their* 13. *his
or her* instead of *their* 14. *his or her seat* instead of *their seats.*
15. *its* instead of *their* 16. *its* instead of *their* 17. *them* instead
of *it* 18. *his* instead of *their* 19. *her* instead of *their* 20. *they*
instead of *she or he*

Level 3

Worksheet 1

1. Whom 2. whom 3. who 4. whom 5. whom 6. whom
7. Who 8. Whom 9. Who 10. who 11. who 12. who
13. whom 14. who 15. Who

Worksheet 2

1. whoever 2. whoever 3. whomever 4. whomever
5. whoever 6. whoever 7. whoever 8. Whoever 9. whoever
10. Whoever 11. Who 12. who 13. who 14. whoever
15. whom

Worksheet 3

1. Whom 2. who 3. whom 4. whoever 5. whom 6. whom
7. Whoever 8. who 9. who 10. who 11. whom 12. whom
13. Who 14. Whom 15. whomever 16. whom
17. Whoever 18. whom 19. whom 20. whom 21. whose
22. who's 23. who's 24. whose 25. who's

Worksheet 4

1. he 2. she 3. its 4. she 5. us 6. there's 7. he 8. I 9. me
10. her 11. us 12. you're 13. her 14. him 15. yours
16. me 17. he 18. its 19. him or me 20. There's 21. him
22. me 23. I 24. their 25. she 26. I 27. me 28. us
29. she 30. there's

Chapter 5 Self-Help Answers

Level 1

Worksheet 1

1. transitive 2. intransitive 3. linking 4. complements
5. helping 6. I 7. L—Jessica 8. T—addresses 9. I
10. L—consultant 11. T—pants 12. T—application
13. L—better 14. L—he 15. I 16. T—questions 7. T—gifts
18. I 19. L—justified 20. T—expectations

Worksheet 2

1. <u>Mark</u> did not receive the text message until Monday morning.
2. <u>Dell</u> shipped our order last week. 3. <u>Sherri Bradford</u> must
authorize withdrawals beginning next week. 4. <u>Mr. Stern</u> asked
Wyatt to be responsible for turning out the lights at the end of
the day. 5. <u>Management</u> forced employees who travel a great
deal to surrender their frequent-flyer mileage awards.

Worksheet 3

Answers may vary. **1.** We must complete our departmental
report before 5 p.m. **2.** Mr. Smith wrote checks on an account
with insufficient funds. **3.** Judges make decisions in the courts
that affect the daily lives of all Americans. **4.** Management
warned employees working with computers to change their
passwords frequently. **5.** Our CPA scrutinized our accounting
records during the audit.

Worksheet 4

1. is 2. occurred 3. is 4. is 5. is 6. plans 7. will sell
8. supplied 9. studies 10. will analyze 11. applied
12. considered 13. varies 14. insists 15. will appeal
16. requires 17. will demand 18. tried

Level 2

Worksheet 1

1. your passing 2. his investing 3. Mr. Cortina's gambling
4. C 5. your criticizing 6. your calling 7. C 8. my working

Worksheet 2

1. b **2.** b **3.** a **4.** b **5.** a **6.** Completing the examination in only 20 minutes, Maria earned a perfect score. **7.** To locate the members' names and addresses, we used a current directory. **8.** Driving through the desert, we thought the highway seemed endless. **9.** My knees shook and my voice wavered when I addressed the audience for the first time.

Worksheet 3

1. were **2.** was **3.** be **4.** would **5.** be **6.** rest **7.** were **8.** were **9.** be **10.** be

Level 3

Worksheet 1

1. rung **2.** froze **3.** hid **4.** chosen **5.** built **6.** drunk **7.** hung **8.** given **9.** gone **10.** bitten **11.** eaten **12.** sung **13.** swore **14.** sprang **15.** shaken **16.** worn **17.** written **18.** stolen **19.** taken **20.** gone

Worksheet 2

1. laid **2.** lie **3.** lying **4.** laid **5.** laying **6.** lie **7.** lay **8.** Lay **9.** lain **10.** lie **11.** lie **12.** lying **13.** lie **14.** lay **15.** lain **16.** lay **17.** lying **18.** lie **19.** laid **20.** laying

Worksheet 3

1. has opened **2.** is planning **3.** had called **4.** has worked **5.** were seeing **6.** will be signing **7.** had broken **8.** have seen **9.** are considering **10.** were hearing **11.** rung **12.** drank **13.** choose **14.** driven **15.** saw **16.** gone **17.** saw **18.** eaten **19.** written **20.** rose **21.** sworn **22.** sank **23.** shrank **24.** begun **25.** forbidden

Chapter 6 Self-Help Answers

Level 1

Worksheet 1

1. provide (subject: websites) **2.** is (subject: supervisor) **3.** comes (subject: supply) **4.** think (subject: workers) **5.** is (subject: Everyone) **6.** was (subject: table) **7.** is (subject: list) **8.** needs (subject: equipment) **9.** has (subject: One) **10.** are (subject: copies) **11.** is (subject: furniture) **12.** are (subject: Effects) **13.** have (subject: salespeople) **14.** are (subject: Profits) **15.** sounds (subject: one) **16.** was (subject: shipment) **17.** is (subject: Everyone) **18.** are (subject: subsidiaries) **19.** have (subject: Officials) **20.** was (subject: letter)

Worksheet 2

1. travels (subject: flow) **2.** are (subject: newspaper and magazines) **3.** is (subject: Coleman, Harris & Juarez, Inc.) **4.** are (subject: books) **5.** appear (subject: points) **6.** are (subject: stages) **7.** was (subject: No one) **8.** is (subject: member) **9.** are (subject: size and design) **10.** is (subject: unit) **11.** has (subject: American Airlines) **12.** provide (subject: seasons) **13.** Has (subject: van) **14.** is (subject: condition) **15.** is (subject: luggage) **16.** has (subject: salary) **17.** appears (subject: One) **18.** is (subject: American Medical Association) **19.** are (subject: ease and convenience) **20.** are (subject: Aggressiveness and delinquency)

Level 2

1. is (subject: Most) **2.** has (subject: The Committee on Youth Activities) **3.** deserves (subject: Each) **4.** is (subject: one [of your two competitors]) **5.** is (subject: work) **6.** is (subject: Either) **7.** were (subject: members) **8.** mention (subject: invoices) **9.** merits (subject: one) **10.** every one **11.** are (subject: you) **12.** has (subject: Each) **13.** belongs (subject: most) **14.** is (subject: group) **15.** is (subject: Some) **16.** has (subject: staff) **17.** Were (subject: any) **18.** has (subject: union) **19.** have (subject: employees) **20.** is (subject: Most)

Level 3

1. has **2.** is **3.** enjoy **4.** was **5.** was **6.** is **7.** favor **8.** are **9.** are **10.** am **11.** is **12.** is **13.** like **14.** are **15.** is **16.** need **17.** were **18.** are **19.** complain **20.** has

Chapter 7 Self-Help Answers

Level 1

1. more effective **2.** worst **3.** friendlier **4.** least certain **5.** more beautiful **6.** fastest **7.** better **8.** noisiest **9.** quieter **10.** most sincere **11.** most skilled **12.** least **13.** slower or more slowly **14.** more likely **15.** most unusual **16.** fewer **17.** better **18.** more credible **19.** worst **20.** fewest

Level 2

1. loudly **2.** C **3.** an **4.** won't do any *or* will do no **5.** more quietly **6.** bad **7.** conflict-of-interest **8.** C **9.** C **10.** a **11.** These sorts **12.** satisfactorily **13.** house to house **14.** could hardly **15.** C **16.** quietly **17.** didn't say anything *or* said nothing **18.** charge account **19.** not-too-distant **20.** up-to-date

Level 3

1. b **2.** a **3.** a **4.** a **5.** a **6.** fewer (for *less*) **7.** really (for *real*) **8.** surely (for *sure*) **9.** neatly (for *neat*) **10.** well (for *good*) **11.** C **12.** recently enacted **13.** worst (for *worse*) **14.** an (for *a*) **15.** had hardly **16.** round-the-world **17.** bad (for *badly*) **18.** fewer (for *less*) **19.** an (for *a*) **20.** farther (for *further*) **21.** Fewer (for *Less*) **22.** latter (for *later*) **23.** well (for *good*) **24.** further (for *farther*) **25.** C

Chapter 8 Self-Help Answers

Level 1

1. should have (for *should of*) **2.** him (for *he*) **3.** C **4.** me (for *I*) **5.** from (for *off of*) **6.** to (for *too*) **7.** her (for *she*) **8.** could have (for *could of*) **9.** too (for *to*) **10.** him (for *he*) **11.** from (for *off*) **12.** him (for *he*) **13.** from (for *off of*) **14.** C **15.** him (for *he*) **16.** too (for *to*) **17.** could have (for *could of*) **18.** C **19.** could have (for *could of*) **20.** me (for *I*)

Level 2

1. besides (for *beside*) **2.** support for *or* support of **3.** omit *with* **4.** in to (for *into*) **5.** omit *of* **6.** among (for *between*) **7.** as (for *like*) **8.** C **9.** type of software **10.** into (for *in to*) **11.** C **12.** concern for **13.** omit *at* **14.** C **15.** omit *from* **16.** omit *up* **17.** style of furniture **18.** in to (for *into*) **19.** omit *to* **20.** graduated *from*

Level 3

1. b **2.** a **3.** a **4.** b **5.** b **6.** a **7.** b **8.** b **9.** a **10.** b **11.** a **12.** a **13.** b **14.** b **15.** a **16.** a **17.** b **18.** b **19.** a **20.** a

Chapter 9 Self-Help Answers

Level 1

Worksheet 1

The order of Answers 1–4 may vary. **1.** and **2.** or **3.** nor **4.** but (students may also list *yet, for,* and *so*) **5.** b **6.** a **7.** b **8.** a **9.** a **10.** b

Worksheet 2

Answers may vary. **1.** therefore, however, consequently, moreover, then (students may also list *accordingly, also, anyway, furthermore, hence, in fact, in other words, in the meantime, indeed, likewise, nevertheless, on the contrary, on the other hand, otherwise, that is,* and *thus*) **2.** semicolon **3.** commas **4.** planning, nevertheless, **5.** occupancy; that is, **6.** organization, on the other hand, **7.** presentation; then **8.** competitive; however, **9.** résumés; consequently, **10.** letter; therefore,

Level 2

Worksheet 1

Answers may vary. **1.** although, because, if, when, until (students may also list *after, as, as if, as though, before, even though, in order that, provided, since, so that, that, unless, where, whether,* and *while*) **2.** T **3.** T **4.** T **5.** T **6.** F **7.** P **8.** D **9.** I **10.** P **11.** D **12.** I **13.** D **14.** I **15.** D **16.** P **17.** D **18.** I **19.** I **20.** D

Worksheet 2

1. suggestions, **2.** C **3.** completed, **4.** C **5.** C **6.** booklet, which was submitted over six weeks ago, **7.** know, **8.** payments, provided there is no interruption in profits, **9.** necessary, **10.** C **11.** Gilroy, who volunteered to head the program, **12.** C **13.** order, **14.** C **15.** days,

Worksheet 3

Answers will vary.

1. Although never signed, the original agreement was drawn between Mr. Hightower and Columbia Communications.
2. Thank you for informing us that your credit card, which has an expiration date of April 30, is missing.
3. Because your account is four months past due, we will be forced to take legal action unless we hear from you within seven days.
4. Sally Horton, who works as assistant to the manager in the Quality Control Department, won an award as this month's outstanding employee.
5. We are sending you four poster advertisements that will appear in magazines in April, which marks the beginning of a national campaign featuring our sports clothes.

Level 3

1. b **2.** b **3.** a **4.** b
5. You can either e-mail your response or send a text message.
6. Our goals are both to educate motorists and to save lives.
7. Tony has neither a job interview nor even an interview lined up.
8. We knew that we had to either raise more money or begin selling stock.
9. Businesses are looking for employees who can not only work in teams but also learn effectively in teams.

Chapter 10 Self-Help Answers

Level 1

1. (2) teams, Mr. Wilson, **2.** (1) By the way, **3.** (4) successful, however, training, coaching, **4.** (2) Ames, Iowa, **5.** (2) teams, on the other hand, **6.** C **7.** (4) MicroTech Systems, 750 Grant Road, Tucson, Arizona 85703, **8.** (2) appears, sir, **9.** (2) Friday, April 30, **10.** (2) Molloy, who is an advertising executive, **11.** C **12.** 10 p.m., **13.** (2) will, in addition, **14.** (2) airports, shopping centers, **15.** (1) considered, **16.** (2) Hudson, who is a specialist in information systems, **17.** (2) patent, trademark, **18.** (2) convinced, incidentally, **19.** (2) policy, budget, **20.** Italy, Greece,

Level 2

1. (1) practical, **2.** (1) months, **3.** (2) Meyers, employees, **4.** (1) week, **5.** C **6.** (2) appreciate, often, **7.** C **8.** C **9.** (1) calculations, **10.** C **11.** (2) please, calculations, **12.** (1) intelligent, **13.** (1) return, **14.** (1) June, **15.** C **16.** C **17.** (1) Goodell, **18.** (2) when, where, **19.** (3) process, Thursday, June 1, **20.** C

Level 3

1. (2) Ferrari, PhD, **2.** C **3.** (1) 2013, **4.** (1) 2013, **5.** (2) Taiwan, China, **6.** (1) before, **7.** (2) name," said the auditor, **8.** C **9.** C **10.** (2) Feinstein, MD, **11.** C **12.** (1) since, **13.** (1) said, **14.** (2) Samuels, not Ms. Lambert, **15.** (1) nine, **16.** (2) 17,365,000 **17.** (3) supervisor," remarked Sid Stern, results, **18.** (3) way, president, vice president, **19.** (2) diamond," said the therapist, **20.** (1) signs, signs

Chapter 11 Self-Help Answers

Level 1

1. profits; however, **2.** Dallas, Texas; Seattle, Washington; and Miami, **3.** names, envelopes, **4.** order; **5.** space; on the other hand, **6.** remarkable; however, **7.** public; **8.** Roberts, secretary, Legal Department; Lea Lim, clerk, Human Resources; and Mark Cameron, dispatcher, **9.** estate; however, **10.** 10 a.m.; **11.** award; **12.** catalog, selections, **13.** property, **14.** convinced, therefore, **15.** seats; **16.** Hyatt Regency Hotel, Columbus, Ohio; Plaza of the Americas Hotel, Dallas, Texas; and the Brown Palace Hotel, Denver, Colorado **17.** requested, Thursday, May 4; however, Friday, **18.** gathering, recording,

Level 2

1. scrutinized: **2.** C **3.** said: **4.** C **5.** decision: **6.** C **7.** following: **8.** sites: **9.** skills: **10.** C **11.** thought: **12.** factors: **13.** Hofer, Stone, **14.** tennis, **15.** following:

Level 3

1. check; namely, **2.** supplies: cartridges **3.** services, philosophy; that is, **4.** rule: **5.** 2:15 6:45 **6.** C **7.** office; namely, **8.** *Investment: An* **9.** Roberts: **10.** areas; for example, **11.** representative"; that is, **12.** advertising: product **13.** convention, namely, **14.** program; for instance, **15.** office; however,

Chapter 12 Self-Help Answers

Level 1

1. possible. **2.** 10 a.m., didn't you? **3.** Mr. Inc.
4. Donald L. Cullens Jr. job? **5.** Help! jammed! **6.** please,

Ms. Juarez, gift. **7.** been! **8.** AA degrees, BA degrees. **9.** decisions. **10.** Tan, Mr. Roe, and Ms. Rich. **11.** 9 a.m., EST, rate. **12.** Bennett, MD, Caracas, PhD, speakers. **13.** website? **14.** China, France, and the UK **15.** USA. **16.** Adamski, Drive, Rochester, NY 14616. **17.** No. $50,000 coverage. **18.** 5 p.m., PST? **19.** Wow! prize? **20.** MA, DVDs.

Level 2

1. F (use two hyphens) **2.** T **3.** F **4.** T **5.** T **6.** b **7.** c **8.** b **9.** a **10.** b **11.** c **12.** c **13.** b **14.** c

Level 3

1. T **2.** T **3.** F (enclose definitions in quotation marks) **4.** T. **5.** F (enclose in quotation marks) **6.** T **7.** T **8.** T **9.** T **10.** F (use apostrophes to make nouns possessive) **11.** a **12.** c **13.** a **14.** b **15.** a

Complete Punctuation Review

1. "Soaring Salaries of CEOs" *The New York Times*? **2.** This year's last year's; therefore, case-by-case **3.** SEC members: Dr. Carla Chang, Professor Mark Rousso, and Robert Price, Esq. **4.** say, 5 p.m., EST. **5.** fixed-rate, not variable-rate, **6.** invited: Christine Lenski, DataCom Industries; Mark Grant, LaserPro, Inc.; and Ivan Weiner, **7.** Orlando, Florida, **8.** say, "We Friday"? **9.** BA 11 a.m.; MBA 2 p.m. **10.** discussed, Monday, August 8. **11.** feel, however, car's **12.** D. B. Rusterholz. **13.** carefully, "bomb." **14.** weather, stations: KJOW, KLOB, and KOB-TV. **15.** employees—Gregorio Williams—Friday, June 5. **16.** attitude, aptitude, altitude," **17.** cars; by June 15, **18.** studied; **19.** 9 p.m., **20.** Ms. Courtney Worthy, Administrative Assistant, Globex Industries, 7600 Normandale Boulevard, Milwaukee, WI 53202, **21.** (see page 2 for a summary of the report) to the president's Friday, **22.** *Success* "A Venture Expert's Advice." **23.** Zuckerman, our former manager, **24.** weight, things; namely, **25.** expected, this year's heavy; consequently,

Chapter 13 Self-Help Answers

Level 1

1. b **2.** a **3.** a **4.** a **5.** a **6.** b **7.** a **8.** a **9.** b **10.** a **11.** b **12.** b **13.** b **14.** a **15.** b **16.** station county **17.** company's **18.** Securities and Exchange Commission e-mail **19.** winter I English **20.** American Association of Nurses Ballroom Hotel **21.** Persian Russian **22.** summer I Grand Canyon Arizona

23. contract April **24.** Italian Spanish **25.** Kansas City International Airport Alameda Plaza Hotel

Level 2

1. a **2.** a **3.** a **4.** b **5.** a **6.** b **7.** a **8.** a **9.** b **10.** b **11.** a **12.** a **13.** b **14.** a **15.** b **16.** supervisor **17.** president company Do How Do It **18.** East Coast **19.** Highway Exit **20.** state **21.** "Does Your Training Measure Up?" **22.** Ray-Ban Jeep **23.** mother and father Flight 37 Gate 6 Phoenix Sky Harbor International Airport **24.** Task Force Meeting This Friday **25.** bus limousine Ritz-Carlton Hotel

Level 3

1. a **2.** b **3.** a **4.** a **5.** b **6.** a **7.** b **8.** b **9.** a **10.** a **11.** Funds **12.** River **13.** Senator Valley **14.** Professor Earth **15.** organization's Monday **16.** president company countries **17.** Homestead Act westward expansion **18.** English dialect English **19.** Malaysia Muslims Buddhists Hindus **20.** mortgage financing

Chapter 14 Self-Help Answers

Level 1

1. a **2.** b **3.** b **4.** b **5.** a **6.** a **7.** b **8.** a **9.** a **10.** a **11.** A total of 194 December 1 **12.** Two 25th Avenue **13.** $5 $.99 **14.** $100 2nd **15.** February 1 15 departments. **16.** 2 Ford Place **17.** (815) 611-9292, Ext. 3 *or* 805-611-9292, Ext. 3 **18.** May 15 two 2 p.m. 8 p.m. **19.** Three 8 a.m. five **20.** 15th $204 **21.** 15-hour $125 **22.** 1 p.m. **23.** 1762 14th **24.** 25 cents $44 **25.** 3rd

Level 2

1. b **2.** b **3.** b **4.** a **5.** b **6.** b **7.** a **8.** a **9.** a **10.** b **11.** 50 **12.** three 35-passenger 15-day **13.** Fifty-three $1 million **14.** ten 48 five **15.** Chapter 8 Volume 2 **16.** Room 4 8 chairs **17.** 30-inch **18.** 20 requests 5 3 **19.** two loans **20.** twenty-four years **21.** Only 2 **22.** 64 **23.** 15-person $3 million **24.** 52 40 million **25.** 30-year 8 percent

Level 3

1. a **2.** b **3.** b **4.** b **5.** a **6.** b **7.** b **8.** a **9.** a **10.** b **11.** No. 10 4 ½ by 9 ½ inches **12.** Thirty-third **13.** 7/200 **14.** twenty-first **15.** 30 ¾ inches by 60 ½ inches **16.** 30th 3 percent **17.** 50 blocks Seventh **18.** 100 degrees eight **19.** 7.94 pounds 15 ½ inches **20.** two-thirds **21.** 9 by 12 two thirds **22.** Form 1040 $800 **23.** 2014 fifty-five 52 percent **24.** 100,000 **25.** 15 gallons 1 quart

UNIT REVIEW ANSWERS

Unit 1 (Chapters 1–2)

1. T **2.** F **3.** T **4.** T **5.** F **6.** T **7.** T **8.** F **9.** F **10.** T **11.** b
12. c **13.** d **14.** b **15.** a **16.** c **17.** a **18.** d **19.** c **20.** a
21. b **22.** d **23.** b **24.** c **25.** b **26.** a **27.** c **28.** b **29.** a
30. c **31.** b **32.** b **33.** c **34.** d **35.** a **36.** c **37.** b **38.** a
39. d **40.** c **41.** c **42.** a **43.** b **44.** b **45.** c **46.** b **47.** b
48. c **49.** a **50.** c

Unit 2 (Chapters 3–4)

1. b **2.** b **3.** a **4.** a **5.** b **6.** a **7.** a **8.** a **9.** b **10.** b **11.** a
12. a **13.** b **14.** a **15.** a **16.** d **17.** c **18.** b **19.** b **20.** d
21. b **22.** b **23.** c **24.** b **25.** b **26.** a **27.** d **28.** c **29.** a
30. b **31.** c **32.** b **33.** a **34.** b **35.** a **36.** b **37.** a **38.** a
39. b **40.** a **41.** b **42.** c **43.** b **44.** a **45.** c **46.** a **47.** a
48. b **49.** a **50.** a

Unit 3 (Chapters 5–6)

1. a **2.** b **3.** a **4.** b **5.** c **6.** b **7.** c **8.** a **9.** a **10.** a **11.** c
12. a **13.** b **14.** b **15.** b **16.** a **17.** a **18.** b **19.** a **20.** b
21. b **22.** b **23.** a **24.** a **25.** b **26.** a **27.** b **28.** b **29.** a
30. b **31.** b **32.** a **33.** b **34.** b **35.** a **36.** a **37.** b **38.** a
39. b **40.** a **41.** a **42.** a **43.** b **44.** b **45.** a **46.** b **47.** a
48. b **49.** b **50.** c

Unit 4 (Chapters 7–9)

1. b **2.** a **3.** a **4.** b **5.** a **6.** a **7.** c **8.** a **9.** b **10.** a **11.** b
12. b **13.** a **14.** b **15.** b **16.** b **17.** a **18.** b **19.** a **20.** b
21. b **22.** a **23.** a **24.** b **25.** a **26.** a **27.** b **28.** b **29.** a
30. b **31.** a **32.** b **33.** a **34.** b **35.** a **36.** a **37.** b **38.** b
39. a **40.** b **41.** a **42.** b **43.** a **44.** b **45.** a **46.** a **47.** b
48. b **49.** c **50.** a

Unit 5 (Chapters 10–12)

1. (1) people, **2.** (1) searches, **3.** (2) Professor, job? **4.** (2) Monday, May 2, **5.** (3) "telesensing," pulse, relatives, **6.** (2) Sizer, Labs, **7.** C **8.** (2) phones, however, **9.** c **10.** b **11.** a
12. a **13.** b **14.** c **15.** a **16.** c **17.** a **18.** a **19.** b **20.** a
21. c **22.** a **23.** c **24.** b **25.** a **26.** b **27.** c **28.** a **29.** c
30. a **31.** b **32.** b **33.** b **34.** c **35.** a **36.** c **37.** c **38.** b
39. a **40.** c **41.** b **42.** b **43.** a **44.** b **45.** a **46.** b **47.** a
48. b **49.** a **50.** b

Unit 6 (Chapters 13–14)

1. b **2.** b **3.** b **4.** a **5.** b **6.** a **7.** b **8.** a **9.** b **10.** b **11.** b
12. a **13.** a **14.** b **15.** b **16.** b **17.** a **18.** a **19.** a **20.** b
21. a **22.** a **23.** b **24.** a **25.** a **26.** b **27.** a **28.** b **29.** b
30. a **31.** b **32.** b **33.** b **34.** a **35.** a **36.** a **37.** b **38.** a
39. b **40.** b **41.** b **42.** a **43.** a **44.** a **45.** b **46.** b **47.** b
48. a **49.** a **50.** b